CW00403322

The King and His Fortresses describes Prussian fortifications during the reign of Frederick the Great – the historical background, the experience of attacking the fortresses captured by the Prussian king, and the theory of fortification. At the book's core are two extensive chapters describing the fortresses built and modernised by the Prussians in two periods – 1740–1756 and 1763–1786, separated by the Seven Years War.

The King and His Fortresses provides a comprehensive overview of Prussian fortifications during the reign of Frederick the Great. The first three chapters briefly describe the Prussian state, European fortification in the late seventeenth and early eighteenth centuries, and the state of Prussian fortifications when Frederick the Great took power. Chapter four details Frederick the Great's experience in fortress warfare, including his education in the field, the fortress exercises he conducted during peacetime, and the sieges he led or observed. Chapter five covers Prussian fortification theory during the Frederician period, including both the king's own ideas and the texts written by his engineers.

The heart of the book lies in chapters six and seven, which describe the fortresses built and modernised by Frederick the Great. Chapter six covers the design and construction of fortresses between 1740 and 1756, including detailed information about fortresses in Silesia, Glogau, Neisse, Glatz, Cosel, Schurgast, Brieg, Schweidnitz, and Breslau. Additionally, the chapter describes the different types of fortress used in Prussian fortification during this time, including the use of advanced works and forts and the subject of caponiers. Chapter seven covers the years between 1763 and 1786, detailing the construction of fortresses on the Oder and in the mountains of Silesia and other provinces of the Prussian state. New solutions used in fortresses are discussed separately; artillery casemates are extensively described, including specific Prussian solutions in the form of casemates with arcaded walls open from behind and so-called Hangars – free-standing casemates serving as shelters for guns firing from open positions.

Chapter eight provides a collective overview of various aspects of the design and construction of Prussian fortresses during the Prussian period, including the most influential designers, the organisation of construction, workers, contractors, and issues related to financing the construction of fortresses and controlling expenditure.

Grzegorz Podruczny was born in Zgorzelec in 1977 and is an art historian and historian. His doctorate, *Pruskie budownictwo wojskowe na Śląsku w latach 1740-1807* (Military architecture in Silesia in the years 1740–1806), was defended in 2006 at the University of Wrocław followed by a postdoctoral work, *Król i jego twierdze – Fryderyk Wielki i pruskie fortyfikacje stałe w latach 1740-1786* (The king and his fortresses. Frederick the Great and Prussian permanent fortifications 1740-1786), was defended in 2014 at the Adam Mickiewicz University in Poznań where he has been employed since 2006.

He deals with the history of fortifications in the modern period, military architecture, and battlefield archaeology, and has been researching the Kunersdorf battlefield (12 August 1759) since 2009. He is the author of six books (including monographs dealing with the fortresses of Silberberg/Srebrna Góra and Glatz/Kłodzko), editor and co-editor of six collected works, and the author of dozens of scientific articles.

The King and His Fortresses

Frederick the Great and Prussian Permanent Fortifications 1740–1786

Grzegorz Podruczny

Helion & Company

Helion & Company Limited
Unit 8 Amherst Business Centre
Budbrooke Road
Warwick
CV34 5WE
England
Tel. 01926 499619
Email: info@helion.co.uk
Website: www.helion.co.uk
Twitter: @helionbooks
Visit our blog at http://blog.helion.co.uk/

Published by Helion & Company 2024
Designed and typeset by Mach 3 Solutions (www.mach3solutions.co.uk)
Cover designed by Paul Hewitt, Battlefield Design (www.battlefield-design.co.uk)

Text © Grzegorz Podruczny 2024
Cover: Frederick II, King of Prussia (Public Domain), Neisse fortress (Geheimes Staatsarchiv Stiftung
Preusischer Kulturbesitz)
Illustrations © as individually credited

Every reasonable effort has been made to trace copyright holders and to obtain their permission for the
use of copyright material. The author and publisher apologise for any errors or omissions in this work,
and would be grateful if notified of any corrections that should be incorporated in future reprints or
editions of this book.

ISBN 978-1-804514-35-1

British Library Cataloguing-in-Publication Data.
A catalogue record for this book is available from the British Library.

All rights reserved. No part of this publication may be reproduced, stored in a retrieval system,
or transmitted, in any form, or by any means, electronic, mechanical, photocopying, recording or
otherwise, without the express written consent of Helion & Company Limited.

For details of other military history titles published by Helion & Company Limited, contact the above
address, or visit our website: http://www.helion.co.uk

We always welcome receiving book proposals from prospective authors.

Contents

List of Illustrations

Preface

The book you hold in your hands is the English edition of my monograph, published in Poland in 2013. However, it is not merely a translation of it. Over the decade that has passed, I have found numerous documents that have resulted in changes to the detailed findings of the various fortresses described in this book. My research attitude has also changed. Ten years ago, I was still an art historian with barely a passing interest in fortifications. For this reason, the book published in 2013 was a monograph on architectural history – specific, very niche (especially for 'ordinary' art historians), but nevertheless drawing strongly on the tradition of civil architecture research. I have now had a decade of research experience in the field of military history, my work having been conducted both in military archives and in the field (an archaeological research project of the Kunersdorf (1759) battlefield). The English version of my book on the fortresses of Frederick the Great therefore had to reflect this change in research attitude. In particular, it resulted in a significantly expanded subsection on Frederick the Great's siege warfare experiences.

At its core, this book is still an attempt to provide a monographic account of Prussian defensive architecture during the reign of Frederick the Great. In it, I have tried not only to present the history of the individual fortresses built and modernised on the initiative of this king, but also to introduce the individual builders – both the king and his engineers – and to shed some light on the organisational and economic conditions of fortress construction in eighteenth-century Prussia.

This book would not have been written if it were not for the help of people to whom thanks are due. First of all, I would like to express my gratitude for the invaluable help of Mariusz Wojciechowski, who is the author of several dozen drawing reconstructions of the defensive works published in this book. Mariusz not only draws superbly, but also understands fortifications, thanks to which he is able to draw a defensive structure that no longer exists, only on the basis of archive plans I have found. To him, as well as to Marcin Wichrowski, I would like to thank him for his numerous substantive comments on this book. Discussions with them have allowed me to draw many important conclusions that have enriched this book. I would also like to thank the people and institutions who provided illustrations and photographs: Daniel Jakubowski, director of Twierdza Kłodzko; Grzegorz Basiński, Head of repairs and renovations of Twierdza Srebrna Góra; Patrycjusz Malicki; Krzysztof Czarnecki; Zofia Woźny; and Robert Maziarz.

Warm thanks are due to the staff of two Berlin institutions – the Geheimes Staatsarchiv and the cartographic collections (Kartenabteilung) of the Staatsbibliothek. I have been conducting research in both of these places for more than 20 years, and without the professional help of their staff, this and my other research projects would not have been successful.

I would also like to thank Profesor Zbigniew Pilarczyk, Chair of Military History, Department of History, Adam Mickiewicz University, Poznań, for the impetus to write the Polish edition of this book, as well as for his subsequent assistance.

Separate thanks are also due to the publisher of this book, Helion & Company, both to its owner, Duncan Rogers, for seeing the potential of a book published 10 years ago in Poland, and to the two editors working on the English edition – Andrew Bamford and Rob Griffith.

Finally, I would like to thank my family, especially those closest to me – Natalia, Antoni, Helena and Ignacy – thanks for keeping me coming back to you after every trip back in time!

Glossary

Avant fosse: An external moat preceding the envelope, usually shallower and narrower than the main moat.

Bastei: A defensive work on a circular or polygonal plan, adapted for defence with firearms, built in northern and central Europe from the fifteenth to the seventeenth century, predecessor of the bastion.

Bastion: A five-sided defensive work, used extensively from the sixteenth to nineteenth centuries. A bastion, like other defensive works similar in outline, consists of a gorge, two flanks and two faces.

Batardeau: A transverse wall (masonry or wood) placed across the moat. In water moats it was used to keep the water level in the moat high, in waterless moats it made it difficult for a possible opponent to move across the moat bottom.

Battery: A position for cannon, either within a defensive work or detached (in the case of a siege battery).

Blockhouse: A small, free-standing defensive structure, usually a reinforcement of a larger defensive work, rarely an independent structure. Originally, the name referred only to wooden structures with walls made of beams. Later on, small masonry structures were also called blockhouses.

Bombproof vault: A vault resistant to being hit by mortar bombs or howitzer shells. This resistance was achieved by the considerable thickness of the vault's roof. It was usually provided with a dosdan (see below) and covered with an additional, thick layer of earth.

Bonnet: A triangular work placed in front of the salient angle of a ravelin.

Breastwork: A parapet, the upper part of the rampart, directly covering the defenders.

Caponier: Originally this term was used to describe a passage through a waterless moat, protected on two sides by a flattened rampart. In the second half of the seventeenth century, a caponier was a low defence structure, often in the form of a blockhouse, built inside another defence structure, a covered way, ravelin, or moat. From the second half of the eighteenth century, caponiers were been defined as low, masonry defensive works erected in the moat, attached to the main rampart, defending its base and the moat bottom.

Casemate: A room, usually located in a rampart, sometimes free-standing, resistant to the impact of mortar bombs or howitzer shells. This resistance is provided by bomb-proof vaults covered by a layer of earth. Casemates can be divided into parallel casemate (a single room covered by a long vault whose axis runs parallel to the front wall) and perpendicular casemate (a row of rooms covered by separate vaults whose axis runs perpendicular to the front wall). With regard to their function, casemates are divided into passive (storage, residential) and active (defensive – casemated batteries, coffers).

Cavalier: A high platform on the defensive work, on top of which is an additional exposed artillery position.

Coffer: A defensive casemate designed for defence by small arms.

Communication: A type of defensive work, usually elongated, whose main function was to connect two other works. Usually, communications connected works located in front of the glacis with the covered way or works extended in front of the core of the fortress.

Countermine gallery: An underground passage for defence against a mine attack.

Counterscarp: The outer wall of the moat, between its bottom and the covered way.

Couterscarp gallery: A gallery located in the moat counterscarp.

Couvreface, counterguard: An external defensive structure built in front of a bastion or ravelin, shielding its fronts.

Covered way: A way running on the outer side of the moat, sheltered from the foreground by a palisade and glacis. The covered way allowed safe movement of the fortress defenders and access to the outer defensive works, and at the same time was the first line of defence of the fortress.

Crownwork: A defensive structure consisting of three bastions (or two half-bastions and one bastion) connected by two curtains.

Cunette: A small ditch located at the bottom of a moat. It usually served as a drainage for moats that were supposed to be waterless, sometimes also as an additional obstacle.

Curtain: A straight section of rampart connecting two bastions or half-bastions.

Dead ground (angle): A fragment of the foreground of a defensive work that cannot be hit by flanking fire from neighbouring defensive works.

Defence gallery: A vaulted corridor inside a defence work used for defensive purposes.

Defence work: A general name for defence facilities

Demi-lune: A detached defensive work on a pentagonal plan, consisting of two faces and two flanks, usually with the gorge open from the interior of the fortress.

Demolition gallery: A mine corridor used to blow up a defensive work abandoned by the defender and captured by the attacker.

Detached bastion: A bastion protruding in front of the curtain, detached from it.

Detached work: A defensive work located in front of the main rampart.

Donjon: A keep, in medieval France, a tall, free-standing tower, serving as a place of defence, but also providing the possibility of long-term housing, located inside the castle. In the eighteenth century, a Donjon was sometimes referred to as the central part of a fortress that was captured at the end of a siege.

Dosdan: (French, dos d'âne) The upper part of a bombproof vault in which the bricks form the shape of a gabled roof. This facilitated the drainage of water and protected the interior of the casemate from dampness.

Embrasure: An opening in a parapet or wall for a cannon.

Envelope: An outer rampart, surrounding all or most of a defensive work (or fortress), separated from the main rampart by a moat, preceded by its own moat, usually narrower and shallower than the main moat.

Esplanade: A deliberately left open space between two defensive works or between fortress fortifications and an area of civilian development.

Face: The side of the defensive work on a pentagonal plan, facing the foreground.

Fausse braye: A rampart, situated at the foot of the main rampart, usually lower and thinner than it. Originally, in the seventeenth century, it served as a rampart for infantry defending the moat.

Firing step: A step made of earth, located on the inside of a rampart or on a covered way, on the glacis side, allowing infantry to fire at the foreground.

Flank: The side of any defensive work on a pentagon plan, located between the face and the gorge.

Flèche: A free standing, detached defensive work on a plan of a redan, consisting of two faces.

Foreground: The open area in front of the defensive structure.

Fort: A large defensive work, set back from the main defensive perimeter or completely independent.

Fortress perimeter: The entirety of the fortifications surrounding a fortress.

Fortress: A vast complex of defensive works combined into a single functional structure, the conquest of which requires the commitment of considerable forces and lengthy preparation.

Gabion: A type of high, cylindrical basket, used to secure siege works or to repair damaged defensive works. Gabions were woven from wicker, were bottomless, and filled with earth.

Glacis: A very wide, flattened rampart covering the covered way.

Gorge: The side of a defensive work on a pentagonal plan, facing the interior of the fortress. Usually, the gorge is unbuilt or has much weaker defences.

Gunpowder magazine: A special magazine used to store gunpowder. These ranged from free-standing masonry structures with thick walls reinforced by buttresses and covered by a thick bombproof vault with a dosdan, to massive casemates inside a larger defensive work.

Half-bastion: A defensive work in the form of half a bastion.

Hangar: A type of casemate with bombproof groin vault supported by thick pillars.

Hornwork: A defensive structure consisting of two half-bastions connected by a curtain.

Loophole: A hole in a wall through which small arms were fired.

Lunette: A detached triangular work on or beyond the glacis, or a small work to the side of a ravelin.

Mine gallery: The general name for underground passages used by fortress miners to defend themselves against mine attack.

Moat: A type of ditch, usually wide, surrounding a defensive work. A moat filled with water was called a water moat, or wet moat, one devoid of water was a dry or waterless moat.

Orillon: The projecting part of a bastion flank, usually ending in a semicircle, which partially screens a retired flank from fire. Orillons were commonly used in the first period of bastion fortification, in structures built in Italy and by Italian engineers in northern Europe. After a hiatus of several decades, they began to be used again from the 1660s, influenced by the design and theoretical activity of Vauban and Coehoorn.

Outer work: A defensive structure situated in the foreground, some distance from the fortress, just outside the glacis.

Outline: A plan of the defence work.

Palisade: A row of piles, driven vertically into the ground, sharpened at the top, forming a wall. Palisades were usually used with other defensive elements as a reinforcing element of a covered way, or a moat, or to close the neck of a work, and sometimes as an independent defensive line.

Parados: An earth rampart erected at the rear of a defensive position, serving as protection for the defenders from projectiles flying from behind.

Parallel: In a regular siege, a trench running parallel to the fortress front under attack. It serves as a defensive facility with which to repel counterattacks from the fortress, as a communication route between individual artillery batteries firing on the fortress and as a base for further approaches.

Place of arms: A section of the covered way, noticeably wider than the rest of the way, where the fortress garrison gathered before making their sorties into the foreground. Places of arms were located at the end of a salient of the covered way or between the two salients. In the latter case, the places of arms formed a smaller salient.

Postern: A vaulted passage or crossing over the main rampart.

Rampart: A defensive work made of earth, a basic component of most early modern fortifications, both permanent and field. The rampart is usually steep, making it difficult to conquer by assault.

Ravelin: A triangular or pentagonal defensive structure located in the moat opposite the centre of the curtain. It protected the curtain from being breached during a siege and enabled better fire coverage of the fortress foreground.

Redan: A defensive work with a triangular outline, consisting of two faces, attached to a curtain.

Redoubt: A closed defensive structure without a gorge, usually with a polygonal outline.

Reduit: A smaller defensive work located inside a larger work, allowing the defence to continue the resistance after the attacker has captured the first rampart.

Regular siege: A method of attacking a fortress in which the primary means of conquering it is the digging of trenches, under cover of which the defensive work under attack is approached, and simultaneous artillery fire, the aim of which is to eliminate the guns defending the fortress and to fire a breach in the main rampart.

Retrenchment: A section of rampart erected behind the main rampart to serve as an additional line of defence. Retrenchments were mainly erected as a makeshift defensive work to continue the defence after a breach in the rampart had been made during a siege, and were less frequently built in advance as a permanent solution.

Revetement: the outer layer of a fortress rampart's slope by which the steepness of the rampart is imparted. The revetment can be made of turf, wooden logs, or masonry.

Salient: a defensive work consisting of two faces and a gorge, lacking flanks. The two salient form a tenaille.

Scarp gallery: A gallery located in rampart scarp.

Scarp: The inner wall of the moat, between its bottom and the rampart of the fortress.

Sconce: The general name for earthen, field defence works irrespective of their outline.

Siege: A military operation to capture a fortress.

Swallowtail: A type of horn work in which, instead of two half-bastions joined by a curtain, there are two salients, forming tenaille.

Tenaille: A defensive structure consisting of two sections of rampart meeting at a concave angle.

Tête de pont: A defensive work defending a bridge. They usually took the form of a single work (ravelin, horn or crown work), but sometimes took a more complex form.

Traverse: A short section of rampart erected at right-angles to the main alignment of the work, designed to shield defenders from ricochet fire conducted along the defensive line under attack. Originally, traverses were made of earth; in the second half of the eighteenth century masonry traverses covered with earth appeared. The latter solution became widespread in the second half of the nineteenth century.

Violent siege: A method of attacking a fortress that employs an organised and pre-prepared storming of enemy fortifications.

1

The Prussian State During the Reign of Frederick the Great

A Brief History of Prussia up to 1740

Frederick II, king of the Hohenzollern dynasty, inherited the medium-sized European state of Prussia from his father, Frederick William I. It had been a kingdom for a relatively short period of less than 40 years, from 1701 when the Elector of Brandenburg, Frederick III, crowned himself king in Prussia. In German it was 'könig in Preußen' and not 'König von Preußen'. A minor difference, but from a legal-historical point of view an important one. The name Prussia itself was derived from the geographical land now located in north-eastern Poland and within the present Kaliningrad Oblast, inhabited until the thirteenth century by the Prussians – one of the last non-Christian peoples of Europe. As a result of the conquest of their lands by the knights of Christian Europe, the state of the Order of the Holy Virgin of the German House, popularly known as the Teutonic Knights, was founded there around 1230. This state reached the height of its power in the fifteenth century, after which it began to decline as a result of two conflicts with neighbouring states ruled by the Jagiellonian house of Poland and Lithuania. First, after the Thirteen Years' War with Poland (1454–1466), its southern part (the so-called Royal Prussia, Prusy Królewskie) was absorbed by Poland, and then, in 1525, under the influence of another unsuccessful war with Poland and the Reformation movements, the Grand Master of the Teutonic Order, Albrecht Hohenzollern, secularised the Order and took over the princely rule of the former monastic lands, from then on called Ducal Prussia. Importantly, he was not independent in his power, as his country was formally part of Poland (later the Polish-Lithuanian Commonwealth), and Albrecht was a vassal of the Polish king. Another important moment in the history of the Prussian state was in 1608, when another representative of the Hohenzollern family, the Elector of Brandenburg, John Sigismund, took over the guardianship of the mentally ill Prussian Prince Albrecht Friedrich Hohenzollern, who thus personally took power in Prussia after 1618, therefore creating the Brandenburg-Prussian state. A special feature of this state was its partial dependence on the Polish-Lithuanian Commonwealth – the rulers of Brandenburg-Prussia had to pay homage to the Polish kings for the Prussian part of their country. This was changed by the Elector Frederick William, who later historians referred to as the Great Elector. This ruler not only gained a favourable outcome for Brandenburg-Prussia in the Thirty Years War, which brought part of Pomerania under his rule, but also to its independence from the Polish-Lithuanian Commonwealth in 1657. In addition, he transformed his country in the spirit of absolutism, part of which was the creation of a standing army, which grew steadily. When he took the throne in 1640, he had only 4,000 soldiers; by 1688, he had 31,000. As a result, he was able to play the role of ally to larger countries in numerous European conflicts, as well as acting independently. For example, the defeat of the Swedish army, hitherto the military hegemon in Central Europe, at Fehrbellin in 1675. His successors kept Prussia on the course outlined by Frederick William. His son, Frederick III, famously acquired the title of king, and his grandson, Frederick William I, further expanded his army (by 1740 he had 80,000 men under arms), and became known as the sergeant king. Under Frederick I and Frederick William I, the Prussians fought, as allies of the larger powers, in the major European conflicts – the War of the Spanish Succession, the War of the Polish Succession and the Great Northern War. Only in the latter conflict did they succeed in gaining territorial gains – in 1713 they captured Stettin, an important trade centre, and in 1721 they captured most of Vorpommern.[1]

Wars Waged by Frederick the Great[2]

At the time he assumed the royal throne in May 1740, Frederick II was the ruler of a signifi-cant European state, but it was far from being called a great power. It was the foreign policy, and, above all, the wars waged by this ruler, who early in his reign became known as the Great, that made Prussia a European power. The first opportunity arose in the autumn of 1740, when the German Emperor Charles VI Habsburg died. He was succeeded by his daughter, Maria Theresa, which was guaranteed by the so-called Pragmatic Sanction; an agreement signed by most European states, including Prussia. However, the new Prussian ruler did not respect the agreement signed by her father and entered Silesia with his troops in December 1740. This populous and rich land had been under Habsburg rule since 1526, but Frederick II had certain rights to parts of it. Above all, however, he had an army ready to fight, something that could not be said of Maria Theresa. On entering Silesia, the province was almost cleared of Habsburg troops, so that the Prussians quickly occupied it. Their attack gave a signal to the rest of Europe, which, seeing Maria Theresa's weakness, moved on her lands, starting the War of the Austrian Succession, which lasted until 1748. As part of it, Prussia fought two separate Silesian wars – the first (1740–1742) and the second (1744–1745). The first began in December 1740, but its key caesura was the Battle of Mollwitz fought on 10 April 1741. This was the first major clash of field armies from which, after initial setbacks,

---

1   Stanisław Salmonowicz, *Prusy. Dzieje państwa i społeczeństwa* (Warsaw: Książka i wiedza, 1998), pp.27–33, 38–42, 54–58, 60–63, 89–100, 102–108, 168–170.

2   The literature on the wars waged by Friedrick the Great is enormous, so it is only appropriate to limit ourselves to the basic study, which is the monumental series of *The Wars of Friedrich the Great*, published by the Prussian Grosser Generalstab from the 1890s to the period of the First World War. This series included volumes devoted to the First (*Die Kriege Friedrichs des Großen*, Th. 1, Der Erste Schlesische Krieg, Bd.1–3, Berlin 1890–93), the Second Silesian War (*Die Kriege Friedrichs des Großen*, Th. 2, Der Zweite Schlesische Krieg, Bd.1–3, Berlin 1895) and the Seven Years War from the beginning to 1760 (*Die Kriege Friedrichs des Großen*, Th. 3, Der Siebenjährige Krieg 1756–63, Bd.1–13, Berlin 1901–1914).

the Prussians emerged as victors. After this battle, other countries (France, Saxony, Bavaria) joined the war against Maria Theresa's army. In October 1741, after a series of setbacks in the war, Maria Theresa concluded a secret convention at Klein Schnellendorf, in which she agreed to surrender Lower Silesia, including the fortress of the Neisse, in return for Prussia's withdrawal from the war. As her armies continued to suffer defeats and were close to losing Bohemia and Moravia, Frederick II broke the convention he had signed and returned to the war, entering Moravia and Bohemia. There, after a setback involving an attack on Brno, he managed to beat Maria Theresa's army again, on 17 May 1742 at Chotusitz. These defeats resulted in the signing of the Peace of Breslau, in June 1742. As a result, Prussia gained all of Lower Silesia and most of Upper Silesia, except for its southern edge. In addition, the Prussians took over the Glatz County (*Graffschaft Glatz, Hrabstwo Kłodzkie*), hitherto belonging to the Bohemian kingdom.

Peace between the two countries did not last long. In 1744, fighting broke out again, which went down in history as the Second Silesian War. Maria Theresa's situation was already decidedly different – her troops had defeated most of the attackers, so they could think about retaliating against Frederick II and retaking Silesia. Before this could happen, however, the Prussians launched a pre-emptive strike and attacked Bohemia again. However, after initial successes they had to retreat back to Silesia. The Austrians, allied with the Saxons in the meantime, followed them in the spring of 1745 and entered Silesia, but were stopped and beaten by the Prussians on 4 June 1745 in a major battle at Hohenfriedeberg. The only Austrian success was the capture of the unfinished fortress of Cosel, located in Upper Silesia, which was lost in the autumn of the same year. Two further Prussian victories over the Austrians at Soor in September and the Saxons at Kesselsdorf in December resulted in the conclusion of peace, on 25 December 1745, which made no changes to the borders.

The next largest and longest of Frederick the Great's wars was the Seven Years War. The battles fought by the Prussian army in central Europe were only part of a worldwide conflict. On the Prussian side, Britain was involved, in addition to a small number of German states (Hesse-Kassel and Hanover). On the Austrian side were Russia and France, as well as the German Reich countries and smaller states such as Sweden and Spain. The war in Europe was triggered by Frederick the Great, who in the summer of 1756 advanced on Saxony, which was allied with the Austrians, seized its capital, and took the Saxon army, which was surrounded in a camp near Pirna. The Saxon soldiers were later forcibly conscripted into the Prussian ranks. In 1756, the Prussians also re-entered Bohemia, where they were confronted by an Austrian army led by *Feldmarschall* von Browne, with whom they fought a bloody battle at Lovositz. The full-scale invasion of Bohemia, however, did not occur until 1757, when the Prussians approached Prague and, in the largest battle of the entire war, fought on the outskirts of that city, again defeated the Austrian army. However, this victory was extremely costly, with the Prussians losing several thousand soldiers, including *Generalfeldmarschall* Kurt Christoph von Schwerin, one of Frederick the Great's most talented commanders. The attempt to capture Prague that followed the battle was unsuccessful; the Prussians were forced to retreat from under the city by an advancing army led by *Feldmarschall* von Daun. At Kolin, this commander managed to beat back the Prussian army led by the King himself on 16 June, forcing the Prussians to leave Bohemia. The Austrians followed them into both Silesia and Saxony. In the former they succeeded in capturing the fortress at Schweidnitz and defeated the Prussian army at Breslau (22 November 1757) and captured the Silesian capital, but on 5 December they suffered defeat at the hands of Frederick the Great in the most famous clash of Frederick the Great's wars, the Battle of Leuthen. In Saxony, von Daun defeated the Prussians at Moys on 7 September, but on 5 November Frederick the Great spectacularly smashed the Franco-German army at Rossbach. In 1757 the Russians also actively joined the war and carried out an initially unsuccessful invasion of the motherland of the Prussian state – East Prussia.[3] Although they occupied part of this territory and defeated the defending troops at the Battle of Gross Jägersdorf (30 August 1757), they later retreated, but not for long, as by January 1758 they had occupied East Prussia, and held it until the end of the war. Despite this loss, the initial success of the war effort in 1758 was on the Prussian side. Frederick the Great made another invasion of the Habsburg countries, this time intending to conquer Moravia and then Bohemia. The main target was the fortress of Olomouc, the siege of which lasted from 4 May to 2 July. The Habsburg troops succeeded in paralysing the supply lines of the Prussian army besieging this fortress, much to the credit of *Generalfeldwachtmeister* von Laudon, the rising star of Maria Theresa's army. The Prussians were forced to retreat from under Olomouc and then leave Moravia, and thus Frederick the Great's last attempt to gain new ground on the Habsburgs failed. In the meantime, the Russian army moved from East Prussia through the neutral, but favourable to the anti- Frederick coalition, Polish-Lithuanian Commonwealth and entered the central lands of the Prussian state.[4]

In August 1758, the Russians unsuccessfully besieged the fortress at Küstrin, which was situated on the Oder River, and in order to repel them, the Prussians marched from Bohemia towards Küstrin. On 25 August, at Zorndorf, a few kilometres north of the fortress, another Prussian-Russian clash took place. This time neither side emerged a clear winner, although both claimed it for themselves. However, the Russians were halted in their march on the Prussian capital, but part of their army moved north and made an unsuccessful attempt to capture the important Baltic port of Kolberg. The Prussians, after the Battle of Zorndorf, moved into Saxony to confront the Austrians. There the two sides manoeuvred for a long time until finally on 14 October von Daun beat the Prussians at Hochkirch. Despite these generally unfavourable battle results for Frederick the Great's army, by the end of 1758 little had changed – the Prussians still controlled Silesia and most of Saxony, the Russians – apart from East Prussia – were unable to occupy Frederick the Great's possessions.

The following year, 1759, was a year of crisis. Frederick concentrated on defending his possessions. He was with his main army in Silesia, where he checked von Daun's army. His brother, Prince Henry, commanded troops in Saxony, while against the still underestimated Russians he sent a small army commanded by *General-Lieutenant* Carl Henrich von Wedel, standing on the Prussian-Polish border. After a war of position and manoeuvre throughout the spring and early summer, in July and August the Russian army, with a little Austrian help, inflicted two major defeats on the Prussians – at Kay on

---

3   This is how the former Ducal Prussia was described in the eighteenth century.
4   The King of Poland, August III Saxon, was at the same time, as Frederick August II, Elector of Saxony.

24 July and at Kunersdorf on 12 August. For Frederick, the second battle was a particularly heavy blow, as he commanded personally there, and his army lost as many as 25,000 soldiers, half of its original strength, killed, wounded, and taken prisoner. Despite these heavy blows, the Prussians fought on, partly due to the mistakes of their enemies. The Austrians were unable to supply the Russian army, which, after several months of marching and encamping in Brandenburg, northern Saxony, and Silesia, departed in the autumn towards the Vistula. The Prussians retook most of Saxony, but suffered another defeat in November when, at Maxen, the entire 14,000-strong Prussian corps was taken prisoner. This was not the last reversal On 23 June 1760, at Landeshut, von Laudon took most of a 13,000-strong Prussian corps defending the passage from Bohemia to Silesia, and then a month later captured the important fortress at Glatz, allowing him to detach the Glatz County from Prussia by the end of the war. The Austrian success ended there, as von Laudon's army failed to capture the capital of Silesia, Breslau, and later, after combining with the main army commanded by von Daun, was beaten by Frederick on 15 August at Liegnitz. A further period of manoeuvre warfare on the Saxon-Silesian borderland was followed by the Battle of Torgau on 3 November, a bloody but indecisive Prussian victory.

The Russian army was not very active in 1760; only in late August and early September did it make another attempt, also unsuccessful, to capture the fortress at Kolberg. The war slowly exhausted all warring parties and in the following year, 1761, no more major battles took place. Nevertheless, important events did occur that year. In the summer, the main Russian and Austrian armies were finally brought together in Silesia. Both surrounded the main Prussian army standing in a fortified camp at Bunzelwitz near Schweidnitz in late August and early September. However, the Allies decided not to attack and had to disperse due to food shortages. The Prussians were in a better position, being supplied from the well-stocked warehouses of the Schweidnitz fortress. For this reason, the loss of this fortress, captured by a sudden attack on 1 October by troops led by von Laudon, was an unexpected blow to Frederick. Moreover, by the end of the year he had also lost another important stronghold – Kolberg, besieged, for the third time, since August 1761. Thus, his power shrank to central parts of Silesia, northern Saxony, Brandenburg, and parts of Pomerania. Luckily for him, the Empress of Russia, Elizabeth Petrovna, died on 6 January 1762. Her successor, Peter III, represented a radically different approach to war, for he was a great fan of the Prussian king and immediately after taking power, he withdrew from the anti-Prussian coalition, signed a peace treaty with Prussia and then sent the Prussian ruler some of his troops. This enabled Frederick the Great's army to achieve its last successes in the war. In Silesia, it beat the Austrians twice at Burkersdorf and Reichenbach and then, after a long siege, took the fortress of Schweidnitz with difficulty. He did not have enough strength for further victories. The Peace of Hubersusburg, signed on 15 February 1763, ended the seven-year conflict between Frederick and his opponents on the basis of the *status quo ante bellum*. The Russians relinquished their conquests in East Prussia and Pomerania, while the Austrians surrendered the Glatz County, captured in 1760, in exchange for the Saxon lands occupied by the Prussians.

Frederick the Great's last war, the War of the Bavarian Succession, lasted less than a year, from July 1778 to May 1779. Unlike the previous wars, no battles were fought during it, and it consisted of manoeuvring, camping and a few skirmishes fought in the border areas of Silesia and Bohemia.

Economy and Society

The conquest of Silesia in the first years of the reign of Frederick the Great, and Prussia's participation in the First Partition of Poland (1772), resulted in a significant increase in the territory and population of the Prussian state. The annexation of Silesia was particularly important. It increased the territory of Prussia by 31 percent, (38,200 km^2) and its population by as much as 60 percent (1.5 million). Moreover, in 1750, the province accounted for 44 percent of all Prussian exports. It is therefore not surprising that Silesia's capital, Breslau, acquired the status of Prussia's third capital city after Königsberg and Berlin. The territories of the Polish-Lithuanian Commonwealth occupied as a result of the First Partition totalled 36,000 square kilometres and over 620,000 people. These two major acquisitions were joined by several smaller ones, and as a result, during the reign of Frederick the Great, the territory of the country he ruled increased from 122,200 km^2 to 199,000 km^2. Thanks to these territorial acquisitions and a high birth rate, the population of Prussia rose from 2.25 million in 1740 to 5.63 million in 1786. The demographic policy pursued by Frederick the Great played an important part in this. It was a continuation of the activities of his predecessors and consisted of importing population groups not tolerated in other countries – mainly Protestant dissidents, such as the Moravian Brethren. A significant difference was the opening up of Prussia under Frederick II to religious groups other than Evangelicals. It was during his reign that religious tolerance was established, thanks to which Catholics also gained freedom to settle and function. An important element in strengthening the demography of the Prussian state were planned settlement campaigns. They were mainly carried out in Brandenburg, along the Oder and Wartha rivers, where hundreds of new settlements were established as a result of the drainage of river areas.

In terms of fiscal policy, Cameralism – a Prussian variant of mercantilism – introduced by Frederick II's predecessors, was consistently implemented in Frederick Prussia. In addition, emphasis was also placed on foreign trade as a source of state revenue. The main objective of the Prussian king's financial policy was to achieve a surplus in foreign trade, high tax revenues (excise duties), and the constant possession of financial surpluses by the state. Thanks to the territorial expansion of the country and a consistent economic policy, the revenue of the Prussian state increased from 7 million thalers in 1740 to 23 million thalers in 1786.

The policy was entirely directed towards military objectives – constant readiness for war both by having an ever-growing army and an adequate supply of cash. In the 1770s, with a total state revenue of 21.7 million thalers, as much as 13 million was spent on the military, which accounted for 60 per cent of the budget.[5]

---

5   Andrzej Kamieński, Grzegorz Kucharczyk, Zygmunt Szultka, Dariusz Łukaszewicz, Bogdan Wachowiak, *Dzieje Brandenburgii-Prus, t. 2: Prusy w okresie monarchii absolutnej (1701–1806)* (Poznań: Wydawnictwo Poznańskie, 2010), pp.418–421, 430, 435, 437–438, 470–472, 592; Christopher Duffy, *Friedrich der Große und seine Armee* (Stuttgart: Motorbuch, 1978, p.196.

The Military

Frederick the Great expanded his armed forces at a similar rate to his predecessors. In 1740, when he assumed the throne, he had 80,000 men under arms. Two years later, the army numbered 117,600, and at the beginning of the Seven Years War, 153,000. In 1763, after demobilisation, only 130,000 men served in the army, but in 1784 the army had been enlarged to 188,500, and at the time of Frederick II's death to as many as 190,600.[6]

The majority of the Prussian army was infantry. In 1784 it numbered 149,100, while the cavalry numbered only 39,400.[7] Technical units consisted of four field artillery regiments with a total of 8,600 men,[8] 14 garrison artillery companies and four miners' companies of 100 men each.[9]

The infantry was divided into field and garrison units. The former category were fully-fledged units, used both in the field and to man fortresses. Garrison units consisted of less valuable soldiers and officers, who were only intended to man fortresses. A Prussian field regiment at the end of Frederick II's life numbered 1,729 men, including officers, non-commissioned officers, and auxiliary services, of which there were 1,220 musketeers and 218 grenadiers.[10] It consisted of two battalions, each with five companies of musketeers and a company of grenadiers. An infantry company in the mid-eighteenth century consisted of 114 to 122 soldiers, and about 20 officers and non-commissioned officers. After 1768 its numbers increased by 40 soldiers.[11] A garrison regiment consisted of four battalions of five companies each, with a total of 2,804 men (2,440 soldiers, 200 non-commissioned officers, 80 officers and 84 auxiliaries).[12] Garrison companies were smaller, numbering about 110 soldiers. The last and least common type of infantry were the so-called *Freibataillone* – units composed mainly of volunteers and formed only for auxiliary purposes during the war.[13] In 1783, three so-called *Freiregiment* were formed to exist also in peacetime.[14]

The cavalry had a different organisation. Its most common types were cuirassiers, dragoons and hussars – these types of cavalry differed both in their armament and in the tasks for which they were intended in battle. The cuirassiers were heavy cavalry, equipped with the largest horses, so that they could be used in battle to break the enemy cavalry. The cuirassiers were distinguished from other types of cavalry by their distinctive half-armour (cuirass), in addition to being armed with a backsword and a short carbine. Dragoons used

6   Salmonowicz, *Prusy*, p.86, 186; Olaf Groehler, *Die Kriege Friedrichs II* (Berlin: Militärverlag, 1966), p.80; Memoire sur L'armee Prusienne en 1784, GStA SPK I HA, Rep.94, II M 13, p.1; Duffy, *Friedrich der Grosse*, pp.245, 318, 329.
7   GStA SPK I HA, Rep.94, II M 13, p.1.
8   Duffy, *Friedrich der Grosse*, p.165.
9   Anon., *Kurzgefaßte Stamm und Rangliste der Königl. Preußischen Armee für das Jahr 1792* (Berlin: Christian Friedrich Himburg, 1792), pp.13, 116; Wollmann Ernst, *Geschichte des Brandenburgischen Pionier Bataillons nr. 3* (Minden: Bruns, 1888), p.6.
10   Duffy, *Friedrich der Grosse*, p.100; Anon., *Rangliste 1786*, p.9.
11   Duffy, *Friedrich der Grosse*, p.100.
12   Anon., *Kurzgefaßte Stamm und Rangliste der Königl. Preußischen Armee von deren Stiftung an bis Ende 1785* (Berlin: Christian Friedrich Himburg, 1785), p.9.
13   Duffy, *Friedrich der Grosse*, pp.110–112.
14   Kurt Jany, *Geschichte der Preussischen Armee vom 15 Jahrhundert bis 1914, V.3 1763–1807* (Osnabrück: Biblio Verlag, 1967), p.131.

lighter horses and had no armour, but their firearms were longer, equipped with bayonets, and the dragoons, unlike other cavalry formations, had cartridge pouches typical of infantry. In the period in question, dragoons were no longer treated as infantry on horseback, as they had been before, and were used in battle for similar tasks as cuirassiers. The last cavalry formation, the hussars, were light cavalry, equipped with the smallest horses. They were used for reconnaissance, patrolling and other tasks.[15]

A regiment of cavalry ranged from 861 men (cuirassiers), to 886 (dragoons), to 1,515 men (hussars), including officers and support staff. The basic unit was the squadron, with about 185 men including officers.[16]

Of the technical units, artillery was the most numerous. As with the infantry, there was also a division into field and garrison units, differing in the quality of the men. A field artillery regiment consisted of 2,050 men, including officers and support staff.[17] An artillery company consisted of approximately 194 soldiers.[18] Garrison artillery units consisted of soldiers unfit for field service. They were not combined into regiments and consisted of companies, each of which varied in size depending on the size of the fortress in which they were stationed.[19]

The Prussian army in the eighteenth century was an assemblage of men from different countries, held together by common drills and regulations. Soldiers were divided into 'foreigners' and *Landeskinder*. The former were a remnant of the previous mercenary armies; soldiers in this category were enlisted into service by recruiting officers operating mainly, but not exclusively, abroad. Engaging recruits from the country's own population was done in a different way. The country was divided into cantons, or districts, with a certain population. Each of these districts was assigned to a specific regiment. The entire male population of a canton, above a certain age, was enrolled in a cantonal list, which regulated when they were called up for service. The cantonal system was introduced in Prussia in 1721–1733. At that time, exemptions from military service were also defined – population from economically important areas (Berlin, Potsdam, Brandenburg, etc.) and certain population groups, regardless of residence (merchants, craftsmen, fathers of families, sons of widows, etc.).[20] Significantly, in areas of the Prussian state exempted from the cantonal system, recruitment was allowed, so some of the 'foreigners' were subjects of the Prussian king.

---

15   Duffy, *Friedrich der Grosse*, pp.140–150.
16   Anon., *Rangliste 1786*, pp.9–10.
17   Anon., *Rangliste 1792*, p.13.
18   Duffy, *Friedrich der Grosse*, p.165.
19   Duffy, *Friedrich der Grosse*, p.166.
20   Salmonowicz, *Prusy*, p.165; Duffy, *Friedrich der Grosse*, p.77.

2

Eighteenth-Century Defensive Architecture

The defensive architecture of the European continent at the end of the seventeenth and early eighteenth centuries was overwhelmingly influenced by concepts developed and realised in France. Military engineers from other countries – the Netherlands, Italy, Sweden or the German Reich – were far inferior to those from France. Prussia, a medium-sized European country that slowly grew into a European military power during the first half of the eighteenth century, was not initially involved in the development of fortification architecture.

Vauban's Legacy

The most important figure for the defensive architecture of the eighteenth century – both French and European in general – was Sebastian le Prestre de Vauban. Although the majority of the great fortification architect's life was spent in the seventeenth century, the appreciation of his work mainly took place after 1700. His work fundamentally changed both defensive architecture and the ways in which fortresses were conquered.

The fortresses created in the course of his prolific building activity were later divided by scholars of Vauban's work into three groups called manners or systems, corresponding to the three, distinctly different, outlines used in them. In the fortresses assigned to the first manner, large bastions were used, provided with orillons. Between them, in front of the curtain were tenailles protecting the bottom of the moat. In front of the tenaille a large ravelin was erected, preceded by three smaller lunettes. The whole was surrounded by a covered way with a large place of arms. The fortress of Huningue is an example of such a fortress.

Other features characterise the second Vauban manner. The most important is the use, instead of large bastions, of small, casemated bastion towers. In front of these were large counter-guards shielding them. In front of each curtain, as in the first manner, there were tenailles defending the moat, with a ravelin in front of them. This one differed from the one described above, as it was additionally equipped with its own reduit, thanks to which it could be defended after a breach was fired in the front of the ravelin. The last difference was the elimination of the outer works protruding in front of the ravelin. Among the fortresses included in this group are Landau and Belfort.

The third Vauban manner was in practice limited to a single fortress; Neuf Briesach. It differed from the previously described manners by one feature only – the bastion towers

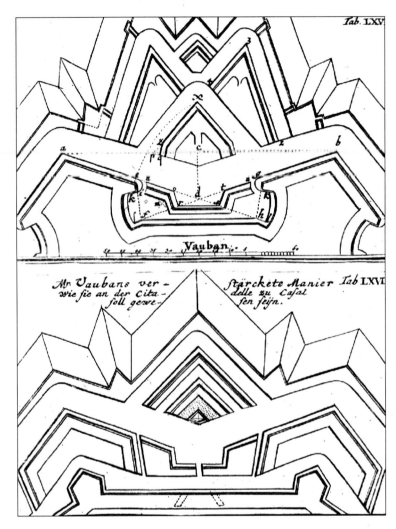

Vauban's first and second manners. (Sturm, *Architectura militaris hypothetico-eclectica*, tab. LXV, LXVI)

were located at the corner of the large, flattened bastions. Their shoulders, like those of the bastion towers, were casemated, so that the moat was covered by many cannon.

One of Vauban's more interesting inventions were the aforementioned bastion towers. These were small masonry bastions, two storeys high. They had artillery casemates and bombproof rooms that served as shelters for the crew. Such towers were built at several of Vauban's strongholds – Belfort, Landau, Neuf Briesach – and became a feature heavily commented on by theorists of the period, although outside Vauban's projects they were not used in practice. Another feature he liked to use were citadels. Here he did not introduce anything new, except perhaps to change the function of the citadel. It ceased to be a facility for the potential domination of the civilian population and acquired a strictly military function. His most famous citadel, which is still standing today, is the one in Lille.

Another element that Vauban introduced into the range of defensive architectural solutions was the external works he often used. Usually these were small lunettes extended in front of the battle slope, as at the fortresses of Mons (after 1691), Namur (after 1692), Landau (1702), Le Quesnay). But sometimes they were larger structures such as the Redoubt du Marais at Dunkirk.

During his lifetime, Vauban was involved in the rebuilding of more than 300 fortresses and the construction of more than 30. Most of these were built in France, some were built on the basis of his designs beyond that country's borders (Turin), while others found themselves outside France as a result of border shifts while he was still alive (Landau, Breisach). In other words, Vauban made an extremely strong mark on the fortified landscape of western Europe.

Vauban's ideas on defensive architecture were not presented in a theoretical work published by him, but throughout the eighteenth century, various authors published dozens of treatises presenting his principles of fortification.

Vauban improved upon the siege techniques previously used and created a coherent method of besieging a fortress – the regular attack. Vauban's fundamental innovation was the introduction of 'parallels' – trenches parallel to the fortress front under attack, which were both defensive positions and communication trenches. Parallels replaced the redoubts used earlier, in which the besiegers protected themselves against sorties by the defenders. As they were much lower, they were not threatened by fire from the fortress, and they were long, so they could accommodate enough men to repel any attack from the fortress. The parallels provided support for the siege batteries built in or near them.

The principle of the Vauban attack was to approach the fortress by zigzagging trenches and establishing further parallels closer to the fortress. There were to be three in all; the last was to be at the foot of the fortress' glacis. The approach to the fortress was linked to an artillery attack on the fortress works. Here, too, Vauban had great merit. He introduced a new way of firing – ricochet firing. The ricochet batteries were placed so that the shells thrown from them shot longitudinally across the fronts of the works under attack and entire sections of the covered way. A higher elevation angle of the cannon and reduced charges were used for this firing. In this way, the projectile flew over the front of the work under fire and then lost momentum in ever-shorter 'jumps', hitting further targets. He was keen to use howitzers for this type of fire.[1] In addition to these innovations, Vauban organised the actions of the artillery, specialised the batteries, and linked their activities to the progress of the trench attack. He first implemented all these elements in the sieges he conducted and then presented them in a separate treatise on the attack and defence of fortresses, published posthumously in 1737.[2]

The last element of siege warfare modernised by Vauban was mines. Thanks to Vauban's efforts, the first permanent company of miners was formed in France, serving as a prototype for units formed in other European countries in the eighteenth century. In addition, Vauban published in print a treatise on mines, in which he not only set out the principles

---

1   Hermann Müller, *Geschichte des Festungskrieges seit allgemeiner Einführung der Feuerwaffen bis zum Jahre 1892* (Berlin: Mittler und Sohn, 1892), p.39.
2   Sébastien Le Prestre de Vauban, *De l'attaque et de la defense des places* (La Haye: Pierre de Hondt, 1737).

of the art of mining, but also described the results of his experiments in blowing up older defences and the effectiveness of demolition mines.[3]

France in the Post-Vauban Period

After Vauban's death, his legacy was critically analysed by his successors and transformed in France into a kind of binding doctrine. The first to develop Vauban's legacy was Louis de Cormontaigne. In a book he published anonymously in The Hague in 1741, he created his version of a bastioned, post-Vauban fortress.[4] In his treatise, he presented a drawing based on Vauban's most famous fortress, Neuf Briesach, but with significant modifications. The most important was the removal of the bastion tower and the counter-guard covering it, and the replacement of these structures with a traditional bastion.

Marc Rene de Montalembert was, after Vauban, another French engineer who exerted a tremendous influence on the development of the field. His activity was in the fourth quarter of the eighteenth century, and his ideas were not put into practice until the nineteenth century, but he should nevertheless not be overlooked in the presentation of the dominant trends in eighteenth-century fortification. His ideas were first published in print in 1776 in the first volume of *La fortification perpendiculaire*. His subsequent books contained additions to his ideas and polemics, with numerous critics, were published until 1793.[5]

The novelty of this Frenchman's ideas lay in proposing a completely new outline for the fortress. Montalembert was a strong opponent of the bastion outline that had been in force until then. He proposed replacing it with a tenaille or polygonal outline, in which the long curtains were defended by flanking fire from caponiers set low in the moat. An important element of the system he proposed was the casemating of the ramparts and the mass use of multi-storey artillery casemates. Montalembert was also a forerunner of the nineteenth century fortification with girdle of forts – he presented designs of such a set-up for Cherbourg and La Hougue. An extremely important feature he invented was the multi-storey, casemated, circular, artillery towers, which he proposed both as an element of reinforcement for older fortifications and as independent defensive works.

Montalembert's ideas attracted enormous interest. In France they were widely criticised, while outside France they were appreciated. One of the first countries where his ideas were recognised was Prussia.

---

3   Sébastien Le Prestre de Vauban, *De l'attaque et de la defense des places, par monsieur le marechal de Vauban; tome second contentant un traite pratique des mines* (La Haye: De Hondt, 1742).
4   Louis de Cormontaigne, *Architecture militaire, ou l'art de fortifier, Qui enseigne d'une manière courte et facile,* (La Haye: Neaulme et Moetiens, 1741).
5   Marc René de Montalembert, *La fortification perpendiculaire, ou Essai sur plusieurs manieres…* (Paris: Philippe-Denys Pierres; Alexandre Jombert, 1776–1798), 11 vols.

The Netherlands

An individual whose work had a similar impact to Vauban's on the development of European defence architecture was the Dutch military engineer Menno van Coehoorn. He was also active as a builder of fortresses, as well as defending and attacking them. He developed a fortification system different from Vauban's, as well as a significantly different method of conquering fortresses.

Coehoorn's fortifications were characterised on the one hand by the use of solutions that were traditional for the Netherlands, such as wide water moats and numerous outer works, but on the other hand by numerous new solutions developed by him. New to the Dutch tradition was the massive use of masonry. The fortresses erected by Coehoorn usually had masonry revetments, which greatly strengthened their resistance to assault during the winter, after the moats had frozen over. In addition, Coehoorn did not shrink from using casemates, although the gun emplacements in his fortresses were always on the ramparts, under the open sky. Coehoorn, like Vauban, left behind three patterns of fortresses. The basis in all of them was the use of a large bastion with retired, concave flanks, protected by orillons. Such flanks contained doubled positions for cannons.

The first type was, as it were, a transformation of the first Vauban manner. Instead of the tenailles found in the French engineer's work, in front of the fortress curtain, Coehoorn used a wide fausse-braye. In addition, he transformed the bastions and ravelins. In the bastions, the faces were separated by a dry moat from the rest of the work, thus creating a permanent retrenchment, which was covered by fire from casemates for small arms placed in the orillons. The ravelin was treated in a similar way, except that its inner part was connected to the fronts by three caponiers, from which the inner moat of the ravelin could be fired upon.

The second of Coehoorn's manners was to be more complicated. The core of the fortress had a standard bastion outline, but large detached defensive works were located in the moat in front of the ravelin. They were placed where ravelins were usually inserted, but in terms of outline and construction they were the same as the bastions known from the Dutch engineer's first manners. Works identical to the ravelins described above were to stand between these works and in front of the corners of the bastions of the main circuit.

Coehoorn's second manner. (Coehoorn, *Nieuwe Vestingbouw*, Fig. M)

Completely different from those described, the third manners presented by Coehoorn in his treatise were the most interesting. The most important novelty was the double main rampart. It consisted of an inner bastion rampart, identical in outline to that of the previous manners, and a lower, outer rampart with a tenaille outline. Only in front of it was the moat. Another innovation was the combination of all the outer works in the moat into an envelope – a trace – a continuous defensive structure located between the main rampart and the covered way, separated from them by two independent moats. All the solutions described above were personally presented by Coehoorn in the form of an architectural treatise published in 1685. This text was quickly translated into other European languages.[6] As a result, Coehoorn's ideas were quickly recognised and began to be implemented in fortresses all over Europe, and this Dutch engineer became as well known as Vauban, even though his practical building activity was extremely modest compared to that of the French *maréchal*. Coehoorn rebuilt only a few fortresses, the most famous of which were Naarden and Bergen op Zoom.

The Coehoorn method of conquering fortresses was diametrically opposed to the one invented by Vauban. It was characterised by much greater violence, and the general difference was in the way artillery was used. Instead of small batteries, specialised for their task, Coehoorn used batteries consisting of numerous cannon, firing at the section of the fortress under attack. Plunging firing played a prominent role. He favoured the use of large mortars, throwing several hundred-pound shells, and an unusually large number of hand mortars, invented by him. These mortars threw 2½-pound grenades and were small enough to be carried by soldiers. In addition, it was possible to accumulate large numbers of them – several hundred at a time – and seed the attacked front with huge numbers of small shells. Thanks to the rapid covering fire, the close siege-work, unlike in the concept of Vauban and his imitators, could also be carried out during the daytime.[7]

Other European Countries

The other countries and their traditions of defensive architecture were far less important for the development of fortifications at the dawn of the Frederician period. Nevertheless, they should also be mentioned, as interesting ideas in the field of defensive architecture also emerged outside of the Netherlands and France. Italy should be mentioned first and foremost. As is well known, the Apennine Peninsula was the cradle of modern defensive architecture. The bastion was invented there and the architects who spread this invention throughout Europe originated there. By the first half of the seventeenth century, however, the Italian military engineers had already lost their importance and were no longer reckoned with. It got to the point where, after 1668, the Duke of Savoy-Piedmont asked Vauban to rebuild the fortress in Turin.[8] The French engineer rebuilt the Turin citadel, which in the

---

6   Menno van Coehoorn, *Nieuwe Vestingbouw* (Leeuwarden: Rintjes, 1685), Menno van Coehoorn, *Nouvelle fortification tant pour un terrain bas et humide que sec et élevé* (La Haye: Van Buldern, 1706), Menno van Coehoorn, *Neuer Vestungs-Bau* (Wesel: Kattepoel, 1708).

7   Müller, *Geschichte des Festungskrieges*, pp.49–53.

8   Pierre A. Allent, *Histoire du Corps Impérial du Génie* (Paris: Magimel, 1805), vol.1, p.696.

sixteenth century had been the prototype for citadels all over Europe, including France. Nonetheless, it cannot be said that Italian defensive architects no longer played a role in the development of fortifications. One example is the work of two Piedmontese engineers, Ignazio Giuseppe Bertola and Bernardino Pinto di Barri. Both made great contributions to the development of mountain fortifications. The former started the Fenestrelle fortress – the largest mountain fortification built in modern Europe – and the latter completed it. Both engineers also contributed to the construction and modernisation of the fortresses of Exilles, Demonte, and the citadel of Alessandria. Barri additionally erected the fortress at Tortona.[9]

Another place in Europe where interesting things, from a fortification point of view, were happening at the time was Sweden, which was at the height of its military importance in the seventeenth and early eighteenth centuries. During this period, in addition to the numerous wars waged by Swedish rulers, there was also intensive fortification of both Sweden and its possessions on the southern and eastern Baltic coasts. The most important figure for Swedish defensive architecture of this period was Erik Dahlbergh. His work included both full urban circuits (Wismar, Gothenburg, Karlskrona) and single forts. The hallmark of this engineer were forts with towering, casemated cores, such as Kronan Fort and Göta Lejon, and the towers protecting Gothenburg, erected in the 1680s.[10]

The German states were of little importance in the development of defensive architecture. Although fortresses were built there, the vast majority were realisations of concepts invented elsewhere in Europe. Germany did, however, make some contribution to the dissemination of defensive architecture theory. This was thanks to the activity of Leonhard Christoph Sturm, a mathematician and professor of Viadrina University at Frankfurt an der Oder. One of Sturm's fields of activity was architectural theory. His writings mostly dealt with civil architecture, but he also published several works on defence architecture. The most important is the volume *Architectura Militaris Hypothetico-Eclectica, Oder Gründliche Anleitung...*, first published in Nüremberg in 1702. This work presents dozens of fortification systems by various authors. Sturm presents both plans (and sometimes cross-sections) of the defensive works and offers, in the form of a conversation between an engineer and a noble amateur, the advantages and disadvantages of each system. This work had five editions between 1702 and 1755.[11]

---

9   Micaela Viglino Davico, *Fortezze Sulle Alpi. Difese dei Savoia nella Valle Stura di Demonte* (Cuneo: L'Arciere, 1989), pp.207–208, 298–303.

10   Christopher Duffy, *The Fortress in the Age of Vauban and Frederic the Great 1660–1789, Siege Warfare Volume 2* (London: Routledge & Kegan Paul, 1985), p.191; Josef von Xylander, 'Festungstürme in Schweden. Ein Beitrag zur Geschichte der Befestigungskunst', *Militaerische Mittheilungen*, vol.1 (1828), p.71.

11   Leonhard Christoph Sturm, *Architectura militaris hypothetico-eclectica, Oder Gründliche Anleitung zu der Kriegs-Baukunst: Aus denen Hypothesibus und Erfindungen derer meinsten und besten Ingenieurs dargestellet* (Nürnberg: Monath, 1702).

3

Prussian Defensive Architecture Before 1740

On ascending to the throne, Frederick inherited a relatively well fortified country. Although Prussia was not on a par with France or the Netherlands in this respect, it fared well in comparison with its neighbours (especially the Polish-Lithuanian Commonwealth). Frederick the Great inherited some 13 fortresses and a dozen more fortified points from his predecessors. However, only a few of these were modern structures, the vast majority having been built during the Great Elector's period of fortifying the country, after the Thirty Years War. Some fortresses were even older – Spandau, Küstrin and Peitz dated back to the mid-sixteenth century.

Pomerania

The region was supplied with two strong and several weaker fortresses. The most important Prussian fortress in the region was Stettin. This fortress had only been in Prussian posses-sion since 1718, when it was captured by the forces of King Frederick William I as a result of a siege during the Great Northern War. Within a short period of time, the town and fortress had risen to become the military and civilian capital of Prussian Pomerania. Great credit for this was due to Cornelius Walrave, who designed and carried out an enormous modernisa-tion of the local fortifications. The work lasted from 1725 to 1740 and involved a great deal of money (costing more than 900,000 thalers) as well as manpower. The earthworks alone involved 500 soldiers as labourers every day; the works were supervised by up to 18 mili-tary engineers – half of the entire Prussian engineering corps of the time.[1] The result of the 15-year reconstruction was an extremely strong fortress. It consisted of extensive defences around the city, the fortifications of Lastadie, and one large, advanced work – Fort Prussia. The main perimeter consisted of a string of eight bastions connected by curtains, largely a remnant of the activities of Swedish engineers. The designer of the Prussian reconstruc-tion, Cornelius Walrave, erected a continuous tenaille counterguard in front of the main perimeter, which bulged out at the two corners of the fortifications to form the intricate outline structures called Forts Wilhelm and Leopold. The only structure that fully deserved

---

1   Udo von Bonin, *Geschichte des Ingenieurkorps und der Pioniere in Preussen* (Berlin: Mittler und Sohn, 1877), vol.1, pp.39–40.

this name, Fort Prussia, was a self-contained defensive structure erected to the south of the town. Its core was in the shape of a five-pointed star, a separate full counterguard was erected in front of it, and it had a continuous covered way. The interior of this small fortress was filled with residential buildings. The last element of the defences was the fortifications of Lastadie. Their shape was generally reminiscent of fortifications from the period of Swedish rule. The Prussian builders' contribution was to transform the outline, which after reconstruction acquired a consistently tenaille character.[2] At the outbreak of the Seven Years War, Stettin had the reputation of being one of Europe's most modern fortresses.

The Kolberg fortress, unlike Stettin, was not in the first league of Prussian fortresses. In 1740, it consisted of a main bastion core, a few outer works and only one advanced work – the Münde Sconce. The core was supplemented with three full bastions, one half-bastion and a small defensive work – the *piatta forma*. These structures were connected to each other by an earth rampart, which, however, did not run all the way around the fortress – its perimeter lacked sections on the Persante River and at Mill Island. The bastion core dated from the time of the fortress reconstruction in 1655–1715, although it was built on the basis of works erected during the Thirty Years War.

In describing the individual works, it is necessary to start with the north-east corner, which was the Halberstadt half-bastion. This structure had an unusual form, with the addition of a redan to the south. The interior of the bastion was filled with a narrow and long cavalier, which housed a gunpowder magazine converted from an old circular medieval bastion. A similar magazine was also located inside the redan. The next bastion, Preussen, had a more typical outline, although it too was far from textbook perfection. It was spacious, and its interior was filled with a narrow cavalier, with an irregular outline that did not repeat the plan of the bastion. This bastion also had a gunpowder magazine, but a more modern one in the form of a small casemate covered with a bomb-proof vault, dating from 1693.[3] The other two bastions, Neu Mark[4] and Pommern, were already devoid of cavaliers. The former had a gunpowder magazine similar to that of the bastion Preussen, but was built in 1715.[5] The curtains connecting the bastions were also an important part of the defence. Almost all of them were double and had a low outer rampart, a fausse-braye. It was missing only at the section between the Halberstadt Bastion and the Münde Thor, but there were fragments where it was doubled. This was the case at the right shoulder of the bastion Preussen and the left flank of the Neu Mark bastion. In addition, in the middle of the curtain between the aforementioned bastions there was a small, four-sided defensive work in the shape of a *piatta forma*. The whole was surrounded by a wide water moat fed by water from the Persante River. The inner perimeter was completed by a weak defensive

---

2   Description of the fortress based on Plan der Vestung Stettin, Geheimes Staatsarchiv Preußischer Kulturbesitz (GStA SPK) XI HA, ref. F 71291.

3   This storehouse, after the reconstruction of 1770–1774, was incorporated into the casemate for the crew of the bastion. During the siege of the fortress in 1807, it was used as quarters for the fortress commander; among others, Gneisenau lived there during the siege. Rubow Otto, Stadt und Festung Kolberg, *Blätter aus Kolbergs Geschichte* (Kolberg: Prangersche Buchhandlung, 1936), p.18.

4   The Neu Mark Bastion originally had a cavalier; it was not removed until 1735, Archiwum Państwowe w Szczecinie, Akta Miasta Kołobrzeg (APS, AMK) ref. 65/202/0/3657, p.23.

5   Anon., *Denkwurdigkeiten der drey Belagerungen Colbergs durch die Russen in den Jahren 1758, 1760 und 1761*, (Frankfurt – Leipzig: Unknown Publisher, 1763), p.12.

Fortress Stettin. (GStA SPK, XI HA ref. F 71291, Plan der Vestung Stettin)

structure protecting the Mill Island, called ravelin Magdeburg. Neither the form nor the location of this structure corresponded to its name – it was an irregularly shaped structure similar to a half-bastion, separated from the main perimeter by the mill canal, without its own moat.[6] The main circuit of fortress Kolberg was covered by several external works. The most important was the Hornwerk Münde, an extensive structure shielding the Münde Thor, as well as the curtain between the bastions Halberstadt and Prussia, which was too long and curved to be protected by a simple ravelin. Such works were sufficient to shield two other curtains – the one between the bastion Preussen and Neu Mark was shielded by the Ravelin Büttow, and the curtain between the bastion Neu Mark and Pommern and the Lauenbourg Thor by the Ravelin Lauenbourg. Both the Hornwerk Münde and the two ravelins dated from the period of the reign of Elector Friedrich Wilhelm and were built from 1655 onwards.

The fortifications on the western side of the Persante river were a separate complex of external works. There was the Hornwerk Geldern, unusual in shape, as it consisted of one half-bastion provided with a cavalier and one full bastion. Its spacious interior was filled with barracks. In addition to the hornwork, this sector of the fortifications included a small structure covering the buildings of the Little Mill – the Ravelin Kleve. The defence works on the west bank of the Persante river were built after 1693 during the reign of Elector Frederick III, later the first king of Prussia, on the site of earlier fortifications dating from the 1630s. The last element of defence was a covered way, occurring both in front of the town fortifications and in front of the fortifications on the west side of the Persante. The section there was particularly interesting, as north of the Hornwerk Geldern there was a wide and long section of covered way reinforced with two extensive redans.

An important source of strength for the Kolberg fortress was the wide moats. The water in them was kept at the right height thanks to masonry batardeau. There were two of them in the moat in front of the main circuit, the first was located at the Halberstadt bastion, the second at the Pommern bastion. The moats of the works on the other side of the Persante were provided with as many as four masonry batardeau. All of them dated from the period of construction of the main defence perimeter, the oldest was in the moat in front of the Halberstadt bastion erected in 1684. [7]

The only advanced work of the Kolberg fortress was the small Münde sconce, defending the entrance to Kolberg harbour. This work was built in 1709, on the site of an older blockhouse destroyed by a storm.[8] It had the outline of a rectangle open from the back, and in its interior, apart from positions for the cannon, there was a building for the crew.[9]

All of Kolberg's defensive facilities had one thing in common – they were made of earth whose ramparts only had masonry revetement in the lower parts. In the fortress there were, apart from the four gunpowder magazines mentioned above, no facilities resistant to artillery bombardment.

---

6   In its place, the Magdeburg Bastion was built during the modernisation after the Seven Years War, which is the only remnant of the inner perimeter of the Colberg fortress preserved today.

7   APS, AMK ref. 65/202/0/3657, p.22.

8   Rudolf Stoewer, *Geschichte der Stadt Kolberg* (Kolberg: Postsche Buchhandlung, 1897), p.133.

9   Description based on a 1768 plan of the work, Plan de La Fortresse de Colberg e de Ses Environs, fait a Potsdam le 6 Octobre 1768, d'Heinze, SBB PK, ref. X 22011.

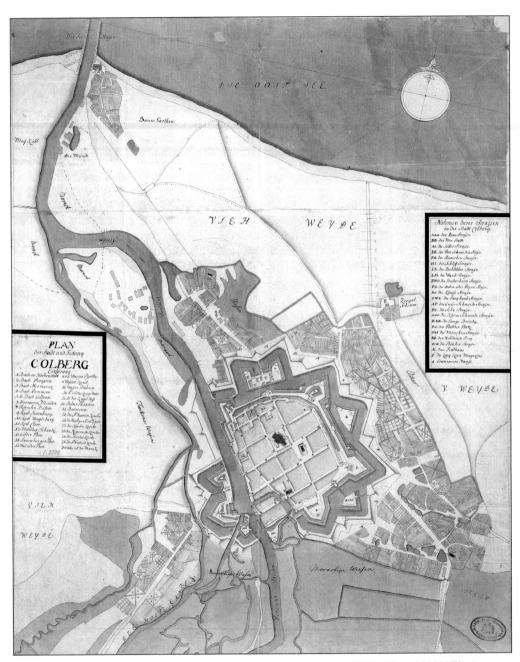

The fortress of Kolberg before the Frederician reconstruction. (SBB PK, Kart. X 22003/2)

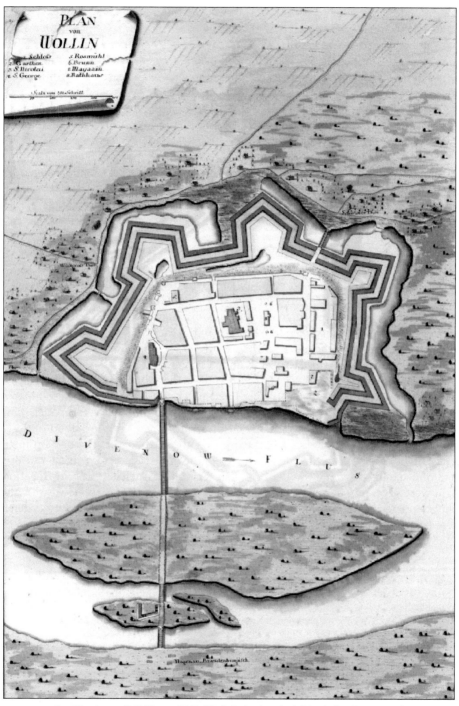

Fortifications of Wollin ca. 1740. (Sächsische Landesbibliothek – Staats- und Universitätsbibliothek Dresden (SLUB, HS Mscr.Dresd.R.30.m,III, p.48)

In addition to fortresses, Pomerania abounded in numerous fortified points, which were a legacy of the wars with the Swedes. The towns of Wollin, Damm, Cammin, Demmin and Anklam all had bastion fortifications. The first town, Wollin, situated on the river Divenau, was surrounded by an earth rampart reinforced with five bastions of different sizes. In front of the rampart was a moat, originally water, but more of a swamp by 1740. Wollin defended a bridge over the river, so in the seventeenth century there were repeated plans to erect strong fortifications on the other bank of the river as well; one design was even made in 1686 by the famous Swedish engineer Eric Dahlberg.[10] In the end, they comprised of just a few small field works.[11]

The next town, Damm, was considered to be the 'tête de pont of Stettin'. Its fortifications consisted of medieval wall and extensive modern fortifications, comprising an eight-bastion main rampart and numerous outer works. In front of the northern bastions there were half-moons and in front of each curtain there were ravelins (seven in total). The whole was surrounded by an almost complete covered way.[12] However, these fortifications were in very poor condition.

The next centre, Cammin, was defended by an extensive rampart reinforced by two large bastions, one half-bastion and one bastion with tenaille. This defensive line stretched from the banks of the Cammin Lagoon south of the town to the marshy meadows north of it. The ramparts were located in front of the suburbs and cut them off, along with the core area of the town, from the surrounding terrain. These fortifications were erected by the Swedes under the command of *Marskalken* Johan Banér in the early 1640s.[13]

The towns to the west of the Oder line had somewhat stronger fortifications. The town of Demmin was defended by a medieval wall and bastion fortifications. The earthen rampart was reinforced by seven bastions. The bastions and the three shorter curtains were provided with a fausse-braye, the rest of the fortified perimeter consisted of a single rampart. The two longer curtains were additionally reinforced by redans, which were smaller than the bastions. Of the few outer works, the ravelin in front of the Kühthor stood out, as well as the tête de pont in the form of a hornwork over the Peene river. The bastion fortifications described were quite outdated at the dawn of the Frederician era, as they were erected in 1648 and designed by the Swedish colonel, Konrad Mardefeld.[14] The fortifications of Anklam were of a similar nature. This town was surrounded by a medieval wall and an incomplete modern rampart (missing on the side of the Peene). The rampart was defended by three bastions, two ravelins and one extensive hornwork. In addition, the section of the

10   Geometrisch Plaan af Staden Wollin, <https://sok.riksarkivet.se/bildvisning/K0039167_00001>, accessed 29 March 2023. Other earlier designs for the reconstruction of the fortifications are also available there.

11   Plan von der Stadt Wollin welche vo. den Königl. Schwedische Tropuppen mit stürmend. Hand… 1759, Książnica Pomorska, ref. K293.

12   I-re Projet sur Damm, 1769, Staatsbibliothek zu Berlin, Preußischer Kulturbesitz, (SBB PK), ref. X 22241–4.

13   Rudolf Spuhrmann, *Geschichte der Stadt Cammin i. Pommern und des camminer Domkapitels* (Cammin i. Pom.: Verlag Von Formazin & Knauff, 1924), p.33.

14   Wilhelm Carl Stolle, *Beschreibung und Geschichte der uralten, ehemals festen, grossen und berühmten Hanseestadt Demmin, wie auch der daran liegenden festen und berühmten Burg Haus Demmin genannt* (Greiswald: Rose, 1772), pp.80–84.

town fortifications on the river side, which lacked a rampart, was protected by two redans extending in front of the medieval wall. The whole was surrounded by a water-filled moat. The bridge over the river was protected by a fortified tête de pont in the form of a lunette reinforced with its own narrow half-moon.[15]

All of these urban fortifications were old and of relatively little use. Some of them, for example Damm, the King allowed to be dismantled before the Seven Years War, others survived longer – until the Seven Years War (Demmin, Anklam). The rest were either demolished after the Napoleonic Wars (Cammin) or underwent a process of natural deterioration. A much more serious role than the aforementioned town fortifications was – paradoxically – played by a small fortified point, the rampart in Peenemünde. This too was a remnant of the wars with Sweden, but its condition was better than that of the previously described fortifications. It was located on the island of Usedom, at the mouth of the Peene into the Baltic Sea. It was of great strategic importance, as it controlled one of the three channels through which ships passed from the Stettin Lagoon to the high seas. This structure, like the vast majority of fortifications in the region, was a remnant of the long-running conflicts with the Swedes that marked the history of Pomerania in the seventeenth and early eighteenth centuries. The fortress was built in 1626 and changed hands several times before 1715. The Prussians finally took control of it after a siege in 1715, as a result of the Great Northern War. At the time of the Prussian takeover, it was a simple four-sided redoubt surrounded by a tenaille counterguard. Inside the work were small barracks for the garrison, a bakery, a brewery, a gunpowder store and numerous cannon and mortar batteries, facing both the land and the waterway. In the 1730s, the rampart was rebuilt on the basis of designs of Cornelius Walrave. The counterguard was re-erected and considerably enlarged. In addition, external works were created – three of the corners of the counter-guard were secured with irregular half moons.[16] These works cost 3,980 thalers.[17]

The other entrenchments defending the river mouths to the Baltic were already in much worse condition. All that is known about the fortifications in Swinemünde is that in 1742 there was one redoubt on the western bank of the Swine river and a battery attached to it, both in poor condition.[18] Cartographic sources from the early eighteenth century still show traces of two similar structures on the east bank. The entrenchments in Divenau were two small, earth and wood structures with a tenaille-bastion outline, located near the mouth of the Divenau river to the sea, on the western bank. They were built by the Swedes during the Thirty Years War and captured by the Prussian army in 1659. Little is known about their condition in 1740, nevertheless they must have existed, since they were still manned by the army during the Seven Years War.[19]

---

15 Plan von Demmin, Plan von Anklam, Johann Georg Maximilian von Fürstenhoff, Sammlung von Festungsplänen. III. Grundrisse von denen Festungen in Teutschland nach seinen X. Hauptcreisen eingetheilet, SLUB, HS Mscr.Dresd.R.30.m,III Bl. 40.

16 Bonin, *Geschichte des Ingenieurkorps*, p.43; Walrave's Plan of the Wall after reconstruction – Peenemünde Plan af Penemündes Skants på Öen Ysedom, <https://sok.riksarkivet.se/bildvisning/ K0006458_00001>, accessed 29 March 2023.

17 Burchardi, Notizen über Festungen, GStA SPK, IV HA, Rep.15 A, No. 806, pp.145–155.

18 von Suchodoletz, Situations Plan von Swinen Munde, SBB PK, ref. X 34845.

19 Die Divenau Schantz 1659, <https://sok.riksarkivet.se/bildvisning/K0007604_00001>, accessed 29 March 2023; vol.d. N., *Geschichte des preußisch schwedischen Krieges in Pommern, der Mark und*

Electoral March

The best fortified land of the Prussian kingdom was, of course, its core – the Electoral March. It was there that the largest number of fortresses, five, were located. The province's defence was also supplemented by numerous towns with bastion fortifications.

By far the strongest stronghold of both the region and the entire kingdom was Magdeburg. The city had belonged to Brandenburg since 1680, but a Brandenburg garrison had already been there from 1666. As early as 1679, *General-Lieutnant* de Maestre drew up the first project to modernise the fortifications, resulting in a large, five-bastion citadel between the city and the Elbe, erected by the engineer *Kapitän* Schmutzen between 1680 and 1702. In the same year, another modernisation began, initiated by Prince Leopold von Anhalt-Dessau, then governor of the city. His plan was to make Magdeburg the strongest fortress in the Prussian state. Based on blueprints drawn up by him, the city was fortified between 1702 and 1713, which resulted in a regular defensive perimeter consisting of 11 bastions (three linked to the rampart and eight detached) and numerous outer works – ravelins and counterguards.

The modernisation began in 1717 on the orders of Frederick William I and was substantially completed in 1725, although due to manpower shortages finishing work continued until the late 1730s. Work on the modernisation was carried out by *Kapitän* Preusser and *Oberst* Walrave, who was designed the reconstruction. According to his plan, a wide envelope consisting of numerous interconnected lunettes was erected in front of the older bastion fortifications of the town. Furthermore, between 1721 and 1725, a star-shaped work, called Fort Berge, was erected south of the town in the suburb of Sudenburg. This structure, on the plan of a four-pointed star, had a redoubt inside whose rampart a casemate for the garrison was built in. This innovative solution became a model for the Frederician modernisation of the Silesian fortresses, carried out two decades later. Another important structure was the Thurm Schanze, a tête de pont completed in 1731, housing a settlement inside, named after the King – Friedrichstadt. This defensive establishment had an irregular hexagonal plan. The main rampart was defended by five small, rounded defensive structures, which can be described as bastei or roundels. They were protected by large half-moons, between which were 4 spacious bastions. The whole was surrounded by a moat, with a covered way in front of it. Particularly interesting features of the Thurm Schanze were these roundels, works which were completely different in outline from the then prevailing fashions and schools of defensive architecture.[20]

A much weaker fortress, although not that inferior to Magdeburg in terms of importance, was Spandau. Its fortifications consisted of a strong citadel and relatively weak city fortifications. The first structure was built between 1560 and 1578, based on the plan and under the supervision of Francesco Chiaramella de Gandino, who designed a small four-bastion defensive structure. Between 1578 and 1583, the work was carried out under the supervision

---

Mecklenburg 1757- 1762: Zugleich als Beitrag zur Geschichte des Siebenjährigen Krieges (Berlin: Mittler und Sohn, 1858), p.81.

20   Bonin, *Geschichte des Ingenieurkorps*, p.39, Friedrich Wilhelm Hoffmann, *Geschichte der Stadt Magdeburg* (Magdeburg: Verlag von Albert Rathte, 1885), pp.258, 358, 372–373; Erich Wolfrom, *Die Baugeschichte der Stadt und Festung Magdeburg* (Magdeburg: Stadt Magdeburg, 1936), pp.28–33.

of Count Rochus zu Lynar, who not only transformed the design of his predecessor, but also planned the erection of extensive new external works. The latter were not erected as planned, with only two small ravelins being built in 1590.[21] The much weaker city fortifications were mostly a remnant of the Thirty Years War, although the first modern fortifications were built as early as the sixteenth century. Substantial reconstruction, however, began in 1627; between 1631 and 1634 it was carried out by the Swedes, then again by the Brandenburgers until the 1640s.[22] At the time of Frederick the Great's assumption of the throne, the fortress consisted of two components: the citadel and the city fortifications. By far the more important of the two was the citadel, a four-bastion defensive structure created in the sixteenth century as a result of the conversion of a medieval castle into a modern fortress. The new Italian School bastions were equipped with cannon casemates in retired flanks, while the citadel's interior was filled with military buildings – barracks, an arsenal and warehouses. The citadel was distinguished by two elements: a high, medieval keep, preserved and integrated into the new defence perimeter, and a beautiful renaissance gate, with brick decorations. The citadel was surrounded by an incomplete envelope, missing only on the side of the Havel lagoon. The town was defended by a medieval wall, in front of which was a straight rampart with two unevenly sized bastions and one salient, in front of which was a moat and an irregular covered way. The strength of this fortress was its location. The citadel to the north, and also partly to the east and west, was protected from regular attack by the floodplain of the Havel and the numerous arms of the Spree there. Only to the south was there a patch of land potentially threatening this fortress.[23]

Together with Spandau, Küstrin was among the oldest bastion fortresses in the Prussian state. It was erected as a refugium for the Elector's family and his officials. A bastion city perimeter was built there from the mid-1560s until the 1590s.[24] The location was perfect for this purpose – the fortress was built on a relatively small, dry islet at the mouth of the Warthe into the Oder. The area was unregulated at the time, so the fortress was surrounded by vast swampy floodplains in addition to the streams of the rivers. The first designs were made by the same Italian architects who built the fortress in Spandau – Chiaramella and Lynar. The core of the fortress, consisting of five bastions, came from the early construction period. All were casemated, with high masonry revetments. The only uncasemated bastion, the Brandenburg, located in the middle of the Oder front, was built between 1672 and 1676 and was the work of the Dutch builder Cornelius Ryckwaert. In the seventeenth century, numerous external works were created in front of the bastion perimeter: in the 1630s and 1640s the ravelins Albrecht and August Wilhelm; and between 1644 and 1645 the new bastion fortified tête de pont. The most important external work was the large hornwork erected between 1688 and 1689 on Gorin, a dry promontory north of the town. This defensive work too had a high masonry revetment, only the casemates were missing. As part of the reconstruction of the fortress from the 1670s to the 1690s, the former fortifications

21   Daniel Burger, *Landesfestungen der Hohenzollern in Franken und Brandenburg* (München: Beck'sche Verlagsbuchhandlung, 2000), pp.295–325.
22   Anton Krüger, *Chronik der Stadt und Festung Spandau* (Spandau: Verlag von Karl Jürgens, 1867), pp.268–270.
23   *Spandav*, 1739, SBB PK, ref. X 33876/10.
24   Burger, *Landesfestungen*, pp.220–232.

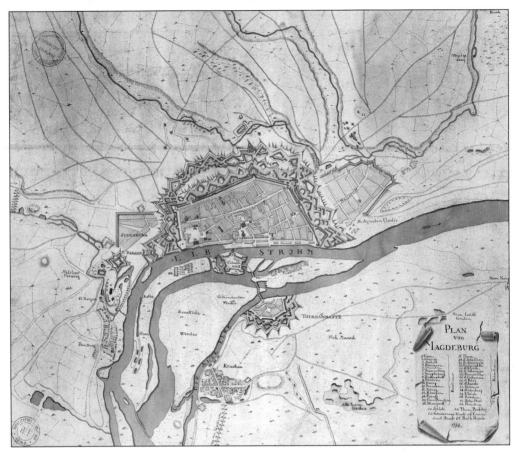

Plan von Magdeburg, 1774. (Bibliothèque nationale de France (BNF), département Cartes et plans, GE DD-2987)

of the fortress's main perimeter were also transformed – the previously open flanks of the bastions were covered with vaults to form closed artillery casemates. At the turn of the seventeenth and eighteenth centuries, another modernisation was carried out; based on the plans of the French military engineer Jean Louis Cayart, the course of the covered way was regularised, the ravelin Christian Ludwig was erected, and the ravelins previously erected were also revetted with masonry. This work was finally completed around 1710. The last work carried out in the fortress before Frederick the Great ascended to the throne was the demolition and rebuilding of the flood-damaged Brandenburg bastion in 1736.[25]

Another town fortress was Peitz, located in the Brandenburg enclave surrounded by Lusatian lands belonging to the Electorate of Saxony. The fortress, founded on earlier

---

25   Grzegorz Podruczny, Marcin Wichrowski, 'Kostrzyn i jego satelity. Brandenburskie fortyfikacje stałe w dorzeczu środkowej Odry od wojny 30-letniej po wojny śląskie', in Bogusław Mykietów, Katarzyna Sanocka, Marceli Tureczek (eds), *Dziennik jeńca i inne szkice. Twierdza Kostrzyn w przeszłości* (Zielona Góra: Księgarnia Akademicka, 2006), pp.14–23.

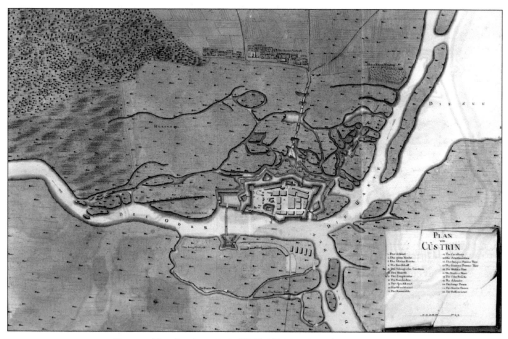

Fortress Küstrin circa 1740. (SLUB, HS Mscr.Dresd.R.30.m,III, 51)

medieval fortifications, was built between 1559 and 1596 as a result of reconstruction work carried out by Duke John of Küstrin and Elector John George of Brandenburg on the basis of designs by the now well-known Italian architects Chiaramella and Lynar. Chiaramella erected the citadel between 1559 and 1562, and also began and led the construction of the town's fortifications until 1570. Lynar rebuilt and strengthened the city's fortifications between 1590 and 1595, rebuilt the citadel's fortifications and planned and partly realised the extensive counterguard surrounding the entire defensive establishment. When completed, the fortress consisted of the Upper Fortress – a citadel defended by four half-bastions provided with retired flanks and artillery casemates – and the Lower Fortress – the town fortification. The town was defended by an earthen, bastioned perimeter consisting of five curtains and four different sized, irregular bastions. In addition, behind each of the bastions there were cavaliers, also of bastion outline, but unlike the ramparts they were masonry and partially casemated. The fortresses was sheltered by numerous external works. The Lower Fortress was sheltered in its entirety by a tenaille and fausse-braye, while a section of the town fortifications was protected by a series of works consisting of irregular ravelins and half-moons. At the time of Frederick II's seizure of power the fortress was already in relatively poor condition.[26]

Driesen stood out from the fortresses already described. This regular, five-bastion fortress was built between 1602 and 1605 as the first defensive structure in Prussia made according to

---

26   Burger, *Landesfestungen*, pp.250–275.

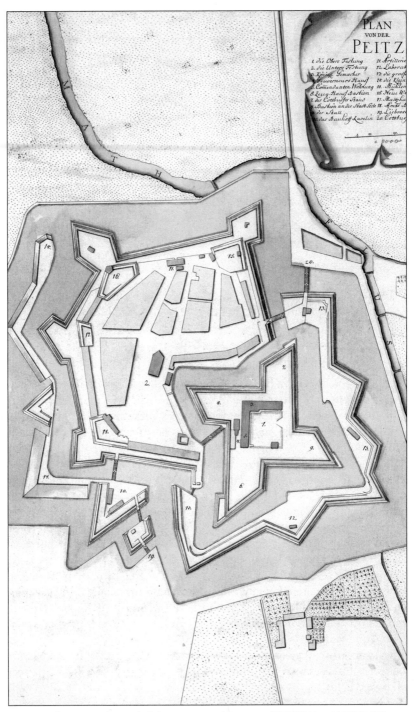

Peitz fortress at the end of the seventeenth century. (SBB PK, Kart. X 31958/17)

the principles of the Old Dutch School of fortification. It was designed by Dutchman Johan de Kampa, who worked for the Brandenburg Electors at the time. However, his fortress turned out to be as misconceived as it was poorly constructed, and shortly after its construction it had to be modernised by erecting two large cavaliers in the middle of the curtains. It underwent further modernisation during the Swedish occupation during the Thirty Years War; among other things, the Swedes erected a wall to protect the chemin des rondes at the base of the ramparts. After the Prussian army took over the fortress again, the cavaliers were removed, and the first external work was erected – a half-moon in front of one of the bastions. Around. 1700, the French engineer Cayart wanted to modernise the fortress and planned to insert tenailles in front of the two curtains, establish a new, regular covered way and build a new tête de pont to defend the bridge over the Netze River.[27] Of these plans, only the last point was realised. The last attempt to modernise the fortress was a project created before 1737 by engineer *Major* Preuss. He proposed to surround the main perimeter with a string of outer works – ravelins and half moons – and to establish a new tenaille defence line to the east of the fortress, but these plans were not realised.[28]

The last Brandenburg fortress was Berlin. This city had extensive bastion fortifications built under Elector Frederick William. They were built on the basis of a design drawn up jointly by the Elector, assisted by his *Generalfeldmarschall* Sparr, and the engineer Memhardt. The fortifications of Berlin were an extensive defensive establishment, incorporating Berlin, Cölln and the suburb of Werder. The defensive perimeter of the capital consisted of 13 bastions connected by curtains. In front of these were five ravelins and a wide moat, in front of which extended a broad covered way. The rampart showed the characteristics of an Old Dutch fortification – it consisted of a main rampart and a lower fausse-braye. Its construction was earthen, only the fausse-braye was provided with sandstone slab revetment. Moats fed by the waters of the Spree were an important part of the defence. The proper water level was maintained by masonry batardeaux, one of which, the Wusterhausener Bär, has been partially preserved to this day. Work on the fortifications began in 1658 but continued until 1683. The main problem was the soft ground, sometimes the ramparts had to be built on marshes.[29]

There were various reasons for the construction of these defences; the most important were the need to protect the capital and the economically important city from devastating events such as those which occurred during the Thirty Years War, and the desire to give it a setting worthy of a European capital. The first reason ceased to play a role during the construction of the fortifications, as in 1675 the Great Elector defeated the Swedes at the Battle of Fehrbellin, thus removing the main threat to the capital. The second lost its importance through the rapid urban development that Berlin experienced at the turn of the seventeenth and eighteenth centuries. As a result of the efforts of Elector Friedrich Wilhelm,

---

27   Plan et Profil de Driesen, Cayart, SBB PK, ref. X 23169/10, X 23169/10 A, B.
28   Podruczny, Wichrowski, 'Kostrzyn', pp.23–25; Marcin Wichrowski, 'Narodziny fortu. Budowa i utrzymanie twierdzy drezdenko w latach 1603–1606', in Grzegorz Podruczny (ed.), *Między zamkiem a twierdzą. Studia nad dziejami fortyfikacji w Drezdenku* (Gliwice: Inforteditions, 2011), pp.26–30.
29   Friedrich Holtze, 'Geschichte der Befestigung von Berlin', *Schriften des Vereins für die Geschichte Berlins*, vol.10 (1874), pp.45–67; Julius Mebes, *Beiträge zur Geschichte des Brandenburgisch-Preussischen Staates und Heeres* (Berlin: Lüderitzsche Verlagsbuchhandlung, 1867), vol.2, pp.189–192.

Driesen fortress at the beginning of the eighteenth century. (SLUB, HS Mscr.Dresd.R.30.m,III, 50)

numerous settlers began to arrive in the city, resulting in the construction of new towns in the immediate foreground of the fortifications. As early as 1673 the town of Dorotheenstadt was founded to the west of the fortifications, and in 1688 another town, Friedrichstadt, was founded to the south of it. Only the first town was integrated into the defence system; in 1688 it was covered by a large hornwork, facing the Tiergarten with a short, two-bastion front, and provided with an unusually long, straight curtain to the south.[30] These new fortifications complicated the defence of the city, as they seriously distorted the hitherto fairly regular defensive perimeter. The quality of the defensive works of this complex was also poor. The southern curtain, which was more than a kilometre long, was not protected by flanking fire for almost its entire length. Although Dorotheenstadt's building regulations still forbade the development of land directly adjacent to the urban fortifications, one cannot help but feel that the defence of Berlin was no longer a priority.[31] This is shown by Friedrichstadt, which did not have any fortifications built to defend it. Due to the successively emerging districts of the rapidly growing city, the belt of fortifications very quickly began to become an obstacle to the free development of Berlin. The first to disappear between 1734 and 1737 were the sections bordering Friedrichstadt.[32] However, the vast majority of the fortress still existed at the time of Frederick's accession to the throne. Its fate, however, was a foregone conclusion, as Frederick the Great considered Berlin's fortifications to be of poor quality.[33]

Fortified towns were an important part of the fortified landscape of the Electoral March. As in Pomerania, they were a legacy of the seventeenth-century wars with Sweden.

The first example is Frankfurt an der Oder. Modern, bastioned fortifications were built here during the Thirty Years War. In 1626, the existence of a fortified tête de pont in the suburb of Dammvorstad (modern Słubice) was mentioned.[34] Between 1626 and 1630 ravelins were erected in front of the Lebuser and Gubener Gates, a rampart between the Lebuser Gate and the Oder and two ravelins extended in front of the line of older fortifications in the section between the Gubener Gate and the river. In 1663, in place of the older work on the at the head of the bridge, construction began on a closed, spacious five-bastion rampart with two gates.[35] A guardhouse was built in its courtyard, as well as two blockhouses and a lazarette building.[36] At the end of the seventeenth century the first sections of the bastion city fortifications were dismantled, only a fragment of the rampart between the Lebuser Gate and the Oder survived, as well as the ravelins in front of the gates, which were not

30   Helmut Zschocke, *Die Berliner Akzisemauer: Die vorletzte Mauer der Stadt* (Berlin: Berlin Story Verlag, 2007), p.13; Hermann von Gansauge, *Das brandenburgisch-preussische Kriegswesen um die Jahre 1440, 1640 und 1740* (Berlin: E. S. Mittler, 1838), pp.73–74.
31   Erika Schachinger, *Die Dorotheenstadt 1673–1708. Eine Berliner Vorstadt* (Köln: Böhlau, 2001), p.84.
32   Carl Eduard Geppert, *Chronik von Berlin von Entstehung der Stadt an bis heute* (Berlin: Ferdinand Rubch Verlag, 1840), vol.2, p.483.
33   Frederic II, *Friedrichs des Zweiten Königs von Preussen bei seinen Lebzeiten gedruckte Werke* (Berlin: Voß und Sohn, Decker und Sohn, 1790), vol.1, p.300.
34   Joachim Schneider, 'Über das Militär in der Dammvorstadt und die Spätere Entwicklung der historischen Militärbauten in Słubice', *Mitteilungen Historischer Verein zu Frankfurt (Oder)*, vol.2 (2005), p.15.
35   Johann Christoph Beckmann, *Kurze Beschreibung der Alten Loeblichen Stadt Franckfurt an der Oder* (Franckfurt an der Oder: Unknown Publisher, 1706), p.96.
36   Wilhelm Jung, Willy Spaß, Friedrich Sloger, *Die Kunstdenkmäler der Stadt Frankfurt a. O.* (Berlin: Meisenbach Riffarth & Co., 1912), p.126.

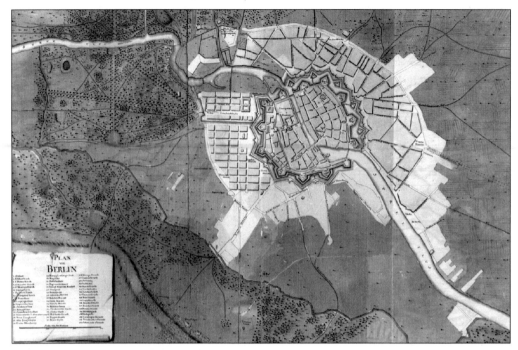

Fortifications of Berlin. (SLUB, HS Mscr.Dresd.R.30.m,III, 53)

dismantled until 1733.[37] At the time of Frederick II's accession to the throne, the fortifications of Frankfurt were reduced to a tête de pont on the west bank of the Oder.

The modern fortifications of another of the March's cities, Landsberg, also date back to the Thirty Years War. At that time, successive Imperial, Swedish and Brandenburgian garrisons turned defences of the city, originally fortified only with a medieval city wall, into a rather strong set of bastion fortifications. The first ones were built in 1631, after Landsberg had been occupied by imperial troops.[38] In 1639 a new fortification was most probably created near the outlet of the bridge on the left bank of the Warthe.[39] This four-sided plan was defended with four bastions, a moat, and palisades. However, the greatest work was carried out by the Swedes, who modernised the fortifications between 1639 and 1650. These defensive works did not last long, but their most important element – the bastion sconce defending the bridge – was still in place when Frederick II took the throne.

Another former fortified town, Crossen, lies at the mouth of the Bober where it flows into the Oder. The floodplains of both rivers provided it with outstanding defensive qualities.

37   Karl Seilkopf, *Frankfurt (Oder) als feste Stadt* (Frankfurt/Oder: Trowitzsch & Sohn, 1932), p.13.

38   Teresa Frąckowiak-Skrobała, Teresa Lijewska, Grażyna Wróblewska, Gorzów Wielkopolski, *Przeszłość i teraźniejszość* (Poznań: Wydawnictwo Poznańskie, 1964), p.63.

39   Bonin, *Geschichte des Ingenieurkorps*, p.7; Galland Georg, *Hohenzollern und Oranien, Neue Beiträge zur Geschichte der niederländischen Beziehungen im 17. und 18. Jahrhundert* (Strassburg: Heitz & Mündel, 1911), p.12.

Its modern fortifications, as in previous cases, were linked to the period of the Thirty Years War. They were built by the Swedes in 1633, 1639 and 1640.[40] The most important work they erected was the regular four-sided tenaille-bastion fortification around the castle. In addition to this, bastion fortifications were also built in front of the medieval walls; a hornwork in front of the Glogau Gate and bastions on the old dyke running around the town. The fortifications here were of a similar scale to the two towns described above. In the middle of the seventeenth century, a project was conceived to transform the town into a regular bastion fortress, but it was not realised.[41] The defences here did not last long. In 1700, part of the fortifications near the castle were demolished.[42] The final dismantling was determined after the occupation of Silesia by Frederick II in 1741. The cannon were transferred to the Silesian fortresses, and the ramparts, which had already been partially removed, were dismantled, retaining only the rampart surrounding the castle.[43]

Western Provinces

Strong Prussian strongholds were also located in the western provinces of the Prussian state – three located on the periphery, close to the border with the United Provinces (Wesel, Jülich and Geldern) and two closer to the centre of the German-speaking area – Minden and Lippstadt in Westphalia.

By far the strongest was the fortress at Wesel, in Prussian possession since 1680. Before 1689, its fortifications were built by the French engineer Dupuy l'Espinasse, who, in addition to strengthening the town's defences, designed a large, regular five-bastion citadel, construction of which began in 1687. From 1689 to 1699, the work was led by the French engineer Corbin, who gained some infamy for embezzling materials intended for the construction of a fortress. In addition, other French architects worked there – Louis de Cayart at the turn of the seventeenth century and Jean de Bodt from 1719 onwards. Work on the fortress was then taken over by Cornelius Walrave, who was brought to Prussia in 1720.[44] The work carried out by these engineers turned Wesel into a powerful fortress. By 1740, the town was defended by five bastions of different outlines and two half-bastions. All, except one, were provided with retired, concave flanks and orillons. The citadel, a regular work of the Vauban school, had smaller, though similar in plan, bastions. In front of its curtains there were tenailles and ravelins. Both the city and the citadel were surrounded by counter-guards. The citadel had a single counter-guard on the river side, and a double and in some places even quadruple one on the foreground side. The counterguard surrounding the city was also single on the river side and double or triple on the foreground side.[45]

40   Eduard Ludwig Wedekind, Geschichte der Stadt und des Herzogthums Crossen, (Crossen: Verlag von J.C. Riep, 1840), pp.120–121, 124.
41   Stadt Crossen 1649, SBB PK, ref. X 22170.
42   Carl Obstfelder, Chronik der Stadt Crossen, (Crossen, Verlag von Richard Zeidler, 1895), p.93.
43   Wedekind, Geschichte, p.168.
44   Priesdorf, Soldatisches Führerthum (Hamburg: Hanseatische Verlagsanstalt 1937–42), vol.1, pp.230–232.
45   Plan der Stadt und Citadelle Wesel c. 1739, SBB SKP X 3608/8.

The fortress of Geldern was not as strong as Wesel, but it also deserves attention. It was captured by the Prussians in 1703 and officially granted to them in 1713 as a result of the Peace of Utrecht. The improvements made afterwards made it a strong fortress. By 1704, the town was surrounded by a regular bastion rampart equipped with nine large bastions, with a ravelin in front of each curtain. A regular covered way, in front of which another moat was dug, was established around the entire fortress. In front of it, during the siege in 1703, large redoubts, later preserved as permanent works, were erected. Bomb-proof gunpowder magazines were created in two bastions and three ravelins, and in front of the covered way on the side of the road to Wesel was a string of tenaille counter-guards betraying some similarity to the later Fort Leopold in Stettin[46]. The modernisation of the fortress was led by the engineers Lancizolles and Petri, and, after the latter's arrest, Balbi and Foris. Work was still in progress in 1737.[47]

Another fortress, Jülich, was, together with Spandau, Kostrzyn and Peitz, among the oldest bastion fortresses of the Prussian state. The defences of Jülich consisted in 1740 of a town fortification and a citadel. The citadel was a four-sided defensive work defended by four bastions with retired flanks. A ravelin was erected in front of each of the citadel's curtains, and in front of two of the bastions were extensive half-moons. The city was defended by three bastions and one half-bastion, while the curtains were protected by four ravelins. The whole – both the city and the citadel – was surrounded by a common strong covered way.[48]

Lippstadt was also a strong fortress. Its defences in the mid-eighteenth century consisted of 12 bastions connected by curtains. The ramparts were built according to the principles of the Old Dutch School; they were earthen, with a fausse-braye, preceded by a wide moat. The curtains were protected by ravelins, and the fronts of some bastions were covered by counter-guards. The whole fortress was surrounded by an elaborate covered way, double in places, preceded by a moat. In front of this belt of fortifications were several small, advanced works.[49]

By far the weakest of the fortresses in the western Prussian possessions was Minden. The town had a main rampart, erected in front of the old medieval wall, defended by 10 bastions of varying size and outline. In addition, there were older defensive works. The bridge over the Weser was defended by a large bastion, and smaller bastions were located in the northern curtain. The rampart was preceded by a moat of varying width, in front of which five ravelins were placed. A covered way ran in front of the moat, but large sections were missing on the river side and in front of the northern curtain. In the northern part of the fortifications, in the corner between the riverbank and the northern curtain, there was a separate settlement, Fischerstadt, which also had its own fortifications, although only on the foreground side – a bastion, two half-bastions, a moat fed by the waters of the Weser, and a full covered way. The stone bridge over the river was defended on the far bank by a crownwork surrounded by a moat and a full covered way.[50] In the 1730s

---

46   Plan de la Forteresse de Güeldren, SBB PK, ref. X25048.
47   Bonin, *Geschichte des Ingenieurkorps*, pp.41–42.
48   Explication du plan de la ville et forteresse de Juliers avec la citadelle. SBB PK, ref. X 27527.
49   Plan der Festung Lippstadt, c. 1750, SBB PK, ref. X 28908.
50   Plan de Minden dans l'etat on cette place se trouvet actuelement, SBB PK, ref. X 30239.

there were plans to strengthen Minden's fortifications. One surviving design envisaged surrounding the entire fortress with a wide, strong, and regular covered way;[51] the other, by Walrave, envisaged more serious transformations. The engineer was commissioned by the King to redesign the city's fortifications so that they could be defended with the strength of just one battalion. In his plan of October 1729, he proposed abandoning the town's fortifications, transforming Fischerstadt into a kind of citadel and, above all, completely rebuilding the defences across the bridge. These were to be replaced by a large fort with a five-pointed star plan. Its corners on the side of the river and the bridge were to take the form of half-bastions – retired and with concave flanks, and orillons. In front of these, tenaille were to be built, with a semi-circular roundels in front of them to cover the bridge. In front of the fort, an extensive envelope consisting of two ramparts was to be built. In addition, short sections of covered way were to be built in front of the sections of the envelope that met the river.[52]

East Prussia

East Prussian was by far the least fortified of all Prussian territories at the time. It had two weak fortresses, Pillau and Memel, and few fortified cities, of which the capital Königsberg should be mentioned as the most noteworthy.

The most important stronghold was Pillau. Its first bastion fortifications were built at the beginning of the seventeenth century, when the local strait leading from Vistula Lagoon to the Baltic was secured with a sconce. This structure is known from to two drawings made in 1604. It was a four-bastion, square in plan sconce, whose ramparts were reinforced by a lining of wooden beams.[53] Later, another sconce was erected on this site by the Swedes, after Gustavus Adolphus with his army landed at Piława in 1626. The permanent fortress, however, was built during the reign of Elector Frederick William, between 1636 and 1651, at a cost of 250,000 thalers. It was a regular five-bastion enceinte, reinforced by five ravelins. The main rampart had a fausse-braye. The bastion core and two of the ravelins had masonry revetment. In later years, after the completion of the fortress, work was done to supplement and repair the revetment, damaged by water. In the years 1688–1698, a half-moon was erected in front of the King bastion, and masonry revetments were added to two more ravelins, a gunpowder storehouse was built in the King bastion, casemates constructed in the curtain between the King and Queen bastions, as well as numerous buildings inside – the gate, soldiers' barracks and the commandant's house. Further reconstruction was carried out on the basis of a design created after 1702 by the French engineer Peter de Montargues. This project included the regulation of the covered way and glacis, the erection of further external works – three lunettes and a half-moon, and the transformation of some already

51   Minden, SBB PK, ref. X 30239–1.
52   Minden, SBB PK, ref. X 30239–3.
53   Blockhauss oder Vöstung Bülaw genandt. Zwischen dem Königsberger Hafen, und der offenbarr See. 1604, Herzog August Bibliothek Wolfenbüttel, Handschriften, Signatur/Inventar-Nr.: 1.6.1a Aug. 2°, Bl. 21–22.

existing buildings. In addition, before 1740, new structures were built inside the fortress – an arsenal, a garrison church, and a food storehouse.[54]

Memel had a slightly larger defensive complex. The fortifications consisted of the castle and the defences of the city. The first modern fortifications were built by Elector George William, who surrounded the castle with a rectangular rampart with four bastions after 1625. A new rampart was also built at this time to surround the town. These first fortifications were earthen; it was not until the second half of the seventeenth century that they were secured with masonry by order of Elector Frederick William. The result was an earthen rampart with a fausse-braye, defended by three bastions and two half-bastions.[55] In the first decade of the eighteenth century, a major expansion of Memel's fortifications began; as with Pillau, the designer was Montargues.[56] The plan was to erect a tenaille-bastion envelope in front of the bastion fortifications of the castle and to seriously strengthen the city defences. The plan was to extend the perimeter by one bastion, ravelins were to be built in front of the curtains of the city ramparts, and a half-moon was to be built in front of one of the bastions. An extensive covered way was to be created in front of the whole; near the river, one of the protruding corners of the covered way was to be greatly extended. On the other side of the river, the ravelin defending the bridge was to be reinforced with two more, linked by an extensive covered way. In front of these fortifications, another work was planned – an extensive tenaille, provided with its own covered way.[57] However, little of these plans were realised, and by 1740 it had only been possible to rebuild half of the envelope in front of the castle fortifications, to delineate the outer works in front of the town, and to begin to raise them up. The condition of the older fortifications also left much to be desired – one of the bastions had a large breach in the corner.[58]

One of the largest defence complexes of the Prussian state was Königsberg. Indeed, this city was surrounded by an extremely long rampart with a total length of almost 15 kilometres. The city was defended by 26 bastions and eight half-bastions. The works were made of earth, the rampart was provided with a fausse-braye preceded by a wide, moat, in front of which there was a covered way. The fortifications were designed by the mathematician Professor Johann Strauß and built from 1626 onwards. Despite their extent, the town's defences were not strong, quite the contrary. Indeed, to fully man the fortifications would have required far more manpower and materiel than was available in the fortress. In addition to the main ramparts, Königsberg also had the Friedrichsburg citadel, also sometimes referred to as a fort, located at the exit of the Pregel river from the city. It was built after 1657 and based on a design by Christian Otter.[59] In 1740, the condition of the Königsberg fortifications was

---

54   Hoburg R., 'Geschichtlich-militärische Nachrichten über die Festung Pillau', *Der neuen Preußischen Provinzial Blätter dritte Folge*, vol.2 (1858), pp.232–238.

55   Kurt Burk, *Handbuch der Festungen des Historischen Deutschen Ostens* (Osnabrück: Biblio Verlag, 1995), pp.37–38.

56   Plan de la Ville et de la citadelle de Memel, dans l'estat que les Ouvrages sont a present avec a luy des nouveaux Ouvrages que l'on projette du faire suivant les orders de sa Majeste pour mettre cette place dans un bon Estat de defence, Montargues, 15.10. 1701, SBB PK, ref. X 29956.

57   Plan de Memmel, SBB PK, ref. X 29960/3.

58   C. Rucker, Plan und beschreibung der Vestung und Citadelle Memmel, SBB PK, ref. X 29961.

59   Erhardt Traugott, *Die Geschichte der Festung Königsberg/Pr 1257–1945* (Würzburg: Holzner Verlag, 1960), pp.14–18.

poor – the rampart was indeed fully preserved, but the entire southern section, up to Fort Friedrichsburg, had no moat or fausse-braye at all. In other sections the outer works were poorly preserved.[60] The only real defensible work was the citadel, a four-bastion structure defended by an earth rampart provided with a fausse-braye on the town side. The whole was surrounded by a moat, fed by the waters of the Pregel. Two of the bastions had cavaliers, there was a gate in the curtain on the town's side, and a ravelin in front of it. In one of the curtains there was a casemate. The inner courtyard was filled with garrison buildings: gunpowder store, arsenal, church, commandant's house, smithy, prison.[61]

Conclusion

The section above has described the fortifications of previous periods of Prussian defensive architecture and illustrated that it was extremely varied. The existing fortress complexes were one of the important factors that shaped the development of Prussian fortifications during the reign of Frederick II. The most important were, of course, those fortresses that were modernised in the first decades of the eighteenth century – Stettin, Magdeburg and Wesel. The ideas applied there were developed in Neisse, Glogau, Glatz and other fortresses built and modernised by Frederick the Great. This does not mean, however, that the older fortresses contributed nothing to the development of Frederician fortified architecture. On the contrary, the fact that Frederick was familiar with the heavily fortified strongholds at Küstrin or Spandau, certainly influenced the renaissance of interest in casemates that occurred during his reign. Doubtless other older fortresses also had elements of potential interest that inspired the King and his engineers during the intensive expansion of fortresses after 1740.

---

60   Plan der Stadt Königsberg in Preußen, SBB PK, ref. X 28073.
61   Plan und beschreibung der Vestung und Citadelle Memmel, C. Rucker, SBB PK, ref. X 29961.

4

Frederick the Great's Experience of Fortress Warfare

The role of fortress warfare during the period in which Frederick II acted as a military commander, compared to the previous era, diminished considerably. As late as the time of Louis XIV and Vauban, the capture of fortresses was often the main objective of campaigns, the siege of Turin in 1706 being the best example. However, during the wars waged by Frederick II, field battles were the most important events. Nevertheless, the Prussian ruler was not only a practitioner of manoeuvre warfare, but he also acquired some skill in siege warfare. This chapter will outline his experiences that had a particularly strong influence on the formation of Prussian fortress architecture in the period under discussion.

Frederick's Education in Fortification

Before describing the King's practical experience in this field, it is necessary to show what he learned about it during his education. As a prince and heir to the throne, Frederick was introduced to military matters from a very early age. At the age of seven, he was given two tutors to introduce him to various sciences useful in warfare. According to his father's instructions, Frederick was to learn mathematics, drawing and making plans, the essentials of fortification, setting up camps, and other military science. He was introduced to subjects relating to fortifications by an officer from the engineer corps, who seems to have been the military tutor that stayed with Frederick the longest. This was *Major* Wilhelm Senning, who was by the prince's side from the time he was seven years old until he assumed the throne. Moreover, he was also to remain Frederick's companion during the Rheinsberg period of his life, and to accompany him in his military studies.[1] Unfortunately, very little is known about this figure, who seems to have had a very strong influence on the King's knowledge of fortifications.

---

1   Friedrich Wilhelm Schubert, 'Beiträge zur Erziehungsgeschichte Friedrichs des Grossen', *Preußische Provinzial-Blätter*, vol.4 (1830), p.18; Johann David Erdmann Preuss (ed.), *Oeuvres de Frederic le Grand* (Berlin: Decker, 1846–1856), vol.27, pp. XII-XIII; Heinrich Rütjes, *Geschichte des brandenburg-preußischen Staates: von d. ältesten Zeiten bis auf unsere Tage* (Schaffhausen: Hurtersche Buchhandlung, 1859), p.355.

Another person who played an important role in the young Frederick's education about fortifications was Prince Leopold von Anhalt Dessau. It is worth taking a closer look at Prince Leopold, as the experience he gathered was, in some respects, crucial to Frederick the Great's later activities. The prince took part in 16 sieges, which in itself testifies to the fact that he had accumulated a great deal of experience which he was able to pass on to the young student of the art of war. Even more important is the fact that during four of these sieges – Namur in 1695, Venloo and Roermonde in 1702 and Bonn in 1703 – he had the opportunity to watch one of the most important military engineers of the time, Menno van Coehoorn, at work. As we shall see below, the methods of capturing the fortress used by Frederick II and his officers were a creative development of Coehoorn's ideas. Importantly, Prince Leopold did not just theoretically introduce the later king to the arcana of siege warfare. Indeed, he accompanied him on his expedition to the Rhine in 1734, during the War of the Polish Succession. Frederick II then observed his first ever siege, a French attack on the imperial fortress of Philipsburg. However, the event did not add much to his education, as the actions of the Imperial troops, which included a Prussian contingent, were limited to blocking the French siege corps to no avail. That same year, Old Dessauer accompanied Frederick, on what appears to have been more than one occasion, to Stettin, where Frederick viewed the newly built fortifications. During these visits, Leopold was to teach the young heir to the throne about fortress warfare – the attack and defence of fortresses. These teachings were to appeal to Frederick so much that he asked the prince to write them down.[2] The result was the work *Deutlich und ausführliche Beschreibung, Wie eine Stadt soll belagert werden*, published in Dessau in 1737. This text is very informative. It is no work of a fortification theorist or even an engineer, but merely a meticulous instruction of all the actions of an entire siege army during a hypothetical siege, spread over 85 pages.[3]

Peacetime Siege Exercises and Experiments

Frederick the Great only acquired practical skills in fortress warfare in the period after his accession to the throne. For the most part, this happened through the sieges in which he took part, and to a lesser extent as a result of peacetime exercises and experiments. However, the latter will be presented first.

The most important exercises that influenced the formation of the Frederician practice of siege warfare took place during the peace between the Second Silesian War and the outbreak of the Seven Years War. On at least two occasions, siege exercises initiated by the King and partly also conducted by him, took place around Potsdam. The first involved an artillery attack, the second a mine war.

---

2   Max Jähns, *Geschichte der Kriegswissenschaften vornehmlich in Deutschland, Bd.3, Das XVIII. Jahrhundert seit dem Auftreten Friedrichs des Großen 1740–1800* (München-Leipzig: Verlag von Oldenbourg, 1891), pp.1922, 1739; A. von Witzleben, 'Das Verhältniss des Fürsten Leopold von Anhalt zu Friedrich dem Großen', *Jahrbücher für die Deutsche Armee und Marine, Bd.8*, Berlin 1873, p.94

3   Leopold von Anhalt-Dessau, *Deutliche und ausführliche Beschreibung, Wie eine Stadt soll belagert werden* (Dessau; Unknown Publisher, 1737).

The 1752 Potsdam siege exercises were organised between 24 and 31 July 1752. On the engineering corps side, they were commanded by *Oberst* Johann Friedrich von Balbi, who was assisted by *Kapitän* Simon Lefèbvre. The artillery was represented by 25 officers and non-commissioned officers and 72 lower-ranking soldiers; they had six 3-pounder guns and two 10-pounder mortars at their disposal. Nineteen infantry battalions also took part in the exercise. A pre-erected practice fortress polygon with bastions and ravelins was attacked.

The exercises were intended to be a kind of review lesson for Prussian officers rather than an experiment or exercise for the King himself. All the officers who were in Potsdam at the time turned up for the exercises as observers. At the very beginning, the King gave them a short lecture on how fortresses were captured, and the mistakes made by the commanders who had defended the fortresses captured by him. In order for the officers to understand the workings of a siege, the King ordered that all the related activities be carried out during the daytime and not, as in a real siege, after dark. Also, the start of the practice siege could not commence without royal participation. Frederick inspected the fortification under attack and pointed out to the engineers the points from which they were to plot the course of the first parallel; thereafter, the King's activity did not slacken either.

The exercises simulated a typical Vauban regular siege. Successive parallels were built, various types of approach trenches were dug, and batteries (dismounting, ricocheting, breach) were established, from which test shots were also fired. In addition, various forms of active attack and defence of the fortress were practised – sorties and their repulsing, and storming the breach. The simulated attack was concluded with a formal surrender with its terms defined as if it were a real siege. The King, extremely pleased with the results of the exercise, distributed expensive gifts to the outstanding officers. The artillery commander, *Major* von Dieskau, received a gold snuffbox and the Order Pour le Mérite. He gave the highest marks and rewards to the engineers: *Oberst* von Balbi, to whom he awarded an annual salary supplement of 500 thalers, and *Kapitän* Lefèbvre, who received an allowance of 300 thalers.[4]

In the exercises described here, all types of attack on the fortress were utilised, except for a mine attack. Its only element was a demonstration of the operation of a fougasse, which, on the King's orders, was carried out on the penultimate day of the exercise. This demonstration was intended to teach officers where to plant such mines and the effect of their use.

Two years later, another exercise was held in Potsdam, which this time focused mainly on mine warfare. Actually, this was not an exercise, but more of an experiment to demonstrate the effectiveness of a new mine technique newly invented in France – the globe of pressure (*globe de compresion*). This technique had been experimentally validated in France in 1753 by its creator, Bernard Forest de Belidor, and the trial carried out in Potsdam was to confirm the results of the French experiment. Interestingly, Belidor corresponded with the Prussian king and engineers even before the results of the trials were published, so that the Prussians gained access to this knowledge very quickly and from the source. The experiment was carried out on Frederick's orders and in his presence by a participant in the previous 1752 exercise, Simon Lefèbvre, who also corresponded with Belidor. The rehearsal consisted of detonating a charge of 3,800 pounds of gunpowder, set about five metres underground.

---

4   Louis von Malinowsky, 'Friedrichs des Großen praktische Instruktion im Festungskriege im Jahre 1752', *Archiv für die Officiere der Königlich Preußischen Artillerie und Ingenieur Korps*, vol.3 (1836), pp.234–242; Bonin, *Geschichte des Ingenieurkorps*, pp.211–212.

Prior to this, three timber-lined underground galleries were made to mimic sections of countermine galleries. The explosion formed a six-metre-deep crater, more than 20 metres in diameter, and caused the complete or partial destruction of the test galleries. The results of this experiment pleased the King, who gained a new and effective method of capturing the fortress, and the engineer who carried out the experiment thus gained royal favour.[5] Both the method and the engineer were to be tested in practice just eight years later, during the siege of Schweidnitz in 1762.

Both of the events described above were perfectly in line with the Frederician practice of regular military manoeuvres, through which the Prussian army maintained a high level of combat training. However, while the annual great infantry and cavalry manoeuvres – which took place in the vicinity of both Berlin and Silesia – resulted in the creation of excellent infantry and cavalry, which in battles and skirmishes was unrivalled in the whole of Europe at the time, the technical army manoeuvres did not result in a significant increase in the fortress warfare competence of either the King or his engineer and artillery corps. This is perfectly demonstrated by the events of the Seven Years War. Before turning to this, however, it is appropriate to say a few more words about siege warfare exercises after 1763.

During this period, simulated attacks on fortresses were definitely more common. However, in the first years after the war, despite the demonstrated inexperience of some siege personnel, exercises did not take place. Miners, whose competence was at its lowest, were again – as before the Seven Years War – thrown into fortress construction work, as happened with the construction of the fortress at Silberberg, whose moats almost had to be made entirely by blasting. The miners had even more tasks than before the war. So, there was not enough time to improve their skills in mine warfare. It was only in the 1770s, after the main wave of construction work had passed, that regular, annual mine exercises began to be organised.[6] The first took place at Potsdam in 1774, followed by those at Glatz in 1775, 1776, 1780 and 1784, at Neisse in 1777 and at Berlin in 1782.[7] The latter, which was conducted by *Major* Georg Friedrich Tempelhoff at the King's behest between the villages of Gesund Brunen and Reinikendorf, were combined manoeuvres – the artillery exercises in the attack on the fortress were complemented by a mine attack.[8]

Siege Warfare

During the reign of Frederick the Great, his army was involved dozens of times in battles for fortresses. The Prussian king, as commander-in-chief of the army, was of course more or less involved in each of them, but his personal participation was limited to a few instances.

5   Bonin, *Geschichte des Ingenieurkorps*, p.68; Simon Lefèbvre, *Versuch über die Minen* (Wien: Trattnern, 1785), pp.126–136.
6   Eugen Polap, 'Die Anwendung von Minen im Belagerungskrieg. Betrachtungen aus der Sicht des 18. Jahrhunderts', in Volker Schmidtchen (ed.), *Sicherheit und Bedrohung – Schutz und Enge. Gesellschaftliche Entwicklung von Festungsstädten. Beispiel Stade* (Wesel: Deutsche Gesellschaft für Festungsforschung, 1987), pp.195 et seq.
7   Lahr, Versuch über die Anwendung der Minen im Belagerungs Kriege oder militairischer Theil der Minierkunst, rkps. 1798, copy from the archives of the TTPF in Toruń.
8   SBB PK, ref. Man 1692.

During the First Silesian War, he took part in two sieges of Neisse and one of Brieg in 1741, while during the Seven Years War, on the other hand, he was involved in attacks on the fortresses of Breslau (1757), Olomouc (1758), Dresden (1760) and Schweidnitz (1762).

The Sieges of Neisse

His first personal experience of fortress warfare was the brief siege of Neisse in January 1741. The Prussian army attacked this fortress less than a month after the attack on Silesia. On 12 January 1741, the Prussians had it encircled and were preparing to capture it. However, instead of following the procedure of a regular attack, Frederick ordered the bombardment of the city. He expressed his motives in a letter to Prince Leopold: 'I am now in Neisse, which, owing to the time of year, I cannot besiege regularly; all that remains for me is to bombard, as it is a nest of papists and is poorly garrisoned with troops'. From 14 to 19 January the construction of the first siege battery continued. On 18 January, the Prussians demanded the surrender of the fortress, which the Austrian commandant refused. As a result, the bombardment began on 19 January, initially with two 12-pounder cannon and two 50-pounder mortars, but the battery was soon reinforced with another six cannon and eight mortars. The following day, in order to increase the effectiveness of the shelling, the battery was moved closer to the city, to the site where Fort Prussia was erected two years later. The attack lasted only a short time, until 21 January, but during those three days 1,200 mortar bombs and more than 3,000 incendiary projectiles fell on the city, causing numerous fires. In spite of this, the fortress did not surrender, and the King had to abandon the siege due to the time of year.[9]

Slightly longer was the second siege of this fortress, which took place in the autumn of the same year. It occurred after the signing of the so-called Klein Schellendorf Convention. This was a secret agreement between the Prussians and Austrians, under which the latter were to surrender the fortress of Neisse and part of Upper Silesia after a sham siege, while the former undertook not to attack Maria Theresa's troops so that they could concentrate on fighting the remaining enemies. Immediately after the signing of the convention, preparations began for the sham defence of the Neisse. Maintaining the secrecy of the agreement on the division of Silesia and the fate of the city was vital. The Austrians wanted to redeploy as many troops as possible to threaten Bohemia (without alerting the attackers), and the Prussians feared a break with France. As a result of the agreement, some ammunition supplies were sent back from Neisse to Glatz, and it was also almost completely cleared of troops. The new commander of the fortress, *Oberst-Lieutenant* Maximilian von Krottendorf, initially had only 733 soldiers at his disposal. He was unable to man all the positions and put up even a pretence of resistance, so on 14 October he received a small reinforcement of 200 soldiers. The Prussians approaching the fortress and demanded its surrender. After the commandant refused, they began preparations for the siege. Flooded foregrounds were drained, work was done to divert the flow of the Biele river to the Glatzer Neisse, and the siege entrenchments were begun. The first of these was completed on 20 October, and immediately began firing

9   Ferdinand Minsberg, *Geschichtliche Darstellung der merkwürdige Ereignisse in der Fürstenzhums Stadt Neisse* (Neisse: Verlag von Wangenfield, 1834), pp.180–182; Grosser Generalstab, *Die Kriege Friedrichs des Großen, Th. 1, Der Erste Schlesische Krieg* (Berlin: Königliche Hofbuchhandlung, 1890), vol.1, pp.266–271; Samuel F. Seydel, *Nachrichten über vaterländische Festungen und Festungskriege* (Leipzig Züllichau: Darmannsche Buchhandlung, 1819–24), vol.2, pp.275–278.

towards the town. *Generalmajor* Cornelius Walrave, who later became the engineer behind the rebuilding of its fortifications, arrived at Neisse that day and took command of the siege work. Along with him, an artillery park arrived from Brieg, including 15 mortars weighing 50 pounds. On 22 October the Prussians received another shipment of guns, this time four-teen 24-pounder cannon.

On the night of 23–24 October, the formal siege began with the digging of the first parallel. A large artillery battery was also built, which was initially armed with 15 guns (five mortars and 10 cannon) and later 42 guns (10 mortars and 32 cannon). After the intense shelling of 29 and 30 October, Frederick II renewed his proposal for the honourable surrender of the fortress. The commandant initially rejected the proposal, but the next day, the 31st, after a brief resumption of fighting, he acceded to the offer. Neisse was to pass into Prussian hands on 2 November, thus fulfilling the commitment to a 14-day defence. A company of Prussian grenadiers garrisoned the Customs Gate on the 1st, while the garrison left the city the following day, leading four 6-pounders and two 10-pounders.[10] During this siege, the Prussian ruler was present in the Neisse area, but had limited influence. Before the shelling began, he gave orders to his artillerymen to spare the city buildings as far as possible, which was obvious in view of the already agreed handover of Neisse to the Prussians; moreover, he was involved in setting the terms of surrender.

The Siege of Brieg

Much more serious was the siege of Brieg. This fortress was in a poor state in 1741. It consisted of two masonry bastions connected by a curtain, built in the mid-sixteenth century by Italian architects; the rest of the fortress perimeter was erected during the Thirty Years War, and was mostly earthen. The fortress was not particularly strong, as the end of hostilities in the second half of the seventeenth century saw only basic repair work, with no decision made to extend it or strengthen it. Nevertheless, it was one of the most important fortresses in Silesia, mainly due to its location on the Oder, the region's most important navigable river.[11]

The first Prussian troops arrived on 10 January, three weeks after the Prussians entered Silesia. The fortress, which initially had a rudimentary garrison of one infantry company, was reinforced and by early January had 2,000 men and was defended by 61 guns and nine mortars.

The first blockade of the fortress lasted to 7 April, when *General-Lieutenant* Kleist's troops were recalled from under Brieg due to the approaching Austrian army of *Feldmarschallleutnant* Wilhelm Reinhard von Neipperg. The break in the blockade was used by the fortress commander to bring in additional supplies, although the fortress was well enough supplied anyway to be able to supply the troops of the main Austrian army.

---

10   Carl von Duncker, *Oesterreichischer Erbfolge-Krieg 1740–1748* (Wien: Velrag von L. W. Seidel & Sohn, 1896), vol.2, pp.528–536.

11   The description of the siege of the fortress is based on the most detailed one in Grosser Generalstab, *Die Kriege 1890–93*, vol.1, pp.255–256, 280–281, 378, and Grosser Generalstab, *Die Kriege 1890–93*, vol.3, pp.22–33. It is supplemented by information from Seydel, *Nachrichten*, vol.2, pp.285–288, Louis v. Malinowsky, Robert v. Bonin, *Geschichte der brandenburgisch-preussischen Artillerie* (Berlin: Verlag von Duckner und Humbolt, 1840–42), vol.2, pp.198–199.

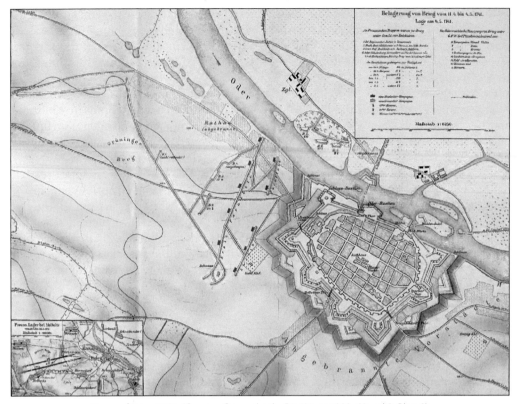

Siege of Brieg 1741. (Grosser Generalstab, *Die Kriege 1890–93*, vol.3, Plan 3)

After the Battle of Mollwitz, which was fought not far from Brieg, and the Austrian defeat, the Prussians again surrounded the fortress and began preparations to capture it. The siege corps was commanded by *General-Lieutenant* von Kalckstein. It consisted of nine infantry battalions and six cavalry squadrons.[12] The bulk of the force had already appeared at the fortress on 11 April. Most of the corps' troops stood on the south bank of the Oder, with two battalions and two squadrons on the north bank. Two bridges across the Oder were established for communication between the groups. The siege corps was protected from a possible attack by the main Prussian army, which was camped in the area. The camp is well known through surviving cartography and iconography. It was protected on the south side by a belt of field fortifications having the form of an earth rampart, reinforced at regular intervals with redans and works with a tenaille outline. These works were permanently manned with artillery. The rampart of the camp near the village of Paulau reached the bridge over the Oder, which was additionally fortified, with a thick wall on the southern bank, and a simple redoubt on the northern bank.[13]

---

12   According to Seydel, *Nachrichten*, vol.2, p.287, The Gotz andGravenitz regiments, plus battalions from Alt-Bork, Kalckstein, Buddenburg, Reibniz and Saldern regiments.

13   Plan von der Belagerung der Festung Brieg, SBB PK, ref. Da 13.25 k/4.

Generalleutnant Linger was in command of the siege artillery, the siege works were commanded by Walrave. Unlike at Neisse, the Prussian king played a significant role in the siege from the start. His first act was to make a reconnaissance, after which the sovereign decided which front was to be attacked. He chose the narrowest of the fortress fronts – the north-west. The main reason was that this location was optimal for the storage of equipment and materials necessary for the siege. Besides, this front was the narrowest and could be attacked from both sides of the Oder. Finally, one of the surrounding hills that overlooked this front offered a site for a siege battery, which, in the King's opinion, could conduct breaching fire. As soon as this decision was made, preparations for the siege began. The plan was to establish the first battery on a hill near Grüningen, 800–900 metres from the fortress, and another on the other bank of the Oder, opposite the burnt village of Rathau. However, the first parallel was to be only 300 metres away from the fortress in order to reach the objective as quickly as possible. Under the protection of two battalions of musketeers and three companies of grenadiers, 2,000 infantry soldiers were to dig the first parallel, while 1,200 were to construct the artillery batteries. The construction of positions on the other bank of the Oder was to be carried out by 200 soldiers. The fascines for the batteries would be brought up by 300 dragoons. The manner in which the attack on the fortress was to be carried out was planned by the King, based on the instructions of Prince Leopold published a few years earlier.[14]

All preparations for the siege had been completed by 25 April and the work was due to begin as early as the night of 26th to 27th, but sudden rain caused a one-day delay. The construction of the parallels and batteries was not carried out until the following night. First, the infantry assigned to cover the construction moved against the fortress. After approaching 170 metres from the moat, the soldiers formed a long line and lay down on the ground. They were followed at a distance of 20 metres by the workers, who immediately set about marking out and digging parallels. Despite the moonlight, the defenders of the fortress did not realise that the work had begun until around 1:00 a.m., but by then the parallels were already far enough advanced to offer cover for the attackers. By daylight, the work was already so advanced that it was defensible and the troops covering the construction could be withdrawn. To the left the parallel touched the Oder, to the right it was completed with a sconce. The total length was about 800 metres. The communication trench had a total length of 1,600 metres. The trenches (parallels and communication) were 2.3 metres wide and 1.3 metres deep, the excavated earth formed a breastwork, and the interior trench wall was protected with sandbags. The exits were reinforced with fascines. Also, on the other bank of the Oder a short line of 250 metres was dug.

Construction of the battery progressed much more slowly, due to the heavy, clay soil, soaked with water after heavy rainfall, as well as the soldiers' inexperience in the construction of such facilities. It was not until the afternoon of 28 April that Battery No. 5 was completed, which was manned with six mortars. The construction of Battery No. 1 on Grüningen hill was poorly advanced, but in the end the King decided to stop its construction. It was decided that more batteries would be erected the following night, closer to the town. As soon as Battery No. 5 was completed, it began firing. Shots were to be directed only

---

14   von Anhalt-Dessau, *Deutliche und ausführliche Beschreibung.*

at the defensive works, as by order of the King the town was to be spared. About 90 bombs were fired with little effect, and only one of the enemy mortars was damaged.

The soldiers working in the trenches changed every 24 hours. One company of grenadiers manned the entrenchment at the end of the parallels, musketeers sat in the parallels, and two companies of grenadiers manned the trenches on the right bank of the Oder.

During the night of 28–29 April, bad weather hampered further expansion of the parallels. It was only possible to erect two further batteries, Nos 6 and 7, which were ready to fire on the morning of 29 April. These batteries were armed with 12-pounders, which took up firing on the fortress during the day. The defenders responded with a strong fire; nevertheless, during that day the Prussians managed to render some of the fortress guns unusable. In addition, Prussian bombs flying too far damaged the castle, which burned down completely the next day. According to some accounts, the Prussians were said to have refrained from firing, on Frederick's orders, so as not to impede the extinguishing of the fire. The following night the attackers succeeded in completing the mortar battery on the left bank of the Oder, and the number of guns in the previously built battery was increased. As a result, on 30 April, a heavy shelling of Brieg also began from this side. The defenders responded with a fire that lasted all day.

The following night, from 30 April to 1 May, Prussian troops completed a third mortar battery and a second with 24-pounders. As a result, on 1 May the town was under fire from 52 guns. At first, the defenders responded with a lively fire, which, however, diminished during the day and at around 4:00 p.m. became completely silent. The siege artillery fire was extremely effective – most of the cannons standing on the ramparts were dismantled and the embrasures destroyed. The shelling continued over the next two days. From 2 May onwards, it intensified, as eight more 24-pounders were added to Battery No. 2. Although the defenders succeeded in placing seven new guns on the ramparts, four of these were destroyed during the day.

On 3 May, the 60 cannon besieging the fortress opened a rapid fire, to which this time there was no response from the enemy. In the evening, the construction of the second parallels began, with 300 workers at work. Communication ditches were brought out from the first parallels. The construction of another siege battery also began. On 4 May, the Prussian guns fired shells, to which, as on the previous day, there was no response from the enemy. The Prussian shelling was very effective, as it was very difficult for the defenders to stay on the rampart under constant fire, due to the lack of traverses. Although the several days' shelling did not weaken the ability of the fortress to repel the assault – the palisade was mostly intact, and no breach was opened anywhere, it was no longer possible to conduct a defence with the fortress artillery. Besides, the commandant had no confidence in the garrison, due to frequent desertions, and was also under pressure from the townspeople, who wanted to avoid further losses to the town buildings. As early as 2 May, their delegation appeared to the commandant with a petition to surrender the fortress. These requests had an effect on 4 May, when at 2:00 p.m. a white flag was raised on one of the bastions. This ended the shelling. Frederick first wanted to take the entire garrison prisoner, but due to the news that the enemy army was approaching Brieg with the intention of relieving the fortress, he agreed to release the garrison, with arms and the honours of war, on the condition that these soldiers would not serve against the King of Prussia for two years.

On the evening of 4 May, a Prussian company of grenadiers occupied the bridge in front of the Breslau gate and the ravelin there. The next morning, the mines were removed, and the arsenal, guns and gunpowder were handed over. At 10:00 a.m. Prussian soldiers entered the fortress, and at noon the Austrian garrison left the fortress.[15] Around 400 of the Austrians volunteered to serve in the Prussian army after marching out. The total losses of the siege were small. The Prussians lost five gunners, the Austrians nine soldiers and a number of wounded.

The Prussians seized 61 cannon, nine mortars, 2,500 shells, 260 *cetnar* of gunpowder, 3,000 muskets, 63 *cetnar* of lead bullets, 1,200 *wispel* of grain and some supplies of flour. Interestingly, seven small-calibre bronze cannons captured from the fortress were given by the King to the engineer in charge of the siege, Cornelius Walrave.

Despite the quick capture of the fortress, the King was not entirely satisfied with the course of the siege, specifically with the effectiveness of the artillery fire. According to him, they fired too high and, although they dismantled some of the cannon, destroyed the palisades and the rampart in some places, they did not cause a breach in the rampart, at least this is how the King's feelings are presented in the literature describing the siege. However, one can judge that the King was quite satisfied with the results of the siege and the work of the artillerymen. Shortly after the fortress was captured, he decided to distribute a considerable sum – more than 2,000 thalers – as rewards for the conquerors. Of this, 1,000 thalers were to go to the engineers, the same amount to the artillerymen, half of which – 500 thalers – to the artillerymen from *Major* Holzmann's battery.[16]

The Siege of Breslau, 1757

During the fortress exercises in 1752, the King placed himself before his officers in the role of teacher. However, analysing his personal experience in siege warfare, which he gathered during the First and Second Silesian Wars, we see that it was in fact very small. The King was actually only present during three sieges: twice at Neisse in 1741, and Brieg in the same year. In none of these three cases could he gain any meaningful experience, as the sieges were short-lived, and the fortresses attacked were mostly outdated. Neither could the peacetime siege exercises described above bring real, combat experience. This was only to be gained by the King during the Seven Years War. The first real attack on a fortress was carried out by the King in Breslau, from 10 to 19 December 1757.

The attack on this fortress, seized by the Austrians less than a month earlier, was led by the King just after his spectacular success in smashing the Austrian army at the Battle of Leuthen. Five days after this great battle, the Prussian army stood at the walls of the Breslau fortress. Inside there was an Austrian garrison of between 12,000 and 18,000 soldiers.[17] The defenders had more than 150 guns at their disposal, for which there was

---

15   According to Malinowsky, Bonin, *Geschichte*, vol.2, p.199, only 1,006 soldiers left the fortress.
16   Letter from the King to Walrave of 10 May, GStA SPK, I HA Rep.96 B Abschriften von Kabinetsordres, Bd.23 p.87.
17   The discrepancies are due to the different data given by those writing about the battle. For detailed information on this, and on the siege itself, see: Grzegorz Podruczny, Twierdza Wrocław w okresie fryderycjańskim. Fortyfikacje, garnizon i działania wojenne w latach 1741–1806, (Wrocław: Atut, 2009), pp.117–123.

a full complement of 250 Austrian and Dutch artillerymen.[18] The Austrians also had an abundance of food – supplies in the warehouses could last for five to six months of a siege. The Prussian siege corps numbered around 12,000 men. At first, it had at its disposal only field guns, captured from the Austrians during the Battle of Leuthen,[19] and later a park of siege artillery was also brought in from Neisse and Brieg. Eventually, the Prussians had 95 guns at their disposal.[20]

The siege began on 10 December. During the first few days, the main siege works were established, including a huge battery for 20 heavy cannons and seven mortars located in the Ohlauer Vorstadt, which began firing on 13 December. The Prussian siege works, as well as Austrian attempts at defence, continued until 19 December, when the Austrians decided to surrender.[21] The main reason for the rapid success was the destruction of the gunpowder magazine in the Taschen Bastion on 16 December, which allowed the Prussians to make a breach in the wall less than six days after the siege began. This fact and the severe frost, which covered the moats with ice, forced the Austrian commander, *Feldmarschalllieutenant* Sprecher von Beregg, to capitulate.[22] The siege was formally led by *Oberst* von Balbi, praised by Frederick for his efficient handling of the Potsdam fortress manoeuvres in 1752, but the King himself played a major role. Balbi claimed that, thanks to the presence of the King, the siege works were run smoothly.[23] From other accounts, it is known that Frederick also influenced the course of the siege with his decisions. One of these was to be of crucial importance: the decision to fire on the Taschen Bastion. Having been told by the Prussians that there was a large supply of gunpowder there (300 barrels, about 15 tonnes), Frederick gave the order to shell the storehouse with mortars. After many unsuccessful attempts, the bomb pierced the vault and caused an explosion.[24] According to Prussian accounts, more than 800 people lost their lives, including an entire battalion of Grenzer constituting the bastion's garrison. In addition, a breach in the curtain more than 30 metres long was created.[25] However, the

---

18   D' Aymée, Memoire sur Breslau relativement a sa Defence, Service historique de la Défense (SHD Vincennes), Article 14 Places Etrangeres, carton n 1, I Breslau, Dossier et plans, 1752–1912, 1 V M 56, no. 4, p.3 verso.

19   Seydel, Nachrichten, vol.3, p.128.

20   In the siege they used 40 12-pounder guns, 20 24-pounder guns, 13 10-pounder howitzers, 17 50-pounder mortars, 2 75-pounder mortars and 3 5-pounder mortars. See Kurd Wolfgang Wilhelm Georg von Schöning, Historisch-biographische Nachrichten zur Geschichte der Brandenburgisch-Preussischen Artillerie, vol.2 (Berlin: Mittler, 1844), pp.80–81.

21   A detailed description of the siege can be found in the siege diary, Diarium der Belagerung von Breslau und Capitulations-Puncte von der Übergabe an Seine Königliche Majestät in Preussen…, (Berlin: Unknown Publisher, 1758).

22   In his official reports, Sprecher also said he had an insufficient garrison to defend the vast fortress. Verantwortung des Generals Sprecher, Österreichisches Staatsarchiv, Kriegsarchiv (OStA KA), Alte Feldakten, Nr. 623 Siebenjähriger Krieg Hauptarmee 1757 XIII (503- Ende) Faszikel 604.

23   Bonin, Geschichte des Ingenieurkorps, p.76.

24   Seydel, Nachrichten, vol.3, pp.130–131, and 'Anon., 'Friedrich der Große als Ingenieur", Archiv für die Officiere der Königlich Preußischen Artillerie und Ingenieur Korps, vol.12, no.1, (1841), p.37, regarding the King's order to target the gunpowder magazine.

25   Seydel, Nachrichten, vol.3, pp.130–131; Colmar Grünhagen, Schlesien unter Friedrich dem Grossen (Breslau: Verlag von Wilhelm Koebner, 1892), vol.2, p.62. Information on the effects of the explosion is quoted by both authors from Anon., Diarium der Belagerung von Breslau und Capitulations-Puncte von der Übergabe an Seine Königliche Majestät in Preussen (Berlin: Unknown Publisher, 1758), p.4.

King himself, who was supposed to have ordered the destruction, writes that the hit on the magazine was accidental.[26] *Lieutenant colonel* d'Aymée, the French engineer in charge of the defence of the fortress, saw the matter even differently. In his description of the siege, he reports that the explosion could have been caused either by Prussian bombardment or by an error of the staff working in the gunpowder magazine. D'Aymée also gives a much smaller loss, about 60 dead, but describes greater damage with a nearly 60-metre section of the curtain being destroyed.[27] It is difficult to determine which version is closer to the truth. The probability of a deliberate attack on the gunpowder magazine is high. It would be an application of the methods of Menno van Coehoorn and frequently used by Dutch engineers in the second half of the seventeenth century. One of the elements of his method was the persistent shelling with heavy mortars of those parts of the fortifications where gunpowder magazines were located, combined with the 'sowing' of the targeted magazines with small hand grenades thrown by extremely numerous (usually in numbers of several hundred) hand mortars, named after their inventor.[28] This method was also readily used by the Prussians, a perfect illustration of which is the siege of Stettin in 1677.[29] This tradition was strong in Prussia, thanks both to the person of Old Dessauer and other Prussian military men educated in the Netherlands. An excellent example of this Coehoornian method of capturing a fortress was the siege of Cosel in 1745, led by the Dutch-educated Walrave, when mortar bombardment played a major role. However, at Breslau the Prussian army had completely different artillery equipment than the Coehoorn method envisaged. The only mortars that were available were, from a seventeenth-century point of view, medium-sized – two 75-pound mortars and 17 mortars throwing 50-pound bombs.[30] The likelihood of a projectile fired from such a mortar piercing the vault of a powder magazine was not great. And there is much to suggest that the vault of the magazine was not actually penetrated. This is because the magazine, which according to the siege accounts was hit, was located in the interior of the Taschen Bastion and, had it exploded, the entire bastion would have been destroyed. However, according to the siege plan drawn up by d'Aymée, only the left flank of the bastion was damaged, along with the adjacent curtain. Presumably, therefore, some gunpowder supplies stored behind the walls of the left flank artillery positions had exploded, which did not require piercing the magazine vault.

The use of a modified Coehoorn method in this siege may be surprising if one considers the siege exercises held five years earlier at Potsdam, where Prussian artillerymen practised in the Vauban method which, unlike the Coehoorn method, required more training in conducting a regular approach attack, including in the disposition of artillery fire. It could be said that the rapid success achieved by makeshift means gave the King the impression that a siege was a relatively easy and ordinary thing to do. In fact, this was the view

---

26   Gustav Berthold Volz (ed.), *Die Werke Friedrichs des Großen*, vol.3, pp.1, 110–111.
27   D' Aymée, Memoire sur Breslau relativement a sa Defence, SHD, Article 14 Places Etrangeres, carton n 1, I Breslau, Dossier et plans, 1752–1912, 1 V M 56, no. 4, p.5 verso. In the original, 30 toise.
28   An example of a successful siege of this kind is the shelling of Namur in 1692, when a magazine containing about four tonnes of gunpowder was hit. Müller, *Geschichte des Festungskrieges*, p.38.
29   The Prussians then used 10 heavy mortars, some of which were designed to throw bombs weighing 6–7 cetnars, see Seydel, *Nachrichten*, vol.1, pp.194–195; Müller, *Geschichte des Festungskrieges*, p.38.
30   Schöning, *Historisch-biographische*, pp.80–81.

he expressed in his most important work on military theory, the *Basic Principles of War*, written in 1748. At the beginning of chapter 24 on fortresses, he writes: 'The art of besieging has become a craft, like carpentry or watchmaking. Certain undeniable rules have developed by which everything always has a similar course. The same theory applies in the same cases'.[31] How wrong the King was, was shown by the siege of Olomouc in 1758.

The Siege of Olomouc, 1758

Frederick II's siege of this Moravian fortress in the spring of 1758 was associated with the Prussian army's last attempt to seize the operational initiative during the Seven Years War. The capture of Olomouc may have provided the King of Prussia with a longed-for opportunity to conquer and permanently occupy Bohemia, and thus achieve a territorial advantage in this war.[32] However, the task set before the Prussian engineers was not easy, as the Austrians had spent 15 years rebuilding this urban centre into a large and strong fortress. The fortification, designed by the French Baron Pierre Bechade de Rochepine, was completed a year before the siege. The new fortress had a strong main core and numerous outer and external works. Of the latter, the most important were the Imperial Redoubt and the three Salzer Redoubts, located on an island between two arms of the Morava River. An important feature of Olomouc's fortifications were the numerous artillery casemates, which provided the fortress's guns with cover when fighting siege artillery.[33]

Prussian troops surrounded the fortress as early as the beginning of May, but the siege work was held up for a long time, waiting for the arrival of the siege artillery park brought from Brieg and Neisse. The regular attack did not begin until 27 May, with the opening of the first parallel located on the hill called Tafelberg (Tabulový vrch) more than 200 metres from the fortress works. Subsequently, siege batteries containing a total of 42 cannon of various types were erected and on 31 May the firing of the town began. It was immediately apparent that the chosen positions were too far from the fortifications. Moreover, they were positioned so that they themselves were vulnerable to fire from the fortress. To improve the situation, on 1 June the parallel was extended by a further 700 paces, which, however, did not have the correct effect and even increased the annoyance of the fire from the fortress. Particularly dangerous was the fire from the Salzer Redoubts, which was enfilading the approach works from the side. To protect themselves from it, the gunners had to build special shields. In the meantime, the trenches progressed. On 4 June, a second parallel was made, 800 paces distant from the fortress works, and by 12 June new siege batteries had been constructed on it. This improved the effectiveness of the shelling towards the fortress but did not increase the safety of the besiegers, who constantly suffered losses from the fire of the Salzer Redoubts. The safety of the attackers was also threatened by the numerous sorties made by the defenders; the one on 12 June not only caused significant casualties but also the destruction of 11 guns. Nevertheless, the approach work continued. On 14 June a third parallel was established and on 22 June a double sap was brought out

---

31   Volz, *Die Werke*, vol.6, p.55.
32   The motivations for the attack on Olomouc are explained in detail by Frederick in his 1775 text, 'Betrachtungen über die Feldzugspläne', Volz, *Die Werke*, vol.6, p.201 et seq.
33   Miroslav Kuch-Breburda, Vladimir Kupka, *Pevnost Olomouc* (Dvur Kralove nad Labem: FORTprint, 2003), pp.80–102.

towards the covered way. Meanwhile, both sides conducted a powerful cannonade. On 16 June the besiegers managed to make a breach in the rampart, and destroyed numerous defensive works, most notably those adjacent to Catherine's Gate. This, however, failed to dampen the firepower of the defenders, who responded effectively. On 14 June they hit a Prussian bomb magazine, and a day later a gunpowder magazine. The approach works were also effectively shelled using, among other things, mortars throwing baskets of stones and Coehoorn mortars throwing hand grenades. Despite this, the siege works were advancing, and by 26 June the besiegers had managed to reach a distance of 100 metres from the palisades of the covered way. A day later, the Prussian sappers came within a metre of the glacis preceding the covered way, and in the following days they began to cross this last obstacle separating them from the fortress.

In the meantime, the main defensive installations had been destroyed by heavy artillery fire, and the defenders prepared to repel the assault inside the city by preparing a retrenchment. However, this attack did not take place, as on 30 June the Austrian field troops destroyed or intercepted a Prussian convoy with supplies for the siege corps during a skirmish at Guntramovice and Domašov. As Frederick II's army was already running out of gunpowder as well as ammunition and food, the King had no choice but to lift the siege. After almost two months of surrounding the fortress and after five weeks of a regular siege, the Prussian army had to leave from under a fortress that had cost the Prussian troops a great deal of effort in their attempt to capture it. The Prussians fired as many as 103,000 cannonballs and more than 25,000 bombs and howitzer grenades into the city. The Austrians answered them with 58,000 cannonballs, 6,000 bombs, 2,700 stone projectiles, 51,000 projectiles from wall guns and 472,000 musket bullets. The Prussians lost 1,139 soldiers, the Austrians almost 900.[34]

The Prussian failure was the result of numerous mistakes made. In the older, primarily German literature on the subject, the most notable errors and their consequences are attributed to *Oberst* von Balbi.[35] Through his error, the first parallel was to be located at Tafelberg, almost twice as far away as was accepted at the time. Because of this, the cannon from the siege batteries established there were unable to fire effectively on the city fortifications. Probably the main responsibility for such a decision lies with the engineer in question; however, the fact that the artillerymen agreed to establish the batteries so far away does not put their skills in a good light. Besides, it is difficult to accept that such an important decision was taken solely by the engineer in charge of the siege, without consulting the siege commander, *Generalfeldmarschall* Keith. Moreover, there are indications which lead one to believe that the King was informed of this intention. Before the siege began, he visited the fortress from Tafelberg at least twice, on 5 and 18 May; the first time von Balbi

---

34   Seydel, *Nachrichten*, vol.3, pp.191–213; Josef August Bartsch, *Olmütz im Jahre 1758 und seine frühere Kriegsgeschichte: Denkschrift zur hundertjährigen Jubiläumsfeier des Entsazes von Olmütz am 2. Juli 1758* (Olmütz: Slawik, 1858), pp.41–70; Grosser Generalstab, *Geschichte des siebenjährigen Krieges: in einer Reihe von Vorlesungen, mit Benutzung authentischer Quellen* (Berlin: Grosser Generalstab, 1826), vol.2, pp.178–186; Henry Lloyd, Georg Friedrich von Tempelhoff, *Geschichte des siebenjährigen Krieges in Deutschland zwischen dem Könige von Preußen und der Kaiserin Königin mit ihren Alliirten* (Berlin: Johann Friedrich Unger 1783–1801), vol.2, pp.49–84; Bonin, *Geschichte des Ingenieurkorps*, pp.80–83; Grosser Generalstab, *Die Kriege* , Th.3, vol.9, pp.66–106.

35   This is the allegation made by both Tempelhoff and Seydel and Bonin.

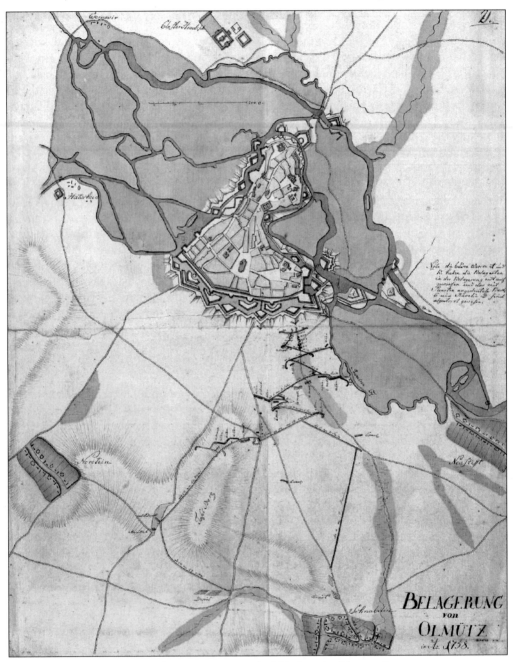

Siege of Olomouc 1758. (Vědecká knihovna v Olomouci)

was present.[36] It is unlikely that on these occasions he did not express his opinions on where the siege should begin. Interestingly, Frederick, in his history of the Seven Years War, identifies as a reason for the failure of the siege the too distant locations of the parallels, but does not direct accusations at specific individuals.[37] Frederick's only personal accusations in this regard were articulated by him in his correspondence with Keith. In a letter of 2 June, he accuses another of the engineers, *Oberst* Wrede, of having allegedly miscalculated the distance from the defences.[38] Despite this, it was von Balbi who was responsible for the failure of the siege – he was not actively employed again after 1758. Although he remained in the army and even retained his post as chief of the engineer corps, he was not involved either in combat operations or, after the war, in the construction of fortresses.

Another mistake made by the engineers was to ignore the threat from the Salzer Redoubts. These defence works had been conducting a murderous flanking fire on the Prussian siege batteries from the beginning. While von Balbi was aware of this threat when he chose the starting point of the siege works, he thought that these defence works could be quickly neutralised. As it turned out, despite directing numerous Prussian cannon against them, it was not possible to suppress their fire, which hampered the progress of the attack until the end of the siege. However, it is difficult to point solely to the fault of the Prussian engineer here. The exceptional resilience of the artillery of the Salzer Redoubts was due to their placement in bombproof, casemated batteries, which remarkably prolonged their service life.

Arguably, much of the blame for the failure of the siege can be attributed to the King himself. For obvious reasons, this is not exposed in early studies on the history of the Seven Years War. The most serious and strongest-sounding accusation was made by the Prussian military theorist Gerhard von Scharnhorst. In one of his writings, he draws attention to what, in his opinion, was a decisive error on the outcome of the siege, namely that the siege began too late. Instead of, as was customary at the time, starting siege work as soon as the fortress was approached, the King ordered the siege to wait until the heavy artillery arrived, which delayed the attack by 15 days. According to Scharnhorst, this loss of time was unnecessary, as the Prussians had enough heavy guns (albeit field guns and not strictly siege guns) to begin the approach works under their cover.[39] Another Prussian theorist, Carl von Clausewitz, criticised the King for not cutting off the fortress sufficiently and leaving an enemy army in the area.[40] In fact, during the siege there were events that were unusual in such circumstances. For example, for most of the siege there were markets in the besieged town, attended by peasants from the surrounding area who managed to evade the Prussian outposts; and the chroniclers of the siege point out that this

---

36   Grosser Generalstab, *Geschichte des siebenjährigen Krieges*, vol.2, p.178; Bartsch, *Olmütz im Jahre 1758*, p.50.

37   'Probably the siege would have gone more happily if the parallels had not been established so far away and if the batteries already erected had not had to be abandoned, as their fire was ineffective and led to useless consumption of ammunition', after Volz, *Die Werke*, vol.3, p.130.

38   Letter from Frederick II to Keith of 2 June 1758, Johann Gustav Droysen (ed.), *Politische Correspondenz Friedrich's des Großen* (Berlin-Leipzig-Oldenburg: Duckner & Humbolt, 1879–1939), vol.17, p.45.

39   Kunisch Johannes, Sikora Michael, Stieve Tilman, *Gerhard von Scharnhorst. Private und dienstliche Schriften* (Köln: Böhlau, 2005) vol.3, p.703.

40   Carl von Clausewitz, *Hinterlassene Werke über Krieg und Kriegführung* (Berlin: Ferd. Dümmler's Verlagsbuchhandlung, 1863), vol.10, pp.62–65.

kept food prices in the town low all the time. The fortress garrison also received constant (and substantial) reinforcements from Austrian troops operating in the vicinity.

In the literature describing the siege, one can find several more mistakes allegedly made by the King. Christopher Duffy, accuses the King of the following omissions: issuing an order to use reduced artillery charges in order to reduce the consumption of gunpowder; issuing an order to establish a second battery on the slope of the Tafelberg, which was in fact located further away than the one established by von Balbi; issuing an order to establish a battery in front of – and not behind – the parallel. These allegations are mostly substantiated in the sources, but not all can be confirmed.[41] The issue of the use of reduced artillery charges is the most questionable. In the surviving correspondence of the King related to the siege, this topic does not appear.[42] Tempelhoff raises the issue in his description of the siege, but not as an accusation against the King, but as evidence of von Balbi's lack of professionalism. According to Tempelhoff, the Prussian engineer was said to have suggested using 13-pound charges for 24-pound guns and seven-pound charges for 12-pound guns, while the firing was done using 10-pound and 5-pound charges respectively.[43] These charges were the standard weight used by Prussian artillery at the time.[44] So, von Balbi called for an increase, which, as Tempelhof rightly points out, would only have resulted in more powder consumption, with no increase in the range of the artillery.[45] The other allegations seem to have confirmation. Everything points to the fact that it was the King who ordered the construction of a second battery on the first parallel, which instead of helping, harmed the siege. Frederick, although not initially personally present at the siege, wrote Keith's instructions for its conduct. One of these, expressed in a letter of 30 May, suggests precisely the establishment of a new battery near the village of Povel.[46] As a direct witness to the events, the Duc de Ligne, quoted by Duffy, notes, this battery was further from the fortress than the one established by von Balbi. The author also draws attention to the third of the King's errors – the location of the siege batteries behind the parallel instead of in front.[47] The batteries established on the second and third parallels were so located, which contradicted both the prevailing theory and practice. This solution, too, was probably dictated by the King. In Frederick's letters to Keith in early June, detailed instructions for the conduct of siege work, including the newly established batteries, appear several times.[48]

The siege described above, although unsuccessful, was a very important lesson for both the Prussian engineers and the King himself. The batteries of the Salzer Redoubt, which

---

41   Duffy, *The fortress in the age of Vauban*, pp.123–124; Duffy, *Friedrich der Grosse*, p.280.

42   The entire exchange of letters relating to the participation of the artillery during this siege is quoted by Schöning, *Historisch-biographische*, pp.383–389.

43   Lloyd von Tempelhoff, *Geschichte des siebenjährigen Krieges*, vol.2, pp.59–60.

44   Malinowsky, Bonin, *Geschichte*, vol.2, pp.441–442.

45   By the mid-eighteenth century, it had already been proven that, with a charge greater than half the mass of a propelled ball, part of it is shot out of the cannon uncombusted along with the ball instead of exploding.

46   Letter from Frederick II to Keith, 30 May 1758. In a further letter, dated 2 June, he mentions the corrections he made to the siege plan sent to him, Droysen, *Politische Correspondenz*, vol.17, pp.38–39, 45.

47   Charles-Joseph de Ligne, *Mon journal de la Guerre de Sept Ans. Campagne 1757 et 1758. Mélanges militaires, littéraires et sentimentales* (Dresden: Walther, 1796), vol.14, pp.117–118.

48   In a letter of 30 May, the King formulates his ideas on the direction in which the siege work should continue and indicates sites for a new battery. Droysen, *Politische Correspondenz*, vol.17, pp.38–39.

caused such great difficulties for the Prussian troops, became an inspiration for Prussian fortress builders, as well as for the King himself. Frederick, who became convinced of their effectiveness with his own eyes, ordered similar casemates to be made in his fortresses shortly after the end of the war.

The Siege of Dresden, 1760

As was evident from the sieges in which Frederick II took part, the Prussian army was far from perfect in the art of conquering fortresses. These sieges were definitely not masterpieces of that 'craft' which, according to the King's words in 1748, was the art of siege warfare. Numerous errors in the conduct of approach works and the use of artillery show how far the Prussian engineers were from the level of their colleagues in the French engineering corps. What distinguished the Prussians from French siege warfare theory and practice was above all the indiscriminate use of mortars, which, as already stated, indicates the influence of the Dutch tradition in Prussian siege warfare. However, whereas in the sieges described above, bombardment was – like that used by the Dutch – only an element of the siege and its purpose was primarily to damage the fortifications, in the siege of Dresden in 1760, bombardment was aimed solely at destroying the city and thereby – and not through a prolonged regular attack – forcing the commandant to surrender. Such ruthless use of force, without the application of the precise tools of war, contrasts sharply with the image of eighteenth-century war as a 'tamed Bellona', in which armed conflict does not affect the lives of civilians.

The siege lasted between 15 and 23 July, although the Prussian army was at Dresden for much longer; it had already surrounded the city on 13 July and did not leave until 29 July. The Prussians had a small park of siege artillery, consisting of only twenty 12-pounders and 12 mortars. Despite this weakness, Frederick decided to attempt to capture the city. As early as 15 July, the first siege battery was erected and it immediately opened fire. Three more were erected over the next 24 hours, and on 18 July, after all the planned seven batteries had been completed and equipped with guns, full bombardment began. Due to the location of the siege batteries (in the suburbs under the cover of their buildings), the batteries were erected in a makeshift manner, mounded only with earth. In addition, only plunging firing was used, both from mortars and cannon, which certainly did not have a good effect on the precision of the shelling. The bombardment of the city continued until 20 July, when, due to the approaching relief of the Austrian army, the guns were removed from most of the batteries. The only remaining one was still firing on 22 July. The Prussian army stood at Dresden until 23 July, when it withdrew due to the advancing Austrians. The result of this brief event was massive destruction of civilian buildings. These were mainly caused by Prussian artillerymen, who fired on both military and civilian targets. One of the tragic images of this siege is the destruction of the Church of the Holy Cross, under the guise of firing at cannon placed on its tower. The bombardment of Dresden brought neither effect nor glory to the King. Even Archenholz, a participant in the Seven Years War on the Prussian side and author of a popular study of the history of that war, who usually praised the King, this time criticised him.[49] Of course, this historian and other authors

---

49   Johann Wilhelm von Archenholz, *Geschichte des Siebenjährigen Krieges in Deutschland* (Berlin: Haude und Spener, 1793), vol.2, pp.73–75.

attribute part of the blame for the destruction of the city to the Austrian garrison, which was supposed to have burned down the suburbs (according to Archenholz, the grenzer in the Dresden garrison looted and burnt the houses in the suburbs), and the King supposedly ordered that the civilian buildings be spared. However, a brief glance at the way the siege was carried out shows that Frederick assumed in advance that the urban buildings could be destroyed. Indeed, in sieges of the time, artillery was only a means to support the main attack on the fortifications carried out by means of ground works; digging trenches with which to approach the fortress fortifications. At Dresden in 1760, not even a single parallel was made, the construction of which was usually the signal that marked the beginning of a siege. The batteries stood free, unconnected to each other. Nor was any approaching work done; the entire siege effort was focused on bombarment. The King's aim was clearly to force the commandant to surrender the fortress; indeed, he directly articulated this intention in his history of the Seven Years War: 'Although the governor of Dresden, General Macquire had 6,000 men, it was thought that he would sooner surrender the city than allow it to be turned to ashes.'[50] In these circumstances, Frederick's explanation that his subordinates disobeyed explicit orders and fired on the city instead of the fortifications is not credible.[51]

The King's actions were not only immoral but also ineffective, as historians writing about the event have emphasised. Success in this siege was not possible, any more than during the Russian siege of Küstrin in 1758, which was very similar in methods and effects. Both of these fortresses had a strong garrison determined to defend themselves, so that despite the burning of the city, it could not be conquered. However, the bombardment of Dresden was an important lesson – both for Frederick and for other military officers. The King was probably aware that by burning Dresden he had thus set an example that would probably be replicated. This bombardment, like those carried out during his other sieges, was the impetus for a significant acceleration in the construction of bombproof buildings in Prussia. After the Seven Years War, numerous casemates appeared not only in existing fortresses, but two fortresses were also erected on Frederick's orders which had no civilian buildings in them at all (Silberberg and Graudenz) and whose rooms were all bombproof. This clearly shows that Frederick was aware that his enemies might try the same thing by bombing the fortress cities and destroying the property of their civilian inhabitants to try to force their surrender. This was in fact what happened half a century later, during the Franco-Prussian War of 1806-1807. It is symptomatic that both of Frederick's fortresses, which were fully casemated and devoid of civilian buildings, defended themselves.

The Siege of Schweidnitz, 1762
The fourth siege of Schweidnitz during the Seven Years War the most important example of fortress warfare in the Friedrician period. The siege was extremely long, lasting 62 days, and bloody. Moreover, all means of defence and attack known to the military of the time were employed there. The attackers shelled the fortress, approached it with ground works, mines and also made assaults. The besiegers also defended themselves in every possible way, not

---

50   Volz, *Die Werke*, vol.4, p.44.
51   Report of Grun, 19 July 1760, Letter from the King to Prince Henry, 23 July 1760; Letter from the King to Minister von Finckenstein, 23 July 1760, Droysen, *Politische Correspondenz*, vol.19, pp.510, 514–517.

only firing cannon and small arms, but also using sorties and mine warfare. Furthermore, during this siege, innovations in fortress warfare were tested. For the first time on a real battlefield, the Prussians used a solution invented and experimentally tested a decade earlier – a powerful mine called a globe of pressure. In turn, the commander of the fortress artillery, French *Generalfeldwachtmeister* Jean-Baptiste Vaquette Gribeauval, fighting on the Austrian side, tested and perfected during the siege the innovative fortress gun carriage he had invented in 1749.[52] This siege also had another aspect – the Prussians were conquering their own fortress, built according to completely new ideas (a fort fortress) just before the war and improved in the meantime both by the Prussians (after the siege in 1758) and by the Austrians, who had been working for almost a year since the capture of the fortress in October 1761 to strengthen the fortifications. So, it was also a test of innovative defensive architecture. Finally, one should not forget the role of Frederick II, who was involved in the siege from the beginning and even took charge of it towards the end.

The siege of the Schweidnitz was the final event of the entire 1762 campaign in Silesia. In order to besiege the fortress safely, Frederick II was forced to attack the Austrian army standing in the nearby Owl Mountains (Eulengebirge, Góry Sowie). His success in capturing the strongly fortified Austrian defensive positions at Burkersdorf and Leutmansdorf on 21 July 1762 enabled the siege to proceed in safety. In the fortress under attack stood a garrison of over 12,000 soldiers, most of whom were specially selected for the task, and the best soldiers from the Austrian army in the Owl Mountains. The siege corps, commanded by the commander of the Breslau fortress, *General-Lieutenant* Tauentzien, numbered about 10,000 soldiers, but not far from him was the main royal army, which could provide the besiegers with any necessary assistance if required.[53]

The Prussians had already cut the fortress off from the Austrian troops supporting it on the day of the Battle of Burkersdorf, but the ring of encirclement was not finally closed until 4 August.[54] The actual siege did not begin until the night of 7 to 8 August, when the

---

52   The gun carriage made it easier to operate the cannon, reduced the number of personnel required to do so and provided greater safety for the crew from enemy fire due to the possibility of using smaller embrasures. It performed very well during the siege of Schweidnitz and was introduced permanently in France in 1774. Gerhard von Scharnhorst, *Handbuch für Offiziere in den angewandten Theilen der Kriegs-Wissenschafften* (Hannover: Verlag der Helwingschen Hoff Buchhandlung, 1815), pp.36–38; Louis de Tousard, *American artillerist's companion: or Elements of artillery. Treating of all kinds of firearms in detail, and of the formation, object, and service of the flying or horse artillery, preceded by an introductory dissertation on cannon* (Philadelphia: Conrad and Co, 1809), vol.2, pp.312–315.

53   Prussian historiographers often seem to forget this fact, writing that at Schweidnitz the Prussian siege corps captured a fortress manned by a stronger garrison than themselves, explaining this fact, for example, by the heroism of Prussian soldiers. Meanwhile, the royal army repeatedly supplied soldiers, for example, during the construction of the first parallel more than 2,000 soldiers were brought in from the main army for earthworks, Johann Gottlieb Tielke, *Beytrage zur Kriegskunst und Geschichte des Krieges von 1756 bis 1756, IV Stück, Die drey Belagerungen und loudonsche Ersteigeung der Festung Scheridnitz in dern Feldzeügen von 1757 bis 1762* (Wien: Trattnern, 1786), p.221.

54   The siege of the fortress has an extensive literature. The most important texts for establishing the histography were written as early as the eighteenth century, these are first of all the 'Journal du Siege de Ville de Schweidnitz', published by the engineer attacking the fortress, Lefèbvre: Simon Lefèbvre, *Oeuvres completes* (Maastricht: Dufour & Roux, 1778), vol.1, pp.281–329, as well as an extremely detailed description of the siege in the work of Johann Gottlieb Tielke, *Beytrage zur Kriegskunst*, pp.199–429. The account of a participant in the event, Lloyd, von Tempelhoff, *Geschichte des*

construction of the first parallel was undertaken. This work was about 750 metres from the fortress fortifications, was over 4.5 kilometres long and was completed within the next day. The attack was directed at Jauernicker Fort, and the parallels were located so that the batteries formed on them could fire from two sides at both the object under attack and the lines connecting it with neighbouring forts. Already on the first day of the siege, the defenders showed that capturing Schweidnitz would be a very difficult task. Taking advantage of the fact that the parallel was not yet fully completed and that the artillery batteries had not yet been armed with guns, the defenders left the fortress with a formidable sortie of 2,500 infantry and 130 cavalry. The Austrians not only inflicted heavy losses on the Prussians (around 300 killed, wounded, and taken prisoner),[55] but also destroyed some of the approach works they had made. Nevertheless, after repelling the Austrian attack, the Prussians completed both the parallel and the first five siege batteries, which began firing on the fortress on 9 August. The construction of further batteries also began immediately.

A day later, two saps were brought out from the parallels towards the fortress, on which three more siege batteries were established, already located 150 metres closer to the fort under attack. As more batteries were armed, more cannonballs and mortar bombs were sent towards the fortress. The besiegers responded with the same, and also tried to defend actively – on the night of 14-15 August they again made a sortie and, with a force of 1,400 men, sent the workers digging approach ditches back to the first parallel. The efforts of the defenders hampered the progress of the attack; nevertheless, on the night of 16-17 August, the Prussians built a second parallel, already less than 200 metres distant from the glacis of the fort. The Austrians repeated the sorties, albeit with smaller forces; they also fired heavily at the advancing saps. The closer the diggers got, the slower their work progressed. This situation was to be changed by Lefèbvre, who decided to attempt an assault on the Jauernicker Flèche, a defensive work located in front of the fort under attack.[56] This assault failed, so they had to return to strenuous digging. This task was exceptionally hard, as the defenders had unusually intensified their fire. Not only were the saps shot at with small arms and artillery; they also began to be pelted with stones thrown from pierriers (similar to those in Olomouc), as well as pelted with hand grenades thrown from Coehoorn's mortars. Moreover, the effectiveness of the defenders' artillery was improved by the introduction on 19 August of cannon on new gun carriages invented by Gribeauval, which, as already noted, were, by their design and size, easier to handle and more difficult to detect and destroy by the besiegers' artillery. For the next few days little changed in this situation – the attackers advanced laboriously through trenches towards the fortress, the defenders combating this work with artillery fire from the fortress, which in turn was endeavoured to be suppressed by the fire of successive siege batteries, established ever closer to the city.

---

siebenjährigen Krieges, vol.6, pp.122–219. Studies by nineteenth-century German military historians, also contribute relevant information: Seydel, Nachrichten, vol.3, pp.514–529, Malinowsky, Bonin, Geschichte, vol.3, pp.315–341, and the historians of the Prussian General Staff, Grosser Generalstab, Geschichte des siebenjährigen Krieges: in einer Reihe von Vorlesungen, mit Benutzung authentischer Quellen (Berlin: Grosser Generalstab 1841), vol.6, pp.253–359. Historical-military literature abounds, moreover, with extremely numerous references to the siege as a whole or analyses of its individual aspects (especially mine warfare), but it is unreasonable to list them all.

55   According to various accounts, total Prussian losses from this event ranged from 280 to 340 men.
56   This work was built just before the formal siege began, ordered by Gribeauval.

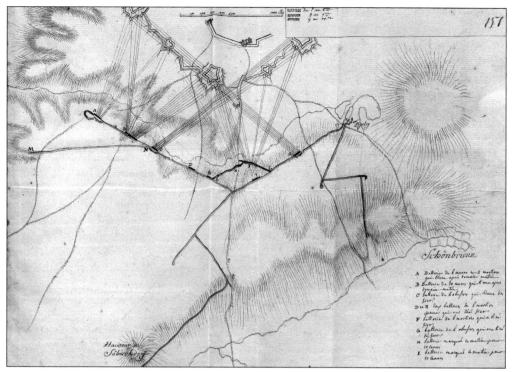

Siege of the fortress of Schweidnitz in 1762. (GStA SPK, I HA Rep 96, Tit 86 B – Lefebure, k. 151)

It was not until 22 August that a new element appeared – mine warfare. Due to the proximity of the defensive works under attack, the King ordered preparations to lay a mine to trigger the first of the globes of pressure. After a third parallel had been laid 150 metres from the fort's covered way, a mine tunnel was dug. From now on, the fortress was attacked on three levels – artillery shells were flown at it from above, at ground level it was approached by saps (the attack had changed direction in the meantime – instead of the fort, the Jauernicker Flèche located next to it was attacked), and miners tunnelled from below. However, the change of attack did not speed up the siege, on the contrary; the work underground was very arduous. Within the first 24 hours the Prussian miners had only made a three-metre-long gallery, by 26 August they had advanced another 15 metres. The trench attack, which was conducted on the surface, was effectively stopped by the Austrians, who pelted the saps with hand grenades, fired on them and finally destroyed them in repeated sorties. In the days that followed, the underground attack encountered more and more difficulties, including groundwater and lack of air.

Despite these difficulties, by the end of August they had managed to build a gallery almost 32 metres long, allowing them to plant the first of the big mines. It exploded on 1 September, creating a crater over 30 metres in diameter and nine metres deep. While the explosion did not damage the counter-mine corridors in front of the fort under attack, it did allow the attack on the surface to advance significantly. Over the next 24 hours, the attackers dug into the crater, established fighting positions on it, and on 3 September began digging another gallery out of it to lay a second large mine. The Austrians made this work difficult – bombarding the crater, shelling it with flat-trajectory artillery, and trying to impede the progress of the mine work by detonating their own mines. The resistance put up by the defences, as well as the trouble caused by nature (groundwater), twice forced the attackers to abandon the galleries they had started and start mines elsewhere. The second time, the Austrians destroyed the entire 20-metre-long gallery with their mine. The Prussians were only able to detonate the second globe of pressure on 16 September, more than two weeks after the first. The crater created by the explosion was smaller, only 20 metres in diameter, yet its locations was already only 15 metres away from the palisades of the covered way. In the following days, the siege dragged on at a steady rhythm – the Prussians established battle positions inside the crater and undertook the construction of another gallery. Although the Prussian siege batteries (their number had risen to 19) destroyed the defenders' artillery, the remaining cannon continued to fire intensively into the crater, making work on the surface extremely difficult. The Austrians were also successful in their underground defence – three times they forced the Prussians to abandon the mine galleries they were building. These failures prompted the King on 21 September to replace *Major* Lefèbvre and to lead the siege himself. Initially this made little difference – a day later the Austrians destroyed the Prussian mine gallery for the fourth time with their mines. By 24 September, however, a third mine of 3,600 pounds of gunpowder had already been laid, the explosion of which made a 20-metre diameter crater, the edge of which was barely four metres away from the covered way palisade. Over the next two days, the Prussians captured the third crater, erected battle positions there and began digging two more galleries. However, despite the prolonged shelling, the destruction of the fortress guns and the explosion of three large mines, the Austrian defence did not lose strength. On the contrary, the Prussian positions in the new crater came under even heavier mortar fire, more counter-mines exploded, until finally, on 26 September, the defenders undertook an sortie that drove the Prussians out of the third crater and destroyed all the positions established there and both mine galleries. The Prussians had to retreat to the second crater and from there start a new mine. Its construction continued until 8 October, when the last of the big mines (6,000 pounds of gunpowder in all) exploded, not only destroying the covered way but also piling up a ramp to enable the fort's reduit to be taken by storm. On the same day, the Prussian artillerymen were also lucky – one of the bombs hit the gunpowder magazine in the Jauernicker Fort. The explosion not only killed 200 of the crew, but also severely damaged the fort's redoubt. Both powerful explosions forced the commandant to decide to surrender the fortress. The defenders' forces and resources were, moreover, exhausted; the fortress already lacked gun carriages, most of which had been shattered by Prussian battery fire. In addition, the two months' shelling had resulted in great damage to the defensive works; Gribeauval, in his report, drew attention to the masonry caponiers in the places of arms in front of Jauernicker Fort, the destruction of which made it impossible to defend the covered way into which the Prussians had penetrated with a mine attack.

On 9 October, after 61 days from the opening of the siege works, the commandant of the fortress signed the surrender. The siege claimed 6,400 casualties on both sides in wounded and killed; almost 300,000 artillery shells of various types and calibres were fired during the siege, ranging from small hand grenades thrown by Coehoorn mortars to 75-pound bombs, as well as almost one million small arms rounds.

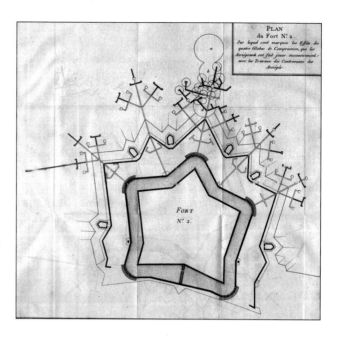

Mine warfare around Jauernicker Fort.
(Lefèbvre, *Oeuvres completes*, Pl. III)

As in previous sieges, the Prussians did not manage to avoid numerous errors in this one either. In the literature to date, these errors are mostly blamed on Simon Lefèbvre, who led the siege of the fortress. This engineer was alleged to have chosen the wrong element of the fortifications to attack, to have set up the siege batteries incorrectly, and finally to have been too slow in carrying out the ground works and mine attack.[57] There is some truth in these allegations and the siege of Schweidnitz was the first that Lefèbvre had led independently. Evidence of his lack of wartime experience was to be found, for example, in the breakdowns he suffered on several occasions when the Austrians destroyed the siegeworks he was conducting. This trait of the engineer is, moreover, pointed out by Frederick in his description of the siege of Schweidnitz in his 'History of my time', where he writes that Lefèbvre 'lost his head' after Gribeauval's miners detonated two mines.[58] The King's opinion was patently unfair. It is sufficient to note that the mines that the Austrians detonated were many more than the two mentioned by king (in fact there were about 15) and that, in addition to counter-mines, the Austrians made excellent use artillery fire to halt the progress of the Prussian approach works. Nevertheless, the engineer's inexperience was a fact. Lefèbvre's contact with mine warfare had actually only amounted to correspondence with Belidor and to a single test explosion made during an exercise near Potsdam. The effectiveness of the technique tested at the time, the globe of pressure, was the same as in the real war (at Schweidnitz it was even possible to create larger craters than at Potsdam), and yet the effectiveness of the mine attack in the real war was already quite different from what Frederick wanted. However, it was not only the engineer commanding the attack, but also his subordinates, who showed a lack of adequate training. It was the weakness of the engineering troops in general and not the weakness of a particular engineer

---

57   Seydel, *Nachrichten*, vol.3, pp.514–529.
58   Volz, *Die Werke*, vol.4, p.160. During the siege he spoke even worse of Lefèbvre, describing him as 'a stupid devil who does not understand the art of miners' and 'a stupid engineer who does not understand tactics', von Schöning Kurd Wolfgang Wilhelm Georg, *Militairische correspondenz des Königs Friedrich des Grossen mit dem prinzen Hienrich von Preussen* (Potsdam: Verlag von Ferdinand Riegel, 1852), vol.3, p.458.

that was the real reason for the delays in the siege of the fortress. The weakness of the engineering troops was also highlighted by Lefèbvre explaining to the King that he had too few engineers to carry out the work and that the number of miners was insufficient. The King was aware of the paucity of engineers, as he acknowledged in a letter to the engineer in charge of the siege.[59]

At the beginning of the siege, he had 15 engineers, some of whom 'could at best draw a plan and had never seen a siege'. Moreover, 11 of them were killed or wounded during the siege and by the end the King had to send those infantry officers who had some understanding of military engineering to supervise the approach works.[60] As for the miners, the attackers had only three officers and 40 men who had to build galleries from scratch for a month and a half. The skills of the miners' personnel were also poor. Both Lefèbvre and *General-Lieutenant* Tauentzien, who commanded the defence, complained about them. The latter even threatened *Major* Castillhon, commanding a group of miners, with arrest for, as he put it, 'extraordinary procrastination'.[61] However, it was difficult to expect any extraordinary skills from the Prussian miners when the only opportunity for them to gain mine experience was the Potsdam experiment. Of course, in peacetime these soldiers were not idle, they were even very busy – they built numerous counter-mine galleries in Silesian fortresses, including those in Schweidnitz. But at that time, they were something like specialised builders and did not have the opportunity to gain any combat experience. What is more, they even lacked the usual military familiarity and discipline, because, due to an excess of work, drill was not practised with them, as their officers complained.[62] No wonder, then, that the mine warfare caused them so much trouble. The problems were even greater because the opponents of the Prussian miners were the experienced Imperial miners. This applied not only to the commander-in-chief, Gribeauval, but also to the lower staff. In the countermines of the Jauernicker Fort was *Kapitän* Josef Pabliczek, for whom the Seven Years War was the fifth in which he took part. His skills, which caused the Prussians such great difficulties, were recognised a few days after the siege by the Empress, who awarded him the Order of Maria Theresa.[63]

Of course, the mistakes of the royal subordinates were not the only reason that made the siege last more than two months. Nor can the impact on the course of the siege of the decisions taken by the King be left without comment. Throughout its duration, Frederick received regular, almost daily updates from Tauentzien on the progress of the siege, as well as receiving plans for future action for his perusal. In addition, he did not confine himself to approving Lefèbvre's ideas; from the very beginning of the siege, he himself took the important decisions. It was on the basis of his decisions that Jauernicker Fort was attacked, not Galgen Fort (Fort Gallows) as Lefèbvre wanted.[64] Moreover, the siege could have ended much sooner, as

---

59   Letter from the King to Lefèbvre dated 18 August 1762, Droysen, *Politische Correspondenz*, vol.22, p.148.
60   Grosser Generalstab, *Geschichte des siebenjährigen Krieges*, vol.6, p.354; Schöning, *Militairische correspondenz*, pp.458–459, 462.
61   Schöning, *Militairische correspondenz*, p.420.
62   Bonin, *Geschichte des Ingenieurkorps*, p.191.
63   Jaromir Hirtenfeld, *Der Militär-Maria-Theresien-Orden und seine Mitglieder* (Wien: Kaiserlich-Königliche Hof- und Staatsdrukerei, 1857), pp.166–167.
64   Grosser Generalstab, *Geschichte des siebenjährigen Krieges*, vol.6, p.258.

early as 22 August, when the commandant of the fortress, *Feldmarschalllieutenant* Guasco, offered to surrender Schweidnitz on the condition that the entire garrison was released. The King, however, did not want to let go of the 10,000 Austrians he was about to take prisoner.[65] The King's greed cost him over a month's delay, the lives of several hundred of his soldiers, and the loss of a mass of materiel.[66] A reading of the letters that Lefèbvre received from the King shows that Frederick often gave him hints and even corrected drafts of his intentions, including in the field of mine warfare.[67] On 23 September Frederick arrived at the siege corps and eventually began to command the siege himself. He gave instructions as to what new batteries were to be laid, parallels to be extended, and more, but, as already stated, his activity did not have a particular beneficial effect. The two mines that were blown up during his command would not have led to the surrender of the fortress had it not been for a lucky hit on the powder magazine on 8 October.

The siege of Schweidnitz was the last act of fortress warfare in which the Prussian army took part, during the lifetime of Frederick the Great. The experience gained during it influenced the development of defensive architecture in various ways in the period following the Seven Years War. First and foremost, the influence on the architecture of the Schweidnitz fortress should be pointed out. The long siege, and especially the bombardment that took place during it, clearly showed the shortcoming of the fortress, which was the lack of bomb-proof rooms. It is therefore not surprising that its post-war modernisation saw the addition of numerous casemates for the garrison. The accumulation of experience from the sieges of Schweidnitz and Olomouc meant that it was in the Schweidnitz fortress that artillery casemates were first constructed. They were built in the Neumühl Flèche, which was one of three works erected to replace those ordered to be built by Gribeauval during the siege. Further structures were put in front of the flèches so that the third belt of defences was created, after the main perimeter and the ring of forts.

The long-lasting mine war, which despite its difficulties ended with the right result of breaking into the fortress, demonstrated the sense of building complex counter-mine systems. This had an impact on all Prussian fortresses built and modernised afterwards. This is demonstrated by the gigantic networks of counter-mine corridors of Glatz or Graudenz, preserved to this day, which would not have been built had it not been for the Schweidnitz experience.

Other Sieges

Described above are only those events of the fortress warfare in which Frederick directly took part. In addition to these, there were several others in which the King did not participate himself, but which he knew, and which influenced his thinking about fortresses. The vast majority of the sieges in which his troops were involved brought no other experiences, other than those described above. However, three other sieges deserve mention. The first is the 1745 Austrian siege of Cosel, during which Maria Theresa's soldiers quickly captured a

---

65   Schöning, *Militairische correspondenz*, pp.408–409.
66   By the end of the siege, at least twenty 24-pounder cannons were worn out. Schöning, *Militairische correspondenz*, p.458.
67   Letter from the King to Lefèbvre dated 11 September 1762, Droysen, *Politische Correspondenz*, vol.22, p.208.

fortress whose fortifications were not yet fully completed. A key factor was the participation of Austrian irregular troops (grenzer), who penetrated the fortress with a sudden, stealthy attack and enabled it to be captured without much resistance.[68] Two successful attacks carried out by the Austrian army under *Generalfeldmarschall* Ernst Gedeon von Laudon – on Glatz in 1760 and Schweidnitz in 1761 – were of a similar nature. The masterpiece was the capture of Schweidnitz, which took Laudon's troops two hours.[69] This instant success had a strong effect on the imagination of the King, who in his written statements about the fortresses often emphasised the issue of their resistance to assault. The King's reaction to the successful assaults carried out by von Laudon also had a material form – the unusually deep moats of Silberberg or Glatz were clearly intended to prevent their capture by a sudden attack, while the caponiers defending the covered way, later built at Glatz, Cosel and Brieg, were intended to enable the covered way to be defended, should it be suddenly seized by the enemy. In the case of the Graudenz fortress, there is even a hint from the King, who forbade the supplying of the casemates of the fortress core with embrasures, because 'where there is a hole, there the Grenzer will crawl'.[70]

---

68   Hans Alexander, *Friedrich der Große und Cosel* (Berlin: Schlieffen Verlag, 1936), pp.30–35.

69   von Tempelhoff, *Geschichte des siebenjährigen Krieges*, vol.5. pp.327–349; Tielke, *Beytrage zur Kriegskunst*, pp.101–162.

70   ‚Wo ein Loch ist, da kriecht ein Kroat hinein'. Wilhelm Adolf Ernst von Kamptz, *Grundsätze zur Ermittelung der artilleristischen Bewaffnung einer Festung* (Potsdam: Rieglesche Buchhandlung, 1862), p.10.

5

The Theory of Defensive Architecture in Prussia During the Frederician Period

Although no outstanding theoretical writings were produced in the country of Frederick the Great, Prussia was not an intellectual desert in this respect. There were several people living and active there who can be described as theorists of defensive architecture. The most important of these was the King himself; besides him, there were also several military engineers who made their name as theoreticians.

Royal Concepts as Expressed in Theoretical Writing

Frederick the Great made his mark in military history not only by his activity in the field, but his writing activity also played a major role. Among the texts he wrote, instructions of various kinds predominate, but there are several that have a theoretical dimension, led by the most important – *Generalprinzipien des Krieges*.

Looking through all the surviving texts of the King on military matters, it is noticeable that issues related to fortifications play a minor role in them. For the most part, they are concerned with the conquest and defence of fortresses, as well as field fortifications. Statements on fortresses themselves – their construction or function – are extremely rare, but are of great importance for our deliberations.

Basic Principles of War, 1748
Generalprinzipien des Krieges und ihre Anwendung auf die Taktik und Disziplin der preußischen Truppen, the first 'theoretical treatise' written by Frederick contains 31 chapters, of which only one, the 24th – 'Attack and defence of fortified places' – deals with the subject matter of interest to us. This small chapter takes up only two and half pages of the pre-First World War edition of Frederick's 'Collected Works' and is divided into three paragraphs: on attacking fortresses, on defending them and on defending against a sudden attack.[1] A comparison of the length of this chapter to the next one on battles (18 pages) clearly illustrates the minimal role of fortress warfare in Frederick's doctrine. The content of chapter 24,

---

1   Volz, *Die Werke*, vol.6, pp.55–57.

on the other hand, shows that Frederick had only a theoretical (and superficial) knowledge of fortress warfare methods at the time of writing this text. In the very first sentences, he likens it to a craft, such as watchmaking, which has developed unchanging rules of operation, applied in the same way every time. In a few words, he recalls the basic elements of a siege, while stating that it is such a repeatable and calculable process that, even without being present at the siege, it is possible to determine when a fortress will fall. Not surprisingly, Frederick, representing such an attitude, was annoyed with his engineers, who, in his opinion, prolonged the sieges they conducted too much. Frederick presented the Dukes von Anhalt-Dessau and Vauban as models of military men capable of conducting sieges. With regard to attacking the fortress himself, he had only one innovation – he proposed attacking the fortress from two sides and, if necessary, launching an assault from a third side at night. Many more practical remarks, testifying to the King's own thoughts, are to be found in the paragraph devoted to the defence of the fortress. It is actually a whole series of reflections by the King on the appropriateness of choosing particular types of defence. First of all, he draws attention to the caution with which sorties should be used. According to him, the possible loss of life that occurs in such situations is not replenishable by the defender. Instead of such dangerous sorties with large forces, he recommends smaller but more frequent forays – so that by disturbing the workers doing the approach works, the progress of the siege is slowed down. He devotes a separate list of advice to ways of protecting against an unexpected assault. In 1752, he added one more piece of advice to these that should be noted – he recommended erecting caponiers manned by a garrison of 12 on the covered way and the advanced salients of defensive works. The date of this correction is significant, as it shows that in this case practice was ahead of theory. Friedrick first introduced caponiers on the covered way with his design for the fortification of the city of Glatz in September 1751.

Political Testament, 1752

Much more thought on fortresses is contained in the chapter dedicated to them in the 1752 Political Testament.[2] It opens with a long passage on the operational role of the fortress. In it, Frederick explains in a few clear sentences the role that a fortress should play in a defence system:

> Fortresses are like powerful nails that hold the province to the ruler. In times of war, they are points of support for the armies that stand near them. They are grain stores for troops. Belts of their strong fortifications shield the stores, the sick and wounded, and the ammunition of the armies. Border fortresses form advanced quarters where a large corps can assemble to winter there, either to carry the war into hostile country or, finally, to encamp in safety while waiting to link up with other troops.[3]

As can be seen, for Frederick fortresses fulfilled a servile role in relation to the field army, which fitted perfectly with the ideas of the time about the role of the fortress.

---

2   Volz, *Die Werke*, vol.7, pp.176–179.
3   Volz, *Die Werke*, vol.7, p.176.

He then directs his attention to the considerations related to the expansion of the fortress system and the construction of new fortresses. In his view, the only argument that justifies the decision to build a new fortress is the occupation of a new province by the state; beyond this case, the expansion of the fortress system is unreasonable. The argument against such an expansion is the costs involved in building and maintaining a fortress. The financial aspect also runs through Frederick's other guidance. He recommends that when fortresses are established, they should be adapted to the terrain and exploit all its advantages, rather than erecting artificial, extensive fortress complexes. This is because the latter will require larger garrisons, which will affect the field army. He also draws attention to other means of securing the fortress without incurring additional costs. Instead of securing the hill over-looking the fortress with a new fortification, he recommends blasting the top of the hill and artificially shaping its slopes in such a way as to prevent it from being used by the siege batteries of a potential attacker.

As for the means used to defend the fortress, he suggests the use of two of the most impor-tant – water and fire. The former involves the use of wide outer moat and artificial inunda-tions, of which the Neisse fortress is said to be the best example, while the latter involves counter-mine systems, the best of which were to be those at Schweidnitz and at Neisse, in front of Fort Prussia.

It also introduces a brief overview of particular forms, particularly good for defensive works. He recommends the use of caponiers on covered ways and in the advanced sali-ents of defensive works to defend them against sudden attack. In addition, he distinguishes defensive works, double covered ways, narrow envelopes, bastions, and ravelins with retired flanks. He particularly recommends his own invention, which was introduced in Glatz – the covered way, which instead of running in a straight line, runs in a broken line, which makes it difficult to target longitudinally.

The King's Instructions for his Quartermasters, 1757

Another statement by the King on the subject of fortifications can be found in volume 30 of his collected works. This is the 'Instruction des Königs für seine Quartiermeister', which Frederick is said to have dictated in 1757, after losing the Battle of Kolin.[4] It contains numerous recommendations for the defence of fortresses, the establishment of fortified camps, and their fortification. As in the other texts, comments on fortresses are in the minority. Everything the King wanted to say on this subject is contained in nine points occupying little more than a page of text, while he devoted eight whole pages to the issue of fortified camps. Nevertheless, these nine points probably constitute the longest statement made by a king on the subject of fortifications, their role, shape, etc. Therefore, this state-ment should be quoted in full.

1. When building a fortress, it is important to adapt to the terrain so that the characteristics of the terrain reinforce the fortifications.

---

4   Preuss, *Oeuvres de Frederic le Grand*, vol.30, pp.238–239; Auszug aus einer Instruktion des Königs Friedrich II über Verschanzte Stellungen', *Archiv für die Offiziere der Königlich Preußischen Artillerie und Ingenieur Korps*, vol.3 (1836), pp.243–245.

2. Each stronghold must be given detached works to keep the attacker at a distance and the enemy must be forced to attack the stronghold from more than one place.

3. These forward works must be well covered by the fortress and arranged so that the enemy cannot get a foothold in them.

4. All these external works must be secured against all *coups de main*, and it must not be possible to take them through the Gorge.

5. All works must defend each other strongly, both from the front and from the flanks.

6. None of the defensive lines must be exposed to longitudinal fire from any hill, still less must they be penetrated from behind. If this cannot be avoided, strong traverses and bonets, or breastworks in the shape of a saw (*en crémaillère*), must be made.

7. All detached works must have secure covered communication.

8. The commander must try to extend the defence by setting up advanced flèches. Then the opponent will have to open up his first trenches further away, and protect them from enfilade fire.

9. If a fortress is located on a river, safe communication should be put across it, and a solidly fortified tête de pont should be established in front of the bridge.[5]

Military Testament, 1768

The King's next statement on fortresses comes from the Military Testament of 1768.[6] Although the chapter on fortresses is just as short there as in the Political Testament of 16 years earlier, we find far fewer statements of a general, theoretical nature, and there are interesting general remarks only in the opening paragraph of the chapter. The lessons learned from the experience of the Seven Years War can be seen very strongly in it. 'My system is based on the defence of defensive works on the covered way and on the depth of moats, both water and dry, and I make every possible effort to avoid taking the fortress by storm.'[7] The second part of the quoted sentence is clearly inspired by the events of the siege of Glatz in 1760 and Schweidnitz in 1761, when the Austrians captured the fortresses in this very way. In turn, the following sentence echoes the 1762 Schweidnitz events: 'The defence of the covered way consists mainly in mines and certain advance works, which keep the enemy at bay and force them to lay siege before they reach the glacis.' As can be seen, king did not introduce many new ideas here about the role of the fortress and its parts. He had already written about the importance of the covered way in a previous testament, as he had the mine war. The experience of the Seven Years War only resulted in him drawing attention to the depth of the moat as a decisive factor in defending against assault. Previously, it had seemed to him that caponiers would be a sufficient remedy.

The rest of his chapter contains brief descriptions of individual Prussian fortresses, together with mentions of their current or future expansion. They do not carry any significant concepts, only the hierarchy of Prussian fortresses outlined is noteworthy. Although, as we read, the vast majority of modernisation work is to be carried out in the fortresses of Silesia, and outside this province only Kolberg and Stettin, threatened by the Russians in

---

5   Preuss, *Oeuvres de Frederic le Grand*, vol.30, pp.238–239.
6   Volz, *Die Werke*, vol.6, pp.243–244.
7   Volz, *Die Werke*, vol.6, p.243.

the previous war, should be modernised, none of these fortresses is considered the most important in the eyes of the King. The primacy among Prussian fortresses was to be held by the Magdeburg fortress, as a refuge for the royal family and 'the last point of resistance for the state.'[8] Interestingly, despite this, the King did not want to expand it much and only wanted to make minor adjustments.

The King's Instructions to Fortress Commanders

An important part of the King's writings are his numerous instructions addressed to specific military officers. Only four have survived, which were addressed to the commanders and governors of the fortresses of Cosel, Schweidnitz and Magdeburg. It is known, however, that in addition to these, the King also issued similar instructions regarding the fortresses at Glogau, Neisse, Glatz and Silberberg.[9]

The oldest is the instruction for the commandant of Cosel, *Oberst* Lattorff, written in 1753.[10] In it, the King discusses in detail each phase of a regular siege and indicates the measures to be taken by the commandant during it. Frederick does not introduce any new thread there that was not present in the military writing of the time; his recommendations are completely typical. The only interesting passage is the order to garrison the caponiers of the covered way and the Weigschützer redoubt with a permanent garrison, before the enemy even appeared near the fortress. It can be seen that the King took the threat of a sudden, unexpected attack very seriously. The next instruction was written in 1755 and was intended for the governor of the Magdeburg fortress, Prince Ferdinand von Braunschweig.[11] It contains more recommendations of an organisational rather than a military nature. It is interesting to note that the King separately draws attention to keeping a particularly close eye on state prisoners during the war, especially *Generalmajor* von Walrave.

There are considerably more unique elements in two instructions concerning the fortress of Schweidnitz. The first was written by the King in 1778, during the War of the Bavarian Succession; it was intended for *Generalmajor* Anton von Otto von Buddenbrock.[12] The King, as in his instruction to another commandant of Cosel in 1753, gives instructions on how to proceed in the event of a regular attack. In doing so, he considers from which side the enemy might attack and in what order the fortress works will be attacked. It is clear that the King envisages a long and persistent defence of this fortress and successive, regular approach attacks on the defensive works: first on the advanced redoubts, then on the forts (two at a time) and finally on the main rampart. Interestingly, the King noted that the siege proper would only take place after the enemy had taken the outer redoubts. Another interesting detail is the recommendation that two large retrenchments (*Abschnitt*), or temporary defensive lines, be made in advance to hold the remaining forts once one of them has been captured. Ideas from this instruction are developed in another, written in 1781.[13] It partly repeats what the King had formulated three years earlier, but is much more detailed. It contains both organisational and strictly military

---

8   Volz, *Die Werke*, vol.6, p.244.
9   Preuss, *Oeuvres de Frederic le Grand*, vol.30, p.XXX; Anon., 'Friedrich der Große als Ingenieur', p.6.
10   Volz, *Die Werke*, vol.6, pp.341–346.
11   Preuss, *Oeuvres de Frederic le Grand*, vol.30, pp.213–216.
12   Preuss, *Oeuvres de Frederic le Grand*, vol.30, pp.375–379.
13   Preuss, *Oeuvres de Frederic le Grand*, vol.30, pp.413–422.

recommendations. It again includes considerations about the side from which the enemy will attack and what steps should be taken to slow the progress of his attack. Frederick includes in his considerations the factor of the newly erected artillery casemates. He writes that it will take the enemy a long time to capture facilities equipped with them. Using the example of under-ground communication galleries connecting the advanced works (Ziegelei, Jauernick Flesche and Jauernick Hangar) with the interior of the fortress, he emphasises the role of this solution in prolonging the defence and security of the garrison of these works. As for the defence of the fortress, he elaborates on the retrenchment to be made in the space between the line of forts and the city. Retrenchment themselves were nothing new, having been used in the defence of fortresses since the sixteenth century. Here, however, what draws attention is the scale and – at least in theory – the effectiveness of this solution. According to the instructions, simply making them and manning them will force the enemy to laboriously capture the defensive works adja-cent to the already captured fort. All of these measures involving the appropriate use of the Schweidnitz defence works will, according to the King's calculations, allow the defence of the fortress to be extended for a period of more than three months.

As can be seen, these texts bring relatively little new information about the fortifica-tions themselves, mostly discussing their use in defence. However, one can conclude from their content that Frederick was deeply convinced of the effectiveness of the new solutions in the fortresses he built and partly designed. This can be seen particularly in relation to the fortress of Schweidnitz. As is well known, this fortress defended itself for two months in 1762 against an attack by Prussian troops. According to the instruction of 1781, it was assumed that this fortress could defend itself for more than three months, which meant that the newly introduced modernisations would allow the siege to be extended by one month.

Engineer Theoreticians

Abraham de Humbert
The most prominent theoretician among the military engineers active during the reign of Frederick the Great was Abraham de Humbert. He is one of the rare cases of an officer known more for his theoretical works than for the buildings he actually constructed. He was the author of several scientific publications, including those on fortifications. Some of these he published in print before 1740, these were polemical writings in which he dealt primarily with the reception of Rimpler's fortification concepts.

His first publication during the reign of Frederick the Great was his translation of *Maréchal* Vauban's work on fortresses defence and attack. This work in itself adds nothing new; what is important about it is mainly that Frederick took a personal interest in the work. In the spring of 1744, he promised the author his support in its publication by financing the printing of the illustrations.[14] The work was eventually published three times: twice in Berlin (1744–1745 and 1751) and once under a changed title in 1747 in Potsdam.[15]

---

14   Letters from the King to Humbert of 5 and 9 March and 12 April 1744, GStA SPK, I HA Rep.96 B
      Abschriften von Kabinetsordres, Bd.29, pp.288, 305, 370.
15   Abraham von Humbert, *Der Angriff und die Vertheidigung der Festungen durch den Herrn von Vauban*
      (Berlin: Bergmann, 1744–1745); (Berlin: Laude und Spener, 1751); The 1747 edition could not be

Humbert's own treatise is *L'art du Genie pour l'instruction des gens de guerre*, published twice in Berlin in French (1755 and 1760) and once in German (Bernburg, 1756).[16] It is the only work published in Frederician Prussia that can be compared in terms of content with other major European theoretical statements on fortification of the time. Of course, there is little novelty in it, as the author himself acknowledges in the introduction to his book. Humbert built on the theoretical achievements of the French, above all Vauban and Belidor, as well as the Dutch, especially Coehoorn. The author's aim, as he emphasised in the preface to the book, was not to create a novel theory, but more of a work that would have a didactic value. The author paid a great deal of attention to building technology specific to the construction of fortifications. He discussed in detail the types of soil and their suitability for erecting ramparts, the types of stone and bricks, the method of erecting masonry and grass revetments, and foundations. In addition to this, he detailed all types of fortress defences – bastions, retrenchment, moats and all types of outer works, and presented the advantages and disadvantages of each type of structure. He devoted a large chapter to the topic of irregular fortification, which is essentially a list of practical methods of strengthening existing defences. In addition, he has filled a separate part of the book covering garrison buildings; barracks, powder stores, guardhouses and other such facilities. Humbert displays great expertise and detailed knowledge, although the examples points out relate to the vast majority of solutions applied in fortresses rebuilt at the turn of the seventeenth and eighteenth centuries by the French. There is only one point where one can see a certain influence of the developing Prussian tradition – when writing about model gates he mentions not only French examples (such as the gates at Lille), but also numerous Prussian examples, such as the Berlin gate at Wesel or the Berlin and Anklam gate at Stettin.

Johann Friedrich von Balbi

Balbi is the author of only one work, and an unpublished one at that, drawn up in 1750.[17] As the author himself states in the title, it was intended as a kind of manual for infantry officers. It is a purely practical handbook that discusses in detail the entire course of a siege. The author describes all the steps to be taken during an attack on a fortress – starting with its surrounding, the preparation of siege materiel, the selection of the site to be attacked, the demarcation and execution of the first parallel, the establishment of batteries, subsequent parallels and batteries (ricochets, mortars), the mine battle for the glacis, the launching of the breach, and its assault. The fortress that Balbi depicts attacking is a completely theoretical creation, with no connection to any existing defensive work. All the descriptions of the

---

found, it is mentioned by Jähns Max, *Geschichte der Kriegswissenschaften vornehmlich in Deutschland, Bd.3, Das XVIII. Jahrhundert seit dem Auftreten Friedrichs des Großen 1740–1800* (München – Leipzig: Verlag von Oldenbourg, 1891), p.2823.

16   Abraham de Humbert, *L'art du Genie pour l'instruction des gens de guerre* (Berlin: Laude und Spener, 1755); Abraham de Humbert, *Vollkommener Unterricht der zur Kriegs-Kunst gehörigen Wissenschaften* (Bernburg: Coemen, 1756).

17   Abchandlung, Wie eine Vestung ordentlich anzugreifen und zu belagern sey, welche in geuten Verteidigungs Stande ist, und nebst einer hinlänglichen Besatzung, auch einen geschickten und erfarenen Commendanten hat, Zum Unterricht derer Officier von der Infanterie, hauptsachlich aufgesetzet, durch Herr Obrist Lieutnant Balbi 1752, SBB PK, Handschriften Abteilung, Ms. Boruss. fol.733.

various actions to be taken are concerned with details related to the works of the imaginary fortress and the surrounding, also imaginary, terrain. The author extremely rarely refers to real experiences; when he does, these are mostly experiences relating to the French siege of Bergen op Zoom.

Gerhard Cornelius von Walrave

The most important Prussian engineer of the early days of the reign of Frederick the Great is mainly known as a practitioner. Walrave wrote only one work (in November 1747), which can hardly be regarded as the work of an architectural theorist – *Memoire sur l'attaque et Defence des Places*. This text has never been published. A copy of it, probably dating from the nineteenth century, is held in the collection of the Geheimes Staatsarchiv in Berlin and comes from the legacy of Gerhard von Scharnhorst.[18] Another copy, described by Klaus Jordan, probably the original, is in private hands.[19] A third copy is held in the archives in Potsdam. This one is devoid of the title, author references and plans, but its contents clearly indicate that it is a copy of the Walrave text.[20] There is probably also a fourth copy of this manuscript, as there is a copy of the memorandum from a different original to the three previously described in the archives of the Society of Friends of Fortifications in Toruń.[21] All versions of the text are in French. The Berlin and Potsdam versions are devoid of illustrations, the former is 31 pages long, the latter 41. In both, there are numerous references to plans for fortresses. The second known version has 56 pages of text and contains 10 illustrations. The third, which was transcribed from an unknown source by Krzysztof Biskup, was 92 pages long.[22]

This text – like the Balbi text described earlier – is a detailed description of the siege, from the preliminary work to the general assault on the breach. But that is where the similarity ends, for Walrave is not concerned with didacticism or with detailing all the steps to be taken by the commander in charge of the siege work. He addresses his text to the King, who, according to Walrave, knows the art of war well. Consequently, he has concentrated on presenting those solutions that are of particular importance for the success of a siege operation. In addition, Walrave devotes just as much space to the attack as to the measures used in the defence of a fortress. In this respect, too, his work is not a textbook, but a chronologically ordered overview of the particularly relevant and useful defensive solutions of a typical

---

18   De Walrave, Memoire sur l'attaque et Defencela des Places, GStA SPK, VI HA Familienarchive und Nachlässe, Nl Scharnhorst, no. 314.

19   A description of this copy was given in Klaus Jordan, 'Gerhard Cornelius Walrave und sein Vorschlag zur Verbesserung des Festungsgrundrisses der Festung Wesel von 1747', *Festungsjournal*, (2009), pp.66–72. There are discussions of a possible second version of Walrave's work.

20   Brandenburgisches Ladneshauptarchiv, sing. 8 Soldin 827, Abschrift einer Denkschrift eines preußischen Ingenieur-Offiziers über den Festungskrieg (in Französisch). For information about this source, I thank Alexander Burns

21   This copy was made in the 1980s by Krzysztof Biskup. Unfortunately, the TTPF archive contains the copy itself, with no reference to the source.

22   It is likely that there were other references; Preuss writes about a copy that was in the archives of the Prussian General Staff, which ran to 83 pages, Johann David Erdmann Preuss, 'Friedrich der Große und der General v. Walrave', *Zeitschrift für Kunst, Wissenschaft, und Geschichte des Krieges*, vol.1 (1859), p.45.

siege. What is more, Walrave draws on his vast experience as a fortification builder and siege participant. He illustrates the various solutions and the steps to be taken by the attacker or defender with numerous examples from sieges of the late seventeenth and early eighteenth centuries.

The most interesting parts of the text are those in which the author refers to defensive architecture. When describing the various phases of defence, he often draws attention to the appropriate architectural solutions. He is very keen to praise those solutions that were used in the fortresses he built. Among other things, he emphasises the role of the outer moat, which, in his opinion, makes a fortress very difficult to conquer. He singles out those at Wesel and especially at Neisse as particularly well-made. He finds it impossible to pass through them using a regular attack because of their width and depth. For dry moats, he recommends the use of counterscarp galleries, as well as coffers similar to those used in Neisse at Fort Prussia and in Magdeburg at Fort Berge. He also singles out the construction of bastions, which he erected at Magdeburg and Wesel.

Walrave's memorandum had little influence on later defensive architecture. It was a study intended for the King; the author even expressed the wish that it not be published. It is known, however, that the text had some influence on the instructions for fortress commanders issued by Frederick and Scharnhorst.[23] For our consideration, the most important is its influence on the royal writings. It can be demonstrated in several places, most notably in the Military Testament in 1752, which recommends the use of outer moats and artificial inundations similar to those in the Neisse.[24] Elsewhere, in a 1757 instruction to his quartermasters, he recommends that commanders erect flèches in the foreground of the fortress, which will force the attacker to begin his approach work further away from the fortress.[25] Walrave's recommendations were also incorporated by king into the instructions he wrote in 1753 for *Oberst* Lattorf, commandant of Cosel. An entire paragraph on the division of the garrison and the tasks for which soldiers are to be used is based on Walrave's advice, as are the recommendations on the means to be used by the commander of the fortress to detect the true location of the start of the approach attack.[26]

Johann Karl Dietrich Pirscher

Another engineer worth mentioning who commented on the theory of defensive architecture was Johann Karl Dietrich Pirscher, who came from Wolfenbüttel. Little is known about his service in the Prussian army other than that during the Seven Years War. He was posted to the corps of Prince Ferdinand of Brunswick and was dismissed from the service due to numerous reprimands given to him by supervising officers. He returned to the Prussian army, however, and in 1777 attained the rank of *kapitän* and retired in 1787.[27] More is known about his work as a fortification theorist. He published a total of three books, the most interesting of which is *Anweisung zum Festungsbau mit verdeckten Flanken und zur Defense en revers, als dem einzigen Mittel den Belagerern lange zu widerstehen*, published in Berlin in

---

23   Jordan, *Gerhard Cornelius Walrave*, p.70.
24   Volz, *Die Werke*, vol.7, p.177.
25   Preuss, *Oeuvres de Frederic le Grand*, vol.30, p.XXX.
26   Volz, *Die Werke*, vol.6, p.343.
27   Bonin, *Geschichte des Ingenieurkorps*, p.301.

1776.[28] The book is interesting for its innovative approach to fortress outline. The models he proposes consist of a main perimeter with either a circular or polygonal outline, with detached works as the main element of defence. Artillery fire conducted from the flanks of these works would primarily cover the moat in front of the main rampart and between the main rampart and the neighbouring detached works. This interesting and innovative concept has some parallels in the Prussian fortifications of the time. A similar principle of operation as well as a fortress outline can be found in the fortress in Graudenz, which was under construction at the time. The date of publication of Pirscher's work rather rules out that the fortress designs were modelled on the text. The idea that Pirscher was somehow inspired by the Graudenz fortress is more likely, although difficult to prove due to the fact that his name never appears in the context of the Graudenz fortress. However, something must have inspired Pirscher to come up with such ideas in the run-up to the book's publication, since his previous publication of 10 years earlier, contains quite traditional ideas for the fortress outline.[29]

Ludwig Müller

The last theorist to be mentioned is Ludwig Müller. This Prussian engineer is the author of only one, but extremely important, book – *Versuch über Verschanzungskunst auf Winterpostierungen*.[30] Although this work is devoted to field fortification, a subject outside the scope of this text, it nevertheless needs to be discussed, at least briefly, as it was something of a revolution in the approach to this subject. The author, having analysed both the experience of the war so far and the types of field works used, proposed his own, completely innovative form. This was a polygonal, wood and earth redoubt, defended by small, bomb-proof caponiers. Thanks to these, the guns defending the redoubt were protected from howitzer fire, which seriously prolonged their life. There is no doubt that the concepts introduced by Müller, although so innovative, were firmly rooted in the wartime practice of the Frederician period. One of the prototypes of this form was the wooden blockhouse from Oberschwedeldorf (Szalejów Górny), which offered prolonged resistance to the Austrian corps in the winter of 1779. It was captured only after several hours of shelling by 6- and 12-pounder cannon and 7-pounder howitzers.[31] The site was probably well known to Müller, who was involved in the construction of outposts in the County of Glatz during the War of the Bavarian Succession.[32]

Müller's ideas were only known to the Prussian military in the eighteenth century, as the book was published in a limited edition, available only to Prussian officers.[33] His ideas were not realised during his lifetime, even though the King planned to fortify some of the points where the battles of 1779 took place, including Oberschwedeldorf. Nevertheless, the Müller

---

28   Johann Karl Dietrich Pirscher, *Anweisung zum Festungsbau mit verdeckten Flanken und zur Defense en revers, als dem einzigen Mittel den Belagerern lange zu widerstehen* (Berlin: Schropsche, 1776).
29   Johann Karl Dietrich Pirscher, *Kurzer Unterricht von den Anfangsgrunden der Kriegs Baukunst* (Berlin, Verlag der Buchhandlung der Realschule, 1767)
30   Ludwig Müller, *Versuch über Verschanzungskunst auf Winterpostierungen* (Potsdam: Sommer, 1782).
31   Seydel, *Nachrichten*, vol.3, pp.168–170.
32   Bonin, *Geschichte des Ingenieurkorps*, p.108.
33   Jähns, *Geschichte*, p.2740.

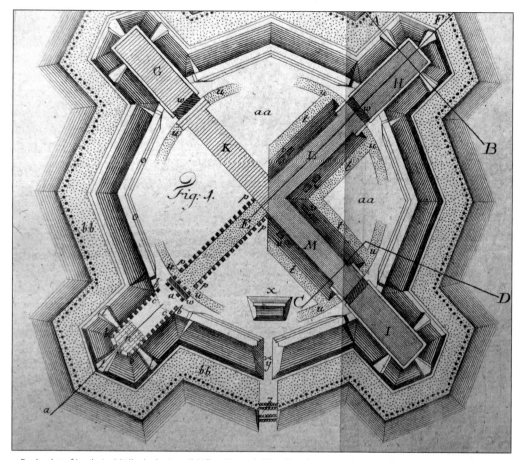

Redoubt of Ludwig Müller's design. (Müller, *Versuch über Verschanzungskunst auf Winterpostierungen*, Pl. I)

redoubt had a considerable influence on later defensive architecture. The Wolfsbergschanze in Kolberg, which was modelled on it, performed excellently in the defence of that city during the French siege in 1807. This building, in turn, strongly inspired the luminaries of nineteenth century Prussian defensive architecture, with Johann Leopold Ludwig von Brese-Winiary at the forefront.[34]

As can be seen from the examples given above, not many theoretical works on defensive architecture were produced in Frederick's Prussia. Those that were produced were either secondary, or they were not published, or they did not generate much resonance. The situation was different with the fortifications actually constructed during this period.

---

34   Johann Leopold Ludwig von Brese-Winiary, *Drei Vorlesungen ueber das Entstehen und das Wesen der neueren Befestigungsmethode, M. bes. Beziehg. auf d. in preuss. Staate seit d. letzten Kriegsjahren z. Ausführg. gekommenen Festgs-Neubauten, gehalten in d. milit. Ges. i. J. 1844* (Berlin: Unknown Publisher, 1856), pp.61–62.

6

Fortifications During the Silesian Wars (1740–1756)

In the first period of the development of fortifications during the reign of Frederick the Great, most investments were made in Silesia. This province, incorporated into the Prussian state in 1742 as a result of the Peace of Breslau, attracted almost all the King's interest. As a result of his and his engineers' activities, between 1740 and 1756 five fortresses (Glogau, Breslau, Brieg, Neisse, Glatz) were substantially modernised, two more were erected (Cosel, Schweidnitz), and one was planned but not realised (Schurgast/Skorogoszcz). The remaining fortress complexes in Prussia were of less immediate importance; apart from minor repair and modernisation work, an attempt was made to strengthen one fortress in the Electoral March (Peitz) and to rebuild one fort in Pomerania (Peenemünde).

Silesia, at the time when the Prussian army entered its territory, had a relatively numerous range of modern fortifications. The most important of these were rebuilt by Frederick, as will be shown below. Before doing so, however, at least a brief mention should be made of the other fortifications which were not modernised. The most important of these was the fortification of the town of Liegnitz (Legnica). This town had a full perimeter of sixteenth century bastion fortifications and a castle fortified in the same way. During the Thirty Years War these fortifications were reinforced with two crown works and single ravelins extended in front of the town ramparts. These fortifications were still in place when the Prussian army entered Silesia but were of little significance. Frederick decided in 1742 only to repair the old medieval walls. Nevertheless, the fortifications of Liegnitz must have been of some value, since the Imperial army occupied the place in autumn 1757 and decided to defend it on the basis of the old ramparts. After the rapid surrender of the garrison in December 1757, the King decided to dismantle the local fortifications.[1]

Ohlau (Oława) also had strong modern fortifications. They were younger than those of Liegnitz, as the bastion fortifications of this town were built during the Thirty Years War by the Swedes. They took the form of four bastions connected by curtains, surrounding the

---

1   Fritz Pfeiffer, 'Liegnitz als Festung', *Mitteilungen des Geschichts- und Altertumes-Vereins zu Liegnitz*, vol.10, (1926), pp.264–271; Kurt Bimler, *Die Schlesische Massive Wehrbauten* (Breslau: Heyderbrand Verlag, 1940–44), vol.4, pp.24–26; Seydel, *Nachrichten*, vol.3, pp.125, 138.

town and an extensive horn work defending the castle. They were poorly preserved earthen fortifications that were of little value in 1740.[2]

Namslau's (Namysłów) fortifications were also built during the Thirty Years War. However, in 1740 they were in better condition, as they had been extended in the 1650s. After this expansion, the fortress consisted of the town's fortifications protected by ramparts with five bastions and one redan, and the medieval castle was defended by a large hornwork. Nevertheless, this fortress too was not able to defend itself for long against the Prussian army. The town surrendered to them without a fight on 11 January 1741, the castle held out for three weeks.[3]

In addition to these three cities, there were other numerous centres in Silesia that had once been strongly fortified. Towns where medieval walls were reinforced with some earthworks in the modern period were not rare. However, none, apart from the towns mentioned above, had any defensive significance in the eighteenth century.

Glogau

The fortress of Glogau was the first Silesian stronghold that Frederick encountered. As early as 28 December 1740, his troops approached its walls, and captured it by storm on the night of 8–9 March the following year. It was therefore natural that Glogau was the foremost Silesian stronghold to acquire a new appearance.

Main Enceinte
The state the Prussians found Glogau in 1741 is very well known, not least from the plan drawn up by Cornelius Walrave. This engineer took measurements of the existing defences before he set about designing the new fortifications.[4] The drawing is preserved in the Berlin Staatsbibliothek and covers only the fortifications of the south bank of the Oder. It shows the town surrounded by a medieval wall with a bastion front. The perimeter had six bastions with a regular outline, three heavily deformed, of which the two adjacent to the Oder had a tenaille outline. In the middle of the Oder front was another very flattened bastion. Of the city's bastions, as many as six had cavaliers. The fortress in 1741 had only one ravelin, between Loewen and Dominikaner Bastion, but it was provided with a full covered way with mostly small places of arms, both in the retreating salients and in those protruding in front of the bastions.

A major drawback of the fortifications here was their poor state of preservation. This was proved by the Prussian assault that led to the capture of the town in March 1741. Therefore, after the seizure of the fortress, the most important task for the Prussians was to secure the existing fortifications against assault by temporary means. As early as 10 March 1741, Walrave drew up a plan for palisading, as mentioned by Prince Leopold von Braunschweig

2   Willy Klawitter, *Geschichte der schlesischen Festungen in vorpreußischer Zeit* (Breslau: Trewendt & Granier Verlag, 1941), pp.75–76.
3   Klawitter, *Geschichte der schlesischen Festungen*, pp.41, 57–58, 121–128.
4   Plan der Vestung Glogau wie selbige bey der Eroberung gewesen, SBB PK, ref. X 25132.

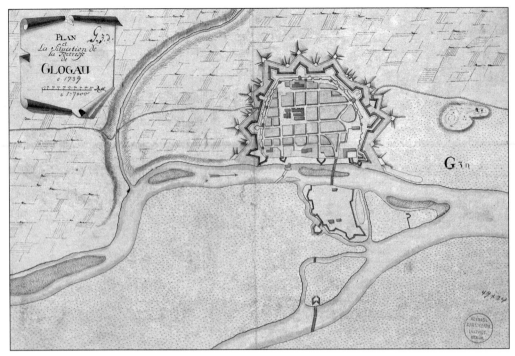

Fortress Glogau in 1740. (SBB PK, Kart. X 25131/10)

in a letter to the King on 12 March 1741.[5] The King liked Walrave's proposals very much.[6] According to other accounts, the project for securing the fortress was to be carried out by *Leutnant* Foris on the King's orders, and the entire work was to cost 49,2477 thalers.[7] Foris seems to have supervised preparations for the reconstruction of the fortress in Walrave's absence. Among other things, he was to organise the stone for the fortress construction in the autumn, and at the beginning of 1742 he drew up a plan of its surroundings.[8] However, in the latter task he showed off too much independence – he drew up the plan without royal permission or an approved cost estimate. Consequently, in the spring of 1742, the work was continued by *Major* Unfried, who drew up a cost estimate for the modernisation of the fortress amounting to 138,673 thalers. He, too, failed to consult the King about his plans, for which he was rebuked by the sovereign. Frederick immediately ordered Walrave, who was overseeing work on the fortresses at Neisse and Brieg, to thoroughly check the afore-

5   Ferdinand Minsberg, *Geschichte der Stadt und Festung Groß Glogau* (Glogau: Julius Gottschalk, 1853), vol.2, p.269.

6   Letter from the King to Walrave of 15 March 1741, GStA SPK, I HA Rep.96 B Abschriften von Kabinetsordres, Bd.23, pp.25–26.

7   Burchardi, Uber die Preussischen Festungen, GStA SPK, IV HA, Rep.15 A, no. 806, p.75.

8   Letter from the King to Foris of 12 October 1741, GStA SPK, I HA Rep.96 B Abschriften von Kabinetsordres, Bd.23, p.315; Letter from the King to Foris of 18 January 1742, GStA SPK, I HA Rep.96 B Abschriften von Kabinetsordres, Bd.25, p.80.

mentioned cost estimate and send it to him with a plan and his comments. He also ordered Walrave to control Unfried and report promptly on all design decisions made, so that the King could feed his comments into each of the designs.[9] From then on, responsibility for the project fell to Walrave. Despite this change, work on the fortress did not progress as quickly as the King would have liked, as he expressed in a letter to Walrave dated 24 May.[10] The main task that was carried out in 1742 was the construction of a new belt of outer works, designed by Walrave. This consisted of ravelins in front of each curtain and lunettes in front of each bastion. The ravelins had a retrenchment in form of a tenaille in the middle and the lunettes were offset from the covered way sections behind them. The whole formed a strong new defensive perimeter independent of the inner ring of bastions. Work on this element of the fortress had already been completed in 1742, and in the early spring of 1743 the new fortifications were supplied with palisades.[11]

However, the state that the main perimeter achieved after the Walrave reconstruction quickly changed. As early as 1745, a project was drawn up to rebuild the envelope that had just been erected. The small lunettes in front of the corners of the bastions were to be replaced by extensive, regular counterguards provided with concave retired flank in the Coehoorn style. In addition to this, the project envisaged the reconstruction of the Oder front by erecting two small, but regular and evenly spaced bastions set up in place of one large one.[12] Preparations for the realisation of this project had been under way since September 1746. That month witnessed the King's letter concerning the rebuilding of the lunettes in Glogau (4 September), the cost estimate for one of them (30 September), as well as the final disposition of the King, who granted the sum of 12,719 thalers for 1747 for the rebuilding of the lunettes postulated by the fortress commander, *Generalmajor* Peter du Moulin.[13] The rebuilding of this section of the city's fortifications was carried out in 1747. The lunettes erected by Walrave were connected by traverses of the covered way, which resulted in the creation of extensive counterguards in front of the corners of the bastions. However, the actual structures that were built differed from the design, as they had irregular forms and their shoulders were straight. While the above-described initial design for the reconstruction of the envelope is anonymous, the final realised version was designed by *Oberst* Sers. It is also known that it was the King who had the final say, as the design was authorised by him before commencement.[14]

The transformation of the lunettes was the last work, originally planned, altering the outline of the main perimeter of the Glogau fortifications, but from the designers' point of view it was not the end of the work in this part of the fortifications. In a document describing the activities to be carried out at the Silesian fortresses in 1748, two items related to further

---

9   Letter from the King to Walrave of 2 March 1742, GStA SPK, I HA Rep.96 B Abschriften von Kabinetsordres, Bd.24, p.89.

10   Letter from the King to Walrave of 24 May 1742, GStA SPK, I HA Rep.96 B Abschriften von Kabinetsordres, Bd.24, p.282.

11   Letter from the King to Walrave of 12 November 1742, GStA SPK, I HA Rep.96 B Abschriften von Kabinetsordres, Bd.26, p.72.

12   Nouveau Plan de Glogau... l'anne 1745, SBB PK, ref. X 25132/17.

13   GStA SPK Geheimes Zivilkabinett I HA Rep.96 No. 616 – Schlesische Festungen, Bd.C pp.15–19, 21–22.

14   Letter from Sers to the King of 25 October 1746, GStA SPK Geheimes Zivilkabinett I HA Rep.96 No. 616 – Schlesische Festungen, Bd.C, pp.18–19.

work appeared: the erection of 48 blockhouses in the corners of the covered way, at a total cost of 7,641 thalers, and the construction of gunpowder magazines in three ravelins, for 600 cetnars each, at a total cost of 7,329 thalers. Both of these works were postponed until the following financial year and were finally completed in 1751.[15] Another important defensive work was the counter-mine corridors built between 1751 and 1752 at a cost of 16,100 thalers.[16] This task was completed in the summer of 1752, as they were visited by the King on 3 September during his stay in Glogau.[17] In this period another gunpowder magazine was also erected for 4,000 thalers.[18] Repairs to existing defences were also important works. In 1749 more than 2,000 thalers were spent to repair one of the curtains,[19] while between 1750 and 1751 a strengthening of the defensive works on the Oder side took place, together with protection against the current. This work cost 6,000 thalers.[20]

Fort Stern

One of the most important works created at Glogau during the modernisation of the fortress before the Seven Years War was the Star Fort (*der Stern*, Fort Stern, *Sternschanze*). The King was involved in the construction of this defensive work from the beginning. It was built as early as 1742 at his personal command. Initially it was to be erected as a purely earthen structure, the King planning to reinforce its ramparts with masonry revetment only in the following years.[21] After the Second Silesian War, a food store was erected inside it. However, as early as 1746 it was decided to erect a new, permanent defensive work there. The protection of the storehouse ceased to be of importance, as it had been dismantled. In October 1746, a cost estimate was drawn up for 'A new fort in Glogau, with a bomb-proof casemate for 200-300 men, together with 2 small powder magazines under the rampart.' According to the cost estimate drawn up by *Oberst* Sers, who was probably also the designer of the fort, this work was to cost 72,205 thalers. The bulk of the cost was for the masonry work associated with the construction of the casemates, gunpowder magazines and the construction of the sewer (42,214 thalers), as well as for the earthworks associated with digging the moat, clearing the area for the casemate, making the rampart road, breastwork, glacis and digging the sewer (19,938 thalers). The fort was not built in a single year. In 1747 the King allocated only 12,000 thalers for the creating the communications and 15,000 for the masonry work

---

15   Summarischer Extract der Kosten welche noch zur Forifications Arbeit bey deren Schlesischen Vestungen erfordert werden, GStA SPK Geheimes Zivilkabinett I HA Rep.96 No. 616 – Schlesische Festungen, Bd.E, p.1; Burchardi, Uber die Preussischen Festungen, GStA SPK, IV HA, Rep.15 A, No. 806, p.76.

16   Amount from the statement of expenses for the construction of the Silesian fortifications which the King drew up, GStA SPK Geheimes Zivilkabinett I HA Rep.96 No. 616 – Schlesische Festungen, Bd.F, p.1.

17   Karl Heinrich Siegfried Rödenbeck, *Tagebuch oder Geschichtskalender aus Friedrich's des Großen Regentenleben* (Berlin: Plahnsche Buchhadlung, 1840–42), vol.1, p.235.

18   Burchardi, Uber die Preussischen Festungen, GStA SPK, IV HA, Rep.15 A, no. 806, p.76.

19   GStA SPK Geheimes Zivilkabinett, I HA Rep.96, no. 616 – Schlesische Festungen, Bd.E, p.11.

20   Burchardi, Uber die Preussischen Festungen, GStA SPK, IV HA, Rep.15 A, no. 806, p.76; Minsberg, *Geschichte der Stadt und Festung Groß Glogau*, Bd.2, p.272.

21   Letter from the King to Walrave of 2 March 1742, GStA SPK, I HA Rep.96 B Abschriften von Kabinetsordres, Bd.24, p.89.

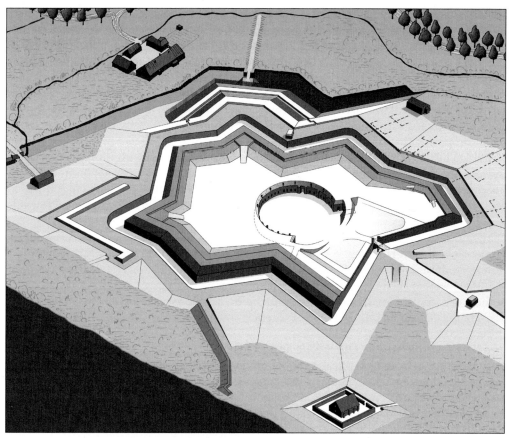

Fortress Glogau's Fort Stern. (Reconstruction by Mariusz Wojciechowski)

in the fort.[22] In the following financial year, a further 40,000 thalers were allocated for 'the masonry revetment of the fort, its casemate and also two powder stores.'[23] According to a letter from the King to Prince Leopold von Anhalt-Dessau, only the casemate for the garrison was remained to be built, which was planned for the following year.[24] As late as July 1749, the King ordered the transfer of 5,000 thalers for the completion of the fort.[25]

As mentioned, the cost estimate for the fort's construction was signed by *Oberst* Sers, the engineer who was in charge of designing the fortress' fortifications at the time, so it

22   GStA SPK Geheimes Zivilkabinett I HA Rep.96 No. 616 – Schlesische Festungen, Bd.C, pp.21–22.
23   Summarischer Extract der Kosten welche noch zur Forifications Arbeit bey deren Schlesischen Vestungeng erfordert werden, GStA SPK Geheimes Zivilkabinett I HA Rep.96 No. 616 – Schlesische Festungen, Bd.E, p.1.
24   Letter from Frederick to Prince Leopold Maximilian on the state of the regiments in Silesia, 21 September 1748, Leopold von Orlich, Geschichte der schlesischen Kriege, vol.2, (Berlin: Verlag von George Gropius, 1841), p.444.
25   GStA SPK Geheimes Zivilkabinett I HA Rep.96 No. 616 – Schlesische Festungen, Bd.E, p.11.

is likely that he was the designer of the fort in the form that was realised. It is not known, however, to what extent his drawing corresponded to the aforementioned provisional structure created while Walrave was still active in design. The determination of the final form of this work was also influenced by king, whose idea was to connect the fort with the interior of the fortress by means of a covered way, provided in the middle of its course with a place of arms with a blockhouse. This idea was presented in the form of a handwritten correction on one of the plans of the fortress.[26] The correction also referred to the outline of the fort, as the King sketched a different shape of the fortifications facing the city than in the original plans, proposing that one of the corners of the fort should be directed towards the ravelin of Breslau Gate. Ultimately, only the way communicating the fort with the city was given a form in line with the King's idea, while the fort itself was given a different outline to both his concept and the original designs. While initially (also on the King's drawing) it was to be a work with a closed perimeter, the final completed structure had a gorge open towards the city fortifications.

There are references in old literature to this fort being based on an ink drawing by Frederick II.[27] Unfortunately – apart from the above-mentioned plan, which contains a minor handwritten correction – no such plan could be found. However, this does not mean that there was no such drawing. In a dossier on Prussian fortresses compiled by one of the authors of a study of Frederick II's wars, Burchardi, mention can be made of as many as two plans of the Glogau fortress drawn by Frederick's own hand.[28]

The Fortifications on the Other Side of the Oder

Very interesting, from a fortification point of view, developements took place on the other side of the Oder. At the time when the fortress was conquered by the Prussians, Glogau was protected on the river side by the bastion fortifications of Dom Insel, as well as by a small tenaille work located on an island in the Oder near the main stream crossing near the village of Zerbau. Both were remnants of a complex set of defensive works that secured the Oder crossing in the seventeenth century. Archival plans show that this part of Glogau's fortifications changed radically, for in addition to the two structures existing in 1740, it is known that a star-shaped entrenchment extended in front of the fortifications of Dom, a small four-sided redoubt at the confluence of the two streams of the Oder, and at least two structures on the northern bank of the main arm of the river. The multiplicity of these defensive works was probably due to the changing hydrographic conditions. Thus, one of the first tasks assigned by Frederick after the occupation of Glogau was to stabilise the bed of the Oder, and in particular to divert the main current, running north of Dom Insel, to the channel immediately adjacent to the town. In addition to the general regulation and taming of the river, the aim of this measure was to strengthen the defensive qualities of the Oder front. In 1742, the King issued an order to deepen the riverbed adjacent to the city, and in 1748 the course of the Oder was regulated by the construction of a new canal, which

---

26   Plan von Gross Glogau, SBB PK, ref. X 25133/2.
27   Eduard Lange, *Die Soldaten Friedrich's des Grossen* (Leipzig: Avenarius & Mendelsohn, 1853), p.396; Johann von Heilmann, *Die Kriegskunst der Preußen unter König Friedrich dem Großen* (Leipzig – Meißen: Goedsche Buchhandlung, 1853), vol.2, p.118.
28   Burchardi, Uber die Preussischen Festungen, GStA SPK, IV HA, Rep.15 A, no. 806, p.75.

brought water to that riverbed.[29] This alone, of course, improved the ability of the town's fortifications to resist assault, but it did not solve the problem of adequately securing the Oder crossing – for the old riverbeds remained. Although less and less water flowed into them and they became muddy over time, they still constituted a terrain obstacle that had to be secured with defensive works.

The first defence structure on the north bank of the Oder, built under Prussian rule, was a tête de pont, which was to surround the village Zerbau. In Frederick's correspondence with Walrave, there are three references to projects for a fortified tête de pont in Glogau: the first is from October, and the other two from November.[30] The project was finally accepted by the King at the end of November.[31] Thanks to the preserved archival cartography the shape of this structure is well known. It was to take the form of a large tenaille securing a bridge over the old Oder riverbed. The structure was to be of enormous size, with the whole village of Zerbau inside. It was planned to be preceded by a moat and a small covered way. In the inner corner of the tenaille the rampart was to be double. One version of the map (held in the Berlin SBB) that describes the work in the legend as 'not yet fully finished', suggesting that its construction had at least begun.[32] However, as the work no longer appears on later plans of Glogau, it must be assumed that its construction was quickly abandoned and never completed. So, the most important protection for the bridge crossing remained the fortifications of Dom Insel. No decision was made to modernise them, only the ravelin in front of the exit gate was enlarged; but a new water-filled moat was dug in front of the whole front. However, the plans to modernise the fortifications in this part of the fortress were not completely abandoned; they were revived a few years later.

At the end of the period in question, a entirely new structure was built: The Water Redoubt – a relatively small but very important defensive work. It was built on the western tip of Dom Insel, at the point where the two streams of the Oder – the old and the new – joined. However, this structure also had its predecessors. Furstenhoff's plan from the first half of the eighteenth century shows a square redoubt at this location.[33] The Prussians also erected a makeshift work there in the first years after the occupation of the fortress, called the Fouqué Redoubt.[34] The idea of a new, permanent redoubt did not appear until the list of planned expenditures for the Silesian fortifications for 1748. As part of the plans for the Glogau fortress, an amount of 21,500 thalers appeared under No. 4 for 'a revetted redoubt on an island, opposite the Jewish cemetery, together with a moat, glacis and palisades'. Interestingly, another 'revetted redoubt above the stream' was planned under No. 5, also

29   Minsberg, *Geschichte der Stadt und Festung Groß Glogau*, vol.2, p.271.
30   Letter from the King to Walrave of 25 October 1742, GStA SPK, I HA Rep.96 B Abschriften von Kabinetsordres, Bd.25, p.848; Letter from the King to Walrave of 12 November 1742, GStA SPK, I HA Rep.96 B Abschriften von Kabinetsordres, Bd.24, p.441.
31   Letter from the King to Walrave of 20 November 1742, GStA SPK, I HA Rep.96 B Abschriften von Kabinetsordres, Bd.24, p.469.
32   Plan von der Vestung Gross Glogau/Wie solche sich an jetzo im stande befindet, SBB PK, ref. X 25133/1.
33   Johann Georg Maximilian Fürstenhoff, Plan von Gros Glogau, c. 1730, SLUB, HS Mscr. Dresd.R.30.m,III, Bl. 66.
34   Burchardi, Uber die Preussischen Festungen, GStA SPK, IV HA, Rep.15 A, no. 806, p.76, Minsberg, *Geschichte der Stadt und Festung Groß Glogau*, vol.2, p.271.

for the sum of 21,500 thalers.[35] In the same spending plan, however, the expenditure on the construction of the redoubts was postponed to later financial years. Clarification of the financial issues continued over the following years. In September 1750, Sers wrote to the King that in his remarks on the cost estimate for new works in Glogau, he had provided for the construction of a redoubt on the Oder River an amount too small by half.[36] Once again, the redoubt appeared in the King's spending plan for the Silesian fortresses for 1752, but not as an expense finally planned for that period, but only postponed to the following financial year.[37] It seems that the construction work on this building did not start until 1754. In the list of expenditures for Silesian fortifications drawn up in November 1753, the amount of 20,000 thalers for a 'casemated redoubt without external revetment', which was to be built in Glogau, is listed under No. 1.[38] Construction work on this redoubt started in the spring of 1754. Sers's report of April 1754 shows that the works were making satisfactory progress, thanks to the good weather. Sers also writes that the redoubt had to be located a little higher because of the water level, but that thanks to this higher position, the casemate and gunpowder store would be dry during floods. The covered way of the redoubt was, according to royal order, placed as close to the water as possible and so regulated that it would survive *horizontales feuer*.[39] In August, the work was slowed down by flooding (as at Cosel), but Sers, who supervised the work, thought that it could nevertheless be completed within the stipulated time – in October.[40] However, the work continued for over a year. As late as October 1755, the building was still not fully completed, with a shortfall of 500 thalers for the necessary carpentry, vaulting and barriers.[41]

The water redoubt was a relatively small rectangular structure surrounded by an envelope and a water-filled moat. Inside it was a circular, masonry casemate housing a garrison of 100. The form of the structure, especially the specific plan of the casemate, reveals analogies with the Capuziner and Cardinal redoubts in Neisse and the redoubt of the tête de pont in Cosel.

Neisse

The fortress of Neisse was the most important defensive complex built during the early years of Frederick the Great's reign. After its Frederician modernisation of the 1740s, it became the second largest and most powerful fortress in the Prussian state, second only

---

35   Summarischer Extract der Kosten welche noch zur Forifications Arbeit bey deren Schlesischen Vestungen erfordert werden, GStA SPK Geheimes Zivilkabinett I HA Rep.96 No. 616 – Schlesische Festungen, Bd.E, p.1.

36   Letter from Col. Sers to the King of 8 September 1750, GStA SPK Geheimes Zivilkabinett I HA Rep.96 No. 616 – Schlesische Festungen, Bd.E, p.36.

37   GStA SPK Geheimes Zivilkabinett I HA Rep.96 No. 616 – Schlesische Festungen, Bd.F, p.1.

38   GStA SPK Geheimes Zivilkabinett I HA Rep.96 No. 616 – Schlesische Festungen, Bd.G, p.14.

39   Letter from Sers to the King of 10 April 1754, GStA SPK Geheimes Zivilkabinett I HA Rep.96 No. 616 – Schlesische Festungen, Bd.G, pp.30–32.

40   Letter from Sers to the King of 3 August 1754, GStA SPK Geheimes Zivilkabinett I HA Rep.96 No. 616 – Schlesische Festungen, Bd.G, p.48.

41   Letter from Sers to the King of 7 October 1755, GStA SPK Geheimes Zivilkabinett I HA Rep.96 No. 616 – Schlesische Festungen, Bd.H, p.27.

to Magdeburg. Moreover, it was here that the King first became a designer of fortifications; his activity in this field concerned practically every building erected in Neisse. The development of Neisse's fortifications in the period before the Seven Years War was linked to another important aspect – the King's cooperation with Cornelius Walrave, at that time the most important military engineer of the Prussian state. Thus far, the literature on this fortress strongly emphasises the personal contribution of the King, while Walrave is presented merely as an executor of his will. However, the nature of the Neisse fortifications and the solutions used there seem to suggest something quite different.

The Main Enceinte

At the time of the Prussian acquisition of Neisse, the defences were limited to the old perimeter of the town's fortifications, which included 10 large bastions connected by curtains. The rampart around the entire perimeter was preceded by a fausse, and four of the bastions had cavaliers. The fortress was surrounded by a wide moat fed by the Biele river. A weakness of the fortress was the earthen construction of the ramparts and outer works (except for a poor covered way). Not surprisingly, shortly after the Prussians took over the fortress, intensive modernisation began. According to some accounts, they got down to it remarkably quickly and Prussian engineers were already marking out new defensive works on the day of the surrender, before the Austrian garrison of the fortress had even managed to leave the town. It is likely that some work was already underway in 1741, since in mid-November the King summoned two more engineers to Neisse.[42]

Frederick allocated as much as 40,000 thalers for these initial works.[43] Most of this sum was probably consumed by the preparations for construction. For in the winter, building materials, especially lime and timber, were intensively procured; the latter task was supervised by all the engineers assigned to the fortress. They also began to employ construction workers, who were needed in exceptionally large numbers, as many as 3,000. The King obliged the states of Upper Silesia to supply them.[44] In addition, in February, Walrave signed a contract with local construction companies for the erection of local fortifications.[45] Design work continued all the time, it was only at the beginning of March 1742 that the King received the designs for both the Cardinal and Capuchin redoubts, from Walrave, for approval.[46] The hiring of labourers to work on the fortress also continued. Most probably there were issues with this, as the King allowed people to be recruited to work not only from the Duchy of Neisse, but also from Münsterberg (Ziębice) and the *weichbilds* of Reichenbach (Dzierżoniów) and Frankenstein (Ząbkowice Śląskie).[47]

The foundation stone for the new defensive works was laid in a ceremony on 29 March 1742 by Walrave. On the King's orders, the entire Neisse garrison took part in the

---

42   GStA SPK I HA Rep.96 B, Abschriften von Kabinetsordres, Bd.23, p.375.
43   Letter from the King to Foris of 26 February 1742, I HA Rep.96 B, Abschriften von Kabinetsordres, Bd.24, p.88.
44   Letters of the King to Field Marshal Schwerin and to General Walrave of 6 January 1742, I HA Rep.96 B, Abschriften von Kabinetsordres, Bd.24, pp.5, 12.
45   King's letter to Walrave of 2 February 1742, I HA Rep.96 B, Abschriften von Kabinetsordres, Bd.24, p.58.
46   King's letter to Walrave of 6 March 1742, I HA Rep.96 B, Abschriften von Kabinetsordres, Bd.24, p.91.
47   King's letter to Walrave of 9 March 1742, I HA Rep.96 B, Abschriften von Kabinetsordres, Bd.24, p.98.

service.[48] In April, work on the new outer moat was mentioned, which would mean that the construction of the structure that constituted the main reinforcement of the fortress – the new envelope – had also begun.[49] There were constant problems with the recruitment of construction workers, so it was decided to use soldiers for this purpose. In August 1742, the King allowed volunteers from the Neisse garrison to be recruited to work on the fortress.[50] The work was intensive and lasted a long time, continuing as late as mid-November.[51] As a result, the progress of the fortification construction was noticeable and in March 1743, during his next visit, Frederick indicated to Walrave his satisfaction with the state of the fortress.[52]

It is not known exactly in what order the various works were built; all that is certain is that in 1745 their construction was, like that of the rest of the Neisse fortifications, essentially complete.[53] Later, minor additions continued. In August 1745, the King dictated a list consisting of a dozen items remaining to be completed at Neisse. Of these, only two related directly to the right-bank fortifications: the erection of works outside Breslau Gate in front of sluice No. 14, together with masonry, moat, and glacis, for which 16,657 thalers were to be spent, and the construction of five new bridges over the moat in front of Breslau Gate, which was to cost 1,299 thalers. The total planned work in the fortress was estimated at 47,300 thalers, which might seem a considerable amount, but was only a trifle compared to the more than 800,000 thalers spent to date on the construction of the fortress.[54]

The works mentioned outside Breslau Gate, in front of sluice gate No. 14, were a short section of fausse-braye and two moats. In other words, relatively small works compared to those already erected. Despite their small size and relatively modest cost, the King decided to economise on their construction; during subsequent visits he decided not to reinforce the new moats with masonry revetment. Finally, work on the structure was completed in 1747, which ended the process of modernising the town's defensive perimeter.

According to Arwed Klose, author of the only monograph on the fortress of Neisse to date, as well as according to Minsberg, nineteenth century author of the Neisse Chronicle, the design of the new fortifications was the work of Frederick, while Walrave, his most important engineer at the time, was left only to implement the project. These statements cannot, however, be accepted uncritically. For if we look at the outline of the works forming the Neisse fortress envelope, we see its unquestionable similarity to the envelopes which

---

48   Rödenbeck, *Tagebuch oder Geschichtskalender*, vol.1, p.66; Seydel, *Nachrichten*, vol.2, p.301.
49   King's letter to Walrave of 18 April 1742, I HA Rep.96 B, Abschriften von Kabinetsordres, Bd.24, p.123.
50   King's letter to Walrave of 16 August 1742, I HA Rep.96 B, Abschriften von Kabinetsordres, Bd.24, p.271.
51   King's letter to Walrave of 16 November 1742, I HA Rep.96 B, Abschriften von Kabinetsordres, Bd.25, p.972.
52   Seydel, *Nachrichten*, vol.2, p.304.
53   Arwed Klose, *Festung Neisse* (Hagen: Werner Dorau, 1980), p.87.
54   According to a statement of 1747, 952,000 thalers were planned to be spent on the construction of the Neisse fortress, whereas by the time it was drawn up, 879,000 had been spent. Summarischer Extract, wegen der Fortifications Bau Rechnungen welche der General Major v. Hautcharmoy den general Major v. Walrave abgenommen hat GStA SPK Geheimes Zivilkabinett I HA Rep.96 No. 616 – Schlesische Festungen, Bd.D, p.7.

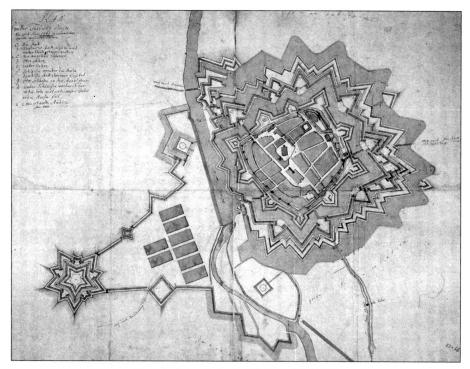

Fortress Neisse in 1748. (SBB PK, ref. X 31028)

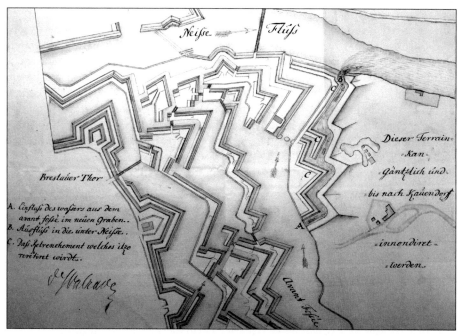

Neisse, fortification design by Walrave, 1747. (GStA SPK, I HA rep 96 no 616 vol. D p.31)

were being built simultaneously in Glogau and Glatz. There the work was led, and designs drawn up by, Walrave. The credibility of the references to royal authorship of the project is further weakened by another piece of information. Both of the aforementioned authors claim that the work on the reconstruction of the city fortifications was carried out by the engineer Rottengatter, which is undoubtedly a misrepresentation. The name appears in the sources several times, but each time in the context of a family of construction entrepreneurs building Silesian fortresses (including Neisse); however, it is missing from lists of Prussian military engineers. If an error may have occurred with the name of the contractor, it may also have occurred in the designation of the designer.

Fort Prussia and Friedrichstadt Redoubts

While the work carried out on the urban perimeter consisted of modernising the old fortifications, the defences built on the northern bank of the Glatzer Neisse (Nysa Kłodzka) river were not connected with the older defensive works, as this area was completely devoid of fortifications before 1740. However, as the terrain on this bank is more mountainous and dominates the town, it posed a potential threat to the town fortifications. It was here that siege batteries were established during the first Prussian attack on the Neisse in January 1741. Although that siege was short and did not result in the surrender of the fortress, the bombardment itself was severe. Not surprisingly, from this experience, it was decided to secure the fortress from this side with new defence works. Another reason was the need to create a new urban district, after the Old Town had been burnt down by a decision of the Austrian commandant in 1740. In 1742, a town was founded on the north bank of the river, independent of the Neisse, and named Friedrichstadt.[55]

The most important element of the new fortifications was the large, self-contained Fort Prussia. Design work on it had already begun in the autumn of 1742, as in November the King received the first draft of this defensive work from Walrave, which was fully approved.[56] Construction work began in the spring of the following year. During a visit to the fortress in May 1743, the King viewed the fortification walls already under construction surrounding the new settlement, and also took part in the ceremony of laying the foundation stone of Fort Prussia.[57] As the pace of work on the fortifications, which had already been carried out on both sides of the river, was deemed too slow, the King decided to increase the number of labourers working at Neisse to 7,000 at a time. Problems with a lack of labour had already arisen, as from March as many as 1,950 soldiers from seven regiments were sent to the fortress.[58] This number was steadily increased, with further regiments (von Groeben, Prinz Heinrich, Hautcharmoy and a pioneer regiment) being sent to work on the fortress. By August 1743, 3,450 soldiers were working on Neisse fortress.[59] As

55   Minsberg, *Geschichtliche Darstellung*, pp.186, 188, 190.
56   King's letter to Walrave of 10 November 1742, I HA Rep.96 B, Abschriften von Kabinetsordres, Bd.24, p.447.
57   Seydel, *Nachrichten*, vol.2, p.304.
58   Letter from the King to Walrave of 8 February and to Kleist of 13 February 1743, I HA Rep.96 B, Abschriften von Kabinetsordres, Bd.26, p.68.
59   Letter from the King to *Generalmajor* Von Groeben and to von Marwitz of 6 August 1743, I HA Rep.96 B, Abschriften von Kabinetsordres, Bd.26, pp.364–365.

a result, work moved more quickly and by the end of 1744 the fort was essentially ready, although finishing work continued until 1745.[60] Finer work was carried out even later. In the already quoted king's order of August 1745 regarding the further construction of the fortress, two points concerning the fort appear – the construction of a bomb-proof well at a cost of 2,126 thalers and the erection of new external works not initially planned. On the glacis of the fort, the King decided to establish two flèches at a cost of 2,349 thalers.[61] These works were not completed until 1747.

As for the other defensive works shielding Friedrichstadt, we have relatively little information about their construction. As is already known, the masonry revetment of the ramparts was being worked on in May 1743. The defensive perimeter was completed before 1745, and consited of two simple curtains defended by a redan, a small star-shaped – Fort Bombardier (east rampart) – and by a single Jerusalem Redoubt (west rampart). Some work was still being carried out in 1745. In the King's order appears: 'The main rampart of the Jerusalem Redoubt must be widened so that the cannons have more room to manoeuvre, this is to be done still with this year's money.'[62] This did not mean the end of the work on this redoubt, for the King also ordered the erection of a guardhouse inside it for 100 men. Judging by its cost – 745 thalers – it was to be a wooden or timber-framed structure. Its construction took place after 1748. The King paid attention not only to the defensive works themselves, but also to their foreground. In the aforementioned disposition, he ordered the filling in of ravines close to the new fortifications. There were to be three: one 550 metres long, nine metres wide and two metres deep, the second 430 metres long, four metres wide and 1.5 metres deep, and the third 300 metres long, 10 metres wide and two metres deep. The entire works were to cost 1,003 thalers.

As in the case of the Old Town fortification project, there are doubts about Fort Prussia and the Friedrichstad fortifications as to who actually designed them. According to some accounts, Fort Prussia was supposed to have been devised by Frederick himself. The fort's foundation plaque describes the King in this way, while Walrave is mentioned on it as the executor of the sovereign's ideas.[63] Arwed Klose saw things in a similar way, claiming that the King was supposed to have drawn up the first design of the fort, which was sent to Walrave in September 1742. This plan was to fall into Austrian hands during the Battle of Soor and was later to be circulated through numerous copies. Interestingly, one of these is in the Berlin SBB.[64] It shows the left bank fortifications in a completely different form than they were later realised. They were to be a bastioned perimeter, equal in area to the old part of the fortress, and Fort Prussia was to be a six-sided citadel. According to Klose, an alternative design to the royal one was to be drawn up by Walrave and submitted to the King. The latter, however, did not accept it, changed it several times and sent his new ideas to Walrave in May 1743.[65] The situation is presented quite differently by Max Jähns, who quotes an exchange of correspondence between the two. It shows that it was Walrave who presented

60   Klose, *Festung Neisse*, p.87.
61   GStA SPK Geheimes Zivilkabinett I HA Rep.96 No. 616 – Schlesische Festungen, Bd.C, pp.1, 31–32.
62   GStA SPK Geheimes Zivilkabinett I HA Rep.96 No. 616 – Schlesische Festungen, Bd.C, pp.31–32.
63   Seydel, *Nachrichten*, vol.2, p.304.
64   Plan von der Vestung Neyß wie solche Ano 1742 ist Fortificirt worden, SBB PK, ref. X 31026.
65   Klose, *Festung Neisse*, p.86.

the first design, which was not accepted by the King. The latter sketched his own design and sent it to Walrave with a request for an honest opinion. Walrave praised the King's idea and confined himself to redrawing it cleanly.[66] The Prussian historian of the engineer corps, Udo von Bonin, saw king's role in a similar way in his 1877 work, *Geschichte des Ingenieurkorps und der Pioniere in Preußen*, and concluded that the King only seriously altered his engineer's design.[67]

Archival sources are sparse on the design process for this element of the fortress. As a matter of fact, only one letter from the King to Walrave, dated 10 November, has survived.

> I have received your letter of the 30th of last month, together with the plan of the fort [planned] to be established near Neisse, sent back here, and I have learned all that you wished to report and show me with it; I give you in reply that, in order to keep the benefit of the land, I would like to keep the previously approved figure of the fort. With your wherefore proposed I am satisfied, for this I have approved and introduced the plan with my own hands. As I have placed your first fort, I have given it only a theoretical figure, how it should look later on is left to you, and I am satisfied with the approved plan all the more so as it moves the fort a little closer to the town, thus they can defend each other better, and the fort can be attacked only on one front; besides, in addition to the cost savings that this will bring. So you can work on the plan, and I want you to copy the plan together with the profiles on a small scale and send it to me as soon as it is ready.[68]

This letter shows that Frederick had indeed drawn up a design for a fort to be away from the town, but did not regard it as a rival proposal to his engineer's design. Moreover, he unequivocally stated that the design drawn up by Walrave was better, cheaper and was fully accepted by him.

There are, however, clues that lead us to believe that the Prussian ruler did have some influence on the design process of Fort Prussia. It is possible to identify at least one element that was introduced into the fort's design through royal interference. These were the counterscarp galleries and the coffers used to defend the moat. Walrave, in his 1747 memorial, stated that they were created at the King's behest.[69] The second element of the fort that can be clearly linked to the King's design activity were the flèches in front of the glacis, which the King had ordered erected in 1747.[70]

A formal analysis of the Friedrichstadt fortifications also supports the thesis of dual authorship of this defensive structure. Looking at the plan of the fort, one immediately notices that it is very similar to Fort Prussia in Stettin, designed and built by Walrave more than a decade earlier, when Friedrich Wilhelm I was still in power. The Neisse fort differs

66   Jähns Max, *Geschichte 1891*, p.2749.
67   Bonin, *Geschichte des Ingenieurkorps*, p.51.
68   King's letter to Walrave of 10 November 1742, I HA Rep.96 B, Abschriften von Kabinetsordres, Bd.24, p.447.
69   De Walrave, Memoire sur l'attaque et Defencela des Places, GStA SPK, VI HA Familienarchive und Nachlässe, Nl Scharnhorst, no. 314, p.12 recto.
70   GStA SPK Geheimes Zivilkabinett I HA Rep.96 No. 616 – Schlesische Festungen, Bd.C, pp.1, 31–32.

Neisse, Fort Prussia. (Zofia Woźny, <https://instagram.com/panizdronem>)

from the Stettin fort only in size, lack of internal civil buildings, lack of a covered way and a main rampart provided with a fausse-braye. On the other hand, looking at the fortifications of the north bank of the Neisse as a whole, we do not see the multiplication of defensive works characteristic of Walrave's manner. The complex consists of a fort and two long curtains reinforced with small redoubts in the middle. This simplification of the outline may have been due to the King's intervention in the design process.

The Cardinal and Capuchin Redoubts

The last component of the Neisse fortress to appear during reconstruction in the 1740s were two large redoubts located on the riverbank. These structures were the last among the Neisse fortifications to acquire their final forms, which, moreover, differed the most from the original designs. The first of the redoubts, the Cardinal Redoubt, is located at the mouth of the Biele to the Glatzer Neisse. This site was ideally suited to the location of a sluice which could form an inundation to protect the foreground of the fortress. Of course, the sluice itself was exposed to destruction, so it was built together with a redoubt protecting it, a four-sided defensive structure with a circular casemate. The second sluice was built on the other side of the town and was also protected by a defensive structure, the Capuchin Redoubt, identical in plan to the previous one. However, the redoubts alone could not provide sufficient defence, so it was planned from the start to surround them with a separate belt of fortifications. The Cardinal Redoubt was originally to be shielded by a work consisting of three sharp corners, located on the other bank of the Neisse. A fourth corner was planned on the other bank of the Biele. The Capuchin Redoubt was to be protected by a regular, elongated structure with a tenaille outline. The rampart of the redoubt was to be directly adjacent to the central corner of the shielding work, which would allow the redoubt to fulfil the function of a reduit. This is how these works were supposed to look like according to the oldest designs. The first designs for the redoubts were made as early as the beginning of 1742. On 24 February, the King received from Walrave 'finished designs for the works in the Cardinal's Garden and at the inundation'.[71] Unfortunately, the drawings the King received have not survived, but there are plans in the holdings of the Berlin Staatabibliothek showing the original appearance of both works. The Cardinal's Redoubt is illustrated in a sketch signed by Cornelius Walrave.[72] The original design of the fortifications of the Capuchin Redoubt is shown by one of the plans of the Neisse created before 1745.[73] The main work on both structures was probably completed in 1744, although it is only with regard to the Cardinal Redoubt that we are certain that it was completed in August of that year.[74]

Around 1745, there was a change in the design involving a complete reshaping of the defensive works covering the two redoubts. It was recorded on the 1746 plan of the fortress.[75] Both were given an irregular, tenaille outline in no way resembling the original ideas.

---

71   King's letter to Walrave of 6 March 1742, I HA Rep.96 B, Abschriften von Kabinetsordres, Bd.24, p.91.
72   Neisse, SBB PK, ref. X 31027- 3.
73   Plan von Neisse/ mit allen neuen Wercken, wie Solche bey Ihro Koniglichen Majestat Hohen Anwesenheit Tractiret worden SBB PK, ref. X 31027 – 1.
74   King's letter to Walrave of 30 July 1744, I HA Rep.96 B, Abschriften von Kabinetsordres, Bd.30, p.167.
75   Plan von der Festung Neisse wie solch Anno 1746 in wircklichen Stande gefunden worden, SBB PK, ref. X 31028.

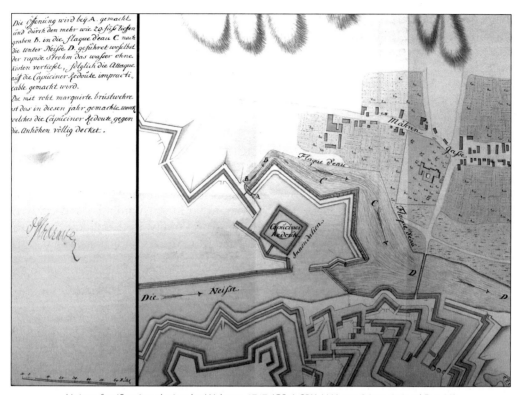

Neisse, fortification design by Walrave, 1747. (GStA SPK, I HA rep.96 no.616 vol.D p.23)

Further transformations of these defensive works were mentioned by the King in an order issued in August 1745. He directed that the old river embankments of the Neisse in front of the Cardinal Redoubt be raised so that the cordon of the redoubt could not be seen from Caninchen Berge, and the corners of the work shielding the Cardinal Redoubt were also to be rebuilt so that they could not be flanked by fire conducted from same location. The King also ordered the work covering the Capuchin Redoubt raised so that the cordon of this redoubt could not be seen from the hills. In addition, the left front of this work was to be given a wall with loopholes, in front of which the King ordered a covered way to be built. In the end, only the river dykes in front of the Cardinal Redoubt were raised and the left front of the work covering the Capuchin Redoubt was rebuilt.[76] This work was carried out in 1747. In May 1747, Walrave, who was in charge of the construction, reported to Frederick that, in accordance with royal orders, the Neisse had been dammed with a weir. The retrenchment, or tenaille shaped shielding work, at the Capuchin Redoubt was mostly in place and had reached such a height that an attacker's guns could not destroy the redoubt or create a breach through it. An inundation had been formed around the redoubt and the water prevented an approach to the redoubt. This retrenchment consisted of five lines, on which

76   GStA SPK IV HA, Rep 96 Nr 616 – Schlesische Festungen, Bd.D, p.13.

48 guns could be placed. Thanks to this work, the redoubt was protected from fire from the surrounding area.[77] In his letter, the engineer expressed the hope that the work would be completed before the King's visit that year, and fortress commander, von Tresckow, wrote in his letter to the King of 17 June that the work would be completed within four weeks.[78] As can be seen, in 1747 the most important fortress in Silesia was completed. The time was ripe for this, as in the same year the construction of the fortress that was to form the next pillar of Silesian defence – the fortress of Schweidnitz – began.

Glatz

The Glatz (Kłodzko) Fortress was of particular importance in the fortification system of Silesia after its Frederician conquest. This was due to both purely military and cultural considerations. From a military point of view, the Glatz County, in the middle of which the fortress was located, was an area strongly isolated from the rest of Prussia. The mountains completely surrounded the area, so communication with neighbouring regions was only possible in the mid-eighteenth century through a few passes. More importantly, those leading towards Bohemia were easier to cross than those through which the roads towards Silesia ran.

Also, when considering cultural factors, it must be said, Glatz stood out strongly from the rest of the Silesian lands. First of all, it should be noted that until the Prussian conquest this area had no connections with Silesia; it belonged to the Kingdom of Bohemia. Moreover, the Glatz County was purely Catholic. Of course, there was no shortage of Catholics in Silesia either, but the local Catholicism was peculiar – the zeal of the faithful was due to the fact of the thorough and effective recatholicization carried out after the collapse of the Protestant revolt during the initial phase of the Thirty Years War. As Glatz was one of the bastions of the anti-emperor revolt, it received particularly strong treatment from the emperor. Among others, the Jesuits, whose local college had for more than a century formed the elite in the spirit of pro-Habsburg Catholicism, helped in the recatholicization. Apparently, these conditions were not conducive to a lasting hold on Prussian supremacy. No wonder, then, that the King decided to build a strong fortress here to help him maintain Prussian power. None of the Prussian fortresses reflected as much as Glatz the royal maxim, which described fortresses as 'a powerful nail attaching the land to the ruler.'[79]

Walrave's Designs
The design for the new fortifications of Glatz was begun by Cornelius Walrave, who in the early 1740s was experiencing the best and most intense period of his career. He corresponded with the King from 1742 onwards on projects for Glatz. Certainly during his activity there, he drew up many plans for the fortress' expansion, but only one has survived,

---

77   Letter from Walrave of 24 May 1747, GStA SPK Geheimes Zivilkabinett I HA Rep.96 No. 616 – Schlesische Festungen, Bd.D, p.21.

78   Letter from von Tresckow dated 17 June 1747, GStA SPK Geheimes Zivilkabinett I HA Rep.96 No. 616 – Schlesische Festungen, Bd.D, p.28.

79   Volz, *Die Werke*, vol.7, p.176.

signed and dated in Neisse on 1 June 1743, and stored in the Berlin Staatsbibliothek.[80] It shows the reinforcement of the defences of the old fortress and a completely new fort on the other side of the Glatzer Neisse valley. The old fortress was to be given an extensive tenaille envelope, built on the basis of the former covered way. In addition, inside the fortress, between bastions Wenclaus and Ludmila and Florian's Sconce, it was planned to erect the Great Tenaille (Grosse Tenaille), a new defence work equipped with a large casemate for the garrison. On the slope between the fortress and the Frankenstein suburb another new structure was to be built, the Small Tenaille (Kleine Tenaille), this time without casemates. On the other side of the river, on Schäferberg (Owcza Góra, Sheep Hill), which dominates the town from that side, Walrave planned an independent defensive work. The new fort was to be given an outline similar to a five-pointed star. Its front section, later named Lower Crown (Dolna Korona, Nieder Krone), was to have two corners, between which a bastion with retired flanks was inserted. The rear part of the fort consisted of three separate works. In the middle was the Upper Crown (Niska Korona, Hohe Krone), with a casemate built into its gorge, and on either side of it were two structures, later called the Right and Left Reduit. An interesting element of the design was the work added to the gorge side of the fort. This structure, called the Horseshoe (Podkowa, *Fer â Cheval*), had the outline of a bastei and was intended to defend the approach to the fort from the steep slope of the Glatzer Neisse valley.

In both parts of the fortress, Walrave designed powerful, extremely elaborate countermine systems. He envisaged two versions of these: a more modest one and a more elaborate one.

According to the project described, the modernisation of the fortress was expected to cost huge sums of money. Unfortunately, we do not know all the assumptions, although Walrave entered something like a cost estimate on the drawing. The new fort was to cost 63,634 thalers, and slightly more for its countermine – 69,629 thalers. It is not known what the cost of modernising the old fort was envisaged to be, as the plan states that for this facility 'his royal majesty has already set aside money, in addition to the sum of 4,900 thalers.' All that is known is that the countermine in this part of the fortress was to cost as much as 77,188 thalers. The total amount for the construction of the new fort and countermines according to the plans was to reach more than 210,000 thalers.

Walrave's Alleged Designs for the City's Fortification

The next phase of the design of the Glatz fortifications was fortifying the town. The subject was already considered in the seventeenth century, and this time the ideas were brought to fruition. Two plans were created. The first was not realised, but more than a dozen copies have survived to this day. The second was carried out, although the plan itself, in paper form with the author's signature, has not survived.

According to the first design, the defences of the town were to consist of four bastions of different outlines and an extensive covered way. Significantly, it was not a classic bastion front, as the curtain was missing, and the bastions were detached. The bastion in front of

---

80   Plan von der Stad und Vestung Glatz, SBB PK, ref. X 25107/6.

Glatz, project for the modernisation of the fortress by Walrave. (SBB PK, ref. X 25107/6)

The siege of Glatz, 1760. (SLUB, ref. KS A9512)

the School Gate had the usual outline, with straight flanks set at an angle of approximately 90 degrees to the moat behind it. The bastion in front of the Green Gate had a completely different outline. Its flanks were drawn in an arc, in addition to which there was to be an cavalier with arched flanks and a front with a dovetail outline. On either side of this bastion were two smaller bastions with retired flanks.

These plans are known from nine drawings stored in the Osterreichisches Staatsarchiv in Vienna, two in the holdings of the Vienna National Library and one from the Sächsische Landesbibliothek – Staats- und Universitätsbibliothek in Dresden. Three of them are simply plans of the Glatz fortress.[81] Another nine depict a real event – the siege of Glatz in 1760 – but the fortifications of the city are shown in a form identical to this unrealized project.[82]

---

81   Plan de la ville et Chateau de Glatz, OStA, G I c 201; Plan der Stadt und Festung Glatz, OStA K II f 23 F–1, Plan der Stadt und Vestung Glatz, OStA K II f 23 F–2.
82   Plans Differens du chateau et de la ville de Glatz avec des Idees d'attaques, OStA, K II f 24 F; two untitled plans, ref. OStA, K II f 23 E; Plan des attaque de Glatz Commencees la nuit du 20 au 21 juillet 1760, OStA H III e 2336–8; OStA H III e 2336–14 untitled plan; OStA H III e 2336–12 untitled plan; Grund-Riss der Vestung Glatz, Österreichische Nationalbibliothek (OsNB) Signatur/Inv-Nr. etc. ALB Port 227,20 KAR MAG; Die Festung Glatz in der Grafschaft gleiches Nahmens OsNB ALB Port 227,21 KAR MAG; Plan de Glatz et des ses Environs avec l'Attaque et Pris par les Truppes Autrichiens sous Commendement du Gen. Bar. de Laudon depuis le 20 jus qu'au 26 Juillet 1760, 1760 SLUB, ref. KS A9512.

These designs are unsigned, but in all probability their author was Cornelius Walrave. His authorship is suggested by the form of the proposed defensive works. The bastions around the town betray a strong resemblance to those in other fortresses designed by Walrave. The two bastions with retired flanks are very similar to works designed by him in Glogau and Neisse, while the central bastion, with its cavalier and shoulders drawn in an arc, is identical in outline to the structures forming Stettin's Fort Wilhelm, also designed by Walrave. The whole is otherwise reminiscent of his designs for the Peitz Fortress. However, it is not only the stylistic similarity that prompts us to attribute to this engineer the unrealised project of the town fortifications in Glatz, suggestions to this effect are also found directly in archival sources. One of the above-mentioned plans showing the siege of Glatz in 1760 bears the pencil signature 'Festung Glatz, gez. Von C. v. Walrave, preussisch. Ing. Lieutnant 1744.'[83] He appears twice more in Viennese archival materials concerning Glatz. These are two letters attached to the plan of Glatz described above. The first is four pages long and is written in German, addressed to an anonymous baroness, and signed 'Gl. d. 29. Octobr 1744, Cornelius v. W, Lieutnant.' The second, entitled 'Remarques de Glatz', is in French, is two pages long, and is unfortunately not dated, but only signed 'C. v. W'. Both letters, like the plan described earlier, have been annotated, or rather a kind of footnote to the abbreviation of the name, by an anonymous archivist which reads: 'Cornelius von Walrave, was a Prussian engineer, lieutenant, went into Austrian service in 1745.'[84] In both cases, the anonymous archivist referred to the records of the Court War Council (*Hofkriegsrath*) from 1745. The annotation quoted above is erroneous, or at least inaccurate, as Cornelius von Walrave was not a lieutenant but a general in 1745, nor did he transfer to Austrian service; he remained a Prussian engineer until 1748 and was arrested and imprisoned by order of Frederick in February of that year. On the other hand, however, one of the charges that led to Walrave's imprisonment was secret contacts with the Austrians and passing information to them about Prussian fortresses. In addition, Walrave's son served in Glatz, as supervisor in the engineering corps.[85] This person does not appear in Prussian archival material after 1744. In other words, it is likely that it was Cornelius Walrave's son who transferred to Austrian service in 1744 and used this opportunity to hand over secret materials to the Austrians, including his father's unrealised project for the fortification of the town.

The hypothesis of the existence of an unrealised design for the city's fortification by Walrave is weakened by the lack of copies of it preserved in Berlin resources. They are not to be found either in the Geheimes Staatsarchiv, or in the cartographic department of the Staatsbibliothek, where dozens of design drawings from the 1740s and 1750s are stored.

Further Projects

While the project for the fortification of the town by Walrave is only plausible (albeit highly so), it is certain that by the 1740s, even before the completion of the work planned in the project of 1743, plans began to be made for another extension of the Glatz fortifications,

---

83   OStA KA KPS LB K II f 23 E.

84   *Cornelius von Walrave war preußischer Ingenieru-Lieutnant, wurde im Jahre 1745 in österr. Dienste übernommen.*

85   Pre-officer rank in the Prussian engineer corps in the eighteenth century. GStA SPK I HA Rep.96 B, Abschriften von Kabinetsordres, Bd.28, p.28.

the main element of which was the construction of fortifications defending the town. The first mention of this appears in a summary of the expenditure on the four most important Silesian fortresses. With regard to Glatz, a note appears in the margin stating that the amounts spent on fortifications do not include 'what his royal majesty still wants to spend on the town and the sluice there.'[86] In parallel, there were probably plans to extend the newly completed fort on Sheep Hill. There is no mention of the project itself, but it must have been conceived in 1747, because in a disposition on the financing of the extension of the Glatz fortifications drawn up at the beginning of 1748, in addition to mentioning the amount of 30,000 thalers for the aforementioned sluice, there appears the amount of 22,000 thalers, which must have been spent on the extension of the fort on Sheep Hill. This was to consist of the construction of the 'lower fausse-braye', commandant's house, the bakery, the piling up of the glacis and the erection of a flèche.[87] Does the erection of the flèche refer to all the flèches erected in front of the fort – Königsheiner, Hassitzer, Neue and Wasser Flèche? Certainly not, for in September of that year Frederick, during his visit to Glatz, ordered the building of 'one more flèche on the glacis of Schäferberg, on the side of the ravine running towards Habelschwerdt, which cannot be fired on from the main fortress'.[88] Unfortunately, none of the Schäferberg flèches fit this description, but the Königsheiner flèches do the most. The rest of the elements listed in the order of early 1748 also need clarification.[89] The 'lower fausse-braye' listed first is probably a new belt of fortifications, an envelope, erected by extending the original covered way. The new defensive work was not preceded by a moat, and only its scarp was provided with low masonry revetment.[90] This structure did not repeat the course of the original covered way in its entirety, and it was not built on the rear of the fort. In front of the envelope, on the other hand, a completely new covered way was constructed, which necessarily repeated the outline of the defensive work in front of which it was erected. More difficult to interpret are the first two buildings – the commandant's house and the bakery. In Johann Gottlieb Kahlo's description of the fort, both buildings are mentioned (in addition to them, there is also a brewery, a powder magazine and casemates), additionally described as bombproof.[91] But there is no trace of them in the later inventory drawings. The only building in its interior was the reduit.[92] On the other hand, the first inventory of the fortress made by the Prussians after their re-acquisition of Glatz in 1763, by Regler, indicates the existence of two more buildings – a semi-circular one, erected between the present Red and White casemates, and a quadrangle near Horseshoe. Could this be the brewery, bakery, and commandant's house? As mentioned above, the Schäferberg fort

86   GStA SPK I HA Rep 96 no. 616 – Schlesische Festungen, Bd.D 1747, p.7.
87   GStA SPK I HA Rep 96 no. 616 – Schlesische Festungen, Bd.E, 1748–50, p.2.
88   von Orlich, *Geschichte der schlesischen Kriege*, vol.2, p.448.
89   An understanding of what was erected as a result of this extension enables a comparison of the design by Walrave with the detailed plans and inventories made by the Austrians during the occupation of Glatz in 1760–1763, the best plan for this is Plan de Glatz avec les nouveaux Ouvrages, mines et le Nouveau Fort, AT-OStA/KA KPS KS G I c 203–10.
90   Rapports Profil lengst ganzer neuen Vostung zu Glatz, AT-OStA/KA KPS LB K II f 26–2 E- no III
91   Johann Gottlieb Kahlo, *Denkwürdigkeiten der Königlichen Preußischen souverainen Grafschaft Glatz* (Berlin: Unknown Publisher, 1757), p.192.
92   Rapports und Projects Plan von der Haupt und Granitz Vöstung und Stadt Glatz pro Anno 1761 u. 1762, AT-OStA/KA KPS LB K II f 26–2.

expansion project was continuing and in September 1748 the King ordered the construction of yet another flèche. At the same time, the idea of reinforcing the main fortress in the same way emerged, the King ordered the erection of a flèche to control the foothills of the Neisse valley.[93] From the description it appears that this work was the structure today called Crane (Żuraw, Kranich).

We learn about another design phase from a document drawn up in December 1749, which was a list of planned works in Silesian fortresses to be completed before 1751. In this document, drawn up by *Oberst* Sers, then responsible for all work on Silesian fortresses, with regard to Glatz, there is an item, for the complete development of new fortresses, according to cost estimates presented by *Generalmajor* Heinrich August de la Motte Fouqué:

1. For a new fort with communications, casemates (souterrains) and mines, together with fields and houses – 77,599 thalers
2. For the works around the town, including land and houses to be paid 12,3905 thalers.[94]

Both projects were expected to consume a significant amount of 201,504 thalers in total.

Let us deal with the first of the tasks indicated in this document. A new fort, sometimes also a new fortress, was referred to as the fort on Schäferberg in the 1740s and 1750s. However, was the author of this document referring to this structure? This is only one possible interpretation. If this was the case, it would imply that a major expansion of this facility was planned and not carried out. As mentioned above, all casemates and defence works that were built in the period before the Seven Years War were included in the plans and cost estimates of the previous year, so the amount of more than 77,000 thalers would have covered facilities that were completely new. Part of it could have been spent on the counter-mine not yet realised but already planned by Walrave, but the rest would have had to be spent on new casemates and also a new defensive perimeter, so extensive that it would have required the purchase of further sections of land around the fort. However, it is just as likely that another brand-new fort was involved. The sum of 77,599 thalers was sufficient to build a sizable fort; after all, according to the first cost estimate, the fort on Schäferberg was expected to cost 63,634 thalers and, with one layer of countermines, 89,426 thalers. Moreover, in the holdings of the Berlin Staatsbibliothek there is a group of design drawings of Glatz fortifications from the period before the Seven Years War. Only some of them show completed structures, the others are drawings, sometimes accurate, of proposed projects never commenced. One of them is a projection of a sizable defensive work, which perfectly matches the building programme contained in a document from December 1749. It shows a large defensive work with the outline of a dovetail. Its core was to be a casemate for the garrison and for storage purposes. In front of it was to be a dry moat and an fausse-braye equipped with mine galleries (demolition galleries). In front of this was to be the main moat, wider than the previous one, with a cunette in the middle. In the counterscarp of the moat there were to be communication galleries and coffers in the corners. From the counterscarp

---

93   von Orlich, *Geschichte der schlesischen Kriege*, vol.2, pp.448–449.
94   GStA SPK I HA Rep 96 no. 616 – Schlesische Festungen, Bd.E, 1748–50, p.13.

galleries and coffers there were to be counter-mine corridors. Above this was to be a typical covered way with places of arms, preceded by a glacis. This drawing is one of the few designs from this collection that has been signed. At its lower edge are the initials, 'F v W'. This was most probably the signature of Friedrich von Winancko.[95] The same engineer signed his name (in the form F. v. Winanco), on the plans for the Glatz garrison bakery from 1756.[96]

Unfortunately, the subject of the new fort was not pursued in later correspondence. This is different from the other project, which was the 'works around the town'. The sum of 123,905 thalers was sizable and suggested a much larger building programme than the one finally realised. It probably did not go down well with the Prussian king, who, as was often the case, forced economies.

The next mention of the town's fortifications comes in early 1751, from a note by Frederick on the further cost of building Silesian fortifications. He allocated 20,000 thalers for Glatz for that year 'to carry out the fortification of the town according to Wrede's plans', and 30,000 for the following year, 1752.[97] This amount, however, was not complete, as we are informed by another letter, written in September 1751. It concerns the project that was finally realised, but it also contains information on the project that was created in 1750. Its author, the Governor of Glatz, *Generalmajor* Heinrich August de la Motte Fouqué, mentions in his covering letter, attached to the cost estimate of the final project, a project from 'last year', 1750, which was to amount to 79,158 thalers and was not to take into account the establishment of counter-mine corridors in front of the town.[98] Unfortunately, nothing more is known about it, in contrast to the project finally realised. We know of this project from a detailed cost estimate drawn up by Christian von Wrede on 19 September 1751. Significantly, we learn from the heading of the cost estimate that it relates to plans, 'by his royal majesty on 10 September 1751 in Glatz…'.[99] So, the King did not like the design of the town fortifications made by the engineer and decided to do it himself, leaving only the drawing up of the cost estimate to Wrede. The royal authorship of the project is also confirmed by a letter enclosed with the cost estimate from La Motte Fouqué.[100]

According to the cost estimate, the project included:

1. Bastion in front of the School Gate with its caponier, gunpowder store, guardhouse and battery, for the sum of 31,625 thalers 6 groschen
2. Bastion in front of the Bohemian Gate with three caponiers, battery, gunpowder magazine and guardhouse – for the amount of 33,529 thalers 13 groschen 4 pfennigs
3. Enevelope's revetment together with the moat wall – for the amount of 2,932 thalers 8 groschen
4. Counter mine gallery with six arms – for the sum of 2275 thalers

---

95   Prussian engineer born in 1723, ranked *kapitän* from 1750, died at the Battle of Landeshut, Bonin, *Geschichte des Ingenieurkorps*, p.297.
96   Plan, Profil et Elevation d'une Boulangerie batie a Glatz l'an 1756, SBB PK, X 25107/6 p.44.
97   GStA SPK I HA Rep 96 no. 616 – Schlesische Festungen, Bd.F, 1751–52, p.1.
98   GStA SPK I HA Rep 96 no. 616 – Schlesische Festungen, Bd.F, 1751–52, p.35.
99   GStA SPK I HA Rep 96 no. 616 – Schlesische Festungen, Bd.F, 1751–52, p.34.
100 GStA SPK I HA Rep 96 no. 616 – Schlesische Festungen, Bd.F, 1751–52, p.35.

5.   Valuation of houses, gardens and fields in front of the Bohemian gate to be removed –
3,702 thalers 16 groschen

In total, all these tasks were expected to cost 74,064 thalers 19 groschen 4 fenigs. As you can
see from the description, this was the design version that was eventually realised.

The project to fortify the town did not end activity in this area in the period before the
outbreak of the Seven Years War, although subsequent ideas for the expansion of the fortress
no longer had such momentum, nor were they implemented. A vestige of the first of these
ideas is the cost estimate for the works planned in Glatz in the following years, created
in October 1753. Two budget items appeared in it, which testified to plans for the expansion of the main fortress: 'a bastion on the old fort' for the sum of 23,808 thalers and 'a
lunette together with a caponier to the right of this bastion for 4432 thalers.'[101] Judging by
the amounts planned, this was to be a significant investment. Unfortunately, it is not known
where this structure was to be located or what it was to look like. The last proposal before
the Seven Years War, also unrealised, came at the beginning of 1756. During the stay of La
Motte Fouqué, in Potsdam, Frederick informed him of plans to casemate all the buildings
in the main fortress. According to the cost estimates made, this investment was to cost
34,675 thalers and would take more than three years to complete. Initially, the King wanted
the work to start in 1756, so the governor asked for the first tranche of a third of the total
amount to be set aside for this task, but in the end the sovereign stated that the start of this
task would be postponed until the following year.[102] As the Seven Years War was in full
swing in 1757, the idea of completely casemating the main fortress was postponed by more
than a decade, only to be realised by building the Donjon.

Chronology of Construction Work

Tracing the stages of Walrave's first project is unfortunately impossible. The archival sources
only provide limited coverage of the main period in which the project was carried out. Only
scraps of information exist for the period before 1746. It is known that as early as June 1742,
Frederick arrived in Glatz, who for two days viewed the works of the local fortress and gave
numerous hints as to its further development.[103] In August some sort of plan of Glatz was
delivered to the King by Walrave, but we do not know whether this was an inventory or a
project for expansion.[104] In April 1743, Walrave made a report on the condition of the fortifications there, which the King approved of. He also requested that Glatz be brought to a
defensible condition by 1743.[105] The fortress expansion project itself was not conceived until 1
June of that year, the date of Walrave's signature. Work on the project started almost immediately, although it amounted to preparatory work. In June and September 1743, clay was

---

101 GStA SPK I HA Rep 96 no. 616 – Schlesische Festungen, Bd.G, 1753–54, p.11.
102 GStA SPK I HA Rep 96 no. 616 – Schlesische Festungen, Bd.H, 1755–56, p.37, 38.
103 He was in Glatz between 27 and 29 June. Rödenbeck, *Tagebuch oder Geschichtskalender*, vol.1, p.70.
104 GStA SPK I HA Rep.96 B, Abschriften von Kabinetsordres, Bd.24, p.285.
105 GStA SPK I HA Rep.96 B, Abschriften von Kabinetsordres, Bd.26, p.182.

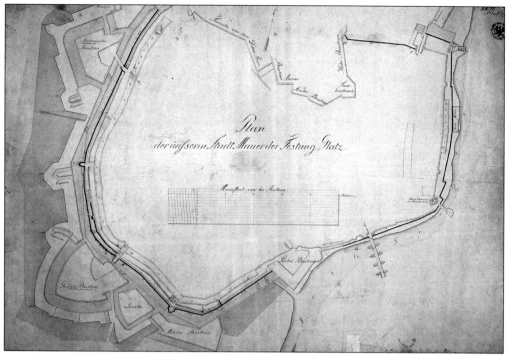

Glatz, fortifications of the Old Town.
(GStA SPK, XI HA ref. E 71977)

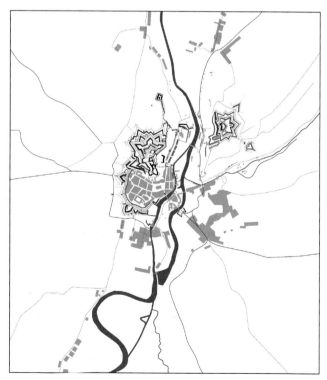

Glatz, fortifications 1756.
(Reconstruction by Mariusz
Wojciechowski)

obtained for the firing of bricks for the construction of the fortifications.[106] While in the autumn the land needed for the expansion of the fortifications was acquired – 20 plots for the expansion of the old fortress, three for the Owcza Góra fort and seven for the fortress brick-works.[107] Within the main fortress, fields of approximately 12 hectares were taken. Within Schäferberg, arable fields with a total area of approximately 14 hectares were acquired, while approximately eight hectares were taken for the brickyard.[108] In autumn 1743 the new fortifi-cations of Schäferberg were also marked out.[109] By 1744 intensive work must have been going on, as 1,000 soldiers were deployed to build the fortress.[110] The only fortification whose date of construction we know precisely was the Small Tenaille, an earthwork defensive struc-ture between the fortress and the Frankenstein suburb, which was built in 1744 and still exists today.[111] In 1746 and 1747 the glacis on the main fortress was also widened, as another six plots of land with an area of approximately 1.6 hectares were acquired at that time.[112] The realisation of the first project, both on the Schäferberg and on the main fortress, was completed in 1747, as according to the summary statement of expenses the entire planned amount – 198,222 thalers – had been spent by that year.[113] We are also able to determine the yearly construction date of the Upper Crown reduit on the site of the Schäferberg fort. The keystone of its entrance gate, around the royal initials, bears the year '1746'.

A little more is known about the subsequent course of the construction work. In 1748–1749, the envelope of Schäferberg, a new covered way and two flèches were erected. In that year 10,000 thalers was allocated for this task, out of a planned 22,000, the rest was to be paid the following year.[114] Certainly in 1748 work was being carried out on the new covered way, as evidenced by the date on the keystone of one of the guardhouses.[115] The Königsheiner flèche, the construction of which was commissioned in September 1749,[116] was certainly being built in 1750. Drawings of two fragments of this structure, revealing features of execution drawings, come from that year – a projection of one of the caponiers defending its covered way (dated 12 May) and a cross-section through one of its unidentified elements (dated 23 April).[117] The work was probably completed as early as 1750; sources from later years do not mention it.

---

106 Archiwum Państwowe we Wrocławiu (APWr), Akta miasta Kłodzka, 5689- Acta von denen zur Fortification ver Vestung Glatz gezogenen burgerl. Grund Stucken und denen Damnificatis…. Bonification von 1743 bis 1752, letters of 26.06.1743 and 05.09.1743.

107 APWr, Akta miasta Kłodzka, 5689, Specification of 28 November 1743 and statement of 8 September 1747.

108 APWr, Akta miasta Kłodzka, 5689, Specification of 28 November 1743 and statement of 8 September 1747.

109 APWr, Akta miasta Kłodzka, 5689, Letter from Joseph Marx, owner of a farm near Schäferberg fort, dated May 1744.

110 GStA SPK I HA Rep.96 B, Abschriften von Kabinetsordres, Bd.28, p.147.

111 APWr, Akta miasta Kłodzka, 5689, letter of 24 May 1748.

112 APWr, Akta miasta Kłodzka, 5689, Statement of 8 September 1747

113 GStA SPK I HA Rep 96 no. 616 – Schlesische Festungen, Bd.D 1747, p.7.

114 For 1748, 10,000 was allocated for this task, out of a planned 22,000; the rest was to be paid the following year, GStA SPK I HA Rep 96 no No 616 – Schlesische Festungen, Bd.E, 1748–50, p.2.

115 Due to the damage the date is barely legible, but it was still clearly legible in the 1960s, Przemysław Wojciechowski, 'Fortyfikacje nowożytne twierdzy kłodzkiej w XVII i XVIII w', Zeszyty Naukowe Politechniki Gdańskiej, vol.122 (1968), p.102.

116 von Orlich, Geschichte der schlesischen Kriege, vol.2, p.448.

117 SBB SKP ref. X 25106 p.17, X 25106, p.24.

The following year, preparatory work for the construction of the town's fortifications probably began. Not only was the sum of 20,000 thalers allocated for that year for the construction of this set of fortifications, but preparations began for the demolition of the burgher buildings in the area of the future defences. This involved as many as 29 properties – houses with gardens, factories and fields.[118] However, it was not until the final design of the town fortifications was created in September 1751 that construction began.[119] In 1753, the cost estimate for the following year's work allocated a total of 20,000 thalers, of which 9,000 thalers was for the bastion in front of the School Gate, 8,583 thalers for the covered way and 2,417 thalers for the counter-mine corridors.[120] These projects took until the end of 1754.[121]

Parallel to these large works, smaller works were in progress, related to ongoing repairs or minor adjustments to the existing defences. In the autumn of 1752, the governor of Glatz drew the King's attention to the poor condition of the gunpowder magazines in the main fortress, which were too damp to store powder.[122] However, it was not until December 1752 that the King created a special fund from which money was to be used annually to finance repairs to the already existing defence works. For 1753 the amount was to be 13,000 thalers for all Silesian fortresses, of which 1,000 was for Glatz.[123] In the first year in Glatz, this budget was slightly exceeded, as 1,088 thalers were spent on repairs. Most of this amount, as much as 932 thalers, was consumed by the rebuilding of the bastion of St Florian – the lowering of the gate, which up to that point had been half visible from the foreground, above the case-mate of the Great Tenaille, as well as the rebuilding of one of the bastion's faces. Significantly, the works would have cost more, but considerable use was made of the labour of the prisoners, who carried out masonry and stone work, paving and earthworks. In addition to the rebuilding of the bastion, two more bridges were made that year at a cost of 156 thalers.[124] The following year the renovation expenditure limit was only slightly exceeded, as a total of 1,002 thalers and 12 groschen were spent. Also in this year, masonry work was carried out on the bastion of St Florian, but this time it cost only 150 thalers. Slightly less, 140 thalers, was the cost of other masonry work on the main fortress – 'the wall opposite the Arsenal, from the *Kreuz Schanze* to the White Tower, including its latrine.' Smaller works – repairs to the breastworks, cordons, barriers and guardhouses on both fortresses cost 206 thalers. More than half of the total repair expenditure (506 thalers 12 fenig) was consumed by the procurement of timber for the palisades, their preparation, and the construction of warehouses for their temporary storage. A total of 920 pieces of palisades were prepared for Schäferberg, and 1,968 for the main fortress.[125] With this expenditure, the preparations for the fortress to be placed in combat readiness began. However, the emplacement of the palisades itself did not begin until June 1756. Just before the war, 18,000 palisades were still missing.[126]

---

118 APWr, Akta miasta Kłodzka, 5689, Letter from Glatz dated 18 December 1750
119 GStA SPK I HA Rep.96 No. 616, Bd.F, pp.1, 22, 23.
120 GStA SPK I HA Rep.96 No. 616, Bd.G, p.12.
121 The last audit of fortification expenditure concerned expenditure from 1 October 1753 to the end of September of the following year, GStA SPK I HA Rep.96 No. 616, Bd.G, p.10.
122 GStA SPK I HA Rep.96 No. 616, Bd.F, p.47.
123 GStA SPK I HA Rep.96 No. 616, Bd.F, p.53.
124 GStA SPK I HA Rep.96 No. 616, Bd.G, p.80.
125 GStA SPK I HA Rep.96 No. 616, Bd.H, p.36.
126 GStA SPK I HA Rep.96 No. 616, Bd.H, p.61.

Unique Solutions Applied During the pre-1756 Modernisation

The new Glatz fortifications built before the outbreak of the Seven Years War had a number of interesting developments that deserve special attention.

The first is the peculiar curvilinear forms of some of the local defensive works. The construction of the time was dominated by rectilinear elements. Regardless of whether a particular fortification theorist or practitioner favoured bastion or tenaille fortification, the defensive works created were devoid of curves. This was, of course, due to the desire to reduce blind spots in the fire conducted from the defensive works. Elements constructed from curved lines appeared extremely rarely; in fact, the only commonly known example are the artillery batteries in the retired shoulders of bastions, which were readily used by one of the most important fortification makers of the seventeenth century school, Menno van Coehoorn. However, they were only a fragment of the entire defensive work, otherwise constructed with straight lines. Meanwhile, several different structures appeared in Glatz that were entirely curvilinear: The Horseshoe on Schäferberg, and the set of fortifications at the Green Gate – the Green Bastion, the adjacent lunette, and one of the caponiers of its covered road. The Horseshoe, a structure that appeared in the original 1743 design, was in fact a large bastion. Its originator, Cornelius Walrave, already had similar structures to his credit in the Thurm Schanze, tête de pont at Magdeburg he designed in the 1730s the main rampart was defended by five similar bastei sheltered by counterguards. It is not known what inspired the Prussian engineer to use such forms. He probably saw somewhere an early modern bastei protected by a later ravelin and liked the form. The lack of such solutions in the contemporary theory of defensive architecture probably did not bother him. As is well known, Walrave was a practitioner, not a theoretician, and was not limited to one trend in defensive architecture – for example, he used bastion forms just as often as he did tenaille forms.

Walrave no longer had anything to do with the second group of 'curvilinear' Glatz structures; the fortifications at the Green Gate were built after his imprisonment. Of the three structures built there, the main bastion is particularly important. This is because it was built on the site of an already existing detached bastion. It is evident that the curvilinear forms of the bastion were consciously applied with the feeling that they were more favourable than the traditional outline. A large, detached bastion with a traditional outline already existed on this site, having been constructed under Austrian rule. The designer – presumably Frederick – did not stop at modernising this structure (which would have been cheaper), but built a completely new structure in its place. Importantly, the Green Bastion is a bastion in name only, as instead of two fronts and shoulders it has two long, arched fronts. The lunette adjacent to the bastion looks similar. The caponier, adjacent to the bastion, has also been given a characteristic curve. The explanation for the use of such forms seems simple; the King probably concluded that defensive works shaped in this way would fit better with the surrounding terrain. And this, as is well known, was one of the few rules of fortification that he recognised. Moreover, in his description of the covered way of the town of Glatz in the Political Testament of 1752, he writes that he ordered it to be set up in such a way as to make it difficult to shoot through it longitudinally.[127] Probably the curvilinear form of the fronts of the defensive works also resulted from similar motivations of the designer.

---

127 Volz, *Die Werke*, vol.7, p.177.

Another theme that emerged during the described modernisation was the caponiers. They were located without exception within the covered way. Four of them were built on the covered way in front of the town fortifications, four on the Königsheiner Flesche, and three more on the Schäferberg covered way. None of these buildings have survived to the present day, but fortunately very detailed drawings have survived, including designs for these works dating from before 1756. Most of them had a rectangular plan, with one of the shorter sides (the one facing the foreground) pointed; the exceptions were the caponier at the Green Bastion described above (arched) and the caponier in the middle of the Königsheiner Flesche communication (both shorter sides pointed). Most of them were made of brick, only those on the covered way in front of Schäferberg were wooden in tie beam construction. These structures were used to defend the covered way with musket fire. However, these facilities were not only intended to help defend this important layer of fortress defence. The caponier located between the Böhmische and Grün bastions was so large (it had a total of 32 musket loopholes) that, together with the large places of arms – in the middle of which it stood – it acted as the equivalent of a small bastion, conspicuously missing at this point.

The last feature of the new fortifications of the Glatz fortress to which attention should be drawn was their heavy saturation with casemates. This is particularly true of the fort on Schäferberg, in which all the rooms, according to Johann Gottlieb Kahlo, who was delighted with this fortress, were to be bombproof.[128] Importantly, the total bombproofing of this work is also the result of modifications to the original design. This is because Walrave only designed one casemate there, albeit a large one, in the gorge of the Upper Crown. The other bombproof structures mentioned by Kahlo – the gunpowder stores, the commandant's house, the bakery, and the brewery – were built later.[129] Casemates also appeared in other parts of the fortress. Both of the main city bastions were equipped with them. The interior plan of one of them, the Bohemian Bastion, is known. It had a large, fortified guardhouse consisting of five rooms on both sides of the gate postern, a handy powder store on the other side of the courtyard and a large powder store in the left shoulder.[130] The largest bombproof facility, the casemate of the Great Tenaille, however, appeared in the main fortress and it is still preserved today. In addition to it, there were other bombproof rooms in the fortress, located in the old castle, but this did not fully suit Frederick. In March 1756, he wanted to proceed with a complete casemating of the works of the old fortress. This was to cost 34,657 thalers and could have started as early as that year. However, the commandant of the fortress believed that the investment could not be completed this year, but in the following three years.[131] The royal desire was only realised after the war, during the construction of the Donjon.

In the context of bombproofing, attention should also be paid to the type of covering used. The vast majority of structures resistant to mortar bomb impact were covered with thick vaults and a layer of earth, which was a typical technique. However, the Glatz caponiers

---

128 Kahlo, *Denkwürdigkeiten*, p.192.
129 The brewery and bakery were located on the site of the now existing Red Casemates, the commandant's house was a characteristic semi-circular casemate between the Red and White Casemates, partly preserved to this day. These structures are shown on the 1779 plan of the fort, *Project des auf den Schäferberg neu zu vertiefenden Grabens...*, SBB PK, ref. X 25107/30.
130 Description based on plan (probably draft), GStA SPK XI HA, ref. G 70791.
131 GStA SPK Geheimes Zivilkabinett I HA Rep.96 No. 616 – Schlesische Festungen, Bd.G, p.37.

achieved their resistance to impacts through the use of a different covering – a wooden ceiling covered with earth! As you can see, we are dealing here with the first example of the use of such a construction for permanent, brick buildings, which came into general use in Prussia only in the nineteenth century, after the Napoleonic Wars. This type of bombproof covering was not a complete novelty; its use was already mentioned by some seventeenth century theorists of defensive architecture.[132]

Fortifications of the Upper Oder River

Schurgast

One of the most important tasks in the first years of Prussian rule in Silesia was the construction of a new fortress on the southern course of the Oder. Work on this project had already begun during the war, before the final borders of Prussian possession in Silesia had been established. The first idea to secure this section was a fortress in Schurgast (Skorogoszcz), at the mouth of the Glatzer Neisse into the Oder. The earliest mention of this fortress dates back to the autumn of 1741, when one of the King's advisors, *Oberst* Karl Christoph von Schmettau, suggested to the King that Schurgast should be fortified instead of Neisse, which was closer to the Oder. The King insisted on extending the fortress at Neisse, but his advisor's arguments convinced him to issue a decision to fortify Schurgast as well.[133] The first mention of the project comes as early as 29 December 1741, when the King sent a letter to Walrave: 'you should make me a plan as to how the town of Schurgast, situated between the Neisse and the Oder, can be fortified at the least expense. My intention is not to make a fortress there like Lile or Tournay, but to make it only a good and strong place.'[134] The King did not have to wait long for his request to be fulfilled, as he received the finished plans for the fortress from Walrave after little more than two months.[135] Doubtless they were not accepted, since less than a year later the King demanded that Walrave provide him with new designs.[136] The final completion of the design work took place in the first half of the year. According to the plans, the larger of the fortresses was intended to be built in 1744, the others in 1745. Some work was even started in 1743 but was quickly abandoned.[137] At the beginning of August, the King abandoned the idea of building a fortress in this location.[138]

---

132 Jacques Ozanam, *Dictionnaire mathematique, ou: Idée genearale des mathematiques dans lequel l'on trouve outre les Termes de cette science, plusieurs Termes des Arts et des autres sciences* (Amsterdam: Huguetan, 1691), p.602; Johann Bernhard Scheiter, *Examen fortificatorium, Darin so wohl Eine gantz newe Art oder Manier vom Festungs-Bau* (Strassburg: Spoor und Wächtler, 1676), pp.2–4.

133 Johann David Erdmann Preuss, *Urkundenbuch zu der Lebensgeschichte Friedrichs des Großen* (Berlin: Nauncksche Buchhandlung, 1832), vol.1, p.4.

134 Letter from the King to Walrave of 29 December 1741, I HA Rep.96 B, Abschriften von Kabinetsordres, Bd.33, p.95.

135 Letter from the King to Walrave of 6 March 1742, I HA Rep.96 B, Abschriften von Kabinetsordres, Bd.24, p.91.

136 Letter from the King to Walrave of 27 January 1743, I HA Rep.96 B, Abschriften von Kabinetsordres, Bd.26, p.39.

137 Paul Kretschmar, 'Schurgast O/S, eine wieder aufgegebene Festung Friedrichs des Großen', *Der Oberschlesier*, vol.14, (1932), p.372.

138 Augustin Weltzel, *Geschichte der Stadt, Herrschaft und ehemaliegen Festung Kosel* (Kosel: Verlag von Paul Mode, 1888), p.348.

No remains of this defensive structure have survived to the present day. It is known only from one design, preserved in the Berlin Staatsbibliothek. It is unsigned and undated but reveals features of the design.[139] It depicts a fortress consisting of three structures separated by the forks of the Oder and Glatzer Neisse rivers. The main work was to be located on the southern bank of the Neisse. It was to be in the form of a five-pointed star, with tenaille retrenchement at each corner. This star was to consist of two parts separated from each other by a moat. Between each corner of the fort was to be a ravelin, and in front of the water-filled moat there was to be a covered way with extensive places of arms. On the eastern bank of the Oder and northern bank of the Neisse there were to be two, almost identical, regular in outline, works surrounded by a moat in the form of a lunette preceded by two symmetrically arranged, trapezoidal flèches. The whole was to be complemented by smaller works and a wide covered way, reinforced with an outer moat.

The fortress at Schurgast, although not realised, is an important structure for considering the Prussian defensive architecture of the early reign of Frederick the Great. The solutions used here betray numerous connections with other completed projects by Cornelius Walrave. The characteristic bipartite nature of the main work finds a parallel in the fort on Schäferberg in Glatz and in the crown work at Teufel Teich in Peitz. The outline of the main section, in turn, betrays similarities with the forts of Schweidnitz in their early design phase. Another motif, used three times in the design of Schurgast, was two trapezoidal defence works symmetrically placed on either side of the capital line of the fort.[140] This was repeated in Walrave's design for the fortified tête de pont at Cosel.

In addition to Schurgast, another location for a fortress on the Upper Oder seems to have been considered. It was Ratibor (Racibórz). As early as June 1742, the King ordered an engineer to be sent there, whose task was to make a plan of the town, to 'thoroughly survey' the town, and to palisade the suburbs.[141] A year later, the King himself appeared at Ratibor and spent a few days there between 29 July and 1 August, among other things familiarising himself with the area.[142] The result of this visit was the choice of Cosel as the new Silesian fortress.

Cosel

The fortress at Cosel (Koźle) is an important defensive ensemble from the time of Frederick the Great. Both the decision to build the fortress and most of the important design decisions are linked to his activities. Before discussing these activities, however, it is necessary to devote some space to unravelling the problem of the date of the fortress. In the last few decades, the dominant view in the literature dealing with the history of the Cosel fortress has been that it has a seventeenth-century origin and is linked to the actions of the troops

---

139 Plan du Fort au Confluant de Neisse et de l'Oder, SBB PK, ref. X 28148.
140 Capital line: a theoretical line running through the centre of a bastion or other symmetrical defensive work.
141 Letter from the King to Walrave, 27 June 1742, I HA Rep.96 B, Abschriften von Kabinetsordres, Bd.24, p.220.
142 Rödenbeck, *Tagebuch oder Geschichtskalender*, vol.1, p.90.

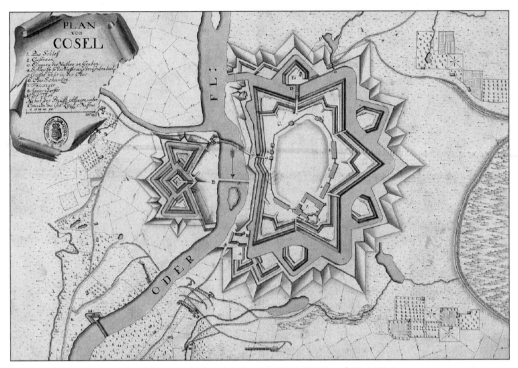

Cosel fortress during the siege in 1745. (SLUB, ref. KS A9324)

occupying Cosel during the Thirty Years War. Moreover, the fortress was said to have been modernised by the Austrians in the early eighteenth century. This information is given by Alexander in his book *Friedrich der Grosse und Cosel*, and later studies on Cosel repeat it.[143] However, this information is incorrect, there was no fortress at Cosel in the early eighteenth century. The creation of this fortress in the 1740s on the basis of the old town, which was fortified only with medieval walls, is consistently written about both in Austrian and Prussian literature.[144] Of the latter group, the most important is the book by Weltzel, the town chronicler, who devoted almost 100 pages to the history of the fortress in his chronicle of the town from 1888.[145] In the twentieth century, Alexander's claim initially went unnoticed. The primary book describing Silesian fortresses in the period before 1740, Willi Klawitter's 1941 work, contains no mention of the existence of the Cosel fortress, yet the author discusses all fortified towns in Silesia.[146] Alexander's thesis became firmly established in the scientific debate only thanks to Janusz Bogdanowski, who presented it in his

---

143 Alexander, *Friedrich der Große*, p.13.
144 Geschichte des zweiten schlesischen Krieges', *Oestreichische militärische Zeitschrift* (1825), vol.3, H.7, p.24; Kosel's entry in: Hirtenfeld, *Der Militär-Maria-Theresien-Orden*, p.618.
145 Weltzel, Geschichte der Stadt, pp.346–443.
146 Klawitter, *Geschichte der schlesischen Festungen*.

1966 article.[147] After Bogdanowski, this thesis was also repeated by other authors, so that it was accepted as a certainty.[148] It was only in 2007 that two publications were published that challenged this idea.[149]

Hans Alexander's claim is based on an archive plan from the collection of the Vienna Kreisgsarchiv. This drawing is not dated in the original, nor does it have the character of a project. Analysing the carefully depicted urban layout of the city, as well as the surrounding area, it is clear that it is far from the actual state. The town has a circular plan (in fact it is an elongated oval), the largest object, which was the castle, is missing from among its buildings, and the hydrological situation, especially the layout of the watercourses, has also been misrepresented. So, what is this drawing? We are probably dealing with intelligence material – a sketch of a Prussian fortress made without measurements. The Viennese archives are full of such depictions of fortresses. The plan was most likely drawn between 1745 and 1750, as its author did not indicate the city walls, which still existed in 1745 but were removed before 1750, nor did he depict the Wiegschützer redoubt, which was such a large structure that it probably could not have been omitted.

The final argument that contradicts the existence of an Austrian fortress in Cosel are two drawings of the town made before 1740 by Friedrich Bernhard Werner, in volume three of his fundamental work on the iconography of Silesian towns: *Topographia oder Prodromus Delinati Silesiae Ducatus...* Both show the town surrounded by medieval walls. The only trace of non-medieval fortifications is a small, single, earthen defensive structure noticeable in the view of the town from the Oder. This was probably one of the relics of Swedish fortifications, similar to the one located at the ford across the Oder, south of the town, marked on some Prussian inventories of Cosel.[150] However, there is no basis for claiming that the Frederician fortress was built on the older fortifications. The actual date from which the history of the Cosel fortress should begin is July 1743. In the summer of that year Frederick travelled through Silesia. On 29 July, he set off from Brieg, via Oppeln (Opole), to Ratibor.

---

147 Janusz Bogdanowski, 'Twierdza Koźle. Problem planu w świetle systemu kleszczowego szkoły staropruskiej i szkoły Arad', *Studia i Materiały do Historii Wojskowości*, vol.12, no.1, (1966), pp.157–158. Bogdanowski's claims were repeated by Jerzy Stankiewicz in his article published in the same volume, Jerzy Stankiewicz, 'Ze studiów nad fortyfikacjami pruskimi na ziemiach polskich', *Studia i Materiały do Historii Wojskowości*; vol.12, no.1, (1966), pp.106–152, p.121.

148 Mention should be made here of the works of Karol Joncy, who wrote several texts on the Napoleonic siege of the fortress of Koźle in 1806–1807, in each of which, when writing about the origins of the fortress, he repeated the claim of the existence of a neglected Austrian fortress in 1740; Karol Jonca, 'Wielka Armia Napoleona w kampanii 1807 roku pod Koźlem', in Stanisław Senft (ed.) Szkice Kędzierzyńsko-Kozielskie, vol.1, (Opole: Instytut Śląski, 1985), pp.9–76; Karol Jonca, Wielka Armia Napoleona w kampanii 1807 roku pod Koźlem, (Opole: Państwowy Instytut Naukowy-Instytut Śląski, 2003); Karol Jonca, 'Strategiczna rola twierdzy kozielskiej w dobie wojen napoleońskich' in Edward Nycz, Stanisław Senft (eds), *Wojna i pokój w dziejach twierdzy i miasta Koźle* (Opole: Państwowy Instytut Naukowy-Instytut Śląski, 2007), pp.33–63.

149 Wojciech Eckert, *Fortyfikacje Nadodrzańskie w procesie rozwoju nowożytnej sztuki fortyfikacyjnej w XVII – XIX w*, (Zielona Góra: Uniwersytet Zielonogórski, 2007), pp.30–33; Grzegorz Podruczny, 'Twierdza Koźle w latach 1743–1806', in Edward Nycz, Stanisław Senft (eds), *Wojna i pokój w dziejach twierdzy i miasta Koźle*, (Opole: Wydawnictwo Instytut Śląski, 2007), p.64.

150 This rampart, with a dovetail outline, was marked by inspector Neuwartz on a project for the digging of a new Oder riverbed in August 1750, GStA SPK, Geheimes Zivilkabinett I HA Rep.96 No. 616 – Schlesische Festungen, Bd.E, p.32.

There he stayed two days, and then set off for Neisse. It was probably during this journey that he decided to abandon the construction of a new fortress in Schurgast and instead decided to fortify Cosel. Although the sources are silent as to when exactly the King was in Cosel, it is possible that it was on 29 July, when he travelled from Oppeln to Ratibor, or on 31 July, which he devoted entirely to familiarising himself with the area around Ratibor.[151] He informed the Minister for Silesia, Count von Münchow, of his decision shortly afterwards, on 5 August 1743.[152]

Construction

Preparations for the construction of the fortress began as soon as the autumn of 1743. In October, the *Landrats* of the Cosel and Ratibor districts were obliged to estimate the price of the land to be bought for the construction of the fortress. Initially, this was not possible, as it was not known what final shape the fortifications would take. It was only after the project was approved in mid-November of that year that the King ordered the minister Ludwig Wilhelm von Münchow to carry out an assessment of the plots of land to be used for the construction of the fortress.[153] The final estimate of the price of the land to be purchased was made in February 1744.[154] At the same time, preparatory work for the start of construction was carried out. In January, engineers were appointed to carry out work on the fortress. The construction of the fortress was prioritised, as the King delegated as many as six engineers to it: *Oberst* Foris, *Kapitäne* Gedeler, Petri and Hohnauer, *Leutnants* Foris and Janitsch and supervisors Wind and Winancko.[155] In March it was decided to send 1,800 soldiers to Cosel to help build the fortress. Following them, a strong detachment of hussars was sent to the Cosel area to make desertion from among the workers difficult. Another 100 military carpenters were assigned to harvest timber for the works.[156] In March, the King finally approved Walrave's design and cost estimate for the fortress. Frederick wanted construction completed in 1744. The work on it was to cost 106,305 thalers.[157] However, in that year probably only one ravelin, the fortifications of the tête de pont– a redoubt with two flèches – and part of the main rampart and moat were built. Three barracks buildings for two battalions were also constructed.[158] The sources include reports of financial difficulties; in September of that year, work on the construction of barracks had to be halted and the money initially earmarked for this purpose was used to build fortifications.[159] Troubles of this kind also plagued the fortress builders in the spring of the following year,[160] moreover, there were also

151 Rödenbeck, *Tagebuch oder Geschichtskalender*, vol.1, p.90.
152 Weltzel, *Geschichte der Stadt*, p.348.
153 Letter from the King to Minister von Münchow, 13 November 1743, GStA SPK, I HA Rep.96 B Abschriften von Kabinetsordres, Bd.29, p.8.
154 Weltzel, *Geschichte der Stadt*, p.264.
155 Letter from the King to Walrave, 11 January 1744, GStA SPK, I HA Rep.96 B Abschriften von Kabinetsordres, Bd.28, p.28.
156 Letter from the King to Marvitz, 9 March 1744, GStA SPK, I HA Rep.96 B Abschriften von Kabinetsordres, Bd.28, p.147.
157 Alexander, *Friedrich der Große*, pp.22–23.
158 Weltzel, *Geschichte der Stadt*, pp.349–350.
159 Letter from engineer Foris, 13 September 1744, GStA SPK, I HA Rep.96 Tit. 83, Hh 2 – Foris, pp.1–2.
160 Letter from engineer Foris, 18 April 1745, GStA SPK, I HA Rep.96 Tit. 83, Hh 2 – Foris, p.7.

difficulties with manpower. Although in April 1745 Minister von Münchow ordered the *Landrats* of the five neighbouring counties to urgently supply 1,000 labourers to work on the ramparts, the required number could not be supplied.[161] Not surprisingly, the fortress was not properly prepared for defence. In May 1745, during the Second Silesian War, the main rampart was still not ready, only two ravelins were completed, and the entire covered way was missing. Only the moat, fed by water from the surrounding marshes, was fulfilling its role.[162] This and other shortcomings resulted in the easy occupation of the fortress by Maria Theresa's army on 25 May 1745. The imperial soldiers continued the work after taking over the fortress. They erected, among other things, the remaining ravelins and the covered way. Although they had only been in possession of the fortress for three months, it must be assumed that they managed to complete its construction to such an extent that the Prussian army, which had already approached the fortress on 26 August, could not risk storming it and was forced to start a regular siege.[163] As a result of this, and especially as a result of the city fire caused by the artillery bombardment of 3 September, the Austrian garrison capitulated. It is worth noting that the siege was led by the designer of the fortress himself, Walrave.[164] The town suffered during the bombardment – both the burgher houses and the newly erected barracks. The fortifications were not damaged.

The takeover of the fortress by the Prussian army was followed by further expansion. This was led from 1746 by *Oberst* Sers. The cost estimate he prepared in 1746 for the construction of the fortress for the years 1747–1748 envisaged both the completion of works previously started and significant modernisation work. The most serious task was to strengthen the fortress' resistance to assault. Up to that point, the fortifications had been purely earthworks, the rampart was only protected from being captured by a sudden attack by means of a wide water moat and palisades. This construction did not fully protect against assault, so it was decided to strengthen the main rampart of the fortress with masonry revetment, at a cost of over 27,000 thalers. Slightly less, at a cost of just under 26,000 thalers, was to be spent on four casemates for 800 soldiers in the fortress. There were also plans to erect a new work, the Wiegschützer Redoubt, with communications and the caponier defending it, at a cost of 9,899 thalers. Sers also wanted to erect five gunpowder magazines, each holding 600 *cetnar*, one of which would be in a redoubt in the tête de pont. In total, the magazines would hold 3,000 *cetnar* and cost a total of 10,597 thalers. These and other smaller works were to cost a total of 92,782 thalers. In addition to this, 10,000 thalers were planned to be spent on an investment not directly related to the fortress, but also of great importance, new flood dykes. In total, the works planned by Sers at Cosel were to cost as much as 102,782 thalers. The King's decision for 1747 allocated 40,000 thalers, out of which the Wiegschützer Redoubt, the flood dykes, two of the four planned casemates, and three of the five planned gunpowder magazines were to be built.[165] The gunpowder magazines were to be completed first. In his letter of 28 February 1747, the King pressed Sers to take care of

---

161 Weltzel, *Geschichte der Stadt*, pp.350–351.
162 Weltzel, *Geschichte der Stadt*, p.351; *Geschichte des zweiten schlesischen Krieges*, p.24.
163 Both the condition of the fortifications and the siege works are depicted on the plan SBB PK, ref. Da 15.163e.
164 Weltzel, *Geschichte der Stadt*, p.354.
165 GStA SPK, Geheimes Zivilkabinett I HA Rep.96 No. 616 – Schlesische Festungen, Bd.C, p.20.

the construction of these facilities first, so that the 1,000 *Cetnar* of gunpowder prepared for this fortress and waiting in Brieg could be transported to Cosel as soon as possible.[166] These facilities were probably completed by 1748. More than 13,000 thalers were budgeted for 1750, for masonry work on the main rampart of the fortress,[167] and another 13,000 thalers for the following year for masonry on the rampart on the Ratibor side, and a further 16,000 thalers for the previously unplanned system of counter-mine galleries.[168] By mid-November 1750, a new bridge over the Oder River had been built, a guardhouse had been erected at the Wiegschützer Redoubt, and half of the masonry revetment had been completed. In November, work was still being done on the rest of the rampart and the necessary clean-up tasks.[169] Cosel appeared twice in the funding schedule for fortress construction for the years 1751–1753, drawn up at the end of the year. For 1751, 8,000 thalers were planned to be spent on mines, while a year later 21,000 thalers were planned to be spent simply on the construction of the fortress. No expenditure was planned for 1753.[170] According to the next plan, this time drawn up at the end of 1751, in 1752 it was planned to spend 8,000 thalers on mines, 13,000 thalers to complete the main rampart's revetment, and 4,000 thalers for two gunpowder magazines with a capacity of 1,000 *cetnar*. This last expenditure was not accepted by the King.[171] In the end, the realisation of these plans dragged on until May 1753. Revetting the rampart cost more than expected (17,187 thalers), while the counter-mine galleries cost less (6,032 thalers).[172]

After the completion of the tasks of Sers' project in 1752, no further work on the fortifications was planned. Cosel does appear in the financial plan of the Silesian fortresses for 1753, but the allocated 9,000 thalers relate to hydrotechnical work on the Oder there.[173] Nevertheless, some work was carried out in 1753, the fortress expenditure report for August 1753 shows an amount of 1,396 thalers for the main rampart.[174] Also for 1754 it was planned to allocate 10,000 thalers: 4,000 for a new casemate in the tête de pont and 6,000 for the foundations of the new barracks.[175] However, these plans were very seriously altered. Indeed, in 1753 the King ordered that another costly reconstruction of the fortress be undertaken. Obviously, this work

---

166 Letter from the King to Sers, 28 February 1747, GStA SPK, Geheimes Zivilkabinett I HA Rep.96 No. 616 – Schlesische Festungen, Bd.D, p.6.

167 GStA SPK, Geheimes Zivilkabinett I HA Rep.96 No. 616 – Schlesische Festungen, Bd.E, pp.7–8.

168 GStA SPK, Geheimes Zivilkabinett I HA Rep.96 No. 616 – Schlesische Festungen, Bd.E, pp.12–13.

169 Letter from Sers to the King, 14 November 1750, GStA SPK, Geheimes Zivilkabinett I HA Rep.96 No. 616 – Schlesische Festungen, Bd.E, p.52.

170 GStA SPK, Geheimes Zivilkabinett I HA Rep.96 No. 616 – Schlesische Festungen, Bd.F, p.1.

171 GStA SPK, Geheimes Zivilkabinett I HA Rep.96 No. 616 – Schlesische Festungen, Bd.F, pp.29–31.

172 Extract der Coselschen Fortifications Bau Rechnung vom 15 Juli 1752 bis ult. May 1754, Gen. Hautcharmoy, GStA SPK, Geheimes Zivilkabinett I HA Rep.96 No. 616 – Schlesische Festungen, Bd.G, p.77.

173 GStA SPK, Geheimes Zivilkabinett I HA Rep.96 No. 616 – Schlesische Festungen, Bd.F, pp.53, 57. Although the term 'glacis coupirung' appears in this document, which would suggest fortification works, *coupirung* was a hydraulic term and meant cutting off the old arm of the river from the new current by means of a dam. Johann Michael Voit, *Technologisches Handwörterbuch oder Beschreibung und Erklärung der gewöhnlichsten Kunstdrücke...* (Augsburg: Jenisch und Stage, 1833), p.36.

174 Monatlicher Extract der Coselschen Fortifications Bau Casse pro Menese Augusti 1753, 1 September 1753, Bosse and Wolf, GStA SPK, Geheimes Zivilkabinett I HA Rep.96 No. 616 – Schlesische Festungen, Bd.G, p.2.

175 GStA SPK, Geheimes Zivilkabinett I HA Rep.96 No. 616 – Schlesische Festungen, Bd.G, pp.13–16.

was seriously beyond what was planned in the aforementioned Silesian fortress expenditure plan for 1754, so the King had to ensure that more funds were available. In a letter to Sers dated 25 December 1753, he tells the engineer that he will receive 6,000 thalers from the Silesian minister Munchow (in addition to that 4,000 for the planned casemate in the fortified tête de pont), in addition to which a further 3,714 thalers would be given to him by the *Geheimrat* Koppen from Berlin. In total, Sers would have 9,714 thalers at his disposal with which to begin the construction of the double covered way ordered by the King. On top of this, the King declared that he would prepare a further 25,000 thalers, with which the entire new covered way, including the masonry of the glacis corners, was to be completed. However, the rest of the tasks listed in the cost estimate would have to wait until 1755.[176]

In fact, the King fulfilled his promise. A total of 30,000 thalers for work on the covered way came in three instalments between May and July. The money for this previously unanticipated expense was set aside by the *Ober Steuer Casse* in Breslau.[177] The work probably started at the end of April; part of it (masonry work) was carried out by the Rottengatter brothers' company.[178] As money was flowing on a regular basis, the work progressed quickly. By the end of August, the southern section (before corners four and five) was almost finished, while the northern section had only just begun.[179] Unfortunately, work slowed down significantly in July. From 25 to 29 July there was heavy rainfall, followed by the Oder breaking its banks. The rains and flooding ruined the freshly laid turf and caused damage to the masonry structures; among other things, the water inundated the countermine corridors.[180] The biggest problem, however, was the disruption to the works, which lasted for more than a week, until 8 August.[181] This, and the need to repair the water-damage, threatened the planned completion date, as Sers reported with concern to the King in his letter of 8 August.[182] However, the improving weather and the employment of an additional 300 workmen enabled the repairs to be made more quickly and the interrupted works to be resumed, so there was a chance that the work could be completed by the end of October.[183] By the end of August, the masonry work on the southern section of the covered way was almost complete, with the exception of two caponiers. There was also little left to complete the earthworks in this section. Overall, work on this part of the fortifications was completed in September. By the end of August, work was fully advanced on the northern section of the new covered way. By the end of September, almost all the masonry work had

---

176 Letter from the King to Sers, 25 December 1753, GStA SPK, Geheimes Zivilkabinett I HA Rep.96 No. 616 – Schlesische Festungen, Bd.G, p.29.

177 GStA SPK, Geheimes Zivilkabinett I HA Rep.96 No. 616 – Schlesische Festungen, Bd.G, pp.36, 37, 46.

178 SBB PK, DPG ref. VII Cosel, 112 – Paginen betrofen bauten in der Festung Cosel 1748 u. 1754, document no. 2.

179 Letters from General Lattorff to the King, 1 and 30 June 1754, GStA SPK, Geheimes Zivilkabinett I HA Rep.96 No. 616 – Schlesische Festungen, Bd.G, pp.35, 38.

180 Letter from General Lattorff to the King, 1 August 1754, GStA SPK, Geheimes Zivilkabinett I HA Rep.96 No. 616 – Schlesische Festungen, Bd.G, p.47.

181 Letters of General Lattorff to the King, 4 and 8 August 1754, GStA SPK, Geheimes Zivilkabinett I HA Rep.96 No. 616 – Schlesische Festungen, Bd.G, pp.51–52.

182 Letter from Sers to the King, 8 August 1754, GStA SPK, Geheimes Zivilkabinett I HA Rep.96 No. 616 – Schlesische Festungen, Bd.G, p.53.

183 Letters of Lattorff and Sers to the King, 11 August 1754, GStA SPK, Geheimes Zivilkabinett I HA Rep.96 No. 616 – Schlesische Festungen, Bd.G, pp.54–55.

been completed, with only three caponiers remaining to be constructed. All the time, earthworks were on going for the turfing of the glacis.[184]

However, the reconstruction of the covered way was only the first element of the rebuilding ordered in autumn 1753. According to the expenditure schedule for that year, the most important task was to rebuild two ravelins, at a cost of 22,000 thalers. In addition, an additional 10 masonry caponiers were to be erected at a cost of 3,000 thalers. There were also plans to rebuild the Kalk Schanze, a small work close to the tête de pont, at a cost of 6,600 thalers. However, there were indications that the works were about to be completed. It was planned to surround the Wiegschützer Redoubt and the fortified tête de pont with a palisade for a total of 3,700 thalers. In total, these works were to cost 35,300 thalers.[185] However, they were not carried out as planned. The reconstruction of the ravelins was not completed; work on them is still mentioned in June 1756.[186] One structure planned for 1755 appeared in the spending plan for the Cosel fortress in 1756 – the Limestone Sconce. Slightly more was planned to be spent on it than in the previous year, 6,800 thalers; the rest – a total of 20,000 – was planned to be spent on mine work at the tête de pont (10,000) and additions to the glacis at the Ratibor Gate were budgeted at 144 thalers. However, the fortress planners were still not satisfied with the state of the fortifications, as the cost estimate included a previously unplanned expense – a small lunette in the northern section of the double covered way, which they wanted to erect for 2,500 thalers.[187] The implementation of these plans in 1756 got off to an exceptionally late start. In early May 1756, *Oberst* Sers wrote of his readiness to start work as soon as the money came in. At the same time, he signalled a problem with workers and asked for 100 supernummary soldiers each from the Lattorf and Blanckensee regiments to be assigned to work on the fortress.[188] In the last months before the outbreak of the Seven Years War, work was mainly carried out installing the palisades,[189] a process that was not completed before the outbreak of war. On 1 August 1756, the palisading of the Wiegschützer Redoubt, Salients No. 3 and 4 as well as the newly constructed sections of the double covered way were in place, but the palisading of the remaining buildings was still in progress. Building work was also underway, with work on the Limestone Sconce in progress, and plans to begin construction in August of the lunette in front of Salient No. 5 and the fougasse in the fortified tête de pont.[190] As can be seen, at the outbreak of war the construction work was not complete.

184 Letters of Lattorff to the King, 31 August and 31 September 1754, GStA SPK, Geheimes Zivilkabinett I HA Rep.96 No. 616 – Schlesische Festungen, Bd.G, pp.59, 70.

185 GStA SPK, Geheimes Zivilkabinett I HA Rep.96 No. 616 – Schlesische Festungen, Bd.G, p.71.

186 GStA SPK, Geheimes Zivilkabinett I HA Rep.96 No. 616 – Schlesische Festungen, Bd.H, p.58.

187 Sers, Summarische Designation der von Ihro Königl. May. pro An. 1756 allergnädigst anbefohlene neue Arbeit bey den Schlesischen Festungs-Bauen, GStA SPK, Geheimes Zivilkabinett I HA Rep.96 No. 616 – Schlesische Festungen, Bd.H, p.33.

188 Letter from Sers to the King, 8 May 1756, GStA SPK, Geheimes Zivilkabinett I HA Rep.96 No. 616 – Schlesische Festungen, Bd.H, p.43.

189 GStA SPK, Geheimes Zivilkabinett I HA Rep.96 No. 616 – Schlesische Festungen, Bd.H, pp.45, 58, 81, 83.

190 Letter from Lattorf to the King, 1 August 1756, GStA SPK, Geheimes Zivilkabinett I HA Rep.96 No. 616 – Schlesische Festungen, Bd.H, p.96.

Project Development

Before the construction of the fortress began, designs were created. Little is known about their progress. What is known is that the King, as soon as he announced his decision to build the Cosel fortress, ordered that the area of the town and the surrounding area be surveyed, and that plans started.[191] By October 1743 there were supposed to be two differing versions, as Foris, who came to Cosel to estimate the price of the land to be purchased, had two, differing plans of the fortress, not yet approved by the King. Approval did not take place until 13 November that year. In a letter to Walrave, the King wrote: 'My dear Sir, I have received your letter of the 8th of this month, together with the plan of Cosel. It is entirely in accordance with my ideas and I assure you that I am satisfied with it. You must now prepare cost estimates so that the work can begin in due course.'[192] As a result, at the beginning of December the engineer Petri, who had arrived from Neisse, was able to outline the extent of the fortress plot.[193] The final project, together with a cost estimate, was presented to the King on 1 March 1744. The King accepted the project and allocated funds for its realisation.[194]

Unfortunately, the original design of the Cosel fortress has not survived. Instead, there are two plans in the collection of the Berlin Staatsbibliotek, which are study works. The first shows the fortress consisting of the main rampart surrounding the town, five ravelins and an extensive covered way. The main rampart has a tenaille outline, the form of a five-pointed star. The rampart is double, and at the corners the upper rampart is retired and forms a kind of tenaille retrenchment. The covered way is extensive, especially on the Oder side; in the sections in front of the corners of Nos. 1 and 5 there are tenaille counterguards. The area on the other side of the Oder River is protected by two works – the Limestone Sconce and an independent defensive work in the form of a square redoubt with two flèches on the sides, flanked all around by its own covered way.[195] The second design is similar in general principles to the first but differs in several important details. According to this plan, the fortress was to receive three additional outer works – two flèches extended in front of the corners of the covered way of the city fortification, connected with them by a communication, and a single, free-standing redoubt placed in the middle of the Oder island, more or less where several decades later the Kobelwitzer Redoubt was built.[196] The first of the described designs is the closest to the version that was constructed. A comparison of this design with the plans of the fortress from 1745 clearly shows the differences in the appearance of the fortifications depicted on it and those actually existing in September 1745. The main difference is the form of the fortified tête de pont. The outline of the lunettes on both sides of the large redoubt differs significantly from the shape known from the plans of the realised fortress. Moreover, in the drawing in question, the whole work is still independent, while the Austrians connected

191 Seydel, *Nachrichten*, vol.2, p.305.
192 Letter from the King to Walrave, 13 November 1743, GStA SPK, I HA Rep.96 B Abschriften von Kabinetsordres, Bd.29, pp.7–8.
193 Weltzel, *Geschichte der Stadt*, p.264.
194 Alexander, *Friedrich der Große*, pp.22–23.
195 Cosel, SBB PK, ref. X 28148.
196 Plan der Stad und Vestung Cosel/In Schlesien gegen Pohlen, SBB PK, ref. X 28148/6b.

it with the Oder bank by means of a covered way, thus giving it the form of a work open with its gorge towards the city. The differences can also be seen by comparing other elements. The ravelins on the design in question had very short flanks, clearly different from those realised. Finally, differences can also be seen in the sections of the covered way on the Oder side.

The most notable feature of the Cosel fortress is its tenaille outline, giving its main rampart the plan of a five-pointed star. This plan distinguishes Cosel from other Silesian and European fortresses. The consistent tenaille pattern was a rarity in the fortress landscape dominated by bastion fortifications in the eighteenth century. It occurred, of course, and even in quite large numbers, but mainly in smaller fortified works. Tenaille forms were common in field fortifications, and even permanent works sometimes adopted such an outline. However, the tenaille outline for an entire fortress was extremely rare, with only a few European fortresses having such fortifications (for example, Hanau). More often such an outline appeared only in the theory of defensive architecture. Of the seventeenth-century architects who proposed it, Alexander von Grotte and Rimpler should be mentioned, and of the eighteenth-century engineers, Hermann Landsberg. The eighteenth century also saw the work of Leonhard Christoph Sturm, a theorist of defensive architecture, who promoted Rimpler's tenaille fortification very strongly. However, it was not architectural theory but the practical experience of the designer of the Cosel fortress, Cornelius Walrave, that was decisive in giving the fortress he designed such an unusual form. Walrave often resorted to a tenaille outline in the fortress works he designed, the best examples being the forts built by him in Stettin, Magdeburg, Neisse and Glatz. Among his designs is also one that should be considered the prototype for Cosel. In 1729, commissioned by King Friedrich Wilhelm I, Walrave prepared a project for the reconstruction of the fortress at Minden.[197] Its most important element was to be the completely new fortifications of the fortified tête de pont. The outline of the fortress was a five-pointed star, the two arms on the river side of the fortress had a considerably larger opening angle than those on the foreground side. Of course, there were some differences between Minden and Cosel, but the similarity is nevertheless clear.

The second phase of design work at Cosel took place after the end of the Second Silesian War. Following the recapture of the fortress from Austrian hands in 1745, not only was the previously started works completed, but its reconstruction was also designed to take into account the events of the war. The new design was created in October 1746. Unfortunately, the drawing part has not survived, only a detailed cost estimate.[198] The author of the new design was *Oberst* Sers, but presumably the King had some involvement in it too, as he is known to have authorised both the design and the cost estimates.[199] The main element of the new project was to locate the Wiegschützer Redoubt in front of the main defensive perimeter. This was to be a strong defensive work connected to the interior of the fortress by a long communication, with a small redoubt in the middle of its length. The described

---

197 SBB PK, ref. X 30239–2.
198 GStA SPK, Geheimes Zivilkabinett I HA Rep.96 No. 616 – Schlesische Festungen, Bd.C, pp.18–19.
199 Letter from Sers to the King, 25 October 1746, GStA SPK, Geheimes Zivilkabinett I HA Rep.96 No. 616 – Schlesische Festungen, Bd.C, pp.18–19; letter from the King to Sers, 28 February 1747, GStA SPK, Geheimes Zivilkabinett I HA Rep.96 No. 616 – Schlesische Festungen, Bd.D, p.6.

work was located exactly in the place where in 1745 the Austrians stormed the fortress. The modification by Sers was therefore motivated by the desire to secure a potentially dangerous part of the foreground. Securing it with a single defensive work, strongly protruding into the foreground and connected to the interior of the fortress, has numerous analogies both in Prussian fortresses (the flèches of Schäferberg in Glatz) and in the Western European defensive architecture of the time.

Seven years later, another project to modernise the fortress was conceived. This time the initiator of the changes was the King himself. Sers only drew up the plans and cost estimates. The basic change was to rebuild the covered way in front of Salient 1 and 2 and 4 and 5. The new one was to be provided with a double glacis, with two rows of palisades and masonry revetment. An important part of the design was the masonry caponiers located in the places of arms and allowing the space between the first and second glacis to be covered by canon. The section of covered way in front of corner No. 3 also needed to be altered; this time the transformation was to involve digging a new outer moat with masonry scarp in front of it. The plan also envisaged the reconstruction of the ravelins between Salients 1, 2 and 4, 5, which were to have a type of cavalier inside, with their slopes revetted in masonry and equipped with their own countermine galleries. Finally, the construction of counter-mine galleries in front of the fortified tête de pont was also planned. In total, all these works were to cost 60,750 thalers.[200] It is not known what was the impetus that prompted the King to plan another reconstruction of the fortress. The reason was unlikely to be his personal acquaintance with the state of Cosel's fortifications, for Frederick had last seen it in September 1752, more than a year earlier. Although he visited Silesia twice in 1753 – from 8 to 12 May he was in Neisse, and from 1 to 5 November in Breslau – nothing is known of his visit to Cosel.[201] However, the King may have met Sers, who was building the fortress, in Breslau, and received information from him that led him to take this decision.

The King's aim with this modernisation is clear. By establishing a double covered way, he strengthened the defence of the section thus secured against both assault and regular attack. This was done at a relatively low cost, as the construction of a double covered way was considerably cheaper than an entire belt of fortifications. It is also quite easy to find analogies for this solution. Indeed, the double covered way appeared quite often in the theory of defensive architecture of the time.[202]

As can be seen, in the 13 years between when the decision to fortify Cosel was taken and the start of the Seven Years War, engineers were involved in designing the fortress as many as three times. As a result, Cosel became an important element in the fortified landscape of the Prussian state.

200 Letter from Sers to the King, 23 December 1753, GStA SPK, Geheimes Zivilkabinett I HA Rep.96 No. 616 – Schlesische Festungen, Bd.G, p.28.

201 Rödenbeck, *Tagebuch oder Geschichtskalender*, vol.1, pp.255, 260.

202 Leonhard Christoph Sturm, *Freundlicher Wett-Streit, Der Französischen, Holländischen und Teutschen Krieges-Bau-Kunst* (Augspurg: Wolfe, 1718), fig.XIV; Sébastien Le Prestre de Vauban, *Oeuvres de M. de Vauban*, (Amsterdam-Leipzig: Arkstee & Merkus, 1771), vol.2, p.18.

Schweidnitz

Schweidnitz was the second fortress to be built completely from scratch during the reign of Frederick the Great. Of course, like Cosel, it was not built completely from scratch; the town had fortifications in 1741. However, these were for the most part medieval walls preceded by an earth rampart, reinforced in two places by a modern defensive work.

The impetus for the construction of the fortress was the role that Schweidnitz played in the Prussian magazine system. Frederick decided on the construction of a grain magazine in Schweidnitz as early as August 1742, and was also personally to determine its location. Construction began in March 1743, and was completed in 1744.[203] The fortress was to be built several years later.

Design Process

The form that the Schweidnitz fortress had at the dawn of the Seven Years War was the result of six years of construction. Before construction started, however, another process took place, which for us is definitely more important; the design process. Thanks to archival material held in Berlin institutions – the Staatsbiliothek and Geheimes Staatsarchiv – we can trace it quite well. At present, it is impossible to determine when the decision to build the fortress was taken. According to the chronicler of Schweidnitz, Schirrman, the King was said to have decided as early as 1743 to erect ramparts covering the Schweidnitz grain magazine, and he was also said to have drawn up a sketch of them, which was a prelude to the construction of the fortress. Some defensive works in Schwednitz were to be erected in May 1745 by *Generalmajor* von Bosse.[204] However, this information can be doubted, as there is an accurate survey of Schweidnitz, drawn up by Wrede in 1747.[205] This plan does not show the existence of defensive structures that could be linked to these works. It only shows a medieval wall reinforced by two, clearly old bastions, remnants of early modern fortifications from the Thirty Years War. The impetus for the actual construction of a fortress in Schweidnitz was probably the Second Silesian War, specifically the Battle of Hohenfriedeberg, which was fought nearby. The first decisions announcing the intention to build a fortress were made in 1746. At that time the King issued a ban on erecting buildings on previously undeveloped plots of land in the suburbs of Schweidnitz.[206] It was not until mid-1747 that the ideas for the fortress finally crystallised. The first document dates back to 13 July 1747 – a letter from the King to Walrave ordering him to send an engineer to Schweidnitz to survey the town and its surroundings and make a model. The King's wish was for an accurate rendering of the terrain including the heights of the hills and a precise representation of the town's fortifications.[207] In fulfilment of the

---

203 Wilhelm Naudé, August Skalweit, *Die Getreidehandelspolitik und die Kriegsmagazinverwaltung Preußens, 1740–1756* (Berlin: Verlag von Paul Parey, 1910), pp.175–176; Wilhelm Schirrmann, *Chronik der Stadt Schweidnitz* (Schweidnitz: Verlag von Georg Brieger, 1909), pp.44, 46.
204 GStA SPK, IV HA Preußische Arme, Rep 15 A Nr. 806 – Notizen über Festungen, p.180.
205 SBB PK, ref. N 15060–68. Dating of this map after Max Hanke, Hermann Degner, *Geschichte der Amtlichen Kartographie Brandenburg-Preussens bis zum Ausgang der Friderizianischen Zeit* (Stuttgart: Engelhorn, 1935), p.249.
206 Schirrmann, *Chronik der Stadt Schweidnitz*, p.46.
207 GStA SPK, Geheimes Zivilkabinett I HA Rep.96 No. 616 – Schlesische Festungen, Bd.D, p.34.

King's order, Walrave sent *Kapitän* Embers to Schweidnitz, who was to do the survey there and finish the model himself in Neisse, under Walrave's supervision.[208] According to the instructions, an area within a radius of 600 Rhine rods (about 2,200 metres) from the centre of the town was surveyed. In the city and the suburbs, the street grid was to be depicted, but not the buildings. The fortifications were to be represented accurately, as well as all elements of the terrain around the city – hills, watercourses, forests, roads, marshes, etc. – 'so that the royal majesty could easily find everything'. These elements were to be rendered in as accurate colours as possible. The model was to be six to seven square feet in area, and Walrave gave his subordinate four weeks to complete it.[209]

First Project

It is not known when the model was completed; however, we do know that it was to play an important role in the design process of the fortress. In a letter dated 24 September, Walrave informed the King that he had ordered a modeller from Glatz 'to set out for Berlin with the necessary instruments, in order to model in the royal presence the new forts around Schweidnitz, as well as the *corps de la place*.' To facilitate the flow of information about his design decisions, Frederick ordered a plan of Schweidnitz to be made on the same scale as the model. This allowed him to add and subtract further objects on it. Walrave, in turn, declared that he would revise the design as often as the King saw fit.[210] There is no plan of the model in the Geheimes Staatsarchiv and Staatsbiliothek collections, but objects have survived which can be linked to the plan of Schweidnitz. These are seven drawings showing the Schweidnitz forts in various stages of design, cut out and kept loose. They clearly served the purpose of being placed on or off the plan when necessary.[211]

In the literature where the the Schweidnitz fortress is mentioned, it is repeatedly stated that the fortress was built on the basis of a design drawn up by the King.[212] Probably, however, the King did not draw up the design drawing himself, but only approved (or not) the ideas presented to him by his engineers. His activity was limited to making corrections in pencil on the plans sent to him, as he did with the designs for the fortresses at Neisse and Glatz. Design in the strict sense of the word was Walrave's concern from the beginning. The first mention of his activity in this matter dates from 23 September 1747. In a letter to the King written after his return from Schweidnitz, where, with Embers and Sers, they had made cross-sections through the city walls, Walrave wrote that 'I am now engaged in making

208 Letter from Walrave to the King, 20 July 1747, GStA SPK, Geheimes Zivilkabinett I HA Rep.96 No. 616 – Schlesische Festungen, Bd.D, p.35.

209 Instruction wie sich der Caipitain Embers bez anfertigung des Models und Nivellirung der Gegend um Schweidnitz zu Verhalten, 19 July 1747, GStA SPK, Geheimes Zivilkabinett I HA Rep.96 No. 616 – Schlesische Festungen, Bd.D, pp.36–37.

210 Letter from Walrave to the King, 24 September 1747, GStA SPK, Geheimes Zivilkabinett I HA Rep.96 No. 616 – Schlesische Festungen, Bd.D, p.48.

211 SBB PK, ref. X 33650.

212 Seydel, *Nachrichten*, vol.3, p.7; Julius Schmidt, *Geschichte der Stadt Schweidnitz* (Schweidnitz: Verlag von Ludwig Hege, 1848), vol.2, pp.256–257; Bonin, *Geschichte des Ingenieurkorps*, p.52; 'Die Erstürmung von Schweidnitz durch den Feldzugmeister Freiherrn v. Loudon am 1 October 1761', *Österreichische Militärische Zeitschrift*, (1860), vol.1, p.267.

cost estimates and plans for the *corps de la place* and other approved *Fortins*.'[213] The oldest documents relating to the fortress and held in the Staatsbibliothek should be linked to his activity. These include three plans for the fortress and more than a dozen cross-sections through the newly designed defensive works. An anonymous, undated and unsigned plan of the fortress should be regarded as the first, starting point for the design process.[214]

It envisaged surrounding the city with a rampart and seven forts on the outskirts. The rampart was to be quite weak, based on medieval walls, defended only by one bastion – the Lower Gate. The forts were to be of two types: a large fort, on the plan of a four-pointed star surrounded by an envelope on a similar plan, with two additional salients, and a small fort, in the form of a four-pointed redoubt with a circular casemate inside and surrounded by an envelope on the plan of an eight-pointed star. There were to be four forts of the first type and three of the second. They were to alternate, with the smaller forts located between the larger ones. Importantly, it was not planned to surround the city with a full perimeter of forts – no structures were to be built on the side of the Weistritz (Bystrzyca) River. The next design phase is presented in another plan.[215] The difference between it and the one described above is insignificant. There is a main rampart, defended by a total of three bastions. A bastion appeared behind the Jesuit church and another by the north-eastern corner of the town's fortifications. The belt of forts had also changed. The larger forts gained circular casemates in the interior, and one of the smaller forts was replaced by a simple lunette preceded by a moat and covered way. Importantly, the plan also shows the fields of fire from the fortress works. The original idea for the defence of the fortress is clearly visible; the forts were to defend each other by covering both the area between the forts and the area in front of and behind the neighbouring forts with their cannon fire. Moreover, the area between the forts was to be additionally shelled by fire conducted from the ramparts of the old town core of the fortress. Thus, at least in theory, the lack of a continuous perimeter was to be counterbalanced by properly organised fortress artillery fire.

The most important of the early plans for the fortress kept in the Berlin library is the one accepted by the King – it was stamped with the royal seal and signed: '*Guht*' and *Friedrich*.[216] The plan is only slightly different from the previous one – the two smaller forts have been replaced by lunettes), but its special significance stems from the fact that the plan is not a working drawing, but a final, though not fully realised, design. What is more, the Staatsbibliothek collection also preserves accurate cost estimates for this project, and not just a collective one, but detailed cost estimates for the individual works. The fortress according to this first draft was to cost a total of 384,907 thalers, of which the core cost 127,813 thalers, the two lunettes 24,491 thalers, the small fort 26,623 thalers, and the four large forts 205,980 thalers (51,494 for each).[217]

213 Letter from Walrave to the King, 23 September 1747, GStA SPK, Geheimes Zivilkabinett I HA Rep.96 No. 616 – Schlesische Festungen, Bd.D, p.41.

214 SBB PK, ref. X 33650-4.

215 SBB PK, ref. X 33650-5.

216 Which, according to the King, probably meant Gut, meaning good. SBB PK, ref. X 33650-8.

217 Summary estimate of fortresses signed by Walrave and Sers, in *Kostenaufschlage, Brouillons zu deren angefertigte Estimations und der… calculiertes alt und neues Mauerwerck der Vestung Schweidnitz*, SBB PK, ref. X 33650, undated, unpaginated collection of documents attached to the plan SBB PK, ref. X 33650.

An important addition to these materials was a series of eight cross-sections through the core of the fortress, mostly signed by the engineers who designed the defences (Sers, Walrave, Embers and Foris). Also among them are cross-sectional drawings bearing the royal seal and signature approving these designs.[218]

All these materials allow us to establish very precisely what, according to the first project approved by the King, the Schweidnitz fortress was to be. Particular attention should be paid to detailed solutions, the analysis of which did not have space in the description of the plans for the entire fortress. Analysing the information on the rampart surrounding the town, it can be seen that it was erected on the basis of the old defensive walls. It was created by filling in the former *Zwinger* (area between the two lines of city walls) with earth, so that the old wall became the revetment of the new rampart. In the process, the walls were subject to alterations. Care was taken to ensure that they were no higher than 12 feet, otherwise they would be vulnerable to destruction by enemy artillery fire. This rule often led to the demolition of taller sections of medieval fortifications. Not only walls were recycled, but also old bastei, which were planned from the beginning to be used as caponier.[219] In addition to adapting the old bastei for moat defence, it was also desired to erect entirely new caponiers. Walrave was the originator of this solution. His proposal for the construction of such structures appears in a letter dated September 1747. According to him, the caponiers could defend themselves well and were covered from hostile fire.[220]

From the documents we also learn details of the intended construction of the outer works. The large forts were to have two ramparts, both reveted in masonry, in addition to a casemate 175 metres long in the interior, and a storehouse for 300 *cetnar* of gunpowder. A puzzling item also appears: two caponiers, which were to be located in the places of arms. There would be nothing strange about this if it were not for their size. According to various concepts they were to have a total of 16 to 24 rods in length,[221] each one was to measure eight to 12 rods (30–43 metres respectively), which is an unusual length for a structure that would be located in a moat. However, an examination of the design drawings clarifies for us what these caponiers were supposed to be. They were simply tenaille, masonry structures enclosing the places of arms in the fort's envelope from behind. They were thus a kind of pre-erected, small retrenchment from which a defence could be carried out once the enemy had captured the place-of-arms.

The small forts, referred to in the documents as the 'Quarree Redoubt', were to have an 87-metre-long casemate in the interior, a main rampart and fausse-braye provided with masonry revetment and, like the larger fort, a caponier. In this case, the caponier was to be a single one, 18-rods (66 metres) long. Thanks to the design drawings, we know that this caponier was to differ from those described above. It was to be a large, tenaille structure

218 Profils des Corps de la place zu Schweidnitz, SBB PK, ref. X 33650–9,10,11,12,13,14,15,16,17,18,19.

219 *Estimation* document, undated, unpaginated text from the collection of documents attached to the SBB PK, plan ref. X 33650.

220 GStA SPK, Geheimes Zivilkabinett I HA Rep.96 No. 616 – Schlesische Festungen, Bd.D, p.41.

221 Even a letter from Embers, one of the engineers active in Schweidnitz, has survived. He writes that, according to him, these caponiers are to be 12 rods long each, while according to Foris (another engineer active in the construction of this fortress) they are only eight rods long. Embers, letter written at Neisse on 5 October 1747, text from the collection of documents attached to the plan SBB PK, ref. X 33650.

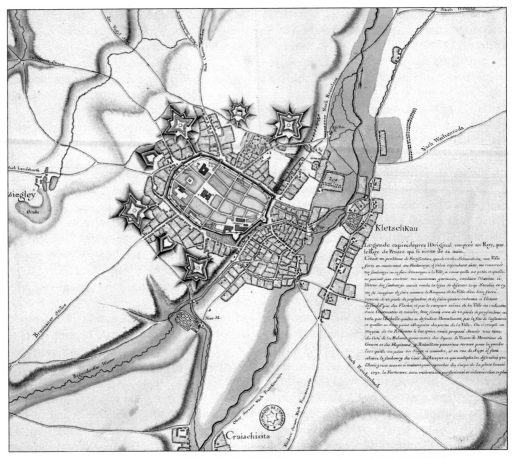

Design for the fortress at Schweidnitz. (BNF, département Arsenal, MS-6463 (673))

located within the fausse-braye on the gorge side of the fort and controlling the moat and the immediate rear of the fort with musket fire.

The final external work – the flèche – was to be the most modest. It was to have a single rampart covered with masonry revetment, a moat with a masonry counterscarp and a covered way. No casemates or caponiers were planned. A simple wall with loopholes for rifles was to be used to defend the gorge of the flèche.

Further Planning Work

The fortress project detailed above was not realised. At present, it is not known what the reason was for deviating from the design already approved by the King but, by incremental steps, the design of the fortress evolved. This is shown by another plan.[222] Compared to the version approved by Frederick, two changes can be seen. The last

---

222 Stadt Schweidnitz, SBB PK, ref. X 33650–7.

'small fort' disappeared, and it was replaced by a flèche. Changes to the large forts also began. In one of them, the later Bogen Fort (Fort Witoszowski), the star corner facing the town was amended – it was given a rectangular outline. In addition, the two places of arms on the envelope facing the town were removed. With these transformations, the fort lost the character of a work capable of defending itself on all sides. The front section facing the foreground and the neck section facing the town, originally identical, acquired a completely different outline. Although it had not yet been decided to open it up so that the fort could be fired on from inside the fortress after it has been captured by the enemy, a clear step had nevertheless been taken in this direction. There are traces on the plan of the next design phase, which led to the final transformation of the Schweidnitz forts into the form we know them. If one were to look closely at this drawing, one would notice handwritten pencil corrections to some of the defensive works. These concern the gorge of the forts, while someone has inserted the inscription 'minen' in front of their fronts. Presumably these are traces of the corrections that the King directly applied to the design. Little is known about this phase of the design, only that changes were still being made during construction. In November 1750, *Oberst* Sers, who took over the role of chief designer of the Silesian fortresses after Walrave's imprisonment, writes to the King that he had made the last change to fort No. 2.[223] And this was, after all, at a time when two forts – Nos. 1 and 4 – were almost complete. From this letter we learn of yet another modification – Sers reinforced the covered way in front of the redoubts with caponiers.

A year later, another modification of the project took place. Two new defensive works were planned; the Jauernick Flèche (Flesza Jawornicka) in front of Fort No. 2 and a new Water Redoubt (Reduta Wodna) protecting the fortress from the river floodplains.[224] This design phase is also documented in a plan kept in the Berlin Staatsbibliothek.[225] The last modification of the project took place in December 1752. The King ordered the erection of another fort, the fifth, at Schweidnitz.[226] In this case, a plan has been preserved which shows that the design of this fort was subject to similar transformations as the designs of the earlier works. In the aforementioned collection of drawings depicting the Schweidnitz forts, there is one drawing that stands out from the others. It depicts a self-contained fort, surrounded by a moat and covered road, which, unlike the others, does not have a star-shaped outline, but only a dovetail form. That it is a water fort is evidenced by the existence of a water moat, marked by a distinctive green colour.[227] The drawing described has another detail worth discussing. Its right flank is marked with 11 gun emplacements. The conclusion is that this fort was originally intended to cover the approach to the Lower Gate. The final realised fort had a completely different form; the outline of a horn work, whose bastions were provided with orillons and concave retired flanks.

223 Sers' letter, 3 November 1750, GStA SPK, Geheimes Zivilkabinett I HA Rep.96 No. 616 – Schlesische Festungen, Bd.E, p.50.
224 GStA SPK, Geheimes Zivilkabinett I HA Rep.96 No. 616 – Schlesische Festungen, Bd.F, p.30.
225 Plan der Stadt und Festung Schweidnitz, nebst dessen Environs, SBB PK, ref. X 33650–6.
226 GStA SPK, Geheimes Zivilkabinett I HA Rep.96 No. 616 – Schlesische Festungen, Bd.F, p.53.
227 SBB PK, ref. X 33650.

Fortress Construction

The course of the building work can only be reconstructed to a limited extent. It is only known that the construction of the fortress began on 8 May 1748 with the demolition of some buildings in the suburbs. A total of three churches and 83 houses were torn down.[228] It is likely that essential construction work was carried out from June onwards. It was decided to start by building the fortifications around the town. A list of planned expenditures in Silesian fortresses, compiled at the end of 1747, indicated that a sum of 60,000 thalers was to be spent in 1748, for which they wanted to build a rampart and moat at the Lower Gate, the Jesuit Bastion and adjacent works.[229] However, it was probably not possible to meet this deadline; by the end of December 1748, only 24,283 thalers, one third of the planned amount, had been spent on work on the fortress.[230] In 1749, earthworks for the fortifications at Schweidnitz started on 6 March, with 800 soldiers from the regiments Dohna (IR 44), Heinrich (IR 42), Nettelhorst (Gar. Rgt. Nr. 8) and Kalsow (IR 43) working on them. As early as 14 March, Sers ordered the commencement of masonry work.[231] These works probably still concerned the main rampart. There is no detailed information on the progress of the works in 1749. All we know is that work on the main rampart was completed, which can be inferred from the fact that on 5 January 1750, 30 cannon arrived from Breslau and were deployed on the new ramparts. The bastion in front of Breslau Gate received six of them, the bastion in front of the Lower Gate, four, and the bastion at the Jesuit cemetery, six. On the curtains near this bastion there were two cannon, on the battery facing Stadt Bau hof, four, and on the batteries on the other side of the garrison church and at Koeppen Gate, four cannon each.[232] In addition, the erection of redoubts between the forts began in 1749, as the cost estimate for 1750 already assumed their completion. In 1749 a total of as much as 132,636 thalers was spent on work on the fortifications.[233]

In 1750, work on the redoubts was completed and the construction of the first two forts was started. Construction started with the two outermost ones – Bogen and Garten Fort.[234] A total of 100,000 thalers was available to the fortress builders that year, to be paid by the Silesian ministry. Interestingly, despite the fact that construction work was usually interrupted for the winter, the ministry paid the money in tranches of 20,000 thalers each, starting in January and continuing until May.[235] According to the surviving reports of Sers, some work was also carried out during the winter between November

228 Schirrmann, *Chronik der Stadt Schweidnitz*, p.46.
229 Summarischer Extract der Kosten welche noch zur Forifications Arbeit bey deren Schlesischen Vestungen erfordert werden, GStA SPK, Geheimes Zivilkabinett I HA Rep.96 No. 616 – Schlesische Festungen, Bd.E, p.1.
230 GStA SPK, Geheimes Zivilkabinett I HA Rep.96 No. 616 – Schlesische Festungen, Bd.E, pp.33–34.
231 Letter from von Kalsov, 19 March 1749, GStA SPK, Geheimes Zivilkabinett I HA Rep.96 No. 616 – Schlesische Festungen, Bd.E, p.3.
232 Letter from von Kalsov, 5 January 1750, GStA SPK, Geheimes Zivilkabinett I HA Rep.96 No. 616 – Schlesische Festungen, Bd.E, pp.14–15.
233 GStA SPK, Geheimes Zivilkabinett I HA Rep.96 No. 616 – Schlesische Festungen, Bd.E, pp.33–34.
234 In most of the archival documentation no information appears as to which forts were built. A reference from which the order of construction can be inferred appears only in Sers' letter, 3 November 1750, GStA SPK, Geheimes Zivilkabinett I HA Rep.96 No. 616 – Schlesische Festungen, Bd.E, p.50.
235 GStA SPK, Geheimes Zivilkabinett I HA Rep.96 No. 616 – Schlesische Festungen, Bd.E, p.16.

1749 and January 1750 – 16,453 thalers were spent on it, and 9,324 thalers in February.[236] By the end of February, a considerable sum had accumulated in the fortress construction fund, more than 30,000 thalers, so that in March, with the onset of good weather, work could be carried out on a large scale. By the middle of February, 160 masons were already on site, working on the redoubts and on the construction of the gunpowder warehouses. The largest of these, the large storehouse in the Jesuit Bastion, was ready, so they set about adapting the old medieval defence towers to function as gunpowder warehouses. For this purpose, bombproof vaults were erected in them. As many as 10 towers were converted in this way, with a total capacity of 2,000 *cetnar* of gunpowder. This task was completed in early April, earlier than intended. The reason for the acceleration of the work was probably an increase in the number of workers. At the beginning of March, 200 masons were working in Schweidnitz. Earthworks were also being carried out, both at the redoubts and at the newly established forts. In March there were 800 men working here, a month later 1,200, and work was progressing rapidly thanks to the good weather.[237] In addition to civilian labourers, military miners also worked on the construction of the fortifications. At Sers' request, the King exempted them, as in the previous year, from having to take part in drills, so that they could get on with the construction work.[238] In 1750, the intensity of construction work peaked in May, when as much as 18,147 thalers were spent. After that, construction activity gradually decreased. In June, 12,748 thalers were spent on the construction of the fortress, in July, 10,722 thalers.[239] In the summer, the work planned for that year was about to be completed, only 5,199 thalers were spent, and only 14,794 thalers remained to be spent from the money allocated for that year.[240] In September, due to the continuing good weather, there was a slight increase in activity on the construction site – 5,683 thalers were spent and Sers hired new workers, mainly bricklayers.[241] A similar pace continued in October, when 5,225 thalers were spent.[242] Work on almost all the structures was successfully completed. On 3 November, Sers reported to the King that the erection of the moat walls at both forts had finished. The last task was to remove the remaining soil from the moat and form it into a glacis.[243] However, this could not be done at the close of the construction season, as Sers reported to the King in a letter of 28 November. The

---

236 GStA SPK, Geheimes Zivilkabinett I HA Rep.96 No. 616 – Schlesische Festungen, Bd.E, pp.18, 21.
237 Sers letters to the King, 17 March and 4 April 1750, GStA SPK, Geheimes Zivilkabinett I HA Rep.96 No. 616 – Schlesische Festungen, Bd.E, pp.22, 23.
238 Sers letter to the King, 14 February 1750 and the King's reply, 19 February, GStA SPK, Geheimes Zivilkabinett I HA Rep.96 No. 616 – Schlesische Festungen, Bd.E, pp.17, 19.
239 Summarischer Extract von die Schweidnitsche Fortification Bau Cassen Rechnung von den 1ten Ferbuary 1750 bis ultimo Decembris 1750, und folglich auf 11 Monethe, von Tresckow, 19 October 1751, GStA SPK, Geheimes Zivilkabinett I HA Rep.96 No. 616 – Schlesische Festungen, Bd.F, p.38.
240 Monatlicher Extract der Schweidnitzschen Fortifications Bau Casse pro August 1750, Sers, 8 September 1750, GStA SPK, Geheimes Zivilkabinett I HA Rep.96 No. 616 – Schlesische Festungen, Bd.E, p.38.
241 Letter from Kalsow, 26 September 1750, GStA SPK, Geheimes Zivilkabinett I HA Rep.96 No. 616 – Schlesische Festungen, Bd.E, p.45.
242 GStA SPK, Geheimes Zivilkabinett I HA Rep.96 No. 616 – Schlesische Festungen, Bd.E, p.38.
243 Sers letter, 3 November 1750, GStA SPK, Geheimes Zivilkabinett I HA Rep.96 No. 616 – Schlesische Festungen, Bd.E, p.50.

weather was no longer favourable, so the engineer completed the work and dismissed the rest of the workmen.[244]

In preparation for the next building seasons, the King drew up a three-year schedule of funding for the construction of the fortifications. It showed that in 1751 the two remaining forts were to be built at a cost of 10,0000 thalers, and in 1752 it was planned to build the counter-mine corridors at a cost of 68,000 thalers, which was to complete the work on the fortifications of Schweidnitz. In the following year, 1753, all that remained was to erect a lazaret and barracks.[245] As is well known, construction plans often change; in this case, it happened exceptionally quickly, for in his report of 24 April 1751, Sers wrote that 'the mine work is already so advanced that, with God's help, it will be completely finished in the month of May.' It would appear from this that the excavation of the countermines had started a year earlier than planned. Intensive work, overdue from the previous year, was underway on the masonry of the envelope of the two forts established in 1750, and earth-works, planned for 1751, were being carried out on the two remaining forts. However, the construction of the fortress encountered a serious problem, a lack of labourers. Although offers of work on the fortress were advertised in all neighbouring counties, not as many applied as in the previous year. Sers explained this by the low bread prices that meant the local population did not need the extra wages. It was necessary to re-commission soldiers for the work, as had been done in 1749. In April 1751, soldiers from the Kalsau (IR 43), Brandeis (IR 38), Nettelhorst (Gar. Rgt. Nr. 8) and the Pioneer Regiment (IR 49) were working on the construction, but a further 200 were needed. Sers asked the King to allocate 100 soldiers each from the Markgraf Heinrich (IR 42) and Blankensee (Gar. Rgt. Nr. 9) regiments.[246]

There were also complications of a different nature. Projects for further facilities, not previously included in the schedules and cost estimates, appeared. The schedule of works drawn up in French on 8 September 1751 in Neisse, under the heading 'Schweidnitz', shows: two forts and a small redoubt costing 70,000 thalers, and a redoubt budgeted at 15,000 thalers.[247] The 'small redoubt' was probably the Jauernicker Flèche (Flesza Jawornicka), located at the Jauernicker Fort, which was under construction. The other redoubt was the Water Redoubt. From the same document we learn that in 1752 it was intended to spend 85,000 thalers to complete the fortress. In October, the work seemed to have already been completed, since Sers was preoccupied with the issue of obtaining timber for the palisades at a cost of 10,000 thalers.[248] However, the plans were changed again; this time the King was responsible. On 10 December 1752, he issued instructions for the expenditure of 1753–1754 on the Silesian fortresses. For Schweidnitz, he allocated 50,000 for another fort, not previously planned, for the purchase of a garden and a square for barracks. This task was to be funded from the surplus of the Silesian budget.[249] As the new fort was a single task, it was

---

244 Sers letter, 28 November 1750, GStA SPK, Geheimes Zivilkabinett I HA Rep.96 No. 616 – Schlesische Festungen, Bd.E, p.53.

245 GStA SPK, Geheimes Zivilkabinett I HA Rep.96 No. 616 – Schlesische Festungen, Bd.F, p.1.

246 Sers letter, 24 April 1751, GStA SPK, Geheimes Zivilkabinett I HA Rep.96 No. 616 – Schlesische Festungen, Bd.F, p.24.

247 GStA SPK, Geheimes Zivilkabinett I HA Rep.96 No. 616 – Schlesische Festungen, Bd.F, p.30.

248 Letter from Kalsow, 28 October 1752, GStA SPK, Geheimes Zivilkabinett I HA Rep.96 No. 616 – Schlesische Festungen, Bd.F, p.46.

249 GStA SPK, Geheimes Zivilkabinett I HA Rep.96 No. 616 – Schlesische Festungen, Bd.F, p.53.

completed fairly quickly. In a letter to the King dated 12 September 1753, Sers reported that 'the Water Fort including the sluice and the caponiers is in a fully finished state'; at the same time he mentioned that 'work on the flèches is nearing completion'.[250] Presumably this refers to some finishing work on the Jauernicker Flèche as well as on the flèche erected near the Gallows Fort (Galgen Fort, Fort Szubieniczny) and defending the ravine near its right shoulder. In total, the works in 1753 (construction of the Water Fort and the Flèche), together with the cost of acquiring plots of land, consumed the sum of 45,129 thalers.[251] The completion of these structures was to be the last act in the construction of the fortress, for Sers began to send away the workmen and ordered a new plan of the fortress to be drawn up.[252] This does not mean that Schweidnitz stopped appearing in the financial plans for fortress construction for the following years. According to the plan for 1754, as much as 30,000 thalers were allocated there. This amount (as well as unused funds from previous years) had already been spent entirely on the construction of the military infrastructure inside the fortress; barracks, arsenal and lazarette. Work on the fortifications was limited to minor repairs, as the fortress was given an annual budget of 1,000 thalers, which was not implemented in full anyway. In 1754, only 347 thalers were spent, including 192 thalers for the repair of the six bridges at the Old Town gates and 154 thalers for the reparation of the two old towers at the Peter's Gate and the Lower Gate.[253]

General Concept, The Genesis of the Schweidnitz Fortress

Created as a result of a lengthy design and construction process, the fortress was an unusual defensive structure that stood out from the fortress architecture of Europe at the time. The most important innovation that is commonly pointed out with regard to the Schweidnitz fortress is its overall plan, in which the relatively weak core is preceded by a ring of advance forts. A fortress formed in this way was first established at Schweidnitz. However, it was not a complete novelty; on the contrary, the constituent elements of this fortress design are well-known in the European tradition of defence architecture. The idea of putting independent structures in front of the main perimeter was encountered relatively often in the modern period.

The first structures of this kind began to be built in the mid-seventeenth century. Single or more numerous works reinforcing the main fortification were often built during the Dutch War of Independence, the Thirty Years War or the English Civil War. From the Netherlands, examples are the fortresses of Aardenburg and Hertogenbosch, where, in the first half of the seventeenth century, in addition to the main, bastion perimeter, also sconces were built extending into the foreground. Of particular interest in the context of Schweidnitz is the second of these fortresses. In the first half of the seventeenth century, two large advancing

---

250 Sers letter, 3 September 1753, GStA SPK, Geheimes Zivilkabinett I HA Rep.96 No. 616 – Schlesische Festungen, Bd.G, p.3.
251 Sers letter, 3 August 1754, GStA SPK, Geheimes Zivilkabinett I HA Rep.96 No. 616 – Schlesische Festungen, Bd.G, p.49.
252 Sers letter, 3 September 1753, GStA SPK, Geheimes Zivilkabinett I HA Rep.96 No. 616 – Schlesische Festungen, Bd.G, p.3.
253 Letter from Kalsow, 3 August 1754, GStA SPK, Geheimes Zivilkabinett I HA Rep.96 No. 616 – Schlesische Festungen, Bd.G, p.50.

structures – the five-bastion Fort Isabel and Fort St Michel – were built there away from the fortress core; a century later, the addition of two further bastion forts and six square redoubts were planned.[254]

Forts protruding into the foreground were also built in German fortresses. The Philippsburg and Mainz fortresses on the Rhine are excellent examples. In the first half of the eighteenth century, forts were built in the foreground there, which betray very close connections with Schweidnitz. The Mainz fortress is particularly important. In the course of modernisation between 1713 and 1728, four lunettes were erected there on the basis of a design by Maximilian von Welsch, which extended relatively far into the foreground. Between 1734 and 1735, during a further reconstruction carried out on the basis of designs by Walrave and Austrian general Gottfried Ernst von Wuttgenau, they were connected to each other by a tenaille defence line, reinforced with additional works set in the gorge of the lunettes, and enclosed by a strong covered way. In this way, a whole new defensive line was created from the four weak lunettes, the main elements of which were strong forts.[255] Both the designer and the solutions used there make us see this fortress as the closest 'relative' of the Schweidnitz fortress.

Fortress of Hertogenbosch. (Mallet, *Kriegsarbeit oder neuer Festungsbau*, vol.2, p.103)

Another trend important for the genesis of this fortress originates from French defensive architecture of the turn of the seventeenth and eighteenth centuries. It consisted of extending in front of the defensive perimeter of the fortress a dozen defensive works, which formed a new, outwardly projecting line.

---

254 Bolsduc, Krigsarkivet Sztokholm, ref. SE/KrA/0406/14/036/007, <https://sok.riksarkivet.se/bildvisning/K0006023_00001>, accessed 29 March 2023.

255 Toll, 'Walrave und die von ihm geleitete Reparatur der Reichsfestungen Philippsburg und Kehl nebst einer Notiz über seine Befestigung Manier', *Archiv für die Offiziere der Königlich Preußischen Artillerie und Ingenieur Corps*, 54, (1863), pp.149; Plan de la ville et citadelle de Mayence, 1758, BNF, département Arsenal, MS–6463(690); Plan de Mayence avec ses nouvelles fortifications 1735, BNF, département Arsenal, MS–6464(691).

Despite the numerous similarities that can be seen between the above-mentioned examples and Schweidnitz, there is one feature that distinguishes it. In all the examples cited above, the external works, even very strong ones, were only an addition, a reinforcement of the main, bastion defensive perimeter. However, as is well known, at Schweidnitz it was different. The core of the fortress was relatively weak, defended only by a simple rampart created on the basis of the medieval walls, while the forts were very strong. Analogies for this solution can be found in British fortifications. On several occasions during the English Civil War, a similar situation to the one that occurred in Schweidnitz took place, when a strip of outer forts was built when fortifications were modernised, and the main perimeter became a superficially modernised medieval wall. An example is Newark, where between 1644 and 1645, in addition to reinforcing the medieval wall with a bastion rampart, two large four-bastion works (Queen's Sconce and King's Sconce) were erected outside the main enceinte. The situation was slightly different at Bristol, where between 1642 and 1644 a new defensive line was erected, independently of the medieval wall, in which the bastioned forts were linked to each other by a straight rampart preceded by a moat.[256] An excellent example of the longstanding tradition of constructing a defensive perimeter in this way was the Halifax, Nova Scotia, fortress, founded by the British in 1749. The fortress in its earliest form consisted of a ring of five bastioned earth and timber forts spread around a new settlement, linked together by a line of palisades. The whole was completed to the design of engineer John Brews between 1749 and 1750.[257]

Another trend in defensive architecture that should be mentioned in the context of possible analogies for the Schweidnitz solutions are the works erected during sieges by the besieged and the besiegers – fortinas. This was the term used by Walrave to refer to the external works of Schweidnitz in one of his letters to the King.[258]

Of course, none of the above examples can be taken as a direct model for Schweidnitz. The advanced defensive works in the previous period, although they appeared, were treated as an exceptional solution, used in very special cases, for example to secure a hill dominating the town or a passage through swamps.[259] In the vast majority of cases, both the theory and practice of fortification were based on the construction of single fortified enceintes. Moreover, it is very likely that Frederick the Great and his engineers were unaware of the examples described above, with the exception of the fortresses of Mainz and Philippsburg, the reconstruction of which involved one of the creators of Schweidnitz's defences – Walrave. However, they were certainly familiar with the trend itself and were able to crea-

---

256 Andrew Saunders, *Fortress Builder. Bernard de Gomme, Charles II's Military Engineer* (Exeter: University of Exeter Press, 2004), pp.56–61, 64–69.

257 Harry Piers, *The Evolution of the Halifax Fortress 1749–1928* (Halifax: The public archives of Nova Scotia, 1947), pp.1–2; Plan of the Town of Halifax in Nova Scotia, BNF, GED–3455, <http://gallica.bnf.fr/ark:/12148/btv1b84422452>, accessed 29 March 2023).

258 Letter from Walrave, 23 September 1747, GStA SPK, Geheimes Zivilkabinett I HA Rep.96 No. 616 – Schlesische Festungen, Bd.D, p.41.

259 In one seventeenth-century fortification manual, the forts at the fortress of Hertogenbosch described above are indicated as an illustration of how the passage through the marshes surrounding the fortress was secured. Allain Manesson Mallet, *Kriegsarbeit oder neuer Festungsbau: so wohl der Lehrsatzmässige als Unlehrsatzmässige, in drei Teilen abgehandel* (Amsterdam: van Meurs, 1672), vol.2, p.103.

tively relate to it. However, this does not detract from their contribution to the development of fortifications, as they created the first fortress in history whose defence was based on forts protruding into the foreground.

It is worth answering the question: what prompted the designers of the fortress to seek a completely new form for the fortress? Several reasons for this can be identified. The most important one, and the one mentioned most often in the literature, was the desire to create a fortress in which there would be enough space to store large amounts of supplies. Schweidnitz, situated in a convenient location in Silesia and in very fertile country, was chosen as the main supply depot for the Prussian army.[260] A spacious fortress interior was essential. The only free space inside the densely built-up city was taken up by the warehouse erected in 1744, so in order to obtain land for further depots, a strip of new fortifications had to be established more widely than just along the perimeter of the old walls. Such a need, however, did not necessarily immediately lead to a belt of forts located at a considerable – for the time – distance from the main rampart. There must have been some reasons why the new line of defence was so far removed from the town. These reasons are known thanks to the surviving plans for the fortress, which Frederick sent to his then ally, Louis XV of France, in 1751. He could not erect a strong enough fortification based on the city wall alone, because then the fortress would be too small for his needs. Nor did he want to erect a new, continuous perimeter around the suburbs, because then in turn the fortifications would have been too extensive. So, the only thing that could be done was to reinforce the fortifications of the old town and in front of this defensive perimeter put up four redoubts and a few flèches.[261]

This care for the existing buildings is also noticeable in the design decisions for the individual fortress buildings. This can be seen in the example of the Capuchin monastery at Striegau Gate, which impeded the erection of a new rampart. Walrave, however, proposed not to demolish it, but only to remove the old slaughterhouse building located at the gate and to erect in its place 'a light work which, with a low flank, would defend the new *corps de la place*.'[262]

The desire to save the urban buildings can be explained in various ways. The King's main motivation was probably cost – demolishing urban and suburban buildings was an expensive endeavour, as it would have necessitated compensation and even the construction of the destroyed buildings on a new site.[263] Another important aspect was probably to spare the famous and important Peace Church for Silesian Protestants. Looking at the plans of the fortress, we can clearly see that, in the vicinity of this church, the line of the new fortifications was moved much further away from the city boundary, thus accommodating both the church and its cemetery.

---

260 Schmidt, *Geschichte der Stadt Schweidnitz*, p.256; Bonin, *Geschichte des Ingenieurkorps*, p.52.
261 Plan de Schweidnitz, BNF, département Arsenal, MS–6463(673). This motivation of the King is also mentioned in later literature. Schmidt, *Geschichte der Stadt Schweidnitz*, p.256.
262 Letter from Walrave to the King, 24 September 1747, GStA SPK, Geheimes Zivilkabinett I HA Rep.96 No. 616 – Schlesische Festungen, Bd.D, p.48.
263 Walrave raised this aspect in connection with the possible demolition of the Capuchin monastery in the letter of 24 September previously cited.

The reluctance to demolish suburbs and important elements of buildings could not have been the only factor that forced completely new fortification solutions. After all, at Glogau, which was being modernised at the same time, the engineers had no qualms about destroying the Church of Peace there; in Glatz, during the expansion of the city's fortifications in the 1750s, the largest and richest suburb was removed, and in Cosel, as part of the construction of the fortress, the Minorite monastery was demolished in order to build it anew with royal money inside the city. There must also have been other factors at play. Certainly, an important one was the desire to secure the high ground towering over the town. However, this reason was not decisive, as there were no particularly high hills around the town. Only the Gallows Fort protected a potentially dangerous hill. Another factor that may have motivated the fortress designers to move the forts significantly away from the core was to increase the area that the fortress could affect. By building a belt of forts distant from the core, but nevertheless remaining within range of the guns of the main rampart, one forced a potential opponent to exert increased effort during a siege. Not only did he have to use a larger force to encircle the fortress, but he was also forced (at least in theory) to extend the regular siege procedure considerably; he had to capture one of the forts first and then attack the main rampart in the same way. This feature of the Schweidnitz fortress was directly highlighted by the King in one of his instructions, where he calculated that due to the layout of the fortifications the siege of this fortress should last a minimum of three months.[264]

As can be seen, it is impossible to pinpoint a single reason why it was decided to use the innovative solution of securing the fortress at Schweidnitz by a belt of forts extended in front of the line of suburbs. Most likely, it was influenced by all the factors described above.

It is also worth noting the effectiveness of the solutions applied here. Although the first three sieges showed its weaknesses, the fourth siege – before which its most important defects were removed – showed that a fortress established in this way could defend itself long and effectively. The fortress was able to accommodate a huge garrison of 12,000 for the time. Importantly, some of the defenders camped in the area between the main rampart and the line of forts, making the fortress literally a fortified camp. In addition, the large garrison could afford to defend itself actively. One of the sorties from the fortress included as many as 2,500 infantry. As can be seen, the experience of the siege of 1762 taught the military that the fortress could not only accommodate a corps of troops, but also left them plenty of freedom and did not limit their ability to manoeuvre. The size of the fortress and the vastness of the terrain it covered also had another benefit for the field troops – the fortress could provide shelter for the army corps, should it suffer defeat.[265]

Of course, one cannot equate the Schweidnitz fortress, a relatively small defensive structure, with the huge fortress complexes of the second half of the nineteenth century, such as the Posen (Poznań), Königsberg or Cologne fortresses. The objectives to be pursued by Schweidnitz Fortress were quite different from those for which ring fortresses were erected

---

264 Disposition für den Gouverneur oder Commandanten der Festung Schweidnitz, im Fall sie sollte attaquirt werden, Preuss, *Oeuvres de Frederic le Grand*, vol.30, p.420. Although this instruction was issued in 1781, when the fortress was much more developed, it also refers to the situation before the expansion.

265 Über die Vestungen in Schlesien, SBB PK, Acta Borussica fol. 531, p.57.

in the nineteenth century, and the demographic and economic realities were also different. Nevertheless, the claim sometimes made in the literature that Schweidnitz is the prototype for the fortresses of the nineteenth century can be considered justified.

Other Strongholds of the Kingdom

During the first period of the reign of Frederick the Great, work was carried out not only on the fortresses described above. There were also numerous smaller or what were considered less important fortresses, where old ones were modernised, and new defences were planned or built.

Brieg, Silesia

The fortress at Brieg should be mentioned first. This fortress was equivalent in importance to that of Glogau, as it was extensively modernised in the first years after the occupation of Silesia by the Prussian army. Moreover, according to accounts by some historians, one of the buildings of the local fortress was supposed to have been built on the basis of a design by Frederick. Unfortunately, due to the paucity of sources concerning the construction of the fortifications here, we shall have to limit ourselves to a brief description.

In 1740, the defences of Brieg consisted of eight bastions connected by curtains, a dry moat, four ravelins and a covered way. The island on the Oder also had fortifications: a section of rampart with a redan and a redoubt. The bridge over the Oder was protected by a small tenaille tête de pont.[266] These fortifications were mostly built in the first half of the seventeenth century. The only older ones, dating from the end of the sixteenth century, were the two old Italian bastions; the Castle Bastion and the one at the Oder Gate.[267]

Shortly after its capture, Brieg began to quickly be transformed. As early as 8 May 1741, four days after the Prussian army entered the city, work was undertaken under the command of Cornelius Walrave, just promoted to the rank of *generalmajor*. The engineer was ordered to restore the fortress' ability to defend itself. This began with the backfilling of the siege works that had been erected earlier, then the covered way was reinforced.[268] The King gave him the sum of 216 thalers to pay the workmen (two groschen each per day) and 2,000 thalers for the rest of the work.[269] Initially, this was limited to repairing the palisades and moats,[270] but the King soon came to the conclusion that the fortress needed to be strengthened significantly. In July he ordered Walrave to make plans to strengthen the fortress in such a way that it could defend itself for two months.[271] However, the major modernisation work was not to take place until 1742. In February of that year, Walrave signed a contract

---

266 Plan de Brig en Silesie, SHD Vicennes, Brieg, Dossier et plans 1757–1808, 1 V M 56, plan no. 1.
267 Bimler, *Die Schlesische Massive Wehrbauten*, vol.2, pp.27–36.
268 Seydel, *Nachrichten*, vol.2, p.289.
269 Letter from the King to Walrave, 10 May 1741, GStA SPK, I HA Rep.96 B Abschriften von Kabinetsordres, Bd.23, p.87.
270 Letter from the King to Walrave, 31 May 1741, GStA SPK, I HA Rep.96 B Abschriften von Kabinetsordres, Bd.23, p.119.
271 Letter to Walrave, 3 July 1741, GStA SPK, I HA Rep.96 B Abschriften von Kabinetsordres, Bd.23, pp.181–182

with the entrepreneur Rottengatter for masonry work on the new envelope and fortified brigdehead.[272] On 23 April 1742, with the ceremonial laying of the foundation stone for one of the defensive structures in front of the Oppeln Gate, construction of the new fortifications designed by Walrave began.[273] An extensive envelope was erected to replace the existing covered way, and another belt of outer works was extended in front of it. One of these, located in front of the Mollwitzer Gate, is said to have been designed personally by Frederick during his stay in Brieg in mid-1742.[274] Work on the modernisation of the local fortifications was probably completed before 1746, as information on the Brieg fortress is extremely rare in the collection of documents on Silesian fortresses dating from 1746–1756. The most important is found in a document from 1747, which listed the amounts spent on Silesian fortresses. According to this document, the total cost of modernising Brieg's defences was to be 102,881 thalers, and by 1747 most of this amount, 92,190 thalers, had already been spent. A sum of 10,691 thalers still remained, which suggested that some significant work would still be done on the fortifications in the following years.[275] However, this did not happen, as the only major work that was done was the building of two new gunpowder magazines in 1747.[276] After this time, there was no further work at Brieg. The fortress was not remembered until just before the outbreak of war, as a list of expenditures planned for Silesian fortresses made by Sers at the end of 1755 included an amount of 28,300 thalers for the reconstruction of the main rampart at Brieg.[277] However, it is not known whether this work was carried out. It is likely that it was limited to repairing the rampart.[278]

An important issue related to the modernisation of the local fortress was the attempt to strengthen it by erecting a new fortified suburb on the north bank of the river. The King decided on such an extension of the fortress in early 1742. In a letter to *Generalmajor* Walrave, he ordered him to go to Brieg and, together with the fortress commander *Oberst* Heinrich Karl Ludwig Herault de Hautcharmoy, choose the most convenient location. The order also required the engineer to draw up a design for the new fortifications and send it to the King for approval.[279] The engineer fulfilled his task remarkably quickly, since on 6 March 1742 the King mentions that he received a design from Walrave for a new suburb in the Brieg.[280] The first concept probably did not satisfy him, as in January 1743 he demanded more from Walrave.[281]

---

272 Letter to Walrave, 3 February1742, GStA SPK, I HA Rep.96 B Abschriften von Kabinetsordres, Bd.24, p.65.

273 Seydel, *Nachrichten*, vol.2, p.301.

274 Bimler, *Die Schlesische Massive Wehrbauten*, vol.2, p.38.

275 Summarischer Extract, wegen der Fortifications Bau Rechnungen welche der General Major v. Hautcharmoy den General Major v. Walrave abgenommen hat, GStA SPK, Geheimes Zivilkabinett I HA Rep.96 No. 616 – Schlesische Festungen, Bd.D, p.7,

276 GStA SPK, Geheimes Zivilkabinett I HA Rep.96 No. 616 – Schlesische Festungen, Bd.D, p.52.

277 GStA SPK, Geheimes Zivilkabinett I HA Rep.96 No. 616 – Schlesische Festungen, Bd.H, p.33.

278 GStA SPK, Geheimes Zivilkabinett I HA Rep.96 No. 616 – Schlesische Festungen, Bd.H, p.86.

279 Letter from the King to Walrave, 11 February 1742, GStA SPK, I HA Rep.96 B Abschriften von Kabinetsordres, Bd.25, p.88.

280 Letter from the King to Walrave, 6 March 1742, GStA SPK, I HA Rep.96 B Abschriften von Kabinetsordres, Bd.24, p.91.

281 Letter from the King to Walrave, 27 January 1743, GStA SPK, I HA Rep.96 B Abschriften von Kabinetsordres, Bd.26, p.39.

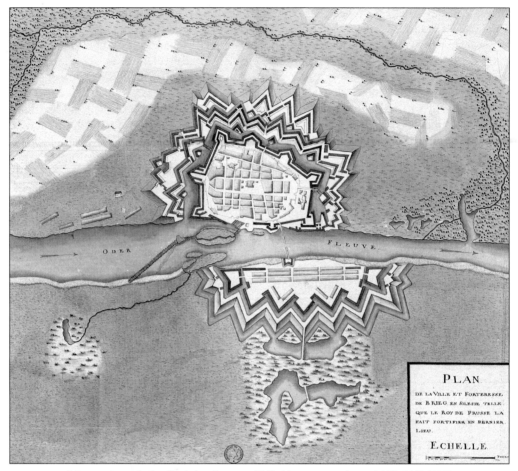

Brieg, project of a fortified tête de pont. (BNF, département Arsenal, MS-6463 (676))

Fortunately, two design versions of these defensive works have been preserved in the resources of the Berlin Staatsbibliothek. The first assumed the construction of an extensive tête de pont in the form of five arms of an eight-pointed star.[282] In front of the main rampart a narrow water moat was to be dug, in front of it a tenaille envelope, also protected by a moat. In addition, on the western side, one corner of the covered way was to be reinforced with a counterguard and a short section of covered way. The entire defensive structure should have been only slightly inferior to the perimeter. The second unrealised project showed a completely different shape for the new fortifications.[283] The tête de pont was to be an elongated, relatively shallow defensive complex. The main front, facing directly north, was to have a tenaille outline and consist of five sharp corners, three of which were provided

282 Plan de Brieg avec Neuve VilleLa , SBB PK, ref. X 20994.
283 SBB PK, ref. X 20994a.

with retired flanks. The two short fronts – east and west – were to be protected by extensive defensive works with a dovetail outline. The whole, as in the previous design, was to be surrounded by two narrow water moats and an envelope.[284]

Both of Walrave's unrealised designs have their equivalents in other defence complexes designed by this engineer at the time. According to the first concept, the tête de pont was to be given an outline remarkably similar to the main rampart at Cosel. In both concepts, the defensive perimeter was established on a star-shaped plan and preceded by only a few outer works. The difference between Brieg and Cosel was to be the construction of the main rampart and the type of external works. In the case of the second Brieg project, looking for similarities with other Walrave projects, we find them in the unrealised plans for the works at Neisse: the Cardinal and Capuchin redoubts. The outline of the Brieg tête de pont from the second project very much resembles the shape of the work covering the Capuchin redoubt – a regular, elongated object with a tenaille outline.[285] The Cardinal redoubt, on the other hand, was originally to be shielded by a work consisting of three sharp corners whose shoulders, like those planned for Brieg, had retired flanks. Its design signed by Cornelius Walrave is preserved in the holdings of the Berlin Staatsbibliothek.[286] Importantly, the redoubt in question was designed at the same time as the Brieg tête de pont.[287]

Breslau, Silesia

Another fortress from a military and economic point of view was one of the key points of Silesia. Breslau was the largest city and at the same time the most important political and administrative centre. Moreover, it was the largest fortress in the region. The fortress consisted of several defensive complexes of varying strength. The most important was the main bastion perimeter surrounding the city. It consisted of as many as 11 bastions connected to each other by curtains. The bastions were erected over a period of more than 100 years: the oldest one, Tenaille Bastion (Scheren Bastion, Bastion Kleszczowy), was built in 1544, the newest one, Dog Bastion (Hunde Bastion, Bastion Psi), only in 1678. In front of them there was an extensive water moat, and also numerous outer works: an extensive crown work in front of the Nicholas Gate (Nikolai Thor, Brama Mikołajska); two ravelins in front of the Schweidnitzer and Ohlauer gates; and a tenaille counterguard in front of the Ziegeler Gate. In addition to the city fortifications, numerous defensive works were located on the Oder islands and on the north bank of the Oder. Of the works erected there, mention should be made of the extensive Oder Crown Works defending the main bridge crossing and the tenaille-bastion fortifications of Cathedral Island (Dominsel, Ostrów Tumski).

---

284 Interestingly, this second design was copied and made its way to France as early as the eighteenth century, as it is preserved in the collection of the French Bibliothèque Nationale, Arsenal branch, in the former collection of Antoine-René de Voyer Argenson, Marquis de Paulmy. Plan de la ville et forteresse de Brieg en Silésie telle que le roy de Prusse la fait fortifier en dernier lieu, BNF, département Arsenal, MS–6463(676).

285 Plan von Neisse mit allen neuen Wercken, wie Solche bey Ihro Koniglichen Majestat Hohen Anwesenheit Tractiret worden, SBB PK, ref. X 31027/1.

286 Neisse, SBB PK, ref. X 31027/3.

287 Letter from the King to Walrave, 6 March 1742, GStA SPK, I HA Rep.96 B Abschriften von Kabinetsordres, Bd.24, p.91.

Despite the abundance of defensive works, Breslau could not be called a strong fortress. Its major drawback was the lack of a covered way. The existing fortifications also needed urgent modernisation.[288] However, as the city had an excellent location in terms of communication – on the Oder River, at the intersection of two important land routes –the decision was taken to strengthen this fortress. As early as August 1741, Prussian engineers made an inventory of the fortifications.[289] This was to be a prelude to major modernisation, as initially Frederick II intended to considerably extend the fortress and wanted to 'bring the fortifications to such a state that they could not be conquered by an army of less than 80,000 men.'[290] However, this intention was quickly abandoned and the focus was changed to repairing the existing facilities. They started with anti-assault installations – palisades and chevaux de frise. Bridges between the defensive works were also repaired, which were then said to be impassable in some places.[291] Repairs were also made to the defence works themselves. In August 1746, 2,438 thalers were allocated to carry out repairs to Matthew's Bastion and 2,473 thalers to Dog Bastion. Two years later, a further 2,000 thalers were spent on the damaged Oder Bastion. Another important modification was the construction of a masonry gunpowder store in the lunette near the Nicholas Crown Works, which was erected in 1751 at a cost of 2,974 thalers.[292] Between 1753 and 1754, repairs were also carried out on the curtain retaining walls in the vicinity of the Nicholas Gate and at the Oder Gate. In addition, one of the oldest structures of the fortress, the Ohlau Gate bastion, was rebuilt. Its characteristic orillons were removed and new, straight flanks were created in their place. In this way, this structure lost its original outline and from then on had the form of a small, rectangular in plan, artillery terrace. The ravelin of the Ohlau Gate was also rebuilt at this time, the flanks of which were extended by seven rods.[293]

Work was equally slow in building the first sections of the covered way and the glacis that preceded it. Admittedly, Walrave, who was intensively modernising the Silesian fortresses, wrote about the necessity of building it in its entirety as early as 1743 (at the time he estimated it at 6,872 thalers).[294] Before the outbreak of the Seven Years War, it had not been completed in its entirety. Only four sections of it were built in front of the city gates. Before 1747, a section was created in front of the Ziegeler Gate, where, in addition to the covered way itself, a ravelin with characteristic retired flanks was built, and another in front of the Nikolai Gate.[295] In 1754 the fortifications of the Ohlau Gate were transformed; the bastion and ravelin defending it were rebuilt, the section of the moat in front of these works was

288 Grzegorz Podruczny, *Twierdza Wrocław w okresie fryderycjańskim. Fortyfikacje, garnizon i działania wojenne w latach 1741–1806* (Wrocław: Atut, 2009), pp.19–26, 29; Plan von der Stadt und Vestung Breslau, SBB PK, ref. X 20663.

289 Hans Henning, *Der Zustand des schlesischen Festungen im Jahre 1756 und ihre Bedeutung für die Frage des Ursprungs des siebenjährigen Krieges* (Jena : Unknown Publisher, 1899), p.39.

290 Quoted from the report of the Saxon minister v. Bülow of 12 August 1741, after Henning, *Der Zustand des schlesischen Festungen*, p.39.

291 The bridge over the Oder was in such a condition that it had to be repaired before the King of Poland used it in 1744. APWr, AmWr, Section XIII, 1656 – Fortifications Acta, vol. 1, 1737–1745, p.53.

292 GStA SPK, Geheimes Zivilkabinett I HA Rep.96 No. 616 – Schlesische Festungen, Bd.F, p.27.

293 GStA SPK, Geheimes Zivilkabinett I HA Rep.96 No. 616 – Schlesische Festungen, Bd.G, p.62.

294 GStA SPK, IV HA Rep 15 A, Nr 806, pp.26–27.

295 APWr, AmWr, ref. 1656, vol.1, pp.70–74.

Breslau fortress, sketch by Walrave. (APWr, AMWr, ref. 12222, p.3)

widened and deepened, and a section of the covered way was built in front of them.[296] A year later similar works were carried out in front of Schweidnitz Gate – the moat of the ravelin defending it was widened and deepened and a section of a covered way was built in front of it.[297]

One of the most important elements of the Breslau fortress, the wide moats, which were constantly silting up, were also kept in good condition. In 1743, this problem was brought to the attention of Walrave, who costed the deepening of the moats at 2,100 thalers. However, this was done almost a decade later, and it was not until 1752 that 5,000 thalers were allocated for the deepening of the moat and the Ohle River.[298] In order to maintain the high water level in the moat, appropriate hydrotechnical equipment was required. In 1751, 3,854 thalers were to be spent on various water facilities.[299] Two years later, in 1753, a new sluice in the moat in front of the Ziegeler bastion was built.[300] In 1755, the Schweidnitzer Ravelin was also rebuilt and a section of covered way was erected in front of it.[301]

The last element of the defences to be worked on in the period before 1756 was the palisades. Just before the outbreak of the Seven Years War, on 30 June 1756, *Generalleutnant* Kaspar Ernst von Schultze reported that cannon had been placed on the ramparts and that palisades had been constructed.[302] However, there was a shortage of palisades and out of 6,616 thalers that it was supposed to cost to make this anti-assault installation, as late as July there was still 3,176 thalers to spend, which shows that the palisading process was only half completed.[303]

As can be seen, despite initial declarations, investment in Breslau fortifications during the first period of Prussian rule was not impressive. It was in fact mostly limited to repairs of existing structures; the construction of new defensive works was an exception. In total, work on the city's fortifications between 1741 and 1756 cost just over 34,000 thalers, a very small sum considering the figures for other Silesian fortresses. These small investments could not significantly change the appearance of the fortress. At the start of the Seven Years War, it differed only slightly from what the Prussian soldiers saw in 1741.

Investments Outside of Silesia

Despite the concentration of almost the entire fortification effort in Silesia, there were also attempts to modernise the older fortifications at important sites outside the province.

In Brandenburg, an example of this was the attempt to significantly strengthen the defences at Peitz. In late 1743 and early 1744, the King decided to modernise this neglected fortress. The design for the completely new defensive works was drawn up by Walrave. It

296 GStA SPK, I HA Rep. 96 nr 616, vol.G, p.62
297 APWr, AMWr, sygn. 1657, vol.2, pp.7, 15, 24–25
298 GStA SPK, IV HA Rep 15 A, No 806, pp 26–27.
299 GStA SPK, Geheimes Zivilkabinett I HA Rep.96 No. 616 – Schlesische Festungen, Bd.F, p.55.
300 GStA SPK, IV HA Rep 15 A, No 806, p.27.
301 APWr, AmWr, ref. 1657 Fortifications Acta, t2, 1754–1757, pp.7, 15, 24–25.
302 GStA SPK, IV HA Rep 15 A, No 806, p.27.
303 GStA SPK, Geheimes Zivilkabinett I HA Rep.96 No. 616 – Schlesische Festungen, Bd.H, p.70.

was ready by the beginning of 1744, and the King received it in early February. However, the decision to accept the designs came later, as the King wanted the modernisation to cost no more than the 60,000 thalers he had budgeted. The cost estimates, on the basis of which the King made his decisions, did not reach him until early March. It seems, however, that the King was not entirely convinced, as he instructed Walrave to go to Peitz once more 'to check everything in a better season.'[304]

According to the surviving plans, this engineer planned to surround the old fortifications with a very extensive, tenaille envelope, reinforced with ravelins. In the north-western corner of the envelope, an extensive set of defensive works was to be created in the form of two interconnected, detached bastions, reinforced by numerous smaller external works. In addition to this, an extensive defensive structure in the form of a tenaille with a retrenchment in the middle was to be extended towards the so-called Teufel Teich, connected to the envelope of the town fortifications by a defensive dyke. In the middle of this was to be a redoubt defending it. In addition to the erection of new works, extensive repairs to older defensive works were planned.[305]

According to the construction cost estimate, the erection of the new works was to cost 35,316 thalers out of the total amount of 69,333 thalers allocated for the modernisation of the fortress. Work on the construction of the new fortifications lasted from February to August 1744; a maximum of 300–500 soldiers and 200–300 civilian labourers worked on the site at any one time.[306] The work was directly supervised by two engineers, *Kapitäne* Fransky and Wolff.[307] The construction work, interrupted by the outbreak of the Second Silesian War, was not resumed after its end. As early as 13 August 1744, the King ordered the two aforementioned engineers to send the plans and drawings of the fortress in their possession to Glatz by post, and then to go there themselves.[308] During these few months of building work, only the construction of a new work on the north-west corner of the envelope was started, for which a total of 11,336 thalers was spent.[309] Not only was this structure not completed, but it was also not brought to a defensible condition. According to one account from 1755, more than 10 years after work had ceased, 'The new works are completely scattered, and in the event of an attack could not be defended, and are even very harmful to the old fortress, so they must be removed.'[310] As can be seen, the fortress at Peitz, after a brief period of interest on the part of Frederick, fell into oblivion again. In the period before the Seven Years War, only the repairs to the defence tower in the citadel had been completed. Not surprisingly, the fortress was occupied effortlessly by Imperial troops in 1758.

---

304 King's letters to Walrave of 12 February and 9 March 1744, GStA SPK, I HA Rep.96 B Abschriften von Kabinetsordres, Bd.28, pp.106, 146.
305 Plan und Project von Peitz, SBB PK, ref. X 31958/10–1, 2.
306 Volker Mende, 'Eine formidable Festung? Die Neuen Werke (1744) der Festung Peitz als Spiegel des Fortifikatorischen Denkens König Friedrichs II', in Göse Frank (ed.), *Friedrich der Große und die Mark Brandenburg. Herrschaftspraxis in der Provinz* (Berlin, Lukas Verlag, 2012), pp.307–325.
307 King's letter to Walrave, 13 August 1744, GStA SPK, I HA Rep.96 B Abschriften von Kabinetsordres, Bd.28, p.298.
308 Letter from the King to the engineers Fransky and Wolff in Peitz, 13 August 1744, GStA SPK, I HA Rep.96 B Abschriften von Kabinetsordres, Bd.28, p.299.
309 Mende, 'Eine formidable Festung?', pp.307–325.
310 GStA SPK, I HA Rep 96 Rep 96 No 616 J Festungen Driesen und Peitz.

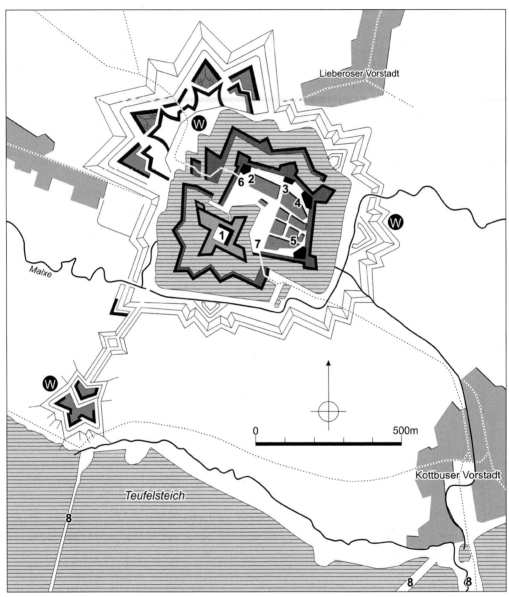

Peitz fortress, unrealised reconstruction project by Walrave. (Drawing by Mariusz Wojciechowski based on SBB PK, project ref. Kart. X 31958/10-1)

Despite the abandonment of modernisation work, the fortress at Peitz is a very important link in the development of Prussian fortifications in the first period of Frederick's reign, between 1740 and 1756. The solutions applied here, on the one hand, indicate the continuation of certain themes present in Prussian fortifications before 1740, and on the other hand, introduce innovations that will only be developed later. The city's fortifications are a reference to already existing developments. The way in which the main perimeter was reinforced by means of an envelope (one section of it strongly extended) closely resembles the solution used by Walrave more than 20 years earlier in Stettin. The outline of the New Work at Peitz is so similar to Stettin's Fort Wilhem that it is safe to refer to it as a copy. In contrast, the defensive work advanced towards Teufel Teich was matched the trends of the time. The outline of this structure is very similar to two structures designed by Walrave a year earlier – the Schäferberg fort in Glatz and the main work of the unrealised Schurgast fortress. What was completely new, however, was the way in which this object was connected to the rest of the fortifications. A long communication was planned, defended in the middle by a small redoubt. This solution was later used many times in other Prussian fortresses, including Glatz, Cosel and Glogau.

Outside Brandenburg, fortress expansion work was only carried out at points in Pomerania. The first was the coastal fort of Peenemünde. The work during this period was a continuation of the fort's expansion carried out under Friedrich Wilhelm I. They were also caused by the deteriorating condition of the structure. In the first half of the 1740s, the need for its repair was mentioned twice. In November 1743 a cost estimate was drawn up by the engineer Wolff, and in February 1745, following storm damage, by engineer de Humbert.[311] A project to reinforce the rampart was made by Walrave in the mid 1740s.[312] It envisaged the construction of new gunpowder stores, barracks and three defensive structures. Two of these were to have the plan of a tenaille hornwork, one was to be a simple salient. According to the legend on the design drawn up by the Prussian engineer, the defensive works were to be approved by the King. Excluding the repairs to the works and the construction of barracks and gunpowder stores, the construction of the three works was to have cost 6,309 thalers. Unfortunately, little information about the construction of this fort has survived. According to *Kapitän* Burchardi, who compiled a report on Prussian fortresses prior to the Seven Years War, all the works envisaged by Walrave were carried out. Further work was carried out in 1748, at a cost of 8,069 thalers, and a further 1,700 thalers was spent between 1755 and 1756. As a result, at the outbreak of the Seven Years War the fort was said to be well maintained and fully ready for defence.[313] However, this information is not confirmed in the surviving source material. There is only one mention of the expenditure of 1,288 thalers for repairs to this fort in the years 1749–1750.[314] In addition, the inventory of the fort, carried out its capture by the Swedes, shows the existence of the defensive works designed by Walrave, but it is clear that they were not completed. The earth ramparts were formed,

311 Letters of the King to Commandant Penemünde of 19 November 1743, GStA SPK, I HA Rep.96 B Abschriften von Kabinetsordres, Bd.29, p.23; Letters of the King to de Humbert of 20 February 1745, GStA SPK, I HA Rep.96 B Abschriften von Kabinetsordres, Bd.30, p.364.

312 Plan von Peenemünde, SBB PK, ref. X 31950/25; Plan von der Penemünder Schanz mit Iren neuen Wercken und dem jenseits der Peene im Schweidschen liegenden Gronswar, SBB PK, ref. X 31950/25.

313 Burchardi, Uber die Preussischen Festungen, GStA SPK, IV HA, Rep.15 A, no. 806, pp.154–155.

314 GStA SPK, Geheimes Zivilkabinett I HA Rep.96 No. 616 – Schlesische Festungen, Bd.E, pp.4–6.

which had an outline according to Walrave's design, but were not given a proper profile. The Swedish plans also show that the barracks and storage infrastructure planned by Walrave had not been erected.[315]

In parallel, work was being carried out on the Anklamer Fehrschanze. This fortress was located on the Peene River near Anklam. It was a small work defending the river channel. Not much is known about it other than the fact that it was mounted with 14 cannon (three 3-pounders, six 6-pounders, three 18-pounders and three 24-pounders). The structure dated from Swedish times; some work was carried out on it twice before the Seven Years War. The first took place as early as 1745; at that time de Humbert drew up a cost estimate for its repair. The work was to be financed by the Stettin fortification fund.[316] It seems that Walrave was also involved in this rebuilding. Another repair took place as early as the 1750s. According to a 1755 report by Prince von Braunschweig, the modernisation of the Anklamer Fehrschanze was carried out at a cost of 2,137 thalers.[317]

The last of the Pomeranian fortified points erected during the first period of the reign of Frederick the Great was Swinemünde (Świnoujście). In 1742 Frederick ordered Johannes Wladimir Suchodloetz, an inspector of hydraulic engineering from Königsberg, to come to Swinemünde and make the Swine River navigable.[318] Suchodloetz obviously focused on strengthening the banks and regulating the river mouth. However, on the plan of Swinemünde drawn up by him shortly after his arrival, in addition to technical projects for strengthening the banks and new breakwaters, one can also see on the western side of the shore one square redoubt with a guardhouse inside, with a short battery next to it.[319] This structure was clearly a remnant of older eras, as according to a report by von Braunschweig in June 1746, this redoubt and battery were in very poor condition and if a fort was to be built there, it would have to be erected completely from scratch. Work on the new fortification of Swinemünde did not start until after the harbour was completed in 1747. The fortification was financed with the proceeds of customs duties charged on goods entering the harbour. On 3 March 1747, a decree was issued that all traffic was to go through Swine river. Immediately, construction of the fortifications began, supervised by the Peenemünde fortress commander, *Oberst* Wobeser. The latter reported on 10 June that the work was going well and that the facilities were armed. The work on the fortifications and the harbour was carried out by engineer *Leutnant* Honeuer and *Oberst* von Balbi and lasted until 1756. There is a lack of concrete data on this, but it is only known that between 1748 and 1749 316 thalers were allocated for the reconstruction of the redoubt and the battery. The fortifications consisted of individual sconces. On the right bank was the star-shaped sconce, in the south the Moevenhaken Schanze, in the east the Ost Swine Schanze, above the Weiche Sandberg Schanze and another sconce. On the left bank was the West Redoubt.[320]

315   Peenemünde Relations Rijtning Öfwer Förrättadt Arbete wid Fortification på Penemünde Skantz åhr 1757, <https://sok.riksarkivet.se/bildvisning/K0006459_00001>, accessed 29 March 2023.
316   Letters from the King to de Humbert, 19 July 1745, GStA SPK, I HA Rep.96 B Abschriften von Kabinetsordres, Bd.30, p.154.
317   Burchardi, Uber die Preussischen Festungen, GStA SPK, IV HA, Rep.15 A, no. 806, pp.15–17.
318   Burchardi, Uber die Preussischen Festungen, GStA SPK, IV HA, Rep.15 A, no. 806, pp.199–200.
319   Situations Plan von Swinen Munde 1742, von. Suchodoletz, SBB PK, ref. X 34845.
320   Burchardi, Uber die Preussischen Festungen, GStA SPK, IV HA, Rep.15 A, no. 806, pp.199–200.

Condition of the Other Prussian Fortresses

As can be seen, in the only case where a major modernisation of a defensive structure was attempted a fortress outside Silesia – at Peitz – there were not enough resources and determination to see it through to completion. The examples of the Pomeranian fortresses show that only small-scale defence works were completed. From around the second half of the 1740s, only Silesia and its fortifications mattered. The work carried out in the other fortresses was of a maintenance nature. There are plenty of examples of this, but we will limit ourselves to a few selected ones.

The work to the fortress at Pillau is perfectly in line with this trend. Between 2 and 13 December 1747, a strong storm took place there, which destroyed a large part of the coastline, as well as a section of the covered way in front of the Albrecht bastion, a section of the covered way in front of the Strohnest ravelin and in front of the Preussen bastion. In the following years, until after 1751, work was done to strengthen the coast and repair the outer fortifications. The coast was sheltered from storm waves by a stone rampart built on a wooden lattice supported by piles driven into the ground. The work, carried out by master builder Betgen, and cost approximately 2,700 thalers. It did not result in any modifications to the fortifications, but only in the reconstruction of the damaged parts and their protection against the action of the sea.[321] The situation was similar at the fortress of Spandau, where in 1743 repairs were carried out on the covered way and the counter-scarp at a cost of 1,546 thalers.[322]

Repairs were also limited to the fortress at Wesel. In 1751, the King ordered the bridges in the fortress there to be repaired. The engineer Balbi, who was to undertake this task, upon seeing the state of these bridges in June 1751, concluded that the 2,500 thalers per year allocated by the King was insufficient. He suggested increasing this amount by another thousand. The King accepted the suggestion, and in a letter of 6 July to the commander of the fortress, *Generalfeldmarschall* von Dossow, he informed him that the Generalkriegskasse had been ordered to increase the funds for the repair of the defence works and bridges in the Wesel fortress by 1,000 thalers a year.[323] The amount of 3,500 thalers per year was not high; it only allowed for ongoing maintenance work. Nevertheless, the commandant of the fortress would have been pleased to have such funds at his disposal. The situation was completely different with the Newmarchian fortress of Driesen. This fortress on the Prussian-Polish border had been in decline since the early eighteenth century, when its previous modernisation took place. It was not until 1754 that the King decided to undertake the necessary repairs there. However, their scale was extremely modest. Three bridges and a warehouse were to be repaired, and a guardhouse erected, at a cost of 237 thalers. However, the documents relating to these repairs provide another important piece of information; the commandant, *Kapitän* von Erlach, was to ask how he was to cover the salaries of the watchkeeper, accountant and chimney sweep, totalling 5 thalers 2 groschen per month? As

---

321 GStA SPK, I HA Rep 96 No 616 J Pillau 1749–51.
322 Letters from the King to de Humbert and to Kleist, 31 March and 12 April 1743, GStA SPK, I HA Rep.96 B Abschriften von Kabinetsordres, Bd.29, pp.328, 370.
323 GStA SPK, I HA Rep 96 No 616 M Festung Wesel und Moers.

it turned out, according to a royal decree, the 200 thalers that were transferred annually for the needs of Driesen were transferred to Silesia.[324]

Specifics of Frederician Defensive Architecture in the Era of the Silesian Wars

There were a few interesting developments in the Frederician fortresses described above. They are worth looking at separately.

Outline

The fortresses rebuilt in the first period of the development of Frederician defensive architecture acquired very characteristic shapes. The literature to date, especially the Polish-language one, on the history of Prussian fortifications has distinguished two types of outline used there in the first half of the eighteenth century: the tenaille and the so-called Mainz-Würzburger, incidentally attributing them to Walrave alone. The issue of the first of the outline has already been discussed in the chapter on the fortress at Cosel, the only location where it was actually used; it therefore remains to deal with the second type. This outline was derived from the fortifications of Mainz and Würzburg, and it was to be characterised by a specific bastion shape, in which the flanks were retired but run in a line almost parallel to the bastion faces. Walrave was said to have become familiar with this solution during his work at Mainz in the 1730s, and to have applied it to the design of the outer works.[325] In fact, both fortresses that appear in the name of this outline have bastions that are quite unusual. Nevertheless, it must be said that the term 'Mainz-Würzburg outline' itself is artificially created and its use in the context of the works created by Walrave is unwarranted. Indeed, defensive works – both bastions and external works, ravelins, lunettes, and others – having retired flanks, running in a line parallel to the faces are not a solution specific to these two German fortresses, and in Prussia it was used not only by Walrave. Bastions with such an outline were proposed by numerous architectural theorists from the seventeenth century, including Griendel.[326] On the other hand, external works with such an outline were used by Menno van Coehoorn. The lunettes defending the covered way, which he presented in the designs in his treatise, as well as in the fortresses he built, were constructed in this way, with the best example being at Bergen op Zoom, in which all ravelins were given this outline.[327] Besides, it was not only Walrave who used buildings with such a plan, the use of which was far more common among Prussian engineers. It was proposed by de Humbert in his treatise published in 1756, and by *Major* Preu in the reconstruction of the fortress of Driesen, which he designed but did not build.[328] It must be admitted, however, that Walrave used this

---

324 Letter written in Berlin, 20 November 1754, GStA SPK Geheimes Zivilkabinett I HA Rep 96 No. 616 J Festungen Driesen und Peitz.

325 Stankiewicz, 'Ze studiów', pp.120–121.

326 Sturm, *Architectura militaris hypothetico-eclectica 1755*, table XXXI.

327 Coehoorn, *Neuer Vestungs-Bau*, p.161, figs. M, L, K, H, Q, O.

328 De Humbert, *Vollkommener Unterricht*, Plan 1–5; Preu, Plan de la forteresse de Drisen, SBB PK, ref. X 23173.

solution with particular fondness; there were 17 defensive works constructed in this way in the Neisse urban enceinte alone.

Envelopes

A much more interesting and important issue related to the Prussian fortresses of this time were envelopes. This term comes from the French and means a defensive work, usually earthen, located in front of the main moat and surrounding and shielding another structure.[329] The envelopes designed in this period were usually a series of defensive works (counterguards, lunettes, etc.) that surrounded the entire front of the fortress or defensive work in question. This is what the envelopes at Brieg, Glogau and Neisse looked like. In two other fortresses, Peitz and the main fortress at Glatz, the envelope was simply a long outer wall with a tenaille outline. Sometimes, but not always, an additional moat – the so-called outer moat (Avant Fosse) – was erected in front of the envelope. This was done at Brieg and Neisse. The latter of the fortresses is particularly important, as both the envelope and the outer moat assumed unusual proportions there. The envelope consisted of dozens of lunettes, counterguards and redans, together forming a veritable labyrinth. The individual works were separated from each other by separate moats, sometimes also by water. What is more, in front of the envelope was a huge outer moat, in some places 125 metres wide

All this gave the designer of this fortress, Cornelius Walrave, the unwarranted opinion that this fortress was the strongest in the world, impossible to conquer.[330] Importantly, envelopes were not only used at the time to strengthen the old fortress. They were also designed and erected to deepen the defences of newly planned defences. An envelope was also envisaged in the fortified tête de pont in Brieg, and envelopes were given to all four star forts at Schweidnitz, as well as Fort Prussia at Neisse.

Obviously, this solution was not invented during the modernisation of fortresses in Silesia, it has an older origin. It was often proposed in his book by Menno van Coehoorn; it was also eagerly used in the fortifications of the Netherlands, as exemplified by the fortresses in Breda, Naarden or Geldern.[331] The solution became established in Prussia thanks to Walrave, and some influence on the spread of this solution also came from the fortresses in the western provinces of the Prussian state, especially the aforementioned Geldern, which came under Prussian ownership after 1713.

Advanced Works

In the Silesian fortresses modernised before 1756, on several occasions fortified works – such as lunettes, flèches and redoubts – were built into the fortress foreground, in front of the main defensive perimeter. Such a solution originated from French defensive architecture

---

329 Antoine Furetière, Pierre Bayle, de Beauval Henri Basnage, *Dictionnaire universel: contenant generalement tous les mots françois tant vieux que modernes, & les termes des sciences et des arts* (La Haye: Arnout & Reinier Leer, 1701), vol.2, entry Enveloppe (unpaginated); Johann Friedrich Pfeffinger, *Nouvelle fortification françoise, espagnolle, italienne et hollandaise* (Amsterdam: Gallet, 1698), p.20. *Dictionnaire de l'académie française* (Paris: Bernard Brunet, 1762), vol.1, entry Enveloppe (unpaginated).

330 De Walrave, Memoire sur l'attaque et Defencela des Places, GStA SPK, VI HA Familienarchive und Nachlässe, Nl Scharnhorst, no. 314, pp.7 verso, 13 verso.

331 Coehoorn, *Neuer Vestungs-Bau*, p.161, fig. L, K, H. p.202 fig. Q, P.

Neisse fortress, envelope of the city fortifications. (GStA SPK, XI HA ref. A 71393)

Envelope according to Coehoorn. (Coehoorn, *Nieuwe Vestingbouw*, Fig. K)

of the late seventeenth and early eighteenth centuries. During this period, French engineers repeatedly designed structures that extended in front of the fortress perimeter to form a new line. The idea first appeared in the fortress of Luxembourg, where between 1672 and 1683 six casemated redoubts were erected in front of the western front of the city's fortifications, based on a design by Charles-Chrétien de Landas, comte de Louvigny. During the siege of the fortress in 1684, these redoubts put up unexpectedly strong resistance, to Vauban's attack. After the takeover of the fortress by the French, the same engineer rebuilt the old redoubts and erected more, between 1684 and 1688.[332] Moreover, he started to apply this idea to other fortresses as well. He erected a range of works extending in front of the glacis in the fortresses of Mons (after 1691),[333] Namur (after 1692), Landau (1702), Le Quesnay.[334] After Vauban's death, this solution was readily applied by his successors. A prime example was the work of Louis de Cormontaigne. This engineer advanced defensive works in front of the main perimeter and was not only keen to introduce them in the fortresses he built (Thionville and Metz), but also promoted them in his theoretical texts. Among the completed projects, the most important was Thionville, where Cormontaigne worked until 1730.[335] His work was to surround the town with a ring of a dozen lunettes extended in front of the glacis of the main defensive perimeter. Importantly, these lunettes formed a full defensive perimeter, and were connected to each other by a second glacis. Far more important than his practical activities were his writings. In a treatise published in 1741, it is possible to read about these lunettes and also see them on two example plans. Although in this treatise he does not use the advanced defensive works as boldly as in the fortresses he built, the attentive reader could not fail to notice this novelty. According to Cormontaigne, the purpose of setting up lunettes was to draw the enemy away from the core of the fortress and force him to prolong the siege.[336]

This solution quickly spread outside France. An excellent example of this was the fortification of the Rhineland imperial fortress; Philippsburg. This type of solution also appeared in Prussian fortresses, as exemplified by the fortresses of Wesel and Lippstadt. It came to Prussia with the French Huguenot engineers. One of them was Peter de Montargues, who designed protruding lunettes connected by a second glacis in 1701 for the fortress of Memel.[337]

Not surprisingly, similar facilities also appeared in the fortresses built and modernised by Frederick. Mention should be made above all of Glatz and Cosel. The best example are the flèches of Schäferberg in Glatz, although only four of them were built, which is a small number in comparison to the above-mentioned Western European examples. These four flèches were advanced in front of a relatively small defence work, which was the Schäferberg

---

332 Friedrich Wilhelm Engelhardt, *Geschichte der Stadt und Festung Luxemburg: seit ihrer ersten Entstehung bis auf unsere Tage* (Luxemburg: Rehm, Buck, 1850), pp.105–106, 126–128, 142, 143–145; Jähns, *Geschichte 1890*, p.1414.

333 Allent, *Histoire du Corps Impérial*, p.253; Arthur Thomas Malkin, *The Portrait Gallery of Distinguished Poets, Philosophers, Statesmen, Divines, Painters, Architects, and Lawyers, Since the Revival of Art* (London, W. S. Orr and Co, 1853), vol.2, p.446.

334 Christopher Duffy, *Fire and Stone* (Edison: Castle Books, 2006), p.68.

335 Guillaume Ferdinand Teissier, *Histoire de Thionville* (Metz: Verronnais, 1828), p.178.

336 de Cormontaigne, *Architecture militaire*, pp.15, 65, 135; ill. 3,11, 31.

337 SBB PK, ref. X 29956 Plan de Villela et de la citadelle de Memel, 1701. The project was not realised.

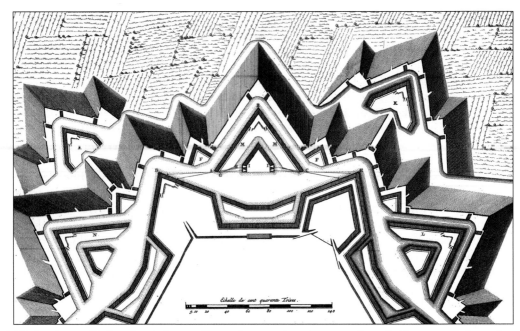

Works advanced before the glacis according to Cormontaigne. (Cormontaigne, *Architecture militaire, ou l'art de fortifier*, il.11)

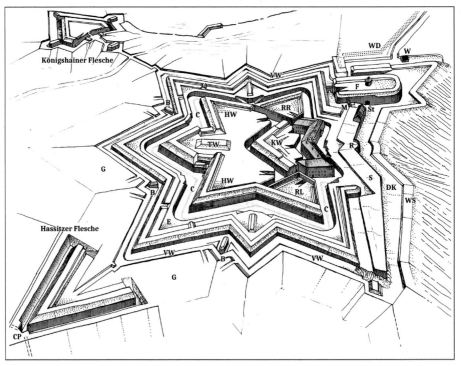

Glatz, fort Schäferberg circa 1756. (Drawn by Mariusz Wojciechowski)

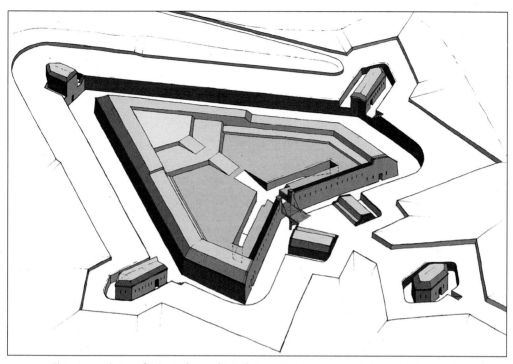

Glatz, Königsheiner flèche in front of Schäferberg fort. (Drawn by Mariusz Wojciechowski)

fort, and they were sufficient to create a second defence perimeter. Only one structure of this type was built at Cosel, although according to the original designs there were to be more. Two small flèches were also built on the foregrounds of Neisse Fort Prussia.

The difference between the above-described examples from Western Europe and the Silesian fortresses was the way in which the structures were linked to each other and to the interior of the fortress. In Silesia, the defensive works protruding into the foreground were not connected by a separate glacis. Instead, they were connected to the covered way in front of the main rampart by means of a communication – a section of road sheltered from both sides by flat rampart. Very often in the middle of this communication another, smaller defensive structure was built to defend the connection between the fortress and the advanced structure. Such a solution was used at Glatz (Königsheiner Flèche), Cosel (Weigschützer Redoubt), and Glogau (Star Fort). It was also planned at Peitz.

New Forts
A separate category of advanced works was forts. Before the outbreak of the Seven Years War, 10 such structures had been constructed in Prussia. The very concept of erecting forts in front of a defensive perimeter, as is already known, was nothing new and numerous examples can be found in older defensive architecture, as discussed in the chapter on the fortress at Schweidnitz. It only remains to look at the detailed solutions used in these forts.

Two of them – Fort Prussia at Neisse and Schäferberg at Glatz – are large, independent works, capable of circular defence. Both of these facilities fulfilled a special role. The Neisse

Stettin, Fort Preußen, fragment of Plan der Vestung Stettin. (SBB PK, Kart. X 34079)

fort, on the plan of a five-pointed star, was capable of defending itself against an attack directed from any direction – both from the foreground and from inside the fortress. Moreover, thanks to its location on a high hill, it was able to control the entire surrounding area, including the city, with the fire of its cannon. This ability makes it similar to early modern citadels. The difference between facilities of this kind and the Neisse fort was its location some distance from the main urban defence perimeter. This, and the outline itself, makes it similar to Stettin's Fort Prussia, of which it is in some respects a copy.

The situation was different with the Schäferberg fort at Glatz. This structure was independent due to its remoteness from the other fortifications at Glatz and due to its size. However, it was designed primarily for defence from the foreground and had a distinct gorge section. Although the gorge was heavily defended, with a covered way and the powerful Horseshoe battery, it nevertheless allowed a view into the interior of the fort from the main fortress area and, if necessary, its targeting. It is questionable, however, how effective it would have been, given the considerable distance between the main fortress and Schäferberg measuring over 500 metres. This facility, unlike the first fort, cannot be compared with older fortifications. Although individual elements of the fort find analogies in Walrave's older designs (the general form of the fort in the form of a five-pointed star with an open gorge is similar, for example, to his design for a fortified tête de pont at Minden in 1729, and the unusual shape of the Horseshoe battery is analogous to the 'bastei' he used at Friedrichstadt in Magdeburg), the fort as a whole is entirely innovative.

The other forts were much smaller. Besides not being self-contained they had an open gorge section, so that their interior could be controlled by artillery fire conducted from the fortress core. In this group, the Schweidnitz structures stand out in particular. In this case, it is necessary to analyse both the solutions that appeared in the original designs and those that were finally constructed. The four main forts of Schweidnitz originally had the outlines of four-pointed stars. Such a shape was extremely popular in defensive architecture, although until then it had mostly been used for field fortifications. In Prussia, however, there were already permanent structures with this outline, for example, Magdeburg's Fort Berge and Neisse's small Fort Bombardier. A particular similarity can be seen with the former. Both the facilities planned for Schweidnitz and the facility at Magdeburg consisted of a core and a surrounding envelope. The difference was in the interior; in Magdeburg there was an even smaller Donjon in the middle of the fort, also with a star-shaped outline, while in Schweidnitz circular casemates were planned.

Looking at the Schweidnitz forts in their final form, one perceives similarities with the forts in the German Rhineland fortresses modernised by Walrave in the 1730s; Mainz and Philippsburg. The former was important for the very concept of a fortress, but looking at the shapes of the forts there, it is difficult to find similarities with those built at Schweidnitz. The structures that were created as a result of the mid-1730s reconstruction have little in common with the Schweidnitz forts. Only the forts of St Charles and St Francis betray some commonalities. When they were rebuilt, Walrave surrounded the older lunette with an envelope, in front of which he extended a covered way that was the same in outline. This gave the outer works a plan similar to that of the Schweidnitz. However, if we look for an analogy for the form of the core of the Schweidnitz forts, we will not find it in the Mainz structures, but in Fort Star, in the Philipsburg fortress. This fort had an outline identical to that of the Schweidnitz forts; a five-armed star, with the gorge open towards the interior of the fortress. However, unlike the Schweidnitz ones, it was surrounded only by a moat and a covered way and lacked an envelope.[338] As can be seen, the Schweidnitz fort in its final version is a compilation of solutions that Walrave knew from his earlier projects.

A completely different site is the fifth Schweidnitz fort, the Water Fort. This structure had the outline of a horn work, whose bastions were provided with orillons and concave retired flanks. This and the curved curtain in the middle clearly indicate the pattern followed by the designers. This fort is almost a pure example of the drawing used by Menno van Coehoorn.

Two further forts were the Star at Glogau and the Crown at Peitz. Both were located close to the main perimeter and connected to it by a communication sheltered on both sides by a flat rampart, in the middle defended by a redoubt. Both also had open gorges so that, once occupied by the enemy, they could not pose a threat to the fortress. The irregular, star-shaped outline of the Glogau fort had no analogues in earlier fortifications; similarities should not be sought either, as the shape of the structure resulted from its adaptation to the terrain. The only element known from other forts was a circular casemate, similar to those

---

338 Plan de Philipsbourg levé en 1734, BNF, GED–7395.

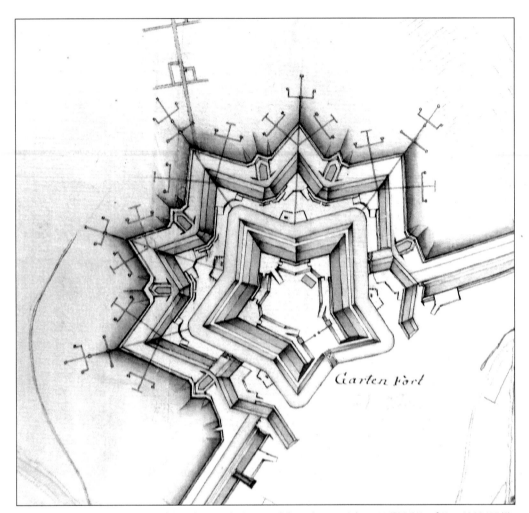

Schweidnitz, Garden Fort, part of the *Plan von der Festung Schweidnitz im Jahr 1766*. (SBB PK, ref. Kart. X 33655/8)

of Schweidnitz. Fort Crown of Peitz, on the other hand, is a smaller and weaker version of the Schäferberg fort at Glatz.

A separate mention should be made of Neisse's Bombardier Fort. It was the smallest among those discussed but should be described as an independent work. Situated in the middle of the rampart connecting Fort Prussia with the Neisse River, it had the outline of a four-armed star. It was capable of defending against both an attack from the foreground and from inside Friedrichstadt.

Rectangular Redoubts
The third category of external works that deserve closer attention are rectangular redoubts. Not many structures of this type were built, only three in Neisse and one each in Cosel and Glogau. In the plans there were three more in Schweidnitz (the form of a rectangular redoubt

surrounded by star-shaped places of arms was, according to the initial plans, intended for small forts designed between large star-shaped forts) and one more in Cosel.

The rectangular redoubt was an frequently constructed type of defensive structure; in fact, it should be considered one of the basic forms in defensive architecture. Redoubts were extremely popular and although they predominated in field fortifications, they were also quite common in permanent fortifications. Facilities of this type were built in almost all of Europe. An excellent example of a large and forward-looking redoubt was one of the defensive works at Luxembourg, the Neipperg redoubt erected in 1730.[339] Structures of this kind were also present in the Prussian tradition. Redoubts protruding in front of the main defensive perimeter were found in the fortresses of Geldern and Lippstadt. A similar facility was designed by Walrave at Philippsburg during his ongoing modernisation of the fortress in 1733.[340]

The element that distinguished the redoubts built and designed in the Silesian fortresses from all the examples presented above were the casemates. Apart from the one on the Oder Island (which appeared in one of the Cosel projects) and the Jerusalem Redoubt in Neisse, all designed and built redoubts were provided with characteristic casemates. In the redoubts of Neisse, Glogau and the unbuilt redoubts of Schweidnitz they had a circular plan, but a semi-circular one in the redoubt of the fortified tête de pont at Cosel. As is already known, identical structures also appeared in forts at Schweidnitz and Glogsu. To date, no direct prototypes for these structures have been found, but similar solutions are known in older European defence architecture. Fort Carre in Antibes, built by Vauban in 1682, has a circular courtyard surrounded by a casemate. Its uppermost casemate protrudes above the rampart.[341] The fort described here differed considerably from the Silesian solutions, but it testifies to the existence of a tradition of using this type of structure. One of the engineers who designed the Silesian fortresses, Walrave or Sers, was probably familiar with this tradition and applied it to the buildings he designed.

Neisse, casemate in the Cardinal Redoubt. (Photo: Grzegorz Podruczny)

339 Engelhardt, *Geschichte der Stadt und Festung Luxemburg*, p.155.
340 Plan der Vestung Philipsburg sambt aller neuen Wercken, wie selbige ins gesambt von dem Obristen von Walraven traciert, BNF, GED–7588.
341 Francois Dallemagne, Jean Moully, *Patrimoine Militaire* (Paris: SCALA, 2002), pp.131–133.

Caponiers

One of the most important phenomena in fortification, which appeared in the forts built and modernised by Frederick the Great in the period before the Seven Years War, were the caponiers. Structures described as such were constructed in Glatz, Schweidnitz, Cosel, as well as Glogau and Brieg. Most of them do not fit at all into the commonly known definition of a caponier as a low structure used for firing at the flanking moat bottom. Only two caponiers located in the moat in front of the main rampart in Schweidnitz fortress had such an appearance and function. In other cases, the caponiers were objects located in the places of arms of the covered way. These structures, like those built in the moat, were called caponiers by their authors. The fact that two different types of structures were referred to by the same name was possible, as the term was very capacious in the eighteenth century. Several different definitions of a caponier can be found in the fortification literature of the time; the most important ones are presented below.

Most commonly, a caponier was defined as a passage running across the bottom of a dry moat, from the centre of a curtain to a ravelin lying in front of it, or to another outer work. Usually, this passage was sheltered on both sides by an earthen slope, which protected passing soldiers from hostile fire.[342] According to another definition, a caponier was a vaulted passage in a moat where soldiers could hide.[343] A good illustration of this definition is at Fort Lambert, Luxembourg, built in 1685.[344] Importantly, these types of caponiers appeared very quickly in Prussia. An example are the four built in the early eighteenth century at the Oderberg fortress. These were long, masonry, vaulted corridors provided with loopholes for small arms, running across a covered way.[345] As can be seen, in both cases the caponiers were active defence facilities – it was possible to fire small arms from them. This is also the function of these structures found in the literature of the time. In some definitions, there is an indication that, thanks to the caponier, soldiers could fire at the area in which this structure was located; sometimes it is specified that from the caponier it was possible to fire without being visible.[346]

According to another definition, a caponier would be a shelter for soldiers, located in a moat or covered way, dug into the ground and slightly protruding above ground level, covered by planks and soil.[347] Elsewhere, a caponier is defined differently as a shelter for soldiers under the glacis.

The meaning of the word caponier in the mid-eighteenth century is best captured by a definition proposed by one of the Prussian engineers, J.D.C. Pirscher. The main function of a caponier was to shield soldiers from plunging fire. This engineer distinguished four types of caponier: wooden and masonry caponiers, as well as full and half caponiers. Full masonry caponiers were to be located in the main moats, places of arms, ravelin gorges, and any low-lying fighting positions. Such caponiers had to be provided with solid bombproof

342 Guillaume Le Blond, *Éléments de fortification* (Paris: Jombert, 1775), pp.96–97; de Humbert, *Vollkommener Unterricht*, pp.193, 234–236.
343 Pierre Richelet, *Dictionaire François* (Geneve: Wiederhold, 1680), p.109.
344 Engelhardt, *Geschichte der Stadt und Festung Luxemburg*, p.143.
345 Podruczny, Wichrowski, 'Kostrzyn', pp.25–26; Fortresse La d'Oderberg, SBB PK, ref. Y 33070; Oderberg, Cayart, SBB PK, ref. X 31685.
346 *Le dictionnaire de l'Académie françoise* (Paris: Coignard, 1694), vol.1, p.145; Francisco Sobrino, *Dicionario Nuevo De Las Lenguas, Española Y Francesca* (Brusselle: Foppens, 1721), vol.2, p.100.
347 Ozanam, *Dictionnaire mathematique*, p.602.

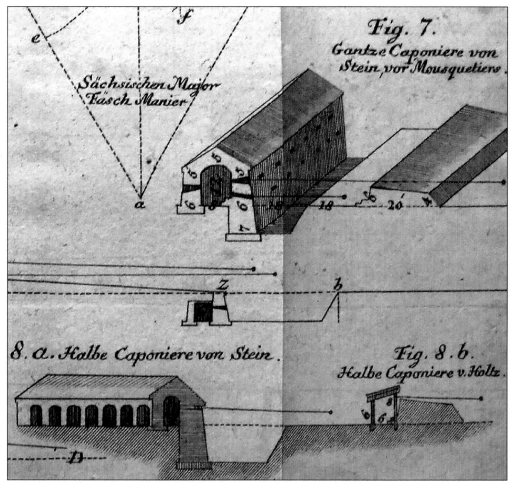

Caponiers according to Pirscher. (Pirscher, *Kurzer Unterricht von den Anfangsgrunden der Kriegs Baukunst*, Tab. I, Figs.7–9)

vaults and were to be located so that they could not be seen from a distance. Masonry half-caponiers, unlike full ones, had an arcaded opening from the inside of the fortress. Wooden half-caponiers were to be located behind the glacis in any type of fighting position regardless of whether it was low or high, as cover for the covered way crew from grenades and stones thrown by the enemy.[348]

The wealth of theoretical models for caponiers is also evident in the structures actually constructed in the Silesian fortresses in the period under discussion. The caponiers built here can be divided into three types: those erected in the places of arms of the covered way, those erected in the salient of the double covered way and those erected in the moat.

---

348 Pirscher, *Kurzer Unterricht*, pp.14–15, Tab. I, Figs. 7–9.

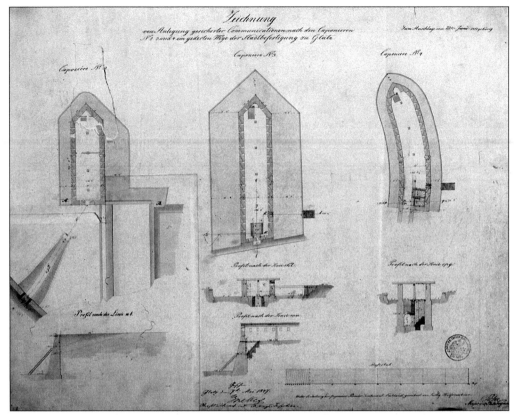

Caponiers on the covered way of the city fortifications at Glatz. (GStA SPK, XI HA ref. F 71797)

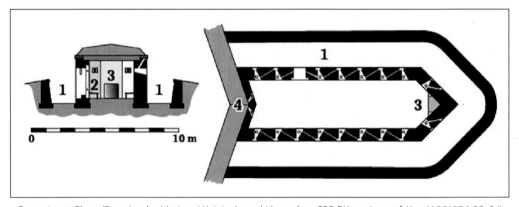

Caponier at Glatz. (Drawing by Mariusz Wojciechowski based on SBB PK, project ref. Kart.X 25107.6-22, 24)

Structures belonging to the first type were erected in Glatz; four on the covered way of the city fortification and three on the covered way of the Königsheiner Flèche in front of the Schäferberg fort. They were also to be found at Schweidnitz, on the covered way of the lunettes between the main forts and on the covered way in front of the Water Redoubt. Of these, the Glatz examples are the best known, as their designs from the time of their construction have survived. They were masonry buildings, provided with a wooden ceiling of thick beams secured by a thick earth embankment. They were located in such a way that their rear wall formed one plane with the wall of the moat counter escarpment. In the walls of the caponiers were loopholes for small arms. The direct prototype for this first group of buildings was the caponier invented by Johann Bernhard Scheiter, one of the seventeenth-century theoreticians of defence architecture. This engineer, based on his experience of defending the fortress of Kandia against the Turks between 1666 and 1669, published an architectural treatise in which he introduced numerous new defensive solutions. Among them were caponiers, which Scheiter called 'caphanaren'. These were relatively small structures located in the middle of the places of arms of the covered way, so that their back wall was adjacent to the wall of the counterscarp. They had masonry walls and wooden, bomb-proof ceilings. They differed from the caponiers built several decades later in Glatz and Schweidnitz only in the proportions of the plan; the Silesian caponiers had a plan similar to an elongated rectangle, those of Scheiter, a square. A more important difference was the two-storey design of Scheiter's buildings. The lower one was to house small arms loopholes, the upper one, gun embrasures.[349]

The use of caponiers to defend the covered way should be linked to the ideas of Frederick the Great. Objects of this type first appeared in the city fortifications of Glatz, a work designed by the ruler. Besides this, it is known that the King was an ardent supporter of this solution; he introduced the recommendation for the use of such facilities into the chapter devoted to the defence of fortresses in his treatise *Generalprinzipien des Krieges*, and also into his Political Testament of 1752. In his opinion, these caponiers were to be an excellent means of protecting a fortress against a sudden attack.[350]

The second type of caponier built in Prussian fortresses between a1740 and 1756 were those defending the double covered way. Unlike the previous type, they were usually small, besides being adjacent to the rampart of the defensive line behind them, and not, like the objects of the type described above, to the moat. As many as 24 structures of this type were built in the forts of Schweidnitz. There were six small, masonry structures each covered with a wooden bombproof ceiling covered with a layer of earth. They were situated within the covered way in front of the retracted corner of the envelope and were connected to the interior of the fort by posterns running under the envelope. Each of these facilities could provide small arms fire at two short sections of the covered way.

Twenty-three caponiers were erected in the double covered way at Cosel, during its construction in 1754. The cost of erecting one was about 300 thalers. They were located in

349 Scheiter, *Examen fortificatorium*, pp.2–4.
350 Volz, *Die Werke*, vol.6, p.57; vol.7, p.177.

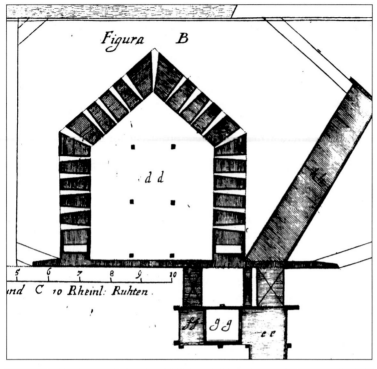

Above: Caponier according to Scheiter. (Scheiter, *Examen fortificatorium*, Bl. 3)

Left: Caponier according to Scheiter. (Scheiter, *Examen fortificatorium*, Bl. 4)

the receding corners of the covered way, but unlike those at Schweidnitz, the Cosel caponiers were erected in pairs, so that one of them fired at only one long section of the covered
way.

Further buildings of this kind were erected at Brieg. Unfortunately, not much is known
about them; their existence is only known thanks to a plan of the fortress from 1766, which
registers seven such objects inserted in the receding corners of the covered way.[351] Unlike in
the cases described above, here the caponiers did not protect the entire defensive line; most
of the corners of the caponiers were missing.

The last type of caponier were structures located in the moat, used to defend its bottom.
Buildings of this type became in later periods the dominant, or even the only, structures
described as a caponiers, but they were very rare in the Prussian fortresses of the first period
of Frederick's reign. While each of the aforementioned caponier types was represented by
a dozen or so structures, the last type was represented by only two. Both were constructed
at Schweidnitz, in the moat in front of the city ramparts. At the same time, these caponiers
are the ones about which the most is known. Their originator was the first designer of the
Schweidnitz fortress, Walrave. In one of his letters to the King, he wrote that, although the
new main rampart would be nice, it would not be possible to flank it because of the houses
close by in the foreground. The solution to this problem, according to Walrave, was to erect
masonry caponiers in the moat, for these, in his view, would provide good defence and at
the same time be covered from hostile artillery fire.[352] Initially it was planned to erect as
many as eight caponiers, but in the end it ended up with just two; some old defensive structures were also adapted for moat defence, among others the bastions of Striegauer, Bogen
and Peters Gates.[353] Flanking in other parts of the main perimeter was solved in other ways:
by building traditional bastions (Jesuit Bastion, Sharp Bastion and the former bastion of the
Lower Gate), by erecting redans (in front of the Bogen Gate) and corners (near the Capuchin
Monastery). As can be seen, the caponiers were only one of several solutions by which the
primary objective – the proper flanking of the moat in front of the main rampart – was to
be achieved.

Counterscarp Galleries

Another noteworthy solution used by designers of Prussian fortifications in the period in
question were galleries located in the moat counterscarp. Such galleries ran at the foot of
the moat's masonry revetment and communicated with the coffers located at the protruding
corners of the moat. The location of the coffers made them particularly durable defensive
installations, as they were situated in a place completely protected from artillery fire. Unlike
caponiers, this solution was not common. it was used only in Fort Prussia in Neisse and
in four star-shaped forts in Schweidnitz. These structures made it possible to defend the
moat bottom; they were particularly effective when the enemy tried to cross the moat with
a regular attack. As such, they were recommended by Walrave in his text on defensive

---

351 Gerhardt, Plan der Stadt und Festung Brieg, 1766, SBB PK, ref. X 20998.
352 Letter from Walrave to the King, 23 September 1747, GStA SPK, Geheimes Zivilkabinett I HA Rep.96
     No. 616 – Schlesische Festungen, Bd.D, p.41.
353 *Estimation* document, undated, unpaginated text from the collection of documents attached to the
     SBB PK, plan ref. X 33650.

The oldest caponier in Schweidnitz, present state. (Photo from the collection of Krzysztof Czarnecki)

Neisse, counterscarp gallery in Fort Prussia. (Photo: Grzegorz Podruczny)

architecture. Everything suggests that the introduction of this solution into Prussian defensive architecture should be traced back to him, as such galleries and coffers also existed in the Magdeburg Berge fort designed by him before 1740. Frederick was also an advocate of such use; according to Walrave, it was on the King's orders that they were applied to the Fort Preussen at Neisse.[354] It was probably also on his initiative that these facilities were created in the Schweidnitz forts, which had already been erected after Walrave's imprisonment.

---

354 De Walrave, Memoire sur l'attaque et Defencela des Places, GStA SPK, VI HA Familienarchive und Nachlässe, Nl Scharnhorst, no. 314, p.12 recto.

7

Fortifications in the Second Phase of the Reign of Frederick II (1763–1786)

The events of the Seven Years War provided the impetus for changes in the defence system of the Prussian state. On the one hand, they resulted in the construction of new fortresses and the modernisation of others; on the other, in the dismantling of outdated and no longer needed fortifications.

Only one fortress was built from scratch – Silberberg (Srebrna Góra), guarding the mountain pass that secured the connection between Glatz and the rest of Silesia. It was established as a direct result of the events of the final phase of the war. The events of the war were also the impetus for the development of two fortresses, previously almost forgotten: Breslau and Kolberg. Both fortresses were repeatedly besieged by the armies of Frederick's opponents, and these sieges revealed numerous weaknesses in their fortifications that had to be secured. The events of the war also confirmed the role of most of the fortresses built or modernised in the previous period. Almost all of the fortresses whose construction or modernisation was described in the previous chapter were besieged, and the experience gained resulted in their further expansion. However, there were also complexes of defensive works that proved to be redundant. These were selected to be dismantled. This was the fate of the fortifications in the west of Prussia, Minden and Gelder, while at Wesel, previously regarded as one of the most important strongholds of the state, the outer fortifications were removed. The fortress at Peitz, near Berlin, was also dismantled, as were the now completely obsolete fortifications of Frankfurt an der Oder and Driesen.[1]

Another impulse for the expansion of the Prussian fortress system was the First Partition of Poland. Although the Prussian state seized the existing fortresses of Elbląg and Malbork as a result, in the strategic situation of the time they were of little significance. The needs of the Prussian state would have been met by Gdansk or Torun, located on the main thoroughfare – the Vistula River – but these cities were not included in the annexation. It was therefore necessary to build a new fortress. It was at first built in the vicinity of Marienwerder (Kwidzyn), but then one of the hills near Graudenz (Grudziądz) was fortified.

---

1 Bonin, *Geschichte des Ingenieurkorps*, p.96; Burk, *Handbuch*, p.107; Jung, Spaß, Sloger, *Die Kunstdenkmäler*, p.126.

The last event that influenced the construction of fortifications was the War of the Bavarian Succession in 1778–1779. It was of lesser importance, and only confirmed the exceptional role of Silesia and the local fortresses in the Prussian state. It only directly influenced the further modernisation of the fortress Cosel, as well as plans for the construction of individual defensive structures.

Strongholds Along the Oder River

During the period in question, work was carried out in all the fortresses along the Oder, but only three – Breslau, Cosel and Glogau – underwent expansion and modernisation. The fortress at Brieg was downsized.

Breslau

As already shown in Chapter 6, in the period before the Seven Years War, Frederick, despite his announcements, did not modernise the fortress of Breslau. Because the fortifications were too weak and outdated, this key communication point (and extremely important magazine), was besieged three times between 1756 and 1763, and once became the target of a brief Russian bombardment. Not surprisingly, the city's fortifications began to be seriously transformed in response to these events.

The first modernisation work was undertaken while the war was still in progress. The task at hand at that time was to complete the missing sections of the covered way and the glacis. Construction started as early as 1757, during the short period when the fortress was occupied by the Austrians, with the section between the Ohlauer and Schweidnitzer Gates being completed.[2] After the Prussians recaptured Breslau, another section, between the Schweidnitzer and Nicolai Gates was completed in 1758.[3]

Subsequent work to extend the fortifications also began before the war ended. It is not known exactly when they started, but it is certain that in July 1762 the Breslau magistrate was informed that a new outer moat would be run across the cemetery, which belonged to the municipality, in front of the Schweidnitzer Gate.[4] This was only a fragment of a larger reconstruction, as we learn from municipal documents from March 1763, when compensation for the land taken for the construction of the new fortifications was estimated. In total, the land covered 23,946 quadrat rod (ruthen), or about 32 hectares. The new defensive works were: the envelope, erected in front of the main urban perimeter along a length of about 3.5 kilometres, from the mouth of the Ohle River to the city moat up to the Oder; a new outer moat (avant fosse), erected in front of the envelope; a single protruding defensive work erected in front of the Ziegeler Gate; and new fortifications at Burger Werder.[5] We do not know the exact dates of the construction of the individual elements of this great expansion of the defences. Certainly, the section of the outer moat in front of the Taschen Bastion was under construction in May 1763, witnessed by one of the owners of the land taken for the

---

2   APWr, AmWr, 1651, pp.1–3.
3   APWr, AmWr, 1651, pp.10–43.
4   APWr, AmWr, 1658, pp.36–38.
5   APWr, AmWr, 1651, pp.55–56.

fortifications.[6] One of the municipal documents from June of that year states that, 'The new fortifications from the Ohlauer Gate to the Schweidnitzer Gate are partly finished, partly still being delineated.'[7] They were probably not completed until 1765.[8] In 1764 construction work was underway on the Burger Werder, where a moat, a new rampart, and work on the foundations of the gunpowder storehouses, were erected in front of the new line of fortifications.[9]

From the early 1770s the fortifications were further developed. New works were created to reinforce the envelope of the city fortifications, the works advanced on Burger Werder, and those located on the north bank of the Oder River – a new envelope and the so-called Silver Sconce were created in front of the Oder Crown Works.[10]

In 1772, the construction of the most important of the new defences, the Springstern, began. According to a letter from the King to *Major* Haab, who was building the fortress, in September 1770 the King received a cost estimate for the construction of this complex (the earthworks alone were valued at 107,000 thalers), and the work was not due to start until mid-1771.[11] It finally started later, in early 1772. On the first day, 7 January 1772, as many as 1,500 men were at work. Construction continued until 1777, and the scope of work included not only the erection of a new defensive work, but also the removal of the northern arm of the Oder.[12] In the meantime, the fortifications began to be filled with military buildings. Between 1773 and 1776 Frederick's Gate was erected there, together with a casemate for the garrison.[13] While between 1780 and 1783 a second casemate was built between the Hundsfeld and Neudorf bastions.[14]

In 1777 a sluice near Scheiting (Szczytniki) was built at a cost of 40,000 thalers, separating the waters of the old Oder riverbed from the main riverbed, as well as a redoubt protecting them, erected at a cost of 16,000 thalers.[15] In 1779 further work was carried out on the Breslau fortifications, of considerable size. They were to cost 32,000 thalers and were to be worked on by as many as 700 labourers, to be supplied by the Silesian Ministry, but it is not known where specifically.[16] In the years 1780–1781 no work was carried out at Breslau,

---

6   APWr, AmWr, 1651, p.64.
7   APWr, AmWr, 1651, pp.76–78
8   APWr, AmWr, 1651, p.117
9   APWr, AmWr, 1651, pp.103–104.
10 APWr, AmWr, 1652 – Acta wegen einiger unterescheidenen Erbsassen vor den Schweidnitzer Thor u. Ohlauischen Thor zur Fortifikation gegebenen Ackerstücker, t2, 1770–1775; 1655 – Acta die Abschätzung und Verteidigung der zur Fortification eingezogenen Fundorum bettrefend.
11 Letter from the King to Haab, 16 September 1770, GStA SPK, I HA Rep.96 B Abschriften von Kabinetsordres, Bd.71, p.469 verso.
12 Karl Adolf Menzel, *Topographische Chronik von Breslau* (Breslau: Gratz und Barth 1805–1808), p.876.
13 Hermann Luchs, 'Über das äußere Wachstum der Stadt Breslau, mit Beziehung auf die Befestigung derselben', *Jahresbericht der städtischen höheren Töchterschule am Ritterplatz zu Breslau*, 1866, p.11; Ernst Kieseritzky, *Das Gelände der ehemaligen Festung Breslau* (Breslau: Morgensterns Verlagsbuchhandlung, 1903), p.12.
14 Luchs, 'Über das äußere Wachstum', p.11.
15 Letter from the King to Regler, 26 December 1776, GStA SPK, I HA Rep.96 B Abschriften von Kabinetsordres, Bd.75, p.911.
16 Letters from the King to Haab, 26 and 29 May 1779, GStA SPK, I HA Rep.96 B Abschriften von Kabinetsordres, Bd.79, p.723, p.848.

but the King did not forget about this fortress. In the autumn of 1781, he requested a new plan from Haab, on which the newly created sluice was to be marked, as well as the area of the foreground that could be flooded thanks to this facility.[17] It is likely that the drawing up of these plans was a prelude to the next stage of the fortress expansion. Indeed, further expenditure on the expansion of the Breslau fortress was planned for 1783.[18] The drawings and cost estimates were received by the King at the beginning of January 1783, the funds for this task (totalling 29,000 thalers) were transferred at the turn of the year.[19] The money was spent on the erection of the so-called communication at the suburb of Hinterdom. This defensive structure took the form of a long rampart preceded by a water moat, with two redans. It ran from the Dom Ravelin up to a redoubt with a casemate at the Pass Brücke.[20]

As well as building new structures, old ones were also repaired. The most urgent was the repair of the damaged flank of the Taschen Bastion. Although it had already been provisionally secured in 1758, permanent repairs were needed, so the damaged flank was rebuilt as early as 1765.[21] Another modernisation of the existing structure was the installation of an artillery casemate in the right shoulder of the Graupen Bastion between 1773 and 1774.[22] This bastion, erected in the second half of the seventeenth century, was originally a purely earthen structure and had only open artillery positions.

Reinforcement of old structures with casemates also took place elsewhere. Between 1773 and 1774 casemates were built at the cemetery by St Barbara's Church, at the Nicholas Gate, at the Ohau Gate, and at the Salvatore Church, and two years later at the rear of the Commandery of the Order of St John, at the curtain connecting the Schweidnitzer and Graupen bastions.[23]

As part of the expansion of the fortifications, further auxiliary facilities were also built, including sluices and bridges. In 1779, for example, a battardeau was constructed at the Alumat on Dom Insel, at the mouth of an arm of the Oder River encircling that island.[24]

Unfortunately, it is not possible to trace the progress of the fortification development in detail. The scarcity of archival sources on the period does not allow this. The small number of surviving documents is offset by the large number of design drawings which show the development of the concept of fortifying Breslau. The cartographic collection of the Berlin Staatsbibliothek preserves six designs of various kinds, which date from 1765 to 1777. From

---

17 Letter from the King to Haab, 20 October 1781, GStA SPK, I HA Rep.96 B Abschriften von Kabinetsordres, Bd.81, p.815.

18 Letter from the King to Haab, 27 September 1782, GStA SPK, I HA Rep.96 B Abschriften von Kabinetsordres, Bd.82, p.919.

19 Letter from the King to Kempf, 1 January 1783, GStA SPK, I HA Rep.96 B Abschriften von Kabinetsordres, Bd.83, p.4.

20 Luchs, 'Über das äußere Wachstum', p.11; Kieseritzky, *Das Gelände*, p.12; King's letter to Regler, 25 December 1775, GStA SPK, I HA Rep.96 B Abschriften von Kabinetsordres Bd.75 p.911.

21 APWr, AmWr, Fortifications Acta, vol. 3, 1758–1808, ref. 1658 (12.197), p.41.

22 Luchs, 'Über das äußere Wachstum', p.11; Seydel attributes the construction of this casemate to Haab, *Seydel, Nachrichten*, vol.4, p.20.

23 Menzel, *Topographische Chronik*, p.896. According to the cost estimate for the construction of Silesian fortresses for 1774, a sum of 40,000 thalers was envisaged for the construction of this casemate, which was to accommodate as many as 800 soldiers. Letter from the King to Regler, 14 October 1773, GStA SPK, I HA Rep.96 B Abschriften von Kabinetsordres, Bd.73, p.314.

24 Luchs, 'Über das äußere Wachstum', p.11.

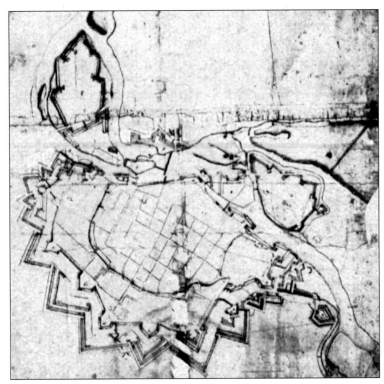

Fortress Breslau, presumed design by Frederick the Great. (Konwiarz, *Die Baukunst Breslaus*, p.51)

the point of view of the subject of this book, however, the most important is the one known only from a reproduction in Richard Konwiarz's book.[25]

This is because this unrealised sketch of the fortification was attributed by him to Frederick. Unfortunately, apart from the caption under the illustration containing this attribution and dating the project to 1770, the author of the architectural guide to Breslau does not refer to this plan in his book. Doubts therefore arise as to whether this drawing is in fact a sketch by Frederick. If one were to consider the drawing itself, the King's authorship would have to be ruled out, as it is too accurate and too precisely executed to have come from the King's hand. All of his known drawings, both of fortifications and of civil architecture, are without exception sketches made by hand. Nevertheless, there is some probability that the drawing presented in Konwiarz's book presents us with the King's ideas, in drawing form, presented by someone more proficient at drawing. Another reason against recognising the drawing as the King's work is that none of the historians to date, whether researching the history of Breslau (apart from Konwiarz) or dealing with the history of fortifications, mentions the King designing the fortifications of Breslau. This, too, need not be a conclusive argument,

---

25   Richard Konwiarz, *Die Baukunst Breslaus: ein architektonischer Führer im Auftrage des Schlesischen Bundes für Heimatschutz* (Breslau: Verlag Grasz, 1926), p.51.

since previous researchers have also made no mention of Frederick's personal participation in the design of Glatz before 1756, or of Kolberg and Silberberg after 1763, for which strong evidence is presented in this book. Thus, it cannot be ruled out that Frederick is associated with the concept presented by Konwiarz. Two indications may support this. Firstly, at the end of the Seven Years War, the King was in Breslau for a very long time, from the beginning of December 1761 to mid-May 1762.[26] He had enough time to familiarise himself with the fortifications there. Secondly, during the period of the post-war modernisation of the Breslau's defences, Frederick exercised his usual intense personal control and influence over the works being built. In this context, a drawing drawn up by the King as a guideline for engineers on how to fortify Breslau seems likely.

Certainly, however, the dating of the plan to 1770 must be rejected. It should be regarded as the first version of the project to modernise the Breslau fortress, created before 1762 and the completion of the final version. It has a very conceptual character and is far from the version that was constructed.

The modernisation of the fortifications outlined in this project was to add a strong defensive line in front of the city fortifications, as well as to strengthen the fortifications of the Oder islands. In the case of the city fortifications, the 'royal' project envisaged the erection of an envelope in front of the bastion core preceded by its own moat. In front of the southern front, the envelope was to take the form of large, spacious salients, while in front of the Nicolai Crown Work, these works were to be much smaller in size; moreover, in the receding salients between the corners, structures resembling small reduits were to appear. On the opposite front, before the Ziegeler Gate, the new envelope was to connect with the counterguard erected before the war during the minor modernisation carried out by Walrave. However, a new structure was planned to be erected there as well. The project described envisaged an outer work to be located more or less where work No. IX was later built. While the city fortifications were eventually completed in a form similar to the 'royal' design, this was not the case with the fortification of the Oder islands. A major change, compared to the status quo, was the plan for a major fortification of Burger Werder. According to the described project, it was to be divided into two parts; the southern part was given a large, relatively regular horn work, while the northern part was completely surrounded by a rampart with a tenaille outline. While the horn work was eventually built on the southern part of the island, structures planned for the northern part were created as three small and unconnected, independent defensive works. In the case of Dom Insel and Sand Insel, the described 'royal' project only involved the modernisation of the fortifications already there. On Sand Insel, a horn work was to be erected, while on Dom Insel, the intention was only to modernise the one that had existed since the 1730s. In place of the small bastions and half-bastions connected by curtains, the intention was to insert a line of tenaille fortifications similar in outline to the fortifications of the northern part of Burger Werder. Later design versions rejected this concept altogether. Instead of strengthening the existing fortifications, it was decided to erect a completely new, large defensive structure to the north of Dom Insel – the Springstern.

---

26   He arrived in Breslau for winter on 9 December 1761 and left the city on 16 May 1762, Rödenbeck, *Tagebuch oder Geschichtskalender*, vol.2, pp.128–149.

As can be seen, the 'royal' project was only a prelude to the planning process that led to the version that was completed. There is little need to describe all the other variants, but it is necessary to mention two further plans at least briefly, created towards the end of 1765. These projects are already much closer to the built version. Both in front of the city's fortifications and on the northern bank of the Oder, numerous outer defensive works were envisaged. In addition to this, a large structure appeared, which formed a large five-bastion defensive work from Dom Insel and the area to the north of it. These drawings, which, like the sketch described earlier, were more of a concept than a project to be realised, were made by a certain *Leutnant* Waldegour.[27]

Cosel

Cosel, as in the pre-war period, played a significant role in the fortress system of the Prussian state. Its importance was confirmed by the events of the Seven Years War, when the fortress was twice blockaded and once, in November 1760, an attempt was made to capture it. At that time, the Austrians under Laudon's command carried out two assaults and an artillery shelling. The biggest battles were fought over the fortified tête de pont, which was attacked by the Grenzer on 26 November.[28] It is therefore not surprising that after the end of the war, it was decided to reinforce this facility in particular. The already existing works were connected by short sections of rampart to the bank of the Oder, thus creating a closed defensive perimeter. In addition, the whole was surrounded by a new counterguard defended by wooden caponiers placed in the places of arms. Furthermore, the main rampart, previously fully earthen, was raised and provided with masonry revetment. Finally, the whole was surrounded by a moat more than 20 metres wide. All this work was completed in 1767.[29] In addition to the transformation of the fortifications, plans were made to erect a new sluice on the Oder, but this was not realised in the 1760s. *Major* von Wins, whose drawings are preserved in the Staatsbibliothek in Berlin,[30] was responsible for the design work. The King played a role in the modernisation, as the plan presenting all the projected works contains a note that these works were 'decided by His Majesty in His Most Excellent Presence'.[31]

After this minor modernisation, no work was carried out on the fortifications for more than 10 years. Only new masonry barracks were built, replacing three older wooden ones destroyed during the Seven Years War.[32] Two more gunpowder magazines were probably built in 1777.[33] It was only after the War of the Bavarian Succession that the local fortifica-

---

27   Plan de la Ville et Faubourgs de Breslau, SBB PK, ref. X 20678, X 20678/1.
28   Weltzel, *Geschichte der Stadt*, pp.366–367.
29   Weltzel, *Geschichte der Stadt*, p.371.
30   SBB PK, ref. X 28150/5, sheet nos. 2, 3, 4, 5.
31   Plan und profil von den Tete du Pont zu Cosel. Was Ihro Majestet bey Aller Höchseter anwesenheit allergnadigst zu Verstärkung des Tete du Pont resolvieret haben, SBB PK, ref. X 28150/5, card no. 2.
32   Weltzel, *Geschichte der Stadt*, p.371; A. Schellenberg, 'Die Evangelische Kirche in Cosel OS. Eine Archivalische Studie', *Der Oberschlesier*, 14, 3–4, (1932), p.151; King's letters to Regler, 22 September and 15 November 1775, GStA SPK, I HA Rep.96 B Abschriften von Kabinetsordres, Bd.74, pp.616, 787.
33   Letter from the King to von Wins, April 1777, GStA SPK, I HA Rep.96 B Abschriften von Kabinetsordres, Bd.76, p.342 recto.

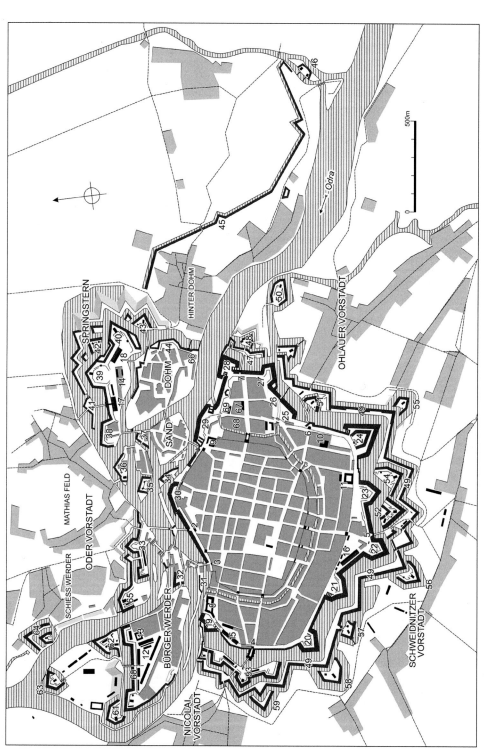

Fortress Breslau in 1786. (Drawn by Mariusz Wojciechowski)

tions began to be transformed anew. The modernisation was designed by *Major* von Haab, whom we have already encountered in the section on Breslau. He drew up the first draft as early as June 1779.[34] He planned an enormous reconstruction. He wanted to significantly change the city defences, transforming the outline of the main rampart of the fortress from a tenaille to a bastion wall. In addition, a new Rogauer Redoubt was to be built in front of the Louis Salient, and the Weigschützer Redoubt was to be completely transformed. In addition to this, Haab was planning to build cavaliers in all ravelins, as well as to strengthen the defence of the entire urban perimeter of the fortress by establishing a wide envelope in front of the main rampart. He also planned to seriously strengthen the fortifications on the other side of the Oder. According to his design, Klodnitzer and Kobelwiter Redoubts were to be built on the Oder island, and a new Adler Redoubt was to be constructed in front of the fortified tête de pont. The changes were also to be noticeable inside the city fortifications, as the construction of four casemates was planned; three for the garrison and one for the bakery. The final element of the project was to be the erection of a large weir.[35]

After receiving the project, the King mostly accepted it, only disallowing the reconstruction of the outline of the main rampart, the elimination of the salients and the erection of bastions in their place. In addition, he stated that the money for this modernisation would not be found until the next financial year.[36] The matter of finances was, after all, the main element that interested the King. The cost of the rebuild was initially set at 189,000 thalers, but the King later sought to reduce it.[37] Initially, Haab also planned to build a masonry storehouse for forage in the fortress, but this was quickly deleted from the cost estimate by the King.[38] The casemates were the first to be built; an amount of over 40,000 thalers for their construction was included in the fortress construction budget as early as 1780, and their construction continued until 1783.[39] At the same time as this first construction the project was being finalised at the end of August 1780. In order to save money, the construction cost estimate was reduced to around 150,000 thalers.[40] The main construction work did not begin until 1781; as many as 2,500 workers and 50 horse-drawn carts were required to carry it out.[41] When the work began, the King had hoped to complete it as early as 1781, but despite the exceptionally long construction season (until the last days of November), this

---

34   Letter from the King to Haab, 28 June 1779, GStA SPK, I HA Rep.96 B Abschriften von Kabinetsordres, Bd.79, p.814.

35   The plan, which probably represents the first reconstruction project for the fortress, is kept in the Berlin Staatsbibliothek, SBB PK, ref. X 28150/9.

36   Letter from the King to Haab, 28 June 1779, GStA SPK, I HA Rep.96 B Abschriften von Kabinetsordres, Bd.79, p.814.

37   Letter from the King to Haab, 5 November 1779, GStA SPK, I HA Rep.96 B Abschriften von Kabinetsordres, Bd.79, p.1126.

38   Letter from the King to Haab, 15 November 1779, GStA SPK, I HA Rep.96 B Abschriften von Kabinetsordres, Bd.79, p.1149.

39   Letter from the King to Haab, 24 April 1780, GStA SPK, I HA Rep.96 B Abschriften von Kabinetsordres, Bd.80, p.244.

40   Letter from the King to Haab, 29 August 1780, GStA SPK, I HA Rep.96 B Abschriften von Kabinetsordres, Bd.80, p.549.

41   Letter from the King to Haab, 15 March 1781, GStA SPK, I HA Rep.96 B Abschriften von Kabinetsordres, Bd.81, p.178.

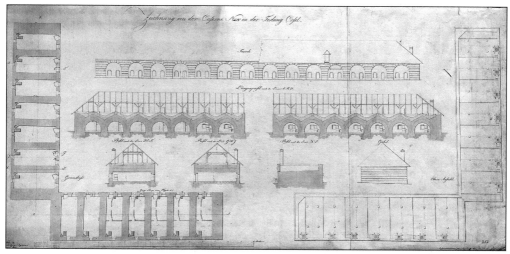

Cosel, Bombproof barracks no. 4. (GStA SPK, XI HA ref. D 70120)

was not done.[42] Nor did the work end in 1782, and presumably its intensity decreased due to Haab's workload with duties at other Silesian fortresses. As the engineer died unexpectedly in December 1782, his duties were taken over by his former subordinate, von Wins, who was charged by the King with the task of building the fortress in December 1782.[43] In March of the following year, we know from his design activity, that he was in charge of the Kobelwitzer Redoubt together with the hangar.[44]

He is also known to have designed the fortress, which differs in certain details from Haab's project. According to his design, a different form was to be given to the Adler Redoubt and the Weigschützer Redoubt, and defensive lines connecting the Klodnitzer and Kobelwitzer redoubts were planned. In the latter, a hangar appeared, which Haab had not envisaged.[45] Wins, however, was in command of the construction of the fortress for quite a short time. In August of that year, the King showed his dissatisfaction with his work. Wins sent him cost estimates, which outraged the King. Not only were the sums that this engineer planned to spend on the construction of the fortress 'impertinent', but the solutions that Wins proposed were mostly rejected by the King. Frederick started looking for another designer.[46] In September he ordered *Kapitän* Harroy to go to Cosel and survey the fortifications there. The cost estimate drawn up by this engineer appealed to the King, and the latter

42 King's letters to Haab, 26 April and 5 November 1781, GStA SPK, I HA Rep.96 B Abschriften von Kabinetsordres, Bd.81, pp.283, 870.

43 Letters from the King to von Saas, 15 December 1782, GStA SPK, I HA Rep.96 B Abschriften von Kabinetsordres, Bd.82, p.1184.

44 Letters from the King to Wins, 24 March 1783, GStA SPK, I HA Rep.96 B Abschriften von Kabinetsordres, Bd.83, p.204.

45 Project plan von Cosel, SBB PK, ref. X 28150/5–1.

46 King's letters to Wins, 22, 26 and 31 August 1783, GStA SPK, I HA Rep.96 B Abschriften von Kabinetsordres, Bd.83, pp.715, 725, 739.

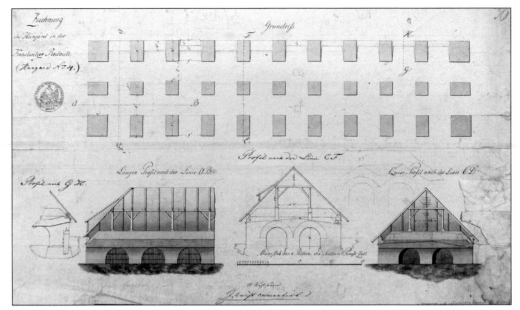

Cosel, hangar in the Kobelwitzer Redoubt. (GStA SPK, XI HA ref. F 72358)

gave him supervision of further work at the fortress.[47] At the time when Harroy took over supervision only the Kobelwitzer Redoubt was almost finished; the Klodnitzer and Rogauer Redoubts and the curtains between the redoubts on the island had only just been started, while the Adler Redoubt had still to be begun.[48] In the literature on the Cosel fortress it appears that Harroy erected the Rogauer, Adler, Klodnitzer and Kobelwitzer Redoubts.[49] However, according to the above-mentioned sources, Harroy's activity was limited only to the completion of the Klodnitzer and Rogauer Redoubts and the erection of the Adler Redoubt from scratch. All the personnel changes obviously prolonged the length of the project. In the early spring of 1784, the King again set a deadline for the completion of the works, this time it was to be at the end of that year.[50] However, the deadline could not be met this time either, with work still continuing in 1785, which saw a piecemeal reconstruction of the main rampart involving partial replacement of salients to bastions.[51] Some work is also known to have been carried out within the fortified island.[52] It was probably not until 1785 that the construction work was completed. In 1786 only repair work was carried out on the

---

47   King's letters to Harroy, 3 September and 8 November 1783, GStA SPK, I HA Rep.96 B Abschriften von Kabinetsordres, Bd.83, pp.750a, 831.

48   Kosel im Novembre 1783, SBB PK, ref. X 28150/10.

49   Weltzel, *Geschichte der Stadt*, p.373.

50   King's letter to Harroy, 10 April 1784, GStA SPK, I HA Rep.96 B Abschriften von Kabinetsordres, Bd.84, p.310.

51   SBB PK, DPG ref. VII Cosel, 89 I – Memoires über die Festung Cosel 1797, text no. 1, Memoir über die Festung Cosel und ihre Einrichtung zu einem Waffenplatz, erster Abschnitt, p.4.

52   King's letter to Harroy, 14 April 1785, GStA SPK, I HA Rep.96 B Abschriften von Kabinetsordres, Bd.85, p.374.

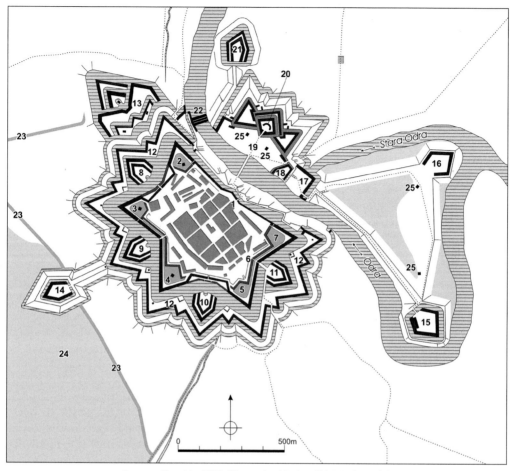

Fortress Cosel in 1786. (Drawn by Mariusz Wojciechowski.)

weir recently erected by Haab. This structure had suffered damage and the King allocated more than 34,000 thalers for its repair.[53]

Glogau

Serious work was also carried out on the fortress at Glogau, even though the Seven Years War showed no gaps in its defences. Indeed, the fortress was not conquered and was only threatened once, in September 1759, by a Russian attack. For the modernisation, the emphasis was on strengthening the resistance to assault of the main defensive perimeter. The King was

---

53   King's letters to Harroy, 30 January and 16 July 1786, GStA SPK, I HA Rep.96 B Abschriften von Kabinetsordres, Bd.86, pp.103, 655.

the initiator of this reconstruction; the project was handled by *Kapitän* Freund, who was working in Glogau at the time. The first project and cost estimate for the modernisation of the fortress was drawn up as early as September 1769 and the King, on receiving it, expressed his satisfaction.[54] Apart from the fact that it was drawn up, we know little about it; only that it concerned the raising of some works and the strengthening of the main moat with a wall. A year later, further alterations were made, the inference being that the King, despite his satisfaction, did not accept Freund's ideas. We know much more about the new project. There were plans to erect a 24-foot-high masonry revetment of the moat counterscarp from the Breslau Gate to the Preussen Gate, to reshape the outline of some of the defensive works between the Schloss Bastion and the ravelin in front of the Breslau Gate, to erect gunpowder stores and guardhouses in the ravelins, to reshape some of the defensive works which were set too low, and to erect a new moat in front of the Oder Redoubt.[55] This, plus various minor works, was to cost the sum of almost 130,000 thalers.[56] However, this was not the final cost estimate, as another cost estimate has survived, unfortunately undated. It concerned only the masonry revetment of the moat, 24 feet high, along the shorter section from the Breslau Gate to the Preussen Gate, at a cost of 131,674 thalers. The design work dragged on to such an extent that it did not come to fruition until 1775–1777.[57]

One more element that was intended to be transformed was sketchily marked on the plans – the front of the Dom Insel fortifications. A new section of the rampart was to be built there, together with a bastion. Another bastion was to be created from the former ravelin, incorporated into the defence perimeter. A cost estimate from 1770 allocated a sum of 12,000 thalers for this purpose. Its author, Freund, justified the rebuilding of the front by the royal desire to preserve the defences of Dom Insel, weakened by the decreased flow in the old Oder riverbed, which had supplied the moat until then. This project was not realised.

The above-described modernisations and projects did not satisfy the King, who planned further transformations of the local fortifications in the early 1780s. This was to be overseen by *Major* von Haab, to whom the King had already announced the commission of modernisation in the autumn of 1780.[58] He did not reveal the details until the following spring. In a letter of 1 March 1781 written to Haab, he criticised the fortifications there.[59] The main problem he noted was the inappropriate height of the outer defensive works. According to the King, they were too low. The enemy could see into the interior of the defensive works and set up a battery from a distance of 1,000 paces, conducting effective ricocheting fire along the defensive lines. The reason for this defect in the defences of Glogau was poor workmanship by the local engineers. Therefore, the King wanted his

54   King's letters to Freund, 17 September 1769, GStA SPK, I HA Rep.96 B Abschriften von Kabinetsordres, Bd.71, p.215 verso.

55   Plan von Glogau, SBB PK, ref. X 25134/10–1.

56   Cost estimate of the works drawn up by Freund in Glogau, 9 September 1770, Plan von Glogau, SBB PK, ref. X 25134/10–1 pp.1–3.

57   Minsberg, *Geschichte der Stadt und Festung Groß Glogau*, vol.2, p.274.

58   Letter from the King to Haab, 20 October 1780, GStA SPK, I HA Rep.96 B Abschriften von Kabinetsordres, Bd.80, p.665.

59   Letter from the King to Haab, 1 March 1781, SHD Vincennes, Article 14 Places Etrangeres, XVII Glogau, dossier et plans 1760–1909, 1 V M 131, no. 6; A copy of this letter is also in GStA SPK, I HA Rep.96 B Abschriften von Kabinetsordres, Bd.81, p.141.

engineer to rectify the mistake of his predecessors. The glacis was to be elevated so that only the earthen slopes of the fortress could be seen from outside, which were to look like a meadow from a distance. The King instructed his engineer to go to Glogau, personally inspect the problem and make a cost estimate for the work so that the following year the work could be carried out. Another modification to the fortifications, which the King orders in the aforementioned letter, is the construction of countermine corridors. They were to be built around the town fortifications from the castle up to the Fort Stern.[60] The King did not want to have such extensive counter-mine corridors at Glogau as at his other fortresses, because at Glogau the risk of mine attack was not as significant. Interestingly, the King mentions in the letter that he is also sending his design for a mine system along with it. Unfortunately, unlike the letter, the drawing has not survived, and we are unable to ascertain whether and to what extent the Glogau counter-mine corridors, which after all already existed, were rebuilt after 1781.[61] A project implementing the King's directives was presented by Haab as early as April of that year, but its implementation was postponed until 1782. At that time, some work began, which the King intended to be completed within one year. However, this did not come to fruition, as Haab, who was overseeing it, died unexpectedly and the perturbations that are natural in such situations followed.[62] The money left over from the previous year and intended for the completion of the work at Glogau was transferred to Cosel in February 1783, in order to speed up work on the fortifications there. As a result, the King decided to suspend the work for that year.[63] Preparations for the resumption of work did not start until December 1783; at that time, the King ordered the Glogau Chamber (Kammer) to provide for work on the fortifications, starting from 3 May 1784 with 500 labourers and 14 four-horse carriages.[64] The King again estimated that the planned work should be completed within a year and was to cost around 24,000 thalers.[65] However, he was wrong again, further work was planned for this fortress at the end of the year.[66] There is unfortunately no information about their progress.

Probably connected with the end of Frederick's reign is the project to rebuild the fortifications of Dom Insel carried out by Harroy. It should be dated to circa 1784, as this engineer also began working at Glogau at that time. In his correspondence with the King there is no shortage of references to various design work for Glogau; unfortunately, there is no mention that could be linked to the Dom Insel project. The project described envisaged a complete transformation of the fortifications there. Instead of a perimeter made up of small tenaille

---

60   Interestingly, the King uses the name Fort Preussen in the letter instead of the correct one.
61   Plan de Glogau, 1811, SHD Vincennes, Article 14 Places Etrangeres, XVII Glogau, dossier et plans 1760–1909, 1 V M 131, no. 11.
62   Letters from the King to Haab, 26 April 1781 and 20 February 1782 and to von Rüts of 15 December 1782, GStA SPK, I HA Rep.96 B Abschriften von Kabinetsordres, Bd.81, p.283; Bd.82 pp.162 i 1184.
63   Letters from the King to Kleist and von Rüts, 2 February 1783, GStA SPK, I HA Rep.96 B Abschriften von Kabinetsordres, Bd.83, p.97.
64   Letters of the King to Kleist and the Glogau Chamber, 17 December 1783, GStA SPK, I HA Rep.96 B Abschriften von Kabinetsordres, Bd.83, p.953.
65   Letters from the King to Harroy and Kleist, 10 and 12 April and 4 August 1784, GStA SPK, I HA Rep.96 B Abschriften von Kabinetsordres, Bd.84, pp.310, 322, 712.
66   Letter from the King to Kleist, 5 December 1784, GStA SPK, I HA Rep.96 B Abschriften von Kabinetsordres, Bd.84, p.1102.

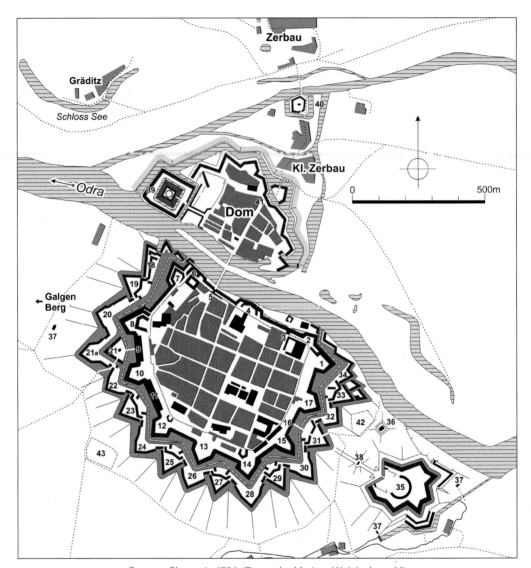

Fortress Glogau in 1786. (Drawn by Mariusz Wojciechowski)

and bastions, he proposed that the whole Dom Insel should be made into a gigantic horn work. With its left flank it was to meet the Oder Redoubt, reinforced with a new ravelin. In front of the curtain, between the two main half-bastions, there was to be a ravelin equipped with its own counterguard. The Zerbauer Redoubt, which extended in front of the Dom fortifications, was also to be transformed.[67]

---

67 Project Tete du Pont von Glogau vom Major Harroy, SBB PK, ref. X 25134/7.

Brieg

Brieg was one of those fortresses where modernisation work was also carried out during the Seven Years War. The most important measure was to continue palisading the defence works. On 1 December 1756, the commander of the fortress, *Generalleutnant* de Hautcharmoy, reported that palisading had to be carried out on the covered way in front of the envelope. However, the King did not grant money for this task, explaining the omission by the insignificance of the fortress in the war situation at the time. Much more work was carried out in 1757. Their extent is known thanks to a report by the then commandant, *Leutnant* von Sas. Some reinforcements were made to the main rampart – the fausse-braye were provided with gabions and the breastworks of the fausse-braye were repaired. In some places a palisade was erected at the base of the fausse-braye. Care was also taken to maintain an adequate water level in the moats. For this purpose, batardeau were erected, which were protected by palisades, chevaux de frise, and wooden caponiers at their rear. They were located between the Brandenburg and Pommern bastions, in front of the corner of the Pommern bastion, between the Mark and Magdeburg bastions, in front of the corner of the Halberstadt bastion and between it and the Westfalen bastion. The outer works were also reinforced. The covered way was palisaded and wooden caponiers were erected in the places of arms. The outer works were already weakly palisaded. In addition, the mill island was reinforced; a low rampart was built there, as well as two batteries for eight guns each. In total, 6,065 thalers were spent on work on the Brieg fortifications in 1756–1760, not including the amounts spent on palisades. As for the latter, it is only known that 1,147 thalers were spent on them in 1757–1758. The most important reinforcement of the fortress during the Seven Years War was the construction of a small earthen redoubt in front of the tête de pont, towards Schreibendorf (Pisarzowice). It was not erected until 1761.[68] It had a quadrilateral ground plan and consisted of an earth rampart with gun platforms in its corners. It was surrounded by a water moat 48 feet wide. In addition, it was encircled by a glacis reinforced with a palisade. Inside the redoubt there was a small masonry guardhouse containing two rooms; the smaller one for officers and the larger one for soldiers. The appearance of Brieg's fortifications after the Seven Years War is well known thanks to a 1766 plan by *Kapitän* Gerhard, engineer of the fortress.[69]

   After the end of the Seven Years War, the fortress at Brieg stagnated. This should come as no surprise as the fortress was not attacked once during the war, so there was no immediate reason to invest in it. The fortress appeared several times in Frederick's correspondence related to fortifications, but no investments were made there involving the construction of new defensive facilities. It was not until the mid-1770s that work was resumed. From 1775, a large sum for work on the fortifications at Brieg – 95,000 thalers – appeared several times in the budgets, but was mentioned only in the general financial plans; moreover, the expenditure was postponed several times. The King's correspondence lacks any detailed mention of the actual expenditure of this amount. Nevertheless, it is possible to guess what

---

68   GStA SPK, IV HA Rep. 15A, no. 808 pp.29–30.
69   GStA SPK, XI HA ref. G 70752, Redoute, C.V Gerhardt, 1766; Plan der Stadt und Festung Brieg / so wie Selbige mit seinem Environs sich gegenwartig befindet, in November 1766 leve et dessine par Gerherdt, SBB PK, ref. X 20998.

this considerable sum was spent on. For it is known that Gerhard carried out extensive work on the fortress from 1774 to 1780, initially involving 500 workers, and from 1775, 800, and in 1780 as many as 1,000. These works, however, rather than building new defences, were primarily aimed at the decommissioning of the old ones, specifically the removal of the envelope and the belt of outer works designed by Walrave. As a result, a huge area of 22,353 square rods (rute, about 317,000 square metres or 32 hectares) of the land seized in 1742 for the fortifications was returned to the original owners.[70] However, this process was not carried out completely. Later cartography shows traces of the old defence works. There was still a several hundred metre-long section of moat in the suburb of Mollwitz in 1860, a remnant of Walrave's reconstruction of the fortress. The work carried out by Gerhard, however, did not just consist of removing the fortifications. The covered way in front of the moat, provided with places of arms, was made anew, and the main rampart was corrected. The biggest changes were made to the bastions of the Oder front. The oldest bastions, Schloss (Preussen) and the Oderbrücke (Hautcharmoy) bastion, were thoroughly rebuilt. In the former, the left orillon was removed, in the latter both orillons were built over, thus increasing its surface area somewhat. In addition, an additional extensive defensive work was created in front of the curtain connecting the two structures. Furthermore, the Oder (Westphalen) bastion was given a tenaille outline and the Oppeln (Halberstadt) bastion was given a similar outline and profile to the neighbouring bastions; a rampart with a surrounding fausse-braye (originally the fausse-braye was only in the shoulders of the bastion, in the left one it was even doubled).[71]

The reconstruction of the Oder fortresses after the Seven Years War had relatively little relevance to the development of fortifications under Frederick the Great. The structures that were erected there did not introduce any new threads into the history of Prussian fortification. Both the external works – so numerous in Cosel and Breslau – and the envelopes were nothing new; facilities of this kind had also been built in the previous period. An important phenomenon was the increasing role of bombproof structures in fortresses; buildings of this type were created in each of the described fortresses. Their role in Glogau, Cosel and Breslau was, however, minor compared to Glatz and Silberberg. The most interesting phenomenon was the peculiar criticism of Walrave's ideas made by *Major* von Haab with his reconstruction project at Cosel. He planned to completely reshape the original star outline of the main rampart and replace the salients with traditional bastions. Although the King did not agree with this at first, the idea was partially realised in the course of implementation.

Strongholds in the Mountains

Silberberg

The only new fortress to be established in Silesia after the end of the Seven Years War was the Silberberg stronghold. The permanent fortification of the Silber Pass was determined

---

70   Karl Friedrich Schönwälder, *Geschichtliche Ortsnachrichten von Brieg und seinen Umgebungen* (Brieg: S. Falsch, 1847), vol.2, pp.38–39

71   Description based on a comparison of the state of the fortress as depicted on Gerhard's 1766 plan with Rüdgisch's 1802 plan (GStA SPK, XI HA ref. F 71687).

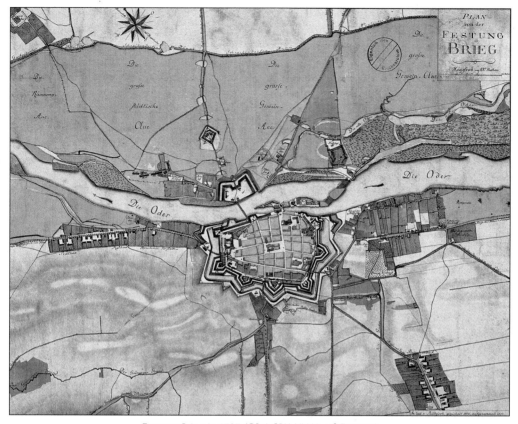

Fortress Brieg in 1797. (GStA SPK, XI HA ref. F 71687)

by the events of the second half of the Seven Years War. In 1760, after the capture of Glatz, the Austrian army, on the orders of *Feldzeugmeister* Laudon, garrisoned the Silber Pass and the Wartha (Bardo) Pass.[72] From that time until the end of the war, the area was the site of minor or major concentrations of imperial troops. In the same year, the area around Silberberg and Wartha was occupied by *Generalmajor* Franz Maximilian Janus von Eberstädt with the task of covering Glatz County during the retreat of the Imperial army after the lost battle of Liegnitz.[73] The Austrian positions were strongly manned and when the Prussian commander, Prince Franz Adolf von Anhalt-Bernburg, attacked the Austrian position near Silberberg in March 1761, he captured as many as eight guns.[74] From March 1761 until May 1762, *Feldmarshalllieutenant* Josip Kazimír Drašković von Trakošćan's corps, consisting of five infantry battalions, 500 Grenzer, five cavalry squad-

---

72   Anon., 'Friedrich der Große als Ingenieur', p.18.

73   Preuss, *Oeuvres de Frederic le Grand*, vol.5, p.80.

74   Grosser Generalstab, *Geschichte des siebenjährigen Krieges: in einer Reihe von Vorlesungen, mit Benutzung authentischer Quellen* (Berlin: Grosser Generalstab, 1836), vol.5, p.1, der Feldzug von 1761, p.168.

rons and a regiment of hussars, were stationed there.[75] The troops, in a camp between Wartha and Silberberg, not only protected the Austrians from a possible Prussian attack on Glatz County, but also enabled their own troops to use these two places as a gateway to Silesia. During the almost three-year stay of the imperial army in the area, a huge complex of field fortifications was built, linked to camps in the vicinity of the Silber and Wartha Pass. It consisted of outposts near Silberberg, Wartha and in the Harthe Berg. Laudon's army encamped around this mountain several times in 1761.[76] These individual positions were not combined into one large camp until 1762. *Feldmarschallleutnant* Philipp Lewin Beck's corps manned the Harthe Berg, *Feldmarschalleutnant* Joseph von Brentano-Cimaroli's corps manned the area of Schönwalde (Budzów), *Generalmajor* Christian Jacob von Vogelsang's corps manned the Silberberg area, and the main mass of the army under *Feldmarschall* Daun stood near Wartha.[77] The whole area was heavily occupied with troops, but the fortifications were concentrated in selected places. The first belt stretched along the foot of the mountains. It started in front of Silberberg, closed the entrance to the Herzogswalde (Żdanów) Basin and reached as far as Niklasdorf (Mikołajów). The second cluster stretched from the Wartha in a three-kilometre arc across the mountains to the Harthe Berg. The third, smallest group of fortifications was located between the villages of Grahau (Grochowa) and Baumgarten (Braszowice), primarily on Grahe Berg. These fortifications were mostly in the form of single lunettes, placed one next to the other. A few places were sheltered by a continuous tenaille line. The least numerous were the star-shaped fortifications. Two such structures stood in the vicinity of Fuchs Berg, and the third on the Wacht-Berg near Baumgarten.[78] The latter of the entrenchments was also supposed to be the largest of the field works erected in this camp.[79]

The King was well aware of the defensive positions occupied by the Austrians between Wartha and Silberberg. He described the camp near Wartha in a letter to his brother of 22 September 1762 as 'unattackable', while regarding the camp on the summit near Silberberg, occupied by seven battalions, he wrote that he 'finds no way to attack it.'[80]

The strength and importance of the camp described above was also said to have been felt by the King himself, for while staying at the palace at Schönwalde around 1761, he was fired upon from the fortifications of Silberberg. It is said that at that time he announced in anger the building of a fortress with these words: 'I'm already going to get you scoundrels out of there and erect such a fortress on the mountain that you will never conquer!'[81] The King's anger was all the greater because strong Austrian fortified camps defended the entrance to the County of Glatz, and until the end of the war Frederick's troops failed to recapture this border country. They only succeeded in doing so during the peace negotiations, when the

---

75 Grosser Generalstab, *Geschichte des siebenjährigen Krieges 1836*, p.171.

76 20–21 July, 27 July, 5 August, among others. Grosser Generalstab, *Geschichte des siebenjährigen Krieges 1836*, pp.224, 242, 270.

77 Lloyd, von Tempelhoff, *Geschichte des siebenjährigen Krieges*, vol.6, p.155; SBB PK, ref. Db 1.33 1930b.

78 The appearance of these fortifications is shown in archival plans: GStA SPK, XI HA, ref. F 70320 and SBB PK, ref. Db 1.33 1930b.

79 OStA KA, ref. G I c 203.

80 Letter from the King to Prince Henry, 22 September 1762, Schöning, *Militairische correspondenz*, pp.448–449.

81 Anon., 'Friedrich der Große als Ingenieur', pp.18–19.

King threatened not to surrender the part of Saxony he had captured. Not surprisingly, as soon as the peace was concluded, the King began to try to fortify the connection between Silesia and the county. Initially, however, he wanted to fortify the area around Wartha. This place was of special importance, as the main road communicating Glatz County with Silesia led there. Besides, there were at least two places where this road could be blocked; the bridge over the Glatzer Neisse and the Warthe Pass. Both of these places had already been protected by field fortifications on several occasions; the pass was fortified by the Prussians at the end of 1756, when, on the orders of *Feldmarschall* Kurt Christoph von Schwerin, and miners from Glatz under the command of *Leutnant* Paul von Gontzenbach worked there.[82] The fortifications were still visible in 1764, marked by *Oberst* Ludwig Wilhelm von Regler on a map of Glatz County of his authorship.[83]

Using his previous experience (which showed that the Wartha area was of the greatest importance for the county's communication with Silesia), the King decided to secure the area with a permanent defence. However, he did not want to build a large fortress there but limited himself to erecting a single fort. The assessment of the possibilities and the selection of the site for the new defence work was entrusted to Regler, who at the time was engaged in surveying Glatz County and designing the extension of the fortress at Glatz. This engineer carefully analysed the terrain conditions and concluded that it was not possible to secure the road running through the village with just one fort. Although his analysis showed that such a fort could be conveniently placed on Rosenkranzberg, a second fort would have to be built at the same time, on Kapellenberg, which dominates the area. However, even in such a situation, the enemy would be able to block both forts by building a chain of outposts surrounding Wartha in an arc from Briesnitz (Brzeźnica) through Giersdorf (Opolnica), Morischau (Morzyszów), Nieder Eicheu (Dębowina), Gierswalde (Laskówka), all the way to Johnsbach (Janowiec). In order to prevent this, a third fort had to be erected in the vicinity of Klapperberg (Kłapacz).[84] As can be seen, the potential defensive establishment controlling the passage through the barrier of the Warthagebirge (Góry Bardzkie) and Eulen Gebirge (Góry Sowie) in Wartha was, in the initial plans, to be extensive. Its additional disadvantage was that in the event of the loss of one of these forts the rest would be useless.[85] Not surprisingly, the fortification of this site was abandoned and the search for a new location began. Regler played a major role in this search. He led, together with lower-ranking engineers, the survey of the county with the aim of making a precise military map of the area. In doing so, he conducted a search for a convenient location for a new fortress. Two locations caught his eye; Hummrich (Wilczak) Mountain between Wiltsch (Wilcza) and Niclasdorf, and the Brand Lade hill near Silberberg. Just two months after drawing up a report negatively assessing the logic of building a fortress in Wartha, Regler sent detailed plans of the area to the King.[86] Both locations were carefully analysed by him. Indeed, the plans show not only the relief of the terrain, the layout of roads, watercourses and buildings, but also

82   Bonin, *Geschichte des Ingenieurkorps*, p.73.
83   SBB PK, ref. N 16992/2–4.
84   This analysis can be found in a report drawn up in Glatz on 12 May 1763, GStA SPK, I HA Rep 96 No 94, Bbb Regler, pp.3–4.
85   Bonin, *Geschichte des Ingenieurkorps*, p.97.
86   SBB PK, ref. N 19055/1; GStA SPK, I HA Rep 96 No 94, Bbb Regler, pp.31–32.

such information as the thickness of rock rubble and earth lying on solid rock. It is clear that in July 1763 both sites were being considered as potential locations for a new fortress. However, as other locations were still under consideration, construction work at Silberberg did not begin until 1764.

Preparatory work for the construction of the fortress lasted from the autumn of 1764 to the spring of 1765. The forest on the site of the future fortress was cut down, the sites for the future fortress core were marked out in the field and materials were collected for the construction of a brickworks.[87] In May the essential phase of construction began, as evidenced by the substantial funds allocated for this purpose from the coffers of the Silesian Ministry. On 4 May Minister Schlabrendorf paid Regler 10,000 thalers out of the 50,000 earmarked by the King for this purpose.[88] As a result, at the end of the month blasting work began on the site where the Donjon was to be built. In 1766 the buildings surrounding it began to be erected: the Tenaille, Stadt Bastion and Neudorfer Bastion. Work on the core of the fortress continued for a very long time. In the autumn of 1767, the King received a status report from the two officers working at Silberberg, Vincent Pinto and Ludwig Wilhelm von Regler, from which he concluded that work on the core (described in the letter to Pinto as *corps de la place* and in the letter to Regler as *Hauptwerk*) would be completed in the spring of 1768.[89] In that year, only the Donjon was ready; the construction of the rest of the buildings surrounding it dragged on until 1769. The reason the work took so long was because of the arduousness of the blasting work with which the moats were made. Although there were already foreign miners working at Silberberg, it is evident that their number was not sufficient, since the King ordered more to be brought in, and also ordered the recruitment of more stone cutters in Piedmont who were already experienced in this kind of work.[90] The King was very keen to progress the construction of the fortress; this is evidenced not only by the large sums he allocated it (in 1768 it was as much as 180,000 thalers), but also by his appeals to engineers carrying out work at other fortresses not to let their activities interfere with the construction of the Silberberg stronghold.[91] In 1768, the concept of the fortress changed, as detached works began to be built outside the core. The first to be constructed was the Horn Work, built between 1768 and 1771. The construction of two further structures – the Hohenstein and the Spitzberg – lasted from 1769 to 1772. In the same year, the fortifications on Kleine Strohhaube were also completed, the construction of which began in 1771. Information on the scale of the works is scarce. It is known that in late 1770 and early 1771 there were 350 labourers and 34 carts working at the fortress.[92] In March 1771, this number was said to have risen to 800 workmen and 40 carts, and in April to 1,800

---

87   Wolfgang Bleyl, *Silberberg, die Passfestung Schlesiens* (Breslau: Flemings Verlag, 1939), p.75.

88   Letter from Minister Schlabrendorf, 4 May 1765, GStA I HA Rep 96 No 94, Bbb Regler, p.28.

89   Letters of the King to Pinto and Regler, 15 October 1767, GStA SPK I HA Rep.96 B Abschriften von Kabinetsordres Bd.70, vol.II 1767, pp.353–354.

90   Letters from the King to Regler,31 June 1768, 3 and 24 May 1769 and to Count Finckenstein, 10 October 1768, GStA SPK, I HA Rep.96 B Abschriften von Kabinetsordres, Bd.70 vol.III, pp.282, 366; Bd.71, pp.120 recto and 136 verso.

91   Letters of the King to Minister Schlabrendorf, 3 May 1768 and to Lefèbvre and Daries, 13 December 1768, GStA SPK, I HA Rep.96 B Abschriften von Kabinetsordres, Bd.70 vol.III, pp.207, 428.

92   Letter from the King to Hoym, 10 October 1770, GStA SPK, I HA Rep.96 B Abschriften von Kabinetsordres, Bd.71, p.491 verso.

workmen.[93] In that year the cost of the work in the fortress was to be 22,000 thalers.[94] In the following year, 800 labourers and 30 carts were to work in the fortress, the works (specifically earthworks) were to cost 30,000 thalers.[95]

The fortress continued to be expanded. In 1773 the idea of fortifying further hills on the western edge of the fortress appeared. In 1774, these ideas were realised with the construction of the Flügel Redoubt and the Casemattierte Batterie in the Grosse Strohhaube fortification complex. These were the last major works to be erected in the fortress; over the next decade work was done to strengthen the earlier structures. In 1775, new sections of moats were erected on the southern and western slopes in front of the Horn Works to impede any possible assault. The works in 1776 cost 18,385 thalers.[96] Archival documents do not provide any information on the intended scope of the works; all that is known is that supplementary work was carried out on the fortifications of Grosse Strohhaube, where two stone caponiers were erected to defend the approach from the Mannsgrund valley. As the construction of the fortress had been underway for more than 10 years, the King showed signs of impatience. In March 1776, he told Regler that he expected the fortress to be completed in the spring.[97] He also ordered an audit of the construction finances for the entire previous decade. The audit showed that from May 1765 to October 1775 the fortress construction had been credited with 1,297,867 thalers, of which 1,297,856 thalers had been spent on the construction of the fortifications, with 11 thalers remaining.[98] However, the King's patience was put to a further test, as there was no indication when the work at Silberberg would cease. Although the main facilities had already been completed, further sections of escarpments (artificial slopes) and moats were being built all the time. In 1777 further escarpments were made in front of Grosse Strohhaube, and it is likely that the amount of 8,767 thalers allocated by the King for Silberberg in 1777 was related to this task.[99] However, it also was the case that already erected facilities were in very poor condition. In December 1776, the King received a report from the commandant of the fortress on the state of preservation of the local fortifications, which left him astonished at the extent of the damage. The veracity of the report was confirmed by Regler, who put the cost of repairs at 14,000 thalers. The damage was particularly to the bridges. In the end, the King allocated the sum

93   Letter from the King to Hoym, 10 February 1771, GStA SPK, I HA Rep.96 B Abschriften von Kabinetsordres, Bd.72, vol.VI 1771, p.56.

94   Letter from the King to Regler, 3 July 1771, GStA SPK, I HA Rep.96 B Abschriften von Kabinetsordres, Bd.72, vol.VI 1771, p.253.

95   Letters from the King to Regler and Hoym, 2 and 19 February 1772, GStA SPK, I HA Rep.96 B Abschriften von Kabinetsordres, Bd.72, vol.VII 1772, pp.49, 75.

96   King's letter to Regler, 24 September 1775, GStA SPK, I HA Rep.96 B Abschriften von Kabinetsordres, Bd.74, p.621.

97   Letter from the King to Regler, 27 March 1776, GStA SPK I HA Rep.96 B Abschriften von Kabinetsordres Bd.75, p.249.

98   Letter from the King to Regler, 24 April 1776, GStA SPK I HA Rep.96 B Abschriften von Kabinetsordres Bd.75, p.339.

99   We do not know the exact date of construction of this fragment, but it must have existed already in 1777. This is because the fragment can already be seen on the Plan de la Fortresse de Silberberg 1777, GStA SPK, XI HA, ref. B 70001; King's letter to Regler, 25 December 1776, GStA SPK, I HA Rep.96 B Abschriften von Kabinetsordres Bd.75, p.911.

of 11,000 thalers for repairs and the work was to be carried out in 1778.[100] However, it is not known whether this happened, as the War of the Bavarian Succession broke out in that year. Probably so, as the King did not return to this topic later. After the end of the war, work was again undertaken on the construction of escarpments and moats; this time a moat was erected between the Kleine Stohhaube and the Casemattierte Batterie. The work was carried out between 1781 and 1782. The latter year also saw the construction of the Brunnen Casematte, a new structure extending in front of the main moat; the Fuchs Brücke was also built to guard the passage through the north-eastern section of the moat surrounding the Strohhaube fortifications. This work was initially carried out by Regler, later taken over by *Major* von Haab, and completed by Regler after the *major*'s death. One hundred miners from Glatz worked on the blasting work.[101] Finally, in the years 1782–1784, the covered way linking the Casemattierte Batterie with the Flügel Redoubt was rebuilt. A moat was built directly in front of it, and a new section of embankments was erected to the east of the Brunnen Casematte. The last structure erected during the construction of the fortress was the terraced battery on the Mittel Strohhaube, which was completed in 1785. Work on the fortress after the War of the Bavarian Succession cost about 80,000 thalers. In June 1781, 32,000 thalers were allocated for it, and in September 1782, 12,000 thalers, but in December of that year the amount had risen to 23,000 thalers. In April 1784, further work at Silberberg was valued at 16,000 thalers, while in August 1784 the cost of building a new battery of the Mittel Strohhaube was set at 11,637 thalers.[102]

In addition to the defensive structures, others were built to serve the garrison. The most important of these were the barracks, which were built around 1770.[103] Around 1774, four large gunpowder magazines were also erected on the slopes in front of the fortress to store gunpowder during peacetime.[104]

The fortress was designed by the same officers who were active in its construction; Vincent Pinto and Ludwig Wilhelm von Regler. Pinto is more important for the origins of the fortress, as he made the first design.[105] This officer proposed the construction of a single,

100 King's letters to Regler and Rossieres, 2,3 and 18 December 1776, 3 January and 11 December 1777, GStA SPK I HA Rep.96 B Abschriften von Kabinetsordres Bd.75, pp.870, 871, 897; Bd.76, p.56 recto; Bd.77, p.180 verso.

101 King's letters to Regler and Haas, 23 July and 5 August 1781, GStA SPK, I HA Rep.96 B Abschriften von Kabinetsordres, Bd.81, pp.542–543, p.584; Bd.84, p.724.

102 Letters from the King to Regler, Breslau Kammer and Harroy, 23 July and 5 August 1781, 8 September 1782, 7 April and 26 August 1784, GStA SPK, I HA Rep.96 B Abschriften von Kabinetsordres, Bd.81, p.420; Bd.82, pp.857, 1184; Bd.84, pp.310, 724.

103 The year 1774 appears in the literature to date as the date of the erection of the Silberberg barracks. This is contradicted by some sources. As early as October 1770, Regler asked for money from the King to equip the barracks. However, these funds, amounting to 7,632 thalers, were not made available until 1772. Since the subject of this correspondence was money for equipment, we can conclude that the construction of the barracks had been completed earlier. Letters from the King to Regler, 25 October 1770, GStA SPK, I HA Rep.96 B Abschriften von Kabinetsordres, Bd.71, p.423 verso and Bd.72, vol. VII 1772, p.223.

104 The chronology given below is based, except for source-confirmed facts, on: Bonin, *Geschichte des Ingenieurkorps*, p.98; Anon., 'Friedrich der Große als Ingenieur', p.19.

105 We will say more about this officer and also about his ideas and connections with the King in subchapter on Glatz fortress in the period after 1763.

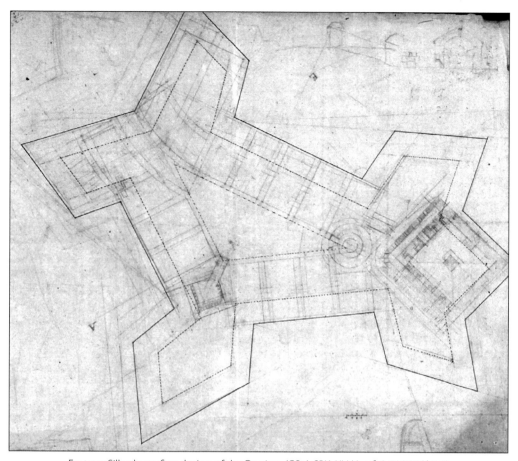

Fortress Silberberg, first design of the Donjon. (GStA SPK, XI HA ref. A 70007 Bl.5, 8)

relatively small defensive work on top of the mountain Brand Lade. This work was to have a plan similar to a triangle. One of its corners was to be defended by two half-bastions, the other corner was defended by a bastion, traditional in form, while the third corner was defended by two half-bastions divided by a triangular corner. The entire structure was to be fully casemated. Another interesting element was the well-tank, located in one corner of the triangular courtyard of the fortress.[106] Pinto's ideas did not find royal approval and the project was not realised. However, Pinto remained at Silberberg and still participated in the design process. In March 1768, he presented the King with another design for a work that was intended to defend the fortress against attack from the Fuchsberg mountain. However, the King also criticised this idea, describing Pinto's proposed work as 'useless and unnecessary'.[107] Unfortunately, it is not known which defensive work this might have been.

---

106 *Les Idees de S. De Ms. Le Capit. De Pinto,* GStA SPK, XI HA, ref. A 70007;5, 8.
107 Letter from the King to Pinto, 18 March 1768, GStA SPK, I HA Rep.96 B Abschriften von Kabinetsordres, Bd.70 vol. III, p.107.

After Pinto, the fortress was designed and built by the same engineer who was involved in the process of selecting the site for it, von Regler. However, there is every indication that he did not carry out this project on the basis of entirely his own ideas. In the holdings of the Berlin Staatsbibliothek there is a handwritten sketch of the fortification of Silberberg, which appears to have been a conceptual drawing preceding the essential design work.[108] The drawing shows the future fortress. In the centre of the foundation is a four-sided structure with four corner towers. It is surrounded by a moat and there is a large ravelin in front of one of its curtains. Two covered ways diverge from this main work, one short, running south towards a small five-sided redoubt, and the other north, defended by two four-sided structures, ending with a small triangular-plan building. The structures depicted on this plan are fairly well identifiable. The central work is obviously the later Donjon, with the rest of works reduced to a ravelin. The structure to the south is located on the site of the later Horn Work, and the structure to the north of the Donjon, at the end of the road with two four-sided redoubts, sits on the site of the unrealised work on the Klosenberg. Note also the two hills that are highlighted in the drawing – one 800 and the other 1,200 paces away from the core of the fortress. The sketch is accompanied by a legend giving details such as the depth of the moat (100 paces, counting to the top of the rampart), its width (10 rods), the garrison (2,000 men), and the manning of the redoubts advanced in front of the core (30–50 soldiers). In addition, there is also information about the construction in progress; that 4,000 labourers work there daily, each of whom got four *groschen* a day, and 1 thaler for a cart with two horses. Six engineers with the rank of *leutnant*, two with the rank of *kapitän* and one *oberstleutnant* were involved in the works.

The drawing described is anonymous but can be regarded with a high degree of probability as the work of Frederick. Although it is not signed by the King, the royal signature is absent from all the sketches of fortifications to which his authorship is attributed, with the famous sketch of the fortifications of Graudenz, published several times, at the forefront. The drawing described has, moreover, a characteristic clumsy style similar to other known sketches by Frederick – of both military and civilian buildings. Frederick's authorship is also suggested by the way in which the Donjon is depicted. The work appears here as a four-sided castle with four towers. Such a medieval form was unusual for defensive architecture of the time. However, Neo-Gothic was making its appearance in works of civil architecture in this part of Europe in the second half of the eighteenth century. The first work of its kind in Prussia was the Nauener Tor in Potsdam, a gatehouse established in 1755, which owed its Neo-Gothic form precisely to the ideas of Frederick. It was one of the first Neo-Gothic works in Prussia, and even one of the first on the European continent.[109] So, it is likely that the form of the newly designed Silberberg fortress was also influenced by the new fashion for the Gothic era prevailing in civil architecture, the manifestations of which were noticed and appreciated by the Prussian king. The search for analogies and inspirations for the Silberberg Donjon in the Neo-Gothic architecture of the time is all the more justified, as some eighteenth-century commentators described this object as a work of art, rather than a

---

108 SBB PK, ref. X 33811–4.
109 Hans-Joachim Giersberg, *Friedrich als Bauherr: Studien zur Architektur des 18. Jahrhunderts in Berlin und Potsdam* (Berlin: Siedler, 1986), pp.183–187.

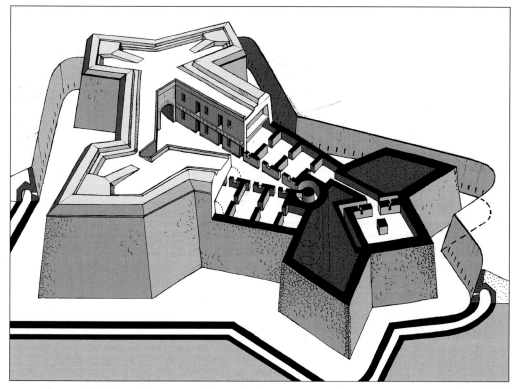

Fortress Silberberg, Donjon according to the first project. (Study by Mariusz Wojciechowski)

fortress actually guarding Silesia.[110] Moreover, the form of the Silberberg Donjon is drastically different from the fortifications designed by Prussian military engineers of the time. Military engineers, unlike civilian architects, had no reason to be interested in the Gothic. Therefore, Frederick seems to have been the only person to have influenced the form of the newly built fortress who was not constrained by schemes derived from the traditions of defensive architecture and knew and appreciated the emerging Neo-Gothic style.

There are (or were in the eighteenth century) a number of medieval and late medieval structures that can be considered as inspirations for the Silberberg Donjon. Previous literature has pointed out, among other things, similarities to the English sixteenth-century coastal fortifications of Henry VIII and to Italian castles (Castello in Casale).[111] However,

---

110 Rudolph Wilhelm von Kaltenborn, *Briefe eines alten Preussischen Officiers, verschiedene Characterzüge Friedrichs des Einzigen betreffend: Mit Rücksicht auf das Zimmermannsche Werk über eben diesen Gegenstand* (Hohenzollern: Schulbuchhandlung, 1790), vol.1, p.79.

111 Maria Lewicka-Cempa, 'Twierdza w Srebrnej Górze: Problemy ochrony konserwatorskiej, Dzieje warowni', in Maria Lewicka-Cempa, Waldemar Brzoskwinia (eds), *O skuteczną ochronę fortyfikacji historycznych* (Warszawa–Kraków: Agencja wydawnicza Zebra, 1995), p.65; Grzegorz Bukal, 'Idea donżonu w pruskie fortyfikacji XVIII wieku', in T. Przerwa, G. Podruczny, (eds), *Twierdza srebrnogórska* (Srebrna Góra: Srebrnogórska Oficyna Wydawnicza, 2006), p.47.

it should be stressed that English forts were not widely known in the eighteenth century; the same was true of most of the medieval fortresses mentioned. When looking for other medieval models, attention should be paid above all to those structures that were well known at the time, especially buildings known from graphic representations. Such buildings, which not only show a formal convergence with the Silberberg stronghold, but were also famous, were medieval French strongholds. The Silberberg Donjon bears the greatest resemblance to that of the chateau of Vincennes, the sub-Parisian residence of the Kings of France. Although Frederick never visited the chateau, he was probably familiar with it. In the eighteenth century, this fortress was considered the prime example of a Donjon – as such, it was presented by Belidor in his dictionary for engineers and artillerymen.[112] Another building with similar formal features and commonly associated, even perhaps more so than Vincennes, was the Bastille in Paris. This building was also often depicted in the pre-revolutionary period, as it was famous as a prison; there were even several books written in the eighteenth century describing it.[113] The building was also very prominent in the Paris skyline, as it was located at the city's border, at St Anthony's Gate. In the field of French medieval architecture, it is of course possible to identify a number of other Donjons that show similarities to the Silberberg; the castles of Etampes, Provins or Arques. However, it is the Donjon at Vincennes that is the most likely model for the Silberberg one.

Remaining within the realm of medieval architecture, we must necessarily draw attention to two more buildings, the late medieval castles of Navaigne and Franchiment on the Belgian-French border. Although these buildings are not as well-known as those described above, they may have had just as great an influence on the form of the Silberberg fortresses, as their plans were included by Vauban in his architectural treatise. These fortresses are not his design proposals, but merely serve to demonstrate his mining techniques, for they were decommissioned by Vauban at the behest of his king.[114] As Vauban's treatises were extremely influential on the defensive architecture of the eighteenth century, it is therefore extremely likely that the medieval buildings depicted in one of them as objects of mine experiments inspired Frederick and influenced the final form of the Silberberg Donjon.[115]

The long list of potential inspirations for the Silberberg stronghold is rounded off by an eighteenth-century building; Scotland's Inveraray Castle. This building was rebuilt in Neo-Gothic style in the 1740s and is one of the earliest examples of British Gothic Revival. This building – four-sided in plan with cylindrical towers on each corner – was well known to the Prussian king, Frederick having been inspired by it already when designing the

---

112 Bernard Forest de Bélidor, *Dictionaire portatif de l'ingenieur et de l'artilleur* (Paris: Jombert, 1768), p.229.

113 J. A. d'Archambaud Bucquoy, *Événement des plus rares, ou L'histoire du Sr abbé Cte de Buquoy: singulièrement son évasion du Fort-l'Évêque et de la Bastille* (Bonnefoy: Unknown Publisher, 1719); René Auguste Constantin de Renneville, *Inquisition Françoise ou l'historie de la Bastille* (Amsterdam-Leide: Lakeman, Verbeek, 1740), among others.

114 In addition to the plans for these castles, Vauban's book describes the technical issues involved in blowing them up. See Vauban, *De l'attaque et de la defense des places*, pp.26–31.

115 This problem has already been written about by Ms Lewicka-Cempa, but she erroneously suggested that these objects were Vauban's design proposals. Lewicka-Cempa, 'Twierdza w Srebrnej Górze', p.65.

Potsdam Nauener Tor; it can certainly be assumed that the object also influenced the form of the Silberberg Donjon.[116]

As can be seen, numerous analogies for the Silberberg Donjon can be found in medieval architecture. Their search was justified not only by the nomenclature associated with the building – after all, names such as castle, Donjon had medieval connotations then, as now. The medieval character of the fortress was already perceived by people in the eighteenth century; the German geographer Anton Friedrich Büsching first drew attention to this feature in his 1786 description of Silesia, followed by Mirabeau in his 1788 description of the Prussian army. In both of these works, the Donjon is described as follows: 'The main work is a castle of Gothic architecture, with great towers.'[117]

Unfortunately, the drawings described – both those of Pinto and those attributed to Frederick – are not dated. We can only assume that they were drawn before 1766, as work on the core of the fortress was already being carried out on a large scale at that time. At that time there must have been at least a preliminary design, close to the completed one.

The Grosse Strohhaube fortifications extending beyond the core of the fortress – the Hochenstein, the Horn Work, the Spitzberg and the Kleine Strohhaube – owe their creation to Regler's designs. There is no strong evidence for this, as the designs of the fortress preserved in the Berlin Staatsbibliothek are not signed by this engineer. However, the surviving letters of the King concerning the fortress of Silberberg leave no doubt in this regard. The King addressed his letters exclusively to Regler. There is even one letter preserved in which the King mentions a plan of Silberberg made by Regler.[118] Probably in the case of these works, the King refrained from any interference in the project, as we have no indication of this. The situation was completely different in the case of the set of fortifications of Grosse Strohhaube, which owed their shape to the King's designs. While in the case of the Donjon the authorship of Frederick is plausible, but nevertheless a hypothesis, in the case of the fortifications of the western part of the fortress we do not have to prove anything, as planning materials have been preserved which explicitly state this. Frederick designed two elements there; the layout of the fortifications of Grosse Strohhaube and the course of the defensive works which connected Grosse and Kleine Strohhaube.

The first idea for solving the problem of the Grosse Strohhaube appeared on one of the plans presenting the second conception of the shape of the fortress.[119] It proposed blasting a long moat in the rock, running in an irregular line from Mittel Strohhaube through the described flat elevation in front of Grosse Strohhaube. Such a solution would certainly have made it difficult for a potential attacker to occupy the area and use it to build siege batteries, but it was provisional and would not have secured the fortress sufficiently. It was necessary to erect a defensive work there. As with the earlier projected structures, there were various ideas for erecting a fortification at this location. Fortunately, a plan

116 Giersberg, *Friedrich als Bauherr*, pp.183–187.

117 Anton Friedrich Büsching, *Große Erdbeschreibung* (Brunn: Traßler, 1786), vol.12, pp.567–568, Honoré Gabriel Riquetti de Mirabeau, *De la monarchie prussienne: sous Frédéric le Grand* (Londres: Unknown Publisher, 1788), vol.4. pt.II, p.297.

118 Letter from the King to Regler, 19 January 1769, GStA SPK, I HA Rep.96 B Abschriften von Kabinetsordres, Bd.71, p.19 recto.

119 SBB PK, ref. X 33807–5.

Fortress Silberberg, unrealised project with two communications, fort on Kleine Stochhaube and Klosenberg but without fort on Spitzberg. (GStA SPK, XI HA ref. A 70001)

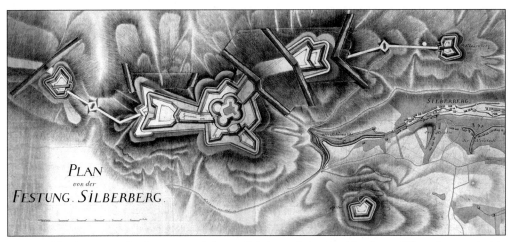

Fortress Silberberg, unrealised project with fort on Spitzberg, Kleine Stochhaube and Klosenberg and with two versions of the fortification of the fortress core – with and without Communications (on tabs). (GStA SPK, XI HA ref. A 70003)

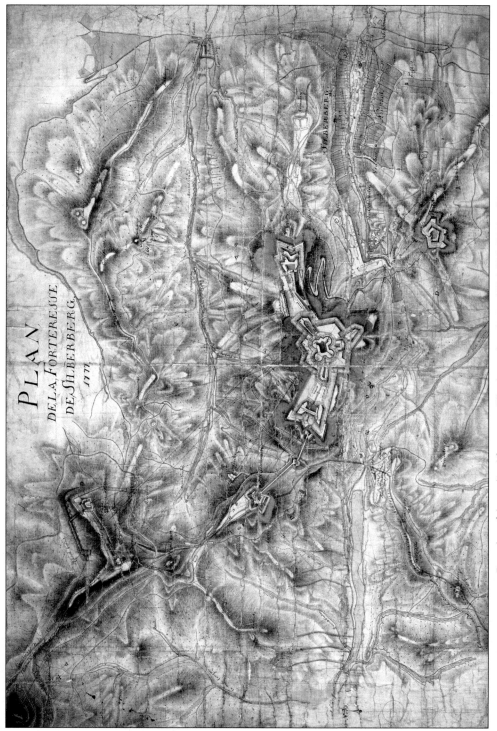

First plan of the realised fortress at Silberberg, dated 1777. (GStA SPK, XI HA ref. B 70001)

showing two concepts for the fortification of this place,[120] as well as a letter from the King concerning the choice of one of them, has survived.[121] The author of one concept is Frederick, and the other is *Generalmajor* Franz Ludwig von Rossieres, a commander on the fortress. Both concepts were conceived in the spring of 1773. The designs differ considerably. Rossieres proposed the erection of a single polygonal redoubt at the very top of the Strohhaube. The King, on the other hand, had a different idea. He ignored the main summit and proposed to erect two small works connected by a curtain, occupying the entire width of the plain below the main summit. Both solutions had their good and bad points. The King's idea maximised the protection of a potentially dangerous point for the fortress. The construction of the two redoubts was a safeguard against the loss of this point in the event of a surprise attack by the enemy. Even if one of the redoubts was successfully captured, the other remained to effectively control the area. The problem, which was not solved in this version, was the threat coming from the neighbouring, even higher hill – Hahn Kuppe – which was the location of a potential siege battery, this time attacking the works of Grosse Strohhaube. Rossiere's idea was based on neutralising this threat. He positioned his redoubt so that one of the redoubt's defence lines faced this hill. In addition, he planned to remove the summit of Hahn Kuppe and shape it in such a way as to make the establishment of a siege battery impossible. His final idea was to cut a deep moat in the rocks, located between the redoubt and Hahn Kuppe. The location proposed by Rossieres also had the advantage of affecting not only the aforementioned hill, but also other potential approaches. There was, however, a significant drawback to this idea; it was a single site, isolated and far removed from the other works of the fortress, making it vulnerable to capture by sudden attack. Besides, as the King emphasised in his letter, the erection of a defensive work on Hahn Kuppe would result in the forces available in the Silberberg garrison being too dispersed. Guided by these considerations, the King ordered his concept to be realised.

The erection of these two works as conceived by Frederick did not completely secure the fortress. Although the new works moved the location of potential siege batteries to a safe distance from the core of the fortress, another threat remained. Due to the nature of the defensive works built on the western side of the fortress, as well as the nature of the terrain, sites such as the Horn Work, Kleine and Grosse Strohhaube, were at great risk of being stormed. This was particularly a problem for the Casemattierte Batterie and Flügel Redoubt, which were relatively small and did not provide sufficient control over the surrounding terrain. There was, moreover, the possibility of bypassing these redoubt facilities and capturing them by assault from the neck of the road. Thus, the next task, after the construction of the fortifications, was to create suitable obstacles against a sudden attack. This task had already been under way since the late 1760s, the first mention of the creation of escarpments (artificial slopes) dating from as early as January 1769. In a letter of the 15th of that month, the King ordered work on the fortress to continue, but ordered the suspension of blasting work on the escarpments, which he

120 SBB PK, ref. X 33811–7,8.
121 King's letters to Regler, 24 March 1773, GStA SPK, I HA Rep.96 B Abschriften von Kabinetsordres, Bd.73, p.80.

wished to examine in person.[122] As can be seen, Frederick was personally involved from the start in the creation of this element of the defences. The erection of artificial obstacles continued in subsequent years, with as much as 20,000 thalers allocated for their construction in 1774.[123] It was then that the construction of the largest section of these obstacles began, which eventually reached a length of almost two kilometres. This line starts from Kleine Strohhaube, encircles the hill of Mittle Strohhaube and circles a wide arc around the fortifications on Grosse Strohhaube. At least five people were involved in establishing its final shape. Rossiere probably initiated it. His projects are connected with the first examples of the application of this solution to the Silberberg fortress and he proposed shielding the fortress core with strings of escarpments and an outer moat.[124] It was during his command at Silberberg that the first section of the anti-assault obstacles in front of Grosse Strohhaube was created; the section of the outer moat running in front of the front of the fortifications, from the Casemattierte Batterie to the Flügel Redoubt.[125] Frederick was again personally involved in the further development of this line of obstructions. In a letter to Regler dated 4 November 1779, the King announced that he wanted to connect the fortifications of the Grosse Strohhaube, hitherto only connected to the rest of the fortress by a line of palisades, with the fort on the Kleine Strohhaube by means of a long line of escarpments. In addition, he wanted to extend the moat surrounding Grosse Strohhaube from the north. He ordered Regler to make a design and cost estimate with the commander of the fortress, *Major* de Haas.[126] The King, as was common for him, could not wait for his engineers' proposals and decided to draw up a design for the new line of fortifications himself.[127] This drawing is still preserved today; it shows the course of the old and new moats and escarpments, a cross section through the escarpments, and a brief description.[128] The engineers, however, did not need to be urged; Regler had already made his estimate on 18 November, but it only reached the King after the sovereign had sent a letter urging him to do so.[129] However, even if it had arrived sooner, it would have been of no use, as the King did not like Regler's proposal very much. The cost estimate of 48,690 thalers was considered by the King to be far too high; an acceptable amount for him was 20,000 thalers.[130] A cost estimate drawn up by

---

122 Letter from the King to Regler, 15 January 1769, GStA SPK, I HA Rep.96 B Abschriften von Kabinetsordres, Bd.71, p.19 recto.

123 Letter from the King to Regler, 14 October 1773, GStA SPK, I HA Rep.96 B Abschriften von Kabinetsordres, Bd.73, p.326.

124 GStA SPK, HA XI, ref. A 70003.

125 We do not know the exact date of construction of this fragment, but it must have existed already in 1777. Indeed, this fragment can already be seen on the plan: GStA SPK, XI HA, ref. B 70001.

126 Letter from the King to Regler, 4 November 1779, GStA SPK, I HA Rep.96 B Abschriften von Kabinetsordres, Bd.79, p.1124.

127 Letters from the King to Regler, 21 November 1779, GStA SPK, I HA Rep.96 B Abschriften von Kabinetsordres, Bd.79, pp.1158, 1161.

128 SBB PK, ref. X 33811–5.

129 Anschlag des bey der Festung Silberberg nach Sr. Majestät Allerhöchsten Idee zu construirenden Escarpements, und zu verlängenden Grabens, Glatz 18 November 1779; SBB PK, ref. X 33812–3;

130 Letter from the King to Regler, 24 November 1779, GStA SPK, I HA Rep.96 B Abschriften von Kabinetsordres, Bd.79, p.1165; Letter from de Haas to the King, 5 December 1779, SBB PK, ref. X 33812–5.

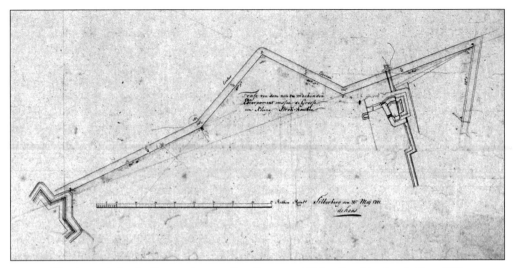

Silberberg, design for the moat connecting Grosse and Kleine Strochhaube, de Haas, 1781.
(GStA SPK, XI HA ref. D 70011)

Major de Haas at the beginning of December that year, amounting to 32,000 thalers, also failed to meet the royal conditions, but was decidedly better.[131] Above all, Haas proposed a different profile for the escarpments, which were to be slightly shallower and narrower than those proposed by Regler.[132] Also, the outer moat near the Flügel Redoubt was to be shallower. Changes were also made to the alignment of these fortifications. In the case of the escarpments, he proposed bypassing the hill of Mittel Strohhaube with a wider arch than in Regler's design; in the case of the outer moat, he proposed significantly curving it towards the south, so that it could be shot through by cannon situated on the right flank of the central corner of Kleine Strohhaube.[133] The start of the implementation of the projects was protracted, and the money for these facilities was not budgeted by the King until 1781. From the amount granted (32,000 thalers), it can be inferred that Haas's design was selected for implementation.[134]

In 1781, another person – *Major* Haab – began to of design new facilities in the fortress. This officer had already presented his proposals for improvements to the Silberberg fortress on his own initiative in November 1779, but the King did not decide at that time to include this officer in the work at Silberberg. This did not happen until August 1781. At that time,

---

131 Plan des bey der Vestung Silberberg nach Sr. Königl. Maj. Allerhöchsten Idee zu construirenden Escarpements und zu verlängenden Grabens, SBB PK, ref. X 33812–3; Anschlag des bey der Festung Silberberg nach Sr. Majestät Allerhöchsten Idee zu construirenden Escarpements, und zu verlängenden Grabens, Silberberg 5 Dezember 1779.

132 The proposals of both engineers are presented in the drawing: SBB PK, ref. X 33812–2.

133 The course of these lines compared to Regler's proposal is shown on the plan: SBB PK, ref. X 33812–3.

134 Letter of the King to Haab, 20 October 1780, GStA SPK, I HA Rep.96 B Abschriften von Kabinetsordres, Bd.80, p.665; Letter of the King to Haab, 21 February 1781, GStA SPK, I HA Rep.96 B Abschriften von Kabinetsordres, Bd.81, p.123; King's letter to von Hoym, 15 June 1781, GStA SPK, I HA Rep.96 B Abschriften von Kabinetsordres, Bd.81, p.420.

the King informed the fortress commander, Haas, that Haab would come to the fortress and make a more detailed estimate.[135] Haab's final takeover of the work at Silberberg took place a year later, in August 1782.[136] He did not lead the work for long, as he died suddenly in December of the same year. However, during this short period he not only carried out work on the basis of earlier designs; he also managed to add further modifications. The modifications included the rebuilding of the covered way linking the Casemattierte Batterie to the Flügel Redoubt, the construction of a moat in front of this covered road, and the erection of a new section of embankment to the east of the Brunnen Casematte. All of this new work was to cost 23,000 thalers. This further expansion was to be carried out by Regler after Haab's death.[137] The same engineer also continued his design work. In 1783, he drew up a design for the Fuchs Tor, a small structure guarding a bridge over one of the moats covering the fortifications of the Grosse Strohhaube.[138] He also planned further works; all that is known about them is that the King did not like the cost of their implementation (6,000 thalers), and that he ordered the ravelin and rampart road to be abandoned for the time being.[139] Regler was also involved in the planning of the last investment in the fortress under Frederick. In August 1784, the King approved his designs for the works on Kirch-Berg and the Kleine and Mittel Strohhaube. This most likely involved the completion of the moats and the erection of artillery batteries on the Mittel Strohhaube. The King not only approved Regler's ideas without reservation, but also allocated additional funds, not provided for in the fortress construction budget for that year, in the amount of 11,637 thalers.[140] With this project, completed in 1785, Regler finished the development of the fortress. During the last two years of Frederick's reign, work at Silberberg, carried out by the next engineer, *Major Harroy*, concerned only repairs to existing structures.[141]

135 Letter from the King to Haab, 11 November 1779, GStA SPK, I HA Rep.96 B Abschriften von Kabinetsordres, Bd.79, p.1143; Letter from the King to Haas, August 1781, GStA SPK, I HA Rep.96 B Abschriften von Kabinetsordres, Bd.81, p.653.

136 Letter from the King to Regler, 19 August 1782, GStA SPK, I HA Rep.96 B Abschriften von Kabinetsordres, Bd.82, p.789.

137 Letters from the King to Regler, 15 December 1782 and 1 January 1783, GStA SPK, I HA Rep.96 B Abschriften von Kabinetsordres, Bd.82, p.1184, Bd.83 p.4; GStA SPK, I HA Rep 96, No 94, Bbb, Regler, Ludwig Wilhelm, p.26.

138 Letter from the King to Regler, 22 August 1783, GStA SPK, I HA Rep.96 B Abschriften von Kabinetsordres, Bd.83, p.712. The King sent this engineer to make a design for a 'wall with loopholes'. The only structure in Silberberg that can be characterised in this way is the Fusch Thor.

139 Letter from the King to Regler, 25 August 1783, GStA SPK, I HA Rep.96 B Abschriften von Kabinetsordres, Bd.83, p.720.

140 Letter from the King to Regler, 26 August 1784, GStA SPK, I HA Rep.96 B Abschriften von Kabinetsordres, Bd.84, p.724.

141 King's letters to Harroy, 20 February, 13 March, 28 August and 28 September 1785, GStA SPK, I HA Rep.96 B Abschriften von Kabinetsordres, Bd.85, pp.175, 247, 897, 1016.

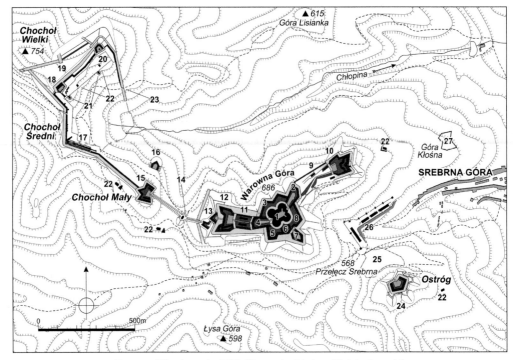

Fortress Silberberg, in 1786. (Drawn by Mariusz Wojciechowski)

View of the fortifications of Srebrna Góra fortress in 1786. (Drawn by Mariusz Wojciechowski)

Fortress Silberberg, Donjon and surrounding bastions, present state. (Photo: Grzegorz Basiński)

Fortress Silberberg, view of the Horn Work, its esplanade and core with Donjon, present state. (Photo: Grzegorz Basiński)

Glatz

A few years after work began at Silberberg, the rebuilding of Glatz, a mountain fortress with an older provenance, was undertaken. The two fortresses are linked, both by the designers and by the nature of the buildings under construction.

During the Seven Years War, in 1760, Glatz was captured by the imperial army commanded by Laudon. As a result, Glatz County came under Habsburg rule for three years; it did not return to Prussia until 1763, as a result of the Peace of Hubertusburg. For three years the Austrians not only maintained a garrison in the fortress, but also undertook its expansion. They managed to reinforce the older structures (the Neue Flèche in front of the Schäferberg fort and the Kranich), as well as carrying out new projects. The most important was the connection between the main fortress and Schäferberg by means of two lines of fortifications. The eastern, stronger one, consisted of two half-bastions. The first, St Theresa's, reached from the fortifications of Schäferberg up to the bank of the Neisse; the new Theresa's Gate was located in the adjacent section of the curtain. The second bastion, St Francis's, sheltered the Franciscan monastery and the fortress bakery, and together with two sections of curtains connected the main fortress to the riverbank. The second defensive line was of lesser importance. It was a wall with loopholes connecting the covered way in front of a Fer á Cheval with the bank of the Neisse. In this way, all the fortification complexes in Glatz were combined into one defensive system. An project of lesser importance was the erection of a small earthen defensive work near the mills and the Glatz water tower.[142] As can be seen, by the time the Prussian army re-entered Glatz the fortress was in good condition. It is therefore not surprising that its reconstruction was carried out as a second priority. The King rightly stated that priority was to be given to the stronghold at Silberberg, which – should a situation similar to that of 1760 be repeated – would allow Glatz to come to its aid. Modernisation of the defences at Glatz therefore did not begin until 1770.[143] Preliminary work was carried out as early as 1769, when the King ordered Regler to travel to Glatz and examine whether the stonework in this fortress would cause much trouble.[144]. However, the main work began in 1771. At that time Glatz became the most important fortress construction of the Prussian state. For 1770, it was planned to spend as much as 100,000 thalers on the fortifications there, half the amount earmarked for Silesian fortresses. The following year, expenditure on Glatz doubled, to 200,000 thalers.[145] A further increase was recorded in 1772. It was initially planned to spend as much as 300,000 thalers on Glatz, but eventually the amount was 241,800 thalers.[146] In the following year, expenditure on this fortress fell

---

142 Rapports und Projects Plan von der Haupt und Granitz Vöstung und Stadt Glatz pro Anno 1761 u. 1762, OStA KA, ref. K II f 26–2.

143 Anon., 'Friedrich der Große als Ingenieur', p.17; Bonin, *Geschichte des Ingenieurkorps*, p.104.

144 Letter from the King to Regler, 4 March 1769, GStA SPK, I HA Rep.96 B Abschriften von Kabinetsordres, Bd.71, p.65 recto.

145 Letters from the King to Minister Hoym, 14 May and 19 September 1770, GStA SPK, I HA Rep.96 B Abschriften von Kabinetsordres, Bd.71, pp.394 verso, 473 recto.

146 Letter from the King to Regler, 17 January 1772, GStA SPK, I HA Rep.96 B Abschriften von Kabinetsordres, Bd.72, p.24; letter from the King to Minister Hoym, October 1772, GStA SPK, I HA Rep.96 B Abschriften von Kabinetsordres, Bd.72, p.223.

slightly and amounted to approximately 200,000 thalers.[147] Data on the cost of building the fortress for later years is incomplete, but shows that the work had lost its intensity. There is only one mention – in 1776 only 21,000 thalers were planned to be spent on the fortifications there.[148] In the spending plans for Silesian fortresses in 1774–1775 and in 1777, Glatz does not appear. The intensity of work at the fortress in the early 1770s is also evidenced by data on the number of workers involved in the works. In the winter season of 1770–1771, as many as 1,000 labourers with 66 carts were supposed to work there; in the spring, this number probably increased significantly, unfortunately there is no information on this.[149] In 1772, initially 1,500 workers and 70 carts were to be involved, and from 5 April 2,500 workers.[150]

Chronologically, the first element transformed at Glatz was the inner part of the main fortress. The builders first dealt with the removal of the old castle, in whose place a completely new defensive work was created, called, as in Silberberg, the Donjon. The work was supposed to be completed as early as 1772, at least that is what the King expected from his engineers.[151] However, this did not happen; after 1773, the Crown Work was rebuilt, and after 1776 the Kranich was modernised, with a new casemate for the garrison and a masonry shelter for the guns – a hangar. The entire work was presided over by Regler, who had been commandant of the fortress since 1773. After the War of the Bavarian Succession, the works of the Schäferberg were also modernised, with a new envelope, an outer moat and a new garrison casemate.[152] Work on these works began in June 1780; 200 workmen were employed to rebuild the fort, and 10 four-horse carts were used.[153] The King had hoped to complete the work quickly, but in the meantime it took more than a year; it was not completed until August 1781. The King blamed Regler and in February 1781 he wrote, among other things, that the work should have taken a few weeks, and Regler was already extending it into a second year.[154]

This was not the end of it, as in 1782 further works were carried out there; the Hassitzer and the Neue Flèche were rebuilt. In both, the moat was improved and the neck section rebuilt. In addition, in the former, musket coffers were created to defend the moat bottom. Another investment made by Frederick, both on Schäferberg and at Glatz in general, was

---

147　The cost estimate for the work on the Silesian fortresses for 1774 was 274,698 thalers. Of this, 60,000 thalers was to be allocated to the fortresses in Silberberg and Breslau. The entire remaining amount of 214,000 thalers was probably allocated to Glatz, as no major work was being carried out on the other fortresses at that time. Letter from the King to Regler, 14 October 1773, GStA SPK, I HA Rep.96 B Abschriften von Kabinetsordres, Bd.73, p.326.

148　King's letter to Regler, 24 September 1775, GStA SPK, I HA Rep.96 B Abschriften von Kabinetsordres, Bd.74, p.621.

149　Letter from the King to Minister Hoym, 10 October 1770, GStA SPK, I HA Rep.96 B Abschriften von Kabinetsordres, Bd.71, p.491 verso.

150　Letter from the King to Minister Hoym, 19 February 1772, GStA SPK, I HA Rep.96 B Abschriften von Kabinetsordres, Bd.72, vol.VII 1772, p.75.

151　Letter from the King to Regeler, 2 February 1772, GStA SPK, I HA Rep.96 B Abschriften von Kabinetsordres, Bd.72, vol. VII 1772, p.49.

152　Anon., 'Friedrich der Große als Ingenieur', p.17, Bonin, *Geschichte des Ingenieurkorps*, p.104.

153　Letter from the King to Regler, 25 May 1780, GStA SPK, I HA Rep.96 B Abschriften von Kabinetsordres, Bd.80, p.404.

154　Letters from the King to Regler, 21 February and 5 August 1781, GStA SPK, I HA Rep.96 B Abschriften von Kabinetsordres, Bd.81, pp.123, 584.

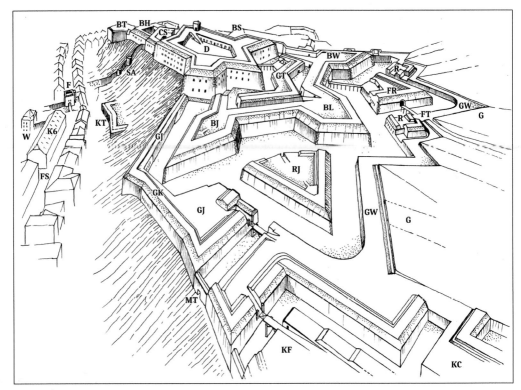

Fortress Glatz in the 1780s. (Drawn by Mariusz Wojciechowski)

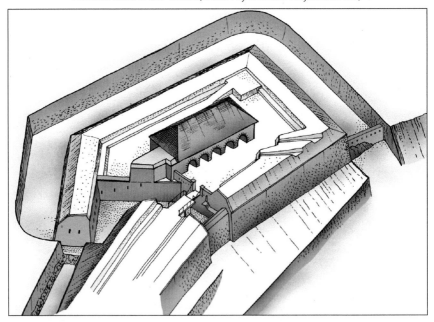

Fortress Glatz, crane with hangar, circa 1780. (Drawn by Mariusz Wojciechowski)

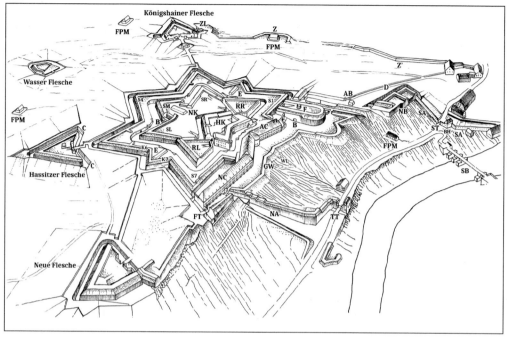

Fortress Glatz, fort on Schäferberg circa 1786. (Drawn by Mariusz Wojciechowski)

the construction of the Neue Batterie. This was planned in 1785, and is known from the King's letter to Regler, in which the sovereign traditionally criticised his engineer for the excessive costing of this facility. In 1785 there were 300 workers and 30 four-horse carts in Glatz.[155]

The construction of Neue Batterie was completed before August 1786, as it was to be visited by one of the aides-de-camp, an *Oberst* Ernst Friedrich Karl von Hanstein, who was to make a tour of Silesia on behalf of the sovereign, which Frederick, lying on his deathbed, was for the first time unable to carry out himself.[156]

In addition to the works on Schäferberg, a small modernisation of the city's fortifications is also known. In 1780–1781 an extension of the Mühlen Bastion, built 40 years earlier, was planned and in 1782 realised.[157]

Some work was also carried out on the main fortress in 1783–1786, but the sources found do not allow us to say what it consisted of.

Despite the late start of construction work, conceptual work on the modernisation of the local fortifications began very quickly. In fact, Regler's memorandum of May 1763,

---

155 Letter from Regler to the King, 15 February 1785, GStA SPK I HA Rep 96 no 94, Bbb Regler, pp.30–31.
156 Letters, 25 July and 4 August 1786, GStA SPK, I HA Rep.96 B Abschriften von Kabinetsordres, Bd.86, p.682, 708.
157 Letters from the King to Regler, 3 January 1780 and 30 August 1781, GStA SPK, I HA Rep.96 B Abschriften von Kabinetsordres, Bd.80, p.9; Bd.81, p.653; Letter from Regler to the King, 2 July 1782, SBB PK, Denkschriften des Preußischen Generalstabes, XXXII Schlesien, 90.

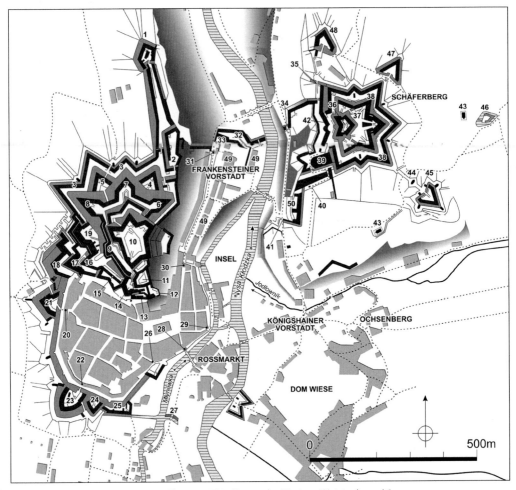

Fortress Glatz in 1786. (Drawn by Mariusz Wojciechowski)

mentioned in the previous section devoted to Silberberg (in which he spoke of the possibility of building a fort on the Warthe Pass) was mostly devoted to proposing strengthening the fortifications of Glatz.[158] Regler proposed the erection of a new work in front of the old fortress, the strengthening of the Kranich and the Neue Flèche in front of the Schäferberg and also the rebuilding of the cemetery church in front of the town fortifications into – as he put it – a 'Caponiere â Canon'.

The desire to erect a new flèche was the King's idea, as Regler himself wrote: 'In accordance with his royal majesty's brightest idea, I have searched 150 paces in front of the centre of the old fortress for a place for a new flèche, from which it will be possible to

---

158   Happily, both the cost estimate and the design drawings have survived. The cost estimate is held in the collection of GStA SPK, I HA Rep.96 No 94 Bbb Regler, pp.1–6, while the designs are held in the collection of the Berlin Staatsbibliothek, SBB PK, ref. X 25108/1–3.

flank the Böhmen Bastion to the left, together with the cemetery, and to the right to see the greater part of the Haasengraben.'[159] The new work, according to the surviving design drawing, was to be an irregular structure (the right face and flank longer than the left) surrounded by its own moat. In its gorge there was to be a small gunpowder magazine. In the middle of the courtyard there was to be a small Reduit, identical to the caponiers built before 1756 in the covered way of the city's fortifications and the Königsheiner flèche. This is also how, as a caponier, this structure is described in the design drawing. This reduit was intended to defend both the interior of the work and its foreground with small arms fire. With its short countermine corridors, the structure was also to be protected against mine attack. The entire works were to cost 15,045 thalers.[160] In the case of the Kranich, the project envisaged extending one of the flanks so that it would cover the entrance bridge and at the same time the foreground of the new flèche could be more easily covered from it. In addition, a casemate for 40 men and a powder magazine were to be inserted into the new flank. An important part of the project was also to erect a masonry revetment for this work. In total, the modernisation was to cost 11,448 thalers.[161] The most expensive work was to be the modernisation of the new flèche in front of Schäferberg. The erection of a small casemate for the garrison, together with latrines and a gunpowder store, and the construction of the masonry revetment of the main rampart and counterscarp were to cost a total of 18,159 thalers. The last and least costly task planned by Regler was the conversion of the church into a caponier, with the surrounding covered way preceded by a glacis, which was to cost 4,800 thalers. In total, the four planned works were to cost a total of 49,453 thalers.

The most interesting object seems to be the new flèche. It combines ideas already known from the pre-war period. At that time, it was often decided to erect works protruding from the core of the fortress – as in Glatz and elsewhere. Such structures were reinforced with caponiers. In the aforementioned flèche, these two elements were combined into a new whole, as the caponier was placed not on the places of arms of the fortress's covered way, but to the interior. It was located in the middle of the courtyard, thus the caponier took on the function of a masonry reduit, which was a completely new idea.

The 1763 planned modernisations mentioned above were not realised. The new defensive work in front of the main fortress was not built, and the new flèche on Schäferberg did not gain casemates. The Kranich was rebuilt on the basis of Regler's designs, but a decade later and differently than originally planned. Construction work in Glatz did not start until seven years later and was associated with the most important structure built after 1763; the Donjon. It is at the same time one of the most important defensive structures built in Prussia in the Frederician period.

Unfortunately, due to the lack of documentation relating to the construction of this fortress (as well as other fortresses built with funds from the Silesian Ministry), factual information

---

159 Haaasengraben – a ravine, or valley, to the north-west of the main fortress; nowadays this ravine in its northern part can be identified with the section of Półwiejska Street parallel to Nowy Świat Street, its southern part is still undeveloped and stretches as far as the allotment gardens on Noworudzka Street.
160 Plan der neu projectirten Flèche vor der Mitte der alten Festung, SBB PK, ref. X 25108/1.
161 From this it can be seen that the Kranich was previously not a masonry structure, but merely created by cutting moats into the rock and piling a rampart of earth.

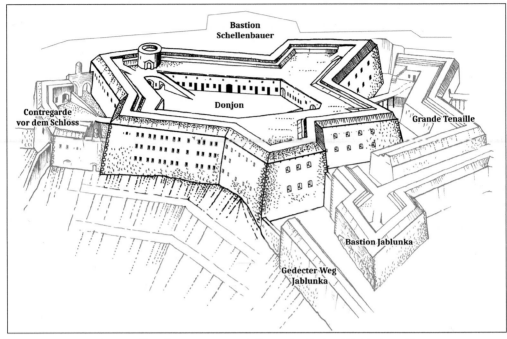

Fortress Glatz, Donjon circa 1786. (Drawn by Mariusz Wojciechowski)

concerning both the construction and design of this important work is extremely poor. Also, little is known about the scale of royal involvement. Only minor mentions in royal writings shed some light. The earliest was recorded in a military will of 1768: 'As soon as the fortress in Silberberg is completed, the old castle in Glatz should be improved. The old walls threatening to collapse must be demolished, strong casemates established and the plan of Lieutenant Colonel Pinto partially implemented.'[162] From this first reference we learn the name of the designer of the fortress. However, this name is not that of Vincent Pinto, known from Silberberg (who was a *major* until the end of his service in Prussia), but his brother Franz Ignatz. The project of this engineer is mentioned again in the King's letter of March 1769. The King chose Regler, an engineer already experienced in stonemasonry, to check at Glatz whether Pinto's project could be easily accomplished.[163] It was to this engineer that the King entrusted the project in the spring of 1770.[164] The appointment is mentioned again in the King's letter to his brother, Prince Henry, in March 1770: 'I have summoned here [to Potsdam] Colonel Regler to prepare everything necessary to begin in the month of June the construction of the castle in Glatz, more or less on the basis of the plan which you my brother

---

162 Volz, *Die Werke*, vol.6, p.243.
163 Letter from the King to Regler, 4 March 1769, GStA SPK, I HA Rep.96 B Abschriften von Kabinetsordres, Bd.71, p.65 recto.
164 Letter from the King to Regler, 2 February 1770, GStA SPK, I HA Rep.96 B Abschriften von Kabinetsordres, Bd.71, p.324 verso.

have seen.'[165] This mention, in addition to confirming Regler's appointment as builder of the fortress, may also suggest the King's mode of working with the engineer carrying out the construction of the fortress while seeking the King's agreement on construction issues. We know of at least one such consultation which took place several months earlier between the King and *Leutnant* Franseky who was to build the fortress of Kolberg. It may well have been similar in the case of Glatz.

The first building that we know of in which the King was personally involved in its design was the Kranich, the reconstruction of which began to be attempted as early as 1773. Regler planned to enlarge this defensive work considerably, but the King did not agree. According to the sovereign, the covered way between the main fortress and the Kranich could accommodate 40 guns, so he considered the enlargement of the Kranich to be completely unnecessary.[166]

Another work in Glatz associated with Frederick's activity was the modernisation of the fort on Schäferberg, which followed the War of the Bavarian Succession. The King was the initiator of this reconstruction. In a letter to Regler in September 1779, he noted that the moats surrounding the fort were too shallow and ordered Regler to draw up a plan and cost estimate to deepen these moats by six to eight feet.[167] Regler quickly completed the task, the design was ready as early as 8 October and, happily, has survived to the present day; it is stored in the Berlin Staatsbibliothek.[168] A close comparison of this design with earlier plans for the fortress shows that, when writing about deepening, the King had in mind the construction of a new moat. Indeed, Regler's design shows a moat running in front of the fort's envelope, which originally had no moat. In other words, the modernisation was of a more serious nature than the content of the King's first letter suggests. Regler's design was received by the King a few days after it was made; on 14 October he wrote to the engineer that the plan was good. Its implementation was scheduled for 1780 and the sum of 48,745 thalers was allocated.[169] Looking closely at the outer moat of the Schäferberg fort, one can notice the coffer located in the salients of the envelope. These facilities enabled firing on the bottom of the moat. Unfortunately, there is no mention of them in the surviving sources. There is some probability that they were built at the time of the modernisation; the amount of over 48,000 thalers was quite high and the erection of several coffers could fit into this. However, this was probably not the case. On close inspection of the building, it is easy to see the distinct change in the stonework of the revetment where these coffers are located. They were most likely introduced during another modernisation of the building at the end of the Frederician period. After the reconstruction of 1780–1781, the outer moat of the fort was

---

165 Letter to Prince Heinrich of Prussia to Rheinsberg, from Potsdam, 14 March 1770, Droysen, Politische Correspondenz, vol.29, p.386.

166 Letter from the King to Regler, 20 October 1773, GStA SPK, I HA Rep.96 B Abschriften von Kabinetsordres, Bd.73, p.331.

167 Letter from the King to Regler, 25 September 1779, GStA SPK, I HA Rep.96 B Abschriften von Kabinetsordres, Bd.79, p.1032.

168 Project des auf den Schäferberg neu zu vertiefenden Grabens, der mit einer hell gelben Farbe angedeutet ist SBB PK, ref. X 25107/30.

169 Letters from the King to Regler, 14 November 1779 and to Hoym of 5 November 1779, GStA SPK, I HA Rep.96 B Abschriften von Kabinetsordres, Bd.79, pp.1072, 1125.

only a passive obstacle preventing the enemy from taking the envelope by assault. In this respect, the solution is reminiscent of that used by Regler at Silberberg.

At the same time as the investment in the defences on Schäferberg, the King planned to further strengthen the main fortress. He stated that a new moat was needed there too, which would further protect the fortress from the city. In this case, the King did not limit himself to the initiative alone. After Regler provided him with a design that did not meet his expectations, he corrected it himself and sent it back.[170] Unfortunately, this project was not realised, and no drawings related to it have survived; therefore, nothing more can be said about it.

The moat project in front of the main fortress described above was not the last action initiated by Frederick at Glatz. In 1780, another appeared. In a letter of 3 January to Regler, the King mentions some work on the Neisse. More details on the subject come from a letter more than a year later, in which the King asks his engineer for a cost estimate for a flèche, located in front of the town fortifications, near the mill.[171] As stated above, this is most likely to be the final completion of the Mühlen Bastion extension.

In the following year, 1782, the King again turned his attention to the main fortress. He wanted to make some modifications to several of the works there; these included the insertion of buttresses on the ramparts of the Donjon, the raising of the curtains near the Schellenbauer and Alarm Bastion, and the rebuilding of the communication linking the fortress to the Kranich. According to the King's intentions, this was to be a minor modernisation, but the cost estimate that Regler prepared was as high as 25,000 thalers. The King criticised his engineer for this and ordered him to prepare another, more economical cost estimate.[172]

A year later, a major expansion, estimated at up to 70,000 thalers, was planned. It is not entirely clear with which part of the fortress this modernisation was connected. Presumably, it was work on the main fortress, as this was the only place where improvements were made on a significant scale in the second half of the 1780s.[173]

The last work of the Glatz fortress associated with Frederick is the so-called Neue Batterie within the fortifications of Schäferberg. As stated above, the battery was created on the King's initiative.

As can be seen, the King's involvement in the design of the fortress at Glatz continued after the Seven Years War. In the case of most of the modernisations, Frederick was involved at least as an initiator, and in some cases, he also drew up the designs. However, little is known about the King's involvement in the design of the fortress's most important structure, the Donjon. However, what is certain should suffice; the King chose for Glatz a design

---

170   Letters from the King to Regler, 14 October and 10 November 1779, GStA SPK, I HA Rep.96 B Abschriften von Kabinetsordres, Bd.79, pp.1072, 1142.

171   Letters from the King to Regler, 3 January 1780 and 30 August 1781, GStA SPK, I HA Rep.96 B Abschriften von Kabinetsordres, Bd.80, p.9, Bd.81 p.758.

172   Letter from the King to Regler, 29 August 1782, GStA SPK, I HA Rep.96 B Abschriften von Kabinetsordres, Bd.82, p.810.

173   Letters from the King to Regler, 26 August 1783, GStA SPK, I HA Rep.96 B Abschriften von Kabinetsordres, Bd.85, p.891.

Fortress Glatz, view of the Donjon's elevation from the attack side. (Photo: Grzegorz Basiński)

by a Piedmontese engineer. As we shall see, this simple decision influenced the direction of Prussian defensive architecture in the coming decades.

It is worth taking a closer look at this unique building. It is fortunate that the Glatz Donjon has survived to the present day in a relatively unchanged condition; moreover, several plans of this structure from the late eighteenth and early nineteenth century have survived, so we can examine its appearance from before the changes made later. There are three features of this structure to which attention should be drawn: the plan, the use of casemates, and the function of the structure within the fortress as a whole.

The first is the outline; the Donjon has a characteristic, irregular and tenaille plan. This in itself is not a novelty, fortifications with a such outline were often built in the period before the Seven Years War, of which the forts Presussen in Neisse and Stettin and Fort Stern in Glogau are excellent examples. However, the analogy with Glatz's Donjon should not be sought in the defences constructed in Prussia. The only structure which resembles Glatz's Donjon in plan is the Donjon at Silberberg, described in an unbuilt project by Vincent Pinto. Analysing the preserved design sketch by Pinto, we can see a very clear resemblance to the plan of Glatz's Donjon. The main front of both objects consists of two half-bastions divided by a triangular corner.[174] This is not surprising, as both Pinto brothers represented the same Piedmontese tradition of defensive architecture. They were the sons of Lorenzo Bernardino Pinto di Barri, head of the Piedmontese engineering corps, and were very familiar with the solutions used by him, indeed they even copied some of them. The tenaille-bastion, irregular defensive structures are typical of Piedmontese Pinto designs.

Even more important parallels with Piedmont relate to the way the casemates are used. The Glatz building is completely bombproof, moreover the interior is in places as high as three storeys. The use of casemates was not a novelty in Prussia, and its scale also found analogies in the Silberberg Donjon, built a few years earlier. There was a major difference between the Glatz structure and the Silberberg one, as the Donjon at Glatz had as many as 42 artillery casemates, while the Silberberg one had none. The sheer number of secure artillery emplacements is impressive, as it was the largest (apart from those at Graudenz) of all the defensive works built during Frederick's lifetime which were equipped with casemated batteries. However, this is not the most important aspect, as the number of gun positions in

---

174 *Les Idees de S. De Ms. Le Capit. De Pinto*, GStA SPK, XI HA, ref. A 70007;5.

the casemates of Prussian fortresses steadily increased. The first structure of this kind that was completed, the Neumühl Flèche of 1768–1770, had only a few embrasures. Garden Fort, rebuilt in 1786, had 16, and in the core of the fortress at Graudenz there were more than 50 (adding up all the casemated batteries in the fortress). However, only in Glatz's Donjon were the artillery casemates built on top of each other in such a way that the gun embrasures were located in two rows, thanks to which two guns in safe positions could fire at the same point. It is this multi-storey nature of the artillery casemates that is evidence of the influence of Piedmontese examples, drawn on by Franz Ignatz Pinto. In the fortresses built by his father, multi-storey artillery casemates were the rule; moreover, there were three-storey casemates in the Tortona fortress and even four-storey casemates in Demont.[175]

The final element worthy of note here is the role the building was intended to play during a siege. Its common name – Donjon – refers to the tradition of medieval defensive architecture, where the Donjon was a tower in which the defenders took shelter in the last phase of defence. The Glatz structure did fulfil this function, but it was more than just a place of refuge for the last survivors of the garrison. The 42 fortified defensive positions allowed not only for prolonged resistance to enemy attacks, but also for effective control of the surroundings by artillery fire. The then commandant of the fortress, Friedrich Benignius von Schmidthenner, wrote explicitly about this a decade after the completion of the Donjon:

> In my opinion, the castle is difficult to take, its walls are so high that it is impossible to climb them, it is founded on rock and its walls are 24 feet thick. Its two-storey casemated batteries can again chase the enemy away from the works in front of them, hence it will never succeed [in them] in arranging a breakout battery. The Schellebauer Bastion and the Alarm Bastion, with their curtain, match the castle in height and thickness of walls. In any case, by constantly throwing bombs, grenades and stones, the enemy's work can be made more difficult, especially when he can go no further.[176]

The Glatz Donjon, extremely difficult to capture by the enemy and capable of influencing its surroundings until the last moments of the siege, should be considered one of the prototypes of the nineteenth century reduits, which were characteristic elements of New Prussian fortifications. Of course, the main model for them was the solutions proposed by Montalembert, with his 'tour angulaire' at the forefront. However, the fact that Prussian engineers were the first to fully accept the ideas of the French engineer was largely due to the Glatz Donjon.

Schweidnitz

The events of the Seven Years War clearly demonstrated the key role of the fortress at Schweidnitz (Świdnica) for the Silesian theatre of war. Its importance as a fortified magazine was confirmed by the events of 1761, when the fortress's stores allowed the royal army

---

175 Viglino Davico, *Fortezze Sulle Alpi*, p.168, ill. D 13d.
176 Disposition zur Defension einer bevorsehen belagerung der Vestung und Stadt Glatz, SBB PK, DPG ref. 118, pp.7–8.

to survive in the fortified camp near Bunzelwitz (Bolesławice). Its location close to the most important routes leading from Silesia towards Bohemia meant that Schweidnitz was besieged four times, the most of all the Prussian fortresses affected by the war. The last of the sieges can even be described without great exaggeration as a key event in the final phase of the conflict. Not surprisingly, the fortress was rebuilt again after the end of hostilities. Of course, the transformation of the fortress after 1763 cannot be equated in importance with the first construction period, but nevertheless the activities undertaken here up to 1786 must be regarded as very important for the development of Prussian fortification.

The appearance of the fortifications of Schweidnitz at the time of the re-entry of the Prussian army in October 1762, after the last siege of the fortress had ended, was very different from that of 1756, when the war began. And it is not so much the fact that the fortifications were destroyed, but the transformations that were made during the war. The Austrians were the first to begin this process after the capture of the town in 1757. They erected a continuous defensive perimeter with a bastion outline, so that the corners of the bastions met the gorges of the forts, and the forts became a kind of outer works for the new defensive perimeter. These fortifications were not completed when the fortress was recaptured in 1758 and the Prussians did not continue their construction. Instead, they connected the individual forts and redoubts to each other by means of a simple rampart, defended by redans, and preceded by a dry moat. The next expansion of the fortifications took place during the almost year-long occupation of the fortress by the Austrians. As part of preparations for the siege in 1762, two flèches were erected; the Neumühl, which was intended to deflect the threat from the Bogen fort, destroyed by the explosion of the powder magazine, and the Galgen Flèche.[177]

Just four days after the siege of the fortress had ended, *Major* Simon Lefèbvre, who had been in charge of the siege works up to that point, drew up the first project. It related more to the reconstruction of the destroyed works than to modernisation. The cost estimate amounted to 20,962 thalers. The largest item on this estimate was the transportation of earth to the gorge of some unnamed work (probably the Jauernicker Fort), which was to cost 3,332 thalers. The repair of the rampart was to cost 1,800 thalers, the repair of the Jauernicker Flèche, 1,660 thalers, the repair of the breastworks, 1,500 thalers.[178]

Substantial modernisation work did not begin, however, until after the end of hostilities and was, essentially, completed before 1770.

The first works that were undertaken were the construction of five so-called 'tête de ponts', defence works protecting the gates in the main perimeter of the fortress, the reconstruction of the casemates in two forts that had been blown up during the sieges of 1761 and 1762, the bringing of the two flèches erected during the war up to permanent fortification standard, the construction of masonry revetments in the ramparts connecting the forts, and the construction of new counter-mine corridors. Unfortunately, the surviving documents allow only a fragmentary description of the progress of construction. According to *Oberst* Daries' report to the King of 17 July 1764, the masonry revetment of the rampart between the Bogen Fort and the Kirchen Redute was to be ready by the end of the month. Both blown-up casemates in the

177 Tielke, *Beytrage zur Kriegskunst*, pp.212–214.
178 GStA SPK, I HA Rep 96 Tit 86 B – Lefèbvre, p.154.

Bogen and Jauernicker Fort had already been rebuilt, but their vaults had not yet been covered with earth. The Neumühl Flèche (with the exception of its counter-mine corridors) was also to be completed; a section of the moat in the gorge was still missing in the Ziegel Flèche. As for the fortified tête de ponts, the tidying up of the area for the one in front of the Croisch Thor had only just begun. At the end of the month, Daries also planned to start work on the countermine corridors of the two aforementioned flèches. Daries explained the slow pace of construction by the rainy weather and the scarcity of workmen. He complained to the King that, although he was supposed to get 300–400 workers a day according to the royal order, neither the fortress commandant, the *Landrat*, nor the minister Schlabrendorf were fulfilling this obligation. Consequently, the work was only carried out thanks to 180 carpenter-grenadiers from the garrison.[179] In the end, all the work was completed before the end of 1766, as the fortress plan of February 1767 already shows the facilities mentioned above as completed.[180] The two structures in front of the Galgen Fort – the flèche there, together with the Flügel Batterie – are marked as not constructed in the said plan. It is not known exactly when their construction was completed; they were certainly ready before 1770.[181] In 1767, the next phase of reconstruction of the fortress began; the insertion of casemated batteries into already existing structures. The first to receive such a battery was the Neumühl Flèche, which was thoroughly transformed on this occasion. Work on it began in March 1769.[182] The casemate itself was not to be built until the middle of the year. In March 1769, the King wrote to Daries, who was in charge of the works at Schweidnitz, that the money for the casemates would not be allocated until July.[183] The decision, however, was taken earlier, as on 24 June 1769 the King informed his engineer that he would receive the necessary 30,000 thalers for this purpose via a Breslau bank.[184] Work on the building was completed in 1770.[185] In the same year another one was built, in the main rampart, together with the barracks casemates there. The first mention of this task dates from January 1770, when the King criticised Daries for the cost of building casemates in the main rampart, which in his opinion was too high. The amount proposed by the engineer is not known, but according to the sovereign, the task should cost a maximum of 90,000 thalers and should be spread over two years. Another 45,000 thalers were to be spent on the project in 1770 and in 1771, 40,000.[186] Also, new caponiers were erected in the moat to defend it.[187] In 1770 the King

---

179 GStA SPK, I HA Rep 96 Tit 93 B De Daries.

180 Plan von der Festung Schweidnitz im Jahr 1766, SBB PK, ref. X 33655/8.

181 Anon., 'Friedrich der Große als Ingenieur', pp.23–24.

182 Letter from the King to Daries, 11 March 1769, GStA SPK, I HA Rep.96 B Abschriften von Kabinetsordres, Bd.71, p.71 verso.

183 Letter from the King to Daries, 22 March 1769, GStA SPK, I HA Rep.96 B Abschriften von Kabinetsordres, Bd.71, p.79 recto.

184 Letter from the King to Daries, 24 June 1769, GStA SPK, I HA Rep.96 B Abschriften von Kabinetsordres, Bd.71, p.160 verso. The letter indicated an area between the Bogen Thor and the 'Garden Redoute', which would suggest that the works were to concern one of the casemates in the main rampart. However, the matter of financing the construction of casemates in the main rampart is not raised by the King until his letters of 1770.

185 Seydel, *Nachrichten*, vol.2, pp.18–20.

186 Letter from the King to Daries, 14 January 1770, GStA SPK, I HA Rep.96 B Abschriften von Kabinetsordres, Bd.71, p.311 recto.

187 Schirrmann, *Chronik der Stadt Schweidnitz*, p.64; von Rauch, Ueber die Festung Schweidnitz, SBB PK, DPG ref. XXXIV Schweidnitz, no. 97, p.7.

decided to start further work; the erection of a casemate in the Ziegel Flèche. The King had already taken the initiative to build it in the early autumn of 1770. In a letter to Daries of 19 September, he announced that he had decided to allocate 50,000 thalers for the construction of the fortress in 1771, out of which the casemate in the Ziegel Flèche and the counter-mine corridors around the town were to be built.[188] Work on the casemate was to be completed in 1772.[189]

Further defensive works were built before 1778: the Neumühl Hangar (1775–1776)[190] together with the rampart communicating it; the new battery in front of the Neumühl Flèche; and the Neu Jauernicker Flèche. In addition to this, numerous counter-mine corridors were built, in some works also demolition corridors (old and new Jauernicker Flèche, Ziegel Flèche and Neumühl Hangar), new sections of the covered way together with the caponiers defending them and hydrotechnical facilities for flooding the foreground from the side of the Weistritz River.[191] After 1779, further modernisation works were commenced, which were completed by 1785. At that time, a hangar was built in the new Jauernicker Flèche (1780–1781)[192] and new free-standing gunpowder magazines. In addition to this, numerous new sections of counter-mine corridors were constructed in the Galgen Flèche, new and old Jauernicker Flèche, the Neumühl Hangar and the Garden and Bogen Fort. The most important modernisation was the reconstruction of the Garten and Bogen forts, which lasted from 1782 and incorporated casemated batteries for 16 guns connected to a large hangar.[193] The designer of this phase of reconstruction of the fortress was *Major* von Haab; the order to proceed with the drafting was given to him by the King in April 1781.[194] After the death of this officer in December 1782, the plans and cost estimates for the new works were taken over by *Oberst* Daries, who also completed the modernisations of these structures.[195] The modernisation of each fort was to cost 48,000 thalers, with more than 300 workmen working on each fort at a time. According to a report from May 1783, 349 labourers (64 of them qualified), 25 soldiers from von Erlach's regiment and 260 labourers supplied by the county were working on the Garten Fort. Only 21 soldiers from von Erlach's regiment and 254 labourers supplied by the county were working at Bogen Fort at the same time.[196] After the casemated batteries had been inserted into the forts, it became apparent that their embrasures were too high and so the King ordered the raising of the forts' breastworks and glacis; the main rampart of the

---

188 Letter from the King to Daries, 19 September 1770, GStA SPK, I HA Rep.96 B Abschriften von Kabinetsordres, Bd.71, p.473 verso.

189 Seydel, Nachrichten, vol.4, pp.18–20; King's letter to Daries, 20 November 1771, GStA SPK, I HA Rep.96 B Abschriften von Kabinetsordres, Bd.72, p.416.

190 King's letter to Daries, 26 October 1775, GStA SPK, I HA Rep.96 B Abschriften von Kabinetsordres, Bd.74, p.715.

191 Von Rauch, Ueber die Festung Schweidnitz, SBB PK, DPG ref. XXXIV Schweidnitz, no. 97, p.7.

192 King's letters to Daries, 7 October 1779, 17 and 18.08.1780 and letter to Hoym of 15 June 1781, I HA Rep.96 B Abschriften von Kabinetsordres, Bd.79, p.1057; Bd.80, p.530; Bd.81, p.420.

193 Von Rauch, Ueber die Festung Schweidnitz, SBB PK, DPG ref. XXXIV Schweidnitz, no. 97, p.9; Seydel, *Nachrichten*, vol.4, p.20; Bonin, Geschichte des Ingenieurkorps p.101.

194 Letter from the King to Haab, 26 April 1781, GStA SPK, I HA Rep.96 B Abschriften von Kabinetsordres, Bd.81, p.283.

195 King's letter to Daries, 15 December 1782, GStA SPK, I HA Rep.96 B Abschriften von Kabinetsordres, Bd.82, p.1185.

196 Rapport von deren Koeniglichen Fortifications Arbeiten zu Schweidnitz, 12 May 1783, SBB PK, ref. X 33655/30–4.

fort also had to be raised. The first task was to be completed by the end of November 1784; the raising of the rampart took longer, as Daries reported in his letter to the King.[197] These works were the last investment in Schweidnitz during the Frederician period.

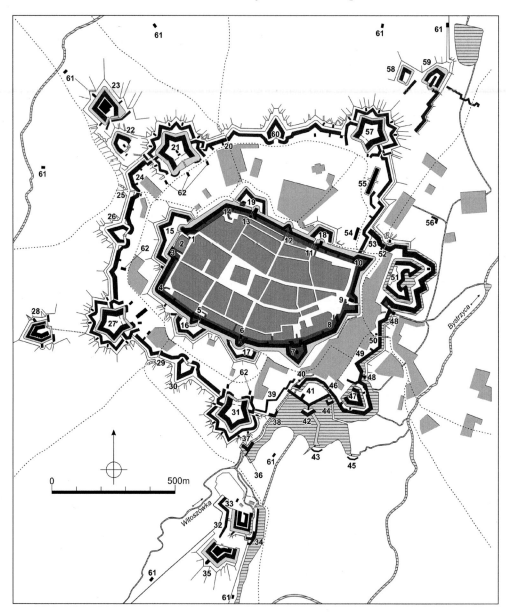

Fortress Schweidnitz circa 1786. (Drawn by Mariusz Wojciechowski)

---

197 Daries' letter, 26 November 1784, GStA SPK, I HA Rep 96 Tit 93 B De Daries.

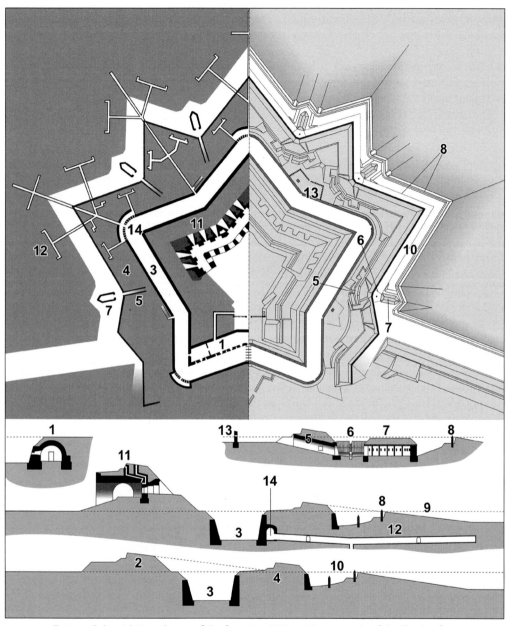

Fortress Schweidnitz, scheme of the fort circa 1786, on the example of the Garden fort.
1) casemates in the gorge, 2) rampart, 3) moat, 4) Fausse braye, 5) postern, 6) palisade with a swinging gate,
7) caponier of the place of arms, 8) palisade, 9) glacis, 10) covered way, 11) casemated battery, 12) courtyard
storehouse, 13) countermine gallery, 14) caponier of the fausse braye, 15) counterscarp gallery. (Drawn by
Mariusz Wojciechowski)

After the completion of the modernisations described above, the Schweidnitz fortress became a fortification complex unique in Europe. It consisted of two continuous defence perimeters: the old, but considerably reinforced city rampart, a strong belt of forts and the advance works. In total, the width of the defence belt that the fortress gained as a result of this modernisation was almost 1,000 metres at its widest point. The general plan of the fortress, although so unique, was, however, not as important to the development of Prussian fortifications as the detailed solutions that were applied to the individual works.

The most important of these were the casemated batteries; however, this issue will be discussed in a separate chapter. Equally interesting were the so called tête de ponts. These were large defensive works, mostly with a tenaille outline, erected in front of the gates in the main urban fortress perimeter. They varied in both size and shape. The largest was the Strigauer Brückenkopf, a tenaille structure with three salients. The next three – Bogen, Croisch and Koppen – were smaller, similar in size and dovetail-like in outline. The smallest was the Peters tête de pont, with a trapezoidal outline. These structures were atypical and had no analogue in the defensive architecture of the period. This was already reflected in the name – tête de pont (brückenkopf) – which until then had been reserved for defensive works protecting a bridge. Here, however, they were erected on the edge of the moat, in front of the gates in the main perimeter, making them similar in function to structures such as horn and crown works. However, a close analysis of these works leads to the conclusion that the Schweidnitz tête de pont did not so much guard the gates as the defensive works guarding these gates – former bastions or completely new caponiers. The novelty of these defensive works can best be seen in the case of the Peters tête de pont. There, a relatively small polygonal structure protected a low-lying caponier. A structure of this type and design could have been successfully constructed in a nineteenth-century fortress built according to the principles of the New Prussian fortification.

Another point to be made about the drawing of the Schweidnitz works created after the Seven Years War is the influence Montalembert's ideas. There are frequent references in the literature to the application of the ideas of this French theorist of defensive architecture at Schweidnitz.[198] These mostly concern hangars, which will be described separately in the chapter on artillery casemates. However, there are still a few structures in Schweidnitz's defensive works which, also by their outline, can be regarded as distant echoes of the concepts developed by Montalembert. Up to this point, the defensive works of fortresses had been constructed on the basis of a bastion or tenaille scheme. They had an outline similar to a pentagon (lunettes, flèches) or, although much less frequently, a star. In Schweidnitz, on the other hand, a few defensive works appeared which had a completely different plan: trapezoidal (the aforementioned Peters tête de pont) or rectangular (Neumühl Flèche and both hangars). This could be considered a reference to the polygonal outline promoted by Montalembert, were it not for the fact that the structures in question were built before 1776, before Montalembert's ideas were presented to the world. The use of the caponiers, and in particular the location of the caponiers in front of the two hangars, could also be related to his ideas. They were built exactly in the middle of the front, where Montalembert suggested, rather than in the corners where they had been located up to that point. However, on closer

---

198 Bonin, *Geschichte des Ingenieurkorps*, p.100; Seydel, *Nachrichten*, vol.4, pp.22–24.

Fortress Schweidnitz, plan of the inner rampart with tête de ponts. (Fragment of plan GStA SPK, XI HA ref. A71278)

examination of the plan of both works, it can be seen that these caponiers are not located at the bottom of the moat, as Montalembert used them, but on the places of arms of the covered way. In this respect, these structures were similar to the caponiers built at Silesian fortresses before 1756. Moreover, like the previously described structures, they were built before the publication of Montalembert's treatise.

The discussion of the use (or not) of the ideas of this famous French engineer at Schweidnitz is related to another issue worth discussing in greater detail; the question of facilities for the defence of one's own work – the defence of the covered way and the moat bottom. At Schweidnitz, during the reconstruction of the fortress after the Seven Years War, several caponiers were built, both ordinary ones defending the moat bottom and those placed in the places of arms of the covered way. Further counterscarp galleries also appeared. The most important facilities of this kind appeared in the Neumühl Flèche after its first modernisation in 1764. The above-mentioned plan of 1766 shows that the flèche was to have two caponiers placed in the corners between the flank and the gorge, defending the bottom of the moat and also the gorge of the facility. The moat in front of the object's face was, in turn, to be defended by a counterguard gallery. This, and the fully revetted scarps and counterscarps, meant that the facility had considerable resistance to assault. This is not surprising; the facility was protruding into the foreground and completely unconnected to the rest of the fortress works. Both the counterscarp gallery and one of the caponiers were later removed during the construction of the Neumühl Hangar and adjacent works, but fortunately the second of the caponiers, located at the north-east corner of the work, has survived to the present day. This small, rectangular, single-storey structure is located at the junction of the flèche's gorge and left flank. It has small arms loopholes in each of its walls, so it could cover both the moat in front of the left flank and the approach to the gorge of the fort. The caponier was connected to the rest of the fort thanks to a communication corridor leading towards the courtyard, now collapsed. The caponiers of the Neumühl Flèche described above were the only examples of this type of structure built in Schweidnitz after 1763. Other examples of structures serving the defence of the moat bottom were built in the Ziegel Flèche. In this facility, the majority of the moat was not defended, but the neck section was defended by two structures, a coffer in the redan defending the gorge section of the flèche and a shooting gallery in the counterscarp. Both of the above-described installations were intended to defend the sensitive area where the underground walkway communicating the flèche with the interior of the fortress. The object was thus to ensure safe communication with the interior of the fortress. After the Neisse Kaninchen Redoubt, it was the second external structure built under Frederick to have a similar underground communication system.

The last element created at Schweidnitz after the Seven Years War to which attention should be drawn is the counter-mine corridors. Such installations had already been created at Schweidnitz in the previous period, and they proved excellent during the siege of the fortress in 1762. They significantly slowed down the Prussian mine attack. Not surprisingly, the counter-mine corridors were extended after the war and also supplied to newly built defensive works. Completely new installations of this kind were built in front of the city ramparts, hitherto devoid of countermines. Extensive countermines were also created in front of the new defensive works. Particularly interesting are the corridors in front of the flèche and the Jauernicker Hangar, where a very extensive and extensive system was created.

Fortress Schweidnitz, caponier of the Neumühl Flèche. (Author's photo)

A potential attacker would have had to reckon with a prolonged mine war, as the counter-mines covered not only the foregrounds, but also the area between them and the interior of these defence works.

A proposal to extend the defences at Schweidnitz, made in 1786, should also be mentioned. According to the project, the fortress was to be strengthened from the east, in front of the Water Fort, with two protruding defensive structures. The plan for this reconstruction, dated 1786, is preserved in the Berlin Staatasbibliothek.[199] This interesting but unrealised project for the further expansion of the fortress raises doubts about its proper qualification. As is well known, the King continued to issue instructions for the expansion, modernisation, and reparation of his fortresses until the last days of his life. His last order in this regard dates from 19 July 1786.[200] As can be seen, almost to his last days, the King took decisions which could result in the construction of new facilities. However, it should be doubted whether this project for the expansion of Schweidnitz is related to Frederick. In his correspondence from 1786, the fortress of Schweidnitz appears extremely frequently, but only in the context of repairs. In March and April, the King corresponded with *Major* Harroy, who was even commissioned to draw up a project for the comprehensive repair of the fortress. Its cost

199 Haupt Plan von denen auf Seiner Koniglichen Majestat Ordre, projectirten veranderungen bei der Festung Schweidnitz,1786, SBB PK, ref. X 33655/35.
200 Letter from the King to Harroy, 19 July 1786 regarding the reparation of the weir at Cosel, GStA SPK, I HA Rep.96 B Abschriften von Kabinetsordres, Bd.86, p.663.

estimate was produced in April, and work was still underway in July. However, these were minor works, as the cost estimate was only 1,300 thalers.[201] Meanwhile, according to the 1786 extension project, both works were to cost over 20,000 thalers, and there is no mention of such sums in the context of Schweidnitz in the surviving letters. In other words, we should assume that the extension project described should be linked to the early period of Friedrich Wilhelm II's reign. There will never be absolute certainty about this, as it is known that the King planned the expansion of fortifications right to the end, as exemplified by the order of 11 August 1786, issued six days before the King's death, informing that *Kapitän* Ruchel had been sent on a study tour to go to Glatz County to see sites in the vicinity of Szczytna (Rückers) and Duszniki (Reiners) where defence towers could be erected.[202]

Neisse

After the Seven Years War, the fortress at Neisse did not attract as much attention from the King as it did in the pre-war period. However, it was an important fortress and extremely interesting processes took place here, from a fortification point of view, in which Frederick was often personally involved.

Work on rebuilding the fortifications had already been carried out during the Seven Years War, when, after the Austrian siege, a rampart was erected on Caninchen Berg on the basis of *Kapitän* Simon Lefèbvre's design.[203] In the late 1760s, another modernisation was undertaken. Preparations had already been made during 1767; in the autumn, the sum of 20,000 thalers was paid to purchase materials and land for the new defensive works.[204] In order to save money on building materials, Lefèbvre wanted to demolish the old city wall, which the King did not agree to, as he stated that 'it always costs more to demolish walls than to collect free material.' So he ordered the collection of stones from the fields around Neisse.[205] The main work was planned for 1768, when the fortress construction funds were replenished with 100,000 thalers.[206] Construction of the casemates began first. In December 1768, the King asked his engineer whether he had sufficient funds to erect three casemates in the town in 1769.[207] Nothing was done on the project that year, however, and it was not revisited until 1770, when detailed plans were drawn up for casemates in Bastion No. 6.[208] At the same time,

201 King's letters to Harroy, 29 March and 23 April 1786, GStA SPK, I HA Rep.96 B Abschriften von Kabinetsordres, Bd.86, pp.326, 402.
202 Letter from the King to Harroy, 11 August 1786, GStA SPK, I HA Rep.96 B Abschriften von Kabinetsordres, Bd.86, p.720.
203 Minsberg 1834, *Geschichtliche Darstellung*, p.197.
204 Letter from the King to Lefèbvre, 12 October 1767, GStA SPK, I HA Rep.96 B Abschriften von Kabinetsordres, Bd.70 vol.II 1767, p.350.
205 Letter from the King to Lefèbvre, 11 October 1767, GStA SPK, I HA Rep.96 B Abschriften von Kabinetsordres, Bd.70 vol.II 1767, p.308.
206 Letter from the King to Minister Schlabrendorf, 3 May 1768, GStA SPK, I HA Rep.96 B Abschriften von Kabinetsordres, Bd.70 vol.III 1768, p.207.
207 Letter from the King to Lefèbvre, 13 December 1768, GStA SPK, I HA Rep.96 B Abschriften von Kabinetsordres, Bd.70 vol.III 1768, p.428.
208 Letter from the King to Lefèbvre, 27 May and 11 June 1770, GStA SPK, I HA Rep.96 B Abschriften von Kabinetsordres, Bd.71 pp.424 recto, 435 verso.

work was planned on the Caninchen Redoubt and on the line of fortifications connecting it with Fort Preussen. An amount of 50,000 thalers was budgeted for the construction of works at the redoubt alone, and an additional 30,000 thalers for the construction of the casemate.[209] At the same time, work was planned on the construction of the Casemattierte Batterie, a structure erected on the site where the Austrians had located the battery shelling the city in 1758.[210] They were started in 1770. Work on these facilities was progressing well, and the King hoped to have them completed as early as 1771.[211] Initially, everything seemed to go well. From March 1771, 700 labourers and 30 carts a day were working on the fortifications at Neisse.[212] However, a major setback occurred in the summer, as the casemate in the main rampart being built by Lefèbvre collapsed on 24 July. The engineer was immediately thrown into custody and the King sent *Major* Daries to Neisse with the task of drawing up a report to answer questions about the cause of the disaster and to determine the possible future risks regarding the construction of the Casemattierte Batterie. Daries' report unequivocally placed the blame for the incident on Lefèbvre. Moreover, according to his analysis, the vaults of the battery that had already been erected were also said to be defective.[213] The incident caused a great deal of confusion and significantly affected the pace of construction. At the time of the catastrophe, the works of the Caninchen Redoubt and the line of fortifications connecting it with Fort Preussen were probably already completed, but work took much longer on the other structures started by Lefèbvre. The battery was not finished until 1774.[214] The casemates in the main rampart were took even longer to build, and work probably continued until after 1775. It is known that finishing work on the casemates was supposed to have been carried out in that year.[215] The year 1775 is also found on the keystone of the entrance gate to the casemate in bastion No. 9.

Other works designed by Lefèbvre were completed around 1776. These include the two free-standing redoubts (Kapellenberg and Ober Kapuziner) on the hills north of the Mahren Gasse and the three flèches in front of Fort Preussen, together with the countermine defences. The works were placed in a design authored by Lefèbvre, but it is likely that he failed to start their implementation. However, this cannot be categorically stated. It is known, for example, that in the spring of 1771 the King was in correspondence with Lefèbvre concerning the flèche.[216] More precise data on the erection of these buildings is lacking. The period of construction of these facilities has so far been assumed in the litera-

---

209   Letter from the King to Minister von Hoym and to Lefèbvre, 14 May and 19 September 1770, GStA SPK, I HA Rep.96 B Abschriften von Kabinetsordres, Bd.71 pp.394 verso, 473 verso.

210   Letter from the King to Lefèbvre, 19 September 1770, GStA SPK, I HA Rep.96 B Abschriften von Kabinetsordres, Bd.71 pp.473 verso.

211   Letter from the King to Lefèbvre, 5 November 1770, GStA SPK, I HA Rep.96 B Abschriften von Kabinetsordres, Bd.71 p.528 recto.

212   Letter from the King to Minister von Hoym, 10 February 1771, GStA SPK, I HA Rep.96 B Abschriften von Kabinetsordres, Bd.72 vol.VI 1771, p.56.

213   Letters from the King to Rothkirch and to Daries, 28 July and 11 August 1771, GStA SPK, I HA Rep.96 B Abschriften von Kabinetsordres, Bd.72, pp.283, 302.

214   Minsberg 1834, *Geschichtliche Darstellung*, pp.198–199.

215   Letter from the King to Regler, 13 February 1774, GStA SPK, I HA Rep.96 B Abschriften von Kabinetsordres, Bd.73, vol.1774, p.63.

216   Letters from the King to Lefèbvre, 24 March and 10 April 1771, GStA SPK, I HA Rep.96 B Abschriften von Kabinetsordres, Bd.72 vol.VI 1771, pp.113, 140.

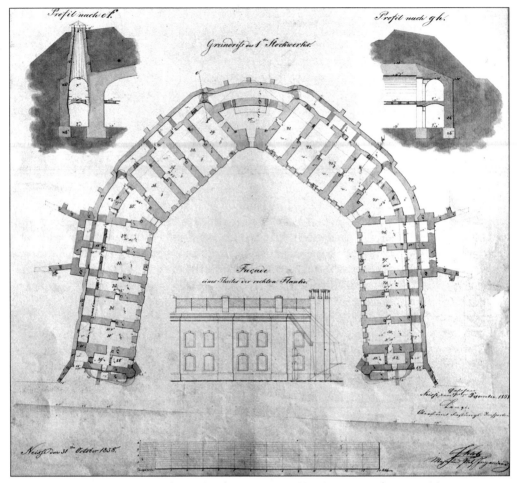

Neisse the bombproof barracks of Bastion No 9. (GStA SPK, XI HA ref. F 717951 bl. 1)

ture to be between 1775 and 1776.[217] However, given the financial data, it must be thought that these facilities were built in 1776. It was only in this year that the fortress construction fund was replenished with another large sum of 102,794 thalers.[218] After the construction of these facilities had been completed, there was a brief hiatus in modernisation work. They were resumed in 1782 with the reconstruction of the countermine corridors in front of the Caninchen Redoubt and Fort Preussen.[219] A minor but significant investment was made between 1784 and 1785, when the Casemattierte Batterie was extended; a smaller section

217 Minsberg 1834, *Geschichtliche Darstellung*, pp.198–199.
218 Letters from the King to Regler of 24 September and 16 November 1775, GStA SPK, I HA Rep.96 B Abschriften von Kabinetsordres, Bd.75, pp.621, 789.
219 Haab's letters, 20 October 1780 and 20 February 1782, GStA SPK, I HA Rep.96 B Abschriften von Kabinetsordres, Bd.80, p.665, Bd.82, p.162.

was added to the main block.[220] Another reconstruction of the fortifications was initiated in the last year of Frederick's reign. At that time, it was decided to incorporate the two originally free-standing redoubts, located to the east of Fort Preussen, into a new, continuous defensive line called the Ober Retranchement.[221] The implementation of this idea dragged on until after 1790.[222]

The construction of the fortress up to 1771 was led by Lefèbvre. After his death, the work was supervised for six months by Regler, then by Freund,[223] and finally by Harroy. In addition to them, *Major* Castillhon from the corps of miners was involved in the work, especially in the construction of the Caninchen Redoubt.[224]

As is already known, the reconstruction of the fortress was initially carried out under the direction of Lefèbvre. This engineer was also the designer of the fortress. We learn of his design activity several times from the King's letters to him.[225] Unfortunately, apart from one plan of the Caninchen Redoubt, described below, no signed designs of the fortress by him have survived. There is, however, a map in the Berlin Staatsbibliothek which should be attributed as a project prepared by this engineer.[226] Although not signed, it is described in French and shows a very early version of the modernisation, never realised in this form. This project involved numerous transformations to the local fortifications. The most important of these was the construction of a new defence structure; a redoubt connected to Fort Preussen by a line of tenaille fortifications. In addition to this, plans were made to rebuild the line of fortifications connecting Fort Preussen with the Neisse River, to erect two new redoubts east of Fort Bombardier, and three flèches in front of Fort Preussen. Relatively minor works were intended to be carried out within the city fortifications; casemates were to be erected there in the four bastions of the city perimeter. Similar plans were also made for the rear of the large barracks at Friedrichstadt. It was also planned to erect two small defensive works connected by a moat in front of sluice No. 10 (on the town side, near the exit road to the south). With the exception of the last structure, all of the elements described were constructed, although mostly in a different form from that planned.

As the first element of the project, the new casemates for the garrison should be described. The fortress has so far had three such facilities: in Fort Preussen for 400 men; and in the Cardinals and Capuciner Redoubts, for 300 men each. In total, a maximum of 1,000 soldiers could take refuge there, at least according to the author of the description to the 1789 plan of the fortress.[227] The designer of the reconstruction of the fortress, Lefèbvre, was of a different opinion. According to the project he drew up for the defence of the fortress in 1760–1761, the two redoubts could accommodate only 80 to 100 men. Considering a wartime garrison

220 King's letters to Harroy, 13 September 1784, GStA SPK, I HA Rep.96 B Abschriften von Kabinetsordres, Bd.84, p.804.
221 Minsberg (1834), *Geschichtliche Darstellung*, pp.198–199, 204.
222 Plan von der Stadt und Festung Neisse 1789, GStA SPK, XI HA, syg. A 71393.
223 Freund took over the construction from Regler on 7 September 1771, King's letters to Regler and Freund, 7 September 1771, GStA SPK, I HA Rep.96 B Abschriften von Kabinetsordres, Bd.72, p.332.
224 Bonin, *Geschichte des Ingenieurkorps*, pp.100–101.
225 Letters from the King to Lefèbvre, 30 May 1767 and 31 October 1768, GStA SPK, I HA Rep.96 B Abschriften von Kabinetsordres, Bd.70 vol.II 1767, p.308, Bd.70 vol.III 1768, p.407.
226 SBB PK, ref. X 31033/2.
227 Plan von der Stadt und Festung 1789, GStA SPK, XI HA, ref. A 71393.

of approximately 4,500 men (seven infantry battalions, 70 miners, 136 artillerymen and 180 cavalrymen), this was far from sufficient.[228] Not surprisingly, as many as five new casemates were planned for the garrison. They were to be erected in bastions 1, 3, 6 and 9 of the fortress's main perimeter, as well as in the Friedrichstadt area at the rear of barracks No. 6. Of these planned casemates, the latter was to be the largest and most interesting, as it was intended to create a compact barracks complex for use in both peace and war. However, in the end only three casemates were built, in bastions 1, 6 and 9. These casemates also differed considerably in shape from what was presented in the project. For example, the casemate in bastion No. 9, which survives to this day, was to have three wings built around a square courtyard. It was eventually given a horseshoe plan, adapted to the shape of the bastion. The King was also involved in the process of designing the casemates. In June 1770, he received a design for them from his engineer. From the context, it is clear that this is another version, as the King described the plan as 'more suitable'. But it did not fully live up to royal expectations, since Frederick sent the engineer the plan with his comments.[229]

The Caninchen Redoubt, the Casemattierte Batterie, and the Aussere Jerusalem Retrenchment

Another element of the project described was the fortification of the north-western edge of the fortress. After the Austrian siege of 1758, Lefèbvre erected a new defensive work on the site where the imperial troops located their siege batteries. There is no fully reliable information with which to reconstruct its shape. However, defensive works that can be suspected to date from the Seven Years War are recorded on the plan described above. Indeed, this plan contains a design for new fortifications stretching from Fort Preussen to the slope of the Neisse valley. This design, marked in yellow according to the design custom of the time, was shown on a tab overlaid on the plan proper. Beneath it, another line of fortifications was drawn, consisting of a covered way covering two larger structures; a redan placed in the middle of the line and a four-sided redoubt at its edge. This line has been drawn in white, which, according to custom, meant a recording of an existing state. It is therefore most likely to be a representation of the defensive structures erected at this location by Lefèbvre during the war.

The newly designed defence line was to follow the shape of the old one, without changing its course or outline. The covered way was to be retained, but the main rampart, which had previously been missing, was to be built behind it. The previously existing redan was planned to be integrated into this rampart. The rampart was intended to be separated from the covered way by a moat. The old redoubt was to be replaced by a new, much larger one, surrounded by a moat and reinforced with countermine corridors. However, like other elements of the project, this too was not realised as originally envisioned. In March 1768, Lefèbvre produced a new, separate project for this section of the fortifications, described as *Plan of the works ordered by His Majesty at Neisse*.[230] The changes from the original design

---

228 Entwurf der Vertheidung der Stadt Neiße durch den Obrist Lieutnant Le Febre anfertigt. Aus den Französischen übersetzt, 1760–61, SBB PK, DPG ref. 100, pp.36, 38.

229 Letter from the King to Lefèbvre, 11 June 1770, GStA SPK, I HA Rep.96 B Abschriften von Kabinetsordres, Bd.71, p.435 verso.

230 Plan de L'Ouvrage ordonne par sa Majeste a Neisse, SBB PK, ref. X 31033.

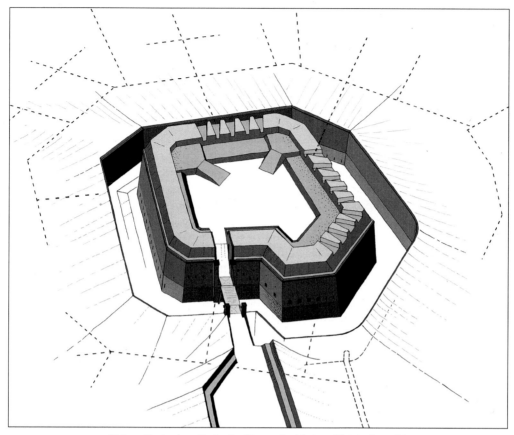

Neisse, Caninchen-Redoubt. (Drawn by Mariusz Wojciechowski)

consisted of simplifying the line of fortifications, as well as separating the redoubt from it, which was extended about 200 metres towards the foreground and located on top of the Caninchen Hill dominating the area. The ramparts consisting of, according to the first project, a rampart, moat and covered way, were deprived of the latter element. However, their characteristic elements were left in place. In the middle of the line there was a large redoubt, and at its southern end half of the old redoubt built during the war was retained (its two sides on the inner side were removed). The abandonment of the covered way did not mean a weakening of the defence. In some places the fortified line was protected by coffers firing from the moat, moreover, it was connected to the new redoubt by a road protected by a slope, so that the foreground could also be defended from this line.

The Caninchen Redoubt is one of the most interesting buildings of the Frederician fortifications of the period after the Seven Years War. It is distinguished from others by its outline, the way it defends the moat and the solution for communication with the interior of the fortress. If you look at the outline, you will see that the left flank with the gorge and face connect at right angles, as in a typical reduit, while the right flank with the right face and gorge is at an obtuse angle. As can be seen, we are dealing with something between a rectangular redoubt and a polygonal lunette. There were no other objects with such a plan in the Prussian fortifications of that time. The solution for the gorge of this defensive structure is also interesting, it consists of two sections which are pinned together. Such a solution facilitated the defence of this part by small arms fire and was encountered, for example, in the forts of Silberberg which were built at the same time. The difference lies in the closure of the gorge with an earth rampart, while in Silberberg the neck was defended only by a wall, relatively easy to destroy with cannon fire from inside the fortress in the event of an enemy seizing the work.

A much more interesting feature of the redoubt were the solutions for defending the moat. Lefèbvre used a gallery here, which ran at the foot of the wall along the entire length of the moat, from which small arms fire could be conducted. This in itself was not new, but the location of this gallery was completely unusual; it was situated at the foot of the redoubt rampart and not, as was customary, at the foot of the counterscarp. The gallery surrounded the entire redoubt, and began in casemates located in the gorge, on either side of the gate. These casemates had a tenaille plan corresponding to the outline of this part of the moat, so that the fire conducted from both wings of the casemates overlapped each other. The moat defence was further strengthened by small-arm coffers located in the corners, at the entrances to the countermine corridor system, and holding two sections of the moat under fire. The coffers were accessible from inside the redoubt via covered passages under the moat. Interestingly, during the course of construction, one of these coffers was significantly expanded and its function partially changed. One room was added to it, which served as a caponier, as it was located at the bottom of a long section of the moat crossing the hillside south of the redoubt.

Another unusual and noteworthy element of the Caninchen Redoubt was the covered communication. Lefèbvre's original design planned to connect this defensive work only by a covered way, sheltered by glacis on both sides. This solution probably did not provide sufficient security, so it was decided to excavate a tunnel more than 200 metres long, which connected the redoubt with the moat in front of the Casemattierte Batterie. This corridor is also part of the countermine system defending this part of the fortress. It is reached by the Commandant's Gallery and the corridor surrounding the entire redoubt. Three other corridors also originate from it, with the longest one protecting against an attack from the south. Of course, this was not the only way into the redoubt, but only a safe communication for the duration of the siege. The main access led over the top and was made possible by a wide esplanade. Outside of Neisse, such a solution was only used in Schweidnitz. When writing about the countermine corridors, it is essential to mention the design activity of another engineer. For two years, between October 1780 and December 1782, the countermines around the redoubt were rebuilt on the basis of a design by *Major* Haab. He had drawn up the reconstruction project in 1780, commissioned by the King.[231]

The last element in this part of the Neisse fortification was the Casemattierte Batterie. This object will be described separately in next chapter, but it is worth devoting some space to it here. This is because the gun emplacement described above was only a fragment of an atypical defensive facility. It had a very irregular (and thus completely unprecedented in

---

231 Letter from the King to Haab, 20 October 1780, GStA SPK, I HA Rep.96 B Abschriften von Kabinetsordres, Bd.80, p.665.

the fortifications of the time) outline. The main part consisted of three terraced defence works, each with a different plan close to a rectangle. A separate defence structure was attached to the upper terrace, while the lower terrace was connected to the flat redan and adjoined the main rampart. The entire structure was concealed from the east by a massive, high, rectangular-shaped rampart with a conical cross-section. It did not serve as a further defensive position but was only a kind of traverse for all the defensive structures that made up the complex of the Casemattierte Batterie.

As can be seen, the fortification complex located to the east of Fort Preussen is a complex defensive installation in its structure. It is extensive, irregular and provided with a detached work. It is clear that the intention of the designers was to make the fortifications fit the terrain as well as possible, in accordance with the demands expressed by Frederick in his theoretical writings. Another feature was to give the works resistance to assault. This was made possible by the use of numerous deep moats, both associated with the structures (the moats in front of the redoubt and in front of the embankment) and treated as an independent structure (the moat south of the redoubt). Resistance to assault was further strengthened by facilities used to defend the moat; galleries and musket coffers. All this makes this fortification complex similar to the fortification complex of the Silberberg Grosse Strohhaube, which was constructed simultaneously, though finally completed a decade later.

Redevelopment of Fort Preussen and the Hohe Retrenchment

Important transformations also took place within Fort Preussen. Up to now, this fort consisted of a core and an envelope built of nine defensive works. There was no covered way in front of the outer moat, only two small flèches in front of two works. It was not until 1775–1776 that the whole fort was surrounded by a full covered way, and in front of the fort, on the north side, five small works were built to deepen the defence of this section. This reinforced the area that was under direct threat during the Austrian siege. Of these works, two were relatively small, and three – Flèche Grand, Lefèbvre and Dierecke – matched the size of the works of the old envelope. The difference were casemates. Like the vast majority of exterior works built in Prussian fortresses after the Seven Years War, these buildings were also provided with the necessary bombproof rooms. Each flèche had a casemate for the garrison and a handy powder magazine. According to some sources, these facilities were supposed to have been built on the basis of an idea of Frederick's.[232]

Two free-standing redoubts were built simultaneously with the flèches on the hills to the east of the fort: the closer Capellenberg Redoubt and the more distant Ober Capuciner Redoubt. These facilities had already appeared in Lefèbvre's original design. According to him, the redoubts were to be very similar; on a rectangular plan with two corners chamfered. There was little difference between them. The Capellenberg Redoubt had a straight front and chamfered corners in the gorge area, the Ober Capuciner Redoubt the opposite. Both redoubts were surrounded by their own moat and their own countermine. According to the original plans, they were not to be linked to the rest of the Neisse fortifications, only to be connected by lines of palisades if necessary. However, after 1780, this changed and a

---

232 Such a reference appears in the legend to the fort plan included on the fortress modernisation project, SBB PK, ref. X 31033/2.

new continuous line of fortifications, called the Upper Ramparts (Hoche Retranchement), was created on the basis of these two structures. One plan of Neisse shows a short section of the tenaille defence line at the Ober Capuciner Redoubt.[233] Before 1783 the fortifications connecting the two redoubts had expanded. One of the plans of Neisse from that year also clearly shows the defensive line connecting the two redoubts, as well as its unfinished section between Capellenberg Redoubt and Fort Bombardier.[234] This line did not form a whole with the rest of the city's fortifications, two long sections were missing. The aforementioned plan also shows a different appearance of the Ober Capuciner Redoubt from that originally designed. It was to have the outline of a flattened lunette, thus differing significantly from that shown on the two previously described plans.

The next step took place around 1786. Unfortunately, in spite of a lot of very interesting material documenting this phase of reconstruction, it is not possible to decipher it with complete confidence. The author of a nineteenth-century history of Neisse – Minsberg – writes that as early as 1786 the Ober Capuciner Redoubt was converted into a bastion and that a gap was filled in the ramparts, which led all the way to the Neisse.[235] However, the only surviving sources claim otherwise. In the legend of the 1789 plan of the fortress we read that the redoubt in question was not to be rebuilt until 1789, while the other redoubt was planned to be converted in 1790.[236] Interestingly, as many as two plans for this reconstruction have survived, both in the collection of the Berlin Staatsbibliothek. Unfortunately, neither of them is dated.

The first, by *Major* Harroy, proposes significant changes. First of all, the two redoubts were to be connected to the rampart and given the form of bastions. Also, the existing rampart was to be reshaped; the short, tenaille section south of the former Ober Capuciner Redoubt was to be re-formed and provided with a regular bastion (later the Bastion Mahren). In addition, the plan was to continue the fortification all the way to the bank of the Neisse River, building a new bastion and a half-bastion connected by curtains. Finally, a gap was to be closed in the defensive perimeter around Fort Bombardier, and to this end two half-bastions and a curtain with a gate between them were to be erected. All these transformations were costed by Harroy at 91,231 thalers.[237] Comparing this engineer's design with later plans for the fortress, we can clearly see that the project was carried out. It is highly likely that this particular project was conceived while Frederick was still alive. Harroy had been carrying out design work on the fortress since December 1782, since the death of *Major* Haab. In turn, following his successor's new division of the engineering service in June 1787, Harroy was given oversight of the other half of the Silesian fortresses to where Neisse was located. Thus, his project to transform the retrenchment must have been conceived before 1787. In this context, Minsberg's account of the reconstruction of the fortifications as late as 1786 sounds more plausible.[238]

---

233 Festung Neisse, SBB PK, ref. X 31033/1.
234 Klose, *Festung Neisse*, il. 47.
235 Minsberg 1834, *Geschichtliche Darstellung*, p.204.
236 Plan von der Stadt und Festung Neisse 1789, GStA SPK, XI HA, ref. A 71393.
237 Project des Major d'Harroy von dem Retranchement bey Neisse, SBB PK, DPG ref. XXIV Neisse 101.
238 Nor does an analysis of royal correspondence clarify the doubts about the dating of the reconstruction. For in 1786, the King did not send any letter to Harroy regarding the works at Neisse,

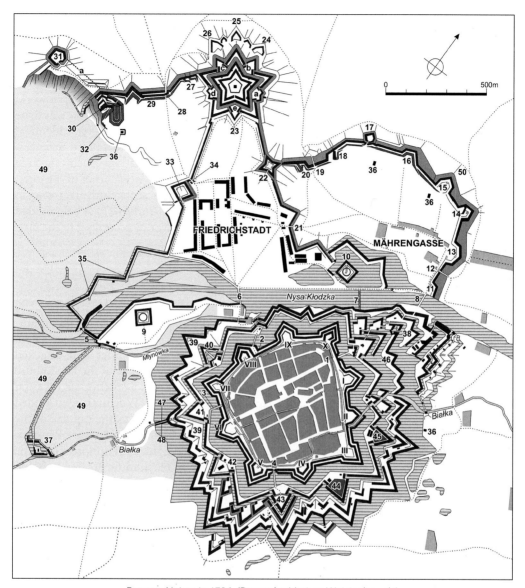

Fortress Neisse in 1786. (Drawn by Mariusz Wojciechowski)

The second of these projects for the completion of the retrenchment is part of the extremely interesting project for the expansion of the fortress at Neisse.[239] This plan, too, may be dated to the end of Frederick's reign or the beginning of that of Frederick William II. This plan

---

although he corresponded with him frequently.
239 Plan von Neisse, SBB PK, ref. X 31035/1.

presents a completely different concept from the previous one for the reconstruction and completion of the ramparts. It assumes leaving the Capellenberg Redoubt unchanged but envisages a much greater transformation of the fortifications in the area around the second redoubt. There the plan was to erect two large bastions, a large ravelin in front of the curtain, and in the foreground, depending on the option,[240] two large, external defence works (roughly on the site of the later Forts I and II built in 1860s), or a large horn work. The section of fortification connecting the existing ramparts with the Niesse River was to be given a tenaille outline. Only the connection to Fort Bombardier was planned to be identical to the above-described design. Importantly, in addition to these two advanced defences, similar works were planned to be erected in front of the town fortifications: one in the area between the Neisse and Biehle rivers, the other in front of the south-west corner of the fortifications. There were also plans to seriously rebuild the Blockhaus sconce. All the works to be built and rebuilt were to be revetted, in addition the advanced works were to be provided with casemates for the garrison and powder stores. The entire works, according to the estimate attached to the project, were to cost 389,500 thalers.[241]

Mountain Forts

Towards the end of his life, Frederick the Great changed his approach to fortifying mountainous areas. The main impetus for this was events of the War of the Bavarian Succession, when relatively small Austrian forces penetrated the mountain border and attacked Prussian outposts. The most famous action of this kind was the defence of the blockhouse at Oberschwedeldorf (Szalejów Górny). In January 1779, there was a small-scale invasion by Austrian troops led by *Generalmajor* Dagobert Sigmund von Wurmser, who raided the territory of Glatz County. The greatest success of the Austrians was the capture of the town of Habelschwerdt (Bystrzyca Kłodzka) and the capture of almost the entire Prussian garrison (714 men), together with its commander, Prince Adolf Hessen-Phillipsthal. At the same time, Austrian forces attacked a small earth and wood blockhouse erected between Glatz and the village of Oberschwedeldorf, defended by 60 soldiers.

The Prussians withstood several hours of shelling from 6- and 12-pounder cannon and 7-pounder howitzers. The defence was ended when a howitzer grenade hit the ventilation chimney, causing a fire and forcing the defenders to surrender. The second, equally important episode, was an attack on a Prussian camp near Dittersbach (Ogorzelec). A major Prussian skirmish from the War of the Bavarian Succession took place near this village, located in the Landeshuter Kamm (Rudawy Janowickie), close to the Schmiedeberger Pass, between Schmiedeberg (Kowary) and Landeshut (Kamienna Góra). A Prussian force of three infantry battalions and a cavalry regiment, located in a fortified camp, were attacked and defeated on 8 November 1778 by a small Austrian corps of 4,000 men, which took the Prussian army completely by surprise. This skirmish, like the events at Oberschwedeldorf,

---

240 The project envisaged two options for upgrading this part of the fortification; both are shown on the inserts pasted onto the master plan.

241 Allgemeine Berechnung von denen Unkosten, die erforderlich seyn könnten, die bei der Festung Neisse projectierte Werke zu erbauen, wie selbige im Plane bezeichnet sind, SBB PK, ref. X 31035/1–2.

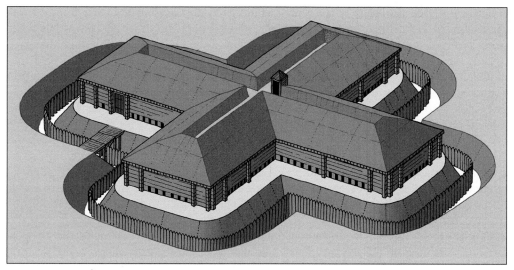

Blockhouse in Ober-Schwedeldorf. (Drawn by Mariusz Wojciechowski)

had little impact on the course of the war. However, it showed that the mountain border was not well protected and that it needed to be secured. In 1781, the King visited the site of the skirmish at Dittersbach and disapproved of the field fortifications erected in 1778.[242] The result of this visit was the first concept of securing this unlucky place with a permanent defence work. As early as October 1781, *Major* von Haab made a design for a blockhouse to defend the site. However, due to financial issues, the King sent the plans for this building back to the designer and decided to return to the subject the following year.[243] The subject returned, but much later, only in 1784. In the autumn of that year, the King ordered *Major* Harroy to draw up cost estimates for the construction of a defence tower. It was to be built on the basis of a plan that the King had sent to his engineer. The tower was, according to the King's wishes, to house a 150-strong garrison and be able to defend itself for four to five days until relief arrived. The King planned to erect several such structures, although he only indicated three specific locations. The first tower was to be built on the site of *Major* Cappeler's blockhouse in Oberschwedeldorf, the second on a hill near Liebau, and the third just near Dittersbach. The King not only presented his engineer with a plan of the structure, but also gave him specific construction guidelines. The basement of the tower could be made of broken stone, obtained during the construction of the moat, but the upper floors were to be made of good, resistant brick. The tower was to be surrounded by a moat, in which a well was also to be established. The King ordered his engineer to see the sites intended for the locations of these towers, and to adjust the cost estimates according to the local

---

242 Theodor Eisenmänger, *Geschichte der Stadt Schmiedeberg* (Breslau: Verlag von Max Woywod, 1900), p.147.
243 Letter from the King to Haab, 3 October 1781, GStA SPK, I HA Rep.96 B Abschriften von Kabinetsordres, Bd.81, p.758.

conditions.[244] The plan sent by the King has not been preserved in the collection of royal correspondence, as this only contains copies of letters and no drawings, but it has most likely survived to the present day. In the collection of the Berlin Staatsbibliothek there are two plans for tower structures for the defence of mountainous areas that have survived, one of which we can identify with high probability as the tower mentioned by the King. This is indicated by several features. Both in the correspondence with Harroy (written partly in French) and on the plan, this structure is identically named: 'tour a machicoulis'. The title of the design additionally has information that it is intended for use in the defence of mountainous areas, which also fits perfectly with the tower mentioned in the royal letters. The details of the drawing also fit. The structure, as described in the letter, is surrounded by a shallow moat and rows of bunks for the soldiers are marked inside, indicating that it was intended to be suitable for permanent residence for the garrison. Furthermore, the drawing is not to scale. We know this because the King sent information about the dimensions of the structure in a separate letter specifically for this reason.[245] Let us therefore look at the design. The tower was to have an eight-sided plan, with three tiers of casemates and an open terrace for cannon on the top tier. The whole was to be additionally surrounded by a dry moat filled with palisades. An important element was to be the machicolations surrounding the artillery platform. Both their form and function were to be similar to those of medieval fortifications. They were to be used to drop projectiles down the tower wall. In this case, however, it was probably not stones that were to be thrown, as in the Middle Ages, but hand grenades. Inside the tower, there were to have been food and gunpowder storerooms, living quarters equipped with long bunks, typical of residential casemates, and positions for small arms.[246]

In addition to the building itself, who designed it is also interesting. This was *Oberstleutnant* comte d'Heinze. The King asked him for the exact dimensions of the tower so that an estimate could be made.[247] Heinze being the designer of this tower should not come as a surprise. He was not valued by the King as a practitioner, but was readily used for purely planning work, such as the execution of a design, later realised by another engineer. Heinze also often sent various proposals for innovative defensive structures to the King on his own initiative.

What was the subsequent fate of the project? Harroy had already drawn up the cost estimates promised to the King for the three towers at the end of December 1784, and the King confirmed receipt of them on the 30th of that month.[248] Thereafter, for more than a year, there was no word of their implementation. It was not until June 1786 that the King issued a decision to build one of the towers, the one located near Dittersbach. The tower was to be

244 King's letters to Harroy, 6 and 24 November 1784, GStA SPK, I HA Rep.96 B Abschriften von Kabinetsordres, Bd.84, pp.998, 1062.
245 Letter from the King to Harroy, 13 December 1784, GStA SPK, I HA Rep.96 B Abschriften von Kabinetsordres, Bd.84, p.1134.
246 Plan d'une Tour á Machecoulis pour Employee a la deffense des Montagnes, SBB PK, ref. N 17915; 17915a; N 17915 a – 3, 4.
247 Letter from the King to Heinze, 13 December 1784, GStA SPK, I HA Rep.96 B Abschriften von Kabinetsordres, Bd.84, p.1133.
248 Letter from the King to Harroy, 30 December 1784, GStA SPK, I HA Rep.96 B Abschriften von Kabinetsordres, Bd.84, p.1184.

Right: A casemated defensive tower on Steiner Berg near Liebau. (Drawn by Mariusz Wojciechowski based on SBB PK, ref. N 17915 a -2,3)

Below: A casemated defensive tower on Steiner Berg near Liebau. (Drawn by Mariusz Wojciechowski based on SBB PK, N 17915 a -2,3)

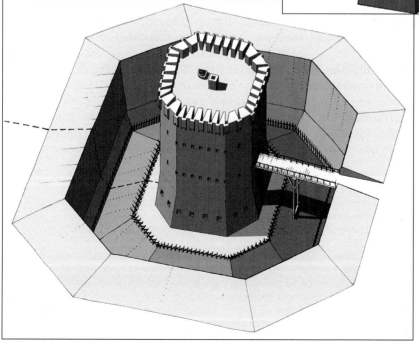

built at a cost of 28,519 thalers, to be paid by Minister von Hoym.[249] Work on the construction of this project occupied the Prussian king literally until the last days of his life. On 4 August, less than two weeks before his death, the King sent a letter to Harroy informing him that on 15 August he would send his two aides-de-camp to make the annual tour of Silesia and review the troops on his behalf. One of them, *Oberstleutnant* von Prittwitz was to go to Dittersbach and see the area where the first tower was planned.[250] What is more, everything points to the fact that the King wanted a whole series of such buildings to be built, according to his first idea from 1784, because on 11 August, that is, less than a week before his death, he informed Harroy that he was sending *Kapitän* Ruchel on a study trip, who was to go to the Glatz County, in the vicinity of Szczytna (Rückers) and Duszniki (Reiners), to examine locations where similar towers could be erected.[251]

The above-described solution seems to be completely archaic and not suited to the realities of modern fortifications. However, as it turns out, similar solutions appeared both in the theory and in the practice of fortifications. The closest analogy are the solutions invented by Vauban. At the end of the seventeenth century, this engineer erected a redoubt at Dunkirk, in the interior of which he placed a single defensive tower. The top storey of the tower had walls slightly overhanging the face of the lower storeys, allowing grenades to be thrown or musket fire to be conducted through the gaps. Importantly, this solution was known in Prussia: at the end of the seventeenth century, a similar tower was planned for the New-Marchian fortress of Oderberg.[252]

The Prussian theoretician of defensive architecture, engineer de Humbert, also presented similar solutions in his 1756 treatise.[253] An important application of the Vauban tower-redoubt for the project described was the Alpine fort of Saint-Vincent. There, in 1692, Vauban designed a tower identical to that for Dunkirk, but with the difference that it was to be located on top of a mountain. The structure within the fort served as a kind of watch-tower and also as a form of Donjon for this small establishment.[254] It is highly likely that the designer of the Lower Silesian towers was familiar with this structure or other similar structures.

Despite significant similarities, the tower designed in 1786 for Dittersbach differed significantly from the Vauban towers-redoubts. First of all, it differed in plan, as it was eight-sided, while the Vauban tower had a square plan with chamfered corners in the upper storeys. The dimensions were also different: the Dittersbach tower was higher and wider than most of the Vauban towers. In addition, it had three tiers of bombproof vaults in the interior, while the Vauban structures had ceilings in the interior. The last difference was the open artillery

---

249 Letters from the King to Harroy and Minister Hoym, 29 June 1786, GStA SPK, I HA Rep.96 B Abschriften von Kabinetsordres, Bd.86, p.608.
250 Letter from the King to Harroy, 4 August 1786, GStA SPK, I HA Rep.96 B Abschriften von Kabinetsordres, Bd.86, p.708.
251 Letter from the King to Harroy, 11 August 1786, GStA SPK, I HA Rep.96 B Abschriften von Kabinetsordres, Bd.86, p.720.
252 Grundriss von der steineren Redouten, so zu Oderberg Soll gebauet werden, sambt der conterscarpa herumbt, SBB PK, DPG ref. XXV Oderberg document no. 1, 2.
253 de Humbert, *Vollkommener Unterricht*, pp.6–7.
254 Thierry Martin, Michèle Virol, *Vauban, architecte de la modernité?* (Paris: Presses universitaires de Franche-Comté 2008), p.122.

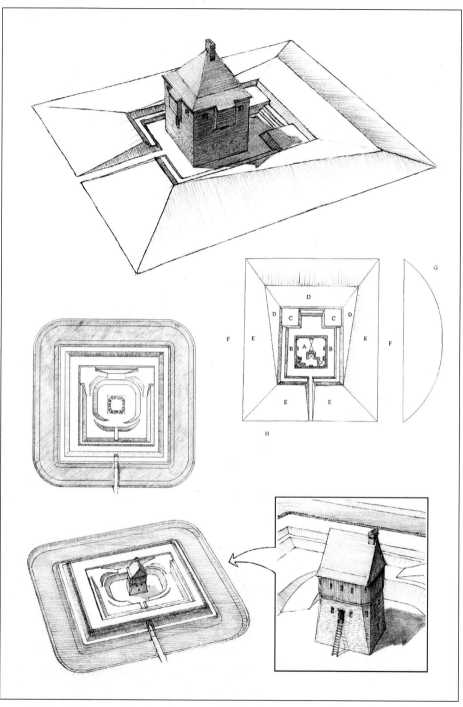

Defensive tower at Oderberg fortress and defensive tower according to de Humbert.
(Drawn by Marcin Wichrowski)

terrace, which was used in Dittersbach. In the Vauban towers-redoubts, the upper storey was consistently covered by a roof. As can be seen, the structure to be built in the Lower Silesian mountains was not a copy, but a creative development of Vauban's ideas.

East and West Prussia

Fortifications located outside Silesia played a much more important role after the Seven Years War than before 1756. The main facilities were established on the Vistula (Wisła) River; these were the fortresses at Grabower Kempe (Kępa Grabowska) and Graudenz (Grudziądz). Compared to them, Fort Lyck, located on Spirdingsee (Lake Śniardwy), had a much lower importance.

Grabow Fortress

After the takeover of the Pomeranian territories seized from Poland during the First Partition of Poland, the Vistula River lands were included within the Prussian state. The need therefore arose to erect a fortress to protect this frontier. Frederick became acquainted with his new dominions during a visit which took place between 1 and 14 June 1773.[255] In preparing for the journey, the King ensured that he was accompanied by the engineer who had hitherto served him as the originator of two major fortress modernisations, at Kolberg and Stettin, comte d'Heinze.[256] On 7 June, the King arrived in Marienwerder (Kwidzyn). It was then that he probably drew attention to a militarily important site, Grabower Kempe, located on the east bank of the river, close to the ford on the Vistula. The officers who were mapping West Prussia at the time (le Clair, Hartmann and Embers) were immediately commissioned to make precise measurements of the area. The work was supervised by Heinze, who, unlike the King, did not return to Potsdam but remained on the Vistula.[257] The King took a keen interest in the new defensive establishment and complained about the slow pace of preparing the plan. In July 1773, he sent two letters urging Heinze to complete the design.[258] Probably the said plan was for the time being a survey of the area for the fortress. However, as early as 1773, design work began, for in October of that year the King was to make a correction to a design by Heinze.[259] As this engineer was not involved with any other fortress at the time, it should be assumed that this concerned the design of a new fortress in Grabow. Preparations for the construction work began in 1774. In March, the King chose Heinze's collaborators. Out of five engineers selected by *Oberst* Regler who had hitherto worked in Silesia, he chose *Kapitän* Gotzenbach and *Leutnant* Maske, who

---

255 Rödenbeck, *Tagebuch oder Geschichtskalender*, vol.3, pp.79–80.
256 Letter from the King to Heinze, 24 May 1773, GStA SPK, I HA Rep.96 B Abschriften von Kabinetsordres, Bd.73 vol.1773, p.155.
257 Troschke, note attached to Plan von denen Durchbrüchen und Eisstopffung der Weichsel bey der Grabower Kempe von 24ten bis 29ten Februar 1776, SBB PK, ref. L 17993; King's letter to Embers, 11 June 1773, GStA SPK, I HA Rep.96 B Abschriften von Kabinetsordres, Bd.73 vol.1773, p.175.
258 Letters from the King to Heinze, 6 and 18 July 1773, GStA SPK, I HA Rep.96 B Abschriften von Kabinetsordres, Bd.73 vol.1773, pp.215 and 233.
259 Letter from the King to Heinze, 12 October 1773, GStA SPK, I HA Rep.96 B Abschriften von Kabinetsordres, Bd.73 vol.1773, p.324.

were to report to Marienwerder on 1 June.[260] In the meantime, Maske had been sent by the King to Glogau and eventually only Gotzenbach was left to assist the count in managing the construction of the new fortress.[261] Too few professionals was something that Heinze complained about throughout his time in Grabow. The King tried to remedy this, but there was not enough engineering staff to meet the needs of building another fortress. In July the King even decided to send two infantry officers to Grabow to support Heinze.[262] Later, *Kapitän* de Legat went there for a while, and at the beginning of October, *Kapitän* Burghesi was permanently posted there.[263] In addition to bringing in engineers, other preparations for construction were being made. In June, the King sent an instruction to the Marienwerder Chamber to transfer 200,000 thalers for the needs of the fortress at Grabow.[264] Presumably these were used to obtain building materials, which were to be collected by the end of the year.[265] Also, in June (between the 5th and 7th of the month) the King was in Marienwerder and again visited the site of the future fortress.[266] In the autumn, planning began for the first building season and Heinze made a request for more funds, this time 400,000 thalers. This sum was to be paid by the Marienwerder Chamber from May 1775 onwards. Heinze wanted to erect barracks in which the workers could live during the construction, but the King categorically rejected this idea.[267] In January 1775, however, the King complied with another, constantly repeated request by Heinze and sent another engineer to help, *Leutnant* Harenberg.[268] In March two more arrived; *Kapitän* Franseky and *Leutnant* Kiestmacher. Although construction work was due to start any day, the final design of the fortress was not ready. The one the King received in early March did not fully satisfy him and he did not like some of the solutions.[269]

Nevertheless, work was set in motion. In addition to the fortress itself, the King also ordered the erection of several wooden gunpowder magazines for 500 cetnars each.[270] For the first year of the construction, the work was led by Heinze. In October, the King sent him to Danzig for a few weeks to familiarise himself thoroughly with that fortress. During the

260 Letter from the King to Regler, 7 March 1774, GStA SPK, I HA Rep.96 B Abschriften von Kabinetsordres, Bd.73 vol.1774, p.89.

261 Letter to Regler, 3 April 1774, GStA SPK, I HA Rep.96 B Abschriften von Kabinetsordres, Bd.73 vol.1774, p.133.

262 Letter from the King to Heinze, 13 July 1774, GStA SPK, I HA Rep.96 B Abschriften von Kabinetsordres, Bd.73 vol.1774, p.268.

263 Letters from the King to Heinze, 19 September and 2 October 1774, GStA SPK, I HA Rep.96 B Abschriften von Kabinetsordres, Bd.73 vol.1774, pp.350, 365.

264 Max Bär, *Westpreussen unter Friedrich dem Grossen* (Leipzig: S. Hirzel, 1909), p.342.

265 Letter from the King to Heinze, 18 December 1774, GStA SPK, I HA Rep.96 B Abschriften von Kabinetsordres, Bd.73 vol.1774, p.453.

266 Rödenbeck, *Tagebuch oder Geschichtskalender*, vol.3, p.97.

267 Letters from the King to Heinze, 19 October, 6 and 20 November and 18 December 1774, GStA SPK, I HA Rep.96 B Abschriften von Kabinetsordres, Bd.73 vol.1774, pp.387–388, 410, 423, 453.

268 Letter from the King to Heinze, 30 January 1775, GStA SPK, I HA Rep.96 B Abschriften von Kabinetsordres, Bd.74, p. XLIII.

269 Letter from the King to Heinze, 8 March 1775, GStA SPK, I HA Rep.96 B Abschriften von Kabinetsordres, Bd.74, p.6.

270 Letter from the King to Heinze, 26 April 1775, GStA SPK, I HA Rep.96 B Abschriften von Kabinetsordres, Bd.74, p.140.

journey, he fell ill and the King ordered him to return to Potsdam for treatment. Gotzenbach was to supervise the work in the Frenchman's absence.[271] However, what was supposed to be a temporary solution turned out to be permanent. Heinze remained in Potsdam and Gotzenbach took command of the works in this part of Prussia. At the time he took over supervision of the construction, the work was not well advanced, in fact the fortress was only delineated and earthworks were being carried out in preparation for the foundation of the masonry lining. It is not known whether the ramparts had already been laid. Moreover, the oldest known Gotzenbach report shows that numerous mistakes had been made in the work to date. Heinze was said to have improperly applied the grate on which the foundation was supported. After taking over the work, Gotzenbach was forced to correct the work, including driving the old piles deeper and hammering in new ones. As a result, the main masonry work could not be started until the following year. As well as improving the foundations, Gotzenbach was also busy preparing for the next building season. He imported tools (these were to be purchased in Elbing) and sourced stone for the masonry revetment.[272] Stone proved to be the biggest problem. Initially it was planned to bring it in by ship from Pillau (Piława, now Балтийск).[273] However, this idea was not implemented. A search was made closer, in a quarry in the village of Jungen (Wiąg near Świecie/Schwetz). No suitable material was found there, but limestone deposits suitable for making lime were discovered. According to Gotzenbach's idea, the missing ashlar stone was to be replaced by field stones. Large stones from fields could be successfully used in the construction of the masonry revetment in the front embankment on the side of the main Vistula stream.[274] The King approved of his engineer's ideas; he also recommended that field stones be obtained in a similar way to what was done in Silesia for the construction of the fortresses at Schweidnitz and Neisse. There the peasants collected stones in the fields in winter, at a time when (according to the King) they had nothing to do, for which they were to receive four thalers per *Klafter*.[275] Gotzenbach, obeying the King's order, sent a request to the local Marienwerder Chamber to organise this activity. However, as it turned out, what was easy in Silesia was difficult to do in Prussia. The chambers – both the one in Marienwerder and the others in Königsberg and Gumbinnen (Gąbin, Гусев) – refused to cooperate in the construction of the fortress. Gotzenbach complained to the King, asking for his intervention, because without the stones the construction could not start in the spring of the following year.[276] In response, the King excused his officials by explaining to the engineer that 'the local chambers are not yet as skilled [as those in Silesia] in fortress construction', but also stressed that he had given them instructions to focus both on the collection of stones and on the other needs of the ongoing construction work. The office appointed to deal with matters of the construction of this

271 Letter from the King to Heinze, 22 October and 8 November 1775, GStA SPK, I HA Rep.96 B Abschriften von Kabinetsordres, Bd.74, pp.694, 758.

272 Letter to Gotzenbach, 12 November 1775, GStA SPK, I HA Rep.96 B Abschriften von Kabinetsordres, Bd.74, p.779.

273 Letter to Heinze, 22 November 1775 and to Gotzenbach of 23 November 1775, GStA SPK, I HA Rep.96 B Abschriften von Kabinetsordres, Bd.74, pp.789, 809.

274 Copy of Gotzebach's letter, 2 December 1775 written in Kl. Grabow, GStA SPK, IV HA Preußische Arme, Rep.1 Geheime Kriegskanzlei, Nr. 104, p.9.

275 Former unit of volume used in construction work, approximately 3.3m3.

276 Gotzenbach's letter, 23 December 1775, Kl. Grabow, GStA SPK, IV HA Rep.1 Nr. 104, p.12.

fortress was the Marienwerder Chamber.[277] However, despite the royal assurances, the problems with the fortress construction were not over. In a letter dated 13 January, Gotzenbach wrote that the work would only progress well if the chambers cooperated and did not make problems, as they had done the previous year.[278] On 17 January, Gotzenbach reported that the local chamber was only able to deliver 12,000 *Klafter* of field stones and 4,000 *Klafter* of limestone from the Jungen quarries.[279] In order to get the local clerical machine to finally prioritise the needs of the construction work at the fortress, the King gave orders to the head of the local administration, the *Oberpräsident* Domhard of Königsberg, to meet Gotzenbach and set up the administration's activities in such a way that the construction would continue without difficulty.[280]

The needs were great. Besides the stone and limestone, Gotzenbach needed 5,000 workers, 150 four-horse carriages, 100 masons, 70 bricklayers and 40 carpenters every day during 1776.[281] However, as it turned out, the problem was not only the unwillingness of local officials to cooperate, but also the lack of a proper artisan force. Only labourers and transport could be organised in the region, while carpenters and bricklayers had to be brought in from Thuringen.[282]

However, all these problems soon went by the wayside. Mistakes were made in the location of the fortress that resulted in a major building disaster. On 24–29 February, a passing block of ice on the Vistula led to a blockage and the damming of the waters. This resulted in massive damage. Gotzenbach drew up the first report documenting it as early as 1 March, before the waters had completely subsided. Even then, however, the enormity of the force of the water was apparent. It had broken the dykes (old and new), and almost all of the piles that had been driven under the foundation the previous year had been uprooted and torn up by the ice. Nevertheless, Gotzenbach promised to 'work day and night so that not all is lost.'[283] The full extent of the destruction is illustrated by Gotzenbach's report of 16 March. It is all the more important because it includes an attached plan showing the deluge and the damage to the work already done. The engineer reported that the new causeway including bridges had been destroyed along 242 rods (about 880 metres), that 496 foundation piles had been torn out, and that 346 piles had been broken by the water. In total, he valued the losses at more than 90,000 thalers. Furthermore, he drew attention to the further effects of the flood. According to him, more than 1,000,000 thalers more than planned would have to be spent to protect against further similar damage. The reason was said to be the poor ground. The layer of sand was 50 feet thick and even with the use of piles it was not possible to reach solid rock. What is more, securing against the ice would have forced the construction of the masonry revetment to be abandoned in favour of erecting it with stone, which would have posed the risk of the massive walls collapsing.[284] As might be expected, upon receiving

---

277 King's letter, 27 December 1775, Potsdam, GStA SPK, IV HA Rep.1 Nr. 104, p.13.
278 Gotzenbach's letter, 13 January 1776, Kl. Grabow, GStA SPK, IV HA Rep.1 Nr. 104, p.15.
279 Gotzenbach's letter, 17 January 1776, Kl. Grabow, GStA SPK, IV HA Rep.1 Nr. 104, p.19.
280 King's letter, 31 January 1776, GStA SPK, IV HA Rep.1 No. 104, p.20.
281 Gotzenbach's letter, 13 January 1776, Kl. Grabow, GStA SPK, IV HA Rep.1 Nr. 104, p.15.
282 Letter from the King to Gotzenbach, 18 February 1776, from Potsdam, GStA SPK, IV HA Rep.1 No. 104, p.23.
283 Gotzenbach's letter, 1 March 1776, Kl. Grabow, GStA SPK, IV HA Rep.1 Nr. 104, p.26.
284 Gotzenbach's letter, 16 March 1776, Kl. Grabow, GStA SPK, IV HA Rep.1 Nr. 104, p.27.

this news, the King (in a letter of 20 March) abandoned the construction of the fortress at Grabow. He immediately decided on a new location for the fortress – he wanted to build it at Graudenz.[285] As it turned out from later letters, the water did not destroy everything, there remained a lot of materials and tools worth a total of 100,000 thalers which could be used to build a new fortress; moreover, 191,483 thalers remained in the construction coffers.[286]

What was the cause of the destruction of the fortress? Evidently its poor location. In his preliminary report of 1 March, Gotzenbach wrote that the construction of the fortress had narrowed the riverbed by half, causing a blockage during the icy winter. This error is surprising when one realises that the problems of river fortresses were well known to Prussian engineers. In fact, all Prussian fortresses (except the one at Silberberg) were located on a river, which determined the risk of flooding. It follows that the location here was decided by someone who lacked this experience. Suspicion falls on the comte d'Heinze and the King himself. The former may have been an engineer, but he came from France and may not have been familiar with the local conditions. The King, on the other hand, although he had some experience, nevertheless lacked engineering expertise. All the indications are that the King is to blame for this mistake. According to some accounts, Frederick was supposed to have been informed that at the site he had chosen, water would inundate the defensive works during floods, but he refused to believe these warnings and ordered the designer to undertake the work. As the Vistula was not expected to rise much during the first spate, the King scoffed at the warnings made earlier and ordered the work to be intensified. By ignoring the warnings, he made the wrong decision.[287] This is also confirmed in the surviving correspondence. Indeed, the King initially quite calmly accepted the fact of the destruction of the fortress and the associated loss of money and time. This is evidenced by the fact that he did not order the arrest of any of the engineers working in Grabow. Although he did not have to arrest Heinze, as he was under arrest for debt, there is no indication that the King blamed him for the disaster. On the contrary, he wanted to help him out of gaol so that he could draw up the design and cost estimate for the new stronghold.[288] Later, however, he changed his mind. In a letter dated 2 April, he accused Heinze of errors in the conduct of the construction. According to the King, if he had worked conscientiously enough, he would have succeeded in completing the causeway on time, which would have protected the fortress from the ice.[289]

It is worth devoting a few words to the fortress itself. Although it was not completed, and work was abandoned when its construction was very poorly advanced, it should at least be briefly described. We only know the outline, which is plotted on the plan attached to Gotzenbach's report of 16 March 1776.[290] The fortress was located on the east bank of the

---

285 Letter from the King to Gotzenbach, 20 March 1776, GStA SPK, IV HA Rep.1 No. 104, p.29.

286 Letter from the King to Gotzenbach, 9 April 1776, from Potsdam, GStA SPK, IV HA Rep.1 No. 104, p.34.

287 Honore-Gabriel Riquetti de Mirabeau, *Von der Preußischen Monarchie unter Friedrich dem Großen* (Leipzig: Dykische Buchhandlung, 1795), Bd.4, pp.377–378.

288 Letter to Heinze, March 1776, GStA SPK, I HA Rep.96 B Abschriften von Kabinetsordres, Bd.75, p.232.

289 Letter to Heinze, 2 April 1776, GStA SPK, I HA Rep.96 B Abschriften von Kabinetsordres, Bd.75, p.266.

290 Plan von denen Durchbrüchen und Eisstopffung der Weichsel bey der Grabower Kempe von 24ten bis 29ten Februar 1776, 88 x 46 cm, signed Kl. Grabow, den 16 mertz 1776 Gontzenbach, SBB PK, ref.

Vistula. It was an elongated, seven-bastion defensive structure. Two fronts – on the Vistula side and on the land side – were distinctly longer. The northern and southern fronts were short. The eastern front, on the land side, had three large bastions; the western front, on the Vistula side, had four smaller ones; two regular, though flattened, and two with a tenaille outline (in the corners of the front). The western front had no projecting works. Ravelins were placed in front of the curtain of the northern and southern fronts. The eastern front was the most heavily fortified, with a large counterguard in front of the central bastion, extensive ravelins in front of the two curtains, and a large horn work each in front of the corner bastions. The entire fortress was about 800 metres long and 450 metres wide at its widest point. The fortress at Grabow, at least in the shape we know from Gotzenbach's drawing, was a relatively traditional structure. The outline of the defensive works was fairly standard, with only two corner bastions with a tenaille outline standing out. However, such a bastion outline is also known in the Prussian tradition and the bastions located in the corners of the riverside fronts of Breslau and Glogau looked similar. Other analogies that can be found are related to the large horn works that were to be located in front of the corner bastions. A similar design was to be created in Stettin, based on the reconstruction project for this fortress made by Heinze around 1769. It was to replace Leopold's Fort.[291] Similar solutions can also be found in the theory of the defensive architecture of the era, for example this form of riverside bastion was proposed by Menno van Ceohoorn.[292]

Graudenz Fortress

The immediate successor of the fortress on Grabower Kempe was the stronghold at Graudenz. Before it is described, however, the question of the fortified camp there must be raised. The authors of the most recent monograph on the fortress suggest that the idea of a fortified camp was supposedly conceived in July 1776, after the fortress had already begun to be built. The later citadel was to be the nucleus for the whole establishment, while the works of the fortified camp were to be the type of external works often found in Prussian fortresses of the time, but missing in Graudenz.[293] Such a conception seems at first glance to be a questionable one – for it is difficult to regard the irregular, field fortified works as equivalent to works of the kind found in Kozielsk's Larger Redoubt or Kłodzko's Wojciechowicka Fleece or Żuraw. Besides, a careful analysis of the surviving correspondence clearly shows that the concept of creating a fortified camp in the vicinity of Graudenz originated earlier than the concept of a fortress there. This is evidenced by Heinze's letter to the King sent from Grabow on 12 December 1775, in which the engineer speaks of a project for a fortified camp near Graudenz, initiated on the King's orders. This camp was to be defended not only with fortifications, but also with flooding. This, however, according to the French engineer, was impossible due to insufficient water in the River Osa. Heinze also writes in this letter about a military map of the Graudenz

L 17993.

291 Stettin – Plan de fondation, SBB PK, ref. X 34071–4; Stettin 1761, 1er Project, SBB PK, ref. X 34071–3. The authorship of Heinze is suggested by the archive catalogue and also by Hanke, Degner, Geschichte der Amtlichen Kartographie, pp.190–191.

292 Menno van Coehoorn, *Neuer Vestungs-Bau*, Wesel 1708, Fig. P, p.238.

293 Jakub Franczak, Włodzimierz Grabowski, Piotr Nowiński, Mariusz Żebrowski, *Twierdza Grudziądz* (Grudziądz: Wydawnictwo Kalamarski, 2010), p.84.

area made by him, as well as plans to fortify this town and expand it.[294] It is difficult to say anything more about the latter, as it does not appear anywhere except in the quoted letter. The map of the Graudenz area is mentioned several times in the correspondence between Gotzenbach and the King. The first letter mentioning the matter dates from 19 December 1775 and the last, informing of the receipt of the original brief with Heine's measurements, from 16 March 1776.[295] Importantly, the map is believed to have survived in the holdings of the Berlin Staatsbibliothek. Indeed, attached to Heinze's letter mentioned above was a map on a scale of 1:20,000, measuring 115 x 73 cm, showing the Graudenz area on both sides of the Vistula. The map locates numerous field fortifications, some of which it identifies as 'old Swedish entrenchments'. On the eastern side of the Vistula these entrenchments are located near the villages of Klodtken (Kłódka) and Neudorf (Nowa Wieś), and on the western side, near the village of Sibsau (Bdzowo). The map also shows other fortifications, without identification, in the vicinity of the villages of Zakurzewo (Sacrau), Parsken (Parski), Tannenrode (Świerkocin) and the hamlet of Ossa Krug.[296] However, neither on the aforementioned map nor in the King's letters to Heinze does the subject of the fortified camp appear. It does not recur until 20 March in the letter from the King to Gotzenbach, in which the sovereign informed him of the abandonment of further construction of the fortress at Grabow. In it, Frederick decides to fortify Graudenz, and construct a fortified camp. In addition, the King informs his engineer that he is sending him all the plans for the vicinity of Graudenz and the plans for the fortified camp.[297] This means that the fortified camp as a project already existed, so according to the initial concepts it was to be a separate structure from the fortress to be built on Grabower Kempe. The King clearly wanted to create two separate fortified complexes, different in character. Although they would be quite distant from each other (25 kilometres), this did not preclude functional links. Moreover, there were already examples of fortified camps and fortresses being linked in the fortifications of the Frederician period. Frederick, in his *Military Testament* of 1768, comments that the Silberberg fortress covered the flank of the fortified camp at Landeshut.[298] If there was a functional link between the stronghold of Silberberg and the camp at Landeshut (50 kilometres apart), it was all the more possible between the stronghold at Grabower Kempe and the camp at Graudenz.

Something of a return to the fortified camp concept took place in the last year of Frederick's reign. In this year Johann Samuel Lilienthal, a civilian designer of hydrological structures, designed a dozen locks to create a lagoon in front of the fortress fortifications, together with four defending redoubts and lunettes.[299] This project also remained unrealised.

294　SBB PK, DPG ref. XIII Graudenz, 59, 12c.

295　The King first sent Gotzenbach a map. The engineer was then to ask Heinze to send the original measurements, and after receiving a refusal he asked for the King's intercession in the matter. The King gave orders to Heinze to send the original briefs and upon receipt sent them to Gotzenbach. GStA SPK, IV HA Rep.1 No. 104, pp.11, 15, 17, 22, 27.

296　SBB PK, DPG ref. XIII Graudenz, 59, 12c.

297　Letter from the King to Gotzenbach, 20 March 1776, GStA SPK, IV HA Rep.1 No. 104, p.29.

298　Volz, *Die Werke*, vol.6, p.243.

299　Situations Plan von der Gegend um die Vestung Graudentz und der Einzurichtenden Inundation das niedrigen Terrains um selbige vermittelst derer zu machenden Stau-Dämme und Schelusen auch Canähle, SBB PK, ref. N 11125. This plan provided with the date '1774' This is, however, most likely a later annotation. The date clearly differs in typeface from the rest of the legend text. Besides, also the

After the disastrous flood of the winter of 1776. Frederick ordered work on Grabower Kempe to cease, and immediately set about choosing a new location for the fortress. In a letter dated 20 March, the King ordered Gotzenbach to 'prepare a plan and cost estimate for the fortifications near Graudenz, and send everything to me as soon as possible.'[300] In a letter written three days later, he writes, in turn:

> As I have given up the plan to build a fortress in Grabow, due to numerous difficulties and uncertainties, and instead on the hills near Graudenz, specifically on the highest one, I have ordered a fortress to be built. So I order you to see them immediately and to find the highest hill between Graudenz and Neudorf, specifically the one closest to the water, with its back towards the Vistula, and to make a decent plan for it.[301]

Gotzenbach immediately set about implementing the royal ideas. Although he himself had to see to the decommissioning of the construction site in Grabow and take care of the transport of materials to the new site, he assigned two officers to draw up maps of the area around Graudenz so as to present plans and cost estimates to the King as soon as possible.[302] However, the King showed impatience and, without waiting for accurate measurements, designed the fortress himself. He wrote to Gotzenbach about this in a letter dated 9 April: 'Besides, I have already made my provisional plan of the new fortifications. However, in order to establish something concrete, I must have all the exact levels.'[303] The plan mentioned by the King is the same one that has been in general circulation since the 1870s. A copy of it is first published by Udo von Bonin in his book of 1877.[304] The plan itself, however, is mentioned in an article on Frederician fortifications from 1841.[305]

To this day, both the royal original drawing[306] and the copy published by Bonin[307] have been preserved in archival collections. The aforementioned original drawing is in the same sheath as the rest of the correspondence with Gotzenbach, placed among the letters of the early period. Although it is neither signed nor dated, the archival context leaves no doubt that this sketch is that 'provisional plan of the new fortifications' mentioned in the letter. In light of the above, the suggestions of the authors of the 2010 monograph on the fortress that the King was not the author of the original drawing should be rejected.[308] Of course,

---

content of the map, both cartographic and its title, indicates that it was created later than 1774, as the decision to build a fortress in Graudenz was not made until 1776, i.e. two years later. Neither can this plan be regarded as part of an unknown concept of the Graudenz fortress, which was created in 1774. This is contradicted by the wording of the title, which refers to a 'fortress in Graudenz' and not a 'new fortress in Graudenz'. It was most likely written during Lilienthal's stay in Graudenz, between January and July 1786.

300 Letter from the King to Gotzenbach, 20 March 1776, GStA SPK, IV HA Rep.1 No. 104, p.29.
301 Letter from the King to Gotzenbach, 23 March 1776, GStA SPK, IV HA Rep.1 No. 104, p.30.
302 Letter from Gotzenbach to the King, written from Grabow, 3 April 1776, GStA SPK, IV HA Rep.1 No. 104, p.31.
303 Letter from the King to Gotzenbach, 9 April 1776, GStA SPK, IV HA Rep.1 No. 104, p.34.
304 Anon., 'Die Festung Graudenz', *Archiv für die Artillerie und Ingenieur-Offiziere des deutschen Reichsheeres*, 81, (1877), pp.106–107.
305 Anon., 'Friedrich der Große als Ingenieur', p.25.
306 GStA SPK, IV HA Rep.1 Nr. 104, p.16.
307 Capt. Heinle, copy of Frederick the Great design, GStA SPK, XI HA, ref. G 70401.
308 Franczak, Grabowski, Nowiński, Żebrowski, *Twierdza Grudziądz*, p.82.

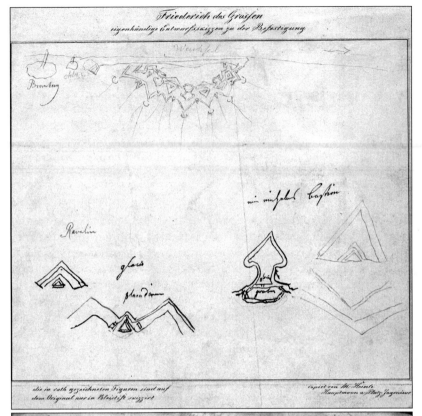

Above: Fortress Graudenz, first known design by Frederick the Great. (GStA SPK, XI HA, ref. G 70401)

Left: Fortress Graudenz, second known design by Frederick the Great. (GStA SPK, IV. HA, Rep. 1, Nr. 104, p.20)

some doubts remain; after all, the drawing is neither dated nor signed. Moreover, none of the surviving drawings have any indication in the title or content that it is a design for the fortress at Graudenz. Doubts may be all the greater as the plan contains unclear topographical information – the only towns located on the sketch are Bromberg (Bydgoszcz) and the smaller town of Ohla. This and the lack of an original signature could suggest that this is a plan for a fortress in the Bromberg area. However, this is not possible. The town lies on the western bank of the river, and the drawing, happily provided with an arrow indicating the direction of the current, clearly shows the foundation located on its eastern bank. Probably the King called Graudenz Bromberg by mistake. An understandable mistake, after all, the area had belonged to the Prussian king for only a few years. The unambiguous identification of this drawing as the design for Graudenz is made possible by the forms of the defensive works that the King depicted in this sketch.

This small sketch was done in pencil and ink. It depicts the fortress in its entirety and with some details – a detached bastion, a ravelin and a glacis with a places of arms. The fortress, drawn in pencil, is depicted as a defensive establishment on the plan of a half (section) of a regular polygon, with its back against the Vistula and its front facing the land. The main perimeter was to be provided with three bastions and two half-bastions (on the border with the river), between the bastions there were to be four ravelins. The whole was to be surrounded by a covered way with places of arms provided with redoubts in the receding salients and with semi-circular flanks located in front of the advanced salients. The fortress was also supposed to be provided with one outer work. South of the corner bastion there was to be a small defensive work with a polygonal outline, probably connected to the core by a covered communication. The ink drawings of the individual elements also give us interesting information. The most important was the detached bastion. It had orillons and also retired and concave flanks. The drawing is devoid of any suggestion of doubled flanks or the existence of a casemated battery there. Importantly, it was separated from the main core by its own moat, as we learn from the caption. Important details are also shown in the second drawing, depicting a section of the covered way. The places of arms in the receding corner were to have a redoubt surrounded by a moat, sheltered from the covered way sections by traverses. The last detailed section of the fortress shown in this sketch is the ravelin. It was drawn twice – in ink and pencil. It can be seen that it was to have a redoubt sheltered by its own moat, and that there was to be an additional defensive work in the form of a tenaille between it and the curtain.

Another suggestion introduced by the authors of the aforementioned monograph is the involvement of Heinze in the initial design of the fortress. To this engineer the authors attribute one of the designs of the fortress, preserved in the Berlin Staatsbibliothek.[309] The design presents a fortress similar in general principles to the constructed one, but differing in important details both from the built version and from all other plans preserved in the Berlin Staatsbibliothek. According to this design, the core was to have a tenaille outline, but with very weakly protruding corners. At a considerable distance from the core were to be detached bastions, with retired flanks protected by orillons. Between the bastions were to be

---

309 Franczak, Grabowski, Nowiński, Żebrowski, *Twierdza Grudziądz*, pp.82, 86. This plan has been published, but with the erroneous information that it comes from the collection of TPF Grudziądz, while it is actually stored in SBB PK, ref. X 25469–1.

ravelins sheltered by counterguards. Finally, there was to be a covered way on the outside, in its places of arms were to be located reduits. All the above-mentioned elements were to be casemated. Both the main rampart and the detached bastions, the ravelin, its counterguards and the reduits of the covered way were to have casemates for the crew. They were all to be single-bay, constructed on the basis of a single module. Attention should also be drawn to the gun casemates, which were planned to be inserted into the retired flanks of the bastions. Unlike the constructed design, these casemates were to be two-storey and integrated into the bastion's earth rampart.

Unfortunately, there is no strong evidence to substantiate the thesis that the author of this plan was Heinze. The plan is not signed, besides, contrary to the claims of the authors of the monograph on the fortress, it is also not dated. The only arguments they put forward about the links between this project and the French designer concern the drawing style which made this project similar to another project by Heinze, the Stettin fortress. These arguments miss the point, for while it is indeed possible to find some graphic similarities the two, the other designs by comte d'Heinze described in the following chapter do not show any such similarities. It is likely that we are dealing here with the work of the same draughtsman, not the same designer.

However, Heinze's involvement in the design of the fortress at Graudenz should not be completely dismissed, as the engineer had considerable connections with the town. As is already known, he drew up measurements and a map of the town's surroundings, as well as designs for the fortification of the town and the fortified camp. Moreover, a letter from the King from the second half of March 1776 has been preserved, which actually suggests the participation of this engineer in the initial design phase of the Graudenz fortress. In it, the King informed the engineer, sitting in jail for debt, that he wanted to help him on his release to make a plan and cost estimate for the new fortress based on the King's idea.[310] However, not much later, in a letter of 2 April, the King blamed Heinze for the disaster in Grabow.[311] It is therefore difficult to suppose that the King would have continued to trust an engineer whom he accused of such glaring errors by allowing him to carry out the project. Moreover, correspondence from the later period concerning Graudenz took place exclusively between Gotzenbach and the King, while Heinze, although he was regularly the addressee of royal letters, this was only in the context of examinations for officer ranks in the engineering corps, which he conducted on the King's commission. However, it cannot be entirely ruled out that Heinze drafted something after the King sent him his first letter (in mid-March). Regardless, the surviving documents clearly point to the King as the person from whose ideas the process of designing the fortress began.

The concepts presented in the royal sketch had already taken the form of a proper building project by the spring; at the end of June 1776 another version was produced.[312] At that time Gotzenbach sent back to the King 'a plan for a polygon with mines based on his majesty's design.'[313] Further ideas of the King appeared in this project. In addition to the introduction of counter-mine corridors, the King decided to build a large casemate in the fortress, on the Vistula side. Both of these modifications significantly changed both the appearance of the

---

310   Letter to d'Heinze, March 1776, GStA SPK, I HA Rep.96 B Abschriften von Kabinetsordres, Bd.75, p.232.
311   Letter to d'Heinze, 2 April 1776, GStA SPK, I HA Rep.96 B Abschriften von Kabinetsordres, Bd.75, p.266.
312   'Die Festung Graudenz', p.18.
313   Gotzenbach's letter to the King, 29 June 1776, GStA SPK, IV HA Rep.1 No. 104, p.39.

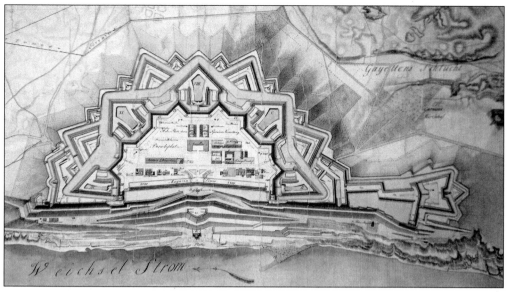

Fortress Graudenz, in 1812. (GStA SPK, XI HA, ref. A 70747)

newly designed fortress and the planned cost of its construction.[314] This was not the last such interference. In 1779, at the King's behest, another novelty was added to the project – adding casemates to the lunettes. Five years later, in a similar fashion, the King decided to casemate the ravelins.[315] Another example of the King's design decision regarding the form of the fortress is the abandonment of the use of cannon embrasures in the core of the fortress. The King forbade Gotzenbach to make them out of concern for the possibility of the fortress being taken by surprise; he stated: 'Where the hole is, there the Croatian will crawl too.'[316]

In addition to imposing specific design solutions, the King also actively influenced the functional programme of the future fortress. In a letter dated 3 July 1776, he writes that the fortress is to have casemates for 2,400 soldiers, 100 miners, 150 gunners and for food for eight months.[317]

The construction of the Graudenz fortress was a long and, as it turned out, very complicated process. According to the first royal assumptions it was to last four years.[318]

The start of construction work was symbolic. On 6 June 1776, during a visit to the site of the future fortress, Frederick personally marked out a point which was to be its centre. This point was to be the place from which the fortress was later demarcated. Essential work began two months later, on 3 August, and lasted until the end of November. Both earthworks (ground levelling) and masonry works were carried out.[319] In the following year, 1777,

314 'Die Festung Graudenz', p.20.
315 'Die Festung Graudenz', pp.29, 43.
316 *Wo ein Loch ist, da kriecht ein Kroat hinein.* Kamptz, *Grundsätze*, p.10 footnote.
317 Letter from the King to Gotzenbach, 9 July 1776, GStA SPK, IV HA Rep.1 No. 104, p.43.
318 Letter from the King to Gotzenbach, 9 July 1776, GStA SPK, IV HA Rep.1 No. 104, p.45.
319 'Die Festung Graudenz', p.22.

the earthworks in the core of the fortress were completed and the foundations were fully established. In addition, the walls of the ramparts began to be erected; the first storey of the casemates was built in one of the bastions. The foundations were problematic, and piling had to be used in some areas, which took a lot of time and money. Fascine retaining walls were also erected to reinforce the bank, which was subsiding into the Vistula. Wells and drainage channels were also constructed to channel water away from the construction site.[320] The War of the Bavarian Succession was fought in 1778 and 1779, which severely restricted construction activity. The number of labourers and the engineering staff serving the construction site decreased significantly. By the end of 1778, it was possible to erect the fortress walls (apart from one curtain) to a height of 18 feet above the level of the moat, to complete the laying of the foundations, and to construct wells and wooden drainage channels.[321]

The builders of the fortress faced numerous complications. Nature posed problems; groundwater made it difficult to lay the foundations, while the unstable Vistula embankment threatened the entire construction. Problems were also caused by the King himself, who, not trusting Gotzenbach, harassed him with inspections, and also insufficiently funded the construction.[322] All this meant that by the end of 1782 only the core of the fortress could be completed; in the bastions either masonry work had just begun or only the foundation excavations had been completed.[323] These were successfully finished in 1783, but all the time work was being done to erect the great storehouse and stabilise the Vistula escarpment. In addition, external works were still missing.[324] Work on the warehouse and the escarpment continued into 1784, and work was also being done on the erection of the ravelins. In 1785, in addition to finishing the storehouse and the Vistula escarpment, work was done on erecting reduits in the ravelins, and masonry for the moat counterscarp and lunettes. It was not possible to complete this work in that year, and the finishing work was still going on in 1786. The construction of the fortress, the erection of the counter-mine corridors planned by Frederick and the new horn works took much longer, and the King did not live to see them finished. Gotzebnach corresponded on the construction of the fortress until 1792 with the King's successor, with some finishing work continuing until 1806.[325]

One of the most important elements that distinguish the fortress at Graudenz from other fortresses in Prussia and even Europe is its unusual outline. This is because the fortress consists of a tenaille, in front of which detached bastions extend. Only in front of these bastions was the main moat located. Such a solution was quite unusual for the time, as the bastion was usually treated as the main defensive structure, so care was taken to ensure its proper functional connection with the curtains. Meanwhile, in Graudenz, the bastions are clearly separated from the curtains, which significantly exceed them in height. Moreover, according to the original designs, the bastions were to be separated from the core by an additional internal moat.

320 'Die Festung Graudenz', p.26.
321 'Die Festung Graudenz', p.28.
322 'Die Festung Graudenz', pp.29, 34–35.
323 'Die Festung Graudenz', p.36.
324 'Die Festung Graudenz', p.38.
325 Franczak, Grabowski, Nowiński, Żebrowski, *Twierdza Grudziądz*, p.96.

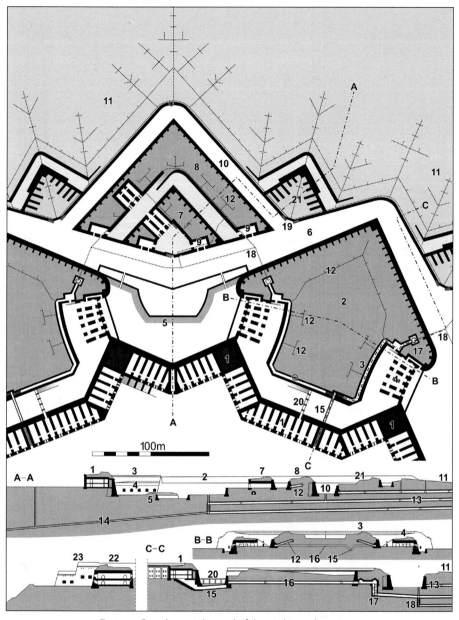

Fortress Graudenz at the end of the eighteenth century.
1) Donjon, 2) bastion, 3) bastion's flank, 4) casemated gun emplacement, 5) tenaille in the main moat, 6) moat, 7) reduit, 8) ravelin, 9) powder magazine, 10) moat in front of ravelin, 11) glacis, 12) countermine gallery, 13) countermine gallery (not all levels completed), 14) drainage canal, 15) postern to the bastion, 16) communication walkway, 17) stairs in the orillon to the postern under the moat, 18) stairs to the lower level of countermine galleries, 19) entrance to the countermine gallery system and counterscarp gallery, 20) bridge, 21) reduit of the place of arms, 22) Vistula River storehouse (off-plan), 23) flanking battery (off-plan).
(Drawn by Mariusz Wojciechowski)

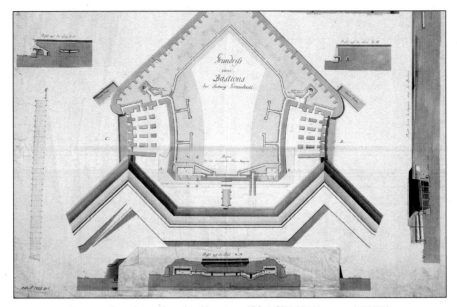

Fortress Graudenz, detached bastion. (GStA SPK, XI HA sygn. A 70751)

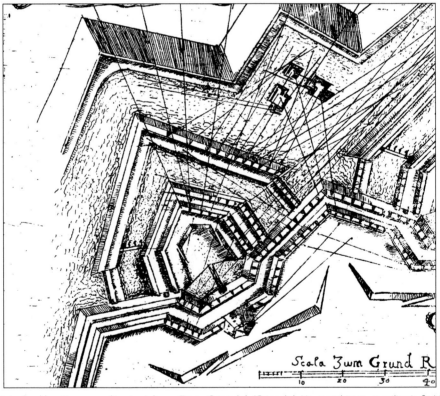

Detached bastion according to Johann Franz Griendel. (Griendel, *Nova architectura militaris*, fig.V)

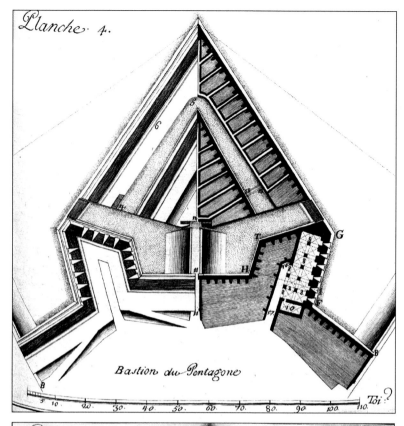

Bastion du Pentagone

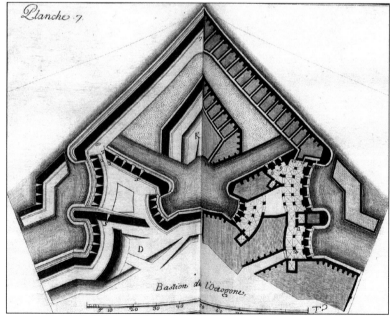

Bastion de l'Octogone

Above: Detached bastion according to Rozard. (Rozard, *Nouvelle Fortification Françoise*, T. 2 Pl. 4)

Right: Detached bastion according to Rozard. (Rozard, *Nouvelle Fortification Françoise*, T. 2 Pl. 7)

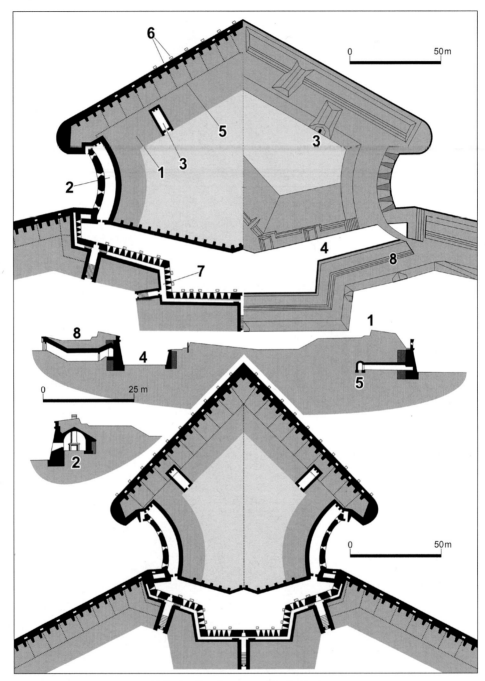

Detached bastion according to Vauban.
1) rampart, 2) casemated lower flank, 3) traverse, 4) moat, 5) countermine galleries, 6) mine chambers established in the masonry revetement and in front of it, 7) scarp gallery. (Drawn by Mariusz Wojciechowski)

Graudenz's detached bastions, although atypical, were obviously not a complete novelty. In the history of defensive architecture, the concept of moving the bastion away from the main rampart appeared several times. Such ideas were already put forward in the seventeenth century by the Italian Alexander von Grotte[326] and by the Germans Johann Franz Griendel[327] and Johann Bernhard Scheiter.[328] In the eighteenth century, on the other hand, Rozard, a French military engineer working for the Elector of Bavaria, presented a somewhat different idea in his treatise – a bastion linked to the rampart, but provided with a tenaille retrenchment and an internal moat. In plan it looked like a ravelin with a redoubt set in front of a small horn work. Importantly, Rozard used artillery casemates located, as in Graudenz, in the flank in these atypical bastions. According to some of his concepts, these casemates were also located in a retired and concave flank and sheltered by an orillon.[329] Another eighteenth-century engineer proposing the use of detached bastions was Johann Karl Dietrich Pirscher, who served in the Prussian army. This engineer published a book in 1777 in which he introduces numerous examples of fortified circuits defended by detached works. Although Pirscher's main concept was the defence of the main moat by means of fire conducted from a battery on the inner side of the flanks of the detached works (so quite differently conceived than in Graudenz), one can nevertheless see some similarity between this engineer's ideas and those of Graudenz.[330] However, the most important model for the fortress at Graudenz are the ideas of Sebastian le Prestre de Vauban. Structures invented by him (and similar to the Graudenz bastions) can be found neither in any of his constructed fortresses nor in any of his printed treatises. The only work where they can be found is a manuscript version of Vauban's treatise, written by him at the end of 1706, a few months before his death. Although this text is dedicated to the defence of fortresses, Vauban also included new ideas from the field of fortification. On three illustrations, he presented new ideas for bastions. Their outline was reminiscent of the solutions from Vauban's so-called First Manner – for they used retired concave flanks, sheltered by orillons. However, unlike those old bastions, the new ones were to have casemates for four guns in the flank, under the open gun emplacements. An even more important difference was that the bastions were cut off from the main rampart by a separate internal moat. This moat was to be covered from inside the fortress by small arms fire from a casemated gallery. In addition, the main rampart of the fortress was clearly higher than the bastions. Finally, there were to be countermine galleries under the faces of the bastions so that, after firing a breach in the rampart, any positions that the enemy wished to occupy in the breach could be destroyed.[331] All these elements bear an extremely strong resemblance to the solutions applied 70 years later at Graudenz. The differences concern only the details and are limited to the outline of the

---

326 Jähns, *Geschichte 1890*, pp.1095–1097; Sturm, *Architectura militaris hypothetico-eclectica 1755*, tab. XXVII.

327 Griendel, Johann Franz, *Nova architectura militaris, das ist: Neuerfundene fortificationes, oder Vestungs Bau* (Dresden: Baumann, 1677), fig. V, VI.

328 Scheiter, *Examen fortificatorium*, figs. 1, 2.

329 Claude Rozard, *Nouvelle Fortification Françoise: Où il est traité de la construction...* (Nuremberg: Lochner, 1731), vol.2, Pl. 4, 7.

330 Pirscher, *Anweisung zum Festungsbau*, especially note plate no. 2.

331 Vauban, Traité de la deffense des places, CNAM Fol Res Qe 3, <http://cnum.cnam.fr/CGI/redir. cgi?FOLRESQE3>, accessed 29 March 2023.

moat and the technical solutions of the casemates in the flanks. The similarities are so great that they entitle one to conclude that the Graudenz bastions are only a slightly altered copy of Vauban's solutions. But how did the designers of the fortress at Graudenz become acquainted with Vauban's ideas presented in an unpublished text? It was possible because this treatise, although unpublished, was circulated in the form of manuscript copies. One of these made its way to Prussia and was still kept in the library of the Prussian General Staff at the end of the nineteenth century.[332] This is probably the same treatise whose translation the King sent to the commanders of all Prussian fortresses in October 1770. Indeed, the text that the King sent to his subordinates with the instruction that it should serve 'for the study and instruction of the officers in the fortress and that it should be constantly in the papers in the fortress' was entitled *Traite de la defence des places* – identical to the aforementioned treatise, and different from the commonly known text published in print in 1737 (*Traite de l'attaque et defense des places*).[333] As can be seen, the Graudenz fortress can be described without great exaggeration as the only realised example of Vauban's Fourth Manner.

Fort Lyck

The vast majority of the permanent fortifications designed and built under Frederick the Great were large fortresses. Permanent, independent defensive structures of small size appeared extremely rarely. The most famous, and at the same time extremely peculiar, structure of the Frederician defence system was Fort Lyck, situated on an island on Spirdingsee. The idea of building a fortified depot for the territory of Masuren (Mazury) originated in 1774, but the King decided to realise it only several years later.[334] The catalyst for this was the decision taken at the end of 1783 to weaken the alliance with Russia, as well as the movements of Russian troops in the borderlands. The task of choosing a suitable location was entrusted to *Generalleutnant* Heinrich Wilhelm von Anhalt, who had served as infantry inspector in East Prussia since September 1783. As early as October of that year, the general made a tour of Prussia, but the King was not satisfied, as he did not make it to the vicinity of Lyck.[335] The reason Lyck was so important becomes clear in a letter in which the King informs the general that he considered the place proposed by him for the establishment of the depot to be good. However, the King wanted the depot to be defended by a rampart with cannon and a casemate for 100-150 men. He also asked for a cost estimate for the construction of all these facilities.[336] Which facilities the King had in mind is explained in correspondence from November, in which the King first asks for a cost estimate for a 'small fortress near Lyck' and then for a small fortress on an island near

332 Jähns, *Geschichte 1890*, pp.1432–1433.
333 Letters from the King to the commanders of fortresses, 9 October 1770, GStA SPK, I HA Rep.96 B Abschriften von Kabinetsordres, Bd.84, p.908.
334 Jany, *Geschichte der Preussischen Armee*, vol.3, p.134.
335 Letter from the King to von Anhalt, 29 October 1783, GStA SPK, I HA Rep.96 B Abschriften von Kabinetsordres, Bd.83 p.801.
336 Letter from the King to von Anhalt, November 1783, GStA SPK, I HA Rep.96 B Abschriften von Kabinetsordres, Bd.83 p.806–807.

Lyck.[337] The plan promised to the King, together with the cost estimate, reached him on 24 November. The royal reply to von Anhalt's letter indicates, for the first time, the exact location of the newly planned defensive establishment; an island on Spirdingsee. In his letter, the King also gives a justification for the construction of this facility, namely the establishment of a warehouse there, which would hold a month's rations for 20,000 soldiers, including *bisquits* for 10 days and flour for 20 days.[338] Planning work on the facility took more than a year. In December 1783, the King received from his general a plan for palisading the island and a study on the cost of building a warehouse, bakery, barracks, and the necessary defensive works. The money for the construction would be budgeted for the following year.[339] In January, the King received another report, in response to which he announced a slight change in the design assumptions; he wanted the warehouse to be able to supply an army of 30,000 soldiers. He also wrote for the first time of the planned armament of the fort (12 iron cannon) and the garrison (100 soldiers).[340] This intensive exchange of correspondence was followed by a nine-month pause and the subject did not return until the end of August, when the King again asked for a cost estimate, this time complete, for all the plans for the island on Spirdingsee. This was ready by the beginning of September and the completed, final version was produced on 21 September.[341] Immediately afterwards, the King asked *Oberst* Regler to choose a good engineer to carry out the work.[342] Regler chose *Leutnant* von Goltz, who had been stationed at Brieg until then. At the same time, the King set the budget,12,769 thalers, and the funds were to arrive on site as early as February 1785.[343] The King was keen to have the building erected quickly. In December he changed his decision and stated that the first tranche of cash would arrive as early as January so that building materials could be gathered. At the same time, he rushed von Goltz to get on site as soon as possible and make a start with the task of harvesting the construction timber, for which the season was supposed to be right.[344] Von Goltz, however, dragged his feet and did not set off for Prussia until early January, when he received a definite order from the King.[345] In turn, the latter handed over the first tranche of funds on 12 January – 6,000 thalers for timber harvesting and promised a further 4–6,000 thalers the following month. In fact, in February he allocated another

---

337 Letters from the King to von Anhalt, 15 and 26 November 1783 GStA SPK, I HA Rep.96 B Abschriften von Kabinetsordres, Bd.83 p.853, 885.
338 Letter from the King to von Anhalt, 29 November 1783, GStA SPK, I HA Rep.96 B Abschriften von Kabinetsordres, Bd.83 p.894
339 Letters from the King to von Anhalt, 20 and 22 December 1783 GStA SPK, I HA Rep.96 B Abschriften von Kabinetsordres, Bd.83, pp.961, 966.
340 Letter from the King to von Anhalt, 17 Janruary 1784 GStA SPK, I HA Rep.96 B Abschriften von Kabinetsordres, Bd.84 p.54
341 Letters from the King to von Anhalt, 28 August and, 11, 14, 26 September, 1784 GStA SPK, I HA Rep.96 B Abschriften von Kabinetsordres, Bd.84 p.734, 783, 802, 847.
342 Letter from the King to Regler, 26 September 1784 r., GStA SPK, I HA Rep.96 B Abschriften von Kabinetsordres, Bd.84, p.850.
343 Letters from the King to Regler and von Anhalt, 11 October 1784, GStA SPK, I HA Rep.96 B Abschriften von Kabinetsordres, Bd.84, p.908.
344 Letters from the King to Regler, von Anhalt and von Goltz, 22 December 1784, GStA SPK, I HA Rep.96 B Abschriften von Kabinetsordres, Bd.84, p.1159.
345 Letter to Goltz, 5 January 1785, GStA SPK, I HA Rep.96 B Abschriften von Kabinetsordres, Bd.85, p.23.

6,000 thalers, and although the sum assumed in the cost estimate had been reached, the King promised another 8,000 thalers in the spring to finish the fort.[346] Work on the fort continued until the autumn. On 17 November, von Goltz reported its completion. At the same time, the construction bills were handed over to Councillor Lilienthal for checking. After more than a month, it appeared that everything was in order in this respect and the King allowed the engineer to return to Brieg.[347] The newly established fort was given a small garrison from the Hallmann garrison regiment and in 1786 received 12 guns.[348]

Its supply base consisted of two warehouses and a bakery with four ovens. The warehouses were to hold 2,400 *sheffels* of flour and 1,800 barrels of *bisquits*. The resources stored there could feed a corps of 30,000 for 4–6 weeks.[349] Transportation of food to and from the warehouses was made possible by a ferry that connected the island to the mainland. Initially the name Fort was an overstatement, but in 1786 the fortifications were erected with the remaining funds.[350] These were six batteries on a lunette plan mounded provisionally from sand, connected to each other by a line of palisades and armed with twelve 12-pounder guns. The defence works were located close to the shore, so that they formed a defensive perimeter. The armament was necessary because, as the fort's builders claimed, the stockade buildings could be set on fire by firing from 7-pounder howitzers erected on the bank.[351] However, as the plan with the fields of fire that could be conducted from the fort shows, the guns set on the batteries could cover the fort all around.[352] As only the batteries near the harbour could reach the mainland, so the others had the task of defending the fort against an enemy approaching on the surface of the lake which would ice over winter. In addition to the batteries and warehouses, inside the fort there was a storehouse for 500 cetnars of gunpowder, barracks for 150–200 soldiers and an officers' barracks. The bakery was made of brick, the warehouses on the ground floor were made of brick, with half-timbering above. The other buildings were half-timbered or completely wooden.

---

346 Letter to von Anhalt, 12 January and 1 February 1785, GStA SPK, I HA Rep.96 B Abschriften von Kabinetsordres, Bd.85, pp.44, 111.

347 Letters to Goltz, 17 November and 24 December 1785 and letter to Lilienthal, 24 December 1785, GStA SPK, I HA Rep.96 B Abschriften von Kabinetsordres, Bd.85, pp.1218, 1365.

348 Jany, *Geschichte der Preussischen Armee*, vol.3, p.134.

349 August Skalweit August, *Getreidehandelspolitik und Kriegsmagazin-Verwaltung Brandenburg-Preußens 1756–1806* (Berlin: Verlag von Paul Parey, 1931), pp.55–56; Adam Żywiczyński, Piotr Olszak, 'Fort Lyck w latach 1785–2004', *Znad Pisy. Wydawnictwo poświęcone Ziemi Piskiej*, 13–14, (2004–2005), pp.226–250.

350 The thesis of a somewhat accidental erection of the fortification was introduced by F. Symanowski, 'Fort Lyck', *Mitteilungen der Literarischen Gesellschaft Masovia*, 8 (1902), p.37, and repeated by Adam Żywiczyński, 'Fort Lyck – fryderycjańskie umocnienie w systemie jezior mazurskich', in Wilkaniec Agnieszka, Wichrowski Marcin (eds), *Fortyfikacje w przestrzeni miasta* (Poznań: Wydawnictwo Akademii Rolniczej im. Augusta Cieszkowskiego w Poznaniu, 2006), p.208. However, in the holdings of the Berlin Staatsbibliothek there is a *Plan einer Insel In der Spirdings See der Teufelsberg gennant*, ref. X 29076 –2, which seems to contradict it. The very title of the plan shows that it was certainly drawn up before 1786, as it lacks the proper name of the fort, which was given to it in 1786. This may indicate that the plan is a kind of project. On the other hand, the fortifications are clearly marked on it, which may indicate that they were planned from the beginning and not created by chance due to the need to spend the funds left over after the construction of the warehouses.

351 Von Hermann letter, 22 June 1787, SBB PK, DPG ref. XIX Fort Lyck, no. 126.

352 Fort Lyck, SBB PK, ref. X 29076 –1.

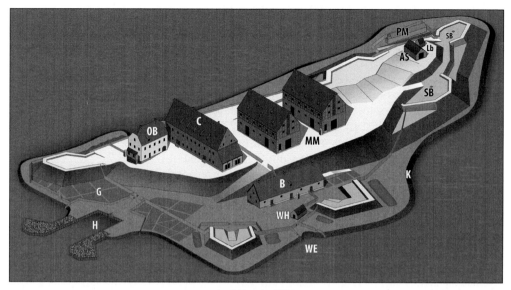

Lyck Fort in 1787.
AS) artillery storehouse (ArtFig. Schup.), B) bakery (Backerey), C) Barracks (Caserne), G) vegetable garden, H) harbour (Haaven), K) stone scarp, Lb) ammunition plant (Laboratory), MM) flour storehouse (Mehl-Magazin), OB) officers' building (Offic. Baraque), PM) powder magasine (Pulver-Magazin), SB) well (Senck Brunnen), WE) winter harbour (Winter-Einfahrt), WH) laundry (Wasch-Haus). (Drawn by Mariusz Wojciechowski)

The makeshift technique used to erect the fortifications led to their rapid destruction, with wind and waves destroying the buildings and eroding the island. It was not until 1787, during the reign of Frederick's successor, that the island's shores and the battery ramparts were secured with a stone wall at a cost of over 3,000 thalers. However, these were makeshift measures, as was realised. In one report on the site in 1787, there was a remark that the fort should be casemated, which would cost around 300,000 thalers.[353] In reality, the budget for the island was far smaller, and finally, in 1793, its military use was abandoned. The facility fell into oblivion, although as late as 1817 *Generalmajor* Karl von Grolman wrote in his report on his travels in East Prussia about the possibility of its re-use as a fortification.[354]

The fort was a unique structure against the background of Frederician defensive architecture. Despite its grand-sounding names (in correspondence, the King referred to it as a fort and even a 'small fortress'), it was simply a field defence facility. The makeshift fortifications might have sufficed if we were dealing with a structure built during the war. Here, however, they were erected in peacetime, to protect the military depot planned by Frederick. Such treatment of the protection of an important facility could be seen as an extreme example of stinginess, a trait often revealed in Frederick's decisions. On the other hand, however, one can see here the King's appreciation of small, permanent defensive facilities

---

353 Von Hermann, letter, 22 June 1787, SBB PK, DPG ref. XIX Fort Lyck, no. 126.
354 Von Grolman, Reisebemerkungen über Ost Preussen, GStA SPK IV HA Rep 15b Nr. 55 pp.50–53.

as a sometimes-sufficient means of safeguarding an important site. The impulse for such statements were the events of the War of the Bavarian Succession and the conclusions drawn from them, formulated in a book by the royal engineer, *Kapitän* Müller, *Versuch über die Verschanzungskunst auf Winterpostierungen*, published in 1782, where the author presents designs for strong earth and timber field forts. Müller took part in the War of the Bavarian Succession, when he built field fortifications in Glatz County. One of his works, a wooden blockhouse near Oberschwedeldorf, equipped with covered gun emplacements, was famed for its long defence against an Austrian attack in 1779. Significantly, similar structures – not fully meeting the requirements of permanent fortification – were also built in the period after 1786, as exemplified by the Glatz County forts erected in 1791.

A separate issue is the authorship of the project. Correspondence shows that the King was heavily involved. A letter dated 1 November 1783 shows that he was the author of the idea of reinforcing the military depot on the island with fortifications. Moreover, in this letter he suggested not only the necessity of a rampart, but also of the casemate that was ultimately not realised. However, it is not known who the author of the project that was finally realised was. In the royal correspondence, the only person who appears in the context of the plans and cost estimates is von Anhalt. Only once is the building councillor Lilienthal mentioned, who is known to have carried out designs for the fortifications, but in the King's letters to Lilienthal from the period of the project's creation the subject of Fort Lyck does not appear. Moreover, the only engineer who was involved in the creation of this work – Goltz – was only concerned with carrying out the construction work; the implementation of the already finished project. In other words, according to the current state of knowledge, the only person who can be regarded as the designer of this building is von Anhalt. Although he was not an engineer, as an experienced military man he was competent enough to design this modest defensive structure.

Pomeranian Fortresses

After the Seven Years War, more was invested in fortifications in Pomerania than before 1756. One large fortress (Kolberg) was thoroughly modernised, a second, smaller one (Damm) was strengthened, and the rebuilding of another (Stettin) was planned.

Kolberg

Kolberg belonged to a group of fortresses that had not been taken care of before the Seven Years War. As in Breslau, the events of the Seven Years War demonstrated the need to modernise the fortress. Three Russian sieges, conducted in 1758, 1760 and 1761, not only demonstrated the poor condition of the fortifications, which had not been repaired since the beginning of the century, but also their obsolescence. They quickly set about transforming the fortress.

The rebuilding of the fortress at Kolberg was initiated by the King himself, who arrived in Kolberg as early as May 1763. On 22 and 23 May, he visited the local fortifications. His attention was drawn to the area around the mouth of the Persante River, which he wanted to secure with a new defence structure. According to accounts, during his stay he was to create a design for this work, which later became known as Maikuhle Schanze.[355] The task of surveying the area for the future defensive work was entrusted to an engineer residing in Kolberg, *Leutnant* Sigismund Cornelius Ludewig von Franseky. Unfortunately, this drawing has not survived. It did, however, initiate other, much more serious design work by von Franseky. He was strongly associated with Kolberg; as one of two engineers of the Duke of Württemberg's corps, he defended the fortress in 1761 and was posted to the garrison in 1763. His project is known only in fragments, as no general plan of his has survived, only a dozen or so detailed drawings and, more importantly, two sheets of text containing detailed cost estimates dated 13 July 1763.[356]

The project, known from the cost estimate, envisaged a significant strengthening of the fortifications at Kolberg. First and foremost, the construction of numerous new defences was planned: two ravelins, seven redoubts, including two near the shipyard, two fortified tête de ponts, one counterguard, one lunette and traverses. Plans were also made to modernise the existing fortifications. Most importantly, repairs were to be carried out to the masonry covering of the fortress ramparts. The plan was to use 400,000 bricks and 500 last of lime for this purpose. Another item mentioned in the cost estimate was the reconstruction of the ruined barriers and palisades at the ramparts, inside the bastions of Halberstadt, Preussen, Neumark, Pommern, Geldern, the Hornwerk Munde and the Munde Sconce. The last defence-related item of the cost estimate was a proposal to build three sections of counter-mine.

The second, extremely important, group of buildings envisaged by Franseky's project were casemates. As many as six such structures were planned: two were to fill the Horn Work, two to fill the Pomeranian Bastion, one was to be built at the curtain of the New March Bastion, and one at Pladder Platz. In addition, numerous hydro-technical and communication works were planned; the construction of four new bridges, a new sluice with a suspension bridge, two new cofferdams (*Wasserbare*) across the Persante and across the moat at the new ravelin, and at the Redoubt, (both 102 metres long), and the reconstruction of 11 other hydro-technical structures destroyed during the Russian sieges.

In addition to the tasks mentioned above, reconstruction of damaged military facilities inside the city was also planned. As part of this, it was planned to renovate the artillery arsenal, in which a bomb had damaged the ceiling and four masonry hatches, to rebuild the completely destroyed laboratory (35 feet long, 18 feet wide), to rebuild the ruined gunpowder tower at the Water Gate (Wasser Pförtchen), the reconstruction of the so-called Blue Gunpowder Tower in the Halberstadt bastion, the reconstruction of the dwelling house in the Munde Sconce, and the masonry revetment of the ramparts in the sconce, which suffered badly during the Russian attack. In addition to this, the author of the cost estimate intended to spend 4,469 thalers on three small dredgers (Baggern) for dredging the old town moat, as well as 2,000 thalers for the purchase of tools that had been taken by the Russians and which were needed in the fortress. All these works were to consume a sum of more

---

355 APS, AMK ref. 65/202/0/3657, p.30; Rödenbeck, *Tagebuch oder Geschichtskalender*, vol.2, p.216.
356 Verschlage von denen Neuzuerbauenden Vestungs Wercken Neuen Brucken, gesprengten Schleussenwerk, Wasser Baren und Casematten; Vorschläge von denen alten, durch die Ruschischen Belagerungen zerschoschenenn und zersprengten Vestungs Werken, Wasser Bären, Pülver Thürmen, Zeug Hauser, Laboratorio, der Benötigten Lagger, Schanz und Arbeits Zeuges, SBB PK, ref. X 22010.

than 350,000 thalers. The casemates were an important part of the project. There were to be four of them, accommodating 750 soldiers. There were also plans to erect a large casemate for 2,000 barrels of flour. A large room in the planned casemate in the Pomeranian bastion was also to be used for food. Such casemated food warehouses were a novelty; fortresses modernised before the Seven Years War did not have them, and it was only after the end of that armed conflict that such warehouses began to be built, as exemplified by the fortresses in Graudenz and Cosel. The Kolberg casemate of this kind, had it been built, would have been the first of its kind.

For reasons unknown today, Franseky's project never materialised. No steps were taken on the Kolberg fortress for the next five years. It was not until 1768 that design work was resumed, this time by an engineer newly imported from France, Madeleine Touros, comte d'Heinze. Kolberg was a kind of test of this engineer's design skills. At the end of June 1768, Heinze made the first sketches of the new fortifications for Kolberg. Having seen them, the King summoned the engineer to himself for a personal interview.[357] Apparently, the King liked the idea, since he ordered Heinze to set off for Kolberg, to make precise measurements of the fortress and its surroundings, and then to make a project for the reconstruction of the fortress, together with a cost estimate. The King gave his engineer several months to complete this task; the whole thing was to be presented to the sovereign after his return from the September manoeuvres.[358] Heinze initially worked alone on the measurements, but in August he got help in the form of the engineer le Clair.[359] The design work took him slightly longer than the King had anticipated. The final design presented is dated 6 October.[360] The King became acquainted with it four days later.[361] Heinze's design, like Franseky's earlier one, envisaged the strengthening of the main perimeter, the construction of numerous external works and new external works. The transformation of the main perimeter was limited. The cavaliers of the Prussian and Halberstadt bastions were rebuilt, the small work (piatta forma) between the Prussian and New March bastions was enlarged, and the Pomeranian bastion was rebuilt and connected to the Magdeburg ravelin. The outer works were also significantly expanded. The works in front of the eastern front of the city fortifications – Ravelin Butow – were heavily rebuilt, and new lunettes were placed on both sides of it. Slightly smaller changes were made on the southern side, they were limited to two lunettes on either side of the Ravelin Lauenberg. The fortifications on the western side of the Persante River were significantly expanded; Bastion Geldern was enlarged, the section

357 Letter from the King to Heinze, 22 June 1768, GStA SPK, I HA Rep.96 B Abschriften von Kabinetsordres, Bd.70 Vol III 1768, p.267.

358 Letter from the King to Heinze, 25 June 1768, GStA SPK, I HA Rep.96 B Abschriften von Kabinetsordres, Bd.70 Vol III 1768, p.272.

359 Letter from the King to Heinze and to Le Claire, 3 August 1768, GStA SPK, I HA Rep.96 B Abschriften von Kabinetsordres, Bd.70 Vol III 1768, p.286.

360 The inventory is the Plan de La Fortresse de Colberg e de Ses Environs, fait a Potsdam le 6 Octobre 1768, d'Heinze, SBB PK, ref. X 22011. The project consists of the Plan de la Fortresse de Colberg relatif au Project, d'Heinze, SBB PK, ref. X 22011–1 (not dated) and 10 detail sheets, which are projects for individual works or fronts of the fortress. All these designs are signed by Heinze, most dated 6 October 1768.

361 Letter from the King to Heinze, 8 October 1768, GStA SPK, I HA Rep.96 B Abschriften von Kabinetsordres, Bd.70 Vol III 1768, p.365.

Fortress Kolberg, Church Sconce. (Gouache from the private collection of Robert Maziarz)

of the covered way north of the bastion was strengthened, among other things by digging a moat. There, three new defensive works were constructed in front of the arm of the Holtz Graben: the polygonal Geldern Redoubt, the Suderland Lunette (exceptionally strong, as it was protected by a counterguard, in front of which there was an outer moat and separate glacis), and the smaller Geldern Lunette. The northern part of the fortifications was most heavily reinforced. A completely new front was created in front of the Munde Hornwork, consisting of a counterguards, lunettes, and ravelins.

Four further defensive works were constructed away from the town: the Kirchhof Schanze, a large, polygonal, tenaille-bastion defensive work surrounding the church of St Nicholas in the suburb of Munde, and a smaller, five-sided redoubt at the mouth of the Wood Canal to the Parsęta (Redoubt Morast) and two large structures protecting the mouth of the Persante into the Baltic Sea; Fort Munde and the irregular defence structure the Maikuhle Schanze (later Heyde Schanze) located on the western bank.[362]

In basic outlines, the project described gained royal approval, but even so, Heinze had to make several more versions of his design. At least two are known. The King received a correction to the design as early as 30 October,[363] while the final, royal-approved design was

362 Description based on Plan de la Forteresse de Colberg relatif au Project, d'Heinze, SBB PK, ref. X 22011–1.
363 Letter from the King to Heinze, 20 October 1768, GStA SPK, I HA Rep.96 B Abschriften von Kabinetsordres, Bd.70 Vol III 1768, p.407.

not to be handed in until 27 December of that year.[364] It is not known which elements of the draft were affected by the royal corrections. However, comparing the project of 6 October with the completed state, we see only a few changes in the outline of the defence works. Significant changes were made in three cases to the works' outline. The first was the lunette on the west bank of the Persante River, in front of the arm of the Holtz Graben, which received a much more elaborate covered way than in the original design, provided with a double glacis and an outer moat. In addition, the outline of the works defending the mouth of the Persante River to the sea was transformed. In the case of Fort Munde, the changes did not concern its core, but only the work added to the fort on the eastern side. Compared to the original design, it was considerably enlarged, and its outline changed. The second structure protecting the estuary, the Maikuhle Schanze, was completely transformed. Its eastern half-bastion was given a concave flank, the curtain (facing the sea), which originally had a tenaille outline, was straightened, and the western edge, previously provided with an elongated 'bastion' and a rectangular bastion, was given a dovetail outline. Interestingly, it is only in the case of this building that traces of design interference have survived. On Heinze's original design, one can clearly see a pencil correction made to the western edge of the work. As the King was interested in this part of the fortress from the beginning and was to design a new defensive work there, it can be assumed that he also made this correction.

Heinze's project contained numerous elements worth describing in detail, but it is necessary to limit ourselves to pointing out the most important ones. Within the city's fortifications, the reconstruction of two bastions – the Halberstadt and Prussian – is particularly noteworthy. In both, the modernisation consisted of building casemates into them. In the first, the casemate was only located in its left flank. It was partially covered with earth but had windows on the courtyard side. It consisted of two parts. The smaller one contained a bakery with three ovens, while the larger part was used for soldiers. The barracks part was connected to the positions on the rampart by a staircase. This detail, and others (buttresses on the courtyard side) resemble the solutions of the casemates described above by Franseky.[365]

In the Prussian bastion the casemate was located inside the cavalier and, unlike its predecessor, it was completely devoid of windows. Interestingly, an old gunpowder magazine was incorporated into this casemate.[366] In 1818, it was described as 'a kind of corridor, which is neither properly ventilated nor illuminated.' Nevertheless, the casemate was intended as a flat for the commandant of the fortress for the duration of the siege and Gneisenau lived there during the siege of 1806.[367]

The most interesting object connected with the Frederician expansion of the fortress was the new Fort Munde with a masonry tower, erected on the site of a small battery from 1708, protecting the entrance to Kolberg harbour. Designed by Heinze, the fort consisted of a semi-circular battery facing the sea, protected from the land side by two bastions. The battery was separated from the bastions by a wall with small-arms ranges. In the middle

364   APS, AMK ref. 65/202/0/3657, p.26.
365   Description based on Grundriss und Profile der Kasematten Halberstadt, inglt. Engelbracht 1826, GStA SPK, XI HA, ref. F 71544.
366   Description based on a plan of the Kolberg fortress from c.1790, SBB PK, ref. X 22012.
367   v. Lützow, Beschreibung der Festung Colberg, 1818, SBB PK, DPG ref. VI Colberg, 95b pp.4v.

of the battery, also called Hufeisen or Donjon in the literature, was a small, circular tower, serving as a kind of cavalier, on top of which was an open artillery platform. In its basement there was also a circular, bomb-proof room used as a casemate by the fort's garrison. This is how the work is depicted in Heinze's design drawings of 1768 and in inventories from the late eighteenth century, and how it was depicted in the 1818 description of the fortress.[368] This object is commonly associated as the 'base' for the lighthouse in today's Kołobrzeg; however, what we can see today is the reduit of Fort Munde created only during its modernisation in the years 1832–1840.[369] In place of the small tower without gun casemates, a new tower with two tiers of artillery casemates was then erected. A remnant of the tower from the Frederician period is the lower, underground storey, originally used as a casemate for the crew of Heinze's tower. The other elements of the fort have also changed since it was built. The semi-circular battery of the fort lost its breastwork and artillery platform (which happened after the fortress was dismantled), and its retaining wall was replaced, which in the 1840s acquired its present-day form with a characteristic arcade frieze. The earthen ramparts of the fort, which have not been preserved (they are replaced by a park and the Maritime Office building), were also rebuilt.

The purpose for which this fort was built was to protect the fortress from bombardment from the sea. The circular battery with a tower was intended to keep bomb-vessels away, so that the events of the Seven Years War, when the fortress was bombarded from the sea by Russian ships, would not be repeated.[370]

Although Heinze did the design of the fortress, the task of building it was delegated to another officer, the engineer Franseky, who had already been associated with the fortress. Moreover, he also had some input into the formation of the project. According to *Leutnant* Woyna, author of a manuscript study on the history of the fortress, the design and cost estimates of the fortress, which were still extant in the mid-nineteenth century, had two versions; the French version bore the signature of a French count, while the German version bore Franseky's.[371] It is possible that the German engineer was merely a translator, but this cannot be determined at the present time. He was certainly the one who carried out the project. Before construction work began, Frederick summoned Franseky to Potsdam and for four weeks they agreed on all matters relating to the construction of the fortress. After these long consultations, the King promoted him to the rank of *kapitän* and made him responsible for the construction of the fortress.

Initially, the King planned to carry out the modernisation work within a year. This short deadline testifies to the desire to erect the fortress as soon as possible. However, this is contradicted by the actual course of the construction work. It is likely that the

---

368 Plan et Profil d'un Fort en maconnerie propose D'etablir sur la rive droitte de L'Entree du Port, SBB PK, ref. X 22011–3; v. Lützov, Beschreibung der Festung Colberg, 1818, SBB PK, DPG ref. VI Colberg, 95b pp.2v–3r.

369 Modernisation began with the construction of the reduit, which lasted until 1836. Reconstruction of the rest of the fort lasted from 1832 to 1840. The total cost of the extension was 15,714 thalers, see APS, AMK ref. 65/202/0/3657, p.34; Zeichnung über den Ausbau des Thurm Reduits im Fort Münde. Müller, Ingenieur Lejtnant, Colberg den 26 Marz 1834, GStA SPK, ref. E 71839; Stoewer, *Geschichte der Stadt Kolberg*, p.185.

370 de Mirabeau, *Von der Preußischen Monarchie*, p.412.

371 APS, AMK ref. 65/202/0/3657 pp.26.

King was unable to decide which of the Pomeranian fortresses should be modernised; Kolberg or Stettin. Eventually, the idea of extending the Stettin fortress was abandoned, and the engineer who was originally to carry out construction work there, *Kapitän* Berger, was sent to Kolberg.[372] It was only then that serious preparations for construction began. In the winter and early spring of 1770, the Pomeranian chamber organised the felling of construction timber for the fortress.[373] It is not known exactly when the construction work started, probably in May 1770. At the end of April, the King was to send an additional 20,000 thalers to Kolberg so that the work could begin.[374] However, the pace of work was relatively slow. In 1770, 500 workers were working on the fortress, and only the Kirchhof Schanze was built.[375] This pace of work did not satisfy Frederick. In October 1770, he decided that the work was to be completed within the next two building seasons. Accordingly, he ordered the number of labourers to be increased to 1,500 per day, in addition to which the construction was to be serviced by 100 carts.[376] A year later, Franseky reported that if the two-year completion deadline was to be maintained, a further increase in the number of labourers and carts would be necessary; to 2,700 and 150 per day respectively.[377] Despite this, it was not possible to complete the work in 1773, and in March 1774 Franseky reported that the deadline had slipped to June.[378] All indications are that this deadline was met.

The main problem that arose during construction was the foundations for the masonry revetment of the ramparts. This problem first arose during the building of the Morast Redoubt. Trouble was also caused by the sea. During the construction of Fort Munde, strong winds blew for a long time, causing elevated water levels, which made it impossible to carry out the work on the foundations. All this caused delays in the construction, as well as a significant increase in the expenses. Initially expected to cost 293,104 thalers, it eventually grew to as much as 486,917 thalers. There is no detailed information on the chronology of the construction. It is not known when the individual fortress buildings were erected (apart from the aforementioned Kirchhof Schanze). This gap in information is due to the fact that Franseky, who led the construction of the fortress, burned all the documentation when the fortress was completed.[379]

The most important fortress structure created during the Frederician reconstruction was Fort Munde. This structure is a close relative of the French coastal forts designed by Vauban

372 Letter from the King to Franseky, 10 January 1770, GStA SPK, I HA Rep.96 B Abschriften von Kabinetsordres, Bd.71, p.286.

373 Letters from the King to Franseky, 2 February and 15 April 1770, GStA SPK, I HA Rep.96 B Abschriften von Kabinetsordres, Bd.71, pp.323, 375.

374 Letter from the King to Franseky, 24 April 1770, GStA SPK, I HA Rep.96 B Abschriften von Kabinetsordres, Bd.71, p.385.

375 APS, AMK ref. 65/202/0/3657, p.30.

376 Letter from the King to Franseky, 21 October 1770, GStA SPK, I HA Rep.96 B Abschriften von Kabinetsordres, Bd.71, p.385.

377 Letter from the King to Franseky, 2 December 1771, GStA SPK, I HA Rep.96 B Abschriften von Kabinetsordres, Bd.72, vol. 1771, p.430.

378 Letter from the King to Franseky, 29 March 1774, GStA SPK, I HA Rep.96 B Abschriften von Kabinetsordres, Bd.73, vol. 1774, p.430.

379 APS, AMK ref. 65/202/0/3657, pp.30–32.

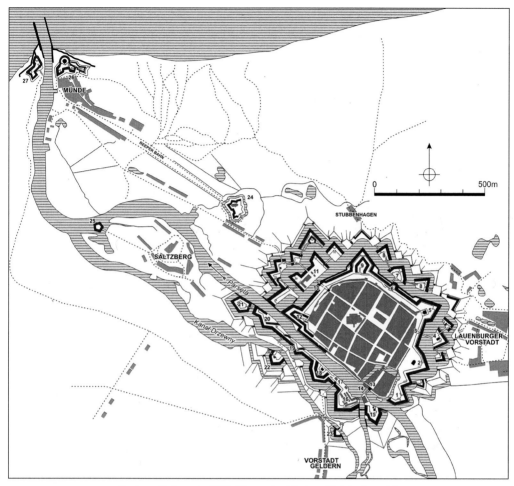

Fortress Kolberg in 1786. (Drawn by Mariusz Wojciechowski)

in the late seventeenth and early eighteenth centuries.[380] Among the structures that Vauban and his successors erected are the Tour Vauban at Camaret sur Mer, Fort Louvois (Chapus) on the island of Orléans, the Risban at Dieppe, Fort Lupin near the mouth of the Charente River and Fort Pate. In the context of Kolberg, Fort Mahon in Ambleteuse (1684–1690)[381] should be mentioned in particular, both because of its location and because of its use of bastioned elements. All of these structures show two features in common with Kolberg's

---

380 This was already pointed out by Stankiewicz in his article (Stankiewicz, 'Ze studiów', p.126). However, this author failed to note that the reduit, which he took to be part of the eighteenth-century complex, was not built until the 1830s.

381 Plan et Profil de la Tour d'Ambleteuse, SE/KrA/0406/13/002/004, <https://sok.riksarkivet.se/bildvisning/K0005504_00001>, accessed 30 March 2023; Jean-Denis G. G. Lepage, *French Fortifications, 1715–1815: An Illustrated History* (Jefferson: McFarland & Co Inc, 2010), p.188.

Fortress Kolberg, Fort Münde. (Drawn by Mariusz Wojciechowski)

Fort Munde. The first is their location – they are erected on a beach or on sandbanks, often close to a harbour entrance (Ambleteuse, Fort Chapus). The second similarity is the form itself – they consist of a low, circular (oval) or horseshoe-shaped battery and a taller tower that serves as a redoubt. Of course, there is a significant difference between the French forts and the Kolberg structure, mainly concerning the casemates. In the buildings designed by Vauban, the redoubt was always casemated, in addition to having artillery casemates. However, Heinze abandoned this solution and the tower he designed at Kolberg could only fulfil the function of a cavalier, while the casemates were limited to a small room in the tower's basement, fulfilling the function of a shelter for the fort's garrison. An element of the Kolberg fort that finds no analogy in France was the large, earthen frontage with a tenaille-bastion outline. It is clear that this work was conceived as a fully self-contained structure that could defend itself from both sea and land attack.

The situation at Kolberg, despite its uniqueness as the only major Prussian coastal fortress at the time, seems to have been typical for Prussia after the end of the Seven Years War. Conceptually, Frederick based the modernisation of the fortress on the ideas of foreign specialists. At both the mountain fortresses already described – Glatz and Silberberg – and at Kolberg, the most important and innovative elements were related to the work of engineers brought in from abroad. In Kolberg, Heinze, who had been educated in France and came from an engineering family, transplanted the Vauban concept of a coastal battery to Prussian soil. The foreign fortification models absorbed during this period became one of the more important foundations on which the school of New Prussian fortification developed in the nineteenth century. In the case of Kolberg, these foundations were even literal

– the New Prussian tower redoubt of Fort Munde stood, after all, on the tower erected by Heinze.

Stettin and Damm

These two Pomeranian fortresses are very interesting cases that need to be written about even though the vast majority of the ideas presented in the projects presented below were not realised. As in the case of other fortresses, the impetus for modernisation was provided by the experiences of the Seven Years War. In the case of Stettin, these were unusual. The fortress was not once actually threatened by enemy troops, but only had plans made against it. This, however, was enough of an impetus for modernisation.

The author of the plans to attack Stettin was none other than Marc-René, comte de Montalembert, a French military man and the most influential fortification theorist of the second half of the eighteenth century. During the Seven Years War, he was the French envoy to Russia and Sweden and, as part of his mission, accompanied the Russian army, among others. One of the ideas he promoted was for the Swedes and Russians to capture Stettin and make it the main supply base for the Russians during the war. This idea runs through his correspondence on several occasions. At least twice, in 1758 and in 1760, Montalembert wrote up a plan to capture Stettin. Shortly after the war, in 1764, one of these was to presented to Frederick.[382] In 1777, Montalembert published the idea in print, in correspondence from the time of his diplomatic mission in London.[383] These plans contain not only a description of a possible attack on the fortress, but also numerous criticisms of the stronghold.

The first of the proposals, made in October 1758, was to capture the fortress by storm. According to Montalembert, the city could be conquered in a single day, as the dry moats and lack of masonry revetment in the defensive works would allow the assault columns to penetrate easily. The outer works were thus too easy to conquer from the gorge. The attack proposed by the Frenchman was to consist of four mutually coordinated assaults, involving a total of 16,000 troops divided into 12 corps of various sizes. The primary siege tool was to be ladders for escalading the defensive works.[384] The second plan, written in January 1760, envisaged a regular attack. Montalembert planned to capture Fort Prussia first, which he saw as the weakest point of the fortress, and then take the town.[385] According to his plan, the fortress would be captured by 25–30,000 troops in three or four weeks. The second plan contains even more, highly critical comments on Stettin's fortifications. Montalembert notes that Stettin is considered to be one of the strongest fortresses in Europe, but upon close examination of its defences, it becomes apparent that it is in fact a very weak fortress, burdened with numerous flaws. Its very location, seemingly favourable, brought, according to Montalembert, many handicaps. Stettin lies on a river, which would normally make it necessary to develop a much wider than usual cordon cutting off the fortress. However,

---

382 Bonin, *Geschichte des Ingenieurkorps*, p.85.

383 Marc-René Montalembert, *Correspondance de Monsieur le Marquis de Montalembert* (London: Unknown Publisher, 1777), vol.1, pp.468–481; vol.2, pp.198–208. A second, German edition was published in Breslau, 1780–1781.

384 Marc-René Montalembert, 'Briefwechsel des Marquis von Montalembert', *Neue Kriegsbibliothek oder gesammlete Beyträge zur Kriegswissenschaft*, vol.8, p.349.

385 Montalembert, 'Briefwechsel des Marquis von Montalembert', vol.9, p.147.

there was only one long causeway on the east bank, linking Stettin with the adjacent area, and blocking it with a small force would have been sufficient to cut off the city from that side. Although this causeway ended at Damm, formally a fortress, this stronghold, reinforced in 1758, was considered by the French to be very bad and easy to take. The greatest flaws, however, were in the fortifications themselves. As in his 1758 siege project, Montalembert highlighted the lack of moats in front of the outer works and the missing (or too low) masonry revetment. Fort Prussia attracted particular criticism for being built 'contrary to all the basic principles of fortified construction'. Defects included narrow moats that lacked revetment or were poorly revetted, the positioning of the defensive works resulting in blind spots, and external works that were very difficult to defend.

Montalembert's plans regarding Stettin were not put into practice. Instead of Stettin, the Russians chose Kolberg as the target of their attacks, which were finally successful in 1761. In his work, Montalembert points out that his proposed method of conquering fortresses by means of a well-organised assault passed the test at Schweidnitz in 1760.

Montalembert's opinions on the weaknesses of the fortress at Stettin, although they were not published in print until 1777, were already known to Frederick; he was to become acquainted with them as early as 1764.[386] For a long time, however, there was no reaction to them. It was not until 1769 that the King ordered comte d'Heinze, who had completed the work at the fortress of Kolberg the previous year, to produce designs for the reconstruction of the fortresses of Stettin and Damm.[387]

The survey work began in June. In addition to Heinze, four engineers were involved: Boulet, Le Clair, Müller and Stein.[388] This team worked on the plans from June to October 1769. The final version of the designs was presented by Heinze, in person, to the King on 11 October 1769.[389] At Stettin, he planned to reshape Fort Leopold and give it the outline of a large horn work, to build a wide moat in front of all the outer works, to add outer works on Lastadie and in the area between Fort Prussia and the Oder riverbed, and finally to make masonry revetments for all the scarps and counterscarps. He also wanted to strengthen Fort Prussia with wide outer moats and a large crown work half the size of the fort. In addition to this, the fort was to be connected to the town by a covered way defended by a redoubt half the distance from the town. As part of these projects, it was planned to add plentiful casemates for the garrison to the defensive work. In addition to the existing ones at the Berlin Gate, a further 47 casemate sections were planned for the main rampart. There were to be new casemates in Fort Leopold, similar ones were planned in the curtains of the new buildings of Fort Prussia.[390]

---

386 de Mirabeau, *Von der Preußischen Monarchie*, p.416.
387 Letter from the King to Heinz, 2 June 1769, GStA SPK, I HA Rep.96 B Abschriften von Kabinetsordres, Bd.71, p.139 verso.
388 Letter from the King to Heinz, of 14 June 1769, GStA SPK, I HA Rep.96 B Abschriften von Kabinetsordres, Bd.71, p.150 verso; Hanke, Degner, Geschichte der Amtlichen Kartographie, p.189.
389 Letter from the King to Heinz, 10 October 1769, GStA SPK, I HA Rep.96 B Abschriften von Kabinetsordres, Bd.71, p.234 recto.
390 Stettin, Plan de fondation, relatif aux Plans et Profils du I Projet sur Laquel sont dessines tout les Cassemattes, Portes, et Communications existantes, et projetees, ainsi que les Galleries de Mines, Contremines et Foqusses, SBB PK, ref. X 34071–4; Stettin 1769, 1er Project, SBB PK, ref. X 34071–3.

As already mentioned, Montalembert pointed out the ease with which Stettin could be blockaded from the east, from the Damm side. Not surprisingly, the project to modernise Stettin also included ideas for strengthening the fortifications at Damm. Of course, they envisaged a lesser transformation. The project planned only a slight correction of the outline of some of the bastions and ravelins of the old main perimeter and, above all, the erection of numerous outer works, especially near the river's exit from the city, in the northern front, and the construction of an extensive horn work in front of the western front. It was also planned to supply the fortress with an adequate number of hydro-technical facilities to provide water in the moats.[391]

Outside the city itself, Heinze planned to erect fortifications to protect the Zollbrucke, on the Große Reglitz, one of the arms of the Oder flowing into Dammscher See (jezioro Dąbie). It was to be in the shape of a tête de pont in the form of a horn work, with two counterguards, a ravelin with a reduit on one side of the bridge and an irregular, tenaille battery facing the inside of this work, on the other side of the bridge.[392] Importantly, there was nothing new in Heinze's idea apart from the drawing, as the site had already been fortified in the seventeenth century.

Once the King had accepted the ideas for rebuilding the fortress, steps were taken to put them into practice. Just four days after the presentation of the designs, the King wrote to *Oberst* Regler to send him a capable engineer to make a cost estimate. This task was charged to *Leutnant* Berger.[393]

Thus, in the autumn of 1769, the King was in possession of designs and cost estimates for two Pomeranian fortresses – Kolberg and Stettin. Probably comparing the designs of the two fortresses drawn up for him by Heinze, he decided that it would be more beneficial to modernise Kolberg. The decision was taken at the end of 1769, and at the beginning of January 1770, the King sent Berger to Kolberg to assist in the construction of the fortress there.[394]

Nevertheless, ideas for the improvement of the defences at Stettin were later revived. In March 1771, the King ordered Freund, the engineer, to go to Stettin and make preparations for the work on the fortress, which was to begin in the spring of 1772.[395] Probably, however, it was only the fortress at Damm that was to be improved, for only there, and only to a very limited extent, were the earlier projects realised. Numerous counterguards were erected between the existing ravelins, connected to some ravelins in such a way that it almost formed an envelope, albeit a very narrow one. On the southern front, a covered way was erected, but this did not encircle the entire town. The fortress also gained one external

391 I-re Projet sur Damm, Profil sur Damm, 1769, SBB PK, ref. X 22241–4, 5, 6, 7, 8, 9, 10.

392 Feuille detachee de la Carte des Environs de Dam sur laquelle est le Projet d'un Tete de Pont au Zoll, et qui fait voir les differents Chemins qui aboutissent au dit Pont, a travers le Marais, sans passer par Damm, SBB PK, ref. X 22241–3.

393 Letters from the King to Regler, 15 October and 1 November 1769, GStA SPK, I HA Rep.96 B Abschriften von Kabinetsordres, Bd.71, pp.237 verso and 249 recto.

394 Letter from the King to Franseky, 10 January 1770, GStA SPK, I HA Rep.96 B Abschriften von Kabinetsordres, Bd.71, p.308 recto.

395 Letters from the King to Freund, 22 March 1771, GStA SPK, I HA Rep.96 B Abschriften von Kabinetsordres, Bd.72, p.198.

work – the four-sided redoubt Micken Schanze located between the detached bastion and the Dammscher See.[396]

Swinemünde

Another interesting, though not realised, proposal were the fortifications of Swinemünde. During the war, a large wooden and earthen redoubt was erected there to defend the harbour on the west bank of the Swine River and several batteries on the east bank. These fortifications were destroyed by the Swedes in 1758. Shortly after the end of the war, in 1766, as part of the planning for the further expansion of Swinemünde's port facilities, a project was drawn up for completely new fortifications for this important location. The new fortifications were to consist of four elements, the most important of which was to be a four-bastion citadel, surrounded by a moat and covered road, located on the eastern side of the Swine, more or less where Fort No. I was later built. On the side of the waterway there were to be two batteries. One in a tenaille outline, in the bottom of the moat between the citadel bastions, the other in the form of a straight line, with the centre curved towards the waterway. The second element of the new fortifications was to be two identical circular forts located at the heads of the breakwaters. Embrasures in the ramparts around these forts allowed both the approach to the harbour and the surrounding beaches to be covered by cannon. The last structure was to be built on the new western breakwater. Roughly in its centre was to be an irregularly shaped fort, half rectangular on the water channel side and curved on the side of the sea. Like the forts on the heads of the breakwaters, it too could fire almost 360 degrees around itself.[397]

This interesting design was drawn up by the Dutch engineer and architect B.R. Bourdet. He was formally a civil architect, and from 1766, the general inspector of hydro-technical structures. Nevertheless, he had, apparently, some knowledge of fortifications; enough to aspire to the Prussian engineering corps. His request to the King in this regard in 1766 was, however, rejected by Frederick, because the King held his qualifications as an engineer in low regard.[398] It is therefore not surprising that the project for the fortification of Swinemünde by Bourdet was not realised.

Bourdet's origins are also revealed by the ideas he presented, which find analogies in the defensive architecture of eighteenth-century France. Similar solutions to those proposed at Swinemünde can be found at the fortress of Dunkirk. There, in the 1680s, Vauban designed a series of forts to protect the entrance to the harbour, including two on the heads of the breakwater and one in the middle.[399]

---

396 Plan der Stadt und Festungswerke von Damm, den 17 August 1786, SBB PK, ref. X 22242.
397 Project pour la perfection du Port de Swinamunde avec les forts et Citadelle propres a sa seurete et deffence projete par l'inspecterur general des Hidrauliques Bourdet au moins d'Aout 1766, SBB PK, ref. X 34847.
398 Hanke, Degner, *Geschichte der Amtlichen Kartographie*, pp.33–34.
399 Bernard Forest de Bélidor, *Architecture hydraulique seconde partie, qui comprend l'art de diriger les eaux de la Mer & des Rivieres a l'avantage de la defence des Places, du Commerce & de l'agriculture, tome premier* (Paris: Jombert, 1750), p.19.

Bourdet's design, although not realised, had some influence on the later development of Swinemünde's fortifications. The location of the citadel on Boudret's design coincides with the location of Fort No. I, which in the nineteenth-century fortress performed precisely the function of a citadel. Also, the second fort, Fort West, was located more or less where Boudret proposed one of his forts. Ultimately, one cannot help but notice some, albeit distant, parallels between the circular-plan forts at the head of the breakwaters and the later Fort No. III at Swinemünde.

Casemated Batteries

Prussian fortifications after the Seven Years War used very similar solutions to those described for the period before 1756. New advance works, including forts, were erected, and fortresses and individual defensive works were reinforced with envelopes. New caponiers and counterscarp galleries were also being built. Nevertheless, the defensive architecture of this period differed significantly from that which had been built earlier. Numerous innovative solutions were used, but these usually appeared only in one fortress and were not copied in others. These facilities have already been described and characterised in the subsections on the history of individual fortresses. The only new solution that became widespread in Prussian fortresses were casemated artillery batteries.

A total of 23 structures were built or modernised in the eight fortresses improved in this period, with the guns placed inside casemates, which made them less vulnerable to the effects of enemy artillery fire. They ranged from small structures, such as the Silberberg Battery, to huge ones, such as the Donjon at Glatz.

The Frederician artillery casemates were not, of course, a novelty in themselves; on the contrary, they were a return to a solution that stood at the origin of modern defensive architecture.

Casemated Batteries in the Tradition of Modern Defensive Architecture

Artillery casemates appeared almost at the same time as cannon began to be used to defend fortresses. With the term being used to describe rooms with gun emplacements found in large numbers in late medieval fortifications. The best illustration of these early artillery casemates are the ideas of Albrecht Dürer in his *Etliche underricht/zu befestigung der Stett/ Schlosz/und flecken*, published in Nuremberg in 1527. Dürer presented numerous designs of low artillery towers equipped with gun emplacements which made it possible to cover a moat.

With the appearance of the first bastion fortifications, there was a retreat from the use of casemates as gun emplacements. These began to be placed either on the ramparts of the fortress or in courtyards located in the flanks of bastions. The latter location was particularly important, both in fortification theory and practice. The flanks were retired and often sheltered by orillons, so that guns placed in the courtyards were shielded from fire from the foreground. Additional cover was provided by a wall separating the courtyards from the moat. The cannon, standing in the open air, fired through holes punched in the wall and, after firing, retreated to a room located at the back of the courtyard. This room was

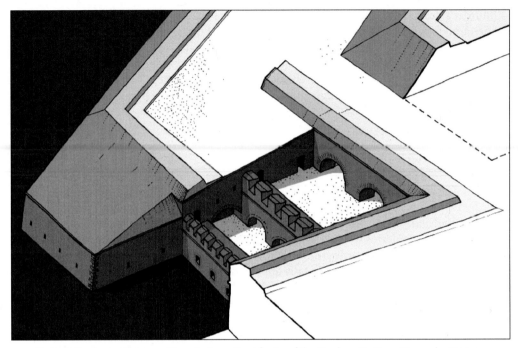

Fortress Breslau, artillery positions in the retired flanks of the Taschen Bastion. (Drawn by Mariusz Wojciechowski)

covered by a bombproof vault and a layer of earth, so that the cannon placed in it were safe from plunging fire. As can be seen, these courtyards were something of an intermediate form between a full casemate and an open fire position. Cannon located in this way were able to cover the bottom of the moat with their fire even when the other cannon placed on the rampart were destroyed, which was particularly useful for repelling an assault on a breach in the curtain made by enemy artillery. This is why defensive architecture theorists, especially the Italians and the French, still considered the retired flanks of bastions as the best possible location for fortress artillery in the second half of the seventeenth century.[400] Interestingly, these very positions in the retired flanks of bastions were called casemates in the literature of the time.[401] Numerous examples of this solution have survived to the present day, and there were even more in the mid-eighteenth century, including in fortresses then belonging to the Prussian state. It is sufficient here to mention examples in Brandenburg, such as the citadel in Spandau, Peitz, the fortress at Küstrin or the Silesian fortresses, for example, Breslau or Brieg.

Much rarer were the true artillery casemates; bombproof, vaulted, enclosed rooms equipped with artillery embrasures. Examples were already to be found in the first period of

---

400   An example is the French theorist and practitioner of defensive architecture, Allain Manesson Malett, who devotes considerable space in his work to arguing for the use of this solution, Mallet, *Kriegsarbeit oder neuer Festungsbau*, pp.28–42.
401   Jähns, *Geschichte 1890*, p.1345.

the development of bastion architecture – casemates were possessed by the bastions of the Poggio Imperiale and Nettuno fortresses, built by architects from the da Sangallo family at the turn of the fifteenth and sixteenth centuries. Numerous casemates were also present in the first bastion fortresses in Poland (Czemierniki, Pieskowa Skała)[402] and also in Germany, as exemplified by the bastions of the Dömitz fortress on the Elbe, Forchheim in Franconia, and Peitz in Brandenburg, from the mid-sixteenth century. Examples of actual artillery casemates can also be found in architectural theory. One example is the artillery casemates proposed by the German fortification theorist and practitioner Wilhelm Dilich. In his treatise *Peribologia Seu Muniendorum Locorum Ratio Wilhelmi Dilichii*, published in 1641, numerous such structures can be found. The closest to the solution described above are his casemates in the flanks of bastions. They look similar to the traditional ones (they are, for example, provided with courtyards); the difference is that the cannon covering the moat were to be located in a full casemate and not in the open.

Another location for artillery casemates according to Dilich was to be fortress gates. In each of his numerous designs for these structures, the gate passage was to have artillery casemates on both sides, capable of firing on the area directly in front of the gate.[403]

The next phase in the development of the artillery casemates was during the dominance of the Old Dutch manner of fortification. This period was very important, as the theoreticians and practitioners of defensive architecture, who were guided by the principles developed at the turn of the sixteenth and seventeenth centuries in the Netherlands, rejected the use of both casemates and masonry structures in fortifications in general. The reason was not only that masonry structures in defensive works were considered more expensive to build, arguments of a different kind were also put forward. The masonry was thought to be more susceptible to damage by shelling than an earth rampart, and the casemates themselves were thought to be harmful to the garrison, as the gunpowder smoke accumulating in the casemate after firing would cause poisoning among the artillerymen, and the concussion of the gunfire might cause the casemates' vaults to collapse. Most of these arguments were erroneous, but in the seveenth century they were widely believed, which led to the abandonment of the use of casemates.

Nevertheless, the idea of the artillery casemate had not been completely forgotten. The best example of this is the aforementioned Dilich, whose book came out at the height of interest in the Old Dutch school of fortification. The breakthrough that brought artillery casemates back into the awareness of fortification scholars was the siege of the fortress of Candia (Heraklion) by the Turks between 1666 and 1669. After its conclusion, two German engineers who took part in the defence of this fortress – Johann Bernhard Scheiter and Georg Rimpler – published treatises in which they summarised their extremely rich experience gained during this siege.[404] Both authors advocated the use of casemates, including

402 Gruszecki Andrzej, *Bastionowe zamki Małopolski* (Warszawa: Wydawnictwo MON, 1962), pp.90–91, 136–138.

403 Wilhelm Dilich, *Peribologia Seu Muniendorum Locorum Ratio Wilhelmi Dilichii* (Fracofurti ad Moenum: Unknown Publisher, 1641), tabs XXIX, XXXV-XXXVII, XXXIX, XLI-LX, CVI, CVII, CIIX, CXIII, CXV, CXVI.

404 Johann Bernhard Scheiter, *Novissima praxis militaris, oder Neu-Vermehrte und Verstärekte Vestungs-Bau- und Krieges-Schuel…* (Braunschweig: Zilliger und Gruber, 1672), Scheiter, *Examen*

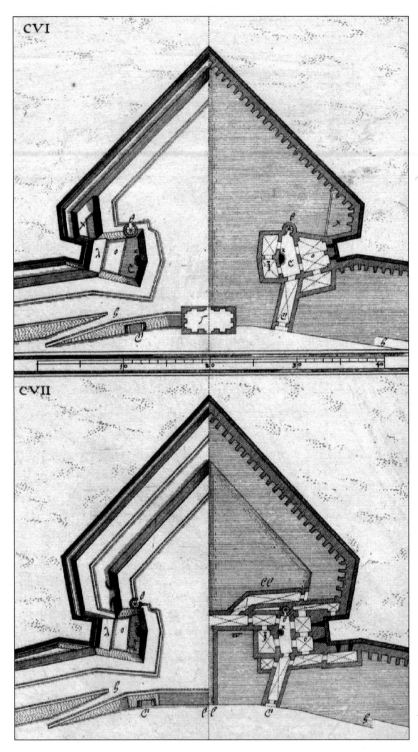

Artillery casemates according to Wilhelm Dilich. (Dilich, *Peribologia Seu Muniendorum*, tabs CVI, CVII.)

artillery casemates. The first author has already been mentioned in the context of caponiers appearing in Frederician fortresses before the Seven Years War, so we will not devote attention to him here. The second author, Georg Rimpler, was much more important, as his ideas were taken up by numerous authors of fortification treatises in the late seventeenth and early eighteenth centuries. He clearly advocated the use of casemates and revetted ramparts. Although he did not include any plans in his text, and also in the description of his new fortification concept he did not introduce any specifics about the location of the casemates,[405] nevertheless his publications represented a very important step in the development of artillery casemates. This was primarily due to the activities of those architectural theorists who took the trouble to explain and illustrate with drawings the ideas put forward by Rimpler. The most important of these was the German mathematician and architectural theorist, professor at the University of Frankfurt an der Oder, Leonhard Christoph Sturm. His main work was published in 1718.[406] In it, Sturm not only describes his version of the Rimpler fortress, but also presents it graphically. Although the main innovation of the Rimpler/Sturm ideas was to be the form of the defensive works (Rimpler departed from the typical bastion outline), the more important aspect for us was the use of artillery casemates. These Sturm located both in the main rampart of the fortress and in the bonnet in front of the bastions and in the curtain.[407]

The real breakthrough in the use of the artillery casemate were those constructed by the most important fortress engineer of the modern era, Sebastian le Prestre de Vauban. This engineer was particularly famous for fortifying the entire border of the French state during the reign of Louis XIV, when he surrounded France with a double belt of fortresses. One of the solutions he used in his fortresses were the so-called bastion towers. These were small, fully-casemated bastions having casemates for the garrison and artillery to defend adjacent sections of the moat. Covering of the foreground was already accomplished from open positions on the crown of the rampart. Such towers were erected at the fortresses of Besançon, Belfort, Neuf Briseach and Landau. The placement of gun emplacements in the flanks was still quite traditional, as it harked back to the function of casemates as flanking devices.

In addition, Vauban was reluctant to knock out embrasures in the bastion faces, as they were vulnerable to direct fire.[408] Nevertheless, at Besançon, the fourth fortress where Vauban placed his bastion towers, this reluctance was overcome.[409] The bastion towers there had artillery casemate ranges facing both the moat and the foreground. An excellent example of this is the Tour de Bregille, preserved to this day, located in the middle of the line of

---

fortificatorium; Georg Rimpler, *Befestigte Festung, Artillerie und Infanterie mit drey Treffen in Bataille gestellen (Beständiges Fundament zu Fortificiren und Defendiren)* (Frankfurt am Main: Unknown Publisher, 1674).

405 Jähns, *Geschichte 1890*, pp.1357–1358.
406 Sturm, *Freundlicher Wett-Streit.*
407 Importantly, some of the gun emplacements were to be directed towards the interior of the fortress, in accordance with the Rimpler principle of 'defence inwards', according to which the fortress was to be defended even after the rampart had been breached by the enemy, who was to be forced to conquer the fortress down to the last work. Sturm, *Freundlicher Wett-Streit*, tab. XIV, XVI.
408 Jähns, *Geschichte 1890*, p.1417.
409 It was erected between 1688 and 1691, Nicole Salat, *Thierry Sarmant, Politique, guerre et fortification au grand siècle: Lettres de Louvois à Louis XIV* (Paris: Société de l'histoire de France 2007), p.12.

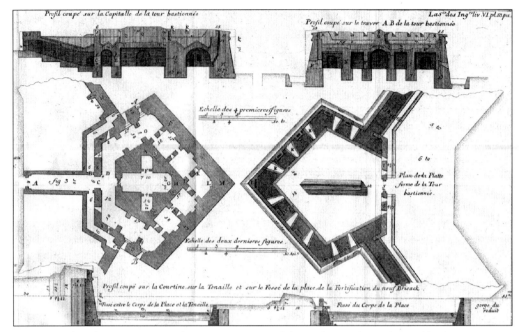

Artillery casemates in the Bastion Tower. (Bélidor, *La Science des ingénieurs*, Pl.53.)

town fortifications on the Doubs River side. This tower had 10 gun emplacements in the lower casemate, including four in the flanks and six in the faces.[410] Vauban used even more interesting artillery casemate solutions in the coastal forts he designed, the best example of which is Fort Mahon in Ambleteuse (1684–1690). This horseshoe-shaped defensive work has a low artillery tower equipped with nine gun emplacements, which made it possible to cover the entire area around the fort with artillery fire.[411]

Vauban's ideas on casemated batteries had relatively little resonance. This was due to the fact that Vauban was more of a practitioner than a theoretician; besides, he did not publish his ideas during his lifetime. Although his innovative ideas on fortification were discussed in the fortification literature of the time, Vauban's imitators focused on other aspects of his work. One of the first, L'Abbe du Fay, barely noticed the existence of bastion towers, although he considered them a very good solution.[412] More attention was paid to the idea by the aforementioned Sturm, who extensively described and illustrated Vauban's ideas on the basis of the Neuf Briesach fortress in his book published in 1718. The book includes a detailed description of the bastion towers there, including construction details, as well as their precise plans and sections. Interestingly, Sturm points out that the towers would have

---

410   Plans de Besançon et de ses travaux de défense par Vauban, BNF, département Estampes et photographie, EST VE–128, pl. 20–26.

411   Riksarkivet, Utländska stads- och fästningsplaner, Ambleteuse, SE/KrA/0406/13/002/004, <https://sok.riksarkivet.se/bildvisning/K0005504_00001>, accessed 1 December 2023.

412   L'Abbe du Fay, *Maniere de Fortifier selon la methode de Monsieur de Vauban…* (Paris: Coignard, 1707), pp.189–190.

served their purpose better if they had gun emplacements in the bastion faces as well, rather than just in the flanks.[413]

The theoretician who was particularly important for the reception of Vauban's ideas was Louis de Cormontaigne. This engineer developed his own system of fortification which was a modification of the ideas of his famous predecessor. One of the most significant modifications he introduced was the abandonment of the use of casemates, of which he was an opponent.[414] He was particularly critical of bastion towers and one of his ideas for rebuilding the fortress of Neuf Brisach was to do away with the towers there and replace them with simple bastions.[415]

Cormontaigne and his theories gained considerable recognition among military engineers, especially in France, where they became the official reference for bastion architecture. This influenced the widespread abandonment by French engineers of the use of the artillery casemate. Despite this, it was the French fortification engineers who were associated with the further development of this type of structure. However, these were military men working abroad, mainly in Germany. A great example of this is Jean de Bodt, a French engineer who was brought from France to Prussia towards the end of the Grand Elector's life. His most important fortifications, however, were created in Saxony. The collection of his designs held in the Dresden State Library contains numerous depictions of artillery casemates. Bodt used them both in the flanks of bastions and in the ravelin redoubt he invented.[416] An even better example of the keen interest in artillery casemates was the work of Claude Rozard, a French-born military engineer active in the electorate of Bavaria. Rozard published an architectural treatise in 1731 in which he presents innovative ideas. The most important novelty, already described in the chapter on the fortress at Graudenz, are the bastions he proposed, the faces of which were cut off from the flanks by a moat. He also proposed interesting solutions for the artillery casemates. In his first bastion concept, he locates a long casemate in its flanks – a two-aisle casemate covered with a bombproof cross vault. Inside it were positions for six cannon, firing through embrasures pierced in the wall. He proposed an even more interesting solution in the second of the bastions he devised. There were three flanks (two on the outer moat side and one on the inner moat side of the bastion) and in all of them he inserted casemated batteries. In total, one such bastion was to have as many as 32 casemated gun emplacements.[417] Rozard used artillery casemates in a different way in the fortress he actually built – the Rothenberg mountain fortress in Bavaria. The outline of this fortress completely deviated from his theoretical ideas, as it was limited by terrain conditions. Nevertheless, he did not abandon the use of artillery casemates. He built a long gallery encircling the fortress around the perimeter of the outer wall and inserted several dozen gun emplacements in it. They were only missing in the curtain wall of the fortress's entrance gate. Thanks to this, the cannon placed in the casemates could cover almost the entire area around the fortress.[418]

---

413   Sturm, *Freundlicher Wett-Streit*, pp.2–3, Tab. II.
414   Jähns, *Geschichte 1890*, p.1758.
415   de Cormontaigne, *Architecture militaire*, pp.75–80.
416   GEL: Bodt Plans de Fortification, SLUB/HS Mscr.Dresd.i.16.
417   Rozard, *Nouvelle Fortification Française*, vol.1, pp.8,9, 17, 18, T. 2. Pl. 4, 7.
418   Sven Thole, 'Die Festung Rothenberg', *Festungsjournal*. vol.42 (2012), pp.16–18.

The last French engineer to influence the widespread use of artillery casemates was Pierre Bechade de Rochepine, designer of the 1742–1757 reconstruction of the fortress at Olomouc. At Olomouc, he used artillery casemates both in the main rampart and in the forward redoubts.[419] The effectiveness of his ideas was encountered by Prussian engineers during the siege of there in 1758.

Before discussing them, however, it is necessary to introduce another, quite separate trend in the history of defensive architecture that was strongly associated with the development of artillery casemates – Swedish artillery towers. The multi-storey defence towers equipped with casemated gun emplacements were a clear indication of the distinctiveness of Swedish defence architecture. Objects of this type appeared in large numbers in the territory belonging to the Swedish kingdom in the second half of the seventeenth century and the early eigtheenth century. The first ideas for this type of fortification were said to have been devised by King Gustavus Adolphus of Sweden in the first half of the seventeenth century, but it was not until the second half of the century that buildings of this type were realised. The vast majority of Sweden's casemated artillery towers were designed by military engineer Eric Dahlberg. The most famous of his works are the towers protecting Gothenburg, erected in the 1680s; Kronan Fort, an artillery tower with a polygonal plan, and Göta Lejon, a circular tower placed on a pedestal in the shape of a four-pointed star.[420] Another important structure was the circular artillery tower that Dahlberg erected between 1682 and 1696 on the island of Walfisch near Wismar. It was the only structure of its kind on the southern shore of the Baltic Sea. Importantly, it has some connection to Prussia as it was that country's army that blew it up after capturing the fortress of Wismar at the end of the Great Northern War, on 2 February 1718.[421]

Schweidnitz

Casemated batteries appeared in a number of Prussian fortresses that were built or rebuilt, but the most important were those in Schweidnitz, as the Neumühl Flèche there began the renaissance of the artillery casemate in Prussia.

The construction of these buildings was inspired by the experiences from the Siege of Olomouc. Under their influence, the King ordered the construction of artillery casemates in Schweidnitz. The first to be built was a battery in the Neumühl Flèche, erected in 1769–1770. Another was erected in the Ziegel Flèche in 1771–1772. A decade later casemates were erected in the Garden and Bogen Forts. Like most of the defences, these structures were blown up by the French in 1807, but we have some data to reconstruct their appearance. The Neumühl Flèche is fragmentarily preserved, while archival plans have been found for the Ziegel Flèche and the batteries of both forts. A comparison of the archival plans with the remains preserved today clearly shows that the batteries in the forts were identical in terms of solutions to those in the Neumühl and Ziegel Flèches.

---

419 Kupka Kuch-Breburda, *Pevnost Olomouc*, pp.83–85.
420 Duffy, *The fortress in the Age of Vauban*, p.191; Xylander, 'Festungstürme in Schweden', p.71.
421 Friedrich Schlie, *Die Kunst- und Geschichts-Denkmäler des Grossherzogthums Mecklenburg-Schwerin. II. Band: Die Amtsgerichtsbezirke Wismar, Grevesmühlen, Rehna, Gadebusch und Schwerin* (Schwerin: Bärensprung, 1898), p.226.

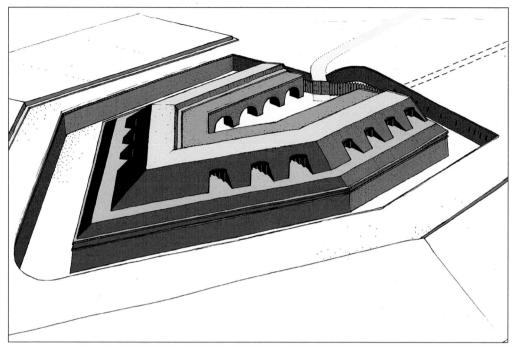

Fortress Schweidnitz, Ziegelei Flèche. (Drawn by Mariusz Wojciechowski)

The casemated batteries known from archive plans took the form of a long parallel casemate, extending along the face and flank of the work. These casemates were connected to the courtyard of the work by wide arcades, so that the back wall was reduced to thick pillars. Similar pillars were located at the front, with bombproof cross vaults spanning them. Unfortunately, there is a lack of archival material with which to reconstruct the appearance of the battery in the Neumühl Flèche. However, there is a thesis in the older literature that this casemate served as a model for those in the Ziegel Flèche. This issue was presented somewhat differently by the King himself. In his order to Daries, in which he directs him to erect a new casemate in the Ziegel Flèche he in no way suggests the need to refer to the solutions used in the casemate completed a few months earlier. He does, however, write about specific models, for he orders Daries to erect the new casemate 'on the Rimpler model'.[422] Unfortunately, he does not specify which specific solution he has in mind, but it is possible to determine this. As is already outlined, Rimpler did not present any of his ideas graphically and also his texts on casemates were very vague. More solutions that could be linked to the Ziegel Flèche casemate are contained in the works of Rimpler's imitators. In Sturm's 1718 work *Freundlicher Wett-Streit*, he proposes the construction of fortifications in front of the corners, which he called bonnets. These structures were to be in the form of an 'Old

---

422 Letter from the King to Daries of 19 September 1770, GStA SPK, I HA Rep.96 B Abschriften von Kabinetsordres, Bd.71, p.473 verso.

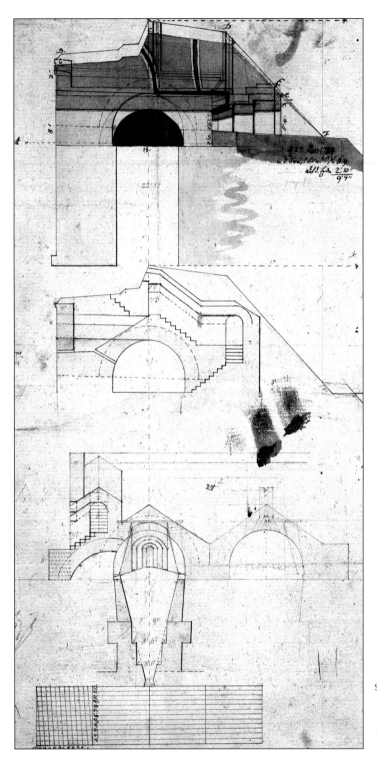

Fortress Schweidnitz, cross-
section through a casemated
battery in the Garden
Fort with a drawing of the
embrasure. (GStA SPK, XI HA,
ref. A 71302, Bl. 2)

Fortress Schweidnitz, Neumühl Flèche, relics of the embrasures of the casemated battery. (Photo from the collection of Patrycjusz Malicki)

Dutch half-moon', to be casemated and provided with gun emplacements for cannon. Moreover, one of the plans accompanying Sturm's book suggests that the casemates were to have arcaded openings on the inside of the work.[423] Similar ideas also appear in the works of the other proponent of Rimpler's ideas, Ludwig Andreas Herlin. Interesting in terms of its similarity to the Schweidnitz flèches is his idea of rebuilding Vauban's Landau fortress in the spirit of Rimpler's ideas, in which lunettes with artillery casemates appear in the flanks.[424] Another solution should also be noted – the so-called half-caponier. Such structures were recommended by Herlin to be erected during a siege under the glacis as good defensive positions.[425] By the mid-eighteenth century, half-caponiers inspired by Herlin's ideas were already commonly presented in theoretical writings. Pirscher, the Prussian theorist of defensive architecture, is an excellent example. In his 1767 book, he presented half-caponiers, which he described as works 'open from the back, from the direction of the fortress.'[426] Arguably, it was these arcaded openings that were to be the solution to the Rimpler designs.

423 Sturm, *Freundlicher Wett-Streit*, p.13, tabs V, VI, VIII.
424 Ludwig Andreas Herlin, *Herrn George Rimplers Sämtliche Schrifften von der Fortification* (Dreßden & Leipzig: Heckel, 1724), tab. IX.
425 Herlin, *Herrn George Rimplers Sämtliche Schrifften*, pp.201, 203.
426 Pirscher, *Kurzer Unterricht*, pp.14–15, Tab. I Fig. 8a.

However, the claim that the casemates of the Neumühl Flèche are similar to those of the Ziegel Flèche is probably also true in older literature. It is most likely that identical and very unusual gun embrasures were used in both structures. According to archive plans depicting the Schweidnitz batteries, from the front side the gun emplacement rooms were enclosed by a relatively thin wall through which embrasures were punched. The casemate was protected by a thick earth embankment, and the earth from the embankment also covered the front wall of the casemates. So that artillery fire could be conducted from inside, four stepped tapering arches were inserted into the frontal embankment, which together with the opening in the frontal wall formed gigantic embrasures. At their highest point, the archways were as much as two metres high and more than two metres wide. Examining the remains of the casemates of the Neumühl Flèche, which have survived to the present day, one can find relatively small, vaulted 'rooms', open to both sides; a careful analysis of these remains and comparison with archival plans makes it possible to identify them as the remnants of these gigantic embrasures.

Casemates with Arcaded Open Rear Walls

Most of the artillery casemates in Prussian fortresses built after the Seven Years War followed a different pattern of construction and interior layout from that of Schweidnitz. These were perpendicular casemates in which the fighting chambers were covered by a separate, bomb-proof barrel vault, while the embrasures were punched into the thick front wall. A distinctive feature of these buildings was the absence of a rear wall enclosing the casemate rooms on the courtyard side. Instead, there were wide, arcaded openings to facilitate the removal of gunpowder smoke from inside the casemates.

Probably the oldest structure of this type was the casemate in the Graupen Bastion in Breslau. There were already quite a few casemated artillery positions in this fortress, located in bastions built during the modernisation of the fortress in the New Italian manner. The most famous were the casemates of the Taschen Bastion, as one of them exploded during the siege in 1757. The other one is known, as its inventory from the end of the eighteenth century has been preserved. The casemates of the Ziegel Bastion have survived to the present day. The multitude of older casemates explains why only one structure of this kind was built during the extensive expansion of the fortress after the end of the Seven Years War. The battery erected between 1773 and 1774 in the right flank of the Graupen Bastion housed four gun emplacements, relatively few compared to the previously described casemates. Nonetheless, the Breslau building should be regarded as extremely important in the context of the development of this type of building. On the one hand, it should be considered traditional, as the casemate was built into the bastion's shoulder and the cannons placed in it could only cover a section of the moat in front of the Hunde Bastion. On the other hand, however, it was innovative, as it had four casemate chambers, the front wall was punctured with embrasures, and the rear wall of the casemate was open. Although the structure no longer exists, as it was destroyed by Napoleon's sappers after the capture of Breslau in 1807, such a technical solution is suggested by an analysis of archive plans of the fortress, the remains of the casemate found during archaeological excavations in 2008, as well as information provided by the French writer Honore-Gabriel de Riquetti de Mirabeau.

Mirabeau, in the fourth volume of his description of the Prussian monarchy under Frederick, published in 1788, devotes a large section of his reflections on Prussian fortresses

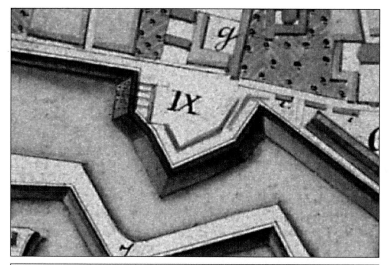

Above: Fortress Breslau, Graupen Bastion with casemated battery, fragment of plan. (GStA SPK, XI HA ref. E 72090)

Right: Fortress Breslau, casemated battery of Graupen Bastion. (Reconstruction by Marcin Wichrowski)

to this very solution, which, according to him, was used for the first time in Breslau. In his opinion, the main problem for gun casemates in general was the removal of gunpowder smoke generated after firing. This author argued that the solutions invented by Montalembert would not be able to solve this problem effectively and that the 'open-back' casemates invented by Prussian engineers were the only way to remedy it.[427] In the context of this remark by Mirabeau, it should be mentioned that there were also those among the Prussian military who had similar doubts when the first casemates were developed in Prussia. This led to an experiment when cannon were fired in the casemates of Schweidnitz in the presence of the King. The experiment was successful, the gunpowder smoke did not impede the work of the gunners.[428] However, Mirabeau was not entirely convinced by this solution introduced by the Prussians; for he stated that its usefulness would only be seen during a future siege of Breslau. As we know, the siege did take place, but this casemate did not do much work, as the city surrendered before the enemy could confront the artillery protected by it.

According to Mirabeau, it was in the Breslau casemate that an arcaded open rear wall was first used. However, there is another casemate in which an identical solution appeared, and whose date of construction is two years earlier than that of the Breslau casemate – the Casemated Battery (Casemattierte Batterie) erected between 1771 and 1774 on the north-western edge of the fortress at Neisse. The structure was started by *Oberst* Lefèbvre and was completed by *Kapitän* Freund after Lefèbvre's suicide in 1771. Unfortunately, it is not known when the casemate acquired its final form, as in 1771, after Freund took over the work, it became apparent that the vaults built under the supervision of the first officer were in danger of collapsing. It cannot be ruled out that this forced far-reaching changes to the design, or even the demolition of the walls already erected. This would explain the unusually long construction period of four years for this building. It is therefore likely that the Neisse building was the first among a group of similar casemates, but this cannot be confirmed. The casemate was finally built as a rectangular free-standing structure, equipped with five embrasures in the front wall and one in the side wall. After it was extended between 1784 and 1785 by *Major* Harroy, a second casemate was added to the first at an angle, creating a two-wing structure. The new wing had identical solutions to the first, with arcaded openings in the rear wall and cannon embrasures in the thick front wall. This allowed the entire structure to control the immediate foreground with artillery fire. The larger casemate directed its fire towards the gorge of the Caninchen Redoubt lying in front of it; the smaller one could shell the foreground between the redoubt and Fort Presussen.[429]

The next structure of this type was the Casemated Battery (Casemattierte Batterie), erected in 1774 within the fortifications of Grosse Strohhaube at the stronghold of Silberberg. It had the same interior layout (perpendicular casemate) and technical solutions (embrasures pierced in the front wall and open arcades in the rear part of the casemates) as the previously described casemates. Some of its special features made it similar to the one at Neisse.

---

427 de Mirabeau, *Von der Preußischen Monarchie*, p.425.
428 Seydel, *Nachrichten*, vol.4, pp.19–20.
429 The building has survived to the present day, but its current appearance differs from its description. In the 1870s, it was rebuilt, with the gun embrasures bricked up and covered from the outside with an earth embankment, and the arcade openings bricked up. The state before the reconstruction is documented in the plan Spezieller Entwurf zur Erdumantelung der kasemattierten Batterie zu Neisse, GStA SPK, XI HA, ref. E 72101.

Fortress Neisse, the Casemated Battery. (Reconstruction by Mariusz Wojciechowski)

However, this casemate was free-standing, and apart from the five gun emplacements in the front wall, it also had one in each of the side walls; as well as the gun emplacements, there were also emplacements for small arms.

All the casemates described above, with the exception of the Breslau casemates, were similar in terms of the function they were intended to perform during a siege. They were not used to defend the moat, but to fire on the foreground. The King himself was to comment on the function of such casemates. According to him, these casemates 'are not to smoke, nor to attract the attention of the enemy; they are not to be used to flank the moat, but to attack, or more to hinder the construction of siege batteries and to shell the whole front.'[430]

Batteries Integrated into the Defence Works

A small but important group of artillery casemates were those that were built as an integral part of a large, multifunctional defensive structure. Other casemates were either built into what was essentially an earthen rampart (Schweidnitz and Breslau), or were small, free-standing casemates that performed the sole function of a bombproof artillery battery. In two cases – the Donjon in Glatz and Fort Spitzberg in Silberberg – it was different. Both of these structures were fully casemated; bomb-proof masonry structures formed the entire

---

430 Seydel, *Nachrichten*, vol.4, pp.13, 18.

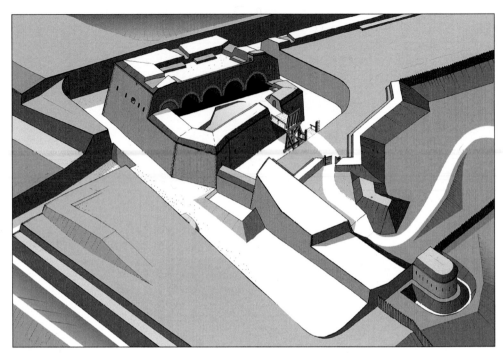

Fortress Silberberg, the Casemated Battery and its immediate surroundings. (Reconstruction by Mariusz Wojciechowski)

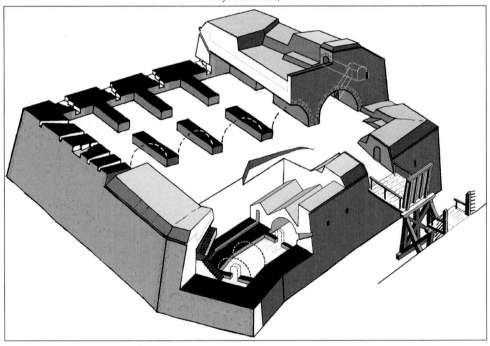

Fortress Silberberg, the Casemated Battery, schematic diagram. (Drawn by Mariusz Wojciechowski)

structure, while the earth did not form a rampart, but only served as an additional protective layer for the vaults. In addition, the casemates stretching around the courtyard housed various functions; the artillery casemates were adjacent to bombproof barracks, kitchens, bakeries, latrines and other such social and living quarters.

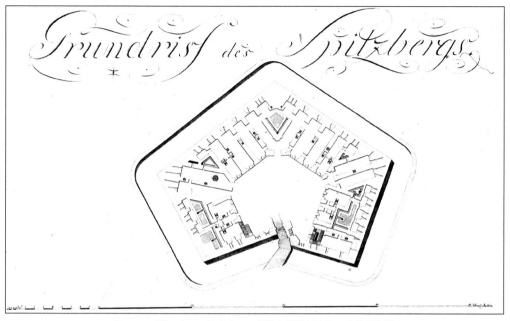

Fortress Silberberg, Spitzberg. (GStA SPK, XI HA, ref. G 70015)

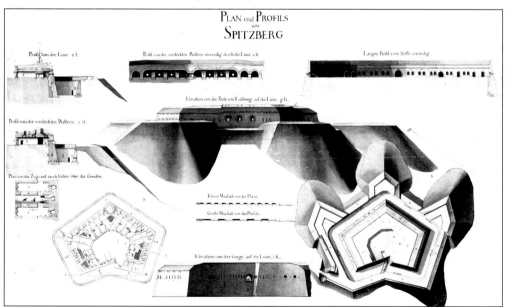

Fortress Silberberg, Spitzberg. (GStA SPK, XI HA, ref. C 70020)

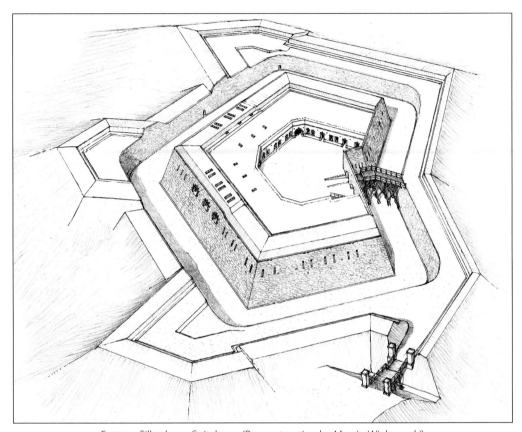

Fortress Silberberg, Spitzberg. (Reconstruction by Marcin Wichrowski)

The first of its kind was Fort Spitzberg, built between 1769 and 1772. It was the second Frederician structure, after the Neumühl Flèche, to use casemated artillery positions. This fort had six gun emplacements placed in both faces of the fort. This structure used solutions completely different from those known from other Silesian casemates. First of all, the case-mate rooms were completely enclosed, unlike most Silesian structures, and the casemate chambers had a wall on the courtyard side. However, even there the designers took proper care of the removal of gunpowder smoke after firing. The casemates used a complex system of ventilation ducts, the inlets of which were located in the casemate vaults. Each casemate had as many as 12 of them, of which as many as six were located near the firing point, where the concentration of gunpowder smoke was highest. These ducts were grouped into seven chimneys, which exited in different places, so as to reduce the risk of their destruction by an accidental hit by a cannonball.

The second structure to be discussed is the Glatz Donjon, built between 1771 and 1773. This structure is of great importance for the Frederician defensive architecture, as are its casemates, but this topic has already been mostly presented in the subsection devoted to the history of the fortress fortress Glatz in the period after the Seven Years War. Here it only remains to present some planning and technical solutions. The most important is the

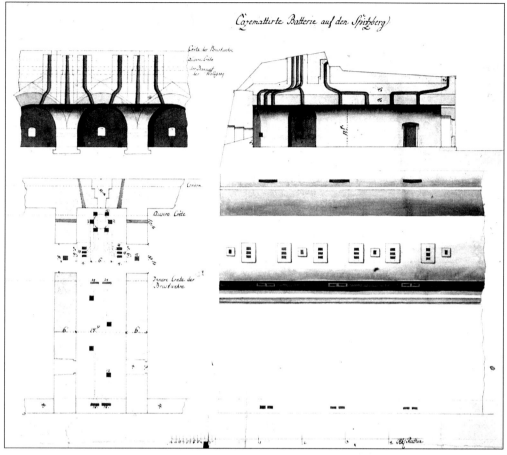

Fortress Silberberg, Spitzberg, details of a casemated battery. (GStA SPK, XI HA ref. G 70047)

integration of the gun casemates with rooms having functions other than combat. The batteries were mainly concentrated in two half-bastions and a north-facing corner, with living quarters placed between them. Between the batteries in the eastern half-bastion and in the corner, were two guard rooms and a room where the fortress commander lived. Between the batteries in the corner and in the eastern half-bastion, were living quarters for the rank-and-file soldiers. Interestingly, these rooms were directly connected to the casemates. In other words, during the siege of the fortress, the soldiers living in these rooms were separated only by a thin door from the dozen or so firing guns. Another important issue concerns the means of removing gunpowder smoke from the casemates. Due to the high saturation of artillery (there were more than 40 gun emplacements in the casemates of the Donjon) and the proximity of the battle and residential casemates, this problem was particularly important, as the possible harmful effects of gunpowder smoke could affect not only the gunners, but also other residents of the Donjon. Unfortunately, materials documenting the course and location of the ventilation chimneys have not survived as accurately

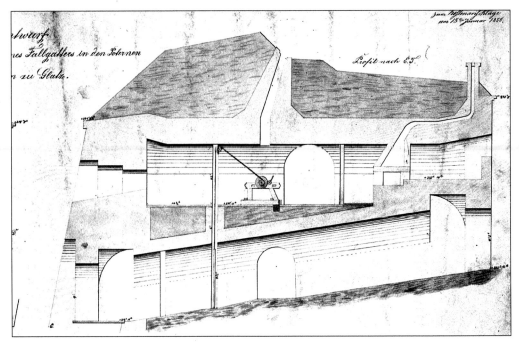

Fortress Glatz, Donjon, cross-section through a casemated battery, fragment of a plan.
(GStA SPK, XI HA ref. F 71761)

as in the case of Fort Spitzberg in Silberberg. However, on the basis of the few archival plans, as well as traces of ventilation ducts preserved to this day, it should be thought that these casemates were ventilated by means of single ducts, but with a much larger cross-section than those of the Silberberg.[431]

Graudenz

The fortress at Graudenz had the largest number of casemated batteries, so it is appropriate to describe them separately, although the technical solutions used there are mostly known from other fortresses. In three bastions and two half-bastions, eight casemates were built, each for five guns. Two artillery casemates, each for six guns, were also located in the extreme (facing the Vistula embankment) sections of the casemated main rampart. In total, there were 10 casemates in the fortress with a total of 52 artillery positions, which in this respect placed Graudenz at the top of Prussian fortresses of the time.

The first type of casemates at Graudenz, those located in bastions, are at first sight very traditional. They are located in the retired flanks of bastions sheltered by orillons. Casemates had been located in this way since the sixteenth century. However, when one does not look at the plan, but at the structure, one can see significant differences. These casemates are in

---

431 The only surviving archive plan showing the course of the chimneys of the artillery casemate is Enwurf über Anlage eines Fallgatters in den Poternen des Dojon zu Glatz, GStA SPK, XI HA ref. F 71761.

fact separate structures from the bastion: each of them is rectangular in plan, almost free-standing, as it meets the bastion with only one wall. In terms of technical solutions, these structures also differ from typical casemates, especially the arcaded openings in the rear part of the casemate. This solution was copied by Gotzenbach from casemates built almost a decade earlier in Silesia.

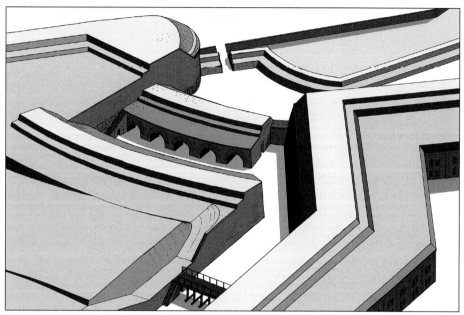

Fortress Graudenz, casemated battery in bastion flank. (Study by Mariusz Wojciechowski.)

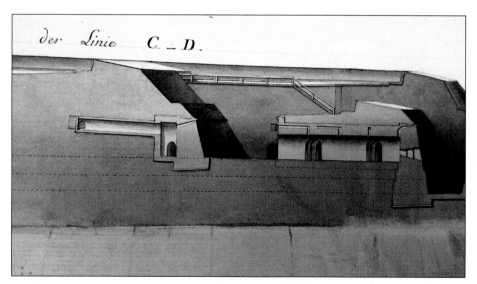

Fortress Graudenz, cross-section through the casemanted battery in a detached bastion, fragment of a plan. (GStA SPK XI HA ref. A 7074)

The second type of artillery casemates at Graudenz was already decidedly more innovative and unique. As already mentioned, they were located in the ends of the casemated main rampart, protruding towards the Vistula escarpment. They had embrasures pointing in two directions: four towards the great storehouse, and two towards the moat in front of each half-bastion. They could control both the approach to the fortress from the Vistula escarpment and sections of the moat with flanking fire. Thus, they can be described as a kind of artillery caponier, although their location in the outermost sections of the casemate also resembles traditor batteries, common in nineteenth-century forts.

A New Casemate Type – Hangars

Towards the end of Frederick the Great's life, another type of artillery casemate appeared – hangars. The first such structures were constructed in Schweidnitz (the Neumühl Hangar ca. 1775–1776, and the Jauernick hangar ca. 1780),[432] in Glatz (Kranich, 1776) and in Cosel (in the Kobelwitzer Redoubt, 1783).[433]

The hangars were fundamentally different from traditional casemates. They were a type of hall in which bombproof cross vaults stood on thick brick pillars. They were devoid of side walls and, of course, had no masonry embrasures. The hangar stood in the middle of the defensive work; between it and the foreground there was space for a cannon position.

Two of the described facilities – in Cosel and Schweidnitz – were used for flat-firing artillery. The Glatz one was to be used as a casemate for mortars.[434] In the first case, the cannon fired through the gun emplacements in the earthen breastwork or above the breastwork, and after firing they withdrew under the hangar vaults.[435] This solution had its advantages. The lack of sidewalls facilitated air circulation and there was no problem with the evacuation of gunpowder smoke after firing. At the same time, the bombproof vaults protected the cannons and their attendants from the effects of plunging fire. The lack of masonry gun embrasures was also not without merit; in the eighteenth century, it was thought that in the event of a direct hit, the pieces of brick and stone from the gun emplacement could injure the gun crew. As can be seen, when building the hangars, the intention was to create an optimal casemate and to eliminate all the inconveniences of traditional buildings of this type while providing artillery with protection from mortar and howitzer fire. However, it is questionable whether this was successful. While the hangar as a type of structure has entered permanent military use, it has not as a defensive post. This is not surprising, the design had significant disadvantages. Firstly: the cannon, when retracted into the casemate, were almost under the key of the vault, which must have been an problematic solution from the point of view of service. The inconvenience of operating in the hangar is mentioned by the authors of the description of the Cosel fortress from 1796.[436] Secondly, as the historical iconography shows, the hangars were too high. The arcade openings alone protruded three

---

432   King's letters to Daries, 26 October 1775 and 6 October 1779, GStA SPK, I HA Rep.96 B Abschriften von Kabinetsordres, Bd.74, p.715, Bd.79, p.1057.

433   Weltzel, *Geschichte der Stadt*, p.373.

434   This is how the engineer Rauch described its function in his 1819 analysis of the fortress, Uebersicht der Befestigungen von Glatz, SBB PK, DPG ref. Glatz, 119, p.7.

435   SBB PK, ref. X 33655/35, Bl. 9.

436   SBB PK, DPG ref., Kosel, 89 I – Memoires über die Festung Cosel 1797, p.8.

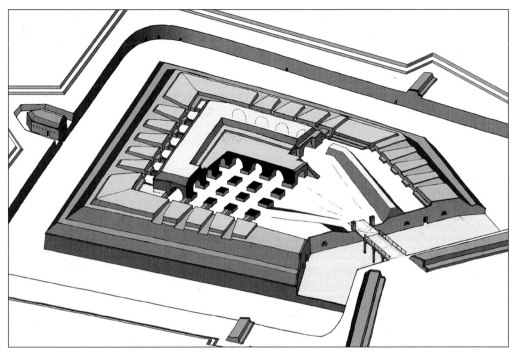

Fortress Schweidnitz, Jauernicker Hangar. (Study by Mariusz Wojciechowski)

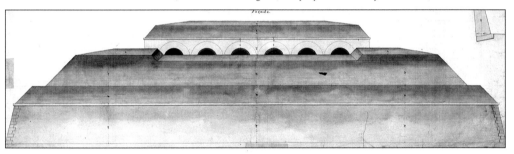

Fortress Schweidnitz Neumühl Hangar. (GStA SPK, XI HA ref. A 71302 Bl.3)

feet above the breastwork, and the hangar wall up to the parapet protruded seven and half feet.[437] Such an exposed wall was easily crushed by artillery fire from a distance. In addition, there was a high probability of a howitzer shell being fired into the hangar through the arcade, which was perfectly visible and unobstructed. As it seems, these drawbacks were recognised fairly quickly. Frederick, in a letter to *Kapitän* Wins, the designer of the hangar in the Cosel redoubt, ordered him to raise the front of the redoubt, so that a potential siege battery set up on the west bank of the Oder could not shell the interior of the work.[438]

---

437 GStA SPK, XI HA, ref. A 71302–3.
438 Letter from the King to Wins, 24 March 1783, GStA SPK, I HA Rep.96 B Abschriften von Kabinetsordres, Bd.83, p.204.

There is one issue related to the hangars that needs clarification. According to the literature to date, these buildings are supposed to have been inspired by the ideas of Marc-René de Montalembert.[439] However, this claim is not supported by the facts. The term 'hangar' does not appear at all in Montalembert's writings, nor is it possible to find structures similar to these unusual casemates. Any connection, or any inspiration, to the writings of the French theorist is also ruled out by the date of construction of the first of the hangars, erected in front of the Neumühl Flèche in Schweidnitz. At the time when the first volume of Montalembert's work went to print (1776), this hangar was already in the process of being finished. Surviving is a letter from Frederick dated 26 October 1775, addressed to the engineer Daries, who was carrying out work in Schweidnitz, in which the King orders that the hangar erected in front of the Neumühl Flèche be completed for the sum of 3,384 thalers.[440] The later hangars are identical to the first one in terms of their construction solutions, so the one in front of the Neumühl Flèche must be regarded as the prototype for the whole group of buildings. As can be seen, the architectural conception of the hangar as a defensive structure was born at least a year before the publication of Montalembert's work, so it is not the result of inspiration by the ideas of this French theorist of defensive architecture. Where, then, did it come from? We are probably dealing with a creative application of a solution hitherto not used in defensive architecture. In the eighteenth century, a hanger or hangar was a type of shed or store open to the sides, with the roof raised on stilts. They were sometimes used as coach houses; some dictionaries also add that hangars were used in naval arsenals as canopies under which gun mounts were stored.[441] Hangars, which were built from 1775 onwards, were also a type of canopy open to the sides but made in such a way that the cannon hidden underneath were protected not only from rain, but also from enemy bombs. It will probably not be possible to determine who was the inventor of this type of facility; it is only possible to identify a group of people who were involved. Among them were Daries, the builder of the first of the Schweidnitz hangars, Regler, the designer of the hangar in Glatz, and King. Although Frederick's involvement was recorded only in relation to the second of the Schweidnitz hangars, built a few years after the first buildings of this type, it was of a special kind, as the King instructed Daries on the technical details of this facility.[442] This shows that the King was very familiar with this structure and its functioning.

439   Bonin, *Geschichte des Ingenieurkorps*, pp.100–101; Seydel, *Nachrichten*, vol.4, p.23.
440   Letter from the King to Daries, 26 October 1775, GStA SPK, I HA Rep.96 B Abschriften von Kabinetsordres, Bd.74, p.715.
441   de Bélidor, *Dictionaire portatif*, p.345; Lukas Voch, *Allgemeines Baulexicon oder Erklaerung der deutschen und französischen kunstwörter in der bürgerlichen, Kriegs und Schiffbaukunst wie auch der Hydrotechnik und Hydraulik* (Ausburg-Leipzig: Matthaus Riegers, 1781), p.262; Nicolas Aubin, *Dictionnaire de marine contenant les termes de la navigation et de l'architecture navale* (Amsterdam: Pierre Brunel, 1702), p.481; Furetière Antoine, *Dictionnaire universel, contenant généralement tous les mots françois…* (La Haye: Arnout & Reinier Leer, 1727), vol.2, entry 'Hangart'; Denis Diderot, Jean le Rond d'Alembert, *Encyclopédie: ou dictionnaire raisonné des sciences, des arts et des métier* (Neufchastel: Samuel Faulche, 1765), vol.8, p.37.
442   Letter from the King to Daries, 17 August 1780, GStA SPK, I HA Rep.96 B Abschriften von Kabinetsordres, Bd.80, p.530.

Conclusion

The casemates built in the Prussian fortresses were only to a limited extent subjected to the test of war. Only those in Schweidnitz and Silberberg were directly involved in a siege. There is more information on the Siege of Schweidnitz in 1807. The several days' shelling of this fortress showed that the gun embrasures used in this fortress were clearly an unsuccessful solution. Although the embrasure itself was not large, the whole, including the window surround, was very exposed, thus clearly visible to a potential observer and a good target. Equipped with such embrasures, the Ziegel Flèche was subjected to a relatively short fire, which nevertheless had serious consequences. According to reports from French artillerymen, after just three days of shelling this facility, it was impossible to fire from it due to the destruction of the embrasures.[443] Hangars probably did not work as fortress artillery structures either, as later defence architecture completely lacked solutions analogous to those of the Silesian fortresses. Hangars were still used, but as a type of non-defensive casemate.

Casemates provided with traditional gun emplacements punched into a solid wall performed better. One of these, the Silberberg casemated battery, came under fire for several hours during the siege of the fortress and there is no record of any damage done. Such gun emplacements became standard in the nineteenth century.

Another solution that was introduced in casemates of this period also had a great influence on the development of defence architecture. It was the wide, arcaded opening at the back of the artillery casemate. This solution is known from numerous casemates in Schweidnitz, Silberberg, Neisse and Breslau. This solution spread throughout the world in the nineteenth century. The French engineer of the Napoleonic period, François Nicolas Benoît Haxo, is generally considered to be the creator of this solution, and the Haxo casemate is the name given to a special type of artillery casemate found in nineteenth-century defensive architecture in France and Great Britain. The prototype was the casemate erected in 1811 by Haxo at Napoleon's Redoubt in Danzig, which had an arcaded open rear wall and embrasure towers sheltered by an earth rampart.[444] Similarly planned casemates, only without the earth embankment protecting the embrasures, were also made in the Napoleon Redoubt in the fortress at Modlin, which was built under Haxo's supervision, with Napoleon's participation. In older German literature as well as in Polish literature, it is often stated that the first Haxo casemate, erected in Danzig, was a copy of the solutions from Schweidnitz. However, this is not true. Contrary to the claim often put forward in Prussian and Polish literature that Haxo was personally acquainted with the casemates erected in Schweidnitz, as he was demolishing them on Napoleon's orders, this engineer could not have been familiar with Silesian examples of casemates with open backs.[445] At the time the French were demolishing the fortifications of Schweidnitz, François Haxo was in Italy and later in Turkey. Haxo was

---

443 Igor Zbigniew Strzok, 'Oblężenie Świdnicy w 1807 roku, jego efekty i wnioski wyciągnięte przez napoleońskich fortyfikatorów', *Rocznik Świdnicki 2007*, (2008), p.74.

444 Lepage, *French Fortifications*, p.153; Strzok, 'Oblężenie Świdnicy', p.75.

445 Reinhold Wagner was the first to introduce this thesis, *Grundriss der Frotifikation* (Berlin: Vossische Buchhandlung, 1872), p.77, then repeated by others, including: Paul Pochhammer, *Friedrich der Grosse und Neisse. Vortrag, gehalten in der Philomathie zu Neisse am 16. Mai 1888* (Neisse: Verlag der Josef Graveur'schen Buchhandlung, 1888), pp. 21–11; Oskar Reuleaux, *Die geschichtliche Entwickelung des Befestigungswesens vom Aufkommen der Pulvergeschütze bis zur Neuzeit* (Leipzig: Göschen'sche Verlagsbuchhandlung, 1913), p.74; Strzok, 'Oblężenie Świdnicy', p.75.

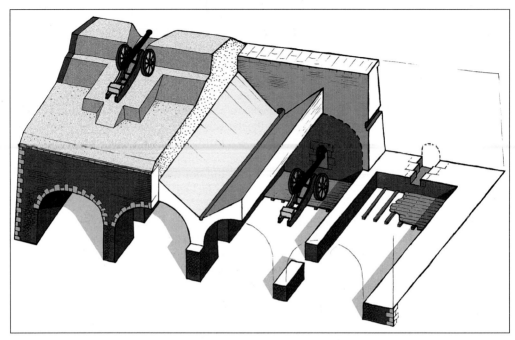

Briançon Fortress, Redoute des Salettes, Haxo casemates. (Study by Mariusz Wojciechowski)

in Northern Europe twice; in 1811, when he inspected several hundred fortified sites in Germany (including Silesia) and Poland, and again, in 1813. At that time, however, he was unable to see any of the Frederician casemates, as the French occupied only one Silesian fortress, Glogau, which had no such facilities. What is more, a decade before his Silesian trip, he designed an artillery casemate, the rear wall of which was open and the front wall protected by an earthen breastwork. He drew up its design for the Rocca d'Anfo fortress in 1801, but it was not realised.[446]

Nevertheless, it is impossible not to notice that the solutions used by Haxo are almost identical to those used in Prussian fortresses from the 1770s onwards. Perhaps their similarity is due to drawing on the same models. Waldemar Łysiak, in his book on Napoleon's fortifications published in 1999 (in which he pushed the thesis that it was the French emperor who invented the arcaded openings of the rear walls of artillery casemates), pointed to earlier models for such casemates by seventeenth- and eighteenth-century theorists.[447] However, while such solutions appeared in architectural treatises, prior to their construction in the Silesian fortresses they were not a solution known and in common use. The French, though not Haxo himself, were familiar with as many as six such structures after conquering

---

446   Yannic Guillou, *Haxo 1774–1838. Successeur de Vauban* (Senones: Edhisto 2015), pp.82, 76–97, 160–161, 438–439; Plan coupe et elevation d'une caseamate sur le terreplein d'un rempart, Anfo, an X, SHD Atlas du génie, La Rocca d'Anfo, XIXe siècle. Cote: atlas 183, pl. 3

447   Waldemar Łysiak, *Napoleon jako foryfikator*, (Warszawa, ExLibris 1999), p.233; Alexis Henri Brialmont, *Études sur la défense des états: et sur la fortification* (Bruxelles: Guyot 1863), vol.2, p.67.

Schweidnitz, Neisse and Breslau. They were probably also familiar with them earlier; after all, this solution was pointed out by Mirabeau, as mentioned in this chapter. Moreover, it was only in Schweidnitz that the French engineers were able to familiarise themselves with the existing, and not merely the projected, casemate, the front wall of which was protected by an earth rampart. What is more, some of the later Haxo casemates can even be described as copies of Silesian solutions, for example the casemates of the Briancon fortress, created in the Redoubt des Salettes as a result of the reconstruction of 1830–1854. In other words, it is highly likely that the Silesian examples of artillery casemates influenced the development of casemates with arcaded open rear walls, including the Haxo casemates.

8

From Design to Implementation

Fortress Planners

The King

Frederick the Great was the central figure in all matters relating to the construction of fortresses in Prussia between 1740 and 1786. He made decisions at the strategic level, deciding on the shape of the fortress and its individual elements, and often on the choice of technology. He decided on the pace of construction, on the number of workers building it, on materials and on budgets.

The most important decisions, of a strategic nature, concerned the construction of new fortresses or the thorough modernisation of old ones. The first such decision was taken by the King at the end of 1741, when the head of the engineer corps, *Generalmajor* Walrave, together with *Generalfeldmarschalls* Kurt Christoph von Schwerin and Samuel von Schmettau, tried to persuade the King to fortify Schurgast instead of Neisse, which according to these military men was supposed to be more favourably located. Schwerin was also said to have drawn attention to the large costs involved in building a fortress in Neisse, which according to him had to be heavily fortified. The King rejected these objections and decided in December 1741 to expand Neisse, claiming that, 'As far as the fortification in Neisse is concerned, it is my idea, and I think I have good reason to believe that this fortification will cost me a good deal, about which I will explain myself to you further when you come here.'[1] However, the Neisse fortress did not fully solve the problem of defending the south-eastern edge of Silesia. The arguments put forward by the royal advisors convinced Frederick and he also agreed to fortify Schurgast. Priority, however, was to be given to the fortresses at Neisse and Brieg.[2] The latter fortress was intensively reinforced from the first days of Prussian rule over it. However, the modernisation of the already existing fortress perimeter was not enough for the King, who considered strengthening the fortress at Brieg with a new fortified suburb. The idea was first mooted in February 1742. In a letter dated

---

1   'Soviel das Fortifizieren in Neisse anbetrifft, so ist solches meine Phantasie, und glaube ich meine guten Ursachen zu haben, daß mir diese Fortifikation was Rechtes kosten lasse, worüber mich gegen Euch weiters expliziren will, wenn Ihr herkommen werdet.'
2   Klose, *Festung Neisse*, p.84; Colmar Grünhagen, 'Die Einrichtung des Militärwesens in Schlesien bei dem Beginne der preußischen Herrschaft', *Zeitschrift des Vereins für Geschichte und Alterthum Schlesiens*, 23 (1889), p.23.

11 February, he wrote to Walrave: 'I have deemed it advisable and necessary to extend the suburb in Brieg, so I want you and Colonel Hautcharmoy, when he is back, to think the thing over well and to have an idea where this suburb, in which place it is best to establish it, and also its plan to be made and sent to me for approval.'[3] The suburb was to be located on the north bank of the Oder River and take the form of a huge fortified tête de pont. According to the surviving designs it was to have an area almost the size of the old part of the fortress.[4] Once it was established, the fortress there would become one of the most important strongholds in the entire Prussian state. The issue of fortifying Schurgast and expanding the fortress at Brieg appears in royal correspondence as late as 1743 and is eventually abandoned. In the case of Brieg, only plans were produced; the construction of the fortress in Schurgast was to be started and abandoned. Indeed, the King changed his idea about fortifying this part of his kingdom, and in August 1743 he decided to erect a fortress at Cosel.[5] This hesitation and change of mind was probably due to Frederick's relatively poor knowledge of Silesia in the early period of his reign. Indeed, he took the decision to build the fortress at Cosel only after travelling along the Oder for several days. Apparently, it was then that he became acquainted with all the advantages and disadvantages of the locations previously considered, with the result that he chose a completely new place in which to establish the fortress.

In addition to making strategic decisions regarding the fortification of a given point, the King also often intervened in the fortification design process itself. This is well illustrated where the King was both the initiator of construction and the author of the concept. This situation is illustrated by the fate of the fortresses at Schweidnitz and Graudenz. In the first fortress, Frederick did not present his design, but intervened in the process of its construction from the outset. He had an accurate model of the area around Schweidnitz made, so that, without travelling to Schweidnitz, he could decide on the location of the new defensive works. This was probably the reason why the design of the fortress took so long and why so many versions, which differed from each other by minor changes, were created. In the case of Graudenz, he also demanded a precise survey from his engineers, but he made a design sketch even before he received the elevation map that he had ordered. This drawing is still preserved today and has already been discussed elsewhere in this book.

Frederick's design activity also concerned individual defensive works, not just whole fortresses. Handwritten sketches have survived on the designs for fortification elements at Neisse and Glatz, which should probably be identified as corrections made by Frederick. The corrections to the Glatz project have already been described; all the indications are that they are some form of representation of the urban fortifications in Glatz designed by Frederick. A correction on one of the designs for Neisse shows a sketch of two external works added in front of the outer moat and envelope designed by Walrave. One was located in front of the south-west corner of the envelope, the other was placed between the Cardinal Redoubt and the River Biehle. This correction was made on the 1745 plan of the fortress, the oldest known

---

3   Letter from the King to Walrave, 11 February 1742, GStA SPK I HA Rep.96 B Abschriften von Kabinetsordres Bd.25, p.88.

4   Plan de Brieg avec La Ville Neuve, SBB PK, ref. X 20994.

5   Weltzel, *Geschichte der Stadt*, p.348.

design. The 1746 plan of Neisse shows one of the works introduced by the pencil correction; the other was not realised.[6]

While in the case of the sketches for the fortifications of Neisse and Glatz the participation of Frederick is only probable, in the case of the fortifications of Strohhaube, the western edge of the Silberberg fortress, there is no doubt. A design drawing has survived, made by a different draughtsman, but in its content showing a design by the King. The same drawing shows his alternative, which was a proposal by *Generalmajor* Rossieres. Thanks to Frederick's surviving letters, we also know the King's motives in choosing the concept. Frederick's drawings and instructions for reinforcing Strohhaube with a system of moats and escarpments have also survived.[7]

Examples of Frederick's interference on an even smaller scale are also known. One of the earliest examples is Fort Stern at Glogau. The opinion repeated in the literature to date is that it was based on a royal drawing. No such drawing has been found, but one of the fortress plans preserved in the Berlin Staatsbibliothek shows handwritten corrections, identified by archivists as alterations made by the royal hand. They concerned only a section of the fort. The King corrected the gorge section of the fort and drew its connection to the fortress core by means of a covered way.[8] Two structures should be mentioned from the period after the Seven Years War: The Maikuhle Schanze at Kolberg and the artillery casemates in Schweidnitz. In the first case, the King was the author of the concept, which was implemented by his engineer;[9] in the second case, Frederick ordered the construction of the casemates and indicated the model to be used by his engineer.[10]

The King influenced not only the design process; sometimes he also dictated the technical and construction details. An example is the fortress of Kolberg, where the King forced the engineer in charge of the construction to use a different type of foundation than originally planned.[11] He also had a huge influence on the organisation of the construction of each fortress, especially in the period before the Seven Years War. This was because, at that time, a large number of soldiers worked on the construction of the fortresses, and their use as labourers required royal permission. However, the King did not limit himself to permissions, when he wanted to finish a project faster, he decided to increase the number of labourers in the fortress, as happened in 1743 at Neisse. This issue will be addressed in more detail below.

However, the aspect of fortress construction in which the King was most heavily involved was finance. The King was involved at every stage of expenditure on fortresses, from costing to settling the accounts. It is no great exaggeration to say that the cost of erecting or modernising a fortress (or part of it) was the most important factor to which Frederick paid attention. A great illustration of this was the modernisation of the fortress at Peitz in 1744. When

---

6   Plan von Neisse/mit allen neuen Wercken, wie Solche bey Ihro Koniglichen Majestat Hohen Anwesenheit Tractiret worden, SBB PK, ref. X 31027 – 1; Plan von der Festung Neisse wie solch Anno 1746 in wircklichen Stande gefunden worden, SBB PK, ref. X 31028.

7   See Chapter 6 of this work.

8   Plan von Gross Glogau, SBB PK, ref. X 25133/2.

9   APS, AMK ref. 65/202/0/3657, p.30; Rödenbeck, *Tagebuch oder Geschichtskalender*, vol.2, p.216.

10   Letter from the King to Daries, 19 September 1770, GStA SPK, I HA Rep.96 B Abschriften von Kabinetsordres, Bd.71, p.473 verso.

11   APS, AMK ref. 65/202/0/3657, p.31.

the King received a draft from the then head of the Corps of Engineers, Walrave, in February of that year, he stated that 'until I get cost estimates, I cannot have any use for these plans' and 'all the time my idea for this fortification is that it should cost no more than the allotted 60,000.'[12] Frederick's austerity and focus on the financial side of fortress construction was also noted by Mirabeau. This French writer further noted the royal habit of halving the cost estimates for the construction of fortresses that he received.[13] This opinion is already exaggerated, but one cannot disagree with the fact that the King frequently forced engineers to seek savings and cut costs. There are many examples of such behaviour on the part of the ruler; one will be presented here, related to the modernisation of the Cosel fortress in the late 1770s and early 1780s. When *Major* Haab presented the King with a project for modernising the fortress, he liked it, except for the cost. The initial sum to be spent on the fortress was 190,000 thalers, but the King ordered savings to be made. He did not limit himself to just an order; he also indicated to his engineer which elements should be dropped and which should be done more cheaply. According to the next cost estimate, dated 25 May 1780, the fortress was to cost only 177,000, which the King described as 'fairer'. In the end (in August 1780), the cost estimate was reduced to just over 150,000.[14]

As can be seen from the examples cited, the King did not leave much room for his engineers to make decisions; he rarely allowed them any independence. Examples of this are abundant. In January 1742, he rebuked *Major* Foris because he had made a plan of the area around the fortress of Glogau on his own. He admonished him that a formal application for permission should have been submitted first, together with a cost estimate for this project.[15] In March 1768, he criticised his Piedmontese engineer, Pinto, for his proposed changes to the design of the Silberberg fortress. He ended the letter with the words 'it is to be implemented as I have ordered.'[16] The situation was similar at Schweidnitz, where the engineer in charge of the construction works, Daries, proposed changes to the Ziegel Flèche. The King rejected them and ordered them to be constructed as already approved.[17]

It is also worth noting the mode in which the King informed his engineers of the decisions he had made. He dealt with issues relating to the financing and organisation of construction by means of cabinet orders. It was different with decisions concerning the choice of particular solutions. Such decisions were often taken by him during a personal meeting with an engineer, often during a visit to the fortress that was being rebuilt. This was already the case in the first period of fortress construction,[18] but the best examples of this mode of informing

12 Letter from the King to Walrave, 22 February 1744, GStA SPK, I HA Rep.96 B Abschriften von Kabinetsordres Bd.28, p.106.

13 Mirabeau, *Von der Preußischen Monarchie*, p.372.

14 King's letters to Haab, 24 April, 25 May and 29 August 1780, GStA SPK I HA Rep.96 B Abschriften von Kabinetsordres Bd.80, pp.244, 321, 549.

15 Letter from the King to Foris, 18 January 1742, GStA SPK, I HA Rep.96 B Abschriften von Kabinetsordres Bd.25, p.80.

16 Letter from the King to Pinto, 18 March 1768, GStA SPK, I HA Rep.96 B Abschriften von Kabinetsordres Bd.70, vol.1768, p.107.

17 King's letter to Daries, 30 March 1771, GStA SPK I HA Rep.96 B Abschriften von Kabinetsordres Bd.72, vol.1771, p.203.

18 King's letters to Walrave, 15 June 1742, 9 March 1744, GStA SPK I HA Rep.96 B Abschriften von Kabinetsordres Bd.24, p.176, Bd.28 p.146.

engineers date from the period after the Seven Years War. In 1769, the King discussed his wishes regarding the design of the fortress at Kolberg with *Kapitän* Franseky in Potsdam over a four-week consultation period.[19] A decade later, he similarly consulted with *Major* Haab on the yet-to-be-formed project for the reconstruction of the fortress of Cosel. As he could not come to Silesia, he asked the engineer to come to the capital as soon as his work at Breslau had been completed, as he wanted to discuss the project with him in person. The matter was so important to the ruler that he wrote as many as three letters to the engineer.[20] Less than two years later, a similar situation occurred. The King commissioned Haab with a project for the modernisation of the fortress at Glogau and also demanded a personal meeting on the matter.[21] Similarly, at the end of 1782, after Haab's sudden death, when ordering Daries to take over this Haab's design for the fortress of Schweidnitz, he stated that Daries must also meet with the King.[22] Sometimes, however, when a meeting was not possible, he conveyed his comments in writing. Then, when this did not yield results, he drew. Very often he applied his corrections to the planning material he received from the engineer. An example of this is the project to make a moat at Glatz between the main fortress and the town. After the engineer proposed a solution that did not fit the royal concept, the sovereign made a pencil correction on the project sent to him, which clarified his idea.[23] Sometimes, however, as at Silberberg, the King made more complicated drawings. In November 1779, he ordered Regler to widen the escarpments and moats surrounding the Strohhaube fortifications. As this engineer again failed to design what the sovereign expected, he made the drawing himself and sent it to his engineer.[24] Luckily this drawing has survived, although unsigned.[25] Similar drawings, attributed to the King, have already been described in this work in relation to the fortresses at Glatz, Neisse, Silberberg and Graudenz.

As can be seen, the King had a personal and active involvement in every stage of the fortress construction process. In this respect, Prussian fortress architecture was no different from any other aspect of life in the Prussian state. The central role in every area was that of an absolute ruler trying, in the spirit of Prussian Cameralism, to control the course of all processes. The role of the subject, in this case the engineer, was to strictly implement royal instructions.

Engineers

Of course, all the King's ideas, orders and regulations would have been impossible to implement had there not been an executive apparatus to do so. This was the engineer corps; a small, specific formation within the Prussian army that consisted solely of officers. What is

---

19   APS, AMK ref. 65/202/0/3657, p.30.

20   King's letters to Haab, 29 June, 3 July and 18 October 1779, GStA SPK I HA Rep.96 B Abschriften von Kabinetsordres Bd.79, pp.816, 822 and 1080.

21   King's letters to Haab, 1 and 11 March 1781, GStA SPK I HA Rep.96 B Abschriften von Kabinetsordres Bd.81, p.178.

22   King's letter to Daries, 15 December 1782, GStA SPK, I HA Rep.96 B Abschriften von Kabinetsordres Bd.82, p.1185.

23   Letter from the King to Regler, 10 November 1779, GStA SPK, I HA Rep.96 B Abschriften von Kabinetsordres Bd.79, p.1142.

24   Letters from the King to Regler, 4 and 22 November 1779, GStA SPK, I HA Rep.96 B Abschriften von Kabinetsordres Bd.79, pp.1124 and 1161.

25   SBB PK, ref. X 33811–5.

more, these officers were rare specialists, difficult to replace. It would seem, therefore, that they would be a well-regarded group of officers. As we shall see, this was not the case and the King was rarely kind to them.

Although there were dozens of engineers in the Prussian corps, only a select few mattered. Initially, the head of the engineer corps, first Walrave, then Sers, was an important figure. It is to them that most of the King's letters concerning fortresses were addressed, and they also mainly made reports to the King. Both of these engineers personally carried out work at one fortress and supervised the others. Walrave's position was much stronger. His activities applied to the territory of the whole Prussian state. Sers was concerned only with Silesian fortresses, and not all of them as Glatz was excluded from his control. After the Seven Years War, the situation changed. Balbi, who was formally the head of the corps, was of no significance. The King, blaming him for the failure of the siege of Olomouc in 1758, ignored him and gave him insignificant tasks. After the Seven Years War, Balbi worked only at Swinemünde, building the port there.[26] However, although the position of corps chief had lost its importance, even after 1763 there were engineers who had a privileged position and, in addition to carrying out work in one fortress, also supervised others. Such a role was initially fulfilled for Silesia by Regler, who not only built the fortresses at Silberberg and Glatz, but also drew up cost estimates for the other strongholds. In the early 1780s, his place was taken by *Major* Haab. Between 1780 and 1782, Haab the reconstruction of the fortresses at Cosel, Neisse, and Glogau, and also supervised the work at Silberberg. After his sudden death in December 1782, the King chose another engineer, Harroy, who supervised work on the most important Silesian fortresses until the end of the King's life. With regard to work on fortresses outside Silesia, there was no one who played a similar role. A status similar to that enjoyed by the Silesian engineers may have been achieved by Heinze, who was involved in the work at four fortresses in Pomerania and West Prussia. However, the King initially only used him as a designer (for Kolberg, Stettin and Damm), and his career as an engineer-practitioner was interrupted by the Vistula's destruction of the fortress at Grabower Kampe. His successor, Gotzenbach, was already in charge of only one fortress: Graudenz. For this reason alone, he cannot be compared to the engineers mentioned earlier. Nonetheless, he was an extremely important person, as the work on the Graudenz fortress almost equalled the scale of the financial and organisational commitment carried out in Silesia at the time. In addition to this engineer, two more engineers from outside the industry elite should be presented – Lefèbvre and Franseky. The first is an example of the difficult fate that some-times befell an engineer; despite his good service, he died in custody, where he was interred by the King. The second is a rare example of an engineer whom the King did not control and whom he trusted.

Gerhard Cornelius von Walrave

This most important Prussian military engineer of the first half of the eighteenth century was born in 1692 in Warendorf near Munster. He was Westphalian, yet he is often wrongly referred to as Dutch, which is due to the fact that he spent the first 12 years of his military

---

26   Letters from the King to Balbi, 17 March 1774 and 21 March 1775, GStA SPK, I HA Rep.96 B
      Abschriften von Kabinetsordres Bd.73, vol. 1774, p.107; Bd.74, p.36.

career in Dutch service, which he joined in 1708 at the age of 16. In 1720 he transferred to the Prussian service, recruited by Prince Leopold von Anhalt-Dessau. Walrave left the Dutch service for financial reasons; interestingly, he joined the Prussian army before he obtained his discharge from service in the United Provinces, which was treated as desertion there.[27] In Prussia, he managed to make a career and achieve social advancement; he was ennobled shortly after entering the service. By 1722 he had been promoted to the rank of *oberstleutnant*, and in 1729 he became chief of the engineer corps. He very quickly attained the status of Prussia's chief fortifier; his work included the modernisation of the country's most important fortresses. Before 1740, the fortresses at Stettin, Wesel and Magdeburg were rebuilt on the basis of his designs; he also made plans for smaller fortresses such as Penemünde and Minden. After Frederick the Great ascended the throne, Walrave carried out designs for all the local fortresses: Neisse, Breslau, Brieg, Glogau, Glatz, Schweidnitz, Cosel and Schurgast. In 1741 he was honoured with a promotion *generalmajor*.[28] In addition to his engineering activities, he was also involved in the creation of an innovative Prussian unit – a regiment of pioneers.[29]

Walrave, as already stated, had undoubted talents in the field of fortress engineering. He was even rewarded twice for these abilities, both during the lifetime of Frederick William I and during the reign of Frederick II. The former conferred Prussian nobility on Walrave and awarded him the *Ordre de la Générosité* (Order of Generosity); the latter appointed him a general and decorated him with the *Order Pour le Mérite*.[30] Despite these honours, Walrave was imprisoned on 10 February 1748 by order of Frederick and thrown into prison without trial. He spent the rest of his life in Fort Berge at Magdeburg, which he built. There are various allegations against Walrave in the literature. The primary one was said to be treason. The engineer was alleged to have been in contact with envoys of foreign courts; Russia, Saxony and Austria. His relationship with a representative of the latter, Count von Berne, proved to be the most serious. Walrave was said to have made a design for the fortification of Vienna for him and to have handed over the manuscript of his work, *Memoire sur l'attaque et la defence des places*.[31] This already qualified as treason. The text had been written on royal orders and handing it over to a representative of an enemy power constituted a serious transgression. Moreover, in this treatise Walrave described in detail sensitive elements of the defences of Prussian fortresses, especially Neisse, Magdeburg and Wesel. Walrave's act

---

27   Christoph Schäfer, *'Krygsvernuftelingen'. Militäringenieure und Forfikation in den Vereinigten Niederlanden* (Gießen: unpublished dissertation, Justus-Liebig-Universität Giessen, 2001), pp.127, 140, 610; <http://bibliotheek.eldoc.ub.rug.nl/FILES/root/UB/2001/SchaeferC-Krijgsvern/SchaeferC-Krijgs-2001.pdf>, accessed 4 September 2012.

28   Priesdorf, *Soldatisches Führerthum*, vol.1, pp.230–232.

29   It was the later Infantry Regiment No. 50 and consisted of 10 companies of pioneers and two of miners. It was an unusual unit, as up to that point technical units in the Prussian army had been few in number. It was an experiment of sorts, abandoned after Walrave's arrest. However, despite its transformation into an actual infantry regiment it was still, as late as the late 1750s, referred to as a pioneer regiment. Johann Friedrich Seyfart, *Kurzgefasete Geschichte aller königlichen preussischen Regimenter...* (Frankfurt am Main: Unknown Publisher, 1759), p.87.

30   Johann Friedrich Seyfart, *Lebens- und Regierungs-Geschichte Friedrichs des andern Königs in Preussen...* (Leipzig: Verlag Adam Friedrich Böhmens, 1784), vol.1, p.69.

31   Bonin, *Geschichte des Ingenieurkorps*, pp.59–61.

cast royal suspicion that the general was also selling other state secrets. Walrave, it seems, noticed the royal distrust, for he tried to leave the Prussian state. In early 1748, he wanted the King to allow him to go to Flanders and take part in the sieges there. He was very keen on this, for through Louis Guy Henri de Valori, the French envoy at the Prussian court, he tried to obtain an invitation from Prince Maurice of Saxony to come to the besieged fortress of Maastricht. Walrave, in his conversation with Valori, was said to have claimed that he 'knows this fortress like his own room.'[32] The King refused Walrave's request and set a trap for him. He summoned Walrave and ordered him to go to Stettin and inspect the fortifications and armament there in preparation for war. The King also revealed to Walrave that he intended to resume hostilities. This information was immediately conveyed by Walrave to the Count von Bern.[33] This became the basis for the general's arrest. On 10 February Walrave was arrested and immediately sent to Magdeburg, where he was confined in the casemate of Fort Berge. The nature of the charges against Walrave, in addition to the above-mentioned facts, is evidenced by the conditions that the King ordered to be fulfilled during his imprisonment. He was allowed to equip and furnish his cell as he wished, he was even allowed to wallpaper the walls. However, under no circumstances was he allowed to possess any material related to writing. Moreover, he was not allowed to meet and talk to anyone in private.[34] As can be seen, the idea was to protect the state secrets that Walrave knew as much as possible, and which he could potentially still pass on to the enemy. Interestingly, Marquis Valori thought that Walrave wanted to go to Maastricht to pass on information about the progress of the siege to the Austrians.

In the context of accusations of contacts with Vienna, two letters and one plan, held in the Vienna Kriegsarchiv, should be mentioned. The first, signed 'Cornelius von W', was addressed to an anonymous baroness. More important is the second, signed 'C. v. W' and addressed to 'Her Majesty the Queen'. It is a description of the fortifications of Glatz, the state of progress of their construction, supplies, arms, and ammunition. The author also describes the garrison and points out that not all roads to the fortress are sufficiently guarded. In addition, he promises detailed information about the fortresses at Brieg and Glogau. In addition to these letters, the collection of material relating to Glatz in the Vienna Kriegsarchiv also contains a plan of the fortress, the author of which, according to the archival catalogue, is Cornelius v. W. Unfortunately, this material does little to answer the question of whether this officer was a traitor and was passing material to Maria Theresa's court. The most important letter, containing a detailed description of Glatz, bears only the initials 'C. v. W'. This signature was elaborated by an anonymous Austrian archivist as 'Cornelius von Walrave, Prussian lieutenant, engineer, who went into Austrian service in 1745.'[35] This identification seems at first sight to be incorrect. As is well known, Walrave was a general and remained

32   Louis Guy Henri de Valori, *Mémoires des négociations du marquis de Valori, ambassadeur de France a la cour de Berlin; Accompagnés d'un recueil de lettres de Frédéric-le-Grand, des princes ses frères, de Voltaire, et des plus illustres personnages du XVIIIe siècle; précédés d'une notice historique sur la vie de l'auteur* (Paris: Firmin Didot, 1820), vol.I, pp.275–276.

33   Preuss, 'Friedrich der Große und der General v. Walrave', p.47.

34   Bonin, *Geschichte des Ingenieurkorps*, pp.56–63; Preuss, 'Friedrich der Große und der General v. Walrave', pp.49–50.

35   OStA KA, ref. K II f 23 E and ref. K II f 23 F.

in Prussian service until his imprisonment in 1748. Besides, there was no lieutenant in the Prussian engineer corps in 1745 who could use such initials and at the same time be familiar with the fortress at Glatz. The lieutenant working at Glatz was Friedrich von Winancko; in his case, the name does not match the initial. In addition to Walrave, the initial matches one other engineer associated with Glatz; Christian von Wrede. However, he was already a major in 1745. The explanation of this riddle may be the existence of a second Walrave. In the King's letter of 11 January 1744, in which he distributed engineering personnel to the various fortresses, there is mention of two supervisors who were to be sent to Glatz. One of them was Daries, later builder of the Schweidnitz fortress, and the other was Walrave.[36] According to information about the family of Cornelius Walrave, this engineer had a son who was an overseer in the engineering corps.[37] So, the letter describing the fortifications of Glatz could be evidence not of the general's treachery, but that of his son.

In addition to treason, Walrave's other, equally serious, offence was said to be financial irregularities. Even before his imprisonment, the King had ordered an investigation into the regularity of the accounts relating to the constructions carried out by Walrave. This investigation resulted in another charge – misappropriation of funds entrusted to him for the construction of fortifications. In Silesia alone, the engineer was alleged to have embezzled 40,000 thalers, and he was also alleged to owe considerable money to contractors; the entrepreneur Rottengatter was alleged to be owed 80,000 thalers.[38]

All of these accusations appear to be valid, and arguably Walrave deserved to be punished. The only question is whether there were also other malfeasances that caused Walrave's career to collapse so suddenly. Historians writing about him often accuse him of a promiscuous and wasteful life. The general lived in luxury. He had a country estate (Lilliput Manor) and two lavishly furnished apartments, in Neisse and Magdeburg. The latter alone was said to contain over 300 paintings. In the context of these descriptions, some of Walrave's statements sound curious. In a letter to the King dated 27 September 1747, Walrave, after describing the design work he had undertaken on the fortress at Schweidnitz, stated that as soon as he had finished this work he would 'obtain permission to lay it at the feet of His Majesty and then to visit my poor Magdeburg and Lilput, which have fallen into decay without my supervision.'[39]

In addition to living a life of excessive glamour, Walrave's social life may have added to his increasingly poor reputation. Despite his professed Catholicism (he had his own chapel in his Magdeburg flat) he had numerous mistresses, which he made no secret of. He lived with the wife of the quartermaster of his regiment as his mistress. In addition, he is said to have committed numerous misdeeds during the war, such as burning down monasteries, or

---

36   King's letter to Walrave, 11 January 1744, I HA Rep.96 B, Abschriften von Kabinetsordres, Bd.28, p.28.

37   Priesdorf, *Soldatisches Führerthum*, vol.1. p.231.

38   Priesdorf, *Soldatisches Führerthum*, vol.1, pp.230–232; Anton Balthasar König, *Biographisches Lexikon aller Helden und Militairpersonen, welche sich in Preußischen Diensten berühmt gemacht haben* (Berlin: Arnold Mever, 1788–91), vol.4, pp.148–151.

39   'Nach deßen Verfertigung würde es mir zu großer Gnade gewesen, die erlaubniß zu erlangen, solches zu allerhöchst deroselben Füßen zu legen, und nachhero meine ohne selbstiges Aufsicht in Verfall gerathener Armuth zu Magdeburg und Lilput zu besuchen.' Letter from Walrave to the King, 23 September 1747, GStA SPK Geheimes Zivilkabinett I HA Rep.96 No. 616 – Schlesische Festungen, Bd.D, p.41.

robbing the palace of Count Gallas in Prague in 1744, the furnishings of which were used to furnish his own homes.[40] Walrave's lifestyle probably did not win him royal sympathy. The final aspect that may have contributed to the punishment meted out to him was the offended pride of the King. Indeed, in his memorial, Walrave reproached the King for his poor preparation for some sieges, when the artillery lacked round shot and bombs of the correct calibres and the bombs were filled with spoiled gunpowder. The memorial containing these allegations was written on 19 November 1747. In other words, the King, in considering the information about this engineer's alleged treachery, certainly had fresh in his mind his remarks reproaching him for his lack of competence.

Phillip Lothar von Sers

The next head of the engineer corps after Walrave was Phillip Lothar von Sers. This officer was born around 1700, and was probably the son of Pether von Sers, a Prussian general of French origin who, as a Huguenot, ended up in Prussia with other religious refugees in the early 1690s.[41] Phillip Lothar entered military service as early as 16 years old. His career was associated with the engineering corps from the beginning. He started in 1716 at the rank of supervisor but was promoted quite quickly. In 1721 he was a *leutnant*, in 1726 a *kapitän*, and in 1734 a *major*. His fortification experience included the modernisation of the fortresses at Magdeburg and Stettin.[42] At the time of Frederick's accession to the throne, he was ranked fifth in the list of officers of the engineer corps. Ahead of him was his boss, Walrave, *Oberstleutnant* Foris and two senior *majors*.[43] Sers, however, was rapidly climbing the ranks. In 1742 he was promoted to *oberstleutnant*, by which he moved up to third in the corps. In 1745, Foris was killed during the defence of the fortress of Cosel, making Sers the most senior engineer after Walrave. Up to this point, Sers had implemented the ideas of others, for example in 1744 he built the fortress at Neisse, the designs for which were made by Walrave together with the King.[44] Towards the end of 1746, his position changed. He was noticed by the King, who charged him with two important tasks – the rebuilding of the fortresses at Cosel and Glogau. In October 1746, Sers drew up plans and cost estimates for new work at both fortresses, which he sent to the King for authorisation.[45] At Cosel he designed the reinforcement of the fortress with casemates, the revetment of the main rampart with masonry, the construction of new gunpowder magazines and the erection of a completely new outer work – the Weischützer Redoubt.[46] At Glogau, Sers also designed a new outer work, the much larger the Fort Stern, and the reconstruction of the outer works located in front of the covered way of the main circuit.[47] In December of that year, Sers was active at Neisse, the fortress where he had worked since 1744. However, while he had

---

40   Preuss, 'Friedrich der Große und der General v. Walrave', pp.44, 45, 56.
41   König, *Biographisches Lexikon*, Bd.V, p.477.
42   Priesdorf, *Soldatisches Führerthum*, vol.2, p.424.
43   Bonin, *Geschichte des Ingenieurkorps*, p.272.
44   Letter from the King to Walrave, 11 January 1744, GStA SPK, I HA Rep.96 B Abschriften von Kabinetsordres Bd.28, p.28.
45   Letter from Sers to the King, 25 October 1746, GStA SPK, Geheimes Zivilkabinett I HA Rep.96 No. 616 – Schlesische Festungen, Bd.C, pp.18–19.
46   GStA SPK, Geheimes Zivilkabinett I HA Rep.96 No. 616 – Schlesische Festungen, Bd.C, p.20.
47   GStA SPK, Geheimes Zivilkabinett I HA Rep.96 No. 616 – Schlesische Festungen, Bd.C, pp.21–22.

previously implemented the ideas of others, he was now involved in design himself. His idea was to build a new arsenal, a fortress laboratory and five gunpowder magazines.[48] As can be seen, Sers was rapidly rising to prominence. In 1747, it was his king who informed on the funding of works in Silesian fortresses.[49] While the engineer had reached a high position, it was still Walrave who was the most important person in the corps – it was he who was in charge of the newly established fortress of Schweidnitz. It was only Walrave's arrest and imprisonment in 1748 that brought Sers to the zenith of his career. He became head of the engineering corps and, until 1756, he designed new facilities in the Silesian fortresses and supervised their construction. His activities at Glogau, Brieg, Cosel, Neisse and Schweidnitz have been mentioned already. His particular achievements from this period include making the final design of the fortress at Schweidnitz and constructing it, designing a new work at Glogau – the Wasser Redoubt, and designing and building another reconstruction of Cosel.[50] His hard work was recognised by the King. In September 1747, he received the order *Pour le mérite*, and on 16 February 1757 he was promoted to the rank of *general-major*. Unfortunately, the collapse of this engineer's career came soon after. The fortress at Schweidnitz, of which he became commandant, fell after a siege of less than two weeks. Sers was taken prisoner, and on his return, he was expelled from the service.[51]

Simon Lefèbvre

In the initial period after the Seven Years War, there was no leading engineer. The officer who stood out and had all, it seemed, the prerequisites for this position was a Frenchman, Simon Lefèbvre. This engineer, born in 1712, entered the Prussian service in 1747, and was probably recruited in the Netherlands by engineer *Major* Johann Friedrich von Balbi. In the 1747 campaign he took part in the famous siege of Bergen-op-Zoom and was also to serve two years as a *lieutenant* in the French army.[52] At the end of the 1740s he was involved in cartographic measurements, resulting not only in maps (of the area between the Spree, the Oder and the Havel), but also in a theoretical work, *Nouveau traite du Nivellement*, published in Paris in 1753.[53] In the 1750s, he took part in a unique event; a mine exercise near Potsdam, in which a new method of blowing up mines, the so-called 'globe of pressure' (*Globe de compression*), was practised. Moreover, on behalf of the King, Lefèbvre corresponded with Bernard Forest de Belidor, the creator of this method and the most important theorist in engineering science at the time.[54] His mastery of the method allowed him to put it into practice during the Siege of Schweidnitz in 1762, already described, which, incidentally, Lefèbvre personally led. The method proved its worth in practice, but the siege itself showed the engineer's practical skills in a poor light. It lasted an exceptionally

---

48   GStA SPK, Geheimes Zivilkabinett I HA Rep.96 No. 616 – Schlesische Festungen, Bd.C, pp.33–41.

49   Letter from the King to Sers, 13 May 1747, GStA SPK, Geheimes Zivilkabinett I HA Rep.96 No. 616 – Schlesische Festungen, Bd.D, p.9.

50   Letter from Sers to the King, 23 December 1753 and 10 April 1754, GStA SPK, Geheimes Zivilkabinett I HA Rep.96 No. 616 – Schlesische Festungen, Bd.G, pp.28 and 30–32.

51   Priesdorf, *Soldatisches Führerthum*, vol.2, pp.424–245.

52   Bonin, *Geschichte des Ingenieurkorps*, p.67, p.297.

53   Hanke, Degner, *Geschichte der Amtlichen Kartographie*, pp.33, 219.

54   Bonin, *Geschichte des Ingenieurkorps*, p.68; GStA SPK, Geheimes Zivilkabinett I HA Rep.96 No. 616 – Schlesische Festungen, Bd.A, pp.30–32.

long time (as long as 48 days for mine warfare alone) and cost the lives of many soldiers. Although the King rewarded Lefèbvre after its successful conclusion, what happened during the siege (including nervous breakdowns) undermined the King's confidence in this engineer. His career stalled, instead of accelerating, after the capture of Schweidnitz defended by the by then well-known Gribeauval. All was not lost for him, however, he was given an important assignment. The King sent him to Neisse, where Lefèbvre was designing a major rebuilding of the fortress. Nevertheless, the perceived lack of progress in his career prompted this officer to become restive, and in October 1768, in a letter to the King, he complained of his rank being too low. The King rebuked him and stated that he promotes officers according to his will.[55] This showed that the King was hesitant towards him. It is not known whether Frederick gave other expressions of dislike to this engineer; he probably did, and this would explain the events of 1771. On 24 July the casemate Lefèbvre was building at Neisse collapsed.[56] The death toll was several dozen.[57] As soon as the King found out, he had the engineer arrested and investigated. It was conducted by *Major* Daries, specially brought from Schweidnitz for this purpose. The investigation clearly established Lefèbvre's sole guilt. Moreover, in addition to the faulty vaults of the garrison casemate, another, the Casemattierte Batterie, also had vaults displaying the same errors.[58] During the King's visit to Neisse to demand an explanation, Lefèbvre committed suicide with a kitchen knife by wounding himself nine times on his stomach and six on his chest.[59] Such an end is surprising in light of the engineer's previously highly-regarded service and high standing. Lefèbvre was, among other things, a teacher of the art of engineering to the later King Frederick William II,[60] as well as a member of the Prussian Academy of Arts for, among other things, his very prolific literary activity in the field of the theory of defensive architecture. Between 1743 and 1778 he published a total of six books which had numerous reprints, the last in Paris in 1808.[61] As can be seen, an excellent knowledge of theory was not enough. The King needed practitioners.

Ludwig Wilhelm von Regler

Such an excellent practitioner was Regler, one of the most important Prussian military engineers of the second half of the eighteenth century. This engineer was born in 1726 in Altlandsberg, near Berlin, and joined the army in 1744. He was a typical example

---

55   Letter from the King to Lefèbvre, 31 October 1768, GStA SPK I HA Rep.96 B Abschriften von Kabinetsordres Bd.70, Vol III 1768, p.407.

56   Letter from the King to Rothkirch, 28 July 1771, GStA SPK I HA Rep.96 B Abschriften von Kabinetsordres Bd.72, Vol 1771, p.283.

57   Accounts give varying numbers of victims, from 12 to 20. Minsberg, *Geschichtliche Darstellung*, p.198.

58   King's letters to Rothkirch and to Daries, 28 July and 11 August 1771, GStA SPK, I HA Rep.96 B Abschriften von Kabinetsordres, Bd.72, pp.283, 302.

59   Johann Georg Zimmermann, *Fragmente über Friedrich den Grossen zur Geschichte seines Lebens, seiner Regierung, und seines Charakters* (Leipzig: Weidmann, 1790), vol.3, pp.307–308.

60   Hanke, Degner, *Geschichte der Amtlichen Kartographie*, p.145.

61   Louis-Gabriel Michaud (ed.), *Biographie universelle, ancienne et moderne: supplément, ou Suite de l'histoire, par ordre alphabétique, de la vie publique et privée de tous les hommes qui se sont fait remarquer par leur écrits, leurs actions, leurs talents, leurs vertus ou leurs crimes* (Paris: L.G. Michaud, 1842), vol.71, p.137.

of a Prussian engineer who started his service at the lowest rank, supervisor,[62] with no specialist training other than his graduation from the mathematics school in Berlin.[63] During his first period of service, before the Seven Years War, he gained experience as a draughtsman (working between 1747 and 1753 on the measurements of Silesia carried out by *Major* Wrede).[64] In 1747 he was promoted to *leutnant* and in 1754 to *kapitän*. In addition, he also worked on the construction of the fortress at Glatz. During the Seven Years War he took part in the sieges of Prague, Breslau, Olomouc and Schweidnitz, but in none of them did he distinguish himself, either positively or negatively.[65] After the end of hostilities, he was an experienced engineer, yet he did not distinguish himself in the eyes of the King. The first task that pushed his career forward was the mapping of Glatz County. The survey was completed in 1763, and by 1770 the engineer was mapping further areas of Silesia.[66] At the same time as surveying Glatz County, he was engaged, at the King's request, in drawing up plans for the modernisation of the fortifications of Glatz, which were ready as early as May 1763.[67] These projects were not realised. From 1763, until the end of Frederick's reign, he was involved in the construction of the fortress of Silberberg. Initially, he took part in the selection of the site for the new fortress (he gave a negative opinion on the idea of building it in Wartha), and then carried out measurements of the area for the future fortress.[68] From 1765, for the first five years of construction, he headed the team building the fortress; his responsibilities ranged from general supervision of the work to issues related to finance and manpower (he supervised the search for qualified specialists such as miners).[69] His work was held in high esteem by the King, who thanked him in 1767 for his progress on the fortress.[70] Furthermore, Regler was also the main designer of the fortress. In 1770, he was given another assignment, even though the fortress at Silberberg had not yet been completed. The King commissioned him to carry out work on a major modernisation of the fortress at Glatz.[71] This involved another promotion; March 1770, Regler was given the rank of *oberst*. His successful completion of this task was rewarded by the King in 1774 with the post of commandant of Glatz.[72] With the assumption of this position, Regler took on many more responsibilities. His tasks no longer included not only continuing the modernisation of the fortress, but also controlling all military affairs inside and outside the fortress. Between 1774 and 1784,

62   Priesdorf, *Soldatisches Führerthum*, vol.2, p.247; Hartmut Niedrich, 'Bedeutende Altlandsberger, Der preußische General und Festungsbaumeister Ludwig Regler', *Altlandsberger Stadtmagazin*, Jg. 5, nr 8, 30 VIII 2007, p.2.
63   König, *Biographisches Lexikon*, vol.3, pp.273–274.
64   GStA SPK, Geheimes Zivilkabinett I HA Rep.96 No. 616 – Schlesische Festungen, Bd.B, p.1.
65   Priesdorf, *Soldatisches Führerthum*, vol.2, p.247.
66   Hanke, Degner, *Geschichte der Amtlichen Kartographie*, pp.269–270.
67   Description and cost estimate of works stored in: GStA SPK, I HA Rep 96, Geheimes Zivilkabinett, No 94, Bbb, Regler, pp 1–4.
68   Regler's letter, 21 July 1763, GStA SPK, I HA, Rep 96 No 94, Bbb, Regler, pp.11–12.
69   Regler letter, 28 January 1769, GStA SPK I HA Rep 96 no 94, Bbb Regler, pp.20–22.
70   Priesdorf, *Soldatisches Führerthum*, vol.2, p.248.
71   Letter from the King to Regler, 3 February 1779, GStA SPK, I HA Rep.96 B Abschriften von Kabinetsordres, Bd.71, p.324 verso; letter from the King to Prince Henry of Prussia, 14 March 1770, Droysen, Politische Correspondenz, vol.29, p.386.
72   Priesdorf, *Soldatisches Führerthum*, Bd.2, p.247.

he also organised mine exercises, mainly in the vicinity of Glatz, but also near Neisse.[73] His responsibilities also included intelligence and counter-intelligence work. He repeatedly informed the King about the situation on the other side of the border, for example very extensively about the journey of Emperor Joseph II in the area of Glatz County. His activities related to the observation of alleged Austrian spies conducting surveys of Glatz County are also known.[74]

Regler was also often asked by the King for his opinion regarding the promotion of engineers or the filling of posts in fortresses. The latter role proved to be particularly important. It was Regler who pointed out Gotzenbach as one of the outstanding officers, as a result of which he ended up in Grabow as deputy to Heinze. Regler also proposed Laurens as Gotzenbach's successor in charge of Graudenz. In 1784 he was charged with a similar task; he was to find a suitable engineer to lead the work at the new fort in East Prussia.[75] He was also constantly involved with fortifications; after 1776 he rebuilt the Kranich at Glatz, and after 1779, the local fort Schäferberg. He was also constantly active at Silberberg: he designed and constructed the moats and escarpments between Kleine and Grossestrohhaube; constructed the fortifications of Mittel Strohhaube; he also issued an opinion on excessive dampness in the casemates there (1785).[76] Until 1780, Regler fulfilled the role of the leading engineer of works in Silesia. In addition to the works mentioned above, he was also involved in works at other fortresses. Although he did not carry out projects, he often drew up annual cost estimates for works at all Silesian fortifications.[77]

Sometimes, though quite rarely, he also dealt with individual structures in other fortresses. In 1771 he briefly carried out works at Neisse, and in 1775 he dealt with the barracks at Cosel

---

73   King's letters to Regler, 13 July and 23 October 1774, 13 December 1775, 21 May and 23 June 1776, 2 February, 31 May and 1 October 1777, 21 May, 9 June and 20 October 1780, 8 and 29 May 1782, 14 August 1784, GStA SPK, I HA Rep.96 B Abschriften von Kabinetsordres, Bd.73 Jg. 1774, pp.270, 393; Bd.74 pp.864; Bd.75 pp.435, 530; Bd.76 pp.114, 380; Bd.77 p.620; Bd.80 pp.395, 445, 451, 475, 665; Bd.82 pp.426, 509; Bd.84 p.694; Regler's documents concerning mine exercises near Glatz in 1775 GStA SPK, I HA Rep 96 No 94, Bbb1, pp.1–3.

74   Regler's letter to the King, 9 October 1783, GStA SPK, I HA Rep 96, No 82 L Politische Nachrichten 1750 – 1783; Regler's letters, 11 and 17 October 1779, GStA SPK, I HA Rep 96, No 259 – E, Den Wiener Hof bert. Nachrichten; letters from the King to Regler, 2, 12, 16 and 19 September and 14 October 1779, 26 January 1780, 8 June 1784, GStA SPK, I HA Rep.96 B Abschriften von Kabinetsordres, Bd.79 pp.973, 1005, 1012, 1021, 1072; Bd.80 p.64; Bd.84 p.478.

75   Letters from the King to Regler, 7 March 1774, 14 December 1777, 24 September 1784, GStA SPK, I HA Rep.96 B Abschriften von Kabinetsordres, Bd.73 Jg. 1774, p.89; Bd.77, p.758; Bd.84, p.850.

76   Anschlag des bey der Festung Silberberg nach Sr. Majestät allerhöchsten Idee zu construirenden Escarpements und zu verlangernden Grabens, cost estimate dated 18 November 1779, SBB PK, ref. X 33812–5; letters from the King to Regler, 25 September, 14 October and 10 November 1779, 3 January and 25 May 1780, 21 February, 5 and 30 August 1781, 29 August and 15 December 1782, 1 January, 22 and 25 August 1783, 26 August 1784 and 26 August 1785, GStA SPK, I HA Rep.96 B Abschriften von Kabinetsordres, Bd.79, pp.1032, 1072, 1142; Bd.80, p.9 pp.404; Bd.81, pp.123, 584, 758; Bd.82, pp.810,1184; Bd.83 pp.4, 712, 720; Bd.84, p.724; Bd.85, p.891.

77   King's letters to Regler, 3 October 1773, 24 May, 24 September and 16 November 1775, 25 December 1776, 28 December 1777, GStA SPK, I HA Rep.96 B Abschriften von Kabinetsordres, Bd.73 Jg. 1773, p.314; Bd.74, pp.244, 621, 789; Bd.75, p.911; Bd.77, p.791.

and the lock at Breslau.[78] Frederick valued all his work and in 1778 Regler was ennobled.[79] However, this was Frederick's last gesture towards this distinguished officer; Regler was not promoted to general rank by Frederick, for whom he had erected two such important fortresses. In 1780, his position in the engineer corps weakened considerably; the tasks he had hitherto fulfilled were handed over to *Major* von Haab. His activities were confined to the fortress in Glatz. In August 1782, the King even deprived him of supervision of the work at Silberberg.[80] Haab's death in December 1782 made little change to Regler's position. Although his supervision of the Silberberg fortress was initially restored, this again passed in 1785 to the supervision of another engineer, *Major* von Harroy, who became the new chief engineer in Silesia.[81] Towards the end of Frederick's life, Regler, apart from designing and constructing more buildings at Glatz, was not given any responsible assignments. The only commission which the King gave him on a regular basis was fairly trivial and consisted of searching for semi-precious stones– initially agates, later chrysoprase.[82] It was only after the death of Frederick that Regler's career, already elderly, gained momentum. As the senior in rank and the most experienced corps officer, Regler had a great influence on the reform of the engineer corps, and with his participation, it was re-organised. Regler's reforms created a clear service structure, which at the same time had control functions. Each engineer in charge of work in a given fortress was subordinate to a sub-brigadier, usually a higher-ranking officer, who supervised work in several fortresses at once. His superior in turn was the brigadier in charge of work on fortifications throughout the province. The highest level of this structure was that of Head of Department IV at the Supreme Military College, controlling all matters relating to fortifications throughout the state. Associated with this function was the concurrent title of Chief of the Corps of Engineers. From 25 June 1787, this function was held by Regler, who had been promoted a little earlier to the rank of *general-major*.[83] He was not able to enjoy this honour for long, as he died on 17 July 1792.[84]

---

78   King's letters to Regler, 30 October 1771, 11 October and 15 November 1775, GStA SPK, I HA Rep.96 B Abschriften von Kabinetsordres, Bd.72 vol.VI 1771, p.387; Bd.74, pp.661, 787.

79   Priesdorf, *Soldatisches Führerthum*, vol.2, p.247.

80   Letter from the King to Regler, 19 August 1781, GStA SPK, I HA Rep.96 B Abschriften von Kabinetsordres, Bd.81, p.789.

81   King's letter to Regler, 15 December 1782 and to Harroy, 20 February, 13 and 30 March and 14 April 1785, GStA SPK, I HA Rep.96 B Abschriften von Kabinetsordres, Bd.82, p.1185; Bd.85, pp.175, 247, 307, 374.

82   King's letters to Regler, 2 April 1784, 2 October, 11 and 29 November 1785, 5 June and 1 August 1786, GStA SPK, I HA Rep.96 B Abschriften von Kabinetsordres, Bd.84, p.291; Bd.85, pp.1035, 1195, 1252; Bd.86, pp.545, 699.

83   The dates of the general's promotion and appointment as head of the Fourth Department are given after Bonin, or more precisely after the instruction of King Friedrich Wilhelm II, quoted by him in full as a source appendix, establishing this institution. These two dates look completely different in the biographical note on the general by Priesdorf, who claims that Regler was promoted to general only in December 1787, and the above-mentioned post only in September 1788. König, on the other hand, writes that Regler arrived in Breslau as head of the Silesian fortresses in 1787, in December of that year he became general, and in December 1788, chief of the engineering services. See Priesdorf, *Soldatisches Führerthum*, Bd.2, p.247; Bonin, *Geschichte des Ingenieurkorps*, pp.278–279; König, *Biographisches Lexikon*, vol.3, pp.273–274.

84   The date of death is certain, only the place is in doubt. According to Priesdorf, the general died at Berlin and was buried in the cemetery at St Sophia's Church; according to Bonin, he died at Glatz. See

In the last years of his life, this distinguished engineer-practitioner still managed to prove himself as a good organiser. Among other things, it was thanks to his efforts that the Engineering Academy was founded in Potsdam; he also succeeded in writing the first regulations for the engineering corps in 1790.[85] Another, though least known, aspect of his activity is his theoretical work. It is known that he produced a manuscript with a treatise on fortifications, unfortunately they have not survived.[86]

Ludwig Wilhelm von Regler's life and career were typical of those of Frederick's engineers who were of Prussian origin. Unlike many foreigners, Regler had no engineering training when he began his service; he learned the ins and outs of the profession during his service. His career started at the lowest level, and he owed his promotions to his conscientious performance of duty. Although he played a key role in major projects, he was promoted slowly after 1763 and had not yet reached the rank of general in Frederick's lifetime, after more than 40 years of service. However, he was fortunate. The foreign officers favoured by the King during the same period either fell into disfavour after a while (Lefèbvre, Heinze) or died (Haab). In other respects, too, his good fortune did not abandon him. He did not participate in any of the actions that ended in defeat and thus did not expose himself to royal disfavour. His experience and talents were only recognised by Frederick's successor.

Caspar von Haab

Another important engineer was the Swiss, Caspar von Haab. From the beginning of his career in the Prussian engineering corps, this officer was associated with Breslau. In the records concerning the extension of the fortifications there, he appears as early as 1762, and worked there until his death in 1782.[87] In the archival sources he is mentioned several times as the author of subsequent plans and cost estimates. In September 1770, the King mentions projects and cost estimates received from Haab for the fortress of Breslau, as well as a cost estimate for the fortifications of Burgerwerder. In 1774 Haab is mentioned as the author of another plan.[88] Frederick valued Haab for his work at Breslau. In a letter to him dated 1 May 1776, he stated that he 'deserves the royal satisfaction' and he therefore increased his salary by 100 thalers. The achievement of rebuilding Breslau's fortress was also highly appreciated later. In a report on the condition of all Silesian fortresses prepared in 1787, on the occasion of Frederick William II's accession to the throne, *Major* Haab was singled out and mentioned by name as the only engineer. Among other things, it contains the following sentence: 'Major Haab has, with all the improvements he has made, given proof of his skill and experience.'[89]

Priesdorf, *Soldatisches Führerthum*, Bd.2, p.247; Bonin, *Geschichte des Ingenieurkorps*, p.297.

85   Priesdorf, *Soldatisches Führerthum*, Bd.2, p.249; Bonin, *Geschichte des Ingenieurkorps*, p.126.

86   Anon., *Katalog der Bibliothek und Kartensammlung der Königlichen allgemeinen Kriegsschule* (Berlin: Schade, 1851), p.1.

87   APWr, AmWr, Fortifications Acta, vol. 3, 1758–1808, ref. 1658 (12.197), p.36; Von Haab died on 8 December 1782 in Cosel, see Weltzel, *Geschichte der Stadt*, p.372.

88   King's letters to Haab, 15 and 16 September 1770, 6 March 1774, 29 May 1779, GStA SPK, I HA Rep.96 B Abschriften von Kabinetsordres, Bd.71, pp.467 verso and 469 verso; Bd.73 vol.1774, p.87; Bd.79 p.723.

89   Über die Schlesische Festungen, SBB PK, Handschriften Abteilung, Ms. Boruss. Fol 431, pp.56–58. This memorial and Haab's high assessment of the modernization of the fortress carried out are also

However, not all aspects of his activities at Breslau were well appreciated. In 1779 he was arrested for accounting irregularities. Problems with the Breslau's finances still followed him in 1780, when it emerged that the construction had generated a debt of over 17,000 thalers.[90] Surprisingly, however, these circumstances did not affect his career, which suddenly accelerated in late 1779 and early 1780. After completing his work at Breslau, Haab set about rebuilding the fortress at Cosel, the design of which he presented to the King as early as June 1779.[91] The project was well received, and Haab pursued it until his death in 1782. During design consultations, Haab often came into contact with the King. In 1781 he was commissioned by him to reshape the outer fortifications of Glogau.[92] In 1782 he implemented the project for the reconstruction of the fortresses in Neisse and Schweidnitz, and took over from Regler to carry out the work at Silberberg. The growing importance of this engineer is also shown by his promotion to *oberstleutnant*. Haab's thriving career was interrupted by his sudden death. He died on 8 December 1782 at Cosel of typhus.[93]

Johann Gerhard Harroy de Techreaux

Another engineer who succeeded in gaining the King's recognition (thus leading and supervising work on several fortresses at once) was Johann Gerhard Harroy de Techreaux. He was Belgian and was born on 21 April 1721 in Liege as the son of Johann Harroy, chief builder of the city and the bishopric of Liege, and Catharina von Moraeu. He received his education from his father, but also at a mathematics school in the Netherlands. In 1747 he entered Dutch service as a cadet in the corps of miners and sappers. In the same year he reached the rank of *tweede luitenant* and took part in the siege of Maastricht. He later worked on the fortifications of Namur. In 1754 he was promoted to *luitenant*, and in 1761 he was recruited into the Prussian service, where he became a *kapitän* in the engineer corps. In 1762 he took part in the famous Siege of Schweidnitz, where he was slightly wounded. After the capture of the fortress, he remained there and until 1763 particpated in the reconstruction of the fortifications there. He was later sent to Neisse, where, among other things, he built the Casemattierte Batterie on Caninchen Berg in the mid-1770s.[94] During this time, he did not stand out much among Prussian engineers. His career breakthrough came in 1783, at which time, after Haab's sudden death, the King resumed his habit of contacting directly the engineers carrying out work at individual fortresses. The initial contact did not look good for Harroy; in April 1783, the King, commenting on what he considered to be an excessively high cost estimate for the rebuilding of one of the sluices at the Neisse, stated that 'it brings no honour to Mr Harroy to make such impertinent estimates.'[95] However, fortunately for Harroy, even more criticism from the King was drawn by the actions of others, notably

---

mentioned in Jähns, *Geschichte 1891*, p.2783.

90 Letter from the King to Haab, 4 June 1780, GStA SPK, I HA Rep.96 B Abschriften von Kabinetsordres, Bd.80, p.433.

91 Letter from the King to Haab, 28 June 1779, GStA SPK, I HA Rep.96 B Abschriften von Kabinetsordres, Bd.79, p.814.

92 King's letter to Haab, 1 March 1781, SHD Vincennes, Article 14, 1 V M 131 Glogau.

93 Bonin, *Geschichte des Ingenieurkorps*, p.103.

94 *Todesfälle, Schlesische Provinzialblätter*, pp.476–477; Bonin, *Geschichte des Ingenieurkorps*, p.102.

95 Letter from the King to Rotkirch, 2 April 1783, GStA SPK, I HA Rep.96 B Abschriften von Kabinetsordres, Bd.83, p.236.

Leutnant Wins at Cosel. In September 1783, the King commissioned Harroy to inspect the work carried out by this officer.[96] The results of the inspection, especially Harroy's new cost estimate for the necessary works at the fortress of Cosel, showed the King that this officer was trustworthy. He was given not only the supervision of Cosel, but the King also ordered him to take care of the works carried out at Breslau.[97] The increase in duties also led to promotion. In December, the King appointed him to the rank of *major*, justifying it by his satisfaction with his work.[98]

Harroy's duties quickly began to apply to other fortresses as well. While in a letter of 5 January 1784 to Harroy the King writes only about Neisse, Cosel and Breslau, as early as April correspondence also mentions Glatz, Schweidnitz, Glogau and Silberberg.[99] However, the engineer's actual design and supervisory activities were not so extensive. In 1784 we know of his activity at Breslau, Cosel, Neisse and Glogau.[100] Silberberg and Glatz were Regler's domain.[101] Clearly, however, Harroy was the more important engineer. This is evidenced by the fact that planning tasks related to new fortification projects were delegated to him, as exemplified by the case of the casemated towers that the King wanted to erect to defend the mountainous areas.[102] In the following year, 1785, Harroy's importance increased further. From February that year, his duties also included planning and designing the works at Silberberg.[103] The last fortress that Harroy became responsible for was Schweidnitz. The King commissioned him to repair the fortifications there in March 1786.[104] Thus, as can be seen, by the end of Frederick the Great's reign Harroy was the most important person in the engineering corps, at least as far as the Silesian fortresses were concerned. However, it is difficult to agree with the sentence placed in the obituary of this engineer that claimed that Harroy 'enjoyed the unbounded confidence of Frederick the Great to the end of his life.'[105] For none of his subordinates had such confidence from the King, and he subjected the engineers working for him to particular scrutiny and criticism. Each cost estimate drawn up by Harroy was analysed in detail by the King, often criticised, and the amount proposed by the engineer was not usually accepted. He considered the cost estimate for the repair of the

96 Letter from the King to Harroy, 3 September 1783, GStA SPK, I HA Rep.96 B Abschriften von Kabinetsordres, Bd.83, p.750a.
97 Letter from the King to Harroy, 8 November 1783, GStA SPK, I HA Rep.96 B Abschriften von Kabinetsordres, Bd.83, p.831.
98 Letter from the King to Harroy, 21 December 1783, GStA SPK, I HA Rep.96 B Abschriften von Kabinetsordres, Bd.83, p.965.
99 King's letters to Harroy, 5 January and 10 and 12 April 1784, GStA SPK, I HA Rep.96 B Abschriften von Kabinetsordres, Bd.84, pp.18, 310, 322.
100 King's letters to Harroy, 5 January, 12 April, 20 June, 12,13 and 29 September 1784, GStA SPK, I HA Rep.96 B Abschriften von Kabinetsordres, Bd.84, pp.18, 322, 519, 792, 804.
101 King's letters to Regler, 25 and 26 August 1784, GStA SPK, I HA Rep.96 B Abschriften von Kabinetsordres, Bd.84, pp.718, 724.
102 King's letters to Harroy, 6 and 24 November and 13 and 30 December 1784, GStA SPK, I HA Rep.96 B Abschriften von Kabinetsordres, Bd.84, pp.998, 1062, 1134, 1184.
103 King's letters to Harroy, 20 February, 13 March, 28 August and 28 September 1785, GStA SPK, I HA Rep.96 B Abschriften von Kabinetsordres, Bd.85, pp.175, 247, 897, 1016.
104 King's letters to Harroy, 29 March and 23 April 1786, GStA SPK, I HA Rep.96 B Abschriften von Kabinetsordres, Bd.86, pp.326, 402.
105 Todesfälle, *Schlesische Provinzialblätter*, p.478.

Breslau Sand Bastion presented to him in April 1784 to be too high, as was the cost estimate for the towers for the defence of the mountainous areas from December of the same year.[106] The cost estimate of June 1785 for the reconstruction of the water-damaged works at Breslau was even described by the King as 'impertinently high'.[107]

Gotzenbach and Franseky

The influence of the engineers described above was limited to the Silesian strongholds. Engineers carrying out work in fortresses outside Silesia were independent of their authority and they corresponded directly with the King. For this reason alone, they should be mentioned. Moreover, these officers also attained a high position. In the case of the first engineer, Paul von Gotzenbach am Berge, this was because the fortresses he built at Grabow, then at Graudenz, were extremely important, and the funds spent on them each year exceeded those available to the Silesian engineers. Gotzenbach was of Swiss origin. He was born in 1722 in Hauptwiel, in the canton of Thurgau. Nevertheless, he spent his entire professional career in Prussia. He started as a non-commissioned officer in a pioneer regiment, from 1747 he was a *leutnant* in the miners' corps, where he served until 1764. He was also a recruiting officer.[108] He learned the craft of engineering in the Prussian army. Initially, as an officer of the miner corps he took part in the mine exercises at Potsdam in 1754.

During the Seven Years War he commanded a mine company that fortified the Warthe Pass. In 1760, he was taken prisoner after the Battle of Landeshut. After the Seven Years War, in 1764 he transferred as a *kapitän* to the engineer corps. Initially, he took part in the construction of the fortress at Silberberg; he was one of the officers building the Donjon there. In 1764 and probably after 1770, when the modernisation of Glatz took priority, he also worked there.[109] His only activity in Glatz we can be certain of is as the supervisor of the construction of new gunpowder magazines around the Schäferberg fort in 1764.[110] He did not leave Silesia until the spring of 1774. In March, the King selected him and *Leutnant* Maske from five engineers nominated by Regler to work on a new fortress in West Prussia. Both were to report to Marienwerder on 1 June, where they were to assist Heinze.[111] A month later, the King changed his mind, and Maske was sent to Glogau. Gotzenbach was to set off alone to Marienwerder.[112] His task was to make, together with Heinze, a cost estimate for the new fortress.[113] Gotzenbach was the first and for a long time the only assistant of the French

---

106 King's letters to Harroy, 12 April and 30 December 1784, GStA SPK, I HA Rep.96 B Abschriften von Kabinetsordres, Bd.84, pp.322, 1184.

107 King's letters to Harroy, 8 June 1785, GStA SPK, I HA Rep.96 B Abschriften von Kabinetsordres, Bd.85, p.592.

108 Bonin, *Geschichte des Ingenieurkorps*, p.307.

109 Bonin, *Geschichte des Ingenieurkorps*, pp.98, 107–108, 192–193, 299; Franczak, Grabowski, Nowiński, Żebrowski, *Twierdza Grudziądz*, p.77.

110 GStA SPK, I HA Rep.96 Gehemies Zivilkabinett, ältere Periode, nr 94 Bbb, letter of 14 July 1764.

111 Letter from the King to Regler, 7 March 1774, GStA SPK I HA Rep.96 B Abschriften von Kabinetsordres Bd.73 vol. 1774, p.89.

112 Letter from the King to Regler, 3 April 1774, GStA SPK I HA Rep.96 B Abschriften von Kabinetsordres Bd.73 vol. 1774, p.133.

113 Letter from the King to Heinze, 18 May 1774, GStA SPK I HA Rep.96 B Abschriften von Kabinetsordres Bd.73 vol. 1774, p.192.

engineer. He also naturally became Heinze's successor for the construction of the fortress at Grabow. This happened by chance. In October 1775, the King sent Heinze to look at the Danzig's fortifications. During his absence in Grabow, he was replaced by Gotzenbach. Shortly afterwards, Heinze fell ill and the King ordered him to return to Potsdam for treatment, and Gotzenbach was still to deputise for the comte.[114] This makeshift situation lasted until the destruction of the fortress under construction by ice in February 1776. The order to build a new fortress, at Graudenz, was given to Gotzenbach.[115] From then until the end of the period in question, Gotzenbach worked exclusively at Graudenz. Despite the fact that he directed the work at the fortress, which turned out to be the largest fortress project of the Frederician era, this did not bring him recognition in the eyes of the King. On the contrary. Every now and then, the construction at Graudenz encountered serious difficulties, usually caused by nature (underground springs, groundwater). This obviously delayed the work and increased the cost of construction. However, the King was of the opinion that Gotzenbach was to blame for the delays and increased expenses. In December 1777, he decided that all work carried out by the Swiss in Graudenz had to be checked by a trusted engineer. He chose Regler for this, whom he ordered to first meet with the King to receive materials from him concerning the fortress, and then to set off for Graudenz to inspect the work in progress within a month. He took the opportunity to betray his unflattering opinion of Gotzenbach, for he stated that 'in matters of fortifications he is usually ignorant.'[116]

In December 1777, everything seemed to indicate that there would be a major collapse in the Swiss officer's career. The King, persuaded by Regler, stated that he would dismiss Gotzenbach from Graudenz and hand over the task of building the fortress to the engineer Freund, whom he even promoted to the rank of *major* for this purpose[117]. In the end, Gotzenbach's dismissal did not happen, for he was exceptionally lucky. Less than a week after issuing this instruction, the Elector of Bavaria died, and the King's attention was drawn to the diplomatic games which ended with the outbreak of the War of the Bavarian Succession. After the war, the King did not pick up the thread about Gotzenbach's dismissal. This did not mean that he began to trust him. As early as the spring of 1779, he ordered him to send the accounts of the fortress's construction to Berlin to be checked by the *Ober Rechnungskammer* there. In turn, in 1784, he appointed a special commissioner to check Gotzenbach's activities at Graudenz. He, however, found no irregularities and even declared that Gotzenbach and his subordinates had worked with the utmost effort.[118] However, this did not change much in Gotzebnach's fate. His long service was not appreciated by Frederick. He waited 22 years for his promotion to the rank of *major*, receiving it only from Frederick William II.[119]

114 Letters from the King to Heinze, 22 October and 8 November 1775, GStA SPK I HA Rep.96 B Abschriften von Kabinetsordres Bd.74, pp.694, 758.
115 Letter from the King to Gotzenbach, 23 March 1776, GStA SPK, IV HA Rep.1 No. 104, p.30.
116 Letter from the King to Regler, 14 December 1777, GStA SPK I HA Rep.96 B Abschriften von Kabinetsordres Bd.78, p.758.
117 Letter from the King to Kriegs Casse and to Regler, 24 December 1777, GStA SPK I HA Rep.96 B Abschriften von Kabinetsordres Bd.78, p.777.
118 'Die Festung Graudenz', pp.29, 45.
119 Bonin, *Geschichte des Ingenieurkorps*, pp.281 and 299; Franczak, Grabowski, Nowiński, Żebrowski, *Twierdza Grudziądz*, p.77.

The second engineer in question is Sigismund Cornelius Ludewig von Franseky, the builder of the fortress at Kolberg. This engineer was born in 1730 in Pomerania and was able to obtain an officer's patent quite quickly; he received the rank of *leutnant* as early as 1750.[120] His activities in the period before 1756 is unknown. During the Seven Years War he served in the corps of Duke Frederick Eugene Württemberg defending Pomerania; in 1761 he took part in the construction of a fortified camp near Kolberg, one of the largest to be established during the Seven Years War. After the end of hostilities, he remained in Kolberg. In 1763, he drew up a design for the Maikuhle entrenchment – according to the King's ideas – and later a project for the extensive modernisation of the entire fortress himself. His ideas were not accepted; the final realised design of the fortress was drawn up by Heinze. However, Franseky enjoyed the royal favour, for in 1768 he was summoned to Potsdam for consultations, where the King discussed the details of Heinze's project with him for over a month.[121] Once these talks were completed, the King promoted Franseky to the rank of *kapitän* and ordered the construction of the fortress at Kolberg. He completed this task between 1770 and 1774; the King exceptionally gave him complete freedom and did not interfere, as was his custom, with the engineer's work.[122] When the work was completed, the King was satisfied with Franseky, despite the fact that he took four times longer to build the fortress than the King had anticipated (originally the work was to be finished in 1770).[123] In addition, he went significantly over budget – instead of the 293,104 thalers originally envisaged, the construction cost 486,917 thalers. Nevertheless, after accounting for the expenses of the fortress construction, the King rewarded Franseky with 300 thalers.[124] Less than a year after the completion of the work in Kolberg, the King sent Franseky to work at the newly built fortress at Grabow near Marienwerder.[125] There he worked until the spring of 1776, when the fortress under construction was destroyed by the Vistula flood. Then, together with other engineers, he was sent to build another stronghold on the Vistula – at Graudenz.[126] In 1778, the War of the Bavarian Succession broke out and Franseky, because of the need to strengthen the engineering staff of the fortresses bordering Austria, was sent to Neisse, where he ended up in August of that year.[127] Shortly after his return from the war, in 1779, Franseky left the service.[128] In March 1779, he settled at the estate he had purchased, Schwessow (Świeszewo) near Greifenberg (Gryfice).[129] The reason for the interruption of this thriving career is not known. Perhaps an incapacity for further service which he had

---

120   Bonin, *Geschichte des Ingenieurkorps*, p.298.
121   APS, AMK ref. 65/202/0/3657, pp.24, 30; Bonin, *Geschichte des Ingenieurkorps*, p.88.
122   Bonin, *Geschichte des Ingenieurkorps*, p.105.
123   Volz, *Die Werke*, vol.6, p.243.
124   APS, AMK ref. 65/202/0/3657, p.31.
125   King's letter to Heinze, 8 March 1775, GStA SPK, I HA Rep.96 B Abschriften von Kabinetsordres, Bd.74, p.6.
126   Gotzenbach's letter to the King, 14 September 1776, GStA SPK, IV HA Preußische Arme, Rep.1, No. 104, p.55.
127   'Die Festung Graudenz', p.28.
128   Bonin, *Geschichte des Ingenieurkorps*, p.298.
129   Ludwig Wilhelm Brüggemann, *Ausführliche Beschreibung des gegenwärtigen Zustandes des Königl. Preußischen Herzogthums Vor- und Hinter-Pommern: Welcher die Beschreibung der zu dem Gerichtsbezirk der Königl. Landescollegien in Stettin gehörigen Hinterpommerschen Kreise enthält* (Stettin: H.G. Effenbart, 1784), p.451.

acquired during the war. This would explain the fact that the King granted him a salary of 50 thalers, which he received after leaving the army.[130] Despite the premature end of his service, Franseky's case must be considered remarkable. The fact that he was personally introduced by the King to the issues involved in the construction of the fortress, and especially the freedom that this engineer had during the construction, find no analogy in the entire Frederician period.

The 'Potsdam' Engineers

One of the more interesting issues related to the designers and implementers of the redevelopment of Prussian fortresses in the Frederician period was that of the Potsdam engineers. This was a group who, unlike other engineer officers, were not permanently assigned to a specific fortress, but based in Potsdam. Such a group appears for the first time in the 1757 census of Prussian engineers when there were four of them at the time. A census compiled a year after the King's death reveals 14 engineers whose permanent posting was Potsdam.[131]

The most interesting person from this group was Madeleine Touros, comte d'Heinze, in 1786 one of the highest-ranking Prussian engineers. He was born around 1730 in France.[132] He came from a family with an engineering tradition, as his father was chief engineer in the French department of Guyenne and carried out the channelisation of the Adour estuary near Bayonne in the 1720s.[133] During the younger d'Heinz's service as a French engineer, he was stationed in Bayonne, Nantes, Bordeaux, ending his career as an engineer in Philippeville. He also served as a military engineer, taking part in 11 sieges (including Mons and Maastricht), most notably during the Flanders campaign of the War of the Austrian Succession.[134] The beginning of his contact with Prussia took place in the autumn of 1767. A letter from the King to Heinze, dated 9 October of that year, shows that he offered Frederick his services. The King, in response to his offer, stated that before accepting it, he needed to see him and talk to him. To this end he ordered him to appear at Potsdam.[135] The beginnings of Heinze's Prussian service are presented somewhat differently in the literature. According

---

130 King's letter to Franzky, August 1779, GStA SPK, I HA Rep.96 B Abschriften von Kabinetsordres, Bd.79, p.961.

131 Bonin, *Geschichte des Ingenieurkorps*, pp.274–275, 280.

132 According to various sources, either in 1729 or in 1731, Hanke, Degner, *Geschichte der Amtlichen Kartographie*, p.149; Priesdorf, *Soldatisches Führerthum*, Bd.2, p.385; Bonin, *Geschichte*, p.299.

133 Jean Baptiste Bailac, *Nouvelle chronique de la ville de Bayonne*, (Bayonne: Duhart-Fauvet, 1827), p.221; Charles Bossut, *Traité théorique et expérimental d'hydrodynamique* (Paris: Unknown Publisher, 1787), vol.2, p.291.

134 Pierre Lemau de La Jaisse, *Cinquieme abrégé de la Carte Generale du Militaire de France sur le terre et sur Mer, Depuis Novembre 1737 jusqu'en Decembre 1738* (Paris: Gandouin, Bauche, Prault, Lamesle, Didot, Morel, Briasson, De Nully 1739), p.26; Lemau de La Jaisse, *Sixième abrégé...* (Paris: Gandouin, Prault, Lamesle, Didot, Morel, Briasson, De Nully, Merigot 1740), p.24; Lemau de La Jaisse, *Septieme abrégé* (Paris: Prault, Lamesle, Lamesle 1741) p.21; André-Joseph Panckoucke, *Calendrier General de la Flandre du Brabant et des Conquetes de Roi* (Paris: Savoye, 1747), p.110; François Edme de Montandre-Lonchamps, *Etat Militaire de France pour l'Anne 1758* (Paris: Guillyn, 1758), p.262; *pour l'Anne 1759* (Paris: Guillyn, 1759), p.389; *pour l'Anne 1762* (Paris: Guillyn, 1762) p.337; Priesdorf, *Soldatisches Führerthum*, Bd.2, p.385; Hanke, Degner, *Geschichte der Amtlichen Kartographie*, p.149.

135 Letter to Heinze, 9 October 1767, GStA SPK, I HA Rep.96 B Abschriften von Kabinetsordres Bd.70, vol.1767, p.366.

to Hanke-Degner, he was said to have been recommended to the King by the quartermaster general, Count von Anhalt, while according to Piersdorf, it was the French-born general, Salemon.[136] All that is certain is that the King accepted him into service and Heinze was a Prussian engineer with the rank of *oberstleutnant* in February 1768.[137]

The first test of the Frenchman's design skills came when the King commissioned him with a project to modernise the fortress of Kolberg. The officer made a sketch for this project at the end of June 1768.[138] This sketch was liked by the King, and the latter ordered him to set off for Kolberg, take detailed measurements of the fortress and its environs, and then make a plan for the rebuilding of this fortress, together with its cost estimate.[139] The design work continued until early October, when the first of the designs presented to the King was produced.[140] The final design, accepted by the King, was not made by Heinze until 27 December of that year.[141] Despite the drafting of the design, the King did not commission him to build this fortress, as he entrusted the construction to Franseky. Such a practice was not unusual; the King had already done the same for Silberberg and Glatz, where the designs were drawn up by the Pinto brothers and executed by Regler. However, this kind of treatment did not please the Frenchman; as late as 1774 he complained that another engineer had realised his project.[142] The King, however, had another task for him. A few months after finishing his design for Kolberg, he ordered him to move to Stettin. There he took measurements of the fortress, on the basis of which he made plans for the rebuilding of the fortifications there, as well as the modernisation of the fortifications at Damm and the erection of a new sconce on the road between Damm and Stettin.[143] Here, too, he was unsuccessful, as the King did not decide to implement the plans. The next, and as it was to turn out, the last, chance to make a name for himself as a fortress builder awaited him in 1773. At that time, after the first partition of Poland, Heinze was sent to West Prussia as the King asked him to accompany him on a tour of the newly conquered territories.[144] The result of this trip was another assignment; a cartographic survey of the new Prussian lands. A particular task was to survey the area around Marienwerder. There,

---

136 Hanke, Degner, *Geschichte der Amtlichen Kartographie*, p.149; Priesdorf, *Soldatisches Führerthum*, Bd.2, p.385.

137 Priesdorf, *Soldatisches Führerthum*, Bd.2, p.385.

138 Letter from the King to Heinze, 22 June 1768, GStA SPK, I HA Rep.96 B Abschriften von Kabinetsordres, Bd.70 Vol III 1768, p.267.

139 Letter from the King to d'Heinze, 25 June 1768, GStA SPK, I HA Rep.96 B Abschriften von Kabinetsordres, Bd.70 Vol III 1768, p.272.

140 The inventory is the Plan de La Fortresse de Colberg e de Ses Environs, fait a Potsdam le 6 Octobre 1768, d'Heinze, SBB PK, ref. X 22011. The project consists of the Plan de la Fortresse de Colberg relatif au Project, d'Heinze, SBB PK, ref. X 22011–1 (not dated) and 10 detail sheets, which are blueprints for individual works or fronts of the fortress. All these designs are signed by Heinze, most dated 6 October 1768.

141 APS, AMK ref. 65/202/0/3657, p.26.

142 Letter from the King to Heinze, 17 July 1774, GStA SPK, I HA Rep.96 B Abschriften von Kabinetsordres, Bd.73, vol.1774, p.276.

143 Letters from the King to Heinze, 2 and 14 June 1769, GStA SPK, I HA Rep.96 B Abschriften von Kabinetsordres, Bd.71, pp.139 verso, 150 verso.

144 Letter from the King to Heinze, 24 May 1773, GStA SPK, I HA Rep.96 B Abschriften von Kabinetsordres, Bd.73 vol.1773, p.155.

on Grabower Kempe, on the Vistula, the King had a new fortress erected. Its Heinze was the designer and this time the King allowed him to oversee the construction. He carried out the work from 1774 until the autumn of 1775. In October 1775, the King sent him to Danzig to reconnoitre the fortress there. During the journey, Heinze fell ill and the King ordered him to return to Potsdam for treatment. He was temporarily replaced by his associate, Gotzenbach.[145] However, the comte did not return to Grabow, as in the meantime it became apparent that he had made numerous errors in the construction of the foundations. There is no information on the date of his final dismissal from his position as builder of the fortress in Grabow; however, this must have happened at the beginning of December 1775, as on 6 December Heinze asked the King to dismiss him from his service, which, however, Frederick did not do.[146] Heinze's situation was further aggravated when, in February 1776, the ice destroyed the fortifications he was building at Grabow. The King did not initially reproach the French engineer or hold him responsible for the disaster, but this soon changed. In a letter dated 2 April, the King blamed Heinze for the disaster, as he had failed to make a dyke in time to shield the fortress from the water.[147] Thus, his career collapsed and the King did not commission any projects from him. He remained in Potsdam, initially unoccupied. In June 1777, he offered to teach officers the science of engineering, but the King refused, claiming that this was already being dealt with by the appropriate person.[148] It was not until mid-1779 that he became active as a teacher and examiner in the field of engineering sciences, a role he continued to carry out until the end of the Frederick's reign.[149] He was even to work on establishing a special engineering school. He included his educational experiences in a textbook he had been working on since 1783. In 1785 he presented the first two volumes to the King, which were well received.[150] Towards the end of the period in question, Heinze managed to make his last appearance as a designer. He was the one who most likely drew up the design for the towers with machicolations that the King wanted to erect at several locations in the mountainous Silesian-Czech borderlands.[151] It was most likely not a design commissioned to him by the King, but his own initiative. Indeed, Heinze quite often sent the King fortification ideas, unrelated to a specific place, which he tried to interest the ruler in.[152] The latter usually politely thanked him; in the case of the tower in question, however, he took steps towards its construction as *Major* Harroy drew up a cost estimate

145 Letter from the King to Heinze, 22 October and 8 November 1775, GStA SPK, I HA Rep.96 B Abschriften von Kabinetsordres, Bd.74, pp.694, 758.
146 Hanke, Degner, *Geschichte der Amtlichen Kartographie*, p.149.
147 Letter from the King to Heinze, 2 April 1776, GStA SPK, I HA Rep.96 B Abschriften von Kabinetsordres, Bd.75, p.266.
148 Letter from the King to Heinze, 17 June 1777, GStA SPK, I HA Rep.96 B Abschriften von Kabinetsordres Bd.77, p.17 recto.
149 Letter from the King to Heinze, 19 June 1779, GStA SPK, I HA Rep.96 B Abschriften von Kabinetsordres Bd.79, p.793, on the examination of the overseer of Roden.
150 Hanke, Degner, *Geschichte der Amtlichen Kartographie*, p.150.
151 Letters from the King to Heinze and Harroy, 13 December 1784, GStA SPK, I HA Rep.96 B Abschriften von Kabinetsordres, Bd.84, pp.1133, 1134.
152 Letters from the King to Heinze, 17 April 1770 and 15–16 April 1771, GStA SPK, I HA Rep.96 B Abschriften von Kabinetsordres, Bd.71, p.377 recto; Bd.72. vol.1771, pp.147–148.

for the construction of these towers for specific locations. The King even ordered one of them to be built, near Dittersbach.[153]

Throughout his service to Frederick, Heinze remained at the rank he had received on his entry into service, *oberstleutnant*. In 1774 the King refused to promote him and told him to wait for 'the effects of his kindness'.[154] In 1786 he refused him again, claiming that the peacetime promotion process was already over.[155] Only after the death of Frederick did his situation change. In 1787 he received a promotion to *oberst*, and a year later he achieved another success as an engineering academy was founded on the basis of his ideas. Finally, in 1793, he achieved the rank of *generalmajor*.[156] As you can see, his career progressed very poorly, which is surprising, as he had several strengths that should have been a great help. He was a French engineer and not only knew a language that Frederick spoke more readily than German, but also represented the French tradition of defence architecture. What is more, he was very active; he very often sent the King all sorts of memoranda concerning the reform of the Prussian engineering services, engineering education or new developments in fortifications.[157] However, the factor that determined the lack of promotion turned out to be the want of practical experience in the field of fortress construction. This was clearly demonstrated by the problems in the construction of the fortress at Grabower Kempe.

The Potsdam officers also included two bearing the surname Pinto: Franz Ignatz and Vincent Pinto di Barri. These officers came from Italy, from the Kingdom of Sardinia-Piedmont. Both were the sons of Lorenzo Bernardino Pinto, one of the most important Piedmontese military engineers of the second half of the eighteenth century. Lorenzo distinguished himself by defending the fortress of Cuneo against a French siege in 1744. After the War of the Austrian Succession, he was active in the construction of the fortresses of Brunette, Exilles, Fort della Madonna la Consolata near Demonte, Fort San Carlo in the Fenestrelle fortress, and Fort San Vittorio in the Tortona fortress. His last known work is the Officers' Pavilion in the Fenestrelle fortress, which he designed before 1780. Lorenzo died in 1798 as head of the Corps of Engineers there. He had seven sons who did military service in Prussia, Austria and Piedmont.[158] Among them were Franz Ignatz and Vincent. The Pinto family descended from the old Portuguese noble family of Pinto, including Emanuel Pinto,

153 King's letters to Major Harroy, 6 and 24 November 1784 and to Hoym, 29 June 1786, GStA SPK, I HA Rep.96 B Abschriften von Kabinetsordres, Bd.84, pp.998 and 1062; Bd.86, p.608.
154 Letter from the King to Heinze, 17 July 1774, GStA SPK, I HA Rep.96 B Abschriften von Kabinetsordres, Bd.73, vol.1774 p.276.
155 Franczak, Grabowski, Nowiński, Żebrowski, *Twierdza Grudziądz*, p.76.
156 Hanke, Degner, *Geschichte der Amtlichen Kartographie*, p.150, Priesdorf, *Soldatisches Führerthum*, Bd.2, p.385.
157 Hanke, Degner, *Geschichte der Amtlichen Kartographie*, p.149; King's letter to Heinze, 17 April 1770, 15–16th April 1771 and 23 June 1773, GStA SPK, I HA Rep.96 B Abschriften von Kabinetsordres, Bd.71, vol.1770, p.377; Bd.72, vol.1771, pp.147–148; Bd.73, vol.1773, p.191.
158 Cesare Saluzzo, *Ricordi militari degli stati Sardi: estratti da parecchie opre si stampate che manoscritte* (Torino: Sebastiano Franco, 1859), p.438; Ferdinando Augusto Pinelli, *Storia militare del Piemonte in continuazione di quella del Saluzo cioè dalla pace d' Aquisgrana sino ai dì nostri, 1748–1796* (Torino: Degiorgis, 1854), vol.1, p.24; Ashleigh Hogg, *The Fortress of Fenestrelle in Detail*, 2004, p.23, <http://www.fortedifenestrelle.com/Pdf/English/The%20Fortress%20of%20Fenestrelle%20in%20Detail.pdf>, accessed 6 December 2012, p.23; Micaela Viglino Davico, *Architetti e ingegneri militari in Piemonte tra '500 e '700* (Torino: Omega Edizioni, 2008), pp.207–208, Carlo Dionisotti, *Notizie biografiche dei*

67th Grand Master of Order of Saint John.[159] The Piedmontese branch of the family was elevated to the rank of count in 1766. Lorenzo was granted the title of Conti di Barri. This title was also used by both brothers in Prussia. In Prussia, it was recognised as early as 1770, confirmation of which took place in 1783, when, on 11 March, Count Pinto, *oberst* and *flügel adjutant,* received the Silesian inkolat.[160] From 1777, the same Pinto was the owner of the Silesian estates of Gallenau (now part of Kamenz/Kamieniec Ząbkowicki) and Liebenau (Lubnów, district of Frankenstein/Ząbkowice).[161]

Franz Ignatz was born around 1725 in Piedmont and died on 28 December 1788 in Potsdam.[162] He entered the Prussian service in the early spring of 1767 with the rank of *major.*[163] Soon he was already an *oberst* and an officer on the staff of the quartermaster general.[164] Around 1768 he drew up a project for a Donjon in Glatz.[165] He was also active in other military fields. He developed an innovation in the 'globe of pressure' technique.[166] He was also involved in experiments in the field of artillery.[167] On 14. November 1786 he was promoted to *generalmajor.* From around 1775 he was married to Katarina Wilhelmina (née von Tarrach). He had as many as four children, the first, Frederike Wilhelmine Charlotte, born on 15 July 1776; the last, son Karl Friedrich, on 2 August 1781. From 1777, he was the owner of the two Silesian estates mentioned above, and from 1783 he was incorporated as a member of the Silesian nobility. He also initiated the Prussian line of the Counts of Pinto.

Slightly less is known about the life and service of Vincent Pinto. He was born in Tortona, where his father was building a fortress, and died in 1800 Turin.[168] He initially served as an infantry officer in the Sardinian-Piedmontese army. He entered Prussian service in 1764, with the rank of *kapitän.* He served in the royal entourage. By 1773 he was promoted to the rank of *major.*[169] From 1766 to 1782 he was at Silberberg, where he took part in the

---

Vercellesi illustri (Biella: Giuseppe Amosso, 1862), pp.168–169; Pio Bosi, *Dizionario Storico, Biografico, Topografico, Militare d'Italia* (Torino: G. Candeletti, 1870), p.460.

159 Ernst Heinrich Kneschke, *Neues Allgemeines Deutsches Adels-Lexicon* (Leipzig: Friedrich Voigt Verlag, 1867), vol.7, p.153.

160 Walter von Heuck, *Genealogisches Handbuch des Adels, Adelslexikon* (Limburg an der Lahn: Starke Verlag, 1999), vol.X, pp.375–376; APWr: Personalia, Rep 47/10, Nachweisung der Personen denen seit Antritt der Königlicher Preusischer Regierung in Schlesien das Incolat verliehen worden, p.94. An inkolat granted a person the rights and benefits of nobility.

161 Priesdorf, *Soldatisches Führerthum*, vol.2, p.244.

162 Priesdorf, *Soldatisches Führerthum*, vol.2, p.244.

163 The King writes about Pinto's employment in his letter to Prince Henry, 17 March 1763. On 23 March 1767, the King grants permission to *Major* Count Pinto to go to Berlin for three days. Certainly, the addressee of this letter was not Vincent Pinto, for to him, *Kapitän* Pinto the King addressed the letter, 15 November 1767. Droysen, *Politische Correspondenz*, vol.26, p.94; GStA SPK, Geheimes Zivilkabinett I HA Rep.96 B Abschriften von Kabinetsordres, Bd.70, vol.II 1767, pp.103, 353.

164 Correspondence relating to this trip was with the quartermaster general, Von Anhalt. GStA SPK, Geheimes Zivilkabinett I HA Rep.96 B Abschriften von Kabinetsordres, Bd.70, vol.III 1768, p.366.

165 Volz, *Die Werke*, vol.V, p.243.

166 von Heilmann, *Die Kriegskunst der Preußen*, p.128.

167 Malinowsky, Bonin, *Geschichte*, vol.2, p.99.

168 Gaspare de Gregori, *Istoria Della Vercellese Letteratura Ed Arti* (Torino: Chirio e Mina, 1824), vol.4, p.274.

169 Priesdorf, *Soldatisches Führerthum*, vol.2, p.244.

construction of the fortress.[170] During the War of the Bavarian Succession, he was initially still stationed at Silberberg, where he was by then in charge of fortifications,[171] and later he was at Broumow.[172] In June 1782 he asked the King for his discharge from service, motivated by his desire to return to Piedmont.[173] On his return to his homeland, he became adjutant-general in the Sardinian-Piedmontese army.[174] Little is known about his private life. The only mention comes from 1779, when he wanted to marry the daughter of the mayor of Silberberg Ruhm.[175] The King advised him against this step, and the wedding probably did not take place.

The Pinto brothers were extremely important for two Silesian strongholds, Silberberg and Glatz. Vincent Pinto was active in the former, and made the design of the Donjon there, already described.[176] The King engaged him because it was his wish that this new Silesian fortress should be influenced by the Piedmontese mountain fortresses. With his background Vincent Pinto was an obvious choice. Vincent Pinto not only had a hand in the design of the fortress but was also active in its construction. The first mention of his stay in Silberberg can be found in a letter he wrote there on 25 February 1766. In it, he asked the King for a loan of 400 thalers to cover his debts. These debts were said to have arisen from, among other things, the purchase of equipment, illness, and theft by servants. In a letter of 8 March of the same year, the King granted the requested amount and at the same time advised him to handle the money better.[177] There are several mentions of Vincent's activity in the construction of the fortress in the following years. On 10 November 1767, he sent the King a report on the status of construction. On the basis of it, the King concluded that the core of the fortress would be finished in the following year.[178] Pinto was still in Silberberg the following March; in his letter, the King was critical of the idea of some new work that Pinto wanted to erect there.[179] In all, Vincent Pinto spent 16 years in Silberberg, as he writes in one of his last letters to Frederick. According to his words, his activity in this fortress, and the advice given to the engineers building it, made it possible to save 150,000 thalers in construction costs.[180] In the literature to date, it has been reported that Pinto also acted as commandant of the Silberberg fortress for several months in 1778, in place of the ailing Rossiere.[181] However,

---

170 GStA SPK, Geheimes Zivilkabinett I HA Rep.96 no. 94 Ss 4 Von Pinto, Vinzent.

171 GStA SPK, Geheimes Zivilkabinett I HA Rep.96 B Abschriften von Kabinetsordres, Bd.70, vol.II 1767, p.353, Bd.79, p.432.

172 GStA SPK, Geheimes Zivilkabinett I HA Rep.96 B Abschriften von Kabinetsordres, Bd.79, pp.571, 605.

173 GStA SPK, Geheimes Zivilkabinett I HA Rep.96 no. 94 Ss 4 Von Pinto, Vinzent.

174 de Gregori, *Istoria*, p.274.

175 GStA SPK, Geheimes Zivilkabinett, I HA, Rep.96 B, Abschriften von Kabinetsordres, Bd.79 p.1066.

176 In the literature to date, Franz Ignatz has been erroneously regarded as the designer of this fortress. Grzegorz Podruczny, Tomasz Przerwa, *Twierdza Srebrna Góra* (Warszawa: Bellona, 2010), p.50; Bleyl, *Silberberg*, pp.18–19.

177 Pinto's letter to the King, 25 February and the King's reply, 8 March 1766, GStA SPK, I HA Rep 96 no 94 Ss 4 Von Pinto, Vinzent.

178 Letter from the King to Pinto, 15 November 1767, GStA SPK, I HA Rep.96 B Abschriften von Kabinetsordres, Bd.70, 1767–68, vol.II 1767, p.353.

179 King's letter to Pinto, 18 March 1768, GStA SPK, I HA Rep.96 B Abschriften von Kabinetsordres, Bd.70, 1767–68, vol.III 1768, p.107.

180 Letter from Pinto to the King, 18 June 1782, GStA SPK, I HA Rep 96 no 94 Ss 4 Von Pinto, Vinzent.

181 Priesdorf, *Soldatisches Führerthum*, vol.2, p.244.

in a surviving letter from the King to Pinto dated 25 June 1778, it appears that the King ordered him to deal in Silberberg only with matters relating to the defence of the fortress, while he temporarily entrusted the function of commandant to a certain *Oberst* Zegelin.[182]

The second of the Pinto brothers, Franz Ignatz, also had some connection with the Silberberg stronghold, and, until now, was thought to be its designer. His only source-confirmed connection with the fortress was in 1768. Franz Ignatz was sent to Piedmont to bring Piedmontese workers to build the fortress at Silberberg. This was because the King was not satisfied with the pace of the stonework (blasting) carried out in this fortress.[183] He therefore instructed him to search in Piedmont for some workmen experienced *dans le metier d'escarper*. In October 1768, it became apparent that these workmen could not leave Piedmont without the permission of the ruler there, so the King involved his minister, Count Karl Wilhelm von Finckenstein, in the whole affair, who was to officially apply for permission to a minister in the government of the King of Sardinia-Piedmont.[184] Eventually they succeeded in bringing the workers and by May 1769 they were already in Silesia.[185] Little is known about their activities: only that the King took a personal interest in how these new workers were performing.

Much more important are Franz Ignatz's connections to Glatz. A work based on his design, the Donjon, has survived to this day in good condition. It is not known when this project was created. It is first mentioned in the military testament of Frederick the Great in 1768, where the King wrote: 'As soon as the fortress in Silberberg is completed the old castle in Glatz should be improved. The old walls, threatening to collapse, must be demolished, strong casemates established and the plan of Lieutenant-Colonel Pinto partially realised.'[186] Pinto, as the designer for Glatz, is mentioned once more, in a letter from the King dated March 1769. In it, the King appointed Regler, an engineer already experienced in stonemasonry, to check at Glatz whether Pinto's project could be built easily.[187]

We do not know many details about the lives of the two Pinto brothers before their arrival in Prussia, but it is certain that they were well acquainted with the fortresses erected by their father. In the two Silesian fortresses they designed, elements of the Piedmontese tradition of defensive architecture were introduced: full casemating of the fortress core including several-storey artillery casemates. Such solutions were characteristic of nineteenth-century reduits, typical elements of New Prussian fortifications. Of course, the main model for them was the solutions proposed by Montalembert, with his *'tour angulaire'* at the forefront. However, the fact that Prussian engineers were the first to fully accept the ideas of the French engineer was largely due to the Donjons at Glatz and Silberberg and their designers, Vincent and Franz Ignatz Pinto.

---

182 GStA SPK, I HA Rep.96 B Abschriften von Kabinetsordres, Bd.79, p.432.

183 Letter from the King to Regler, 31 June 1768, GStA SPK, I HA Rep.96 B Abschriften von Kabinetsordres, Bd.70 vol.III, p.282.

184 Letter from the King to Count Finckenstein, 10 October 1768, GStA SPK, I HA Rep.96 B Abschriften von Kabinetsordres, Bd.70 vol.III, p.366.

185 Letters from the King to Regler, 3 and 24 May 1769, GStA SPK, I HA Rep.96 B Abschriften von Kabinetsordres, Bd.71, pp.120 recto and 136 verso.

186 Volz, *Die Werke*, vol.6 p.243.

187 Letter from the King to Regler, 4 March 1769, GStA SPK, I HA Rep.96 B Abschriften von Kabinetsordres, Bd.71, p.65 recto.

Summary

From the above characterisations of some of Frederick the Great's engineers, it is clear that the lot of the military engineer in Prussia under this ruler was not an easy one. Their careers also tended to develop very slowly, for the King was reluctant to promote them. He rarely granted steps-up and never did so at the request of the subordinate. The two French engineers described here, active in the period after 1763, both asked for promotions and neither received them. Lefèbvre, who complained about not being promoted, was told by the King to calm down, not to complain about his rank, because the King decided promotions in his own way.[188] The same was the case with Heinze. In July 1774 he also complained about his rank being too low, in his opinion. The King, in response to his letter, stated that he was 'to take it easy, do calmly what is ordered of him and let him be convinced that he will be able to try the effects of my kindness.'[189] The kindness came eventually, but only from Frederick's successor, as the promotion for which Heinze asked did not take place until 1787.[190] This does not mean, however, that the King ruled out promotions in the engineering corps altogether. These did happen, but they were usually very slow. Daries, builder of the fortress of Schweidnitz, waited 15 years for his promotion to the rank of *oberst*.[191] Haab was promoted to *major* in 1764, and to *oberstleutnant* shortly before his death in 1782. This slow promotion could be seen as unfair, because, unlike officers in other arms, engineers worked just as hard in peacetime as they did in wartime. Rapid promotions in the engineer corps were the exception, although they did happen. An example was Regler, who in 1760 was a *kapitän*, a decade later already an *oberst*.[192] Regler also illustrates that there was a limit which the King did not cross in promotions. Neither this distinguished officer, nor any other engineer attained the rank of general after 1763. The King did, however, try to value his engineers in a different way. Regler was given the post of commandant of the fortress at Glatz in 1774, in 1776 the King increased his salary by 400 thalers, and in 1778 ennobled him.[193]

As can be seen, the King did not value his engineers; however, this situation did not last throughout Frederick's royal reign. Eventually the first two heads of his engineering corps, Walrave and Sers, attained general rank. It was only the disappointment they caused the King – the former with treachery and his financial embezzlements, the latter with the surrender of the fortress of Schweidnitz, which he had erected, in 1757 – that caused a decline of royal confidence in his engineers. This process continued even in the period after the Seven Years War, even though the engineers no longer gave any compelling reasons for it. By the end of Frederick's life, engineers did not enjoy his respect at all. This is perfectly illustrated by a fact which took place in 1783. At that time, the King appointed Johann Martin Pohlmann, superintendent of construction at the Breslau chamber, to review the

---

188 Bonin, *Geschichte des Ingenieurkorps*, p.68. King's letter to Lefèbvre, 31 October 1768, GStA SPK, I HA Rep.96 B Abschriften von Kabinetsordres Bd.70, Vol III 1768 p.407.

189 Letter from the King to Heinze, 17 July 1774, GStA SPK, I HA Rep.96 B Abschriften von Kabinetsordres Bd.73, Vol 1774 p.276.

190 Bonin, *Geschichte des Ingenieurkorps*, p.298.

191 Bonin, *Geschichte des Ingenieurkorps*, p.297; King's letter to Daries, 17 April 1776, GStA SPK, I HA Rep.96 B Abschriften von Kabinetsordres Bd.75, p.317.

192 Bonin, *Geschichte des Ingenieurkorps*, pp.297–298.

193 Priesdorf, *Soldatisches Führerthum*, vol.2, p.247; King's letter to Regler, 1 May 1776, GStA SPK, I HA Rep.96 B Abschriften von Kabinetsordres Bd.75, p.364.

masonry and earthworks carried out at Glatz, Breslau and Cosel.[194] In militarised Prussian society, the fact that the King commissioned a civilian architect to inspect the work of military engineers must have been an insult to them. However, they had to bear it meekly, as they did the opinions often expressed by the King about the impertinence of the engineers, or the accusations of corruption that appeared. Not surprisingly, engineers treated in this way were not held in high esteem by others either. In a text written down in French in 1784 describing the Prussian army, there is this, partly false and certainly unfair, opinion: 'The corps is composed of French and Portuguese adventurers. Since the death of Monsieur Le Fevre, who proved his talents by fortifying Silberberg and defeating Monsieur Gribauval at Schweidnitz, there is not one officer to be named. This corps has no reputation.'[195]

Fortress Construction

Organisation
The construction of a fortress was a process that required the cooperation of several people and institutions. The central figure was the engineer who ran it. It was he who designed, made cost estimates, corresponded with the King, dealt with the accounts of the fortress, liaised with the civil offices and, in the early days, was also responsible for recruiting labourers. The local civil administration also played an important role. In the early days, its task was limited solely to the provision of cash; after the Seven Years War it had much more to do. Both the Silesian ministry and the Pomeranian and Prussian chambers were tasked not only with providing cash, but also with ensuring an adequate number of labourers, providing the means of transport, and supplying building materials.[196] Certain tasks, especially in the first period of fortress construction, were also carried out by the commandants of fortresses. Their role was limited to acting as an intermediary between the King and the engineer, especially when the engineer supervising the construction was not permanently in the fortress. This was the case before 1756 in Neisse, Glogau and Cosel, where the work was supervised by Sers permanently stationed at Schweidnitz.[197]. At Glatz, too, correspondence with the King was carried out by its commandant, Baron La Motte Fouqué, even though *Major* Wrede was permanently stationed in that fortress.[198] Exceptionally,

194 W. Bode 'Versuch einer Biographie und Charakteristik des verstorbenen Ober Baudirector Pohlmann', *Schlesische Provinzialblätter*, vol.33 no.1 January 1801, pp.24–34; King's letters to Pohlmann, 3 August and 3 September 1783, GStA SPK, I HA Rep.96 B Abschriften von Kabinetsordres Bd.83, pp.738, 750.
195 GStA SPK, I HA, Rep.94 II M 13, Memoire sur L'armee Prusienne en 1784, p.12 recto.
196 GStA SPK, I HA Rep.96 B Abschriften von Kabinetsordres, Bd.70, vol. III 1768, p.207; Bd.71, pp.323, 375, 394, 424, 491; Bd.72, vol. VI 1771 p.56; vol. VII 1772, pp.75, 223; Bd.73, vol. 1773, p.4; Bd.73, vol. 1774, pp.62, 63, 387–388, 410; Bd.74, p. XXVI verso, 322, 622, 789; Bd.75, pp.54, 71, 137, 250, 251, 911; Bd.76, pp.112, 142; Bb. 79, pp.723, 848, 1125; Bd.80, pp.83, 404, 408, 420; Bd.81, pp.123, 156, 178, 420; Bd.82, pp.162, 206, 813, 857; Bd.83, pp.4, 5, 115, 586, 625, 697, 953; Bd.84, pp.724, 792, 804, 1102; Bd.86, pp.608, 654, 655.
197 GStA SPK, Geheimes Zivilkabinett I HA Rep.96 No. 616 – Schlesische Festungen, Bd.C, pp.42, 43, 45; Bd.D, pp.1. 3, 10, 12, 13, 15, 28, 30, Bd.E, p.49, Bd.F, pp.2, 18–20, 33, 37, 40–42, Bd.G, pp.5, 17, 31, 35, 38–40, 47, 51, 52, 54, 59, 60, 70; Bd.H, pp.1, 15, 24, 26, 30, 39, 44, 47, 48, 54, 56, 57, 96, 97.
198 GStA SPK, Geheimes Zivilkabinett I HA Rep.96 No. 616 – Schlesische Festungen, Bd.C, p.27; Bd.D, p.25; Bd.F, pp.21–23, 35, 47; Bd.G, p.81; Bd.H, pp.35, 37, 61.

commandants also had other duties – in Cosel, the commandant there was also in charge of hiring construction workers.[199]

One of the problems that the organiser of fortress construction solved was compensation for building plots taken for new fortifications. This is because they were rarely built on land belonging to the state. Usually the land on which the new fortifications were erected already had an owner, and was sometimes even built on. We have information on this subject mainly for the period before the Seven Years War. The procedure for the valuation of compensation is perfectly illustrated by the example of Cosel. The estimation of land prices was attempted as early as October 1743, even though the fortress plans were not yet ready. It was only after the project was approved in mid-November of that year that the King ordered Minister Ludwig Wilhelm von Münchow to carry out a valuation of the plots of land intended for the construction of the fortress.[200] The final estimate of the price of the land to be purchased was made in February 1744. Numerous fields and gardens were taken over for the new fortifications, and houses, outbuildings, a cemetery, a hospital with a chapel, as well as the Minorite monastery, which had been erected only eight years earlier, were earmarked for demolition. The property seized was initially estimated at 30,500 thalers; this was later reduced to 12,413 thalers. The compensation paid to the owners was even lower, amounting to 6,500 thalers, and did not reach Cosel until August 1748.[201]

A similar situation occurred in Glatz, where in 1751 part of the Neu Land suburb was removed to be replaced by fortifications around the town. Eighteen houses were removed in front of the Schul Thor, for which the King gave compensation to the owners. However, in order to force them to remain in the town (and thus not lose the inhabitants and places for the accommodation of soldiers), part of the compensation amount was paid in cash and the rest in the form of building materials. Out of this, six new houses were to be built in Glatz to accommodate these families. The cost of their erection was to be 16,341 thalers. Of this, 6,574 thalers were to come in cash, 8,085 in the form of new building materials.[202] The buildings in front of the Bohmische Thor were also to be demolished; the cost estimate for the project of Glatz's fortifications estimated them at 3,702 thalers.[203] Some craftsmen's workshops situated in front of the Schul Thor were also destroyed. They too were later rebuilt elsewhere.[204] Two of them – the dyeworks and the linen weaving mill – have survived to the present dayand are located in Malczewskiego Street.

The issue of compensation for seized properties and demolished buildings also played a big role at Schweidnitz during the construction of the fortress. The King ordered the project to be carried out in such a way that the suburbs suffered as little as possible. Instead of erecting a strong fortified perimeter in front of the line of medieval fortifications, it was

---

199 Letter from Lattorff, 11 August 1754, GStA SPK, Geheimes Zivilkabinett I HA Rep.96 no. 616 – Schlesische Festungen, Bd.G, p.54; Letter from Sers, 28 March 1756, Bd.H, p.43.

200 Letter from the King to Minister von Münchow, 13 November 1743, GStA SPK, I HA Rep.96 B Abschriften von Kabinetsordres, Bd.29, p.8.

201 Weltzel, *Geschichte der Stadt*, pp.264–265.

202 Letter from La Motte Fouqué, 16 April 1751, GStA SPK, Geheimes Zivilkabinett I HA Rep.96 no. 616 – Schlesische Festungen, Bd.F, pp.22–23.

203 Wrede, Summarischer Extract…19 September 1751, GStA SPK, Geheimes Zivilkabinett I HA Rep.96 No. 616 – Schlesische Festungen, Bd.F, p.34.

204 GStA SPK, Geheimes Zivilkabinett I HA Rep.96 No. 616 – Schlesische Festungen, Bd.F, pp.44–45.

decided to build a relatively weak rampart and to extend several forts far into the fore-ground. This allowed the majority of buildings to be spared, especially the (particularly important for Schweidnitz) Church of Peace. Demolitions, however, were not avoided; while building the main rampart, some of the suburban buildings had to be removed. In May 1748, three churches and 83 houses were removed in preparation for construction.[205] Clearly, however, the planners were guided by the principle of the 'lesser evil' – they chose design solutions that would result in less destruction of buildings and, consequently, in less compensation. This can be seen in the example of the Capuchin monastery at Striegauer Thor, which impeded the erection of a new embankment. Walrave, the then designer of the fortress, proposed that instead of demolishing the monastery, the old slaughterhouse building located at the gate should be removed and in its place a 'light work which, with a low flank, would defend the new corps de la place.'[206] The appraisal of the plots of land for the new fortifications was carried out in the autumn of 1747. The prices of the properties taken over were to be set 'at the usual rate for the country.'[207] Compensation payments were made at the time of the actual seizure of the plot for the construction of the defensive work in question. For example: in March 1750, when the construction of the Bogen and Garten forts began, 6,197 thalers were spent on plots of land for both structures, which was almost half of the expenditure on the construction of the fortifications in that month.[208]

Much less information on compensation exists for the period after the Seven Years War. This may be due to the fact that new fortresses were established in non-urbanised areas (Silberberg, Grabower Kampe, Graudenz), and the expansion of fortifications mainly concerned areas lying in front of the existing fortifications, which did not entail the need to buy land. Only one example of this is known, related to the fortress at Grabower Kampe. Its construction stood in doubt for some time due to the claims of Count Czapski of Opaleń, who owned the surrounding land. His claims prevented the construction of the bridge over the Vistula which Frederick had planned to erect there in 1754. In 1775 the King expressed concern (in a letter to the designer of the Grabow fortress) that the count's claims might harm the construction of the fortress. As it eventually turned out, the Vistula proved to be the more serious problem, but despite the destruction of the fortress by the waters of the river, the disputed areas were bought by the Prussian state in 1776.[209]

Another issue dealt with by the person organising the construction was the import of materials. The vast majority of them came from the vicinity of the fortress under construction; transporting materials over long distances was expensive. At Grabow and Graudenz, lime from limestone from nearby Jungen near Schwetz was used.[210] At Silberberg the stone

205 Schirrmann, *Chronik der Stadt Schweidnitz*, p.46.
206 Letter from Walrave to the King, 24 September 1747, GStA SPK, Geheimes Zivilkabinett I HA Rep.96 No. 616 – Schlesische Festungen, Bd.D, p.48.
207 Letter from the King to Minister von Munchov, 28 September 1747, GStA SPK Geheimes Zivilkabinett I HA Rep.96 No. 616 – Schlesische Festungen, Bd.D, p.51.
208 Letter from Sers to the King, 4 April 1750, GStA SPK, Geheimes Zivilkabinett I HA Rep.96 No. 616 – Schlesische Festungen, Bd.E, p.24.
209 Franczak, Grabowski, Nowiński, Żebrowski, *Twierdza Grudziądz*, p.75. Letter from the King to Heinze, 15 January 1775, GStA SPK, I HA Rep.96 B Abschriften von Kabinetsordres, Bd.74, p. XXIII.
210 Gotzenbach's letter, 17 January 1776, Kl. Grabow, GStA SPK, IV HA Rep.1 No. 104, p.19; Franczak, Grabowski, Nowiński, Żebrowski, *Twierdza Grudziądz*, p.97.

for the walls came from previously blasted moats, the lime from lime extracted in the vicinity (the nearest lime kiln was several hundred metres from the fortress), while the stonework detail was made from sandstone from Wünschelburg (Radków).[211] The situation was similar with bricks, which were fired locally. The issue of brick procurement hardly appears in the sources; hence the conclusion that it was simply bought. In fact, there were brickworks in most cities; archival cartography shows such facilities at Schweidnitz, Neisse, Brieg, Glogau and Glatz, in the latter city there were as many as three brickworks.[212] Only in the case of the strongholds of Silberberg and Graudenz did the need for a brickyard appear. For the needs of the first fortress, brickworks were established at Silberberg itself, as early as 1765. For Graudenz, brickworks were established both in Graudenz and in nearby Schwetz.[213]

However, some materials had to be imported from distant areas. An example was cement, which for the construction of the Neisse fortress was imported from Stettin in 1744 on the initiative of the King[214]. This was also the case with sourcing timber from Poland for the construction of the fortress on Grabower Kampe in 1775.[215] Sourcing materials from abroad was no exception. In his 1763 cost estimate for the modernisation of the Kolberg fortress, Lieutenant Franseky wanted to import cement from the Netherlands and lime from Sweden's Gotland[216].

It is also worth noting this aspect of fortress construction, which was time. The construction of a fortress was a long-term process and was dependent on natural conditions. In this respect, the most important aspect of fortress construction was its seasonality. The main work (both earthworks and masonry) usually started in March or early April and continued until November. The starting and finishing dates were determined by the weather. In 1771, spring frosts caused a late start to construction work at Neisse.[217] The situation was different at Graudenz, where the work often took less time. In 1776, they started in August, but this was related to the late decision to build the fortress. There were no such reasons in 1780, yet work did not start until mid-July. From 1783 onwards, the short construction season was fixed top-down, by royal order. Frederick ordered that work should not begin until early June and should be completed by the end of September.[218]

There was also some specific work going on outside the main season. These usually concerned the procurement of materials. Trees were felled in winter, which was more a result of technological requirements than organisational issues. The winter period was also

---

211 Podruczny, Przerwa, *Twierdza Srebrna Góra*, p.123.

212 Plan der Stadt und Festung Brieg/so wie Selbige mit seinem Environs sich gegenwartig befindet, in November 1766 leve et dessine par Gerherdt, SBB PK, ref. X 20998; Stadt Schweidnitz, SBB PK, ref. X 33650–7; Plan von der Vestung Gross Glogau/Wie solche sich an jetzo im stande befindet, SBB PK, ref. X 25133/1; Plan von Glatz nach der Aufnahme im Jahre 1763, SBB PK, ref. X 25107–20.

213 Bleyl, *Silberberg*, p.22; Franczak, Grabowski, Nowiński, Żebrowski, *Twierdza Grudziądz*, p.97.

214 Letters of the King to Walrave, von Bredow and Prince von Zerbst, 11 January, 18 April and 4 July 1744, GStA SPK, I HA Rep.96 B Abschriften von Kabinetsordres, Bd.28, p.29; Bd.29, p.381; Bd.30, p.103.

215 Letter from the King to Heinze, 15 April 1775, GStA SPK, I HA Rep.96 B Abschriften von Kabinetsordres, Bd.74, vol.1775, p.115.

216 Verschlage von denen Neuzuerbauende…, SBB PK, ref. X 22010.

217 Letter from the King to Lefèbvre, 24 March 1771, GStA SPK, I HA Rep.96 B Abschriften von Kabinetsordres, Bd.72, vol.VI 1771, p.113.

218 'Die Festung Graudenz', pp.22, 30, 39.

used to procure building stone. For example, between December 1770 and mid-March of the following year, as many as 1,000 people and 66 carts worked in the quarries for the construction of the fortress at Glatz.[219] Also at Graudenz, building stone was gathered in winter, in this case field stone collected by farmers in the fields. This was ordered by the King following a practice previously used in Silesian fortresses, including Schweidnitz and Neisse.[220] Occasionally, essential construction work took place outside the main season. A good example of this is the construction of the fortifications of the Breslau Springstern, which started as early as 7 January.[221] The construction period was also affected by all kinds of violent weather phenomena. The most troublesome was water. In February 1776, an ice march destroyed the fortress under construction on Grabower Kampe. In 1754, July rainfall caused a surge of water in the Oder, which seriously slowed down work in Cosel and Glogau.[222] In the former fortress, the water additionally caused damage that had to be repaired. In coastal fortresses, the sea traditionally caused problems. Not only did it destroy the already existing fortifications (Penemunde in 1745, and Pillau in 1747),[223] but it also hindered work on newly established structures. At Kolberg, during the construction of Fort Münde, strong winds blew for a long time, causing elevated water levels, which made foundation work impossible. Groundwater was also often a problem. Also at Kolberg, too high a water table caused further delays in construction.[224] At Graudenz, on the other hand, problems were caused by underground springs appearing regularly, which flooded construction excavations.[225]

All this meant that construction schedules were very rarely met. As a rule, projects were completed much later than initially planned. The construction at Graudnenz suffered the greatest delays. Work began in 1776 and it was originally scheduled for completion in 1780, but was still underway after the death of Frederick.[226] There was a smaller delay of only three years in the construction of the fortress at Kolberg. According to initial assumptions, it was to be built in a year, but it took four years.[227] Such a protracted period of construction for fortresses was a difficult test for the King's patience. In March 1776, after more than 10 years had passed since the start of work at Silberberg, he wrote to Regler 'Until spring have patience, the fortress will be ready soon.'[228]

219 Letter from the King to Hoym, 10 October 1770, GStA SPK, I HA Rep.96 B Abschriften von Kabinetsordres, Bd.71, p.491 verso.
220 Gotzenbach letter, 23 December 1775, Kl. Grabow, GStA SPK, IV HA Rep.1 Nr. 104, p.12.
221 Menzel, *Topographische Chronik*, p.876.
222 Letters from Lattorff and Sers to the King, 1, 4, 8 and 11 August 1754, GStA SPK Geheimes Zivilkabinett I HA Rep.96 No. 616 – Schlesische Festungen, Bd.G, pp.47, 51–55.
223 Letter from the King to Humbert, 20 February 1745, GStA SPK, I HA Rep.96 B Abschriften von Kabinetsordres, Bd.30, p.364; GStA SPK Geheimes Zivilkabinett I HA Rep.96 No. 616, Bd.J, Pillau 1749–51.
224 APS, AMK ref. 65/202/0/3657, pp.31–32.
225 Franczak, Grabowski, Nowiński, Żebrowski, *Twierdza Grudziądz*, pp.89–91.
226 Letter from the King to Gotzenbach, 9 July 1776, GStA SPK, IV HA Rep.1 Nr. 104, p.45; Franczak, Grabowski, Nowiński, Żebrowski, *Twierdza Grudziądz*, pp.86–96.
227 APS, AMK ref. 65/202/0/3657, p.30.
228 Letter from the King to Regler, 27 March 1776, GStA SPK, I HA Rep.96 B Abschriften von Kabinetsordres, Bd.75, p.249.

Contractors

A topic related to the organisation of the construction of fortresses that requires separate treatment is the question of workers – both ordinary day labourers and specialists. The workforce to be deployed always exceeded local resources, sometimes even those of the region. The King, as the disposer of national resources, played a key role in the process of organising the workforce. His decisions in this area significantly influenced the pace of fortress construction.

1740–1756

During this period, efforts were initially made to build fortresses with the workforce of the local communities. The earliest mention of the organisation of manpower for the fortresses comes from January 1742. At that time, the King decided that 3,000 workers for fortress construction were to be provided by the Upper Silesian states.[229] It is likely that this referred only to labourers for earthworks, as the masonry work at Neisse and Brieg, which had been under construction since 1742, was to be carried out by a private firm, the Rottengatter brothers. In February 1742, the King made his arrangements more specific; workers were to be recruited from Upper Silesia, especially from the Neisse area.[230] However, a month later he changed his mind and ordered that workers should be taken not only from the Neisse principality, but also from the Münsterberg (Ziębice) principality, Reichenbach (Dzierżoniów) and Frankenstein (Ząbkowice).[231] Even with such an extended area it was not possible to recruit sufficient manpower. In August the hitherto untapped resource, troops quartered in Silesia, was called upon. Initially, the scale of this was small. In a letter of 16 August, the King allowed volunteers from the Neisse garrison to be recruited to work at the fortress.[232] However, it soon became apparent that the army was the only source of labourers in large numbers. As early as February 1743, the King allowed the recruitment of 1,950 soldiers from seven regiments (von Roeder, von Rorck, von Lehwaldt, von Borck, von Dohna, von Persode and a regiment of the Duke of Württemberg).[233] This, however, did not satisfy the need for manpower, especially as, during his visit to Neisse, the King decided to increase the number of labourers building the fortress to 7,000.[234] This, of course, resulted in an even greater involvement of the army in the construction of the fortifications. In August 1743, 3,450 soldiers taken from 10 regiments (von Borck, von Lehwald, von Dohna, von Persode, von Roeder, Hautcharmoy, von Groeben, the regiments of Prince Henrik of Prussia, Prince Louis of Württemberg and the pioneer regiment) were already working in Neisse. Most

---

229 Letter from the King to Schwein, 6 January 1742, GStA SPK, I HA Rep.96 B Abschriften von Kabinetsordres, Bd.24, p.5.
230 Letter from the King to Walrave, 3 February 1742, GStA SPK, I HA Rep.96 B Abschriften von Kabinetsordres, Bd.24, p.65.
231 Letter from the King to Walrave, 9 March 1742, GStA SPK, I HA Rep.96 B Abschriften von Kabinetsordres, Bd.24, p.98.
232 Letter from the King to Walrave, 16 August 1742, GStA SPK, I HA Rep.96 B Abschriften von Kabinetsordres, Bd.24, p.271.
233 Letter from the King to Walrave, 13 February 1743, GStA SPK, I HA Rep.96 B Abschriften von Kabinetsordres, Bd.26, p.68.
234 Klose, Festung Neisse, p.87.

of them sent 100–200 soldiers each to the construction, but some (von Groeben and the pioneer regiment) fielded as many as 500 soldiers.[235]

In the following year, the employment of soldiers for fortress work increased further. In 1744 the needs in this respect (3,000 labourers to Neisse, 1,800 to Cosel, 1,000 to Glatz) were to be met by soldiers who were to be treated as on leave.[236]

Even after the Second Silesian War there were instances of soldiers being employed. Numerous soldiers worked at Schweidnitz. In 1749, earthworks on the fortifications there started on 6 March and 800 soldiers from the von Dohna, Markgraf Heinrich, von Nettelhorst and von Kalsau regiments were employed.[237] A similar situation occurred in April 1751, when soldiers from the von Kalsau, von Brandeis, von Nettelhorst and pioneer regiments worked on the construction of this fortress. Sers asked the King to allocate 100 soldiers each from the Markgraf Heinrich and von Blankensee regiments for the construction work. However, it seems that the bulk of the workers were to be civilians. In a letter (in which he asked the King to increase the number of soldiers to work on the fortress), Sers pointed out that 'as bread is very cheap, so people from the villages are not reporting for work in the same numbers as before, even though this has been announced in all the neighbouring counties.'[238]

The same was true in May 1756, when Sers was building the fortifications at Cosel and asked the King for permission to employ 200 'over-complete' soldiers from the von Lattorf and von Blankensee regiments. The soldiers had to be obtained because the labourers, recruited mainly from among the farmers, were leaving for field work.[239]

A separate and even more troublesome group of workers were the construction specialists. Of course, bricklayers were the most in demand. They must have made up a significant group among all the workers; for example, at Schweidnitz in 1750 there were 1,200 workers, 200 of whom were bricklayers. In Silesia as a whole, the number of bricklayers in demand must have been much higher. As in the case of ordinary labourers, workers in this category were also brought in from distant locations. The city of Breslau in 1742 and 1744 was to supply journeyman masons for the construction of the fortresses at Brieg and Neisse. In March 1742 there were to be 100 of them, in April, 200.[240] However, local forces were not enough, and workers from the more distant provinces of the Prussian state had to be sought. In April 1743, 50 apprentice bricklayers were sent to Neisse from Berlin, in May another 50 were supplied by the Neumark.[241]

235 Letters from the King to Von Groeben and Von Marvitz, 6 August 1743, GStA SPK, I HA Rep.96 B Abschriften von Kabinetsordres, Bd.26, pp.364, 365.

236 Letter from the King to Von Marvitz, 9 March 1744, GStA SPK, I HA Rep.96 B Abschriften von Kabinetsordres, Bd.28, p.147.

237 Letter from von Kalsov, 19 March 1749, GStA SPK Geheimes Zivilkabinett I HA Rep.96 No. 616 – Schlesische Festungen, Bd.E, p.3.

238 Sers' letter, 24 April 1751, GStA SPK, Geheimes Zivilkabinett I HA Rep.96 No. 616 – Schlesische Festungen, Bd.F, p.24.

239 Letter from Sers to the King, 8 May 1756, GStA SPK, Geheimes Zivilkabinett I HA Rep.96 No. 616 – Schlesische Festungen, Bd.H, p.43.

240 APWr, AmWr, 1656 – Fortifications Acta, t1, 1737–1745, pp.23–24, 29–34, 40–41, 55–62, 66–69.

241 Letter from the King to Walrave, 27 April and 1 May 1743, GStA SPK, I HA Rep.96 B Abschriften von Kabinetsordres, Bd.29, pp.417, 433.

Also among the specialised workers were soldiers from the corps of miners, who, as is well known, were primarily used for construction work on the fortress in the period before the Seven Years War.

Of course, all these workers, civilians, and soldiers alike, did not work for free. Workers' wages were important components of the fortress construction budget. In Schweidnitz, for example, 15,066 thalers were spent on the construction of the fortress in April 1750, of which 6,197 thalers were spent on compensation for land taken, 5,160 thalers on materials and 3,707 thalers on workers' wages. A year later, when land compensation no longer played a role, 9,140 thalers were spent in the same period, of which 3,471 thalers for building materials and as much as 5,427 thalers for workers' wages.

In addition to the workers building the fortresses and the engineers supervising their work, an important factor were the construction companies operating as part of these major undertakings. In fact, we can only speak of one company, owned by the Rottengatter brothers.[242] Their company was involved in the construction of fortresses at Brieg, Cosel, Neisse, Glatz and Glogau. They were involved in the construction of Silesian fortresses from the beginning. As early as 3 February 1742, Walrave, who was in charge of fortress construction, signed a contract with them for masonry work on a new enclosure and tête de pont at Brieg.[243] Due to the lack of documents, we can say little more about their activity during the construction of the fortifications there. We only know about their erection of one of Brieg's gunpowder warehouses in 1747.[244] In February 1742, a contract for the construction of the fortress at Neisse was signed with a local entrepreneur.[245] Probably the Rottengatters were involved here as well. Their participation in the construction of this fortress is mentioned in the literature; it was they who were to erect the fortifications in front of the main rampart.[246] Apart from that, they also built fortifications on the northern bank of the Neisse River, especially Fort Preussen.[247] Sources mention their activity at this fortress in 1747 when they rebuilt the fortifications in front of the Capuciner Redoubt.[248] Their activity at Cosel is known from 1745. Initially, they were engaged there in rebuilding the town, which had been destroyed by Prussian bombardment.[249] In addition, of course, they also worked on fortifications. In 1752 they were employed on the main rampart.[250] In 1754 they were extending the fortified tête de pont, while in the spring of 1755 they carried out masonry work on

---

242 There were probably two brothers involved, but it is possible that there were more. In 1745, Cosel was built by Caspar and Theodor Rottehengatter, while Carl and Caspar worked on the same fortress in 1754.
243 Letter to Walrave, 3 February 1742, GStA SPK, I HA Rep.96 B Abschriften von Kabinetsordres, Bd.24, p.65. When writing the name of the entrepreneur, the King made a mistake and wrote 'Gathen Gatter'.
244 GStA SPK, Geheimes Zivilkabinett I HA Rep.96 No. 616 – Schlesische Festungen, Bd.D, p.52.
245 Letter to Walrave, 2 February 1742, GStA SPK, I HA Rep.96 B Abschriften von Kabinetsordres, Bd.24, p.58.
246 Minsberg 1834, *Geschichtliche Darstellung*, p.188; Klose, *Festung Neisse*, p.83. Both authors misidentify the Rottengatters and write about the involvement of engineer *Major* Rottengatter in the construction of the fortress.
247 Klose, *Festung Neisse*, p.87.
248 GStA SPK, Geheimes Zivilkabinett I HA Rep.96 No. 616 – Schlesische Festungen, Bd.D, p.19.
249 Weltzel, Geschichte der Stadt, p.273.
250 GStA SPK, Geheimes Zivilkabinett I HA Rep.96 No. 616 – Schlesische Festungen, Bd.G, p.77.

the construction of the new covered way in Cosel.[251] The Rottengatters' business was not limited to Upper Silesia. In 1746 they carried out construction work as part of the reconstruction work at Glogau.[252] They also built the Schäferberg fort at Glatz; sources mention their activity at this site in 1747,[253] and in the period from September 1748 to July 1750.[254]

These entrepreneurs were limited in their activities to masonry work only. The scope of their duties is known thanks to a surviving contract for work on the reconstruction of Cosel's covered way and on the construction of the casemate in the fortified tête de pont. According to this document, the Rottengatters were only to work on masonry. They were not responsible for any other work, neither earthworks nor foundations. The company sourced the building materials itself. For their work they were to be paid monthly in cash at a rate of three thalers for each cubic toise of masonry erected.[255]

There is a suggestion in older literature that they were Walrave's helpers in his fraudulent financial practices.[256] However, this was not the case. It was the Rottengatters who were Walrave's victims, due to his financial embezzlement they were not paid the enormous sum of 80,000 thalers for the construction of fortresses.[257] As late as 1750, the unpaid debt from the state amounted to 47,652 thalers.[258] The repayment still took many years. An amount of 18,000 thalers was received in 1753, another 15,000 in 1754, and in 1755, 14,329 thalers.[259] These sums, in addition to the scale of Walrave's guilt, also indicate the great importance of the work carried out by the Rottengatters' company. This aspect is illustrated in detail by documents relating to the financing of the construction of fortresses. Where there was little masonry work, their pay was a small part of the construction costs. An example of this is the rebuilding in 1746 of the ramparts guarding the Capuciner Redoubt at Neisse. The total cost of the work was 29,450 thalers; the Rottengatters were paid 4,543 thalers of this. However, where the wall was an essential part of the fortification, the share of their wages in the construction was considerable. The reconstruction of the main rampart at Cosel in 1752 cost 17,187 thalers, of which the Rottengatters received 9,440 thalers.[260]

---

251 Paginen betrofen bauten in der Festung Cosel 1748 u. 1754, SBB PK, DPG ref. VII Cosel, 112, document no. 2; GStA SPK, Geheimes Zivilkabinett I HA Rep.96 no. 616 – Schlesische Festungen, Bd.H, p.13.
252 GStA SPK, Geheimes Zivilkabinett I HA Rep.96 No. 616 – Schlesische Festungen, Bd.C, pp.15–17.
253 Letter of 5 December 1750, GStA SPK, Geheimes Zivilkabinett I HA Rep.96 No. 616 – Schlesische Festungen, Bd.E, p.55.
254 GStA SPK, Geheimes Zivilkabinett I HA Rep.96 No. 616 – Schlesische Festungen, Bd.E, p.48.
255 Paginen betrofen bauten in der Festung Cosel 1748 u. 1754, SBB PK, DPG ref. VII Cosel, 112, document no. 2.
256 Bonin, *Geschichte des Ingenieurkorps*, p.58.
257 Priesdorf, *Soldatisches Führerthum*, vol.1, pp.230–232; König, Biographisches Lexikon, Bd.4, pp.148–151.
258 Sers letter of 5 December 1750, GStA SPK, Geheimes Zivilkabinett I HA Rep.96 No. 616 – Schlesische Festungen, Bd.E, p.54.
259 GStA SPK, Geheimes Zivilkabinett I HA Rep.96 No. 616 – Schlesische Festungen, Bd.F, p.53; Bd.G, pp.13–16, 68.
260 Inventory of expenditures for the fortress Cosel from June 1752 to May 1754, Hautcharmoy, GStA SPK Geheimes Zivilkabinett I HA Rep.96 No. 616 – Schlesische Festungen, Bd.G, 1753–54, p.77.

1763–1786

After 1763, there were similar problems relating to contractors. As before, soldiers were resorted to as labour. As early as 1764, the King allowed soldiers with masonry or carpentry qualifications to be employed in the construction of fortifications. Not only were these soldiers on leave, but they were not even called up for the duration of manoeuvres.[261] However, the use of this labour force was relatively rare. In the rebuilding of the fortress at Schweidnitz, 180 carpenter-grenadiers were employed in 1764.[262] In the same fortress in May 1783, in the rebuilding of the forts, 46 soldiers from von Erlach's regiment were used.[263] Soldiers were also utlised during the construction of fortresses on the Vistula. During the work at Grabow in March 1775, soldiers from Stutterheim's regiment worked there.[264] Also, at Graudenz in 1777, due to the shortage of masons, recruitment of labourers was allowed from among the soldiers.[265]

The overall demand for labourers was comparable to that before 1756 and was met by the local civil authorities. The authorities were obliged to organise construction workers and people with horses and carts.[266] Wages of varying amounts were paid for this work. As a rule, it was four *Silber Groschen* per construction worker and two thaler for peasants with four-horse carts who were used for transport work.[267]

In Silesia, workers were organised by the minister there, Count von Hoym. In 1770, he was to supply 1,000 labourers and 66 four-horse carts to Glatz for the winter, and 350 labourers and 24 carts to Silberberg.[268] With the onset of spring, the number of labourers increased. From March 1771, the construction work at Silberberg required the Silesian ministry to supply 800 labourers and 40 carts, from April, a total of 1,800 labourers per day. Fewer were needed at Neisse, where only 700 workmen and 30 carts were to be employed.[269] A year later Hoym was charged with delivering 2,500 labourers and 70 carts to Glatz and 800 labourers and 30 carts to Silberberg.[270] These figures are incomplete, and there is no information about the labourers needed for the work in the other Silesian fortresses under construction at the time. There were certainly a lot of them working, as the civilian population complained loudly about the excessive workload. Discontent was widespread and loudly expressed. In 1769, a complaint about the necessity of work at the Silberberg fortress (calling it the 'Silberberg misery') was lodged by the landrats and peasants of the Strehlen (Strzelin)

261 Bonin, *Geschichte des Ingenieurkorps*, p.100.
262 GStA SPK, I HA Rep 96 Tit 93 B De Daries.
263 Rapport von deren Koeniglichen Fortificatons Arbeiten zu Schweidnitz, 12 May 1783, SBB PK, ref. X 33655/30–4.
264 Letter from the King to Heinze, 8 March 1775, GStA SPK, I HA Rep.96 B Abschriften von Kabinetsordres, Bd.74, p.6.
265 Anon., 'Friedrich der Große als Ingenieur', pp.28–29.
266 Bonin, *Geschichte des Ingenieurkorps*, p.99.
267 Bleyl, *Silberberg*, p.22.
268 Letter from the King to Minister von Hoym, 10 October 1770, GStA SPK, I HA Rep.96 B Abschriften von Kabinetsordres, Bd.71, p.491 verso.
269 Letter from the King to Minister von Hoym, 10 February 1771, GStA SPK, I HA Rep.96 B Abschriften von Kabinetsordres, Bd.72, p.56.
270 Letter from the King to Minister von Hoym, 19 February 1772, GStA SPK, I HA Rep.96 B Abschriften von Kabinetsordres, Bd.73, p.75.

district.[271] In the spring of 1771, complaints about the workload of the population were lodged by the landrats of the Hirschberg (Jelenia Góra), Bunzlau (Bolesławiec), Löwenberg (Lwówek Śląski) and Jauer (Jawor) districts. They complained in particular about work at Glatz, where peasants were engaged in stone quarrying.[272] The complaints were successful and the daily wage for workers was increased.[273]

In Pomerania, the Stettin chamber had only one fortress to service – Kolberg, which took four years to build. For its construction it had to supply 1,500 thousand labourers and 100 carts per day in 1771, and in 1772, 2,700 thousand labourers and 100 carts per day.[274]

The greatest difficulties were encountered in gathering an adequate number of labourers to work on the new fortresses on the Vistula. In the first year of the construction at Grabow, the Marienwerder chamber was to supply as many as 4,000 labourers.[275] Estimating the continuation of the Grabow fortress in 1776, the plan was to employ even more, as many as 5,000 labourers, 150 four-horse carts, and 100 masons every day. The labourers and transport were to be provided by the surrounding war-dominion chambers from Marienwerder, Königsberg and Gumbinnen. Initially there was trouble with this, as the engineer Gotzenbach complained to the King.[276] According to the King, the chambers there were not yet skilled in building fortresses.[277] In the end, in order to facilitate the circulation of orders, the King decided that all needs in this matter should be communicated by the engineer to the First President of East and West Prussia, Johann Friedrich von Domhardt, who, like Hoym in Silesia, was to organise centrally both the recruitment of men and the supply of building materials.[278]

Such an organisation of labour was necessary, because after the location of the new fortress was moved to Graudenz, the demand for labour increased even more. In 1777, 6,981 workers were employed on the construction of this fortress, and in 1778, 5,300.[279] In 1782, more than 7,000 people were working there; 4,180 labourers from East Prussia and 3,282 from Lithuania.[280] A year later, there were initially 2,850 there, and after the annual manoeuvres, 4,520.[281]

Just as before the outbreak of the Seven Years War, after 1763 there was a great deal of difficulty in securing an adequate number of building specialists. In this period, however,

271   Bleyl, *Silberberg*, p.76.
272   Letter from the King to Tauentzien, 19 April 1771, GStA SPK, I HA Rep.96 B Abschriften von Kabinetsordres, Bd.72, vol. VI 1771, p.150.
273   A royal order to this effect has not been found; it is known from the King's letter to Regler, 3 July 1771, in which the King stated that, due to the increase in the day labourers' wages, the new cost estimate for the construction of the fortress exceeds the amount set aside for Glatz for 1771. GStA SPK, I HA Rep.96 B Abschriften von Kabinetsordres, Bd.72, vol. VI 1771, p.253.
274   Letters from the King to Franseky, 21 October 1770, 2 December 1771 and 24 January 1772, GStA SPK, I HA Rep.96 B Abschriften von Kabinetsordres, Bd.71, p.502 verso; Bd.72, p.430; Bd.73, p.4.
275   Letter from the King to Heinze, 21 June 1775, GStA SPK, I HA Rep.96 B Abschriften von Kabinetsordres, Bd.74, p.322.
276   Letter from the King to Gotzenbach, 13 January 1776, GStA SPK, IV HA Rep.1 No. 104, p.15.
277   Letter from the King to Gotzenbach, 27 December 1775, GStA SPK, IV HA Rep.1 No. 104, p.13.
278   Letter from the King to Gotzenbach, 31 January 1776, GStA SPK, IV HA Rep.1 No. 104, p.20.
279   Franczak, Grabowski, Nowiński, Żebrowski, *Twierdza Grudziądz*, p.98.
280   Gotzenbach letter, 20 November 1782, GStA SPK, I HA Rep 96 No 93 Ll1 Gontzenbach.
281   Anon., 'Friedrich der Große als Ingenieur', p.31.

specialists of all kinds – bricklayers, stonemasons, brick makers or miners – became a sought-after commodity. Whereas in the preceding period the need for such workers was met by importing them from various parts of Silesia and Prussia, after 1763 workers from outside Prussia, even from very distant European countries, were used with great frequency.

In Silesia, the largest number of foreign specialists were brought in to build the fortress at Silberberg with 600 masons being brought there from Bohemia.[282] Also, as previously discussed, stone masons were brought in from Piedmont. It is possible that they worked not only at Silberberg, but also at Glatz.

Imported building specialists were also sought for the fortresses along the Vistula. For Grabow, it was planned to bring 100 masons, 70 brick makers and 40 carpenters from Thuringia, however, it is not known how many were eventually obtained.[283] After the work was moved to Graudenz, it was initially planned to maintain this number of specialists. The task of importing 100 journeyman masons from abroad was given to the master masons Mader and Leidhold from Potsdam, who began their search in June 1776.[284] By December, it turned out that they had only been able to recruit 40 masons, whereas in the meantime the needs had increased considerably, as Gotzenbach had placed a demand for 200 journeyman masons for 1777.[285] The recruiters persevered in their search for labour; by April 1777 they had managed to supply a total of 210 masons. However, the building needs continued to grow; in the same month Gotzenbach put the number of masons he needed at 500. The King pressed his recruiters and ordered them to look for masons in Thuringia and Silesia.[286] By June of that year, they had managed to bring in a further 70 masons, but this was still not enough and the King again urged them to search intensively for the remaining 200 craftsmen needed.[287] A different kind of specialist – brick makers – were sought from other areas of Prussia, especially from the Duchy of Kleeve and from around Magdeburg. As it turned out, although there were plenty of this type of craftsmen in Kleeve, it was expensive to bring them in. This was because they were only masters with families, who made their possible arrival conditional on extra money to reimburse their families' travel expenses. Later, the King ordered that a master brick maker with several families of brick makers be brought from Belgium to settle here and train local people in the trade. This did not succeed, however, so 55 brick makers were brought from the Magdeburg area, 45 from Saxony, Mecklenburg and Poland, and 80 from East Prussia. A master bricklayer, Walter, was also brought in from Mannheim.[288]

---

282 Tomasz Przerwa, *Dzieje Srebrnej Góry* (Srebrna Góra: Srebrnogórska Oficyna Wydawnicza, 1998), p.20.
283 Letter from the King to Gotzenbach, 13 January and 18 February 1776, GStA SPK, IV HA Rep.1 No. 104, pp.15 and 23.
284 Letter from the King to Mader and Leidhold, 7 June 1776, GStA SPK, I HA Rep.96 B Abschriften von Kabinetsordres, Bd.75, p.479.
285 Letter from the King to Mader, 19 December 1776, GStA SPK, I HA Rep.96 B Abschriften von Kabinetsordres, Bd.75, p.900.
286 Letter from the King to Mader and Leidhold, 5 April 1777, GStA SPK, I HA Rep.96 B Abschriften von Kabinetsordres, Bd.76, p.284 recto.
287 Letters from the King to Mader and Leidhold, 2 and 16 June 1777, GStA SPK, I HA Rep.96 B Abschriften von Kabinetsordres, Bd.77, pp.37 recto and 53 recto.
288 'Die Festung Graudenz', pp.31–33.

Another group of specialist workers worthy of separate mention were the miners. The first group for the Silberberg fortress was brought from abroad by *Berg Hauptman* von Justi as early as 1766, with *Oberst* Regler also participating in the process.[289] In 1768, the King again ordered miners to be brought in from the Reich. This time the recruitment was handled by *Oberbergmeister* Rück. This official recruited a certain number of miners in Thuringia, with whom the contract was signed on 4 May 1768.[290] Initially the group was small; in November 1769 there were only 26 miners, but the King insisted that as many as 100 be found.[291] This number was reached in early 1770. According to the King's instructions, the miners were to be assigned to work at the strongholds of Silberberg and Glatz, and when the work was completed, to join the ranks of the miners' companies.[292] Silberberg miners also came from the Palatinate, Trier and Nassau.[293] In 1776, the King again reached out to foreign miners. In June of that year, he ordered Regler to bring another 100 miners from the Harz, Freiburg, or the Erzgebirge. These miners were to be brought to Graudenz and, in the King's mind, ultimately to form the 4th Miners' Company.[294] Regler hired the *Oberbergmeister* Rück, already known from Silberberg, for this purpose, and he arrived in Graudenz in October 1776 with a group of 110 miners.[295]

To the miners recruited, the Prussian state not only provided work, but also reimbursed travel expenses. In the case of the first group to reach Silberberg, the amount was 1,500 thalers, in the case of the Graudenz group it was as much as 5,452 thalers. Each miner was to be reimbursed three silver Groschen per mile travelled. They were also better paid than ordinary workers. At Silberberg in 1768, their basic daily wage was six silver Groschen, rising to seven to eight silver Groschen for piecework. The miners at Graudenz were offered a basic rate of eight silver Groschen per day. An additional benefit granted to miners brought to Silberberg with their families was free accommodation, fuel, and lighting materials. The situation was similar in Graudenz, where foreign workers were granted building plots free of charge.[296]

A final, quite distinct category of workers were sculptors. Architectural details, requiring skilled stone carvers, appeared relatively frequently in fortresses, mainly on fortress gates. Examples of this have survived to this day at Glatz and Silberberg, and rich sculptural decorations are also known of at Breslau. Unfortunately, the artists who made these elements are extremely rarely mentioned in the sources. In the period before the Seven Years War, 'the local sculptor Anthon Jörg' is mentioned in the context of work at Neisse.[297] A second

289 Letters from the King to Regler and von Justi, 7, 9 and 29 November 1765 and 30 April 1766, GStA SPK, I HA Rep.96 B Abschriften von Kabinetsordres, Bd.69, pp.40, 48, 49, 120.
290 Regler's letter, 28 January 1769, GStA SPK, I HA Rep 96 no 94, Bbb Regler. pp.20–22.
291 Letter from the King to Regler, 5 November 1769, GStA SPK, I HA Rep.96 B Abschriften von Kabinetsordres, Bd.71, p.252 verso.
292 Letter from the King to Regle, 17 January 1770, GStA SPK, I HA Rep.96 B Abschriften von Kabinetsordres, Bd.71, p.312 verso.
293 Przerwa, Dzieje Srebrnej Góry, p.20.
294 Letter from the King to Regler, 7 June 1776, GStA SPK, I HA Rep.96 B Abschriften von Kabinetsordres, Bd.75, p.474.
295 Letter from the King to Gotzenbach, 28 October 1776, GStA SPK, IV HA Rep.1 No. 104, p.57.
296 Franczak, Grabowski, Nowiński, Żebrowski, *Twierdza Grudziądz*, p.98.
297 GStA SPK, Geheimes Zivilkabinett I HA Rep.96 No. 616 – Schlesische Festungen, Bd.E, p.49.

Fortress Breslau, Frederick Gate. (GStA SPK, XI HA ref. D 70140)

sculptor is noted in the context of the construction of the Frederick Gate at Breslau. The panoplies there were to be made by the Breslau sculptor Stein.[298]

Funding

Financial issues constantly appear in the archival material on the construction of the fortress. The King also took this matter very seriously, as the fate of Walrave perfectly illustrates. Reading Frederick's correspondence with his engineers, one might even get the impression that the cost of a defensive structure was more important to the ruler than its design. Therefore, it is also important to present this aspect of fortification architecture in the Frederician era. Unfortunately, the surviving archival materials allow us to deal with this issue only in a piecemeal way. Relatively abundant information is available for the years 1746–1756, while less is preserved for earlier years (1741–1745) and later years (1763–1786). Nevertheless, the information collected gives some insight into the problem and allows conclusions to be drawn.

---

298 Friedrich Albert Zimmermann, *Beschreibung der Stadt Breslau im Herzogtum Schlesien* (Brieg: Johann Ernst Tramp, 1794), p.437.

1740-1756

It is relatively easy to determine the scale of expenditure on fortification construction during this period. From 1742, the first full construction season, until 1756, a sum of 2,581,000 thalers was spent on Silesian fortresses.[299] Outside of Silesia, only small amounts were spent on the unfinished modernisation of Peitz (11,300)[300] and on the reconstruction of fortresses at Peenemünde, Swinemünde and Anklamer Fehrschanze. Funding for the construction of fortresses came mainly from two sources during this period: the Silesian Ministry and the Berlin *General Kriegs Kasse*. Only for certain years can it be determined how large the contribution of each of these institutions was. In the 1749–1750 season, 216,000 thalers were spent on the construction of Silesian fortresses, 60,000 of which came from the funds of the *General Kriegs Kasse*.[301] In the following season, the Silesian Ministry spent 100,000 thalers on the construction of fortresses, the *Kriegs Kasse*, 60,000.[302] The same amount was spent from this source in the 1753–1754 season, while only 50,000 thalers were spent from Silesian sources. In 1755, the last year for which we have data, 50,000 thalers were spent from the budget of the Silesian ministry, while only 30,000 thalers were spent from the Berlin fund.[303]

It is also possible to determine, to a certain approximation, the amounts spent on individual fortresses. The fortress at Neisse cost by far the most – by 1747 alone, as much as 879,900 thalers had been spent on it. In the same period, 198,000 thalers were spent on Glatz, 137,000 on Cosel and 92,000 thalers on Brieg. In total, approximately 1,307,000.[304] Missing from this list is expenditure on the fortress at Glogau, which should be estimated at approximately 130,000 thalers.[305] How the remaining 1,000,000 thalers spent to 1756 was distributed can only be determined in general terms. A significant part of this amount was spent on the fortress at Schweidnitz. According to the original cost estimate, 384,907 thalers were planned to be spent on it.[306] However, in the end it cost considerably more, nearly 500,000 thalers. Between June 1748 and January 1750 132,636 thalers were spent at Schweidnitz, in 1750 and 1751 100,000 thalers each year, in 1752 85,000 for the completion of the previously

---

299 This sum consists of the amounts actually spent in 1742–1751 and the amounts used to finance the construction of fortresses in 1752–1756. GStA SPK Geheimes Zivilkabinett I HA Rep.96 No. 616 – Schlesische Festungen, Bd.F, pp.1, 29–32, 57; Bd.G, pp.13–15, 68; Bd.H, p.34.

300 Mende, 'Eine formidable Festung?', pp.307–325.

301 GStA SPK, Geheimes Zivilkabinett I HA Rep.96 No. 616 – Schlesische Festungen, Bd.E, pp.4–6.

302 GStA SPK, Geheimes Zivilkabinett I HA Rep.96 No. 616 – Schlesische Festungen, Bd.E, pp.9–10.

303 GStA SPK, Geheimes Zivilkabinett I HA Rep.96 No. 616 – Schlesische Festungen, Bd.F, p.57; Bd.G, pp.13–15.

304 GStA SPK, Geheimes Zivilkabinett I HA Rep.96 No. 616 – Schlesische Festungen, Bd.F, p.57; Bd.D, p.7.

305 This is the only amount we know of in relation to the cost of rebuilding Glogau; this was the cost estimate for rebuilding the fortress by the engineer Unfried. However, this cost estimate was criticised by the King, not so much by the amount, but by the fact that it was not agreed with the King. However, the comments that the King made on this project suggest that also the final cost estimate for the rebuilding of this fortress carried out by Walrave was not materially different. Letter from the King to Walrave, 2 March 1742, GStA SPK, I HA Rep.96 B Abschriften von Kabinetsordres, Bd.24, pp.88–89.

306 Summary estimate of fortresses signed by Walrave and Sers, in *Kostenaufschlage, Brouillons zu deren angefertigte Estimations und der... calculiertes alt und neues Mauerwerck der Vestung Schweidnitz*, SBB PK, ref. X 33650, undated, unpaginated collection of documents attached to the plan SBB PK, ref. X 33650. GStA SPK, Geheimes Zivilkabinett I HA Rep.96 No. 616 – Schlesische Festungen, Bd.E, p.2.

started defence works and the new Wasser Redoubt (two forts, two redoubts), in 1753 45,000 for the Wasser Fort, and in 1754 30,000 for the barracks.[307] Financial plans from the end of 1747 also envisaged spending 110,815 thalers on further work at Glogau, 109,875 thalers on fortifications at Neisse, and 52,000 thalers on work at Glatz. The same document also mentions a sum of 48,274 thalers allocated for 1748 for the completion of works at Cosel. In total, the planned expenditure, apart from on Schweidnitz, was to amount to 319,000 thalers.[308] Of course, the estimates were quickly revised. In the next spending plan for the Silesian fortresses (drawn up in 1749), completely new expenditures appear; over 200,000 thalers for Glatz (instead of the previously mentioned 52,000) and another expenditure at Cosel of 29,000 thalers.[309] At a later stage these estimates changed again. Glatz cost less (instead of the planned 124,000 thalers the town fortifications were cost at 74,000 thalers),[310] while the expenditure on Cosel increased. In December 1753, the King decided to rebuild Cosel once again, which was to cost over 60,000 thalers.[311]

1763–1786

The period after the Seven Years War definitely differs from the previous one in terms of funding. The main difference is the amount of money spent on the fortresses – they were definitely higher than before the war. The fortress at Silberberg alone was to have cost, from the beginning of its construction in 1765 until 1785, the sum of 1,459,973 thalers.[312] The development of the defences at Kolberg was to have cost 479,594 thalers,[313] about 110,000 thalers were lost in the destroyed Grabow fortress,[314] and as much as 3,171,000 thalers were spent in the construction of the fortress at Graudenz.[315] This last fortress cost more than all the fortification works in Silesia in the previous period. The overall cost of works in Prussian fortresses in this period closed with an even higher amount, as, apart from the four mentioned fortresses, serious investments were also carried out in five Silesian fortresses: Glogau, Breslau, Cosel, Neisse, Glatz and Schweidnitz. One nineteenth-century military historian quoted a sum of 4,146,000 thalers to be spent on Silesian fortresses during the entire Frederician period.[316] It is unlikely that this amount is so low. If one were to subtract from it the expenditure in the pre-war period (2,581,000 thalers) and the already

307 GStA SPK, Geheimes Zivilkabinett I HA Rep.96 No. 616 – Schlesische Festungen, Bd.E, pp.7–8, 12–13, 33–34; Bd.F, pp.1, 29–31, 38, 53, 57; Bd.G, pp.13–16, 49.

308 GStA SPK, Geheimes Zivilkabinett I HA Rep.96 No. 616 – Schlesische Festungen, Bd.E, pp.1–2.

309 GStA SPK, Geheimes Zivilkabinett I HA Rep.96 No. 616 – Schlesische Festungen, Bd.E, pp.12–13.

310 GStA SPK, Geheimes Zivilkabinett I HA Rep.96 No. 616 – Schlesische Festungen, Bd.F, p.34.

311 GStA SPK, Geheimes Zivilkabinett I HA Rep.96 No. 616 – Schlesische Festungen, Bd.G, p.28.

312 Anon., 'Friedrich der Große als Ingenieur', p.19. The same amount, only rounded off, is given by Bonin, Bonin, *Geschichte*, p.99. This amount is also confirmed in the sources, in the King's letter to Regler, 24 April 1776, GStA SPK I HA Rep.96 B Abschriften von Kabinetsordres, Bd.75, p.339.

313 APS, AMK ref. 65/202/0/3657, p.32.

314 In 1775, 400,000 thalers were deposited in the building fund; after the catastrophe, 191,000 remained in the fund, as well as tools and materials worth 100,000. GStA SPK I HA Rep.96 B Abschriften von Kabinetsordres, Bd.73, pp.387–388, 410, 423; King's letter to Gotzenbach, 9 April 1776, GStA SPK, IV HA Rep.1 Nr. 104, p.34.

315 By 1790, expenditure on the fortress amounted to 3671,000 thalers, of which 500,000 thalers were spent between 1787 and 1790. 'Die Festung Graudenz', pp.52–53.

316 Anon., 'Friedrich der Große als Ingenieur', p.32.

known expenditure on the fortress at Silberberg (1,459,000 thalers), only 106,000 thalers would remain. Meanwhile, the total expenditure on Silesian fortresses (apart from that of Silberberg), which appears in Frederick's correspondence for the years 1768, 1770–1772 and 1774–1783, amounts to as much as 2,291,000 thalers.[317] Thus, the above-mentioned figure of 4,146,000 thalers as the total expenditure on Silesian fortresses during the entire Frederician period is incorrect. However, looks like it might be the expenditure only in the period after the Seven Years War. Assuming this to be true and adding the sums spent on fortresses outside Silesia, we obtain the sum of 7,906,000 thalers. As can be seen, after the Seven Years War more than three times as much was probably spent on the construction of fortresses as before 1756.

Unlike in the previous period, after 1763 the money came directly from the local administrations. In Silesia the local ministry paid for the construction of fortresses, in the other provinces it was the local *Kriegs- und Domänenkammer.*

Adding up the accumulated data on the financial effort involved in the construction of fortresses in the period before the Seven Years War (2,581,000 thalers) and after the war (7,906,000 thalers) yields a value of approximately 10.4 million thalers. This is how much was spent on the construction of fortresses during the entire reign of Frederick the Great. This amount may seem enormous, especially when compared to the total expenditure of the Prussian state, which amounted to 6,077,000 thalers in 1740 to reach 16,756,000 thalers in 1786. However, it is worth comparing the individual annual fortress expenditures with the annual budgets of the Prussian state. In the financial year 1749/1750, the Prussian state spent 9,309,000 thalers, of which 8,270,000 was for military purposes and 1,039,000 for civilian purposes.[318] An amount of 216,000 thalers was spent on the construction of fortresses in that year, which accounted for 2.3 percent of total expenditure and 2.6 percent of military expenditure.[319] In the period after the Seven Years War (but before work was undertaken on fortresses outside Silesia) expenditure increased slightly. In 1768 it accounted for 2.5 percent of total expenditure and about 3.2 percent of military expenditure.[320] The share of expenditure on fortresses was even more noticeable when work began at Kolberg and especially on the Vistula. In 1780 they accounted for 2.9 percent of general expenditure and 3.7 percent of military.[321]

---

317 GStA SPK I HA Rep.96 B Abschriften von Kabinetsordres, Bd.70, p.207; Bd.71, pp.394, 473; Bd.72, vol. VII, p.223; Bd.73 (vol. year 1773), p.326; Bd.74, pp.244, 621, 789; Bd.75, p.911; Bd.79, pp.723, 1125; Bd.8,0 p.83; Bd.81, p.420; Bd.82, pp.857, 919. The amount of 172,000 thalers planned for 1778 was not included in this account. Due to the war, no work was carried out in the fortresses that year. GStA SPK, I HA Rep.96 B Abschriften von Kabinetsordres, Bd.77, p.791.
318 Annual expenditure data of the Prussian state, Kamieński, Kucharczyk, Szultka, Łukaszewicz, Wachowia, *Prusy*, p.596.
319 GStA SPK, Geheimes Zivilkabinett I HA Rep.96 No. 616 – Schlesische Festungen, Bd.F, p.32.
320 Letter from the King to Minister Schlabrendorf, 3 May 1768, GStA SPK, I HA Rep.96 B Abschriften von Kabinetsordres, Bd.70, vol.II, p.207.
321 In that year 100,000 thalers were spent on the Silesian fortresses and 300,000 on the Graudenz fortress. Letters of the King to Minister Hoym, 5 November 1779 and to Haab, 5 February 1780, GStA SPK I HA Rep.96 B Abschriften von Kabinetsordres, Bd.79, p.1125; Bd.80, p.83; 'Die Festung Graudenz', p.30.

Financial Control

An important part of the process of spending money on the construction of fortifications was the control of accounts. While cost estimates for the construction of fortresses were approved by the King personally, the control of expenditure was carried out by his subordinates. Initially, the King was satisfied with the reports presented by the engineers. This task was entrusted to the engineer Foris, who as early as February 1742 was to provide the King with a financial report on the sum of 40,000 thalers spent in 1741 on the first works at Neisse.[322] Thereafter, Foris was constantly involved in presenting financial reports to the King. The King appreciated his work and trusted him, as he expressed in his letter to Walrave, clearly questioning Foris' work.[323] However, Foris was killed in 1745 during an attack by Imperial troops on Cosel, of which he was commandant, and after his death the accounts were kept, it seems, by Walrave himself. Although he was checked, (for example Hautcharmoy's check showed delays in payments to contractors), he was, as it later turned out, ineffective.[324] Walrave was thrown into prison after being accused of, among other things, misappropriating money intended for fortresses. Following this incident, the King tightened spending controls considerably. From then on, the engineers in charge of the fortress construction sent financial reports to the King every month. A number of such reports are known, including that of Sers for Schweidnitz.[325] Spending controls covered longer periods: usually the entire accounting year, sometimes an even longer period. These audits were carried out by others, usually the commander of the fortress at Brieg, *Generalmajor* Hautcharmoy,[326] or the commander at Neisse, *Generalmajor* Joachim Christian von Tresckow.[327]

In the second period of fortress construction, after 1763, inspections were initially rare. The first information on this subject is related to Kolberg. There, after the work was completed in 1772, the accounts were checked by the Stettin Chamber and the King himself.[328] The frequency of inspections increased after the building disaster of February 1776, when a flood destroyed the fortress under construction at Grabow. As the King found the culprit of this disaster in the form of the officer in charge of the construction, comte d'Heinze, he also decided to check for irregularities in other fortresses. A comprehensive check of the accounts of Silberberg for the entire first decade of its construction has survived. The King ordered it on 27 March 1776, 11 days after receiving

---

322 Letter from the King to Foris, 22 February 1742, GStA SPK, I HA Rep.96 B Abschriften von Kabinetsordres, Bd.24, p.88.

323 King's letter to Walrave, January 1743, GStA SPK, I HA Rep.96 B Abschriften von Kabinetsordres, Bd.26, p.35.

324 GStA SPK, Geheimes Zivilkabinett I HA Rep.96 No. 616 – Schlesische Festungen, Bd.D, p.39.

325 GStA SPK, Geheimes Zivilkabinett I HA Rep.96 No. 616 – Schlesische Festungen, Bd.E, pp.18, 21, 24, 38; Bd.F, p.25; Bd.G, pp.3, 4.

326 GStA SPK, Geheimes Zivilkabinett I HA Rep.96 No. 616 – Schlesische Festungen, Bd.E, pp.33–34; Bd.F, pp.50–51, Bd.G, pp.73–79; Bd.H, pp.16–17, 28–29.

327 GStA SPK, Geheimes Zivilkabinett I HA Rep.96 No. 616 – Schlesische Festungen, Bd.E, p.46; Bd.F, pp.28, 38; Bd.G, pp.17–18; Bd.H, p.10.

328 APS, AMK ref. 65/202/0/3657, p.32; King's letter to Franseky of 29 March 1774, GStA SPK I HA Rep.96 B Abschriften von Kabinetsordres, Bd.73, vol.1774, p.124.

the full report on Grabow.[329] He charged *General der Infanterie* Friedrich Bogislav von Tauentzien, commander of the Breslau fortress, with the task of carrying it out. At the same time, the King pointed to the Silesian Ministry as the institution which was to assist him in carrying out the inspection. Indeed, Count Hoym was to provide Tauentzien with 'several trusted officials who understood the accounts.' The audit did not reveal any irregularities.[330] Announcing the audit, the King said that he would inspect all fortresses in the same thorough manner.[331] And so he did. In October 1777 he ordered Regler to send the accounts for all Silesian fortresses to the Berlin *Ober Rechnungs Kammer.*[332] Information on the results of this inspection is residual; all that is known is that the accounts from the fortress of Schweidnitz, presented by *Oberst* Daries, were considered correct.[333] This engineer was checked again in 1779 when the secret financial councillor Rheden audited his expenditure on the repair of the fortress of Schweidnitz. As part of the King's correspondence with Daries relating to this particular audit, the King revealed his motives for ordering such a frequent inspection of the accounts. Indeed, in one of his letters, he wrote that 'the management by the engineers of the construction of fortresses is useless, and I do not like it because on such occasions they always have sticky hands and something always sticks to them...'[334] The results of most inspections did not confirm the King's concerns. In the period after 1763, only once did a royal engineer get into trouble because of accounting irregularities. This was *Major* Haab, who was taken into custody in 1779 for poorly managed finances.[335] This engineer clearly did not handle money well, since an inspection of the construction of the fortress at Breslau conducted by him in 1780 revealed unpaid bills amounting to 17,274 thalers.[336] Both of these incidents were probably negligent acts that could be explained and justified, since they did not hinder Haab's career.

The most is known about inspections of Graudenz's finances. The first time the fortress accounts were checked was in 1777. At that time, *Oberst* von Rohr checked the finances for the year 1776. In March 1779, all previous accounts were checked by the Berlin *Ober Rechnungs Kammer.* Finally, in October 1784, the King appointed a separate commission headed by Councillor Lilienthal to check the accuracy of the accounts again. Like the previous ones, this last commission also failed to detect any errors.[337]

---

329 Gotzenbach's letter, 16 March 1776, Kl. Grabow, GStA SPK, IV HA Rep.1 Nr. 104, p.27.
330 King's letters to Regler, 27 March 1776, GStA SPK, I HA Rep.96 B Abschriften von Kabinetsordres, Bd.75, pp.250–251, 339.
331 Letters from the King to Regler, 27 March 1776, GStA SPK, I HA Rep.96 B Abschriften von Kabinetsordres, Bd.75, p.249.
332 Letters from the King to Regler, 13 October 1777, GStA SPK, I HA Rep.96 B Abschriften von Kabinetsordres, Bd.77, p.129 recto.
333 Letters of the King to Daries, 4 December 1777, GStA SPK, I HA Rep.96 B Abschriften von Kabinetsordres, Bd.77, p.175 verso.
334 King's letters to Daries, 10 and 22 September 1779, GStA SPK, I HA Rep.96 B Abschriften von Kabinetsordres, Bd.79, pp.1002, 1026.
335 Letters from the King to Regler, 21 November 1779, GStA SPK, I HA Rep.96 B Abschriften von Kabinetsordres, Bd.79, pp.1158, 1161.
336 Letter from the King to Haab, 4 June 1780, GStA SPK, I HA Rep.96 B Abschriften von Kabinetsordres, Bd.80, p.433.
337 'Die Festung Graudenz', pp.26, 29, 45.

9

Conclusion

The death of Frederick the Great marked the end of a long 46-year period of development of Prussian defence architecture. This almost half-century seriously changed the defensive landscape of the Prussian state. In 1786, the most heavily fortified region was Silesia, defended by eight strong fortresses. In the other regions, the saturation of modern fortifications was less. The Elector's March was defended only by the older fortresses at Magdeburg, Spandau and Küstrin, which were not modernised in this period; the other fortifications that existed there in 1740 had been dismantled. Pomerania was protected by a strong fortress at Stettin, strengthened during the reign of Frederick by the modernised fortifications at Damm, and a modern fortress at Kolberg. Other fortifications were dismantled or abandoned. East Prussia was poorly fortified, where, apart from the small Fort Lyck, no investment was made in fortifications. On the other hand, the province of West Prussia, newly conquered from the Polish–Lithuanian Commonwealth, had a new, strong, but not yet completed fortress in Graudenz. The fortresses in the Prussian estates in western Germany lost their importance during the reign of Frederick the Great; not only were they not modernised, but they were also even subjected to partial liquidation.

During this period not only did the number of fortresses change and the saturation of the various regions of Prussia with them; the appearance of the fortifications themselves also changed. At the beginning of the period in question, ideas and concepts which had appeared in Prussia in the 1720s and 1730s were still being developed, on the basis of designs by Cornelius Walrave. Buildings were being erected which differed only slightly from those of Stettin, Magdeburg or Wesel. However, Frederick's increasing personal design interference, which intensified after Walrave's arrest, resulted in new developments. Completely new concepts emerged for the form of the fortress, an example of which was the fortress of Schweidnitz. Novelties were also introduced into individual defence works. Bomb-proof structures such as caponiers, erected both within the covered way and in the moat, began to appear en masse. In addition, outer works were used much more frequently as elements reinforcing the defence of the fortress core.

The innovations in defensive architecture were even more noticeable in the second period of the development of Prussian fortifications, between the end of the Seven Years War and the death of Frederick the Great. The most important innovations used in this period were the artillery casemates, with which fortresses both in Silesia and outside the province were intensively saturated. New types of defensive structures also appeared, for example heavily fortified Donjons, which, on the one hand, were an adaptation of the medieval model to the needs of the modern fortress, and on the other, were related to the influence of the modern defensive architecture of northern Italy. In addition to drawing architectural patterns from traditions and regions that had hitherto been irrelevant to the development of Prussian defensive architecture, patterns were also drawn from countries that had already provided them to Prussia, the Netherlands and France. However, new solutions, not previously found in Prussia, were also drawn from the architectural traditions of these countries. Finally, there were themes and ideas that stemmed from Prussia's own traditions or were a response to the experience gained in the armed conflicts of the Frederician period. As can be seen, defensive architecture in Prussia during the reign of Frederick the Great was characterised by innovation. Both the fortresses themselves and the large amount of experience gained during their design and construction were the King's legacy, which he left to his successors. In addition, Frederick's successor also received a negative legacy. For this is how the practical abolition of the Corps of Engineers must be judged. Whereas in 1740 the engineers formed a small but compact and well-regarded group of professionals, by the end of Frederick's life they were in practice a group of unconnected individuals, heavily burdened with work, and at the same time poorly assessed and poorly paid. This, however, was quickly corrected by Frederick's successors. Frederick William II, lacking the will to personally hold the helm of the state in all its manifestations, enabled a revolution in fortification. Officers of the engineer corps, previously humiliated, overlooked for promotions, often arrested, and generally discriminated against, after 1786 were put on an equal footing with representatives of the other arms. In addition to this, the structure of the Corps of Engineers was put in order, it was given its own regulations, a system of service dependencies was created and, finally, the head of the Corps was appointed from among the engineers, exercising real authority over it. The reformation of the system, combined with the unusually rich wealth of experience and fortification innovations from Frederick's lifetime, allowed Prussian fortification to flourish in the nineteenth century, which, under the name of the 'New Prussian school', dominated Europe in the first half of the century, gaining a status similar to that enjoyed by Dutch fortification in the seventeenth century and French fortification in the eighteenth century.

Bibliography

Archival Sources

Archiwum Państwowe we Wrocławiu (APWr)
Akta miasta Wrocławia, Sekcja XIII, Fortifications Acta, V. 1, 1656; V. 2, 1657; ref. 1658.
Zespół Personalia, Rep 47/10, Nachweisung der Personen denen seit Antritt der Königlicher
  Preusischer Regierung in Schlesien das Incolat verliehen worden.

Archiwum Państwowe w Szczecinie (APS)
Akta miasta Kołobrzeg, Geschichte der Festung Colberg. Bearbeitet im Jahre 1857 durch den
  Ingenieur-Lieutenent von Woyna, ref. 65/202/0/3657.

Brandenburgisches Ladneshauptarchiv
sing. 8 Soldin 827, Abschrift einer Denkschrift eines preußischen Ingenieur-Offiziers über den
  Festungskrieg

Geheimes Staatsarchiv Stiftung Preusischer Kulturbesitz Berlin (GStA SPK)
I HA, Rep.94, II M 13, Memoire sur L'armee Prusienne en 1784.
I HA, Geheimes Zivilkabinett, Rep.96 B, Abschriften von Kabinetsordres, 1740-1786, Bd.23-86.
I HA, Geheimes Zivilkabinett, Rep.96, nr 83 Hh 2 Foris; nr 93, Pp1Von Haab; nr 93, Pp2,
  Dietrich von Haas (de Haas); nr 94, Bbb Regler; nr 94, Ss 4 Von Pinto, Vinzenz.
I HA, Geheimes Zivilkabinett ,Rep.96, nr 616, Bd.B-H. Bd. J; Bd. L; Bd. M
I HA, Geheimes Zivilkabinett, Rep 96, nr 259 E,
IV HA, Preußische Arme, Rep 15 A, nr 806,
IV HA, Preußische Arme, Rep.1, Geheime Kriegskanzlei, nr 104,
IV HA, Rep 15b, nr 55,

Service Historique de la Défense (SHD), Vincennes
Archives du depot des fortifications
1 V M 56, Breslau
1 V M 131 Glogau;
1 V M 260, Silberberg;

Staatsbibliothek zu Berlin, Stiftung Preussischer Kulturbesitz (SBB PK)
Kartenabteilung Unter den Linden
Silberberg

X 33812-1; X 33812-5,
Hauptmann Freund
X 25134/10-1
Kolberg
X 22010
Schweidnitz
X 33650; X 33655/30- 4
Neisse
X 31029; X 31035/1-2

Denkschriften des Preussischen Generalstabes
VI Colberg, nr 95b
VII Cosel, nr 89, nr 112
XIII Graudenz, nr 59, 12c.
XIX Fort Lyck, nr 126.
XXIV Neisse, nr 100, 101,
XXXIV Schweidnitz, nr 91, nr 97,
XXXV Silberberg, nr 124
XXXII Schlesien, nr 127
IX Glatz, nr 118, nr 119,
XXV Oderberg, nr. 1.
XXVI Peitz

Handschriften Abteilung
Ms. Borussica, fol. 531; fol.733,

Österreichisches Staatsarchiv (OStA), Abteilung Kriegsarchiv
K II f 23 E., C. v. W., Remarques de Glatz.
Alte Feldakten, nr 623 Siebenjähriger Krieg Hauptarmee 1757 XIII (503- Ende) *Faszikel 604,*

Cartography

Archiwum Państwowe Opole
Kartografia Rejencji Opolskiej
III 835; III 845, III 846; III 877

Bibliothèque Nationale de France (BNF)
(accessed via gallica.bnf.fr)
Besançon – EST VE-128
Bois-le-Duc – GED-5614
Brieg – MS-6463 (676)
Halifax – GED-3455
Magdeburg – GE DD-2987
Mainz – MS-6463(690); MS-6464(691)

Philipsbourg – GED-7395; GED-7588
Schweidnitz – MS-6463(673)

Geheimes Staatsarchiv Stiftung Preusischer Kulturbesitz (GStA SPK)
XI. HA, FPK Kriegsministerium, Festungspläne; 1763-1914

Breslau – E 72090
Glatz – A 71685; E 71989; E 71990; E 72000; F 71761; F 71771; F 71774; XI HA, G 70779; G 70791
Graudenz – G 70401
Kolberg – F 71544; E 71839
Neisse – A 71393; E 72101, F 717951 bl. 1.
Schweidnitz – A 71302-1–5; E 71953; F 71629; F 71742; G 70777
Silberberg – A 70001; A 70003; A 70007; B 70001; C 70020; E 70001; F 70320; G 70002; G 70032
Stettin – F 71291

Herzog August Bibliothek Wolfenbüttel
(accessed via deutschefotothek.de)
Pillau – 1.6.1a Aug. 2 °, Bl. 21-22.

Krigsarkivet Sztokholm
(accessed via riksarkivet.se)
Ambleteuse – SE/KrA/0406/13/002/004
Divenau Schantz – SE/KrA/0406/25/051/001
Halifax – SE/KrA/0406/08/005/001
Hertogenbosch – SE/KrA/0406/14/036/007
Peenemünde – SE/KrA/0406/25/200/007; SE/KrA/0406/25/200/008
Wollin – SE/KrA/0406/25/303/002

Książnica Pomorska
K293

Sächsische Landesbibliothek – Staats- und Universitätsbibliothek Dresden (SLUB)
(accessed via deutschefotothek.de)
Anklam, Demmin – SLUB/HS Mscr.Dresd.R.30.m, III, 40
Berlin – SLUB/HS Mscr.Dresd.R.30.m, III, 53
BODT PLANS DE FORTIFICATION – SLUB/HS Mscr.Dresd.i.16, GEL:
Cosel – SLUB/KS A9324
Driesen – SLUB HS Mscr.Dresd.R.30.m,III , 50
Glatz – SLUB/KS A9512,
Glogau – SLUB/HS Mscr.Dresd.R.30.m,III, 66,
Küstrin – SLUB/HS Mscr.Dresd.R.30.m,III, 51
Wolin – SLUB/HS Mscr.Dresd.R.30.m,III, p, 48

Service Historique de la Défense (SHD), Vincennes
Archives du depot des fortifications
1 VN 90 Glogau
1 VM 209 Neisse
1 VM 257 Schweidnitz

Atlas du génie
La Rocca d'Anfo, XIXe siècle. Cote: atlas 183, pl. 3,

Staatsbibliothek zu Berlin, Stiftung Preussischer Kulturbesitz (SBB PK)
Kartenabteilung Unter den Linden
Breslau – X 20663/1; X 20678; X 20678/1; X 20679/5; X 20679/10; X 20679/12; X 20679/13; X 20679/14; X 20683
Brieg – X 20994a; X 20994; X 20998
Cosel – X 28148; X 28148/6a, b, c; X 28150/1; X 28150/5; X 28150/5-1; X 28150/9; X 28150/10; X 28150/12; Da 15.163e; Da 15.163k
Crossen – X 22170
Damm – X 22241-2–10; X 22242
Dittersbach – N 17915 a – 2; N 17915 a 3
Driesen – X 23169/10, X 23169/10 A, B; X 23169/16; X 23173
Fort Lyck – X 29076; X 29076 –1; X 29076 –2; X 29076 –4; X 29076 –5; X 29076 –6
Fort Penemünde – X 31950/25; X 31950/25
Frankfurt an der Oder – X 24562
Geldern – X 25047; X 25048
Glatz – X 25107/6; X 25107/6-1 to 44; X 25107/20; X 25107/30; X 25108 – 1; X 25108 – 2; X 25108 – 3
Glogau – X 25131/10, X 25132; X 25132/13; X 25132/17; X 25132/12; X 25133/1; X 25133/2; X 25134/7; X 25134/10; X 25134/10-1
Grabower Kempe – L 17993
Graudenz – X 25469-1; X 25469-2; X 25469-3; X 25470-1; X 25470-2
Jülich – X 27527
Kolberg – X 22003/2, X 22011; X 22011-1; X 22011-3; X 22011-5; X 22011-6; X 22011-7; X 22012-1; X 22012-2
Königsberg – X 28073; X 29961
Lippstadt – X 28908
Magdeburg – X 29087; X 29089
Memel – X 29956; X 29960/2; X 29960/3; X 29961
Military manoeuvres – Man 1692
Minden – X 30239; X 30239-1; X 30239-2; X 30239-3
Neisse – X 31026; X 31026-2; X 31027; X 31027-4; X 31027-2; X 31027-3; X 31028; X 31029; X 31033; X 31033/2; X 31034; X 31035/3; X 31033/1; X 31035/1
Oderberg – X 31688; X 31684; X 31685; Y 33070
Peitz – X 31958/10-1; X 31958/10 -2, X 31958/17
Pillau – X 32070/5
Schurgast – X 31648

Schweidnitz – X 33650-2; X 33650-4; X 33650-5; X 33650-6; X 33650-7; X 33650-8; X 33650-9;
    X 33650-10; X 33650-11; X 33650-12; X 33650-13; X 33650-14; X 33650-15; X 33650-16;
    X 33650-17; X 33650-18; X 33650-19; X 33652; X 33655/8; X 33655/15; X 33655/20; X
    33655/30; X 33655/35; X 33657; Db 1.33 1914 r; N 15060-68
Silberberg – X 33806; X 33807; X 33807/5; X 33811, k. 1, 2, 3, 4, 5, 6, 7, 8; X 33812-1; X 33812-2;
    X 33812-3; N 19055-1; N 19055/2-1; N 16992/2-4; N 19057; Db 1. 33 1930 b
Spandau – X 33876/10
Stettin – X 34071-3; X 34071-4, X 34079
Swinemünde – X 34845; X 34846; X 34847
Wesel – X 3608/8

Österreichisches Staatsarchiv (OStA), Abteilung Kriegsarchiv
Glatz – K II f 23 F; K II f 24 E; K II f 26-2; K II F 26 E; G I c 203

Research Library in Olomouc (Vědecká knihovna v Olomouci)
Belagerung von Olmütz in A[nn]o 1758, ref. M IV 8

Published Sources

Alexander Hans, *Friedrich der Große und Cosel* (Berlin: Schlieffen Verlag, 1936)
Allent, Pierre A., *Histoire du Corps Impérial du Génie* (Paris: Magimel, 1805)
von Anhalt-Dessau, Leopold, *Deutliche und ausführliche Beschreibung, Wie eine Stadt soll
    belagert werden* (Dessau; Unknown Publisher, 1737)
von Archenholz, Johann Wilhelm, *Geschichte des Siebenjährigen Krieges in Deutschland* (Berlin:
    Haude und Spener, 1793)
Anon., 'Auszug aus einer Instruktion des Königs Friedrich II über Verschanzte Stellungen',
    Archiv für die Offiziere der Königlich Preußischen Artillerie und Ingenieur Korps, 3 (1836),
    pp.243–251
Anon., 'Friedrich der Große als Ingenieur', *Archiv für die Officiere der Königlich Preußischen
    Artillerie und Ingenieur Korps*, 12.1 (1841), pp.1–44
Anon., 'Die Festung Graudenz', *Archiv für die Artillerie und Ingenieur-Offiziere des deutschen
    Reichsheeres*, 81 (1877), pp.1–78; 95–162; 189–229
Anon., *Biographie universelle, ancienne et moderne: supplément, ou Suite de l'histoire, par ordre
    alphabétique, de la vie publique et privée de tous les hommes qui se sont fait remarquer par
    leur écrits, leurs actions, leurs talents, leurs vertus ou leurs crimes* (Paris: L.G. Michaud, 1842)
Anon., *Denkwurdigkeiten der drey Belagerungen Colbergs durch die Russen in den Jahren 1758,
    1760 und 1761* (Frankfurt-Leipzig: Unknown Publisher, 1763)
Anon., *Diarium der Belagerung von Breslau und Capitulations-Puncte von der Übergabe an Seine
    Königliche Majestät in Preussen…* (Berlin: Unknown Publisher, 1758)
Anon., *Le dictionnaire de l'Académie françoise* (Paris: Coignard, 1694)
Anon., *Dictionnaire de l'académie française* (Paris: Bernard Brunet, 1762)
Anon., 'Die Erstürmung von Schweidnitz durch den Feldzugmeister Freiherrn v. Loudon am 1
    October 1761', *Österreichische Militärische Zeitschrift* (1860), vol.1, pp.258–287

Anon., 'Geschichte des zweiten schlesischen Krieges', *Oestreichische militärische Zeitschrift* (1825) vol.3, H.7, pp.1–32; H.8, pp.109–150; H.9 pp.254–275

Anon., *Geschichte des preußisch schwedischen Krieges in Pommern, der Mark und Mecklenburg 1757- 1762: Zugleich als Beitrag zur Geschichte des Siebenjährigen Krieges* (Berlin: Mittler und Sohn, 1858)

Anon., *Katalog der Bibliothek und Kartensammlung der Königlichen allgemeinen Kriegsschule* (Berlin: Schade, 1851)

Anon., *Kurzgefaßte Stamm und Rangliste der Königl. Preußischen Armee für das Jahr 1792* (Berlin: Christian Friedrich Himburg, 1792)

Anon., *Kurzgefaßte Stamm und Rangliste der Königl. Preußischen Armee von deren Stiftung an bis Ende 1785* (Berlin: Christian Friedrich Himburg, 1785)

Anon., 'Todesfälle 1789', *Schlesische Provinzialblätter*, 5, May 1789, pp.469–482

Aubin, Nicolas, *Dictionnaire de marine contenant les termes de la navigation et de l'architecture navale* (Amsterdam: Pierre Brunel, 1702)

Bartsch, Josef August, *Olmütz im Jahre 1758 und seine frühere Kriegsgeschichte: Denkschrift zur hundertjährigen Jubiläumsfeier des Entsazes von Olmütz am 2. Juli 1758* (Olmütz: Slawik, 1858)

Bailac, Jean Baptiste, *Nouvelle chronique de la ville de Bayonne* (Bayonne: Duhart-Fauvet, 1827)

Bär, Max, *Westpreussen unter Friedrich dem Grossen* (Leipzig: S. Hirzel, 1909)

Beckmann, Johann Christoph, *Kurze Beschreibung der Alten Loeblichen Stadt Franckfurt an der Oder* (Frankfurt an der Oder: Unknown Publisher, 1706)

de Bélidor, Bernard Forest, *La Science des ingénieurs dans la conduite des travaux de fortification et d'architecture civile* (Paris: Jombert, 1729)

de Bélidor, Bernard Forest, *Architecture hydraulique seconde partie, qui comprend l'art de diriger les eaux de la Mer & des Rivieres a l'avantage de la defence des Places, du Commerce & de l'agriculture, tome premier* (Paris: Jombert, 1750)

de Belidor, Bernard Forest, *Dictionaire portatif de l'ingenieur et de l'artilleur* (Paris: Jombert, 1768)

Bimler, Kurt, *Die Schlesische Massive Wehrbauten* (Breslau: Heyderbrand Verlag, 1940–44)

Biranowska-Kurtz, Alicja, *Świnoujście. Fortyfikacje nowożytne w planach, projektach i rycinach* (Szczecin: Univers, 2005)

Biskup, Krzysztof, 'Der Bau der Festung Lötzen', in Schmidtchen, Volker (ed.), *Festungsforschung als kommunale Aufgabe* (Wesel: Deutsche Gesellschaft für Festungsforschung, 1986), pp.167–168

Biskup, Krzysztof, 'Flesza Nowomłyńska w Świdnicy. Historia i współczesne uwarunkowania konserwatorskie', *Infort*, 1996, no.2, pp.2–12

Bleyl, Wolfgang, *Silberberg, die Passfestung Schlesiens* (Breslau: Flemings Verlag, 1939)

Le Blond, Guillaume, *Éléments de fortification* (Paris: Jombert, 1775)

Bode W., 'Versuch einer Biographie und Charakteristik des verstorbenen Ober Baudirector Pohlmann', *Schlesische Provinzialblätter*, vol.33, no.1, January (1801), pp.24–34

Bogdanowski, Janusz, 'Twierdza Koźle. Problem planu w świetle systemu kleszczowego szkoły staropruskiej i szkoły Arad', *Studia i Materiały do Historii Wojskowości*, vol.12, no.1 (1966), pp.153–162

von Bonin, Udo, *Geschichte des Ingenieurkorps und der Pioniere in Preussen* (Berlin: Mittler und Sohn, 1877)

Bosi, Pio, *Dizionario Storico, Biografico, Topografico, Militare d'Italia* (Torino: G. Candeletti, 1870)

Bossut, Charles, *Traité théorique et expérimental d'hydrodynamique* (Paris: Unknown Publisher, 1787)

von Brese-Winiary, Johann Leopold Ludwig, *Drei Vorlesungen ueber das Entstehen und das Wesen der neueren Befestigungsmethode, M. bes. Beziehg. auf d. in preuss. Staate seit d. letzten Kriegsjahren z. Ausführg. gekommenen Festgs-Neubauten, gehalten in d. milit. Ges. i. J. 1844* (Berlin: Unknown Publisher, 1856)

Brialmont, Alexis Henri, *Études sur la défense des états: et sur la fortification* (Bruxelles: Guyot 1863)

Brüggemann, Ludwig Wilhelm, *Ausführliche Beschreibung des gegenwärtigen Zustandes des Königl. Preußischen Herzogthums Vor- und Hinter-Pommern: Welcher die Beschreibung der zu dem Gerichtsbezirk der Königl. Landescollegien in Stettin gehörigen Hinterpommerschen Kreise enthält* (Stettin: H.G. Effenbart, 1784)

Bucquoy, J. A. d'Archambaud, *Événement des plus rares, ou L'histoire du Sr abbé Cte de Buquoy: singulièrement son évasion du Fort-l'Évêque et de la Bastille* (Bonnefoy: Unknown Publisher, 1719)

Bukal, Grzegorz, 'Twierdza kłodzka 1620-1900', *Kwartalnik architektury i urbanistyki*, vol.31, no.3–4 (1986) pp.279–320

Bukal, Grzegorz, 'Fort "Prusy" w Szczecinie', *Materiały Zachodniopomorskie*, vol.XLVI (2000) pp.433–556

Bukal, Grzegorz, 'Idea donżonu w pruskie fortyfikacji XVIII wieku', in T. Przerwa, G. Podruczny (eds), *Twierdza srebrnogórska* (Srebrna Góra: Srebrnogórska Oficyna Wydawnicza, 2006), pp.39–50

Burger, Daniel, *Landesfestungen der Hohenzollern in Franken und Brandenburg* (München: Beck'sche Verlagsbuchhandlung, 2000)

Burk, Kurt, *Handbuch der Festungen des Historischen Deutschen Ostens* (Osnabrück: Biblio Verlag, 1995)

Büsching, Anton Friedrich, *Große Erdbeschreibung* (Brunn: Traßler, 1786)

von Clausewitz Carl, *Hinterlassene Werke über Krieg und Kriegführung* (Berlin: Ferd. Dümmler's Verlagsbuchhandlung, 1863)

van Coehoorn, Menno, *Nieuwe Vestingbouw* (Leeuwarden: Rintjes, 1685)

van Coehoorn, Menno, *Nouvelle fortification tant pour un terrain bas et humide que sec et élevé* (La Haye: Van Buldern, 1706)

van Coehoorn, Menno, *Neuer Vestungs-Bau* (Wesel: Kattepoel, 1708)

de Cormontaigne, Louis, *Architecture militaire, ou l'art de fortifier, Qui enseigne d'une manière courte et facile* (La Haye: Neaulme et Moetiens, 1741)

Dallemagne, Francois, Moully Jean, *Patrimoine Militaire* (Paris: SCALA, 2002)

Diderot, Denis, d'Alembert Jean le Rond, *Encyclopédie: ou dictionnaire raisonné des sciences, des arts et des métier* (Neufchastel: Samuel Faulche, 1765)

Dilich, Wilhelm, *Peribologia Seu Muniendorum Locorum Ratio Wilhelmi Dilichii* (Fracofurti ad Moenum: Unknown Publisher, 1641)

Dionisotti, Carlo, *Notizie biografiche dei Vercellesi illustri* (Biella: Giuseppe Amosso, 1862)

Droysen, Johann Gustav (ed.), *Politische Correspondenz Friedrich's des Großen* (Berlin-Leipzig-Oldenburg: Duckner & Humbolt, 1879–1939)

Duffy, Christopher, *Friedrich der Große und seine Armee* (Stuttgart: Motorbuch Verlag, 1978)

Duffy, Christopher, *The fortress in the Age of Vauban and Frederick the Great 1660-1789. Siege Warfare Volume II* (London: Routledge & Kegan Paul, 1985)

Duffy, Christopher, *Fire and Stone* (Edison: Castle Books, 2006)

Duncker, Carl von, *Oesterreichischer Erbfolge-Krieg 1740-1748* (Wien: Velrag von L. W. Seidel & Sohn, 1896)

Eckert, Wojciech, *Fortyfikacje Głogowa* (Zielona Góra: Uniwersytet Zielonogórski, 2006)

Eckert, Wojciech, *Fortyfikacje Nadodrzańskie w procesie rozwoju nowożytnej sztuki fortyfikacyjnej w XVII – XIX w* (Zielona Góra: Uniwersytet Zielonogórski, 2007)

Eisenmänger, Theodor, *Geschichte der Stadt Schmiedeberg* (Breslau: Verlag von Max Woywod, 1900)

Engelhardt, Friedrich Wilhelm, *Geschichte der Stadt und Festung Luxemburg: seit ihrer ersten Entstehung bis auf unsere Tage* (Luxemburg: Rehm, Buck, 1850)

du Fay, L'Abbe, *Maniere de Fortifier selon la methode de Monsieur de Vauban...* (Paris, 1707)

Frąckowiak-Skrobała, Teresa, Lijewska, Teresa, Wróblewska, Grażyna, *Gorzów Wielkopolski, przeszłość i teraźniejszość* (Poznań: Wydawnictwo Poznańskie, 1964)

Franczak, Jakub, Grabowski, Włodzimierz, Nowiński, Piotr, Żebrowski, Mariusz, *Twierdza Grudziądz* (Grudziądz: Wydawnictwo Kalamarski, 2010)

Frederick II, *Friedrichs des Zweiten Königs von Preussen bei seinen Lebzeiten gedruckte Werke* (Berlin: Voß und Sohn, Decker und Sohn, 1790)

Furetière, Antoine, Bayle, Pierre, de Beauval, Henri Basnage, *Dictionnaire universel: contenant generalement tous les mots françois tant vieux que modernes, & les termes des sciences et des arts...* (La Haye: Arnout & Reinier Leer, 1701)

Furetière, Antoine, *Dictionnaire universel, contenant généralement tous les mots François...* (La Haye: Arnout & Reinier Leer, 1727)

Galland, Georg, *Hohenzollern und Oranien. Neue Beiträge zur Geschichte der niederländischen Beziehungen im 17. und 18. Jahrhundert* (Strassburg: Heitz&Mündel, 1911)

von Gansauge, Hermann, *Das brandenburgisch-preussische Kriegswesen um die Jahre 1440, 1640 und 1740* (Berlin: E. S. Mittler, 1838)

Geppert, Carl Eduard, *Chronik von Berlin von Entstehung der Stadt an bis heute* (Berlin: Ferdinand Rubch Verlag, 1840)

Giersberg, Hans-Joachim, *Friedrich als Bauherr: Studien zur Architektur des 18. Jahrhunderts in Berlin und Potsdam* (Berlin: Siedler, 1986)

de Gregori, Gaspare, *Istoria Della Vercellese Letteratura Ed Arti* (Torino: Chirio e Mina, 1824)

Griendel, Johann Franz, *Nova architectura militaris, das ist: Neuerfundene fortificationes, oder Vestungs Bau* (Dresden: Baumann, 1677)

Groehler, Olaf, *Die Kriege Friedrichs II* (Berlin: Militärverlag, 1966)

Grosser Generalstab, *Geschichte des siebenjährigen Krieges: in einer Reihe von Vorlesungen, mit Benutzung authentischer Quellen* (Berlin: Grosser Generalstab, 1826)

Grosser Generalstab, *Geschichte des siebenjährigen Krieges: in einer Reihe von Vorlesungen, mit Benutzung authentischer Quellen, der Feldzug von 1761* (Berlin: Grosser Generalstab, 1836)

Grosser Generalstab, *Geschichte des siebenjährigen Krieges: in einer Reihe von Vorlesungen, mit Benutzung authentischer Quellen, der Feldzug von 1762 und der Schluß des Krieges 1763* (Berlin: Grosser Generalstab 1841)

Grosser Generalstab, *Die Kriege Friedrichs des Großen, Der Erste Schlesische Krieg* (Berlin: Königliche Hofbuchhandlung, 1890-1893),

Grosser Generalstab, *Die Kriege Friedrichs des Großen, Der Zweite Schlesische Krieg* (Berlin: Königliche Hofbuchhandlung, 1895)

Grosser Generalstab, *Die Kriege Friedrichs des Großen, Der Siebenjährige Krieg 1756–63* (Berlin: Mittler und Sohn, 1901–1914)

Grünhagen, Colmar, *Schlesien unter Friedrich dem Grossen* (Breslau: Verlag von Wilhelm Koebner, 1892)

Grünhagen, Colmar, 'Die Einrichtung des Militärwesens in Schlesien bei dem Beginne der preußischen Herrschaft', *Zeitschrift des Vereins für Geschichte und Alterthum Schlesiens*, 23 (1889), pp.1–28

Gruszecki, Andrzej, *Bastionowe zamki Małopolski* (Warszawa: Wydawnictwo MON, 1962)

Hanke, Max, Degner, Hermann, *Geschichte der Amtlichen Kartographie Brandenburg-Preussens bis zum Ausgang der Friderizianischen Zeit* (Stuttgart: Engelhorn, 1935)

Hartmut, Niedrich, 'Bedeutende Altlandsberger, Der preußische General und Festungsbaumeister Ludwig Regler', *Altlandsberger Stadtmagazin*,' Jg.5, nr.8, 30 VIII 2007, p.2

von Heilmann, Johann, *Die Kriegskunst der Preußen unter König Friedrich dem Großen* (Leipzig – Meißen: Goedsche Buchhandlung, 1853)

Henning, Hans, *Der Zustand des schlesischen Festungen im Jahre 1756 und ihre Bedeutung für die Frage des Ursprungs des siebenjährigen Krieges* (Jena : Unknown Publisher, 1899)

Henning, Herzeleide, *Bibliographie Friedrich der Grosse 1786–1986: Das Schrifttum des deutschen Sprachraums und der Übersetzungen aus Fremdsprachen* (Berlin: de Gruyter 1988)

Herlin, Ludwig Andreas, *Herrn George Rimplers Sämtliche Schrifften von der Fortification, Dreßden* (Leipzig: Heckel, 1724)

von Heuck, Walter, *Genealogisches Handbuch des Adels, Adelslexiko* (Limburg an der Lahn: Starke Verlag, 1999)

Hirtenfeld, Jaromir, *Oesterreichisches Militär-Konversations-Lexikon, Acht und Dreißigste bis ein und Vierzigste Lieferung* (Wien: Karl Gerold und Sohn, 1853)

Hirtenfeld, Jaromir, *Der Militär-Maria-Theresien-Orden und seine Mitglieder* (Wien: Kaiserlich-Königliche Hof- und Staatsdrukerei, 1857)

Hoburg R., 'Geschichtlich-militärische Nachrichten über die Festung Pillau', *Der neuen Preußischen Provinzial Blätter dritte Folge*, vol.2 (1858) pp.231–238, 279–289

Hoffmann, Friedrich Wilhelm, *Geschichte der Stadt Magdeburg* (Magdeburg: Verlag von Emil Baensch, 1850)

Hoffmann, Friedrich Wilhelm, *Geschichte der Stadt Magdeburg* (Magdeburg: Verlag von Albert Rathte, 1885)

Holtze, Friedrich, 'Geschichte der Befestigung von Berlin' *Schriften des Vereins für die Geschichte Berlins*, vol.10 (1874), pp.45–67

von Humbert, Abraham, *Der Angriff und die Vertheidigung der Festungen durch den Herrn von Vauban* (Berlin: Bergmann, 1744–1745)

von Humbert, Abraham, *Der Angriff und die Vertheidigung der Festungen durch den herrn von Vauban* (Berlin: Laude und Spener, 1751)

de Humbert, Abraham, *L'art du Genie pour l'instruction des gens de guerre* (Berlin: Laude und Spener, 1755)

de Humbert, Abraham, *Vollkommener Unterricht der zur Kriegs-Kunst gehörigen Wissenschaften* (Bernburg: Coemen, 1756)

Hogg, Ashleigh, *The Fortress of Fenestrelle in Detail*, 2004, <http://www.fortedifenestrelle. com/Pdf/English/The%20Fortress%20of%20Fenestrelle%20in%20Detail.pdf>, accessed 6 December 2012

Jany, Kurt, *Geschichte der Preussischen Armee vom 15 Jahrhundert bis 1914*, (Osnabrück: Biblio Verlag, 1967)

Jähns, Max, *Geschichte der Kriegswissenschaften vornehmlich in Deutschland, Bd.2, Das XVII. und XVIII. Jahrhundert bis zum Auftreten Friedrichs des Großen 1740* (München-Leipzig: Verlag von Oldenbourg, 1890)

Jähns, Max, *Geschichte der Kriegswissenschaften vornehmlich in Deutschland, Bd.3, Das XVIII. Jahrhundert seit dem Auftreten Friedrichs des Großen 1740-1800* (München-Leipzig: Verlag von Oldenbourg, 1891)

Jonca, Karol, 'Wielka Armia Napoleona w kampanii 1807 roku pod Koźlem', in Stanisław Senft (ed.), *Szkice Kędzierzyńsko-Kozielskie* (Opole: Instytut Śląski, 1985), pp.9–76

Jonca, Karol, *Wielka Armia Napoleona w kampanii 1807 roku pod Koźlem* (Opole: Państwowy Instytut Naukowy-Instytut Śląski, 2003)

Jonca, Karol, 'Strategiczna rola twierdzy kozielskiej w dobie wojen napoleońskich', in Edward Nycz, Stanisław Senft (eds), *Wojna i pokój w dziejach twierdzy i miasta Koźle* (Opole: Państwowy Instytut Naukowy-Instytut Śląski, 2007), pp.33–63

Jordan, Klaus, 'Gerhard Cornelius Walrave und sein Vorschlag zur Verbesserung des Festungsgrundrisses der Festung Wesel von 1747', *Festungsjournal*, (2009), pp.66–72

Jung, Wilhelm, Spaß, Willy, Sloger, Friedrich, *Die Kunstdenkmäler der Stadt Frankfurt a. O.* (Berlin: Meisenbach Riffarth & Co., 1912)

Kahlo, Johann Gottlieb, *Denkwürdigkeiten der Königlichen Preußischen souverainen Grafschaft Glatz* (Berlin: Unknown Publisher, 1757)

von Kaltenborn, Rudolph Wilhelm, *Briefe eines alten Preussischen Officiers, verschiedene Characterzüge Friedrichs des Einzigen betreffend: Mit Rücksicht auf das Zimmermannsche Werk über eben diesen Gegenstand* (Hohenzollern: Schulbuchhandlung, 1790)

Kamieński, Andrzej, Kucharczyk, Grzegorz, Szultka, Zygmunt, Łukaszewicz, Dariusz, Wachowiak, Bogdan, *Prusy w okresie monarchii absolutnej (1701–1806)* (Poznań: Wydawnictwo Poznańskie, 2010)

von Kamptz, Wilhelm Adolf Ernst, *Grundsätze zur Ermittelung der artilleristischen Bewaffnung einer Festung* (Potsdam: Rieglesche Buchhandlung, 1862)

Kieseritzky, Ernst, *Das Gelände der ehemaligen Festung Breslau* (Breslau: Morgensterns Verlagsbuchhandlung, 1903)

Klose, Arwed, *Festung Neisse* (Hagen: Werner Dorau, 1980)

Klawitter, Willy, *Geschichte der schlesischen Festungen in vorpreußischer Zeit* (Breslau: Trewendt & Granier Verlag, 1941)

Kneschke, Ernst Heinrich, *Neues Allgemeines Deutsches Adels-Lexicon* (Leipzig: Friedrich Voigt Verlag, 1867)

Konwiarz, Richard, *Die Baukunst Breslaus: ein architektonischer Führer im Auftrage des Schlesischen Bundes für Heimatschutz* (Breslau: Verlag Grasz, 1926)

Köhl, Eduard, *Die Geschichte der Festung Glatz* (Würzburg: Holzner Verlag, 1972)

König, Anton Balthasar, *Biographisches Lexikon aller Helden und Militairpersonen, welche sich in Preußischen Diensten berühmt gemacht haben* (Berlin: Arnold Mever, 1788–91)

Kretschmar, Paul, 'Schurgast O/S, eine wieder aufgegebene Festung Friedrichs des Großen', *Der Oberschlesier*, 14 (1932) pp.271–272.

Kroczyński, Hieronim, *Twierdza Kołobrzeg* (Warszawa: Barwa i Broń, 2000)

Krüger, Anton, *Chronik der Stadt und Festung Spandau* (Spandau: Verlag von Karl Jürgens, 1867)

Kuch-Breburda, Miroslav, Kupka, Vladimir, *Pevnost Olomouc* (Dvur Kralove nad Labem: FORTprint, 2003)

Kunisch, Johannes, Sikora, Michael, Stieve, Tilman, *Gerhard von Scharnhorst. Private und dienstliche Schriften, V. 3 Preussen 1801–1804* (Köln: Böhlau, 2005)

Lange Eduard, *Die Soldaten Friedrich's des Grossen* (Leipzig: Avenarius&Mendelsohn, 1853)

Lemau de La Jaisse, Pierre, *Cinquieme abrégé de la Carte Generale du Militaire de France sur le terre et sur Mer, Depuis Novembre 1737 jusqu'en Decembre 1738* (Paris: Unknown Publisher, 1739)

Lemau de La Jaisse, Pierre, *Sixième abrégé de la Carte Generale du Militaire de France sur le terre et sur Mer, jusqu'en Decembre 1739* (Paris: Unknown Publisher, 1740)

Lemau de La Jaisse, Pierre, *Septieme abrégé de la Carte Generale du Militaire de France sur le terre et sur Mer, jusqu'en Decembre 1740* (Paris: Unknown Publisher, 1741)

Lefèbvre, Simon, *Oeuvres completes* (Maastricht: Dufour & Roux, 1778)

Lefèbvre, Simon, *Versuch über die Minen* (Wien: Trattnern, 1785)

Lepage, Jean-Denis G. G., *French Fortifications, 1715–1815: An Illustrated History* (Jefferson: McFarland & Co Inc, 2010)

Lewicka-Cempa, Maria, 'Twierdza w Srebrnej Górze: Problemy ochrony konserwatorskiej, Dzieje warowni', in Lewicka-Cempa, Maria, Brzoskwinia, Waldemar (eds), *O skuteczną ochronę fortyfikacji historycznych* (Warszawa–Kraków: Agencja wydawnicza Zebra, 1995), pp.61–82

de Ligne, Charles-Joseph, *Mon journal de la Guerre de Sept Ans. Campagne 1757 et 1758. Mélanges militaires, littéraires et sentimentaires* (Dresden: Walther, 1796)

Lloyd, Henry, Georg Friedrich von Tempelhoff, *Geschichte des siebenjährigen Krieges in Deutschland zwischen dem Könige von Preußen und der Kaiserin Königin mit ihren Alliirten* (Berlin: Johann Friedrich Unger 1783–1801)

Luchs, Hermann, 'Über das äußere Wachstum der Stadt Breslau, mit Beziehung auf die Befestigung derselben', *Jahresbericht der städtischen höheren Töchterschule am Ritterplatz zu Breslau*, 1866, pp.1–11

Lukoschik, Rita Unfer, *Italienerinnen und Italiener am Hofe Friedrich II (1740-1786)* (Berlin: Duncker & Humblot, 2008)

Łysiak, Waldemar, *Napoleon jako foryfikator* (Warszawa, ExLibris 1999)

Mai, Bernard, Mai, Christine, *Festung Magdeburg* (Dößel, Stekovics, 2006)

von Malinowsky, Louis, 'Friedrichs des Großen praktische Instruktion im Festungskriege im Jahre 1752', *Archiv für die Officiere der Königlich Preußischen Artillerie und Ingenieur Korps*, 3 (1836), pp.234–242

von Malinowsky Louis, von Bonin Robert, *Geschichte der brandenburgisch-preussischen Artillerie* (Berlin: Verlag von Duckner und Humbolt, 1840–1842)

Malkin, Arthur Thomas, *The Portrait Gallery of Distinguished Poets, Philosophers, Statesmen, Divines, Painters, Architects, Physicians, and Lawyers, Since the Revival of Art* (London, W. S. Orr and Co, 1853)

Mallet, Allain Manesson, *Kriegsarbeit oder neuer Festungsbau: so wohl der Lehrsatzmässige als Unlehrsatzmässige, in drei Teilen abgehandel* (Amsterdam: van Meurs, 1672)

Małachowicz, Maciej, 'Historia nowożytnej twierdzy Świdnica', *Rocznik Świdnicki 2007*, (2008), pp.17–29

Martin, Thierry, Virol, Michèle, *Vauban, architecte de la modernité?* (Paris: Presses universitaires de Franche-Comté 2008)

Mebes, Julius, *Beiträge zur Geschichte des Brandenburgisch-Preussischen Staates und Heeres* (Berlin: Lüderitzsche Verlagsbuchhandlung, 1867)

Mende, Volker, 'Eine formidable Festung? Die Neuen Werke (1744) der Festung Peitz als Spiegel des Fortifikatorischen Denkens König Friedrichs II', in Göse, Frank (ed.), *Friedrich der Große und die Mark Brandenburg. Herrschaftspraxis in der Provinz* (Berlin, Lukas Verlag, 2012), pp.307–325

Menzel, Karl Adolf, *Topographische Chronik von Breslau* (Breslau: Gratz und Barth 1805–1808)

Minsberg, Ferdinand, *Geschichtliche Darstellung der merkwürdige Ereignisse in der Fürstenzhums Stadt Neisse* (Neisse: Verlag von Wangenfield, 1834)

Minsberg, Ferdinand, *Geschichte der Stadt und Festung Groß Glogau* (Glogau: Julius Gottschalk, 1853)

de Mirabeau, Honoré Gabriel Riquetti, *De la monarchie prussienne: sous Frédéric le Grand* (Londres: Unknown Publisher, 1788)

de Mirabeau, Honore-Gabriel Riquetti, *Von der Preußischen Monarchie unter Friedrich dem Großen* (Leipzig: Dykische Buchhandlung, 1795)

Montandre-Lonchamps, François Edme de, *Etat Militaire de France pour l'Anne 1758* (Paris: Guillyn, 1758)

Montandre-Lonchamps, François Edme de, *Etat Militaire de France pour l'Anne 1759* (Paris: Guillyn, 1759)

Montandre-Lonchamps, François Edme de, *Etat Militaire de France pour l'Anne 1762* (Paris: Guillyn, 1762)

Montalembert, Marc René, *La fortification perpendiculaire, ou Essai sur plusieurs manière...* (Paris: Philippe-Denys Pierres; Alexandre Jombert, 1776–1798)

Montalembert, Marc-René, *Correspondance de Monsieur le Marquis de Montalembert* (Londres: Unknown Publisher, 1777)

Montalembert, Marc-René, 'Briefwechsel des Marquis von Montalembert', *Neue Kriegsbibliothek oder gesammlete Beyträge zur Kriegswissenschaft*, 8 (1780), pp.1–480 (1781), pp.1–328

Müller, Ludwig, *Versuch über Verschanzungskunst auf Winterpostierungen* (Potsdam: Sommer, 1782)

Müller, Hermann, *Geschichte des Festungskrieges seit allgemeiner Einführung der Feuerwaffen bis zum Jahre 1892* (Berlin: Mittler und Sohn, 1892)

Naudé, Wilhelm, Skalweit, August, *Die Getreidehandelspolitik und die Kriegsmagazinverwaltung Preußens, 1740–1756* (Berlin: Verlag von Paul Parey, 1910)

Obstfelder, Carl, *Chronik der Stadt Crossen* (Crossen, Verlag von Richard Zeidler, 1895)

von Orlich, Leopold, *Geschichte der schlesischen Kriege* (Berlin: Verlag von George Gropius, 1841)

Ozanam, Jacques, *Dictionnaire mathematique, ou: Idée genearale des mathematiques dans lequel l'on trouve outre les Termes de cette science, plusieurs Termes des Arts et des autres sciences* (Amsterdam: Huguetan, 1691)

Panckoucke, André-Joseph, *Calendrier General de la Flandre du Brabant et des Conquetes de Roi* (Paris: Savoy, 1747)

Pfeffinger, Johann Friedrich, *Nouvelle fortification françoise, espagnolle, italienne et hollandoise...* (Amsterdam: Gallet, 1698)

Pfeiffer, Fritz, 'Liegnitz als Festung', *Mitteilungen des Geschichts- und Altertumes-Vereins zu Liegnitz*, 10 (1926), pp.232–274

Piers, Harry, *The Evolution of the Halifax Fortress 1749–1928* (Halifax: The public archives of Nova Scotia, 1947)

Pirscher, Johann Karl Dietrich, *Kurzer Unterricht von den Anfangsgrunden der Kriegs Baukunst* (Berlin, Verlag der Buchhandlung der Realschule, 1767)

Pirscher, Johann Karl Dietrich, *Anweisung zum Festungsbau mit verdeckten Flanken und zur Defense en revers, als dem einzigen Mittel den Belagerern lange zu widerstehen* (Berlin: Schropsche, 1776)

Pinelli, Ferdinando Augusto, *Storia militare del Piemonte in continuazione di quella del Saluzo cioè dalla pace d' Aquisgrana sino ai dì nostri, 1748–1796* (Torino: Degiorgis, 1854)

Pochhammer, Paul, *Friedrich der Grosse und Neisse. Vortrag, gehalten in der Philomathie zu Neisse am 16. Mai 1888* (Neisse: Verlag der Josef Graveur'schen Buchhandlung, 1888)

Podruczny, Grzegorz, 'Twierdza Koźle w latach 1743–1806', in Edward Nycz, Stanisław Senft (eds), *Wojna i pokój w dziejach twierdzy i miasta Koźle* (Opole: Wydawnictwo Instytut Śląski, 2007), pp.64–78

Podruczny, Grzegorz, *Twierdza Wrocław w okresie fryderycjańskim. Fortyfikacje, garnizon i działania wojenne w latach 1741–1806* (Wrocław: Atut, 2009)

Podruczny, Grzegorz, *Twierdza od wewnątrz. Budownictwo wojskowe na Śląsku w latach 1740-1806* (Zabrze: Inforteditions, 2011)

Podruczny, Grzegorz, Przerwa, Tomasz, *Twierdza Srebrna Góra* (Warszawa: Bellona, 2010)

Podruczny, Grzegorz, Wichrowski, Marcin, 'Kostrzyn i jego satelity. Brandenburskie fortyfikacje stałe w dorzeczu środkowej Odry od wojny 30-letniej po wojny śląskie', in Mykietów, Bogusław, Sanocka, Katarzyna, Tureczek, Marceli (eds), *Dziennik jeńca i inne szkice. Twierdza Kostrzyn w przeszłości* (Zielona Góra: Księgarnia Akademicka, 2006), pp.9–48

Polap, Eugen, 'Die Anwendung von Minen im Belagerungskrieg. Betrachtungen aus der Sicht des 18. Jahrhunderts', in Volker Schmidtchen (ed.), *Sicherheit und Bedrohung – Schutz und Enge. Gesellschaftliche Entwicklung von Festungsstädten. Beispiel Stade* (Wesel: Deutsche Gesellschaft für Festungsforschung, 1987)

Preuss, Johann David Erdmann (ed.), *Oeuvres de Frederic le Grand* (Berlin: Decker, 1846–1856)

Preuss, Johann David Erdmann, *Urkundenbuch zu der Lebensgeschichte Friedrichs des Großen* (Berlin: Nauncksche Buchhandlung, 1832)

Preuss, Johann David Erdmann, *Die militärische Richtung in Friedrichs jugendleben* (Berlin: Decker, 1858)

Preuss, Johann David Erdmann, 'Friedrich der Große und der General v. Walrave', *Zeitschrift für Kunst, Wissenschaft, und Geschichte des Krieges*, 1 (1859) pp.40-68

Priesdorf, Kurt, *Soldatisches Führerthum* (Hamburg: Hanseatische Verlagsanstalt 1937–1942)

Przerwa, Tomasz, *Dzieje Srebrnej Góry* (Srebrna Góra: Srebrnogórska Oficyna Wydawnicza, 1998)

de Renneville, René Auguste Constantin, *Inquisition Françoise ou l'historie de la Bastille* (Amsterdam-Leide: Lakeman, Verbeek, 1740)

Reuleaux, Oskar, *Die geschichtliche Entwickelung des Befestigungswesens vom Aufkommen der Pulvergeschütze bis zur Neuzeit* (Leipzig: Göschen'sche Verlagsbuchhandlung, 1913)

Richelet, Pierre, *Dictionaire François* (Geneve: Wiederhold, 1680)

Rimpler, Georg, *Befestigte Festung, Artillerie und Infanterie mit drey Treffen in Bataille gestellen (Beständiges Fundament zu Fortificiren und Defendiren)* (Frankfurt am Main: Unknown Publisher, 1674)

Rozard, Claude, *Nouvelle Fortification Françoise: Où il est traité de la construction...* (Nuremberg: Lochner, 1731)

Rödenbeck, Karl Heinrich Siegfried, *Tagebuch oder Geschichtskalender aus Friedrich's des Großen Regentenleben* (Berlin: Plahnsche Buchhadlung, 1840–1842)

Rubow, Otto, *Stadt und Festung Kolberg. Blätter aus Kolbergs Geschichte* (Kolberg: Prangersche Buchhandlung, 1936)

Rütjes, Heinrich, *Geschichte des brandenburg-preußischen Staates: von d. ältesten Zeiten bis auf unsere Tage* (Schaffhausen: Hurtersche Buchhandlung, 1859)

Salat, Nicole, Sarmant, Thierry, *Politique, guerre et fortification au grand siècle: Lettres de Louvois à Louis XIV* (Paris: Société de l'histoire de France 2007)

Saluzzo, Cesare, *Ricordi militari degli stati Sardi: estratti da parecchie opre si stampate che manoscritte* (Torino: Sebastiano Franco, 1859)

Saunders, Andrew, *Fortress Builder. Bernard de Gomme, Charles II's Military Engineer* (Exeter: University of Exeter Press, 2004)

Schachinger, Erika, *Die Dorotheenstadt 1673–1708. Eine Berliner Vorstadt* (Köln: Böhlau, 2001)

Schäfer, Christoph, *'Krygsvernuftelingen'. Militäringenieure und Forfikation in den Vereinigten Niederlanden* (Gießen: unpublished dissertation, Justus-Liebig-Universität Giessen, 2001)

Scharnhorst, Gerhard von, *Handbuch für Offiziere in den angewandten Theilen der Kriegs-Wissenschafften* (Hannover: Verlag der Helwingschen Hoff Buchhandlung, 1815)

Scheiter, Johann Bernhard, *Novissima praxis militaris, oder Neu-Vermehrte und Verstärekte Vestungs-Bau- und Krieges-Schuel...* (Braunschweig: Zilliger und Gruber, 1672)

Scheiter, Johann Bernhard, *Examen fortificatorium, Darin so wohl Eine gantz newe Art oder Manier vom Festungs-Bau...* (Strassburg: Spoor und Wächtler, 1676)

Schellenberg A., 'Die Evangelische Kirche in Cosel OS. Eine Archivalische Studie', *Der Oberschlesier*, vol.14, no.3–4 (1932), pp.150–154

Schirrmann, Wilhelm, *Chronik der Stadt Schweidnitz* (Schweidnitz: Verlag von Georg Brieger, 1909)

Schlie, Friedrich: *Die Kunst- und Geschichts-Denkmäler des Grossherzogthums Mecklenburg-Schwerin. II. Band: Die Amtsgerichtsbezirke Wismar, Grevesmühlen, Rehna, Gadebusch und Schwerin* (Schwerin: Bärensprung, 1898)

Schmidt, Julius, *Geschichte der Stadt Schweidnitz* (Schweidnitz, Verlag von Ludwig Hege, 1848)

Schneider, Joachim, 'Über das Militär in der Dammvorstadt und die Spätere Entwicklung der historischen Militärbauten in Słubice', *Mitteilungen Historischer Verein zu Frankfurt (Oder) e.V*, 2 (2005), pp.15–24

von Schöning, Kurd Wolfgang Wilhelm Georg, *Historisch-biographische Nachrichten zur Geschichte der Brandenburgisch-Preussischen Artillerie* (Berlin: Mittler, 1844)

von Schöning, Kurd Wolfgang Wilhelm Georg, *Militairische correspondenz des Königs Friedrich des Grossen mit dem prinzen Hienrich von Preussen* (Potsdam: Verlag von Ferdinand Riegel, 1852)

Schönwälder, Karl Friedrich, *Geschichtliche Ortsnachrichten von Brieg und seinen Umgebungen* (Brieg: S. Falsch, 1847)

Schubert, Friedrich Wilhelm, 'Beiträge zur Erziehungsgeschichte Friedrichs des Grossen', *Preußische Provinzial-Blätter*, 4 (1830), pp.8–31

Seilkopf, Karl, *Frankfurt (Oder) als feste Stadt* (Frankfurt/Oder: Trowitzsch & Sohn, 1932)

Seydel, Samuel F., *Nachrichten über vaterländische Festungen und Festungskriege* (Leipzig Züllichau: Darmannsche Buchhandlung, 1819–24)

Seyfart, Johann Friedrich, *Kurzgefassete Geschichte aller königlichen preussischen Regimenter...* (Frankfurt am Main: Unknown Publisher, 1759)

Seyfart, Johann Friedrich, *Lebens- und Regierungs-Geschichte Friedrichs des andern Königs in Preussen...* (Leipzig: Verlag Adam Friedrich Böhmens, 1784)

Skalweit, August, *Getreidehandelspolitik und Kriegsmagazin-Verwaltung Brandenburg-Preußens 1756-1806* (Berlin: Verlag von Paul Parey, 1931)

Sobrino, Francisco, *Dicionario Nuevo De Las Lenguas, Española Y Francesca* (Brusselle: Foppens, 1721)

Spuhrmann, Rudolf, *Geschichte der Stadt Cammin i. Pommern und des camminer Domkapitels* (Cammin i. Pom.: Verlag Von Formazin & Knauff, 1924)

Stanisław, Salmonowicz, *Prusy. Dzieje państwa i społeczeństwa* (Warsaw: Książka i wiedza, 1998)

Stankiewicz, Jerzy, 'Ze studiów nad fortyfikacjami pruskimi na ziemiach polskich', *Studia i Materiały do Historii Wojskowości*, 12:1 (1966), pp.106–152

Stankiewicz, Jerzy, 'Twierdza grudziądzka', *Rocznik Grudziądzki*, V-VI (1970), pp.125–210

Stoewer, Rudolf, *Geschichte der Stadt Kolberg* (Kolberg: Postsche Buchhandlung, 1897)

Stolle, Wilhelm Carl, *Beschreibung und Geschichte der uralten, ehemals festen, grossen und berühmten Hanseestadt Demmin, wie auch der daran liegenden festen und berühmten Burg Haus Demmin genannt* (Greiswald: Rose, 1772)

Strzok, Igor Zbigniew, 'Oblężenie Świdnicy w 1807 roku, jego efekty i wnioski wyciągnięte przez napoleońskich fortyfikatorów', *Rocznik Świdnicki 2007*, (2008), pp.62–76

Sturm, Leonhard Christoph, *Architectura militaris hypothetico-eclectica, Oder Gründliche Anleitung zu der Kriegs-Baukunst: Aus denen Hypothesibus und Erfindungen derer meinsten und besten Ingenieurs dargestellet* (Nürnberg: Monath, 1702, 1720, 1729, 1736, 1755)

Sturm, Leonhard Christoph, *Freundlicher Wett-Streit Der Französischen, Holländischen und Teutschen Krieges-Bau-Kunst* (Augspurg: Wolfe, 1718)

Symanowski F., 'Fort Lyck', *Mitteilungen der Literarischen Gesellschaft Masovia*, 8 (1902), pp.37–44

Teissier, Guillaume Ferdinand, *Histoire de Thionville*, (Metz: Verronnais, 1828)

Thole, Sven, 'Die Festung Rothenberg', *Festungsjournal*, vol.42 (2012) pp.1–62

Tielke, Johann Gottlieb *Beytrage zur Kriegskunst und Geschichte des Krieges von 1756 bis 1756, IV Stück, Die drey Belagerungen und loudonsche Ersteigung der Festung Scheridnitz in dern Feldzeügen von 1757 bis 1762* (Wien: Trattnern, 1786)

Toll, 'Walrave und die von ihm geleitete Reparatur der Reichsfestungen Philippsburg und Kehl nebst einer Notitz über seine Befestigung Manier', *Archiv für die Offiziere der Königlich Preußischen Artillerie und Ingenieur Corps*, 54 (1863), pp.135–150

de Tousard, Louis, *American artillerist's companion: or Elements of artillery. Treating of all kinds of firearms in detail, and of the formation, object, and service of the flying or horse artillery, preceded by an introductory dissertation on cannon* (Philadelphia: Conrad and Co, 1809)

Traugott, Erhardt, *Die Geschichte der Festung Königsberg/Pr 1257–1945* (Würzburg: Holzner Verlag, 1960)

de Valori, Louis Guy Henri, *Mémoires des négociations du marquis de Valori, ambassadeur de France a la cour de Berlin; Accompagnés d'un recueil de lettres de Frédéric-le-Grand, des princes ses frères, de Voltaire, et des plus illustres personnages du XVIIIe siècle; précédés d'une notice historique sur la vie de l'auteur* (Paris: Firmin Didot, 1820)

de Vauban, Sébastien Le Prestre, *De l'attaque et de la defense des places* (La Haye: Pierre de Hondt, 1737)

de Vauban, Sébastien Le Prestre, *De l'attaque et de la defense des places, par monsieur le marechal de Vauban; tome second contentant un traite pratique des mines* (La Haye: Pierre de Hondt, 1742)

de Vauban, Sébastien Le Prestre, *Oeuvres de M. de Vauban* (Amsterdam-Leipzig: Arkstee&Merkus, 1771)

Viglino, Davico Micaela, *Fortezze Sulle Alpi. Difese dei Savoia nella Valle Stura di Demonte* (Cuneo: L'Arciere, 1989)

Viglino, Davico Micaela, *Architetti e ingegneri militari in Piemonte tra '500 e '700* (Torino: Omega Edizioni, 2008)

Voch, Lukas, *Allgemeines Baulexicon oder Erklaerung der deutschen und französischen kunstwörter in der bürgerlichen, Kriegs und Schiffbaukunst wie auch der Hydrotechnik und Hydraulik* (Ausburg-Leipzig: Matthaus Riegers, 1781)

Voit, Johann Michael, *Technologisches Handwörterbuch oder Beschreibung und Erklärung der gewöhnlichsten Kunstdrücke... (*Augsburg: Jenisch und Stage, 1833)

Volz, Gustav Berthold (ed.) *Die Werke Friedrichs des Großen* (Berlin: Verlag von Riemar Hobbing, 1913–1914)

Wachter, Franz (ed.), *Acten des Kriegsgericht wegen der Eroberung vom Glatz 1760 und Schweidnitz 1761* (Breslau: Josef Marx, 1897)

Wagner, Reinhold, *Grundriss der Frotifikation* (Berlin: Vossische Buchhandlung, 1872)

Weltzel, Augustin, *Geschichte der Stadt, Herrschaft und ehemaliegen Festung Kosel* (Kosel: Verlag von Paul Mode, 1888)

Wedekind, Eduard Ludwig, *Geschichte der Stadt und des Herzogthums Crossen* (Crossen: Verlag von J.C. Riep, 1840)

Wichrowski, Marcin, 'Narodziny fortu. Budowa i utrzymanie twierdzy drezdenko w latach 1603–1606', in Grzegorz Podruczny (ed.), *Między zamkiem a twierdzą. Studia nad dziejami fortyfikacji w Drezdenku* (Gliwice: Inforteditions 2011), pp.19–40

von Witzleben, A., 'Das Verhältniss des Fürsten Leopold von Anhalt zu Friedrich dem Großen', *Jahrbücher für die Deutsche Armee und Marine*, Bd.8, (1873), pp.87–95

Wojciechowski, Przemysław, 'Fortyfikacje nowożytne twierdzy kłodzkiej w XVII i XVIII w.', *Zeszyty Naukowe Politechniki Gdańskiej*, 122 (1968), pp.85–119

Wolfrom, Erich, *Die Baugeschichte der Stadt und Festung Magdeburg* (Magdeburg: Stadt Magdeburg, 1936)

Wollmann, Ernst, *Geschichte des Brandenburgischen Pionier Bataillons nr. 3* (Minden: Bruns, 1888)

von Xylander, Josef, 'Festungstürme in Schweden. Ein Beitrag zur Geschichte der Befestigungskunst', *Militaerische Mittheilungen*, 1 (1828), pp.54–74

Zimmerman, Johann Georg, *Ueber Friedrich den Grossen und meine Unterredungen mit ihm kurz vor seinem Tode* (Leipzig: Weidmann, 1788)

Zimmermann, Johann Georg, *Fragmente über Friedrich den Grossen zur Geschichte seines Lebens, seiner Regierung, und seines Charakters* (Leipzig: Weidmann, 1790)

Zimmermann, Johann Georg, *Beschreibung der Stadt Breslau im Herzogtum Schlesien* (Brieg: Johann Ernst Tramp, 1794)

Zschocke, Helmut, *Die Berliner Akzisemauer: Die vorletzte Mauer der Stadt* (Berlin: Berlin Story Verlag, 2007)

Żywiczyński, Adam, Olszak, Piotr, 'Fort Lyck w latach 1785–2004', *Znad Pisy. Wydawnictwo poświęcone Ziemi Piskiej*, 13–14 (2004–2005), pp.226–250

Żywiczyński, Adam, 'Fort Lyck – fryderycjańskie umocnienie w systemie jezior mazurskich', in Wilkaniec, Agnieszka, Wichrowski, Marcin (ed.), *Fortyfikacje w przestrzeni miasta* (Poznań: Wydawnictwo Akademii Rolniczej im. Augusta Cieszkowskiego w Poznaniu, 2006), pp.205–215

Index

From Reason to Revolution – Warfare 1721-1815

http://www.helion.co.uk/series/from-reason-to-revolution-1721-1815.php

The 'From Reason to Revolution' series covers the period of military history 1721–1815, an era in which fortress-based strategy and linear battles gave way to the nation-in-arms and the beginnings of total war.

This era saw the evolution and growth of light troops of all arms, and of increasingly flexible command systems to cope with the growing armies fielded by nations able to mobilise far greater proportions of their manpower than ever before. Many of these developments were fired by the great political upheavals of the era, with revolutions in America and France bringing about social change which in turn fed back into the military sphere as whole nations readied themselves for war. Only in the closing years of the period, as the reactionary powers began to regain the upper hand, did a military synthesis of the best of the old and the new become possible.

The series will examine the military and naval history of the period in a greater degree of detail than has hitherto been attempted, and has a very wide brief, with the intention of covering all aspects from the battles, campaigns, logistics, and tactics, to the personalities, armies, uniforms, and equipment.

Submissions

The publishers would be pleased to receive submissions for this series. Please email reasontorevolution@helion.co.uk, or write to Helion & Company Limited, Unit 8 Amherst Business Centre, Budbrooke Road, Warwick, CV34 5WE.

Titles